Mastering

Active Directory®
for Windows Server® 2008

Mastering

Active Directory®
for Windows Server® 2008

John A. Price

Brad Price

Scott Fenstermacher

Wiley Publishing, Inc.

Acquisitions Editor: Tom Cirtin
Development Editor: Karen L. Lew
Technical Editor: Jim Kelly
Production Editor: Christine O'Connor
Copy Editor: Candace English
Production Manager: Tim Tate
Vice President and Executive Group Publisher: Richard Swadley
Vice President and Executive Publisher: Joseph B. Wikert
Vice President and Publisher: Neil Edde
Book Designer: Maureen Forys, Happenstance Type-O-Rama, Judy Fung
Compositor: Laurie Stewart, Happenstance Type-O-Rama
Proofreader: Sheilah Ledwidge, Word One
Indexer: Nancy Guenther
Cover Designer: Ryan Sneed
Cover Image: © Pete Gardner/Digital Vision/gettyimages

For general information on our other products and services or to obtain technical support, please contact our Customer Care Department within the U.S. at (800) 762-2974, outside the U.S. at (317) 572-3993 or fax (317) 572-4002.

Wiley also publishes its books in a variety of electronic formats. Some content that appears in print may not be available in electronic books.

Library of Congress Cataloging-in-Publication Data

Price, John A., 1970-
Mastering active directory for Windows Server 2008 / John A. Price, Brad Price, Scott Fenstermacher.
    p. cm.
ISBN 978-0-470-24983-3 (paper/website)
1. Directory services (Computer network technology) 2. Microsoft Windows (Computer file) 3. Operating systems (Computers)
I. Price, Brad. II. Fenstermacher, Scott. III. Title.
TK5105.595.P759 2008
005.7'1376--dc22
                    2008014656

10 9 8 7 6 5 4 3 2 1

Dear Reader,

Thank you for choosing *Mastering Active Directory for Windows Server 2008*. This book is part of a family of premium quality Sybex books, all written by outstanding authors who combine practical experience with a gift for teaching.

Sybex was founded in 1976. More than thirty years later, we're still committed to producing consistently exceptional books. With each of our titles we're working hard to set a new standard for the industry. From the paper we print on, to the authors we work with, our goal is to bring you the best books available.

I hope you see all that reflected in these pages. I'd be very interested to hear your comments and get your feedback on how we're doing. Feel free to let me know what you think about this or any other Sybex book by sending me an email at nedde@wiley.com, or if you think you've found a technical error in this book, please visit http://sybex.custhelp.com. Customer feedback is critical to our efforts at Sybex.

Best regards,

Neil Edde
Vice President and Publisher
Sybex, an Imprint of Wiley

For Jul, my best friend—I love you.

—J.A.P.

Acknowledgments

I want to start by thanking my wife and daughter for their patience while I work on yet another project. You two are the motivation to do all the things that I do. I know that I would not be where I am today if it weren't for the love and support you have given me, whether it is for writing, starting a new company, deciding to remodel the house, or some goofy "computer project" that you don't even want to understand. You both make me laugh on a daily basis. Your smiles, hugs, and laughter are all I need to keep me going at this breakneck pace day after day.

I would like to thank my family for giving me support throughout the writing process. There were times when the typical "let's meet in town for dinner" was not an option as deadlines were looming (and often missed). Mom and Dad always understood and were always more than willing to babysit in a crunch. Brian—thank you for taking my mind out of the book and getting me back to reality with random phone calls and lunches to talk about the important stuff in life, like supercharging my GTO or starting a restoration on a diamond-in-the-rough Camaro.

Professionally, I want to thank my brother Brad. Brad—we've worked on a lot of books together, and we've always talked about going into business together. Throughout everything, you've been a great brother, friend, and business partner, and I can't wait to see where this road leads us. A very big thank-you goes out to Scott Fenstermacher and Robin Wright. Both of these talented authors stepped up to provide some great material, most of which was with very tight deadlines. Both of you are amazing and the book is a better product because of your knowledge and writing ability.

To the Sybex crew—a HUGE thank you. Thanks to Tom Cirtin for going to bat and getting the new edition approved and working with us in the early stages; Pete Gaughan for keeping us on schedule and making sure we were not overloading the other editors' schedules; Jim Kelly for making sure everything is technically accurate; and last but certainly not least, Karen L. Lew. Karen is a master at taking my rambling thoughts and actually making me sound like I can write. I called Karen a showoff for taking a paragraph of mine that was close to 30 words and knocking it down to a 9-word sentence that had more power than my initial attempt.

— John Price

The work that I did on this book wouldn't have been possible if not for the support of my family. DeAnn—you have been very patient and understanding when it comes to my long workdays and weeks away from home. One of these days I am going to repay you for all that you have done for me. To my beautiful daughters, Jami and Becca—you both make me so very proud to be your dad. You were great kids and have you have grown up to be intelligent, kindhearted, and honest adults. You have bright futures ahead of you. To Dad and Mom—thanks for your support through everything. It should come as no surprise that I think the world of you. To John—thanks for being the best friend a brother could have. To the rest of my family—I am glad I can call each and every one of you family.

—Brad Price

First I would like to thank the brothers Price for asking me once again to share the book-writing experience with them. They're a couple of really smart guys, so you would think they'd have learned their lesson by now. And you can't write a book without a great publisher and people like Tom Cirtin, Pete Gaughan, Jim Kelly, and Karen Lew, who make it tick, so a big thanks go out to the entire John Wiley & Sons staff for the too-often thankless job of actually producing the book that you now hold in your hands. It's a task with details beyond my comprehension, so I'll just stick to the easy things, like beta software.

The biggest thanks go out to my wife Lori for being supportive through all these late nights at the computer. Between the endless hours of her own job and the endless hours of managing a family, she has managed to keep things together while I mumble incoherently at operating systems and software products that aren't always what they claim to be (perils of beta software). I owe you big-time, and one of these days I know you're going to make me pay for it.

More thanks go out to the mess-makers of the house, Jaina and Shelby. Sometimes I think my best idea was putting your playroom next to my office so I can see you while I work. I said it in the last book, and the sentiment still holds true: you might not have contributed words to the book or work around the house, but everyday you manage to put a smile on my face without even trying. Now go pick up those toys; they wake me up when I'm sleepwalking.

Of course, I wouldn't be who I am today without the molding at the hands of my parents. To Carol, my mother, the words escape me sometimes, but always know that I am proud to call you Mom. To Craig, my father, I miss you. You taught me lessons about life that I'm still just realizing. Your time with us was too short, but you made every moment count. Happy hunting.

And last but not least, the friends that probably think I'm just naturally not right in the head (usually Linux is involved in those conversations), if for nothing else than simply putting up with me. To Jeff Miller and Ken Ratliff for the constant stream of jobs to do. To Michelle Ingram and Penny Morgan for keeping me entertained with the soap opera. To "Fun Aunt Susan" for always being the voice of encouragement. To Phil Feese for the constant stream of jokes to my inbox. And finally to Jay Howerter, Chris King, Tim O'Brien, Paul Emery, Doug Sims, Darrin Bentley, and Mark Feleccia just for being a great bunch of guys to work with.

—Scott Fenstermacher

About the Authors

John A. Price is the Lead Architect for a Microsoft Gold consulting firm in the Midwest. He has 11 years of experience with several Microsoft products, specializing in Active Directory, Exchange Server, and the System Center line of products.

Brad Price is an MCT with 16 years of experience in the IT field, specializing in Active Directory, Exchange Server, Systems Management Server, and Operation Manager. He is the author of several books on Active Directory.

Scott Fenstermacher holds a degree in Computer Science, along with Microsoft certifications for Systems Engineer, Database Administrator and Solutions Developer. Somewhere in there, he even managed to squeak in a Cisco certification. He has worked with networks from Linux to Novell to Windows, and with programming languages from Assembly to C# and Visual Basic.NET. Prior to his current position as a network engineer for a Fortune 500 software and consulting company, Scott taught classes for a Microsoft CPLS ranging from application and database development to Windows and Linux system administration.

Contents at a Glance

Contents

Introduction

As I contemplate what I am going to say in this introduction, I find myself thinking, "Why would I want to buy this book?" And the first thing that comes to mind is a conversation I had with my acquisitions editor Tom Cirtin over the summer. We were discussing the upcoming release of Windows Server 2008 and an update to the *Mastering Active Directory* book. Just as we have done in the past with this book, we went the route of an all-inclusive Active Directory book rather than highlighting just the changes or new features that Windows Server 2008 brings to the table.

This book is a labor of love. I really do enjoy going through the new material and learning what I can do with an operating system. And I didn't have to go through all of it myself. Truth be told, I am not qualified for some of this, especially the scripting section. C+ programming courses in college told me that I am not a programmer or a scripter; I dreaded those courses. On the front of this book there are three authors listed: Brad Price, John Price, and Scott Fenstermacher. We divided up the chores, with Brad and me writing the core of the book, which includes the designing, planning, managing, and troubleshooting sections, while Scott's scripting expertise was being applied to the final section on scripting.

Who Should Read This Book

Anyone responsible for Active Directory, or at least part of an Active Directory installation, needs to learn the lessons taught in this book. If the title alone intrigued you, this is probably the book for you. These pages provide detailed coverage of Active Directory as it is used in Windows Server 2000, 2003, 2003 R2, and now 2008. The topics covered range from the design options you need to consider before deploying Active Directory to management and troubleshooting.

If you are responsible for the day-to-day operations of Active Directory, this book is for you. If you are responsible for designing a new Active Directory rollout for a company, this book is for you. If you need to learn some troubleshooting tips and want to see how some of the utilities work, this book is for you.

But most important, the final part of this book delves into scripting. Smart administrators know that any shortcut you can take to perform an action is helpful, especially because we usually don't have all the time we would like to perform all of the duties for which we are responsible, let alone for the emergencies that arise. These administrative shortcuts can be as simple as creating a Microsoft Management Console (MMC) that includes all the administrative tools you use regularly so that you don't have to open each administrative tool in its own window, or as involved as writing scripts and batch files that will perform those repetitive tasks.

If you have been hesitant to jump into the scripting side of administration, check out Part 5 of this book, "Streamlining Management with Scripts." It starts with the basics and leads you through the steps to create your very own scripts. Scott has included several examples you can use in your environment. What you learn from Part 5 alone will save you more in administrative costs than this book will set you back.

What's Inside

The first part of this book (Part 1, "Active Directory Design") deals with designing and planning your Active Directory rollout. This part is not geared solely toward Windows Server 2008. As a matter of fact, you could use the book's first five chapters to help you design and plan an Active Directory implementation based on either Windows Server 2003 or Windows Server 2008. If you are already familiar with the Active Directory and are ready to introduce it into your organization, check out the chapters dedicated to design and planning. The information in these chapters will help you build a rock-solid design. You will learn the best method of naming your forest, trees, and domains; how to organize objects using containers and organizational units; and how to plan your Group Policy implementation. The following chapters make up Part 1:

- ◆ Chapter 1: Active Directory Fundamentals

- ◆ Chapter 2: Domain Name System Design

- ◆ Chapter 3: Active Directory Domain Services Forest and Domain Design

- ◆ Chapter 4: Organizing the Physical and Logical Aspects of AD DS

- ◆ Chapter 5: Flexible Single Master Operations Design

The second part and third parts of the book deal with managing your Active Directory implementation once it is in place. The day-to-day operations of Active Directory rely on you knowing how to manage Active Directory objects. In Part 2, "Active Directory Object Management," we start with information about Active Directory objects then introduce ways to manage these objects with organizational units and Group Policy, and we finish with securing these objects. The more you know, the easier it is for you to effectively manage your environment. But even more important, the more you know about the inner workings and interoperability of the features, the easier it will be for you to troubleshoot issues effectively. The following chapters are in Part 2:

- ◆ Chapter 6: Managing Accounts: User, Group, and Computer

- ◆ Chapter 7: Maintaining Organizational Units

- ◆ Chapter 8: Managing Group Policy

- ◆ Chapter 9: Managing Active Directory Security

Active Directory Service Management is the core of the Part 3. With the announcement of Windows Server 2008, Microsoft placed all of its "identity" products under the Active Directory umbrella. This includes Rights Management Services, Certificate Services (thanks to the expertise of Robin Wright), Active Directory Lightweight Directory Services, and Active Directory Federation Services. For this reason we have decided to give service management its own part, "Active Directory Service Management," which consists of the following chapters:

- ◆ Chapter 10: Managing Access with Active Directory Services

- ◆ Chapter 11: Managing Active Directory Rights Management Services

- ◆ Chapter 12: Managing Active Directory Certificate Services

- Chapter 13: Managing the Flexible Single Master Operations Roles

- Chapter 14: Maintaining the Active Directory Database

Part 4 is "Active Directory Best Practices and Troubleshooting." As we all know, there is no perfect operating system. And the more complex the operating system, the more likely the chance of something breaking. Your best friend during a crisis is knowledge. If you possess the necessary troubleshooting skills and tools when something goes wrong, you will be able to fix the problem faster than if you were stumbling around in the dark. The chapters in this part cover the tools at your disposal, and provide tips you'll find useful when faced with problems. The following chapters are in this part:

- Chapter 15: Microsoft's Troubleshooting Methodology for Active Directory

- Chapter 16: Troubleshooting Problems Related to Network Infrastructure

- Chapter 17: Troubleshooting Problems Related to the Active Directory Database

As we have already mentioned, the final part of this book is dedicated to administrative scripting. Scott Fenstermacher has brought his scripting expertise to this part. He did a great job on the last revision of the book, and we asked him to work with us on this version as well, adding a chapter on PowerShell scripting.

Building and understanding how scripts work and how they affect Active Directory can make you stand out in the crowd, as well as make your life easier. Using administrative scripts, you can run a script to create several users, have a script inform users who never log off that their password is about to expire, manipulate a groups membership so only authorized users are members, and much more. Once you're comfortable with the scripting basics and the administrative options, you can move on and use scripts to affect other services, not just Active Directory. Following are the final chapters of the book:

- Chapter 18: ADSI Primer

- Chapter 19: Active Directory Scripts

- Chapter 20: Monitoring Active Directory

- Chapter 21: Managing Active Directory with PowerShell

Final Comments

Throughout the book you will see references to zygort.com. Zygort is the fictional company that we have used in all of the books we have written. We decided to capitalize on the name and use it as a central repository for our Active Directory and Windows Server knowledge.

While our website, `http://zygort.com`, will not duplicate the information from this book, we will post updates to the Active directory information presented in the book. Additionally, we'll use the site as a portal to great new Active Directory information we find. We'll also include other topics that might make your life easier, such as tips for anything from server virtualization to application virtualization to product integration. We understand how fast the computing world changes, and we want to keep you as up-to-date as possible.

So sit back and enjoy this ride into the wondrous adventure known as Active Directory. We hope this book helps you in all of your Active Directory endeavors. And we hope we can minimize the amount of time it takes you to perform administrative tasks. We know how much time administrators put in just to stay on top of things; if this book can make your life a little easier and give you a little more free time, we have done our jobs.

Part 1

Active Directory Design

In this part:

Chapter 1

Active Directory Fundamentals

Since the inception of network operating systems, the men and women who are responsible for administering and managing them have wanted an easy way to do so. Networks have gone through a natural evolution from peer-to-peer networks to directory-based networks. Directory-based networks have become the preferred type of network because they can ease an administrator's workload.

To address the needs of organizations, the Institute of Electrical and Electronics Engineers (IEEE) developed a set of recommendations that defined how a directory service should address the needs of administrators and efficiently allow management of network resources. These recommendations, known as the X.500 recommendations, were originally envisioned to include a large centralized directory that would encompass the entire world, divided by geopolitical boundaries. Even though X.500 was written to handle a very large amount of data, designers reviewing the drafts of these recommendations saw merit in the directory and soon the recommendations were adopted by several companies, including the two best known, Novell and Microsoft.

Active Directory is Microsoft's version of the X.500 recommendations. Battles rage between directory services camps, each one touting its directory service as the most efficient one. Because some of the directory services, such as Novell Directory Services (NDS) and eDirectory, have been around longer than Active Directory, those that are familiar with NDS will attack Active Directory. Their attacks are usually focused on the idea that Active Directory does not perform functions the same way that NDS does.

When it is all said and done, companies that develop X.500-based directory services can interpret the recommendations and implement them to fit their design needs. Microsoft interpreted and employed the X.500 recommendations to effectively manage a Windows-based network. Novell did the same for a Novell-based network, and the two for years have been at odds over which is more efficient. All that notwithstanding, Microsoft has enjoyed great success with Active Directory. It has been adopted by thousands of organizations and will more than likely continue to be used for many years to come.

Do I Need Active Directory?

Active Directory is the database (think of a directory as a collection of information, like a phone book), whereas a domain controller is a single computer or server that controls Active Directory. There are typically multiple domain controllers that host Active Directory.

How do you know if you need Active Directory? There are factors that you should address to determine whether you should defer installation of a domain controller. Following are some of the questions you should ask:

Do I want to centrally manage access to resources such as printers, users, and groups?

Do I want to control user accounts from one location?

Do I have applications that rely on Active Directory?

If you answered "yes" to any of these questions, you undoubtedly will want to take advantage of the features that Active Directory provides. Taking each one of the questions into account, you will find that your life as an administrator will be much easier if you use Active Directory over using no directory service whatsoever. The tools that become available when you implement Active Directory will ease your administrative load, although there is an inherent learning curve associated with any new technology.

If you answered "yes" to the last of the three questions just posed, you have no choice but to implement Active Directory. Most of the Active Directory–enabled applications on the market rely on the installation of a full version of Active Directory within your network. There are some Active Directory–enabled applications that can take advantage of using Active Directory Lightweight Directory Services (AD LDS) –based systems. AD LDS is discussed later in this chapter.

The first two questions relate to something for which administrators have strived over the years. Having one central location to manage users and resources makes an administrator's life easier. If you have to continually move from server to server to administer the resources contained on them, you will spend more time tracking down the resources than you would performing your job. If you have to maintain user accounts on several systems, you must make sure you have an efficient method of cataloging the accounts so that you know where they reside.

With Windows 2000 Server, Windows Server 2003, and now Windows Server 2008, you can use Active Directory Domain Services (AD DS) as the central repository for user, group, and computer accounts as well as for shared folders and printers. Having the ability to manage these resources from any domain controller within your domain allows you to greatly reduce your administrative overhead.

The Basics

When you break it down, Active Directory is a type of database, but one built as a "directory." The difference between a relational database and a directory is that the former is optimized for updating, while the latter is optimized for reading. In this manner, Active Directory was developed with the understanding that the objects contained within the directory would not be changing often, but would be used for users, computers and administrators to control, manage, and discover the organization's resources.

One of Active Directory's most basic functions is that it provides a centralized repository for user account information. When an administrator creates a user account, the account information is held on a domain controller within the domain in which the user resides. All of the domain controllers within the domain will receive an identical copy of the user account so that the user is able to authenticate using any domain controller in the domain.

Any changes to the user account are made on one of the domain controllers and then sent to every other domain controller within the domain. This transfer of data is called *replication*. Replication of information can be a burden on the network, especially in environments with several thousand users, groups, computers, and other objects. To alleviate the replication burden on the network, Active Directory replicates only the attributes that have been changed, and not the entire object.

To get a good understanding of how Active Directory works, you must first understand what the schema is and the role it plays in the directory service. The following section will outline the major roles of the schema.

Schema

The *schema* (i.e., a structured framework or plan) acts as the building blocks of Active Directory, much like DNA molecules are the building blocks for our bodies. Just as our DNA holds all of the information necessary to build our leg, ears, hair, ear hair, etc., the schema holds all of the information needed to create users, groups, computers, and so on within Active Directory. The schema defines how each attribute can be used and the properties associated with the attribute. Take, for instance, a child's toy that we have grown up with: LEGOs. When you first take a look at LEGO bricks, you see hundreds of tiny pieces that really don't seem to represent anything. Some are short, some are long, and some are special shapes. These are the individual pieces, or building blocks, that will go into creating the buildings, cars, airplanes, and dioramas.

The Active Directory schema is pretty much the same thing. If you look within the Active Directory Schema snap-in you will see hundreds of entries that are used when creating objects within Active Directory. As you expand the Active Directory Schema section of the tool, shown in Figure 1.1, you will see the window that contains classes and attributes. The entries known as attributes allow you to create new objects or modify existing objects within your directory.

To add the Active Directory Schema snap-in to a Microsoft Management Console (MMC), you will first need to register the dynamic link library. To do so, open the Run line or use a command prompt on the domain controller and type in `regsvr32 schmmgmt.dll`.

FIGURE 1.1
Active Directory
Schema snap-in

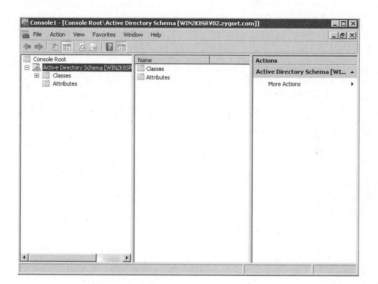

ATTRIBUTES

To standardize Active Directory, the schema defines the attributes that can be used when creating objects. Unlike our LEGO bricks, however, these attributes are defined only once and can be used for any object. Defining the attribute once and using it for multiple objects allows for a standardized approach of defining objects, especially when searching for the attribute. Take the name attribute, for example; whenever an object uses the name attribute you know that the name has to be at least one character in length and cannot exceed 255 characters. You would know this because of the syntax and rules that are applied to the attribute.

The Properties page of the name attribute is shown in Figure 1.2. There is a lot of information within this page, but right now we are interested only in the Syntax and Range area. Notice that the attribute is a Unicode string that has to be at least one character in length and cannot exceed 255 characters. Each attribute within the schema is defined in such a manner, although the syntax for each of the attributes could be different.

The properties for Bad-Pwd-Count are shown In Figure 1.3. This is another attribute that makes up a user object. Notice that the X.500 Object Identifier (OID) is different from that of the name attribute. Each attribute within the schema has to have a unique OID. These are registered and maintained by the Internet Assigned Numbers Authority (IANA). Once assigned, the OID should not be used by any other attribute. Within Active Directory, the default attributes are already assigned OIDs, and those OIDs are protected in a way that will not allow another application to overwrite them.

New attributes will need to be assigned an OID. If you are adding an attribute for use in an object, you should register it with the IANA to safeguard the attribute and to make sure that it does not step on any other attributes. Registration is free, and as long as your OID is unique, you should be issued an OID for your attribute. The attributes that Microsoft uses are all within their own OID range, which starts with 1.2.840.113556. For a complete list of the registered OIDs, visit `http://asn1.elibel.tm.fr/oid/index.htm` and perform a search on the OID. If you have registered an OID, it will appear in this database once the entry is added.

FIGURE 1.2
Name attribute
property page

FIGURE 1.3
Bad-Pwd-Count
attribute
property page

Within an attribute's properties, you will find several check boxes that you can select. Each of them is described in the following list:

Attribute Is Active   You can deactivate attributes that you no longer need within Active Directory. Note that the default attributes cannot be deactivated, nor can attributes that are still in use within an object.

Index This Attribute   If this is an attribute on which you are going to allow searches, you may want to index the attribute to increase the search responsiveness.

Ambiguous Name Resolution (ANR)   When you select this option, you allow a Lightweight Directory Access Protocol (LDAP)–based client to resolve a request when only partial data is available.

Replicate This Attribute to the Global Catalog   Not every attribute needs to reside within the global catalog. The rule of thumb is, if you need to locate an object based on an attribute or if the object's attribute is needed within another domain, you should add it. Otherwise, to reduce the total size of the domain partition you should not add in any superfluous attributes.

Attribute Is Copied When Duplicating a User   When you copy a user account, several attributes are copied from the original account to the new account. If you want the attribute to copy, select the box. Do note that many attributes are unique to a user, so select this option with care.

Index This Attribute for Containerized Searches   If you select this option, the attribute can be indexed for searches within containers, such as organizational units (OUs), in Active Directory.

OBJECT CLASSES

An object class is a defined grouping of attributes that make up a unique resource type. One of the most common object classes is the user class. Use the user object class as the template for a user account. When you create a user account, the attributes that are defined for the user object class are used to define the new account. Information that you populate within the Add User wizard or enter within the dsadd command line become the properties within the attributes.

If we go back for a minute to the LEGO metaphor, you can use some of the brown blocks available to create a roof on a house, some red bricks to make the walls, and tan bricks to make a door. The clear pieces can be used as windows and the white pieces form the porch. Each of these individual items (the bricks, the color of the bricks, the shape of the bricks, and the placement of the bricks) is considered an attribute. Putting these attributes together forms the object class "house." When you build your first house, you have built your first object. Subsequent houses will have the same attributes, but you may build the porch with tan pieces instead of white ones.

So, when I create a user account for Maria, that user account will have unique values stored within the attributes for her user account. Bob's user account will be created using identical attributes, but will not have the same values within each attribute. Maria's phone number may be 555.1234, and Bob's 555.9876.

Not all of the attributes that make up an object class are shown within the administrative tools. Many of them hide behind the scenes and will rarely, if ever, need to be changed. One such attribute is the user's Security Identifier or SID. The user's SID will change when a user is moved from one domain to another, but will not change while the user remains within a domain. The Active Directory Users and Computers management tool does not have the ability to change this attribute. A default set of attribute fields appears within the utilities, and if you decide to make an attribute available for updating, you may need to programmatically add the fields to the utilities.

Attributes are defined as mandatory or optional. Mandatory attributes have to be populated, or the object will not be created. One such attribute is a computer's name. Optional attributes do not necessarily need to have values. Attributes such as Manager within a user object does not need to be populated, but it is always nice to include that information. The more complete the information, the more useful Active Directory becomes.

The Two Sides of AD

Active Directory has both a logical side and a physical side, and each one plays a very important role. The physical side is made up of the domain controllers and physical locations where the domain controllers reside. When you promote a system to domain controller status, you will usually place that domain controller close to the user population that will use it for authentication and access. Domain controllers need to communicate with one another to share the information they have.

The logical side is a little more nebulous; as well as containing the objects that define how the resources are organized and accessed, the logical side contains objects within Active Directory that define how the domain controllers will communicate with one another. Active Directory sites and site links define which domain controllers will replicate directly with each other and which ones will have to communicate indirectly through other domain controllers.

Domains dictate the replication scope. When you create a domain, the domain partition is replicated only to domain controllers from the same domain. The domain partition is not copied to domain controllers outside of the domain. This allows you to partition your directory service and reduce the size of the database file that holds all of the forest's objects. Forests and domains are discussed in greater detail in Chapter 3, "Active Directory Forest and Domain Design."

Organizational units are used to organize objects for easy administration and to manage those objects easily using group policies. To have efficient administration of resources, you should design your Active Directory with administration in mind.

The design of the logical and physical sides of Active Directory is discussed in great detail in Chapter 4, "Organizing the Physical and Logical Aspects of Active Directory." If you are in the process of rolling out Active Directory, be sure to develop a detailed plan for the rollout. Without a good design, Active Directory may not work efficiently for your environment. If your design does not meet the needs of your organization, you may be faced with either suffering through working with an inadequate design or rebuilding your Active Directory infrastructure from the ground up. Neither of these options will sit well with your user base or the management of the company.

What's New in Windows Server 2008?

Windows Server 2003 shipped in the spring of 2003. When released, it was the most advanced network operating system Microsoft had ever developed. The advances that it made over Windows 2000 Server were obvious almost immediately; even though most of the new functionality was seen only by administrators, Microsoft went to great lengths not only to enhance the security and functionality in Windows Server 2003, but also to include additional administrative tools to make an administrator's life easier. And if you know anything about administrators, you know that anything that makes their life easier, they like.

Over the course of the two and a half years from the time Windows Server 2003 shipped and Windows Server 2003 R2 became available, several new technologies developed that Microsoft wanted to take advantage. Also, new codes with patches for new attack vectors that posed security risks to an organization's resources had been developed and needed inclusion.

Several enhancements to Active Directory were included with the R2 release. Those enhancements include Active Directory Application Mode (ADAM)—now known as Active Directory

Lightweight Directory Services (AD LDS), Active Directory Federation Services (AD FS), and Unix Identity Management.

Windows Server 2008 builds on these technologies and incorporates other stand-alone Microsoft products to become the most robust operating system Microsoft has released to date.

What's in a Name?

With the release of Windows Server 2008 and the inclusion of several enhancements to AD, Microsoft has decided to realign all of its "identity" technologies under the Active Directory umbrella. Some items have simply been renamed; other technologies have been moved into the Active Directory Family. With all of these changes, and in typical Microsoft fashion, there are some new names to get familiar with. (These new technologies are discussed in subsequent subsections.)

- ◆ The Active Directory that we've all grown to know and love is now known as Active Directory Domain Services (AD DS). AD DS stores all information about resources on the network, such as users, computers, and other devices.

- ◆ Active Directory Lightweight Directory Services (AD LDS) is the latest version of Active Directory Application Mode (ADAM).

- ◆ Active Directory Federation Services (AD FS) provides Web single sign-on (SSO) technologies to authenticate users to multiple web applications in a single session.

- ◆ Active Directory Rights Management Services (AD RMS) is an information-protection technology that works with RMS-enabled applications to protect and secure information from unauthorized use online and offline, inside and outside of the environment.

- ◆ Active Directory Certificate Services (AD CS) allows the mapping of users and resources to a private key to help secure identity in a Public Key Infrastructure (PKI)-based environment.

Along with renaming and restructuring these technologies, Microsoft (MS) also updated all of the existing Active Directory technologies. Following are some of the major updates to Active Directory:

- ◆ Read -only domain controllers (RODCs) allow organizations to easily deploy a domain controller in locations where physical security cannot be guaranteed.

- ◆ Windows Server Core has introduced a new edition of Windows Server titled "Server Core". Server Core is a Windows 2008 server that is command line–driven and does not possess a GUI.

Active Directory Lightweight Directory Services

Active Directory Lightweight Directory Services (AD LDS) allows administrators to create small versions of Active Directory that run as non–operating system services. Because AD LDS does not run as an operating system service, it does not require deployment on a domain controller. Any workstation or server can host an instance, or multiple instances, of AD LDS. Instead of building a domain controller so that developers have an Active Directory database to work with, you could create an instance of AD LDS on their workstations for them to test against. You could also use it as a repository for data used by a customer-relations management program or an address book directory. If you need a directory to hold data instead of a database, you may want to consider using AD LDS.

One of the biggest benefits of using AD LDS is its administrative benefits. Because AD LDS is a user version of Active Directory, anyone familiar with how to manage objects within Active Directory should be at ease when working with objects in AD LDS. And as in Active Directory, you can control your replication scope and the systems with which you replicate objects. If you have three systems that need to host the directory, you can specify that the AD LDS partitions be hosted on those systems.

Until the release of Exchange 2007, developers were more interested in AD LDS than were most administrators. For developers, the possibilities provided by AD LDS are limited only by imagination. If an application's primary use of data is reading that data and performing queries against that data rather than making mass changes, AD LDS should fit the bill.

Exchange 2007 introduced a new Exchange server role, the Edge Transport role. An Edge Transport server is not a member of your Active Directory domain and usually sits in your demilitarized zone (DMZ). Among other functions of the Edge Transport role, you can configure AD LDS in the DMZ to help facilitate the Active Directory account lookups.

For more information on AD LDS and how to manage it within your infrastructure, turn to Chapter 14, "Maintaining the Active Directory Database."

Active Directory Federation Services

Many organizations are partnering with businesses to efficiently deliver products and services. As businesses form these alliances, there needs to be a secure method of authenticating users from the partners' organizations. Part of the challenge to allowing authentication into your network is the security needed to maintain the connection between partners while keeping hostile entities at bay. In the past, this was possible with several tools and utilities, none of which appeared to work well with each other.

Active Directory Federation Services (AD FS) extends Active Directory to the Internet while guaranteeing the authenticity of the accounts attempting to authenticate. Using this technology will not only enable organizations to work with partner organizations more efficiently; it will also allow interoperability with a with range of applications and platforms, such as Netegrity, Oblix, and RSA, as well as leverage client systems that can utilize Simple Object Access Protocol (SOAP)–based command sets.

When using AD FS, an organization can allow users that exist within separate forests, as well as among partner organizations, to have access to the organization's web applications and use a single sign-on. AD FS is based on the Web Services (WS-*) architecture that is being developed with the cooperation of several companies, including IBM and Microsoft. Chapter 10, "Managing Access with Active Directory Services," will cover managing and maintaining AD FS integration between organizations and within an organization.

Active Directory Rights Management Services

Microsoft released Windows Rights Management Services (RMS) a few years ago. Windows Server 2008 introduces a pretty significant update to this product and has changed the name to Active Directory Rights Management Services (AD RMS).

Chapter 11, "Managing Active Directory Rights Management Services," details AD RMS and all the new features that have been introduced in Server 2008. Previously available as a separate download, AD RMS is now a feature of Active Directory and has been included in the base product.

Active Directory Certificate Services

The Active Directory Certificate Services (AD CS) allow you to create and manage certificates used in environments that employ public-key technologies. AD CS allows you to associate the identity of a person, device, or service to a private key.

AD CS is not a new technology, but it is new to the Active Directory family. This book will dive deep into Certificate Services, as well as highlight the changes that are included in Server 2008.

One of the biggest changes is the addition of Cryptography API: Next Generation (CNG). CNG allows administrators to use custom algorithms with Active Directory, with Secure Sockets Layer (SSL), and with Internet Protocol Security (IPSec). This is accomplished by using the U.S. government's Suite B cryptographic algorithms.

Enhancements such as Online Certificate Status Protocol support, Network Device Enrollment Service, web enrollment, restricted enrollment agent, and PKIView will be discussed in greater detail in Chapter 12, "Managing Active Directory Certificate Services."

Windows Server Core

In keeping with Microsoft's ongoing battle against all things security (whether implied or true), the company has introduced a new type of server for 2008. Windows 2008 Server Core is a Windows server that does not contain a GUI. All administration of Server Core is performed via the command line or via scripting. You may also administer some functions by connecting to Server Core from another server's Microsoft Management Console (MMC) utility.

Server Core was introduced for many reasons:

◆ Reduced maintenance—Server Core installs only what is necessary for the specific server role.

◆ Reduced attack surface—Because Server Core installs only what is necessary for the specific server role, fewer applications are running on the server, and the attack surface is reduced.

◆ Reduced management—Because fewer applications are running on the server, there is less to manage. (Noticing a trend here?)

◆ Less disk space—Server Core can run on less that 5 GB of disk space. Considering that most new servers come standard with 150-plus GB drives now, you may be wondering why this is an advantage of Core Server. Think about what is being done with solid-state drives in the marketplace right now. There may be options for running Server Core on solid-state drives in the very near future.

Read-Only Domain Controller

With the release of Windows Server 2008, Microsoft has introduced the read-only domain controller (RODC). The RODC contains a read-only copy of the Active Directory database that cannot be directly configured. This increases security, especially in areas where the physical security of the domain controller cannot be guaranteed.

A new Domain Name System (DNS) zone was also created to support this new server type. A primary read-only zone contains read-only copies of the domain partition, ForestDNSZones, and DomainDNSZones. More information about the changes to DNS in Windows Server 2008 can be found in Chapter 2, "Domain Name System Design."

Server Manager

At first glance, Server Manager seems to be just another attempt by Microsoft to put some things together that they think would be in our ideal tool chest. I dismissed it in the beginning, but after working with it for a while, it has become one of my favorite new features of Server 2008.

Real World Scenario

RODC IN ACTION

Carlos is an administrator of a small bank with five branch offices. Because of the regulations that banks have to follow, Carlos cannot deploy a domain controller at a remote site unless he can guarantee physical security of the server.

Each of the five branch offices has one room that contains the shared printers, copiers, and all of the office supplies. Carlos decides that this room is the only room he can place the domain controllers.

Carlos installs five new Windows 2008 RODCs on his network, one in each remote branch. This allows Carlos to place domain controllers at the remote site in an unsecured area, and users at the remote sites gain the benefits of having a local domain controller (e.g., faster logon times and faster DNS lookup times).

This functionality is gained by the RODC introducing technologies such as the following:

Read-only AD DS database

Unidirectional replication

Credential caching

Administrator role separation

Read-only DNS

While some of the features are not new, they may be new to the branch office that until now could not host a domain controller.

When you first launch Server Manager, you are greeted with a summary page that displays a high-level summary of the server, the roles on that server, the features that are configured on that server, and resources and support.

We will not get into every component of Server Manager, but we will highlight the Server Manager throughout the book as it relates to Active Directory. You will see that we reference it quite often as we walk through a scenario or discuss steps to perform a task.

As you will see in Figure 1.4, Server Manager contains a wealth of information about your server, specifically in the Reliability and Performance area.

Pre-Design: Microsoft Solutions Framework

When working with any design, make sure you have a good framework from which to work. Throughout the years, Microsoft has identified what it terms the Microsoft Solutions Framework (MSF), which is based on four principles:

Work toward a shared vision.

Stay agile; expect things to change.

Focus on delivering business value.

Foster open communication.

FIGURE 1.4
Server Manager

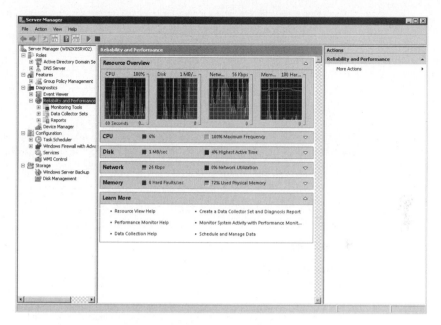

This set of guidelines can be used to control nearly any design and, if used correctly, can help stabilize the operations rollout.

When you adopt MSF, you are taking on a set of principles and models that can aid you in a successful design. When you look at the high-level view of the MSF model, you will see five distinct phases:

Envisioning

Planning

Developing

Stabilizing

Deploying

Each phase within the cycle moves one step closer to the final product, with the Envisioning phase containing the design tasks.

The Envisioning phase can then be broken down into discrete functions, the first of which should be the creation of the design team. This team will be responsible for putting together the initial design specifications and determining if the project should move forward. The roles that will be included within the design team should include individuals within six categories:

Program Management

Product Management

Development

Test

Release Management

User Experience

The Program Management role is responsible for making sure that the project is delivered on time and within budget. The team members that hold this role will need to make sure that they are on top of the overall project and are monitoring the progress. This role becomes the de facto project owner.

The Product Management role is responsible for making sure that the project meets the organization's business needs. The individuals who hold this role are responsible for making sure that the needs of the organization are met and that trade-offs in the plan are handled correctly. They will need to have a good sense of the business and understand what the customers ultimately need.

The Development role needs to have a good technical understanding of the project's design criteria and is responsible for making sure that the technical constraints of the project are met.

The Test role is responsible for making sure that the success criteria of the design is met. The Test role needs to have a good understanding of the business processes and needs to create the milestones that the design must pass to be approved.

Release Management is a role often ignored during the design phase, but it is vital to any technical rollout. The Release Management role is responsible for making sure that the piloting phase of the project moves forward without a problem. If there are problems, the Release Management role can communicate those issues with the rest of the team so that an efficient solution can be devised.

The final role is User Experience. If the users are not happy, your life will not be pleasant. The individuals that hold this role are responsible for making sure that the users' needs are met and that the design will address the need for ease of use.

While each project that goes through the design phase will have these six roles assigned to it, smaller projects may include individuals who are members of more than one team. On larger projects, you may have several members who hold a given role. No matter how many members you have for each role, make sure that the team members can perform the functions for which they are responsible, and that they know what function they are to perform. Set guidelines and, if necessary, train each member so that they have the appropriate skills.

Risk Assessment

Every project has risks involved. Risk is the possibility that you will incur some type of loss. Don't confuse the possibility of loss with the certainty of loss, however. Just because you have identified that a loss could occur doesn't mean that it *will* occur. Many projects have been stopped because nervous program managers and corporate sponsors feared that the project would cause a problem. Instead of pulling the plug on a project, the risk-assessment process should be used so that you have a basis for risk mitigation and management.

If you look at risk assessment as positive instead of negative, you can plan out the requirements to alleviate problems within the project and stop catastrophes from wiping out the budget. However, remember that risk assessment does not stop after you identify the risks. You should continually assess the risks during the entire project life cycle, because you could introduce new risk vectors as you progress.

There are six steps for you to follow during risk assessment and management:

◆ Risk identification—Identify the conditions that could lead to a loss and the ramifications of that loss.

◆ Risk analysis and prioritization—Analyze each risk and determine which risks will be considered the most dangerous or have the highest priority for the design team.

◆ Risk-management planning and scheduling—Develop plans that will address how risks will be controlled.

- ◆ Risk-status tracking and reporting—Continually monitor the process to identify when a risk condition has been triggered.

- ◆ Risk control—Carry out the contingency plans if a risk has been triggered.

- ◆ Risk education—Develop a database of information that will aid in the control of risks in the future.

MICROSOFT SOLUTIONS FRAMEWORK

For more information concerning the Microsoft Solutions Framework, visit `http://www.microsoft.com/technet/solutionaccelerators/msf/default.mspx`.

Once the risk assessment is out of the way, you are ready to begin designing the Active Directory infrastructure. This can be a daunting task to undertake considering there are so many variables to consider. In the next few chapters we will introduce the knowledge necessary to build an effective design.

Coming Up Next

The next few chapters walk you through the criteria for designing a rock-solid Active Directory infrastructure. Without a good design, you will probably not have a stable infrastructure. Of course, everything within an Active Directory environment relies on a solid DNS infrastructure. If your DNS infrastructure is not stable, Active Directory will not be stable and your users will not be happy with the design.

Chapter 2, "Domain Name System Design," outlines the requirements for a viable DNS design that Active Directory can use. The better you understand the design options, the more reliable your infrastructure will be.

Chapter 2

Domain Name System Design

You cannot have Active Directory without having the Domain Name System (DNS) in place. I know that is a blunt way to open, but it is the fundamental basis for this chapter. DNS is required when you implement Active Directory. Although you do not have to run Microsoft's version of DNS, there are many reasons to consider doing so.

You have many options as to how you will implement DNS. You must follow some guidelines to make sure you are taking advantage of the best way to use DNS; failure to do so could cause severe problems with name resolution and Active Directory functionality. Throughout this chapter, we will look at why DNS is required and how you can implement an efficient and secure DNS infrastructure. In Chapter 16, "Troubleshooting Problems Related to Network Infrastructure," we will cover troubleshooting DNS.

In this chapter you will learn the following:

◆ The importance of DNS in Active Directory Domain Services (AD DS)

◆ The different zone types and when to use them

◆ How to protect DNS data and keep them accurate

How DNS and AD DS are Tied Together

When implementing Active Directory within your environment, DNS is required. Active Directory cannot exist without it. The two entities are like trains and railroad tracks. The train's engines are mighty-powerful machines that can pull thousands of tons of equipment, but without the tracks, they cannot move. If the tracks are not aligned correctly, the train may derail. If the tracks are not switched in the right direction, the train will not arrive at the correct destination.

If you haven't immersed yourself in the finer details of DNS, now is the time. If you think you understand how DNS works, you should still review all of the new options that have been added to the DNS service in Windows Server 2003 (including R2) and Windows Server 2008. Where Windows 2000 added some fancy new features into the Microsoft DNS world (such as support for dynamic updates and service locator [SRV] records), Windows Server 2003 upped the ante even more with support for stub zones and the ability to use application directory partitions for Active Directory–integrated zones.

As we mentioned previously, you are not required to use Microsoft's implementation of DNS; UNIX BIND (Berkeley Internet Name Domain) DNS will work just fine as long as it meets certain criteria. As a matter of fact, several companies are already invested deeply in a BIND DNS solution and are not about to completely restructure with a new DNS implementation. As the old saying goes, don't fix what isn't broken. We will look at using BIND within your infrastructure later in this chapter.

Looking at the correlation between your Active Directory and DNS, you will find the two share the same zone-naming conventions. If your Active Directory domain name is zygort.1c1, the DNS namespace will also be zygort.1c1. Notice that the top-level domain (TLD) name for DNS, in this case 1c1, does not have an equivalent domain within Active Directory. That is because, for most companies, the top-level domain is not unique and is not owned by the company. Take for instance a company that is using widgets.com as its Active Directory namespace. The TLD used in this case (com) is owned by the Internet Corporation for Assigned Names and Numbers (ICANN) and is shared by hundreds of thousands of Internet-based websites. When designing Active Directory, the designers decided to make sure that the root of the Active Directory forest could be unique; they required the domain names to take on two domain components: the company's DNS domain and the TLD that it resides under.

As a domain controller comes online, part of its startup routine is to attempt registration of the SRV records that identify the services that are running on the domain controller. The only requirement for a DNS server to work with Active Directory is that the DNS server support SRV records. It does not matter to Active Directory clients if the records are entered manually by an administrator or automatically by the domain controller itself; all that matters is that the records are correct. If the SRV records are not listed within the zone or are entered incorrectly, the client will not be able to locate the domain controller. If the SRV records are correctly listed within the DNS zone, the host name of the server that is providing the service is returned to the client. The client will then query the DNS server for the A record (hostname record) of the domain controller to resolve the IP address.

Resolving the IP Address

The most basic of all DNS services provide the ability for a client system to send a query to the DNS server, asking it to return the IP address of a host system. This type of resolution is referred to as *forward name resolution*. DNS provides this functionality by hosting resource records that specify the IP address for each of the host systems within the DNS namespace. The namespace is referred to within the DNS server as the *zone*. For instance, if your DNS namespace is zygort.1c1, and you have a server named APFS01 with an IP address of 192.168.29.75, your zone name would be zygort.1c1 and the server would have a resource record that tied the name APFS01 to IP address 192.168.29.75. When a client sent a query to the DNS server looking for APFS01.zygort.1c1, the DNS server would reply to the query with a response containing the IP address.

This is the most fundamental purpose of DNS, and probably the most utilized function—finding an IP address when a client sends a query. There is another resolution type known as *reverse name resolution*. Reverse name resolution allows a client to query for a host name when it knows the IP address of the system in question. This works in much the same way as the caller ID system on your telephone. When you receive a phone call, the phone number corresponds to a "friendly" name that you may recognize. Since it is much easier to remember names than a long numbers, this makes it much easier for you to determine exactly who is calling. If a name is not associated with the phone number, then only the phone number will appear. There are several programs and utilities that use reverse name resolution, and you may find it beneficial to make sure you have the correct information included within the zone.

DNS servers will resolve queries within the zones that are configured on them. You can have more than one zone on a server, and the server will accept and respond to queries for records in those zones. When a client sends a query for a zone that is not hosted on the DNS server, the DNS server has to perform additional tasks to respond correctly to the client. The DNS server will search all the way to the top of the DNS hierarchy, known as the *root*, for help. These root DNS servers are listed within the Root Hints tab of the DNS server's properties page. The DNS server will send a query of its own to one of these root servers, asking for resolution. The root servers will refer the DNS server to the appropriate TLD DNS server. The DNS server will then query the TLD DNS server for assistance. The TLD server will refer the DNS server to the appropriate second-level domain DNS server. This process will continue until a DNS server with the resource record resolves the request, either with a successful lookup or a failed one.

There are problems that can be encountered with the typical DNS resolution methods. First off, not every namespace is accessible from the Internet. Our zygort.lcl is a prime example of that. If you were to perform a lookup on a server name within that namespace using conventional DNS methods, the lookup would fail. There needs to be another method of resolving the DNS queries for these zones. The other problem lies with companies that do not want their DNS servers to query outside of their organization. Because DNS servers look to the root of the Internet as the de facto starting point for name resolution, in this case you need a way to keep them from doing so. New options have been introduced to address these issues.

Windows 2000 DNS servers introduced *forwarders* to the Microsoft DNS world. Using forwarders, you can specify another DNS server that will attempt to resolve queries when the local DNS server cannot. By default, a DNS server will use the DNS servers that are configured within the Root Hints tab of the DNS server's properties page. If your DNS server cannot reach the root servers or if you want to control the servers that perform the iterative queries from your organization, you can enter the server's IP address within the Forwarders tab on the properties sheet for the DNS server. Once configured, the queries that cannot be resolved by the DNS server will be sent to the first DNS server listed in the Forwarders tab.

Sometimes when you define a forwarder, the DNS server identified as the forwarder will have to take on the task of resolving all the queries outside of the DNS server's zones. This can be a considerable amount of traffic. Another problem occurs when the forwarder does not have the ability to query for certain zones. Windows Server 2003 introduced another method of forwarding: *conditional forwarding*. Using conditional forwarding, you can specify a DNS server that will be used to resolve queries based on the domain name in question. For example, if a user needs to resolve an address for zygort.local and if a conditional forwarder is created for the zygort.local domain, the DNS server will send a recursive query to the server specified within the forwarder setting. Figure 2.1 shows conditional forwarders configured for the zygort.local zone.

For more information on conditional forwarding, see the TechNet article 304991 at http://support.microsoft.com/default.aspx?kbid=304491&product=winsvr2003.

Another item to note: if a DNS server is configured as the root server for the organization, you cannot configure it to forward requests to another DNS server. If you have a DNS server configured to forward requests to another DNS server, simply delete the root zone from the DNS server, which is specified by the dot (.), as seen in Figure 2.2. In the case of a Windows 2003 or Windows 2008 server, the root zone is designated by .(root), as seen in Figure 2.3. Once the root zone is deleted, you can enter external root servers into the root hints and can configure forwarders.

This "root zone" behavior does not occur within a Windows Server 2008 DNS server when you promote the first domain controller. This doesn't mean that you need let Dcpromo install the DNS service; you could configure the DNS zone first and then promote the domain controller. Doing so will allow you to configure the zone the way you want and then allow the domain controller to register. There are other considerations to take into account if you create the zone first when promoting the first domain controller for your forest, and we will discuss those options later in the chapter. First and foremost, if you create the zone manually, make sure that you configure the zone for dynamic updates; otherwise you will receive an error message stating the domain is not configured.

FIGURE 2.1
Conditional
forwarders

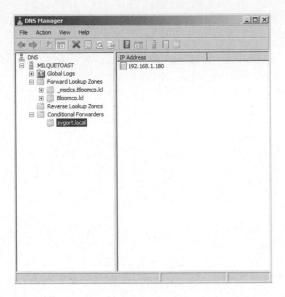

FIGURE 2.2
Root zone in
Windows 2000

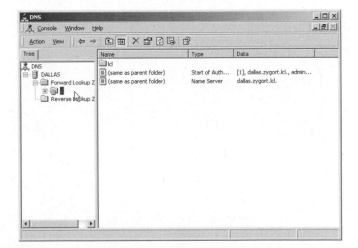

Selecting a Zone Type

For every zone that you use, you will need to determine how you will configure the DNS servers to use it. There are three main zone types within Windows Server 2003 and Windows Server 2008: primary, secondary, and stub. The data for the zone can be contained within a file on the system drive of the DNS server and read into memory at startup, or it can be held in Active Directory. The former option is known as a standard zone type, which uses zone transfers as a means of sending the data to other DNS servers that host the zone. The latter is known as Active Directory–integrated and uses Active Directory replication to send the data. Of the three zone types, you have the choice of making primary and stub zones Active Directory–integrated; however, secondary zones cannot be Active Directory–integrated. Each of them has its place within your infrastructure, but knowing when to choose one over the other can be confusing.

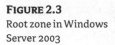

FIGURE 2.3

Root zone in Windows
Server 2003

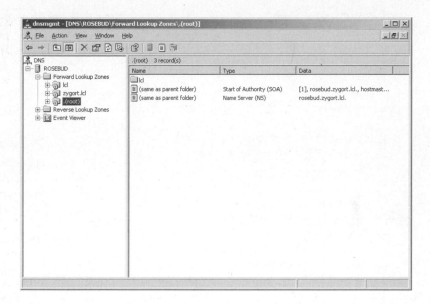

PRIMARY ZONES

Primary zones have traditionally been held on a single system and are known in the Microsoft world as *standard primary zones*. Primary zones are the update points within DNS. The limitation to these zones is their inherent single point of failure. Although the zone data can be transferred to another server that acts as the secondary zone, if the server that holds the primary zone is unavailable, you cannot make changes to the zone. In this case, you must promote a secondary zone to primary if you need to make updates to the zone.

Another limitation to standard primary zones stems from the single update point. When using clients that support dynamic DNS updates, the only server in the zone that can receive the updates is the one holding the primary zone. Whenever a dynamic DNS client comes online, it queries its preferred DNS server for the start of authority (SOA) record for the zone in which it is preparing to register. The SOA record informs the client of the server that is authoritative for the zone. The client then sends the dynamic DNS registration information to the server holding the primary zone. This is not a problem unless the server with which the client is registering is across a slow or overconsumed WAN link. The additional DNS registration traffic may become too cumbersome. In addition, the same data then has to travel back across the WAN link if a server holding the secondary zone requires a zone transfer.

This situation has led administrators to create subdomains within the DNS hierarchy to support the remote locations. In this manner, the remote locations have their own DNS servers to hold their primary zones, with the parent domain holding delegation records to the subdomain. Clients within the zone register locally, and the only data that needs to be sent across the WAN link are the queries for zone information and zone transfers if a secondary zone is configured on another server.

However, this scenario has two problems: you may not have an administrative staff in place at the remote locations, and query traffic could consume more bandwidth on the WAN link than the registration traffic would. So what is an administrator to do?

Besides evaluating the traffic that would be generated from either of the two scenarios to determine which will be the lesser of two evils, you could break away from the archaic DNS methodologies and start using the new-and-improved Microsoft DNS technologies. Using Active Directory–integrated zones greatly enhances your DNS infrastructure. Gone are the days of having one update point and tedious zone transfers. (Do I sound like a salesman yet?)

Active Directory–integrated primary zones store the zone records within Active Directory. Any Active Directory–integrated DNS server can then use these records. The domain controllers that hold the data will replicate changes amongst one another. This allows for any of the Active Directory–integrated DNS servers to be updated and the updates replicated to every other Active Directory–integrated DNS server. Later in this chapter, we will discuss the replication options that are available once you configure a zone as Active Directory–integrated.

Primary Read-Only Zones

With the introduction of the read-only domain controller (RODC), Windows Server 2008 also introduced the primary read-only zone.

An RODC with a primary read-only zone configured will receive a read-only copy of the following application directory partitions in the domain:

◆ The domain partition

◆ ForestDNSZones

◆ DomainDNSZones

This allows the secure RODC to have a very secure read-only copy of the DNS information in the domain. From the RODC, you can view the contents of the primary read-only zone, but you can make changes to only the zones that are located on DNS servers that host the primary zones.

SECONDARY ZONES

Secondary zones have been around as long as primary zones. When an administrator wanted another DNS server to host the same zone information as the primary zone, a secondary zone would be created, which would host identical information as on the primary zone. The zone data within a secondary zone is a read-only copy of the primary zone database.

Secondary zones still have their place within an organization. If you have a remote location where you do not want to support a domain controller but you want to provide local resolution to the clients, you can create a secondary zone on a server within that location. This will reduce the amount of query traffic that has to pass across the WAN link, but you will be required to send zone transfers from a master server across the WAN link to the secondary zone. Typically, there will be more queries sent by clients than there will be dynamic updates from clients. Even so, you should monitor the traffic that is passing across the WAN link to determine if you are using the link appropriately.

STUB ZONES

Although the name may sound a little strange, it does perfectly describe this zone type. Stub zones do not contain all of the resource records from the zone, as the primary and secondary zone types do. Instead, only a subset of records populates the zone, just enough to provide the client with the information necessary to locate a DNS server that can respond to a query for records from the zone.

When you create the stub zone, it is populated with the SOA record along with the NS records and the A records that correspond to the DNS servers identified on the SOA record. All this is done automatically. The administrator of the zone is not required to create the SOA, name server (NS), or A records. Instead, as the zone is created, the DNS server will contact a server that is authoritative for the zone and request a transfer of those records. Once populated, the DNS server holding the stub zone will contact the authoritative server periodically to determine if there are any changes to the SOA, NS, and A records. You can control how often the DNS server requests updates by configuring the refresh interval on the SOA record for the zone.

As a client queries the DNS server to resolve the IP address for a host, the DNS server is going to attempt to locate the A record for the host name. If the DNS server is configured with a stub zone for the domain name contained within the query, the DNS server will send an iterative query directly to an authoritative DNS server for the zone. In Figure 2.4, you will find the common query path that is taken when a client is trying to resolve an address. In this case, the client is trying to locate `server1` `.dallas.bloomco.com`. When the client in `chicago.zygort.com` sends the recursive query to its DNS server, the DNS server will "walk the tree" by sending iterative queries to DNS servers along the path to eventually get to a DNS server that is authoritative for `dallas.bloomco.com`.

In Figure 2.5, we have configured the same server with a stub zone for `dallas.bloomco.com`. When the client sends the recursive query to its DNS server, the DNS server has a zone listed within its database that lets it know which servers to contact when trying to locate `dallas.bloomco.com`. The DNS server can then send a single iterative query to the authoritative server and then send the result back to the client, thereby making the resolution process far more efficient.

Thus you might ask, "Why not use a conditional forwarder instead of the stub zone?" There are two reasons why you would want to use a stub zone instead of a conditional forwarder. First, the stub zone has automatic updating features. When the refresh interval on the SOA record is reached, the server holding the stub zone will contact an authoritative server for the zone and update the list of name servers and their associated addresses. Conditional forwarders rely on administrative staff to keep them updated. Second, conditional forwarders will require more processing power to perform the logic of evaluating the conditions to determine which one matches. Stub zone information is held within the DNS database and can be parsed far more quickly.

FIGURE 2.4
Standard name
resolution

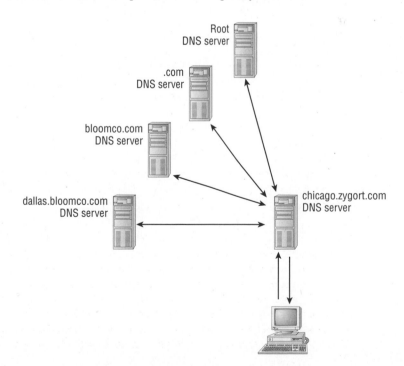

FIGURE 2.5
Name resolution
using a stub zone

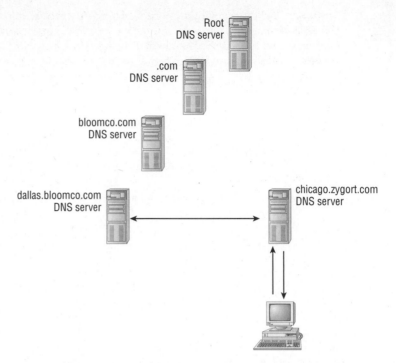

For more information on conditional forwarding and stub zones, see the Microsoft webcast at `http://support.microsoft.com/default.aspx?kbid=811118&product=winsvr2003`.

GLOBALNAMES ZONE

I still remember when Active Directory was introduced with Windows 2000. A lot of consultants and sales people were touting the fact that if you migrate completely to Active Directory and do not have any Windows NT or Windows 9x clients on your network, you can safely rid yourself of Windows Internet Name Service (WINS).

It is now 2008, and WINS is still widely used, even in environments that do not have a single NT or 9x server. These companies like the fact that you can have a collection of static, global records with single-label names. Without WINS, this was not possible.

For those people wanting to move to an all-DNS environment, the GlobalNames DNS zone comes to the rescue. The GlobalNames zone holds single-label names. This zone can then be replicated to other DNS servers in the network, alleviating the typical problems inherent with the WINS push-pull technology.

How to Name a Zone

Determining what to name your zone can be difficult. The name should be descriptive enough to be easily remembered while short enough that it is not too difficult to type. Even though it may sound fun, you will not want to have `supercalifragilisticexpialidocious.com` as a domain name. Or if you do, your users will probably want to torture you for torturing them. If you are using any other DNS servers within your environment besides Windows DNS server, you should follow the DNS naming guidelines, as set forth in RFC 952. This document spells out the characters that can be used within a DNS implementation. Any character within the American National Standards Institute (ANSI) character set is legal to use. You have the option of using any of the following:

◆ Uppercase letters A–Z

◆ Lowercase letters a–z

◆ Numerals 0–9

◆ Hyphen (-)

Other rules:

◆ Every name should start with a letter, not a number.

◆ Names cannot contain spaces.

◆ The period (.) is used as a delimiter between subdomains.

◆ Names should not end with a dash.

◆ Single-character names are not allowed.

However, if your network uses only Windows-based DNS servers or other DNS implementations that support extended character sets, you can use extended characters from the UTF-8 character set. This includes the underscore (_) character that is so popular amongst Windows NT administrators. During migration from Windows NT to Windows 200x, you will not have to rename computers that use an underscore in their name in order for them to be added to the DNS zone. This keeps you from having a domain named `chi-corp.zygort.lcl` as the DNS name, and `CHI_CORP` as the domain's NetBIOS name. Be wary, however. If you have any DNS servers that cannot handle the extended character set, you will receive errors during zone transfers when using UTF-8 characters.

 **Real World Scenario**

MOVING AWAY FROM WINS

Planning to decommission your current WINS environment is easier than ever before. After you config-ure the GlobalNames zone and set the replication scope, you are ready to move away from your existing WINS environment.

From the DNS client side, there is a slight difference in how the name resolution process occurs; how-ever, you will not need to make any changes or updates to your DNS clients to take advantage of this functionality.

When a client requests a single-label name, the client's DNS suffix is added to the request and the request is submitted to the local DNS server. If the fully qualified domain name (FQDN) does not resolve, then the client's DNS suffix search list is submitted with the request. If that fails, the request is sent using the single-label name, and the GlobalNames zone is checked for a match. If this fails, the request is handed over to WINS.

You must register your Internet presence with an Internet registration authority so that you are ensured of owning your domain name. If you do not register your domain name, another company could register it and use it. Even if you do not plan to use the name on the Internet, register it so that it is reserved in case you ever do need an Internet presence.

Internal and External Name Options

Basically, you have two options when you are choosing internal and external namespaces for your organization: using different namespaces or using the same namespace. Each of the options presents its own trials and tribulations for administrators, so take the time to plan which method you will implement. Making changes to an existing namespace is a nightmare that you probably do not want to go through. You should make sure that you design your DNS/Active Directory namespace to support your organization's business needs as well as security requirements.

Keeping Internal and External Names Separate

If you have determined that your organization will need an Internet presence, you need to determine the name with which you will be identified. Your name should identify your company. Users who are accessing your external resources should find your name easy to understand. One guideline is to make your name short yet understandable. The easier it is to remember and type, the easier it will be for users to return to your site. The name zygort.com is much easier to remember and type than zygort-manufacturing-inc.com. Plus, if you are using a subdomain as your internal name, the longer the external DNS name is, the longer the internal namespace will be as you append the subdomain. Users will not appreciate having to enter **accountspayable.accounting.corp.zygort.lcl**.

To keep your internal resources hidden from external users, make the internal namespace different from the Internet namespace. If you want to keep the two namespaces separate, you can make the internal domain name a child domain from the Internet namespace or have two completely different namespaces.

COMPLETELY SEPARATE NAMESPACES

Using a completely separate namespace can help protect your internal infrastructure by having records for external resources stored within the external DNS servers while keeping internal resource records local to internal DNS servers. By hiding your DNS namespace in such a manner, you do not have as much to worry about when it comes to attackers trying to find out how your Active Directory infrastructure is configured.

There are two methods that administrators will use when creating a separate namespace: public namespaces and private namespaces.

Public namespace   When a company uses a public namespace, it will use one namespace that is generally known by the public, and another not made readily available to external users. For instance, a company may have registered zygort.com and zygort.org. Using the zygort.com namespace for the external namespace and zygort.org as the internal namespace keeps the two separate. As long as the internal resources are not registered within the DNS servers that are publicly accessible, the Active Directory infrastructure should be relatively secure.

Private namespace   Let's say the company is using zygort.com as its external namespace. By using an internal namespace of zygort.lcl, none of the resources within the zygort.lcl namespace are accessible from the Internet by default. An administrator would have to configure additional mechanisms for the Active Directory infrastructure and internal resources to be made available externally.

DELEGATING A SUBDOMAIN

Another naming scheme is to create a subdomain beneath the company's Internet presence. While this method does not protect the internal resources as efficiently as a private namespace, you can effectively use the "security by obscurity" method. In other words, if a company uses an external namespace of zygort.com and an internal namespace of internal.zygort.com, the internal namespace should not be available within the external DNS servers. Even if you never add any delegation records to the Internet domain so that the internal domain name is available from the Internet, you will still be using a domain name structure that will make sense to your users. If you decide to make the internal domain accessible, you can add a delegation record to the DNS servers that are used for your Internet presence or create a subdomain to allow specific servers to be accessed.

Internal and External Name Confusion

Using the same name for your internal infrastructure that you are using to identify your organization on the Internet can be very time-consuming and confusing. While users will not have any problem remembering just a single namespace, the administrative staff will have an increased workload to allow users the ability to access both internal and external resources.

A basic rule to protect your resources is to not allow external entities to discover your internal resources. If you want to use the same namespace internally as well as externally, you will have to use two completely different zones with the same namespace to guarantee that they will not share any zone information. Otherwise, zone transfers or Active Directory replication will populate the DNS servers that the external clients use with information about your internal network. Letting anyone outside of your organization access this information is not a good thing.

Therein lies the problem. How do you allow internal clients the ability to access resources outside of your internal infrastructure? For each of the web servers, SMTP servers, and any other server that is part of your Internet presence, you will have to manually enter the records into your internal DNS zones. If anything changes, you must make sure that you update the records accordingly. Missing any updates or forgetting to enter records for resources that the users need to access will cause plenty of phone calls to come your way!

Understanding the Current DNS Infrastructure

DNS has been around for many years, and chances are you already have DNS within your infrastructure. You'll have to determine if your current DNS implementation will support your needs. After all, what works for the Unix or Novell side of your network may not work the best for Active Directory. Case in point: DNS is normally a single-master database. This means that updates and entries into the database can be made on only one server—the server holding the primary zone. Every other DNS server that holds a copy of the zone will use secondary zone types that contain read-only copies of the zone database. In order for clients who support dynamic update to enter their resource records within the database, they have to be able to contact the DNS server that hosts the primary zone. This is an inefficient method of using DNS.

Unix and Novell DNS solutions already in place may not support the Active Directory requirements. At the very least, your DNS has to support SRV records as recorded in RFCs 2052 and 2782. If it doesn't, Active Directory–aware clients will not find Active Directory domain controllers. The best environment would be to have a DNS server that not only supports SRV records, but that also supports dynamic updates as recorded in RFC 2136. If the DNS server does not support dynamic updates, you will have to manually enter the correct information for the domain controllers, which will include all of the SRV records that are found within the NETLOGON.DNS file that is created when the domain controller is promoted. Doing so could be a time-consuming, boring task.

After determining if the current DNS servers will support Active Directory, take a look at where the DNS servers are located, and the client population they serve. You probably retain DNS functionality at those locations. You should also determine whether you want to place DNS servers in locations that are not supported by local DNS servers. Ask yourself if the clients would be better served by having a local DNS server. The answer will be based on the difference between the queries made by the clients and the zone replication between DNS servers. In a large zone, you may have a large amount of zone-transfer data, so you need to weigh that against the numbers of queries the clients are making. Use a network-monitoring tool such as Microsoft's Network Monitor or McAfee's Sniffer to analyze the data that is traveling through your network links to determine the source of the majority of the data.

That Other DNS Server

What do you do if another division is responsible for the DNS infrastructure? Some companies have a complete division of responsibilities, and the DNS servers may not be under your control. People are very possessive of the things they manage, and you may find yourself fighting to get the support you need to implement Active Directory.

The Windows-based DNS service was designed to interoperate with the latest DNS standards. It was also designed to support additional features that are available only to a Microsoft DNS implementation. These additional features are beneficial to administrators who want to have easier administration and additional security options.

Because of Windows Server 2008's compliance with DNS standards, it will interoperate with Berkeley Internet Name Domain (BIND) DNS servers running BIND versions 9.4, 9.1.0, 8.2, 8.1.2, and 4.9.7. Windows Server 2008 DNS is also fully compliant with Microsoft Windows NT 4's DNS service.

As you will note in Table 2.1, Windows Server DNS service and BIND 9.4 support some important DNS features. Other versions of DNS do not support all of the options.

TABLE 2.1:   DNS Features Supported on Multiple Platforms

	SRV RECORDS	DYNAMIC UPDATES	INCREMEN- TAL ZONE TRANSFER	STUB ZONES	CONDITIONAL FORWARDING
Windows Server 2008	x	x	x	x	x
Windows Server 2003	x	x	x	x	x
Windows 2000	x	x	x		
Windows NT 4			x		
BIND 9.4	x	x	x	x	x
BIND 9.1.0	x	x	x	x	x

TABLE 2.1: DNS Features Supported on Multiple Platforms *(CONTINUED)*

	SRV RECORDS	DYNAMIC UPDATES	INCREMEN-TAL ZONE TRANSFER	STUB ZONES	CONDITIONAL FORWARDING
BIND 8.2	x	x	x		
BIND 8.1.2	x	x			
BIND 4.9.7	x				

Additional features are present in a Windows Server DNS environment that are not supported by other DNS servers. Table 2.2 presents a list of additional features.

TABLE 2.2: DNS Features Not Supported on Non-Windows Platforms

	SECURE DYNAMIC UPDATES	WINS INTEGRATION	UTF-8 CHARACTER ENCODING	ACTIVE DIRECTORY—INTEGRATED ZONES	APPLICA-TION DIRECTORY SUPPORT	OBSOLETE-RECORD SCAVENGING
Windows Server 2008	x	x	x	x	x	x
Windows Server 2003	x	x	x	x	x	x
Windows 2000	x	x	x	x		x
Windows NT 4		x				
BIND 9.1.0						
BIND 8.2						
BIND 8.1.2						
BIND 4.9.7						

When attempting to integrate Windows Server 2008 DNS into an existing environment, take into account the interoperability. If the existing infrastructure does not support some of the features you need, you may be forced to upgrade the current infrastructure to Windows Server 2008 DNS.

In many companies, a DNS infrastructure is already controlled by a DNS group. If this group is unwilling to relinquish control of DNS or will not allow you to implement your own Windows

Server 2008 DNS server, you may be forced to use the existing DNS services. Some organizations do have separate divisions that are responsible for specific portions of the network infrastructure. If you are not allowed to implement DNS because of departmental standards and regulations, you will be forced to use what the DNS administrative staff dictates. Be aware of the requirements for Active Directory, however. You may need to convince others to upgrade their existing servers to handle the service locator (SRV) records and dynamic updates that Active Directory uses. (If AD is mandated "from above," there may simply be no room for argument with the administrative staff; you'll have to get upper management to enforce a policy change.)

Propagating the Changes

To have an effective DNS solution, you need to make sure that the clients have access to a local DNS server. To have DNS servers close to the clients, you will probably need to propagate the zone data to DNS servers in several locations. This is accomplished by using zone transfers.

Zone transfers come in two flavors: *authoritative zone transfers (AXFRs)* and *incremental zone transfers (IXFRs)*. An AXFR, sometimes referred to as a complete zone transfer, transfers the entire zone database when the zone transfer is initiated. An IXFR, as defined in RFC 1995, transfers the changes in the zone only since the last zone transfer. The amount of data that is transferred during an IXFR could be substantially less than that of an AXFR.

The choice to use zone transfers is usually made because the DNS servers in your environment are not Windows 200x–based. Third-party DNS servers do not participate in Active Directory replication, nor can they read the Active Directory database to determine the resource records that are used. To keep the network usage as low as possible, make sure the DNS servers all support IXFR. Otherwise, every time a zone transfer is initiated, the complete zone records will be passed to all of the appropriate DNS servers.

Active Directory–integrated zones can take advantage of Active Directory replication to propagate the changes made to resource records. When you use Active Directory replication, not only do you have the additional benefit of having only one replication topology, but the amount of data usually passed across the network is smaller. For instance, take a record that changes a couple of times before the replication or zone transfer occurs. In the case of a zone transfer, if the record changes twice before the transfer is initiated, both changes have to be sent even if some of the data is no longer valid. In the case of Active Directory replication, only the effective changes are replicated. All of the intermediate changes are discarded.

You also gain the advantage of the built-in functionality of replication. Replication traffic between domain controllers is compressed to reduce network overhead. This is significant when you consider an environment where you have multiple sites, many of which could be connected through WAN links. If there are considerable amounts of zone information to be transferred, the replication traffic that is sent between domain controllers in different sites is compressed.

Active Directory–integrated zones boast the benefit of being able to share the responsibility of updating the zone, whether it is from dynamic DNS clients or via manually entered records. The single point of administration and single point of failure disappear. There are, however, limitations to using Active Directory–integrated zones.

First, you can create an Active Directory–integrated zone only on a DNS server that is also a domain controller (and yes, a read-only domain controller counts). At a location where you do not want to place a domain controller, you will not be able to take advantage of Active Directory–integrated zones on a DNS server. Of course, if you do not have enough clients to warrant placing a domain controller at that location, you probably will not have dynamic update client issues either.

The second limitation is only of Windows 2000 domain controllers, and is typically not a problem with Windows Server 2003 or 2008 domain controllers. The zone data is replicated to every domain controller within the domain. Active Directory replication is far more efficient than zone transfers, but there are still some problems with replicating changes. Windows 2000 domain controllers will replicate changes only to other domain controllers within the same domain, and that replication goes out to all domain controllers, not just those that are DNS servers.

Windows Server 2003 made Active Directory–integrated zones more efficient; at the same time, using the zones gave the administrators a little more to think about. Active Directory–integrated zones within a Windows Server 2003 or 2008 environment do not hold the zone data within the domain partition; instead, a separate application directory partition is used. An application directory partition does not rely on any specific domain within Active Directory, and it can be replicated to any domain controller in the forest. If you look at the partitions within a Windows Server 2003 or 2008 domain controller, you will find the typical partitions (Schema, Configuration, and Domain), and you will also find application directory partition for the forest and domain.

When you create an Active Directory–integrated zone on a Windows Server 2003 or 2008 domain controller, you have the option of determining the scope of replication for the zone. Four options are available, as seen in Figure 2.6:

◆ Replicating to all DNS servers in the forest

◆ Replicating to all DNS servers within a domain

◆ Replicating to all domain controllers within the domain

◆ Replicating to all domain controllers defined in the replication scope of a DNS application directory partition

If you choose the first option—replicating to only DNS servers within the forest—every DNS server within the forest will receive the DNS zone information. The zone information will be held within an application partition. This will cause the most replication because every DNS server within the forest will hold the records for the zone, but the only domain controllers that will receive the data will be those that host the DNS service. You cannot have any Windows 2000–based domain controllers in this scenario.

The second option—replicating to only DNS servers within the domain—will reduce the amount of replication traffic because only the domain controllers that are DNS servers for the domain in question will hold a copy of the domain records. As with the previous option, the zone is stored in an application partition. Again, as with the previous option, you cannot have any Windows 2000–based domain controllers within the domain.

The third option—replicating to all domain controllers within the domain—essentially makes all domain controllers within the domain behave as if they are Windows 2000 domain controllers. Every domain controller, whether or not it is a DNS server, will hold the data for the zone. If you still have some Windows 2000–based domain controllers that are DNS servers, this is the option you will choose.

The final option—replicating to all domain controllers defined in the replication scope of a DNS application directory partition—is also an option that is only available to Windows Server 2003 and higher domain controllers. Using an application directory partition, you can choose which of the domain controllers will host a copy of the partition. In this manner, you can control exactly which domain controllers that are also DNS servers will host the zone data. If you do not want to replicate the zone to a server that is across a WAN, you will not have to replicate it.

FIGURE 2.6
Replication scope
options

Protecting DNS

DNS has been a popular service to attack because so many clients rely on it to locate the host systems they are attempting to contact. Without DNS, you would not be able to locate www.microsoft.com. You could call the web server by its IP address, but how many of us have the IP address of the server memorized?

Two methods of attack are usually attempted against DNS servers: denial-of-service (DoS) attacks, and abusing the name resolution. Earlier in this chapter I used an analogy that compared DNS to train tracks. When someone attacks DNS, they are essentially attempting to derail or misguide our trains by adversely affecting the tracks. With denial-of-service attacks, the attacker attempts to block the DNS server from answering client queries, thereby derailing the clients. When abusing the name resolution that a DNS server provides, the attacker either will cause the DNS server to return incorrect results to the client or will gather information about a company from the data that the DNS server returns. This method does not stop the DNS service from responding to the clients; it simply misdirects them, sending them to the wrong destination.

Understanding just how important DNS is to a company's infrastructure, the designers of DNS built the service be redundant and able to withstand attacks that attempt to take down the DNS servers that support a company. Nevertheless, some attackers will try to knock down your DNS so that they can reduce the effectiveness of your implementation, annoy your clients as they attempt to perform their jobs, and just plain dampen your spirits. Denial-of-service attacks can be devastating, but you can take steps to put yourself at ease. The following sections cover practices you should take into account when you are designing your DNS infrastructure. You may not need to implement each of the methods identified here, but you should identify the systems that are at risk and use every precaution to ensure your systems are protected from attack.

Limit the Dynamic Updates

I am going to assume that you are working in an Active Directory environment, because that is the main thrust of this book. An Active Directory–integrated DNS server can be configured so that it accepts dynamic update requests only from authorized systems. Once you configure a zone as Active Directory–integrated, you should change the dynamic updates so that only secure updates are allowed. At that point, only members of Active Directory can update the zone records. Once secure updates are turned on, an attacker will not be able to easily add to your database false records that could cause the domain controller to become overloaded as it tries to replicate the changes. Figure 2.7 shows the zone properties for zygort.lcl. Notice that the Dynamic updates option is set to Secure Only.

In a Windows Server 2003- or 2008-based domain, you can take this one step further by making sure that the DNS data is replicated only to domain controllers that are DNS servers or by specifying that the records are replicated only to the DNS servers that are included within the scope of an application partition. Later in this chapter, we will discuss the replication options that are available when using Windows Server 2003 or 2008 DNS.

FIGURE 2.7

Properties of the zygort.com zone showing secure updates enabled

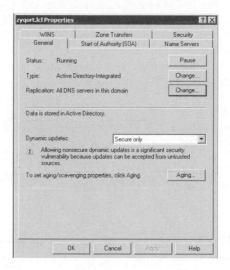

Monitor for Traffic

If the DNS server appears to be overloaded and you believe the resource overhead is due to an attack, you can use a monitoring tool, such as Microsoft's Network Monitor or a product such as Sniffer, to detect where the traffic is originating. If the traffic is from outside of your company, you can assume that you are being attacked. If this is the case, you can attempt to quell the traffic by putting firewall rules into place that will reject packets that originate from the addresses that you identify from the network trace. Most firewalls can be configured to drop spoofed packets. Check with your firewall administrator to determine what you can do with the firewalls in your infrastructure.

Putting rules into place does not mean you will stop the attack. The attacker was probably spoofing his or her address in the first place, so you may end up being attacked again from the same entity but through another address. Some firewalls have intrusion-detection capabilities, and you may be able to have the firewall dynamically drop packets if they are deemed an attack. You should develop a plan for monitoring the traffic that enters your network, whether or not it is bound for DNS. This plan should take into account the necessity of watching for attack types as well as determining how much monitoring you should perform so that it does not adversely affect the network performance.

The DNS monitoring policy should include references to who will be responsible for designing the monitoring solution, who will implement the policy, where the settings will be applied, and who will be responsible for reviewing the data that is collected. In traditional organizations, you may have several individuals who are responsible for each part of the DNS monitoring. There are new monitoring tools available, such as Microsoft Operations Manager, that will consolidate the monitoring of several systems into one cohesive solution.

Set Quotas

In Windows Server 2003- and 2008-based Active Directory domains, you have the ability to set quotas on the number of objects a user is allowed to create within the Active Directory partitions. You can set quotas differently on each Active Directory partition because each partition is evaluated separately. By using quotas you are able to effectively control the number of objects that can be created by an account, thereby quelling any attempt to flood an Active Directory–integrated zone with too many false objects.

You can set a quota limit on either user accounts or group accounts. An account that has been explicitly added to the quota list and is a member of a group that has quotas applied to it will be able to create as many objects as the *least* restrictive of the quota policies will allow. When a user attempts to create an object within the container where a quota limit has been set, the existing objects are compared against the quota limit. If the user has not met the quota, the object can be created, but the user will be denied the ability to create the object if the quota has been met.

The command dsadd is used to create a quota limit for an Active Directory partition. You can set quotas on any of the partitions, schema, configurations, domains, or any application partitions. However, the quota can be created or modified only on a Windows Server 2003 or 2008 domain controller, because Windows 2000 domain controllers are unfamiliar with the command-line utilities used to work with the Active Directory partitions.

Figure 2.8 shows the switches that are available when you are using the dsadd quota command. In its most basic form, you can use it to simply set a quota on a partition. For example, the command dsadd quota -part zygort.lcl -acct zygort\jprice -qlimit 10 would restrict the account jprice so that it is able to create only 10 objects within the zygort.lcl domain partition.

Take note that the quota limit you set on an account will include *tombstoned* objects in the quota count. Tombstones objects are objects that are marked for deletion, but have not yet been purged from the database because a deleted object needs to replicate the deletion action to all domain controllers before purging the object. Once the tombstoned object has met the tombstone lifetime, all of the domain controllers will purge the object during the next database cleanup cycle. If an object were deleted from one domain controller and not marked as tombstoned, the object would simply replicate from another domain controller and reappear in the database.

If you want to ignore tombstoned objects, you can use the dsmod partition command with the -qtmbstnwt switch. If you specify a value of 0, then all tombstoned objects will be ignored when objects are evaluated against a user's quota. If you want to reduce the percentage that a tombstone object counts against a user's quota, you can use a weight percentage between 0 and 100. This percentage is used to relate an active object's full value to a tombstoned object's value. For instance, if you set the -qtmbstnwt switch to 50, each tombstoned object will count as only half of an active object. A value of 10 will count each tombstoned object as one-tenth of each active object.

If at a later time you want to modify the number of objects that jprice could create, you could use the dsmod quota command. The syntax for dsmod quota is shown in Figure 2.9. Notice that you will have to know the fully distinguished name for the quota entry before you can change the quota limit. You can use the dsquery quota command to list the quotas that are set. As you can see in Figure 2.10, nearly all of the same options that are available from dsadd are also available from dsquery.

FIGURE 2.8
Syntax of the dsadd quota command

```
C:\Users\Administrator>dsadd quota /?
Description:  Adds a quota specification to a directory partition. A quota
              specification determines the maximum number of directory
              objects a given security principal can own in a specified
              directory partition.

Syntax:  dsadd quota -part <PartitionDN> [-rdn <RDN>] -acct Name
        -qlimit <Value> | -1 [-desc <Description>]
        [{-s <Server> | -d <Domain>}] [-u <UserName>] [-p {<Password> | *}]
        [-q] [{-uc | -uco | -uci}]

Parameters:

Value                          Description
-part <PartitionDN>         Required. Specifies the distinguished name of the
                            directory partition on which you want to create a
                            quota. If the distinguished name is omitted, it
                            will be taken from standard input (stdin).
-rdn <RDN>                  Specifies the relative distinguished name (RDN)
                            of the quota specification being created. If the
                            -rdn option is omitted, it will be set to
                            <domain>_<accountname>, using the domain and
                            account name of the security principal specified
                            by the -acct parameter.
-acct Name                  Required. Specifies the security principal (user,
                            group, computer, InetOrgPerson) for whom the
                            quota specification is being specified. The -acct
                            option can be provided in the following forms:
                              DN of the security principal
                              domain\SAM account name of the security
                              principal
 qlimit <Value> | 1
                            Required. Specifies the number of objects within
                            the directory partition that can be owned by
                            the security principal. To specify an unlimited
                            quota, specify -1 as the value.
-desc <Description>         Specifies a description for the quota
                            specification you want to add.
{-s <Server> | -d <Domain>} Connects the computer to either a specified
                            AD DC/LDS instance or domain. By default, the
                            computer is connected to an AD DC in the logon
                            domain.
-u <UserName>               Specifies the user name with which user will log
                            on to a remote server. By default, the logged on
                            user name is used. You can specify a user name
                            using one of the following formats:
                              user name (such as, Linda)
                              domain\user name (such as, widgets\Linda)
                              user principal name (UPN) (such as,
                              Linda@widgets.microsoft.com)
```

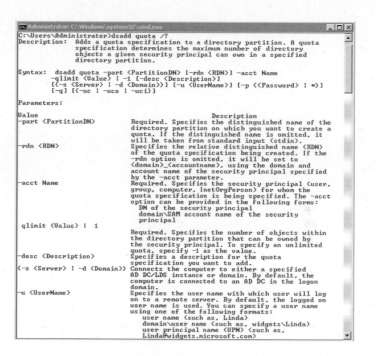

what is a reasonable quota?

FIGURE 2.9
Syntax of the dsmod quota command

```
C:\Users\Administrator>dsmod quota /?
Description:  Modifies attributes of one or more existing quota specifications
              in the directory. A quota specification determines the maximum
              number of directory objects a given security principal can own
              in a specific directory partition.

Syntax:       dsmod quota <QuotaDN ...> [-qlimit <Value>]
              [-desc <Description>] [{-s <Server> | -d <Domain>}] [-u <UserName>
]
              [-p {<Password> | *}] [-c] [-q] [{-uc | -uco | -uci}]

Parameters:

Value                           Description
<QuotaDN ...>         Specifies the distinguished names of one or more quota
                      specifications to modify. If values are omitted, they
                      are obtained through standard input (stdin) to support
                      piping of output from another command to input of this
                      command.
-qlimit <Value>       Specifies the number of objects within the
                      directory partition that can be owned by the security
                      principal to which the quota specification is assigned.
                      To specify an unlimited quota, use -1.
-desc <Description>   Sets the description of the quota specification to
                      <Description>.
{-s <Server> | -d <Domain>}
                      Connects to a specified AD DC/LDS instance or domain.
                      By default, the computer is connected to an AD DC
                      in the logon domain.
-u <UserName>         Specifies the user name with which the user logs on to
                      a remote server. By default, -u uses the user name with
                      which the user logged on. You can use any of the
                      following formats to specify a user name:
                        user name (for example, Linda)
                        domain\user name (for example, widgets\Linda)
                        user principal name (UPN)
                          (for example, Linda@widgets.microsoft.com)
-p {<Password> | *}   Specifies to use either a password or a * to log on to
                      a remote server. If you type *, you are prompted for a
                      password.
-c                    Specifies continuous operation mode. Errors are
                      reported, but the process continues with the next
                      object in the argument list when you specify multiple
                      target objects. If you do not use -c, the command quits
                      after the first error occurs.
-q                    Suppresses all output to standard output (quiet mode).
{-uc | -uco | -uci}   Specifies that output or input data is formatted in
                      Unicode.
                      -uc   Specifies a Unicode format for input from or
                            output to a pipe (|).
                      -uco  Specifies a Unicode format for output to a
                            pipe (|) or a file.
                      -uci  Specifies a Unicode format for input from a
                            pipe (|) or a file.
```

To find the quota entry for the jprice account, enter dsquery quota -acct zygort\jprice at the command prompt. If you want to start your search at a specific partition, you can enter the partition's fully distinguished name in the command by using the startnode option. Of course, the best bet for maintaining your DNS server is to make sure you have good documentation—and we know we all document everything. If you end up having to support an Active Directory implementation that another administrator set up, you will be able to find out what has been set by querying for the information.

Once you know the quota entry, you can issue the dsmod quota "CN=zygort_jprice,CN=NTDS Quotas,dc=zygort,dc=lcl" -qlimit 15 command, which will set a new quota of 15 objects for the jprice account. Note that when you have a space within the fully qualified name of an object, you need to enclose the entire name in quotes.

Disable Recursion

The typical behavior for a DNS server is to take over the name-resolution process whenever a client is attempting to resolve a host name. Clients typically send an iterative query to their DNS server, and the DNS server starts the recursion process to locate a DNS server that can identify the IP address for the host name in question. An attacker can take advantage of this scenario and start attacking the DNS server with several queries in an attempt to limit its ability to respond to valid queries.

When you disable recursion on a DNS server, you are essentially telling the DNS server that it will no longer be a slave to the client, and it should only return a referral to the client. In this scenario, the DNS server takes on a far smaller load, but the client will incur more of the work. As the clients send queries to their DNS servers, the DNS servers will check their zone data for a match. If the DNS server is not authoritative for the zone and has not cached the entry, the DNS server will refer the client to another DNS server to contact.

To disable recursion, open the properties of the DNS server and select the option Disable Recursion (Also Disables Forwarders), as seen in Figure 2.11.

This takes most of the resolution responsibility off the DNS server; however, note that DNS servers that have been stripped of their recursive abilities cannot be configured to forward by using either a standard or conditional forwarder. This is because of the recursive nature of forwarding. The DNS server would normally send a recursive query to the server listed within the Forwarders tab of the DNS server properties.

FIGURE 2.11
Disabling recursion

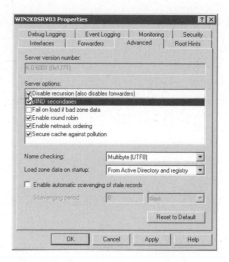

Use Appropriate Routing

There are several ways to resolve a query when it is sent to a DNS server. If the DNS server that receives the query cannot resolve the query from a zone in which the DNS server is authoritative, the server will attempt to locate the host name within the query by asking other servers. As long as you have not disabled recursion, you can still configure a server to act as a forwarder. You can also configure any Windows Server 2003 or 2008 DNS server with a stub zone.

Which routing method should you choose when you are attempting to maintain a secure system? If you are worried about a denial-of-service attack, use the method that is the least resource-intensive. Conditional forwarding is the most resource-intensive of the routing methods because it has to process the conditions before it decides where to forward the query. However, if you have implemented a firewall to block traffic, you may need to use another method besides a stub zone, because stub zones require access to remote systems by using TCP and UDP port 53. Make sure you work in conjunction with the network infrastructure team to determine where you have firewall rules that will block traffic on TCP port 53.

Keeping the System Accurate

Attacks are not always attempts to stop the system from responding. Sometimes attacks are meant to discover information about a company or to redirect clients to incorrect hosts. Two of the most common attacks on a DNS implementation are *database manipulation* and *cache poisoning*. In either of these scenarios, data entered into the DNS do not correspond to the host with which the client is attempting to communicate.

To alleviate attacks on your system, take steps to help guarantee that the DNS database can be modified only by authorized entities and to ensure that the DNS resolver cache does not contain invalid records. The options discussed in the following sections will help you protect your systems and alleviate problems for your users.

Use IPSec

IPSec (IP Security) was developed to secure communication at the IP layer of the Open Systems Interconnection (OSI) model. With IPSec, the two communicating devices must share a public key.

To make sure you have control over the systems that are able to connect to your DNS server, and to ensure that those systems are authorized to do so, you could implement IPSec and use a policy that requires the clients to have IPSec in order to communicate with the DNS servers. You could even go so far as configuring policies that are specific to certain clients in order to allow only a subset of clients to connect to a DNS server. Clients from remote sites, or outside of a specific department, may not have the appropriate settings to connect to a DNS server; meanwhile, authorized clients are allowed to update records within the zone and communicate with the DNS server to query for other hosts.

Create your own IPSec policies that have rules in place that allow only the appropriate clients to access the DNS server. At the same time, you can include a rule that will allow all of the DNS servers that need to communicate with one another to do so. If you are using Active Directory–integrated DNS servers, make sure the IPSec rules that govern the domain controllers are configured to allow any replication partner the ability to connect and communicate.

IPSec is covered in Chapter 9, but you should determine at this point what type of IPSec policies you will need to implement. Not all client types support IPSec, so you should determine if it is supported within your organization. If it is, you will need to make sure that the appropriate level of security is configured via policies. The three basic policies that are preconfigured allow for client, server, and secure server connection types, as seen in Figure 2.12.

FIGURE 2.12
Built-in IPSec
security policies

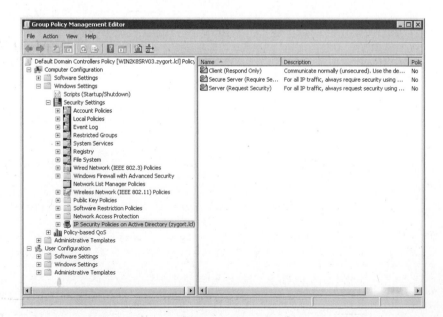

Client The client IPSec policy will not initiate IPSec communication with any other system. Instead, it will enable the system to communicate using IPSec, but only if another system initiates an IPSec-enabled connection. If not asked to talk via IPSec, it will continue to communicate clear text.

Server The server IPSec policy will attempt to initiate IPSec communication with all of the systems with which it is communicating; however, if a system is not configured to use IPSec or if the IPSec policies do not match, the two systems will still communicate using clear text.

Secure Server The secure server IPSec policy is the network equivalent of a snob. Assigning this policy will configure the system to communicate only with other IPSec-enabled systems. If a system is not able to talk via IPSec or if the IPSec policies between the two systems do not match, the systems will not be able to connect to one another.

Use Secure DDNS

As mentioned before, if you want to make sure the records entered within your DNS zones are valid, you can implement the Secure Only option from the General tab of the zone properties, as seen in Figure 2.13. Once enabled, only clients that are members of your AD DS domain can enter records within the zone.

FIGURE 2.13
Enabling secure
dynamic updates

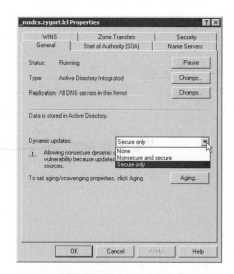

The greatest benefit of using only secure updates is that you can be guaranteed that the records entered are valid. An attacker would not be able to register records that would redirect the client to an invalid host, or bad records that would cause the client's access attempt to fail.

The only way you would be able to make the zone more secure would be to completely disable the ability to use dynamic updates. Usually this is not an option because the administrative staff would have to manually enter every record within the zone. This could be a very time-consuming task, and it would be prone to human error, which could cause the same problems you are trying to alleviate.

If you implement secure updates, make sure that the clients that need to register within your zone are still able to do so. You might need to allow DHCP to register on behalf of some of the clients within your network, and you might have to manually create the records for others.

Avoid Cache Poisoning

An attacker could attempt to populate the cache on your DNS server with incorrect information in an attempt either to stop name resolution or to redirect clients to incorrect systems. If an attacker were able to populate the cache with an entry that would redirect a client to the wrong DNS server, the client could receive a response to their query that redirected them to a compromised host.

To make sure the entries within the DNS cache are complete and accurate entries that are part of the name-resolution path the DNS server has obtained during resolution, you can enable the Secure Cache against Pollution option, as seen in Figure 2.14. You can reach this option by opening the properties of your DNS server and selecting the Advanced tab.

During normal query operations, DNS servers will query other DNS servers to resolve the query. If a DNS server holds the correct information in cache, it can respond with a complete answer to the query, but it is not the authoritative server. Why not? Because if someone wants to cause a misdirection, they could enter information into the DNS server's cache, which would in turn give wrong data back to all other DNS servers that are using that DNS server to resolve. Once this option is enabled, your DNS server will ignore records that were not obtained from the DNS server that is authoritative for the zone in question. This will place additional resource requirements on your DNS server: it will need to perform more queries due to the dropping of records that are not obtained from authoritative DNS servers. However, this method guarantees the authenticity and accuracy of the records.

FIGURE 2.14
Securing against
cache pollution

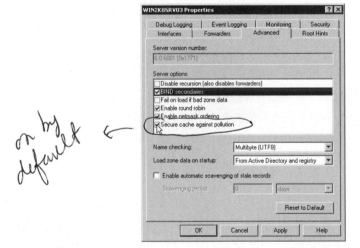

Allow Appropriate Access

Keeping attackers away from the data contained in your database should be of high concern. If an attacker is able to access the records or to damage the database so that it no longer responds correctly to queries, either your clients will become victims of redirection attacks or they will not have the ability to access the hosts with which they were intending to communicate. The following sections cover options that you should consider when attempting to secure both Active Directory–integrated and non–Active Directory–integrated zones.

ACTIVE DIRECTORY–INTEGRATED ZONES

By default, members of the domain groups—Administrators, Domain Admins, Enterprise Admins, and DNS Admins—have the ability to manage DNS zones. If you want to control the administrative staff who can manage a zone, you can configure the permissions on the zone within the DNS console. If special groups are responsible for specific zones, make sure you remove the other administrative groups from the zones' access control lists (ACLs). If you don't, a rogue administrator could make unauthorized changes to the zones.

NON–ACTIVE DIRECTORY–INTEGRATED ZONES

Stub zones, secondary zones, and primary zones that are not Active Directory–integrated do not have associated access control lists. This is not necessarily a bad thing for stub and secondary zones because the records they contain cannot be modified directly (the primary zone's records can be). Non–Active Directory–integrated primary zones are at risk, however. Make sure that you monitor the accounts within the groups that have the ability to work on the DNS server, and consider turning off the option for dynamic update.

Zone data is stored within a file on the DNS server when the zone is not Active Directory–integrated. These zone files are protected using file-system ACLs. The default members of the ACL include the Users and Power Users groups. Typically, neither of these groups needs access to the zone files; therefore, modify the access control list so that only the Administrators group, any special DNS administrative groups, and the System account have access. Remember that any dynamic updates are performed within the DNS service, and it is up to the System account to update the zone's associated file; therefore, users do not need to have access to the these files.

You should also consider moving the zone files to another partition away from the system files. Such a move would effectively reduce the chance of a zone file being compromised by a buffer over-flow and allowing an attacker to browse the files stored on the system partition. Once you move the files to another partition, be sure to adjust the access control list so that only the appropriate DNS administrators and system have access to the files.

Lock Down Transfers

An Active Directory–integrated zone can send zone transfers to a secondary zone if the DNS server is configured to do so. You may want to review your settings to make sure that you only allow zone transfers to DNS servers authorized to receive the transfers. This is especially important if your zones are not Active Directory–integrated. All of the zone information will need to pass between the DNS servers as zone transfers. Make sure all of the DNS servers that need to receive the transfer are listed and that no other servers are allowed to receive a transfer.

If you can be certain that all of the DNS servers listed within the Name Servers tab of the zone properties are valid servers, you can use the setting shown in Figure 2.15. By using the option Only to Servers Listed on the Name Servers Tab, you can allow all servers that have a secondary zone configured for the namespace to receive zone transfers when a change occurs.

However, if you think you might have a rogue administrator or that someone has built a DNS server to capture records for your namespace, you may want to kick up your level of security by using the Only to the Following Servers option. When using this setting, you will need to manually enter the IP address of every valid DNS server that needs to receive a zone transfer. Of course, this will not keep a rogue administrator who has permissions to view the zone data away from your

DNS records. If you have granted such an administrator the privileges, there is not much you can do besides revoke their power.

If your zones are Active Directory–integrated, you can probably use the default setting of not allowing zone transfers. This guarantees that only domain controllers hold the zone records, but limits you if there are any non–Active Directory–integrated DNS servers within your environment.

FIGURE 2.15
Allowing zone transfer to servers listed as name servers

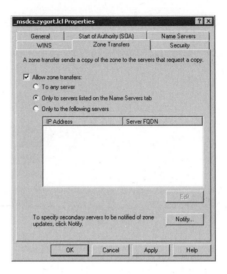

Coming Up Next

Just like the chicken and the egg, the debate rages on about which you should design first: the Active Directory domains or the DNS infrastructure. We decided that, because the AD relies on DNS, we should discuss it first. In Chapter 3, "Active Directory Domain Services Forest and Domain Design," we will go in depth about the criteria you should take into account when designing your Active Directory domains.

The Bottom Line

The importance of Microsoft Server 2008 DNS in Active Directory Domain Services   DNS is the backbone of Active Directory. While other DNS servers, such as BIND, may allow you to run Active Directory, certain Active Directory features are available only with Microsoft Windows Server–based DNS servers.

Master It   You are designing your Active Directory domain infrastructure that consists of multiple physical locations. Your domain will consist of Windows 2008 servers only. You want to implement a DNS infrastructure that provides you with a simple and easy way to manage DNS replication topology.

How to protect DNS data and keep it accurate   As the adage goes, garbage in, garbage out. Protecting DNS data and keeping the data accurate are key to the reliability and performance of your DNS infrastructure.

Master It   You've just completed your DNS design and implementation. You now need to make sure your DNS servers are protected from attack and from data corruption.

Chapter 3

Active Directory Domain Services Forest and Domain Design

As I mentioned in Chapter 1, "Active Directory Fundamentals," there are a lot of changes to Active Directory in Windows Server 2008. One I believe will be the hardest to get used to is a terminology change. What was previously known simply as Active Directory is now Active Directory Domain Services (AD DS).

This chapter uses three different references to "Active Directory." Because the domain services piece has been broken off, we should not reference domain and forest items with the term *Active Directory*. I repeat: what was formerly known as Active Directory is now AD DS. The three items referenced in this chapter are as follows:

- ◆ Active Directory—Active Directory as it was known in Windows 2000 and Windows 2003. When discussing items that relate only to Windows 2000 Server or 2003 Server, we will use the term *Active Directory*.

- ◆ AD DS—Active Directory Domain Services in Windows Server 2008. Again, this is what was formerly known as Active Directory. Forest, domain, resources, objects, organizational units (OUs), sites, etc., all fall under AD DS.

- ◆ Active Directory–enabled applications. This term has not changed as of the writing of this book in early 2008. This is a reference to any application that is Active Directory– or AD DS–aware. See—I'm doing it already.

How do you optimally design a database that replicates only parts of itself to as many as thousands of domain controllers at differing intervals? Therein lies the need for the first section of this chapter. AD DS may very well become one of the largest database implementations within your organization. If you talk to many database administrators, you will see them cringe when you mention that you would like to replicate a database to multiple servers. But that is exactly what you are going to do with AD DS and your domain controllers. In all fairness, the AD DS database is not nearly as complex as you will find with a relational database used for data warehousing, but this kind of replication is still not a trivial task.

AD DS is unlike most directory services in that it is an integral part of the operating system (OS). The many other directory services out there sit on top of the OS. For example, Novell's NetWare Directory Services (NDS), now termed eDirectory, can be upgraded easily, independent of an OS upgrade. But that's not the case for AD DS. To update the directory service on the Microsoft platform, you currently need to upgrade to the latest server OS or service pack. Each service pack brings a host of bug and security fixes for AD DS, as well as additional functionality; therefore, you should apply the latest service pack on all of your domain controllers within a month of its release—although that is easier said than done.

Don't get me wrong; you can extend AD DS to support new attributes and object classes at any time. When you deploy Active Directory–enabled applications, you will usually need to add the additional attributes and object classes to AD DS to support those applications. That is different from making structural changes to AD DS, which requires that you make changes to the OS to support the updates.

Each new version of Windows Server (2003, 2003 R2, and now 2008) has added new administrative tools and functionality to Active Directory. A lot of the added functionality will require you to retire all of your older domain controllers, depending on what features you would like to use. I'll discuss more on that later in this chapter as we review the functional levels for domains and forests.

You should consider moving to Windows Server 2008 for a myriad of reasons, not the least of which is the support-timeline expiration of Windows 2000 and 2003. Mainstream product support expires five years after a product release. After that five-year period, the product enters extended support. Only security hotfixes and paid support are available for a product after it enters extended support. Many in the IT industry will take the conspiracy theorist's stance and accuse Microsoft of retiring products to keep companies on the purchasing side of the table. However, in our industry the technologies that develop over the course of five years tend to make operating systems and applications obsolete. For those of you who have left Windows NT 4 for the greener pastures of Windows 2000/2003 and Active Directory, could you even imagine trying to perform some of the administrative tasks on Windows NT 4 that you can perform with the newer technologies? For more information on the life cycle of operating systems and applications, peruse the article on Microsoft's website at `http://support.microsoft.com/default.aspx?pr=lifecycle`.

In the following sections we're going to look at the criteria you should consider when developing your AD DS design. Most of the information included comes from working with Active Directory over the past eight years, and from reflecting on the methodology that has worked the best. Although some of the information may seem like simple common sense, there are times when common sense seems to take a backseat to the desire to implement technology. Also, this chapter is not going to delve deeply into the technology; we're saving that for the upcoming administration, maintenance, management, and troubleshooting chapters. Instead, in this chapter we concentrate on the requirements and options for a solid forest and domain design.

In this chapter, you will learn:

◆ When to use a single forest or multiple forests

◆ When to use a single domain or multiple domains

◆ Which forest functional level and domain level to choose for your environment

AD DS Forest Design Criteria

AD DS design requires both technical expertise and organizational acceptance. It requires compromise among diverse groups that may be used to doing tasks their own way—Domain Name System (DNS) administrators can use Unix for DNS; Novell NetWare administrators have a different architecture of directory services that they want to implement; enterprise resource planning (ERP) packages use their own directory service; proxy/firewall/Internet access might use its own directory service; email uses its own directory service—you get the idea. How do you please everyone with your design? You probably can't. Start by developing the ideal design by yourself, if possible, and then let each group have its turn telling you what modifications they would like to see or, in a worst-case scenario, why your design won't work. If you let each group try to design AD DS, you will never complete the project.

Get executive sponsorship in the design phase. I cannot stress this point enough. In other words, find an executive to approve the design phase of AD DS. If you make an executive ally within the organization and that executive trusts and likes your plan, you will find that getting the design approved and moving on to the planning stages will be much easier. Of course, you need to make sure that the executive with whom you ally yourself has a basic understanding of the whole picture when it comes to AD DS.

AD DS design is about putting structure around a confused mass of unorganized objects. It's about administrative control and separating the service owners accountable for maintaining AD DS and the services that support it from the data owners who are responsible for maintaining the objects within the directory. It is about building a solution that takes into account the limitations of the technology you are working with (Windows Server and Active Directory) and designing around the organizational day-to-day business. Your design needs to take into consideration speed/latency, name resolution, availability, security, disaster recovery, hardware, and so on.

Forest design should be your first architectural element when designing AD DS. A forest is a single instance of AD DS, and is the topmost container in AD DS. It is scalable beyond 5,000 domain controllers, 5,000 sites, and millions of users, according to Microsoft's Branch Office Deployment Guide. Even the largest organizations should be able to contain all of the necessary objects within a single forest. You will find that other considerations will come into play when developing your design. Legislative, political, or organizational reasons may force you to move to a multiple-forest design, but make sure there is a valid reason to do so. Later in this chapter, we discuss the pros and cons of single- and multiple-forest implementations.

Although a forest is almost insanely easy to build, it is far, far more complex to design. Several options are available, and you need to know what roles forests and domains play within your organization. As you will see in the next section, the domain is no longer the security boundary as it was under Windows NT 4. I will discuss the differences, and the new technologies that make up the security boundary, replication boundary, administration boundary, schema, and global catalog.

Schema

A forest shares a single *schema*, which can be defined as the rules of what can go into a directory service. AD DS is made up of *objects*, which are instances of an object class that have been defined by combining attributes to form what can be allowed within the directory. These rules also define where objects can be created and used within the directory service. Because all of the objects within the forest have to follow the same rules, there can be only one schema per forest.

Because of the important nature of the schema, you should not take its existence lightly. Although you may not have to think about it on a daily basis, you will need to make sure that you do not allow just anyone to have access to the schema. If changes are enacted within the schema, the results could be disastrous. Your organization may be one of the lucky ones that never have to modify their schema, but very few organizations are so fortunate.

Keep your Schema Admins group empty until you are required to make a change to the Active Directory schema. By default, the Administrator account is defined as a Schema Admin. This is the account that you used to install AD DS when you first configured your forest. This account is also listed as an Enterprise Admin.

If you remove this account from the Schema Admins group, an Enterprise Admin can add it back into the group when needed.

Many organizations will modify their default schema so that it will support directory-enabled applications. A common situation is the need to implement Microsoft Exchange. Exchange 2000, 2003, and 2007 servers add many attributes and object classes to the schema. Prior to implementing an Active Directory–enabled application within your production environment, make sure you understand the ramifications of altering your schema. Test the application first in a test environment.

If you would like to see the schema extensions that are installed with Exchange 2000/2003, check out the information at `http://msdn2.microsoft.com/en-us/library/ms985900.aspx`. Information on the schema changes in Exchange 2007 can be found at `http://msdn2.microsoft.com/en-us/library/aa581540.aspx`.

When designing your AD DS infrastructure, determine which Active Directory–enabled applications you will be implementing and determine which of them will extend the schema. You should then determine when you want to extend the schema for each one. Extending the schema is not something that should be taken lightly. You will be adding attributes that will possibly change existing objects, and adding new object classes that will be used to create new objects. As all of these changes occur, consider how much additional replication will occur, which domain controllers these changes will affect, and the additional global catalog replication that will start consuming network traffic throughout every domain within your forest.

Schema Considerations and OID-Issuing Authorities

If you are extending the schema for an in-house application, consider contacting an object identifier (OID) –issuing authority for the proper classification. Failure to do so could cause problems with other applications when they are installed within your environment. If an application needs to use an OID that is already in use, the application will fail to install. Once an attribute is created, you cannot delete it. You can take an existing attribute and reclassify that attribute, giving you an option of "reusing" an existing attribute instead of creating a new one. Windows Server 2003 and 2008 will allow you to reclassify an attribute; however, Windows 2000 will not. As a best practice, you should contact one of the following organizations to verify that the OID is not in use:

◆ The Internet Assigned Numbers Authority (IANA) hands out OIDs for free under the Private Enterprises branch.

◆ The American National Standards Institute (ANSI) hands out OIDs under the US Organizations branch for $1,000.

◆ The British Standards Institution (BSI) hands out OIDs under the UK Organizations branch.

Visit the International Organization for Standardization (ISO) at `www.iso.ch` for information on your country's national registration authority. While you are at it, register the OID so that no one else can use it for their commercial applications. Microsoft will validate all applications that you want to be certified for use within AD DS. If you register your OID and someone else tries to use it, Microsoft will fail the application, and the software vendor will have to change its application accordingly.

For information on registering OIDs for the ISO or if you are registering an OID under Microsoft's branch, see the following websites:

`http://msdn2.microsoft.com/en-us/library/ms677620.aspx`

`http://msdn2.microsoft.com/en-us/library/ms677621.aspx`

For more information on registering OIDs for your AD DS environment, see Chapter 14, "Maintaining the Active Directory Database."

Security Boundary

The rules have changed since Windows NT 4. Under NT, the domain was the security boundary. If you were a member of the Domain Admins group, you had full control of your domain and you were isolated from Domain Admins from other domains. Now with AD DS, the forest—not the domain—is the security boundary. Any Domain Admin on any domain controller throughout the forest can bring down the entire AD forest—either on purpose or by mistake. There are, unfortunately, some simple ways to do this:

◆ Impersonate any user in the forest (in any domain).

◆ Read, change, or delete any Windows-secured resource or configuration setting on any machine (especially domain controllers) in the forest. FSMO roles are an even higher risk because the FSMO roles are, by nature, a single point of failure. There is more information on FSMO roles in Chapters 5, "Flexible Single Master Operations Design," and 13, "Managing the Flexible Single Master Operations Roles."

◆ Modify service accounts that run in the *system context*—that means OS privileges.

◆ Run code in the system context.

◆ Hide (bury) domain administrator–equivalent accounts for later use.

◆ Cause changes to replicate to other domain controllers. This is not a problem with database corruption, but it is for a denial-of-service (DoS) attack, which would be easy with a simple script that added users endlessly.

◆ Take ownership of files, folders, objects, attributes, and, thereby, breach privacy.

These are just a few of the many ways to bring down the AD forest. Granted, being a member of the Domain Admins group from the forest root makes it easier to carry out some of these attacks, but having Domain Admin membership anywhere within the forest could be a potential risk if the user who is granted that level of control is not trustworthy.

When you are creating your AD design, you must account for who will become a forest owner. A forest owner is any account that has full-control access to every domain within the forest. Any Domain Administrator in the root domain of the forest (the first domain created in the forest) is automatically made a member of the Enterprise Admins and Schema Admins groups. Take users and administrators out of this group immediately. You can then create a set of standards and procedures detailing when an account can be added to these groups to perform the administrative duty.

Replication Boundary

AD DS forests provide for a complete replication boundary. Every domain controller within the forest will participate in the replication topology, sharing information among them so that each domain controller can respond correctly when a client requests it. Two AD partitions—the configuration partition and the schema partition (or naming contexts)—will replicate on a forestwide basis. Every domain controller within the forest will share identical data for these two partitions. The schema partition holds all of the rules pertaining to how objects can be created within the forest. If any of the domain controllers within your forest had a different set of attributes or object class rules, the objects that were created by that domain controller would not work with the other domain controllers.

The configuration partition specifies how the domain controllers communicate and how the domain is designed. Other systems, such as Exchange 200x, use the configuration partition to hold data about the systems that provide the email service. Having this information replicated to all domain controllers within the forest gives you the ability to hold the configuration data in one location, AD DS, and allows other systems to look to the domain controllers to find out how they are supposed to run. This also means that you only have to configure one replication topology when synchronizing changes instead of having AD DS–specific data replicating through domain controllers and Exchange data replicating through Exchange servers.

Note that data will not replicate between domain controllers in different forests. Even if you have domain controllers from two forests at the same physical location, they will not share configuration and schema partition data; only those from the same forest will. These servers may reside in the same physical location, but they are in different logical forests and domains.

Another partition type, the application partition, can be configured to replicate to all domain controllers within the forest, but it is not mandatory that it do so. With an application partition, you have the ability to choose the domain controllers to which the partition will replicate, thus giving you a means of controlling some of the replication traffic within your organization. This technology is not available with Windows 2000 systems, but is available when you're using Windows Server 2003 or 2008.

You can control the replication traffic within the partition to all Active Directory–integrated DNS servers within the forest, restrict it to all Active Directory–integrated DNS servers within the domain, host the data within the domain partition, or choose which domain controllers will hold the partition. Later in this chapter we look at how the application partition works and the benefits of using this new partition type.

You can see the naming contexts upon opening Active Directory Services Interface (ADSI) Edit, which is provided on the Windows 2000, 2003, or 2008 CD under \SUPPORT\TOOLS. Figure 3.1 shows ADSI Edit with the naming contexts opened. You can also view the naming contexts that are held on a domain controller using the NTDSUtil command-line utility. For more information on NTDSUtil, see Chapter 12, "Managing Active Directory Certificate Services."

FIGURE 3.1
ADSI Edit and the naming contexts

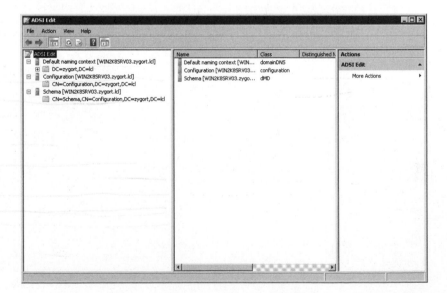

As you'll see in the following chapter, the last partition—the domain partition, or domain-naming context, as it is sometimes called—is replicated only to other domain controllers within the same domain. Although this does improve performance by restricting the amount of replication throughout the organization, it causes issues when users are trying to locate objects within other domains. To alleviate some of the problems associated with partitioning the forest into separate domains, Microsoft introduced the concept of a global catalog.

A Common Global Catalog

A forest also provides for a common global catalog (GC) within the forest. A global catalog is a domain controller that hosts objects from every domain naming context within the forest. At first you might think that could be a lot of data for a domain controller to host. If the GC server were to hold all of the attributes from every domain within the forest, you'd be correct. However, to keep network traffic at a minimum, only about 200 of the 1,700+ available attributes for each object are copied into the GC. The GC is like a giant cache of directory objects and attributes that keep you from needing to query beyond a single domain controller. For example, you could easily take a laptop from domain to domain, country to country inside the same forest and authenticate immediately, because your user object (and every user object in the forest) is cached in the GC, which replicates forestwide.

You can control which attributes populate the GC with the Schema Management Microsoft Management Console (MMC) snap-in. Attributes that are selected to replicate to the GC are referred to as the Partial Attribute Set (PAS). When you load the Active Directory Schema snap-in, you can open the properties of any attribute and view whether the attribute will be part of the GC. Figure 3.2 shows the properties of the Bad Password Count (badPwdCount) Properties attribute. Notice that the check box for Replicate This Attribute to the Global Catalog is not checked. Once it is selected, the attribute would need to replicate to all GCs within the forest.

Be warned, though; in Windows 2000, when you make a change to the PAS, you cause a full GC replication throughout the forest. Windows 2000 domain controllers do not know how to handle the PAS efficiently.

This does not happen in Windows Server 2003 or 2008; instead, only the changed or added attributes are replicated throughout the forest. If you want to maintain efficient control of the GCs in your infrastructure, think about allowing only Windows Server 2003 or 2008 systems to have the GC role.

FIGURE 3.2
Properties of the
Bad Password Count
Properties attribute

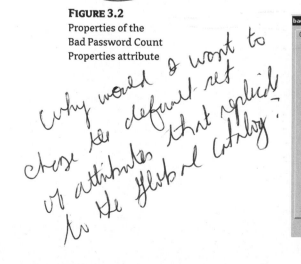

Later, as we determine the placement of domain controllers, we will come back to the GC server. There will be specific locations to place GC servers so that users and applications have access to the GC. For instance, the GC holds the Exchange 200x global address list (GAL), so you need to provide constant access to the GC for all of your Exchange servers.

Always start your design with the most basic design options. If finding a resource easily across domain boundaries and without additional software services is important, consider a single forest. A single forest will allow all of the objects from every domain to be seen through the GC. If you must use multiple forests, there are applications such as Microsoft Identity Lifecycle Manager 2007, formerly Microsoft Identity Integration Server (MIIS) 2003, that can replicate objects and attributes between forests and differing directory services, such as Novell's NDS to Active Directory. These applications have a steep learning curve and will usually require additional design and planning. Make sure you exhaust every other option before deciding to create more than one forest. For more information concerning Microsoft Identity Lifecycle Manager 2007, visit Microsoft's website at http://www.microsoft.com/windowsserver/ilm2007/default.mspx.

When you have multiple domains within your forest, you need to have a method to gain access to the resources in each domain. The GC servers must have the ability to pull data from domain controllers in each of the other domains. To do so, trust relationships are used to determine which domains can contact each other.

Kerberos Authentication and Trust Relationships

Under the Windows NT 4 model, every domain was its own security boundary. To allow users to access resources within another NT domain, you had to create a trust relationship between the two domains. When you created a trust relationship, only one domain was allowed to trust users from the other domain. If you wanted to allow both sets of users to access each other's resources, you had to create two trust relationships. To make matters worse, there was no sharing of trust. In other words, the trust relationships were not transitive. If DomainA had a trust relationship with DomainB, and DomainB had a trust relationship with DomainC, DomainA was still restricted from accessing DomainC until an explicit trust was set up between DomainA and DomainC. Further, these trust relationships were only one-way trusts, so you needed to create two trusts just so that two domains could trust one another. Needless to say, planning and maintaining the correct trust relationships in a large NT infrastructure caused a loss of sleep for many administrators.

AD DS has changed the trust-relationship game. Within a forest, all of the domains are interconnected through two-way transitive trusts. This allows all the users within the forest to access resources from any domain within the forest so long as they have been granted permissions to access the resource. All of this is accomplished using the fewest trust relationships possible. Take a look at Figure 3.3. This is a typical forest that has two trees, and domains within each tree. In an AD DS forest, you will need only the trust relationships, defined as arrows shown in the graphic. If you were to implement the same number of domains within a Windows NT 4 environment, you would need 20 trusts.

In order for the trust relationships to work within our forest, the Kerberos authentication service (the default trust authentication service used by Windows) is used. With Kerberos, each of the domains and all of the security principals within each domain are identified and given access to the resources through a process known as *delegation*. Later in this chapter, as we look at domain design, we take a closer look at Kerberos and how it works across domain boundaries.

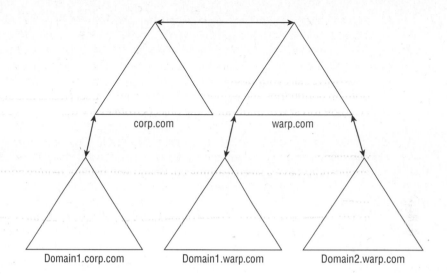

FIGURE 3.3
AD DS trusts within
a forest

Political and Administration Boundaries

These two topics, political and administration boundaries, are tied together because there is usually an underlying political reason for creating separate forests. As I mentioned earlier, the forest is the security boundary. Administrative accounts from the root domain of the forest have the ability to become the forest owners and, as such, can control all of the objects within the forest. Although there are other reasons why you may want to create separate forests, doing so to appease a faction within your organization might be the deciding factor. Some divisions simply do not like allowing other administrators access their data, and they may have a corporate sponsor who has enough power to override your design. The only way that you can isolate those divisions' data is to create a separate forest and assign select users from those divisions as the forest owners.

The drawbacks to giving them their own forest are that you will have additional administrative overhead and you will need to make sure that the users are properly trained to use AD DS. When you have two forests, you have two completely separate administrative structures. If you can get by with a single forest, do so. You will reduce the total administrative costs. In the next section we review the advantages and disadvantages associated with single and multiple forests.

Where the administrative boundaries should be drawn will be dictated by whether you have to isolate services or data from other portions of the organization. You can create a separate forest to truly isolate the domains from users in other domains, whereas creating a new domain in the same forest allows users to access data from the other domain while allowing different administrators to control each domain. Before you decide to create a separate forest, review the arguments from all sides. Autonomy allows the administrators of certain resources to control them, while limiting the access to those resources from the other domains. Weigh the cost of a separate forest where isolation can be granted, against the ease of administration with a single forest where you can apply autonomy. Of course, the political battles will ensue, as each division wants to have complete control over all of its resources. Don't forget what I mentioned earlier about executive sponsorship. If the battles rage on and you need to settle the disputes, there is nothing like having someone with lots of clout in your corner.

Multiple Forests: Pros and Cons

Seeing multiple forests in a medium-sized business is not uncommon. One of my AD DS clients had about 2,000 people and six forests. They used one for production, one for development, two for extranet applications, and two for development that mimicked the extranet production forests. This was a good, secure design for them. Although not every organization will need to go to this extreme, I often recommend that you have a separate forest in which to test changes to AD DS and software interaction. Creating a secondary version of your production environment will allow you to test changes before they are implemented within your production environment. Most companies that have a test environment have far fewer problems within their infrastructure than those that "shoot from the hip." We've all experienced how a service pack or hotfix has caused instability within a network.

I also like to recommend using a development forest if an organization has developers who need to test their software prior to implementing it within the production forest. Developers need their own forest if they require excess privileges or if they touch AD DS. Often developers think they need Domain Admin access and a domain controller under their desk. It is never a good idea to give anyone this much power over your forest. As I mentioned in the "Schema" section earlier, changes to the schema are not easily undone. Although AD DS in Windows Server 2003 and 2008 is a great deal friendlier than prior versions when it comes to modifying the schema, you should never make any changes without first testing the implementation to determine the ramifications.

I always recommend that developers do their work in a separate forest or, if possible, on virtual-machine technology. Running a virtual system on an existing system is an easy way to mimic the production environment. The drawback is that the computer on which you are running the virtual system needs enough horsepower to run multiple operating systems at the same time. Two premier virtual system software applications are available for free. Microsoft's Virtual Server 2005 R2 is available at `http://www.microsoft.com/windowsserversystem/virtualserver/` and EMC's VMWare Server is available at `http://www.vmware.com/products/server/`.

I also briefly mentioned a forest used for extranet applications. This is one area in which you will need to determine the level of security you require for users who access your infrastructure across the Internet. Some organizations will implement for their perimeter network a completely separate forest from the one they use within their internal network. This adds an additional layer of security to your design. If you were to use the same forest in both locations, you could run the risk of exposing information about your internal network if someone were to hack into your perimeter network. There are other options available, depending on the level of access you need to grant to the external users. In later chapters I will discuss Active Directory Federation Services (AD FS) and Active Directory Lightweight Directory Services (AD LDS).

Figure 3.4 is a flowchart that will assist you in making decisions for your forest design. Within this flowchart, take into account isolation and autonomy needs, and choose the best forest design based on the needs of the organization. Table 3.1 shows the advantages and disadvantages of using a single forest. Table 3.2 compares the multiple-forest pros and cons.

FIGURE 3.4
Flowchart to
determine isolated
or autonomous
control

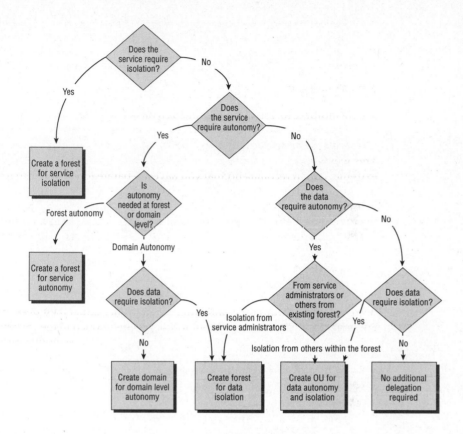

TABLE 3.1: Single-Forest Pros and Cons

SINGLE-FOREST PROS	SINGLE-FOREST CONS
Easier to administer	Less secure for multiple business units with unknown/untrusted administrators
Easier to troubleshoot	Forests cannot be merged or split.
A single security boundary	Domains cannot join other forests.
Single schema	Schema differences are sometimes needed between business units.
Easier to support	Cannot agree on change control within a domain.
	Users cannot search GCs of other forest without additional software.

TABLE 3.2: Multiple-Forest Pros and Cons

MULTIPLE-FOREST PROS	MULTIPLE-FOREST CONS
More secure	More administration
May have different schema in each forest (e.g., one business unit uses Exchange and another doesn't want its schema extended with the Exchange attributes).	Difficult to remember what schema extensions have been added and from which application they were added.
More control over outside trusts	No complete transitive trusts
Trusts between forests in W2003 and W2008 are transitive and Kerberos-secured.	Trusts between two forests are one-way, nontransitive NTLMv2 in Windows 2000.
	Certain Exchange 2000 mailbox features are not available when users exist in a different forest than does their user object.

Most small- and medium-sized companies will opt for a single forest. Following are situations that might call for exceptions:

- Extranet application(s) use Active Directory.

- Acquisitions and/or businesses break off into their own entities.

- Pilot deployments are needed to roll out applications or new systems.

- Network administration is separated into autonomous groups that do not trust one another.

- Business units are politically separated, or geographical separation creates nervousness about availability of technical support.

- Business units must be maintained separately for legal reasons.

- There is a need to isolate the schema or configuration containers.

- There is a need to limit the scope of trusts between domains.

If part of your organization needs to have additional schema attributes and objects, and those attributes and objects are specific to an application, you could be able to use an Active Directory Lightweight Directory Services (AD LDS) partition (to be discussed later in this chapter), sometimes referred to as an application partition, instead of creating a separate forest. Note that if the objects are used for security purposes, they will have to be stored within Active Directory and not as an AD LDS partition.

If you are considering a multiforest implementation, you will need to do special planning for the following:

DNS name resolution Your solution is easy in Windows Server 2003 and 2008 because you can use *conditional forwarding*, which is forwarding to preferred DNS servers depending on the domain name.

Resource sharing   This includ[...]
trust relationships, and access[...]
Manager (ILM) Server.

Network infrastructure   You[...]
single forest configuration, suc[...]
to ensure proper communicati[...]

If you plan to use AD DS in an [...]
you need to synchronize accounts, [...]
windowsserver/ilm2007/defaul[...]
Edition to run it.

To get the most functionality f[...]
est *functional level you can support*[...]
AD to utilize new tools that are [...]
trollers from other operating sys[...]
domain controllers, you will hav[...]

[Handwritten notes overlapping text:]
Windows 2008 stn.
~~2008~~
Sql serve 2008
What is sharpnt
serve (?)

Designing with Change-Control Policies in Mind

This is an often-overlooked planning step. Realize that extending the schema later (to implement or upgrade to Exchange, for instance) affects the entire forest, every object, and the domain controller. Have a change-control policy in place that emphasizes proper operational processes. I know this is boring and a pain to implement, but it is sorely needed. Everything you do should be verified in a lab first, monitored, rolled out to a pilot group, verified, and then deployed in a systematic approach. Anticipate change, reorganizations, politics, and so forth.

Before deciding to make any type of change, make sure you verify the necessity of the change that will be implemented. If you are simply adding an attribute to an object class, make sure none of the existing attributes will support your needs. There are 15 custom attributes that can be used for any purpose. Using these attributes will only cause replication traffic to the domain controllers in the domain where the object exists. If the change needs to be added to the global catalog, the change will replicate throughout the forest. Be aware of the additional replication you will be introducing.

If you do add an additional attribute or attributes to an object class, the new object class will need to replicate to all domain controllers within the forest. If you have wide area network (WAN) links where replication is controlled through a schedule, you could introduce inconsistencies between your domain controllers until the replication has completed. You will also cause additional replication across those WAN links, which could pose other problems for the users who are trying to use them. Make sure you know how you are going to roll out the changes, and the schedule you will enforce.

A well-defined change-control policy will reduce the problems associated with making changes to your infrastructure. Debates will ensue among the administrators of the domains within the forest. The battles that need to be fought to prove a change needs to be put into place are hard enough without having to decide on all of the criteria to include within your policy. The criteria should include the following:

Planning and testing   The planning documents that must be completed and the types of tests that the change will need to pass

Who is able to make the change   The appropriate parties that will be able to enact the change within the schema

The rollout schedule   Project guidelines for how the change will be made

Where the change can be made   The systems that will be used to change the schema

Prior to implementing AD DS, decide who will make up the approval committee. Meet with the administrators of all of the domains within the forest to gain approval of the policy. Everyone who will be affected needs to buy in. Getting them to do so may not be a simple task, especially in an environment where you have service or data autonomy. Some administrators may not have a great deal of trust in other administrators. As mentioned before, make sure you have the appropriate allies so that you can get approval from the highest-level stakeholder.

Building a Design Based on the Standard Forest Scenarios

There are three basic forest-design scenarios: the organization-based forest, the resource forest, and the restricted-access forest. Each of them is used for specific design goals.

Organization-based forest   The organization-based forest is the most common type of forest. Under this design, an organization's resources are placed within the forest and organized so that the appropriate groups have control over the resources they need. One of the primary reasons companies will choose the decentralized model is autonomy of control. If autonomy is required, a department or division could have a domain created for it, or organizational units (OUs) could be built within a domain.

Resource forest   If certain resources need to be isolated from the rest of the organization, a resource forest can be created. A resource forest is one in which the resources (such as shared folders, printers, member servers, etc.) are located within their own forest so that the owners of the resource can control them. Usually, the resource forest will not have any user accounts within it (with the exception of the Service Administrator accounts required to maintain the forest). Using this type of forest, an organization can make sure that the resources contained within the resource forest are not affected by the loss of services in any other forest.

Restricted-access forest   A restricted-access forest creates complete separation of service administrators. Although trust relationships can be built to allow users to access the resources within the remote forest, the Service Administrators from the two forests will not be allowed to administer the other forest services. If there is any need for isolation of services, this is the type of forest structure to be built.

Separating Extranet Applications into Their Own Forest

I can't stress enough that security is too important to take administrative shortcuts. Don't allow an extranet application in your demilitarized zone (DMZ) to use the same forest as do your production users. Simple hacks (such as enumeration, DoS, and elevated-privileges attacks) against your extranet could cause catastrophic damage to your internal network AD structure if the extranet application domain and your internal domain are linked with a single forest.

If Windows Server 2003 or 2008 is the OS upon which AD DS is operating, you will have options (e.g., conditional forwarding) that will make implementing separate forests easier. If you are still running Windows 2000, you should design a secure foundation for your AD infrastructure, even if it will take additional administration and time.

New features within Windows Server 2008 make using multiple forests a little less intimidating. AD FS takes advantage of using a single sign-on for users who are in separate forests. You can extend that functionality to the DMZ by using AD FS to authenticate accounts to your internal AD infrastructure. For more information on working with AD FS, see Chapter 10, "Managing Access with Active Directory Services."

Forest Functionality Mode Features in AD DS

Windows 2000 introduced mixed- and native-mode functionality. When Window NT 4 backup domain controllers were used in conjunction with Windows 2000 domain controllers in the same domain, the domain had to use mixed-mode functionality. This limited what functions were available to Active Directory because every domain controller had to work under the Windows NT 4 domain rules.

Windows Server 2003 brought additional functionality to Active Directory, and in doing so expanded into *forest functionality* and *domain functionality*. Choosing to move your domain or forest to a higher functional level gave you the added benefit of additional AD functionality.

Windows 2008 Server introduces changes at the domain functional level only. No significant changes are achieved at the forest functional level beyond what was provided with Windows 2003 forest functional level.

It is a best practice in any upgrade, migration, or installation to get to Windows 2000 native mode, Windows Server 2003 forest functional, or Windows 2008 forest functional mode as soon as you can. When you switch your domains from Windows Server 2000 mixed mode to native mode, you lose the ability to support Windows NT 4 backup domain controllers. From that point on, the backup domain controllers will not be allowed to participate in replication. When switching from native mode to Windows Server 2003 forest functional level, you excommunicate the Windows 2000 domain controllers from the domain. This also applies to Windows Server 2008. If you switch from native mode or Windows Server 2003 functional level to Windows Server 2008 forest functional level, Windows 2000 or 2003 domain controllers cannot participate in your AD DS forest. In return, because all of the domain controllers are at their highest level, you can take advantage of all of the advanced feature sets of Windows Server 2008.

To switch your forest from Windows 2000 to Windows Server 2003 forest functional level, you must be a member of the Enterprise Admins group. All of the domains within the forest must be at least at the Windows 2000 native mode. As long as all of the domains within the forest are at that level, when you choose to switch the forest to Windows Server 2003 forest functional level, all of the domains will switch at the same time. If any of the domains are still at the Windows 2000 mixed mode, you will not be able to raise the forest functional level. As you can see in Figure 3.5, you will find the Raise Forest Functional Level choice in Active Directory Domains and Trusts. You can, however, also manually edit the functionality levels in ADSI Edit, and/or LDP.EXE, although I don't recommend doing so unless Microsoft support tells you to.

When going to Windows Server 2003 forest functional level, you gain the following features:

Domain rename   This ability is accessed through the netdom command-line utility or the rendom resource-kit utility.

Link value replication   This is the ability, for example, for a group to replicate a single member when a change is made instead of the entire group being replicated each time (which is what Windows 2000 does). This also removes the 5,000-member limit on groups.

The ability to convert a user in AD to INetOrgPerson on the fly   You also gain the ability to put a user password on the INetOrgPerson Lightweight Directory Access Protocol (LDAP) object.

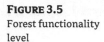

FIGURE 3.5
Forest functionality
level

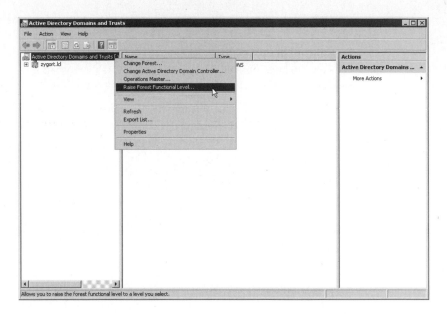

Schema redefine   This is not deletion, though it is the next best thing.

Dynamic auxiliary classes   Use this when you need to have a departmental schema extension that doesn't affect the rest of the forest. For example, use it when a department needs to put employee IDs into Active Directory and you, as the forest owner, don't want to extend the schema for this small department's needs.

Basic and query group types   The basic group types, Security and Distribution, are available with all versions of Active Directory. Query groups types become available when the forest level is raised to Windows Server 2003 functional level. Query-based groups allow you to create an email distribution list that dynamically updates its members based on an LDAP query.

Improved Knowledge Consistency Checker (KCC) algorithms and scalability   This feature is a big deal. In Windows 2000, you were told to turn off the KCC for implementations where you had about 100 DCs in a domain. Now the KCC can scale to more than 4,000 DCs in a domain, although you'd probably never want to have a domain that big.

Additional attributes automatically added to the global catalog   Because forest-level trusts are now available, the global catalog has a few additional attributes that it tracks so that clients can utilize the trusts efficiently.

Inter-Site Topology Generator (ISTG) enhancements   You can allow for complex site designs that have more than 100 sites and the ability to stop replicating automatically with an "offline" domain controller.

Constrained delegation   This allows you to control the service-principle names of the service accounts that another service account has delegated to you.

Application groups   This is a method of controlling the accounts that have access to an application.

Cross-forest trusts   These are perfect for Exchange clients that exist in one forest but have their Exchange mailbox in another forest. They eliminate the need to log in again. Windows 2000 has

NTLMv2 cross-forest trusts. Windows Server 2003 uses Kerberos trusts. (Can you say single sign-on?)

The ability to update logon time stamp as a fast-synching replicated attribute   When a user logs on, the logon time stamp is updated within the domain controller to which the user authenticates, and that attribute is replicated as an urgent update to all of the other domain controllers.

Universal groups   This is the same as in native mode for Windows 2000.

Group nesting   This is the same as in native mode for Windows 2000.

The ability to switch distribution groups to security groups, and vice versa   This is the same as in native mode for Windows 2000.

SID history as an attribute of a user object   This is the same as in native mode for Windows 2000. It is a very important part of migrations that happen over time. An NT 4 or Windows 2000 security identifier (SID) can be brought over during migration so that authentication against resources and objects in the NT 4 or Windows 2000 domain or forest that have not been migrated will still work.

ADDITIONAL RESOURCES

The following are white papers and websites that will help you familiarize yourself with some of the important Active Directory topics:

◆ Multiple Forest Considerations Whitepaper

   www.microsoft.com/downloads/details.aspx?displaylang=en&familyid=B717BFCD-6C1C-4AF6-8B2C-B604E60067BA

◆ Design Considerations for Delegation of Administration in Active Directory

   http://technet.microsoft.com/en-us/library/Bb727032.aspx

◆ Best Practice Active Directory Design for Managing Windows Networks

   http://technet.microsoft.com/en-us/library/Bb727085.aspx

◆ Active Directory Information

   www.microsoft.com/ad and www.microsoft.com/technet/ad

◆ How to Create a Cross-Reference to an External Domain in Active Directory in W2K

   http://support.microsoft.com/kb/241737

AD DS Domain Design

So far we have looked at what goes into a forest design. The criteria I introduced for forests will flow over into domain design. You are still going to base your design decisions on one major design criterion: administrative control. Keep this in mind as you work through the rest of this chapter. All of your decisions will have administrative control as the primary concern, and then group policies and security policies will help you refine your design.

As many administrators will tell you, designing the domain structure can be troubling. If you have separate administrative teams within your organization, you will probably find that they do not trust outside influences and will demand that they have their own forest so that they can have complete control over their resources. Although there may be cases where you will give in and allow them to have their own forest, under most conditions you should avoid creating an additional forest.

To create a forest, you must first promote a stand-alone server to a domain controller. During that promotion, you will specify the details that will control the very destiny of the forest. Think about that for a moment, because that statement does imply the gravity of the design decisions you are making. Creating an AD infrastructure takes planning and understanding of the options you have available to you. We are going to look at the design decisions for domains, which ultimately will affect the forest structure as well.

We start with the design criteria that needs consideration and then move into a discussion of the administrative and replication issues that pertain to domains. From there we go through a quick rundown of the benefits and drawbacks when you have a single domain design as compared to a multiple-domain and multiple-tree design. We examine trust relationships and look at the different trusts that can be built, as well as alternatives to creating additional trust relationships. Because some domains will need to support previous versions of Windows domain controllers, we study the functional modes of Windows 2000 and Windows Server 2003 domains.

AD DS Domain Design Criteria

I'm going to say it again, and you are probably going to tire of hearing this, but administrative control will become the primary domain-design criterion. As you remember from earlier in this chapter, the forest is the security boundary. Because you cannot guarantee that a domain will not be affected by an account from outside the domain, the forest becomes the security boundary within AD DS. Thus, the domain becomes the autonomous administrative boundary. This means that administrators for a domain have control over the resources within their domain, but no other domain; additionally, the resources they control can also be controlled by members of the forest root high-level group Enterprise Admins.

However, before planning multiple domains, you should think about the ramifications of doing so. Later in this chapter, I spell out the advantages and disadvantages of having multiple domains and trees. Always start simple—single forest, single domain—and work from there. You will encounter plenty of political battles as you design your domain structure, so plan well. Create a design that you think will work, and, just as with the forest structure, let others review it so that you can refine it to fit their needs.

Defining Domain Requirements

Effectively, a domain can host millions of objects. Theoretically, you are restricted only by the hardware limitations of your domain controllers. With that said, you will find that other factors will force you to limit the size of your domain to make your AD infrastructure efficient. If all the accounts that you have created within your domain are within a large, well-connected network where you have plenty of available bandwidth for all your network traffic to flow, you could probably get by with a single domain. Problems crop up when you start working with locations that are separated by WAN links that may not have enough available bandwidth to support the replication traffic.

Domain Boundaries

As we mentioned earlier, the domain is the administrative boundary for AD DS. Because the Enterprise Admins group has the ability to affect any domain within the forest, administrators will not have complete isolated control of their domain. The same can be said about the replication boundary.

The schema and configuration-naming contexts are replicated throughout the forest. Application-mode partitions can also be replicated throughout the forest. The domain-naming context, on the other hand, replicates only between domain controllers within a single domain. In this section, we look at how this can affect your domain design.

ACCOUNT POLICY BOUNDARY

An account policy is enforced at the domain level and will not affect other domains within the forest. Account policies are not inherited from domain to domain, so a parent domain's policy will not affect any child domain.

With Active Directory 2000 and 2003, you could not override the account policy within the domain by using another policy that is linked elsewhere within the domain. In other words, you could not set differing password policies at the domain and OU levels; the domain policy will override the OU policy. Windows 2008 changes this behavior and will allow you to set password policies through Group Policy at any level in the domain.

Domain account policies consist of three policy sections: Password, Account Lockout, and Kerberos restrictions. Figure 3.6 shows the sections as found in the Group Policy Management Editor, under Default Domain Policy ➤ Security Settings. When the domain is created, a security template is imported into the default domain policy. Every domain member will be controlled by the policy.

FIGURE 3.6
Default Domain Policy
security options

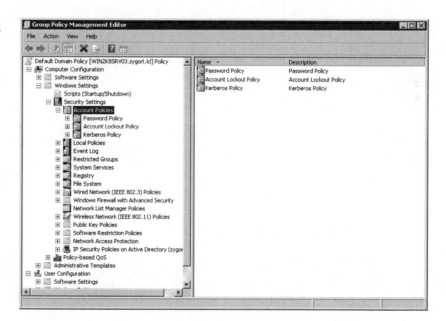

Password Policy

Password restrictions can be set to control exactly how passwords are used within the domain. If you open the Password Policy node, you will see the following options:

Enforce Password History This option specifies how many passwords the system will keep track of and how many unique passwords a user will go through before they are allowed to reuse a password.

Maximum Password Age   This option specifies how long a password will remain valid before the user is forced to change the password.

Minimum Password Age   This option specifies how long a password has to be used before a user is allowed to change it.

Minimum Password Length   This option specifies how many characters a password is required to contain.

Password Must Meet Complexity Requirements   If enabled, the passwords that users generate will need to contain three of the following four criteria: uppercase character, lowercase character, numeral, or special character (i.e., !,@,#,$,%).

Store Password Using Reversible Encryption for All Users in the Domain   When this option is enabled, the user's password is stored within Active Directory in a format that can be used to authenticate users when they are accessing websites that use digest authentication.

Account Lockout Policy

The Account Lockout node contains the options that control when a user's account will be locked out, or disabled from use, if too many password attempts fail. This is used to make sure that a user's account is not easily compromised if an attacker is trying to determine the user's password. Following are the options contained within this node:

Account Lockout Duration   This option specifies how long an account remains in a locked-out state. If it's set to 0, the administrator will have to unlock the account manually. If it's set to any other value, the system will automatically unlock the user's account after the number of minutes specified.

Account Lockout Threshold   This option defines the number of attempts that can be made to enter the correct password. Once this number is exceeded, the account will become locked out.

Reset Account Lockout Counter After   This option defines the amount of time in minutes that must elapse after a failed logon attempt before the counter is reset to 0. After an invalid password entry is made, the account-lockout counter is incremented by 1. If this number is set to 0, the account lockout counter is reset as soon as the password is entered correctly.

Kerberos Policies

Kerberos policies are implemented by the domain's Key Distribution Center (KDC). These policies are configured and applied at the domain level, and can only be changed by members of the Domain Administrators group.

Enforce user logon restrictions   If this setting is enabled, the KDC will validate every request for a session ticket against the user rights policy of the user account. This may slow network access so use with caution.

Maximum lifetime for service ticket   This determines the maximum amount of time (in minutes) that a session ticket can be used to access a particular service. The values for this setting must be between a minimum value of 10 (minutes) and a maximum that is less than or equal to the value defined for "Maximum lifetime for a user ticket."

Maximum lifetime for a user ticket   This value is the maximum amount of time (in hours) that a user's ticket-granting ticket (TGT) can be used before it must either submit a request for renewal or for a new ticket.

Maximum lifetime for a user ticket renewal   This value defines the period of time (in days) during which a user's TGT may be renewed.

Maximum tolerance for computer clock synchronization   This setting defines the maximum time difference (in minutes) that Kerberos will allow between the time in the client object and the time on the domain controller that provides Kerberos authentication.

Within a Windows 2000 or 2003 Active Directory domain, every account within the domain will have to follow the rules set forth under the default domain policy. With a Windows 2008 domain, you can enforce some options on users or groups.

For example, you want to ensure that service accounts are forced to change their passwords on a 30-day cycle, but the account policy for the domain is set so that users will not have to change their password until 60 days have lapsed.

To do so, create a new Group Policy Object (GPO) and link it to the OU that contains your service accounts. Configure the password policy, edit the Maximum Password Age setting, and configure it for 30 days.

REPLICATION BOUNDARY

Domain controllers within a domain will share their domain partition, or domain-naming context, with one another, but will be selfish with domain controllers from other domains. There is a perfectly good reason for this. The domain partition will usually be the largest of the Active Directory partitions and is the one that changes the most frequently. To reduce the amount of replication traffic to be sent to each domain controller within your forest, the domain boundary was defined.

If you have two locations that have very poor network connectivity, or you want to control the replication that is sent across WAN links, you can divide the locations into separate domains to reduce the replication traffic. Once you have separate domains, all of the changes to objects within the domain partition are replicated only to the domain controllers within the domain. The other domains do not "see" the changes. If both domains are still within the same forest, they will share global catalog information as well as the configuration and schema partitions.

Defining Tree Requirements

Every domain within a tree shares the same DNS namespace. A majority of organizations will need to use only a single namespace to define all the units within their organization. If you need to support two namespaces within your organization, and you do not want to support multiple forests, creating another tree within your existing forest will provide additional administrative advantages over the multiple-forest design. Every tree within the forest will still use the same schema and configuration naming contexts. They will also be under the same Enterprise Admins control. Every global catalog will contain the same information so that users will be able to search for resources anywhere within the forest.

At the same time, the administrative staff from the new tree will have autonomous control over their resources only. This can become a political issue if you are working with separate companies all under the same organizational umbrella. However, the administrative costs of maintaining a single forest with multiple trees will usually outweigh the need for complete isolation of resources between divisions of an organization. Remember: always start simple and then add complexity to your design only if you have a valid reason to do so.

Multiple Domains: Pros and Cons

Any time you add domains, whether the domains exist within the same tree or if there are multiple trees hosting the domains, you will have additional administrative requirements. Table 3.3 details some of the advantages and disadvantages of having multiple domains.

If you add several layers of domains within your forest, the resources required to process object access through the transitive trusts could hinder performance of your domain controllers.

TABLE 3.3: Multiple Domains Pros and Cons

ADVANTAGES	DISADVANTAGES
Account policy boundaries in place	Additional administrative overhead
Centralized GPOs, account policies, and administrative delegation	Separate GPOs, account policies, and administrative control at each domain
Active Directory database size reduced	Increase in global catalog size
Reduced domain-naming context replication traffic	Increase in global catalog replication
Less file replication service traffic	Moving user accounts to other domains is more difficult than moving them within a domain

DNS Requirements

The Domain Name System (DNS) design criteria were discussed in the previous chapter; however, any discussion of domains must mention DNS. Active Directory relies on DNS to function, and the domains that make up Active Directory have a one-to-one relationship with DNS. Each of your domains will share a name with a DNS zone. Whenever a domain controller is brought online, service locator (SRV) records are registered within the DNS zone that supports the AD domain. Figure 3.7 shows the correlation between AD domains and the corresponding DNS zones.

Authentication Options

When a domain is in mixed mode, the authentication options are limited. You will have the ability to use only the standard logon method. Once you have cleared your environment of the Windows NT backup domain controllers, you can let your remaining Active Directory domain controllers expand their horizons and start taking advantage of some of the new features. For user authentication, this means that the user principle name can now be used when authenticating.

Standard logon Most users are now familiar with the standard logon method in which you enter your username and password, and then choose the domain to which you are authenticating. Using this method, your username and password are used to create a hash that is sent to the nearest domain controller from the domain that was chosen from the drop-down box.

User principle name A user principle name (UPN) is a user account–friendly name that is shorthand for the user account and the DNS name of the tree where the user object resides. If you choose to use your UPN instead of the standard logon method, after you enter your UPN and password, a global catalog server is contacted to determine to which domain your logon request should be sent. This approach offers several advantages. If your users become familiar with their UPN, they do not have to be concerned about which domain the workstation is a member of when they sit down at a workstation. As a matter of fact, at that point the user doesn't really need to know of which domain his or her account is a member.

Using either of the two logon methods produces the same results when the user is authenticated. Kerberos builds the appropriate tickets for the user so that the user can be authenticated and authorized to access all the resources for which they have been given permission. A global catalog server is required if you are logging in using the UPN. The global catalog server is used to determine in which domain the user belongs, and is required if the domain is in native mode. As we look at global catalog servers in Chapter 4, "Organizing the Physical and Logical Aspects of AD DS," we'll discuss some of the pros and cons of locating a global catalog server within a site.

FIGURE 3.7
Correlation of Active
Directory domains
and DNS zones

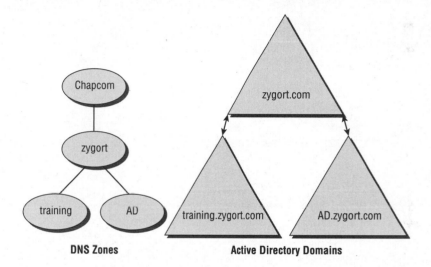

DNS Zones   **Active Directory Domains**

Interforest Trusts

Between domains within a forest, you will find trust relationships that define how the users within the domains can access resources within other domains in the forest. By default, when a domain is created, a trust relationship is built between the new domain and its parent. In a single tree, the trust relationships are parent-child trusts. When a new domain tree is created, a tree-root trust is created between the forest root and the root of the new tree. You cannot control this behavior. The Active Directory promotion tool (dcpromo) is responsible for creating the trust relationships and configuring how they will work. A third type of trust, the shortcut trust, is created manually by an administrator. When the trust relationships are in place, each domain will allow requests to flow up the tree in an attempt to secure Kerberos access to a resource.

Parent-child trust   A parent-child trust is the most basic of the trust types because all the domains share the same namespace. Each trust relationship is configured to allow two-way access to resources and is also transitive, so that users within every domain can access resources anywhere in the tree structure if they have been given permissions to do so.

Tree-root trust   Tree-root trusts share the same behavior as the parent-child trust, but they are used to allow communication between two namespaces. Because of their two-way transitive nature, users from any domain within the forest are allowed to access resources anywhere within the forest, assuming that the administrative staff has given them the permissions to do so.

Shortcut trust Another interforest trust relationship, the shortcut trust, is available to reduce the network traffic that is incurred when a user attempts to gain access to a resource within the forest. By default, when a user attempts to connect to an object and that object resides within another domain, the user's account has to be authorized to access the object. This process has been nicknamed "walking the tree" because the trust path through which the user needs to be authorized could take the user to multiple domains within the forest. A domain controller from each domain within the trust path will be contacted to determine if the user is allowed to access the object in question. In Figure 3.8 you will see that for John, whose account is located in the domain `hr.north.bloomco.lcl` to access a printer in the `hr.east.zygort.lcl` domain, domain controllers from `hr.north.bloomco.lcl`, `north.bloomco.lcl`, `bloomco.lcl`, `zygort.lcl`, `east.zygort.lcl`, and `hr.east.zygort.lcl` will need to be contacted in order for John's account to receive the appropriate Kerberos authentication and authorization to the printer.

FIGURE 3.8
Trust path

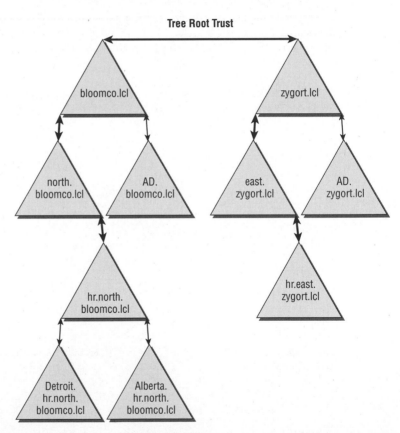

There are a couple of options you can implement that will reduce the amount of Kerberos traffic as John attempts to access the printer. The first is to place domain controllers from each of the domains within the trust path into the same site as John's account. This will alleviate the need to send the traffic across WAN links. However, you will incur additional costs because you will need more hardware, and you may also increase administrative overhead at that site as a result of the introduction of the domain controller hardware at that location. This scenario has a serious drawback. If you have users who frequently access resources from another domain, yet those users are located in different sites, you may be forced to locate domain controllers at each of the sites to optimize your traffic.

As an alternative, you can create a shortcut trust between the two domains. In doing so, you are essentially cutting a path from one domain to another, thereby allowing the two domains' Kerberos subsystems to work together instead of having to pass the data through intermediary domains. Figure 3.9 shows the shortcut trust created between `hr.north.bloomco.lcl` and `hr.east.zygort.lcl`.

There is an advantage to creating a shortcut trust: you have the ability to dictate how the trust will be used. As long as you have the appropriate credentials, you can create the shortcut trust between the two domains so that it is a two-way trust; in other words, both domains can then use the trust path. You can also create the trust as a one-way trust, which will allow only users from one domain to access resources in the other, but not vice versa.

To reiterate the last line of the opening paragraph for this section, when the trust path is used, it flows up the domain hierarchy. In Figure 3.9, users from `hr.north.bloomco.lcl` and any child domain beneath it can take advantage of the shortcut trust path, but the parent domains will still have to take the original trust path.

FIGURE 3.9
Shortcut trust path

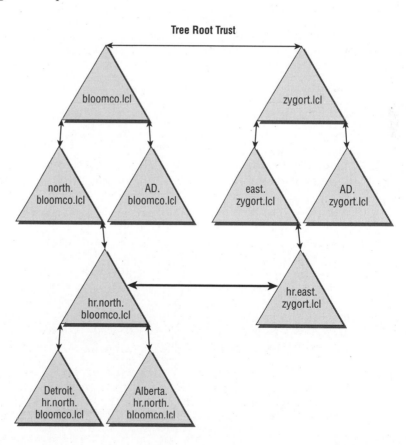

Domain Controller Placement

Domain controllers host the database that is Active Directory. In order for users to log on to the domain, they need to be able to connect to a domain controller. The rule of thumb is to locate a domain controller near any user so the user can log on even if WAN connections fail. There are instances when you will not want to place a domain controller at a specific location. In the following sections, we look at the options for placing domain controllers within your infrastructure and, in some cases, the reasons why you would not.

PHYSICAL ACCESS TO DOMAIN CONTROLLERS

It is rare to meet a developer who doesn't believe he needs to be a member of the Domain Admins group. As a matter of fact, many developers have rogue domain controllers under their desks to use for testing. This is a bad practice because any Domain Admin can bring down the entire forest. A simple power-off on the domain controller immediately causes replication problems in Windows 2000 Server, although Windows Server 2003 and 2008 have mechanisms for just such an occurrence. The solution is to use a separate forest for any developer who either develops on Active Directory or needs elevated privileges. Yes, this increases administrative costs, but it will help secure your forest.

No matter how much time or money you spend securing an environment, it is for naught if your server is physically accessible. If someone is in front of your server, it is not *your* server anymore. Especially take this into account if you have branch offices that may not have a room to lock up the domain controller. Protecting your directory service database should take precedence over making sure that the users will be able to log on if the WAN link fails.

SITE AWARENESS

Active Directory–aware clients (such as Windows Server 2003 and 2008, Windows 2000 Server, Windows XP and Windows Vista), along with operating systems that have Active Directory client software available (such as Windows 98 Second Edition and Windows NT 4) are able to determine whether a domain controller is within the same site as the client. If a domain controller is not located in the same site, the client will connect to a domain controller that is located in a nearby site.

If you have several users within a site, it may be in your best interests to include a domain controller within the site. Of course, you want to make sure you can physically secure the domain controller. After users authenticate and receive an access token and the appropriate Kerberos tickets, they will be able to access resources until the Kerberos ticket expires. However, when users log off during the time a domain controller is unreachable, they will be logged on using cached credentials and will not be able to regain access to resources using their domain account.

If the users require uninterrupted access to network resources within the domain, you should also consider having two domain controllers at their site. Although this is an added expense, you have the peace of mind of knowing that if one domain controller fails, the other will still allow users to authenticate. You also gain the advantage of having an additional domain controller to take on part of the client load.

GLOBAL CATALOG PLACEMENT

Global catalog (GC) servers are domain controllers that take on the additional load of hosting objects from every domain within the forest. You should be familiar with the placement of GC servers within your network. The same basic rule applies to a GC server as it does to a domain controller: one should be placed within every site. Of course, this could be easier said than done. Budget limitations and security practices may prohibit you from placing GC servers everywhere you want. Follow these guidelines for trade-offs:

◆ If the global catalog cannot be physically secured, do not place it in the unsecured location.

◆ If an Exchange 200x system is within a site, it is highly recommended you place a GC server within the same site.

◆ If you have only a single domain, make all of your domain controllers GC servers.

◆ If you have multiple domains, you will need to make sure that the Infrastructure Master role is not on a GC server and that the Domain Naming Master is on a GC server.

GC servers provide functionality to users as well as to applications within the domain. GC servers are responsible for collecting information about the objects that exist in the domain partition of other domains in the forest. Although this is just a subset of the attributes for the objects, this could still be a considerable amount of information. Once a domain controller is specified as a GC server, additional replication will occur so that information from the other domains will populate the database. You need to determine if this additional replication is going to affect the performance of the network links.

Universal group membership caching   One of the features of Windows Server 2003 and higher versions is universal group membership caching. This feature is available only when the domain is in the Windows 2000 native mode or a at higher functional level, and only Windows Server 2003 and 2008 domain controllers provide this functionality. The benefit of using universal group membership caching is that a domain controller does not have to be made a GC server to provide users with their universal group membership, which is required to log on. As users authenticate, the domain controller contacts a GC server from another site to retrieve the required information. The group membership is then cached on the domain controller and is ready to be used the next time the user logs on. Because the domain controller does not have to provide GC services, replication across the WAN link is reduced.

Universal group membership caching is not meant for sites with large user populations, nor is it meant to be used where applications need to access a GC server. A maximum of 500 users is supported using this caching method. Also, the cached data are updated only every eight hours. If you are planning on performing group-membership changes on a regular basis, your users may not receive those changes in a timely manner. You can reduce the time frame for updating the cache, but in doing so you will be creating more replication traffic on your WAN link. Make sure you weigh the trade-offs before you decide where you will place a GC server.

When determining if you should have a GC server placed within a site, you should consider how much the GC server will be used and whether applications within the site need to use a GC server. Ask the following questions to determine if a GC should be placed within a site:

Are any applications, such as Exchange Server 200x, located within the site?   If so, you will want to locate a GC server within the same site as the application, because the LDAP queries being posted to the GC server will probably consume more bandwidth than replication would. Test the network requirements to determine which will consume more bandwidth. If the WAN link is not 100-percent reliable, you should always have the GC server local; otherwise the application will not function properly when the link goes down.

Are more than 100 users located within the site?   If more than 100 users are within a site, you will need to determine if stranding them without having the ability to access a GC server if the WAN link goes down is an acceptable option. You will also need to determine if the query latency is worth the cost savings of keeping the GC server at another location and not dedicating hardware for the site in question.

Is the WAN link 100-percent available? If you need application support and the user base consists of fewer than 100 users, you could have those users access a GC server in the remote site if the WAN link is reliable. Although no WAN link will ever be 100-percent available, the greater the reliability of the link, the better your chances of being able to support the user base from a remote site. If the WAN link is not always available and there are no other applications that rely on the GC server, you could implement universal group membership caching to alleviate some of the problems associated with user authentication.

Are there many roaming users who will be visiting the site? If many roaming users will be logging on at the site, you will want to locate a GC server within the site. Whenever a user logs on, the user's universal group membership is retrieved from the GC server. However, if the user population at the site is relatively static, you may be able to implement universal group membership caching on a domain controller.

Another Active Directory technology whose location needs to be determined is the Master Operations roles (see Chapter 5, "Flexible Single Master Operations Design"). Because only specific servers support the Master Operations functions, you need to know the criteria for their placement.

Domain Functional Levels

As the engineers behind Active Directory build new and better features, administrators are given more efficient and easier tools with which to work. At the same time, the new features in one operating system are not always supported in legacy operating systems. Windows NT 4 had some serious limitations when it came to secure and efficient administration. Windows 2000 addressed many of the limitations and presented Active Directory as the next generation of directory services.

Moving from the original security accounts manager–based directory service within Windows NT 4 to Active Directory was embraced by thousands of organizations once they realized the level of control and security that was built in. The only problem was that the thousands and thousands of Windows NT 4 installations could not simply roll over to Active Directory overnight. There had to be a means of interoperability between the directory services. To complicate matters, some of the features introduced with the Windows Server 2003 version of Active Directory were not supported under the Windows 2000 Server version of Active Directory.

To help with the interoperability issues between the differing directory services, Microsoft created functional levels that essentially put restrictions in place on the newer versions of Active Directory so that they play by the rules of the earlier operating systems. These functional levels come in various flavors: Windows 2000 mixed mode, Windows 2000 native mode, Windows Server 2003, Windows Server 2003 Interim, and Windows Server 2008.

Windows 2000 mixed mode If you need at least one each of Windows NT 4 and Windows 2000 domain controllers within your domain, you will need to maintain a mixed-mode environment. In mixed mode, the domain controllers work under the NT 4 rules for backward compatibility. This is the most restrictive mode, and you do not get all of the functionality of Active Directory. However, you can still use your Windows NT 4 Backup Domain Controllers (BDCs) to authenticate users until you have a chance to upgrade all of the BDCs.

Note that the functional levels apply only to domain controllers. You can still have Windows NT 4 and Windows 2000 member servers within domains of any functional level.

Windows 2000 native mode When you decide that you are ready to move to native mode, you manually set off the update through the appropriate Active Directory snap-ins. How do you know if you are ready? You are ready if you no longer need to have NT 4 BDCs as part of Active Directory. This could mean application needs, political needs, or timidity about moving from NT 4. Basically, if an NT 4 BDC has to be a part of an Active Directory domain, you are not ready to go to Windows 2000 native mode. Moving to Active Directory native mode is a one-time, permanent move. Once you are there, replication to Windows NT BDCs no longer occurs, and you cannot add any new BDCs to the network.

Windows Server 2003   This is the utopia for Windows Server 2003 domain controllers. Once you have raised the domain to this level, the domain controllers no longer need to share their databases with any of the Windows NT–based or Windows 2000–based domain controllers. As with native mode, once you have set the functional level to Windows Server 2003, there is no going back and you cannot install a Windows 2000–based domain controller into your Active Directory infrastructure.

Windows Server 2003 Interim   The Interim functional level assumes that you are migrating directly from Windows NT 4 to Windows Server 2003 without ever introducing Windows 2000–based domain controllers into the mix. You can still implement a Windows 2000–based workstation or server into the infrastructure; they will work perfectly. The major advantage to moving directly from Windows NT 4 to Windows Server 2003 is that the Windows Server 2003 Interim functional level allows you to take advantage of linked value replication (LVR) when replicating the membership of groups. This means that every member of a group is seen as a separate attribute. If you do not choose the Windows Server 2003 Interim level during the upgrade of the PDC to the forest root, or you do not have the forest root domain at the Windows Server 2003 Interim level when you upgrade PDCs to their own domain within the forest, group membership values will be replicated as a single attribute. LVR also removes the 5,000-member limit on groups.

Windows Server 2008   Following are the features that are changed with Windows Server 2008:

- Distributed File System (DFS) replication of SYSVOL. Because DFS is the mechanism used for replication, only deltas (changes) to the SYSVOL are replicated.

- Advanced Encryption Services (AES) support for Kerberos authentication.

- Last-interactive-logon information. Information is retained about the last successful interactive logon, the workstation that was used, and even the number of failed logon attempts for each user.

- Fine-grained password policies. Password policies and account-lockout policies can now be configured for users and global security groups in a domain. In Windows 2000 and 2003 Active Directory domains, there was one password policy and one account-lockout policy that was configured for the entire domain. If there was a need for different settings for any reason, another domain would have to be introduced.

Depending on the version of Active Directory you are running, you will have different methods of changing the functional level of the domain. If you are running Windows 2000's Active Directory, meaning that you have not added any Windows Server 2003 domain controllers, you can change to native mode as seen in Figure 3.10. If you have added a Windows Server 2003 domain controller, you can change to native mode by raising the functional level within Active Directory Users and Computers by right-clicking on the domain and selecting Raise Domain Functional Level, as seen in Figure 3.11. The same procedure can be performed through Active Directory Domains and Trusts. The screen in Figure 3.12 will appear after you have chosen to raise the functional level of the domain. Notice that you do not get an option to change to any other levels except for Windows 2000 native mode and Windows Server 2003.

FIGURE 3.10
Changing to Windows
2000 native mode

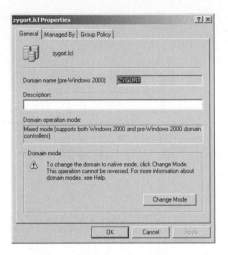

FIGURE 3.11
Choosing to raise the
functional level in a
Windows Server 2003
Active Directory
domain

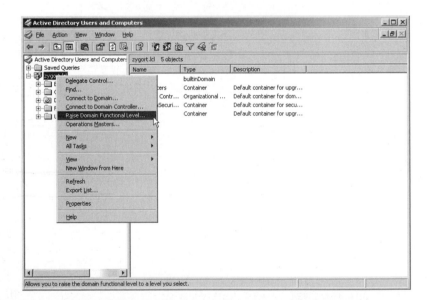

You may have noticed from the previous two functional-level options that you cannot raise the functional level to Windows Server 2003 Interim. You do have the option to set the functional level when you upgrade the domain's Primary Domain Controller (PDC). To set the functional level to Windows Server 2003 Interim after the PDC has been upgraded, you will have to use either the LDP.exe tool or the ADSI Edit MMC snap-in. Using either of these tools, connect to the domain controller that holds the Schema Master role and connect to the configuration naming context. The fully qualified path is CN=Partitions, CN=Configurations, DC=*ForestRootDom*, *DC=tld object*, where *ForestRootDom* is the name of the root domain for your forest and *tld* is the name of the top-level domain you are using within your forest. You need to change the msDS-Behavior-Version attribute. Setting this attribute to a value of 1 will place the forest in Windows Server 2003 Interim. Figure 3.13 shows the ADSI Edit utility being used to change the msDS-Behavior-Version attribute.

FIGURE 3.12
Changing to the
Windows 2000 native
mode functional level

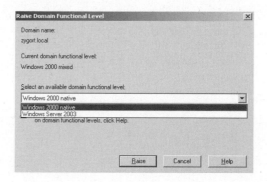

FIGURE 3.13
Using ADSI Edit to
change the functional
level to Windows
Server 2003 Interim

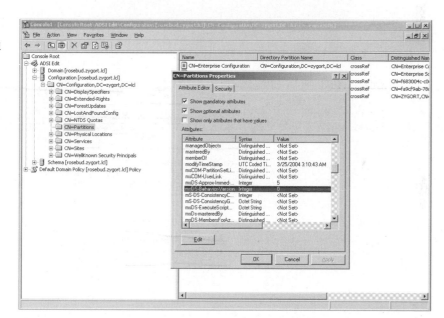

SETTING THE FOREST FUNCTIONAL LEVEL

You can set the forest functional level to any of the four levels by using LDP.exe or ADSI Edit. When you attach to the msDS-Behavior-Version attribute, you have the ability to set the level by entering one of the following values:

◆ Value of 0 or not set = mixed level forest

◆ Value of 1 = Windows Server 2003 Interim forest level

◆ Value of 2 = Windows Server 2003 forest level

◆ Value of 3 = Windows Server 2008

BENEFITS OF NATIVE MODE

Native mode gives you the best options that Windows 2000 has to offer. Once at this level, you will have the ability to use security groups to your advantage. Global and domain local groups can be nested, and universal security groups are available to make administering large organizations easier. Native mode and higher modes allow for the following group functions and features:

- Domain local groups
- Universal groups
- Group nesting
- Switched-off NETLOGON synchronization
- SIDHistory
- ADMTv2

Domain Local Groups

All of the servers within a Windows NT 4 domain and member servers within Active Directory have local groups to access local resources. Using local groups became cumbersome because we had to re-create the group on every server where we wanted it so that users could access similar resources. Now you can share local groups across the entire domain in Windows 2000 native mode. Domain local group membership can include universal groups, global groups, user accounts, and computer accounts from any domain within the forest, in trusted forests, or in trusted Windows NT 4 domains. Domain local groups are able to grant permissions only within their own domain.

Universal Groups

Universal groups were created to address the limitations of global groups within a large environment. Just as local groups had the negative side effect of duplicate groups on multiple servers, a problem that domain local groups alleviate, universal groups alleviate the need to manage several global groups when adding membership to domain local groups.

There are a couple of caveats to using universal groups. First, make sure all domains in the forest are in native mode. Native-mode functionality is controlled on a domain-by-domain basis. Users logging on to domains that are in native mode will have their universal group membership enumerated before they log on; but if they log on to a computer in a mixed-mode domain, the universal group membership is ignored. This can cause problems with the access token when accessing resources, because a user could be denied access to a resource due to their universal group membership.

Another caveat is the universal group membership replication that occurs. Global catalog servers within the forest will receive the universal group's membership through replication. Whenever there is a change to the group's membership, the changes have to be replicated to all of the other global catalogs throughout the forest. Within a Windows 2000 Active Directory domain, the group membership is a single attribute within the Universal Group object. Unfortunately, if you change a single member of the group, all of the members have to be replicated, and a group with a large number of members will cause a considerable amount of replication. Your best bet is to include global groups as the only members of a universal group. Doing so will allow you to add and remove members from the global group, thus not directly affecting the universal group.

BENEFITS OF UNIVERSAL GROUPS

Cheryl is an administrator of an organization that has five domains. Each of these domains has printers for which users from every domain will need to have print permissions. The previous administrator created domain local groups and assigned print permissions to them. Then he created global groups and added user accounts that have the same resource-access needs to the global groups. When Cheryl took over, the domain had 20 domain local groups and 20 global groups.

Through acquisitions, Cheryl's company has added five more domains. During her planning, she determined that if she added one more domain local group, she would have to add in all 20 of the global groups to the new domain local group. Inversely, if she created a new global group, she would have to add it in to 20 domain local groups.

Cheryl decides to incorporate universal groups. Universal groups simplify her administrative overhead by minimizing the number of groups with which she would have to work. After she has assigned permissions to the domain local group and added the users to the global groups, she can create a universal group and add all of the global groups to it. Then, by adding the universal group to the domain local group, all of the users will have access to the printers. If she adds another printer and creates a domain local group for access, all she would have to do is add the universal group to the domain local group's membership, and all of the users would have access. Of course, the inverse works, as well. If she creates a new global group, she can add it to the universal group to give the users access to all printers.

Group Nesting

Nesting groups is immensely helpful. Putting global groups into other global groups can really simplify matters for an administrator. This feature is available once you have moved to Windows 2000 native mode. Windows 2000 has a group limitation of 5,000 members—Windows 2003 has no such limitation. Using nested groups in Windows 2000 helps alleviate the 5,000-member limit by allowing a single group object (which may contain thousands of members) to count as one object in the group in which it is placed.

Group nesting also allows you to apply the "most restrictive/most inclusive" nesting strategy to make administration of resources easier. In most organizations, you will find that there are employees who need access to the same resources. These employees may have different levels of authority within the organization, yet they have similar resource-access needs. After you determine what resources they will need to access, you can develop a nesting strategy that will allow you to control the resource access easily.

Take, for instance, a typical accounting division. Within the division, you usually have at least two departments: accounts payable and accounts receivable. Within each of these departments, you usually find employees who have differing job responsibilities and different resource-access needs—yet there are resources to which they all need access. Managers from all of the departments will need to have access to resources that the accounts payable and accounts receivable employees need to access (such as for customer and vendor contact information). If you create a global group for the accounts payable managers and another for the accounts receivable managers, you can add the appropriate user accounts into the groups so that they can access the confidential resources.

Because accounts-payable employees have different resource-access needs than accounts-receivable employees, global groups should be created for each, and the appropriate user accounts should be added to the global groups. This is where group nesting and the most restrictive/most inclusive method of group creation comes into play. Instead of adding all of the managers from each department to the employees' global groups, simply add the managers' global group to the employees' global group. This has the same effect as adding the managers' accounts into the employees' global groups, but it simplifies group administration later. If you hire a new manager, you simply add the new manager's account into the managers' global group, and the new manager will have access to all the resources from both global groups. Taking this one step further, if there are resources that all the users from both accounts payable and accounts receivable need, you could create an All Accounting global group and add the Accounts Payable and Accounts Receivable global groups to it.

Switched-Off NETLOGON Synchronization

Don't worry about this; it isn't as bad as it seems. It just means that you will not be able to add additional Windows NT 4 BDCs to your domain. Once you have made the commitment to move to Active Directory, you should not need to install additional Windows NT 4 domain controllers to your network. There are cases in which this may not be true, but if you have eliminated all of the Windows NT 4 BDCs from your domain, you can safely make the move to native mode. Windows NT 4 member servers can still be part of the Windows 2000 Active Directory domain.

SIDHistory — used to allow network users to domain resources

Moving user accounts between organizational units (OUs) is a relatively painless operation. Because they are still within the same domain and retain the same security identifier (SID), you need to be concerned only about the effects of Group Policy Objects (GPOs) during the move. Moving the user between domains is another issue altogether. You must use a special utility to move the user accounts, and when an account is moved, its SID is changed. For the user to continue accessing the same resources they had access to within the original domain, you would need to rebuild the access control for every resource.

Active Directory accounts within native mode have an additional attribute: SIDHistory. When an account is moved from a domain, Windows NT 4, or Active Directory to a native-mode or higher Active Directory domain, the SIDHistory attribute is populated with the SID from the previous domain. Almost as if by magic, the user has access to all the resources that were granted to the user's previous account. Every time you move the account to another domain, the previous SIDs are included in the SIDHistory to make the move easy on administrators and users alike.

There is a catch to the SIDHistory attribute: it is deemed a security risk in some environments. See Chapter 10, "Managing Access with Active Directory Services," for more information on how you can limit the use of the SIDHistory attribute.

ADMTv2

The Active Directory Migration Tool version 2 is the best free migration tool around. You can find it on the Windows CD under the i386\ADMT directory or as a free download from the Microsoft website. This is the tool you want if you are moving users between domains. It will allow you to migrate users from a Windows NT 4 domain as well as move users between Active Directory domains. Make sure you get ADMT version 2; it has lots of upgrades, including password migration. The tool also populates the SIDHistory attribute, but you need to be in native mode to do so.

Coming Up Next

Designing the domain structure will force you to have a good grasp of how the organization administers resources. Usually this is not the full story when it comes to administering the resources, however. Nearly every domain will be broken down into smaller administrative boundaries so that the organization does not have to supply every administrator with high-level domain rights and permissions, and to allow a fine level of control over resources.

In the following chapter (Chapter 4, "Organizing the Physical and Logical Aspects of AD DS") we will look at how the resources are organized for administrative control, as well as how the physical side of Active Directory can be organized to control the replication that occurs within a domain and throughout the forest.

The Bottom Line

In this chapter we reviewed AD DS forest and domain design criteria. There are many decisions to be made to help shape the layout of your forest and domain structures.

When to use a single forest or use multiple forests   Forest design is the first step in a very crucial design plan regarding your AD DS environment. Creating a forest design that meets your business and administrative goals is key to a successful design.

Master It   You are creating an AD DS design that consists of five physical locations. You have a centralized administration model, and all AD DS management is done by administrators at your location. You have one business unit that runs an application that requires schema changes upon each update.

When to use a single domain or use multiple domains   The next step in your AD DS design is to determine your domain structure.

Master It   Business requirements state that you must keep a business unit's accounts and information separate from the rest of the company. You want to allow for this requirement while still using a simple administrative model.

Which forest and domain functional levels to choose   If you are upgrading to Windows Server 2008, or you have requirements for Windows 2000 or 2003 domain controllers, you will have to determine which forest and domain functional levels you should use.

Master It   You have an environment that consists of one Active Directory 2003 forest with three Active Directory domains. Three domains were created because of password policy differences between the business units in each domain.

You are planning an upgrade to Windows Server 2008 on all of your domain controllers. Along with the upgrade to the servers, you would also like to simplify administration.

Chapter 4

Organizing the Physical and Logical Aspects of AD DS

At this point, you have had a chance to take a good look at designing some of the most common aspects of AD DS. As we move on, we will be working with some of the important technologies that make up our AD DS infrastructure but that sometimes go ignored until they start causing problems within the organization.

This chapter covers how to use sites for the physical organization of AD DS, and you'll learn some of the criteria you should consider when creating sites. The second part of this chapter discusses organizing AD DS objects logically by using organizational units (OUs).

In this chapter, you will learn how to:

◆ Design an efficient AD DS replication infrastructure

◆ Design an organizational unit (OU) structure that fits your environment

Determining the Site Topology

AD DS employs a multimaster replication technology that allows nearly every aspect of the directory service to be modified from any of the domain controllers within a domain. Changes that are made to one domain controller within the domain are replicated to all the other domain controllers within the domain. This replication allows all the domain controllers to act as peers and provide the same functionality. However, this same replication can cause problems when you are trying to keep WAN traffic to a minimum.

To reduce the amount of WAN traffic generated by replication, you will need to create sites within AD DS that define the servers that are considered "well connected." The domain controllers that are all members of the same site will update quickly, whereas replication to domain controllers in other sites can be controlled via scheduling; you will be able to control when and how often the replication will occur.

Another advantage to using sites is that client traffic can be contained within the site if there are servers that provide the service the user needs. If there is a domain controller for the appropriate domain in that site, user authentication will occur with domain controllers that are located in the same site as the computer the user is logging in to. In addition, you can make queries to a global catalog server and access the *Distributed File System (DFS)* shares within the same site as the user's computer.

Within a site, the *Knowledge Consistency Checker (KCC)*, a background process that runs on all domain controllers, creates connection objects that represent replication paths to other domain controllers within the site to produce an efficient replication path. When the site topology is analyzed, the KCC will determine which domain controllers should replicate to one another and build the connection objects so that no more than three hops are necessary to deliver a new object or updated attribute. This allows for fast and efficient replication within the site, with very little latency.

An administrator can also create connection objects manually. In doing so, the KCC will build other connections around the manual connection to allow for replication redundancy. Do note, however, that if you create a connection object that does not allow for efficient replication, the KCC will *not* override your efforts. As domain controllers are brought online or sites are created, the KCC is responsible for creating the connection objects to allow replication to occur. If a domain controller fails, the KCC will also rebuild the connection objects to allow replication to continue. Figure 4.1 shows two connection objects, one that was automatically created by the KCC (Chicago), the other that the administrator created manually (St. Louis).

The KCC is also responsible for generating the intersite connection objects. When a site connector is created to allow replication between two sites, one domain controller is identified as the *Inter-Site Topology Generator (ISTG)*. The ISTG is responsible for determining the most efficient path for replication between sites. Windows 2000's version of the ISTG did not have a very efficient algorithm for building intersite connection objects, which left many large companies with 100 or more sites creating their own connection objects between those sites. If you have the ability to put your forest in the Windows Server 2003 forest functional level, the ISTG uses a new algorithm to calculate and build the intersite connection objects. You can identify which domain controller is functioning as the ISTG by using the Active Directory Sites and Services snap-in and displaying the properties of the site, as seen in Figure 4.2.

FIGURE 4.1
Connection objects

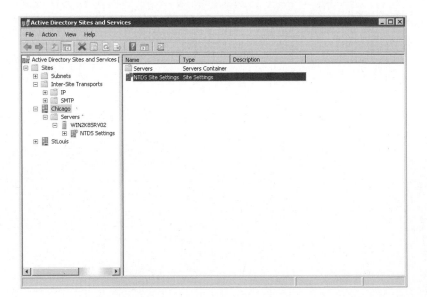

Domain controllers that are placed in different sites do not replicate to one another automatically. Unless a mechanism is put into place to allow replication, changes made to domain controllers in one site do not get replicated to domain controllers in other sites. To give them the ability to replicate objects to one another, you have to configure a site connector. Once the site connector is created, the domain controller defined as the bridgehead server for the site will poll the bridgehead server from the other site to determine if any data need to be replicated. Because data that are replicated between sites are compressed to conserve network bandwidth, you may want to designate a server with sufficient processing power to be the bridgehead server. Bridgehead servers should have enough available resources to perform the compression and decompression of data as well as to send, receive, and redistribute the replicated objects.

Intersite replication compression can be toggled to favor WAN utilization versus CPU overhead on the bridgeheads. See Chapter 14, "Maintaining the Active Directory Database," for more information.

Bridgehead servers are chosen according to their *globally unique identifier (GUID)*. A GUID is a somewhat random object ID that is assign to each Active Directory object when it is created. I say "somewhat" unique because there is an order to the GUID. A timestamp is included in the creation of the GUID, allowing the systems to determine which GUIDs are a newer version (higher number) or an older GUID (lower GUID). If you do not select a domain controller to be a preferred bridgehead server, the domain controller with the highest GUID is selected. The same holds true if you have multiple domain controllers that are configured to be preferred bridgehead servers; the one with the highest GUID is selected. The remaining domain controllers will wait until the bridgehead server goes offline, and then the ISTG will appoint one of the remaining domain controllers according to the GUID value.

Only one domain controller in each site will become the ISTG. Initially, it is the first domain controller within the site. As systems are added to the site, rebooted, and removed from the site, the ISTG will change. The domain controller with the highest GUID in the site will become the ISTG for the site. It is responsible for determining the bridgehead server and maintaining the connection objects between bridgehead servers in each of the other sites.

FIGURE 4.2
Site properties
showing the ISTG

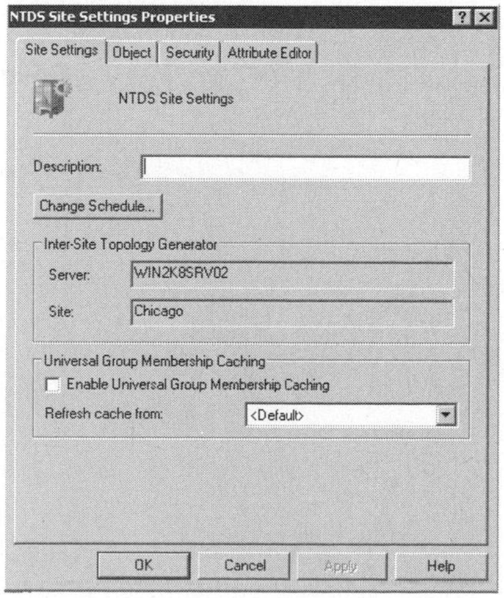

In the following section, we look at the options and strategies you need to consider when designing the site topology to support your AD DS design. You will need to be comfortable with and knowledgeable about all aspects of your current infrastructure before you can implement a stable AD DS infrastructure.

Understanding the Current Network Infrastructure

Very few organizations will be starting fresh with Windows Server 2008. Unless it is a brand-new business, some type of network will already be in place. To build an effective site topology for the AD DS design, you will also need to know how the current infrastructure supports the user and computer base. Once you have identified the current network infrastructure, you can create the site and site link design.

Identifying the Current Network Infrastructure Design

Networks are made up of well-connected segments that are connected through other less-reliable or slow links. For a domain controller to be considered "well connected" to another domain controller, the connection type will usually be 100 Mbps or greater. Of course, that is a generalization. Some segments on your network may have 100 Mbps or higher links between systems, but if the links are saturated you may not have enough available bandwidth to support replication. The inverse is also true: you may have network connections that are less than 100 Mbps that have enough available bandwidth to handle the replication and authentication traffic.

Look over the existing network and draw up a network map that defines the subnets that are well connected. Some organizations have a networking group that is responsible for the network infrastructure and a directory services group that is responsible for the AD DS infrastructure. If this is the case, you have to make sure that the two groups work closely. From the group responsible for maintaining the network infrastructure, find out the current physical topology of the network. Gather information about the location of routers, the speed of the segments, and the IP address ranges used on each of the segments. Also note how many users are in each of the network segments and the types of WAN links that connect the locations. This information will prove useful as you design the site topology.

As an example, consider a company that has a campus in Newark with four buildings and two remote locations: Albuquerque and New Haven. All of the buildings in Newark are connected via a fiber distributed data interface (FDDI) ring. The two remote locations are connected to Newark via T1 connections. Figure 4.3 shows the network map, which also lists the user population at each location.

For organizations that have more than one domain, you will need to determine where the user accounts reside. A site can support users from multiple domains as long as those domains are members of the same forest. On your network map, if you have more than one domain, designate the number of users from each domain. In our previous example, if the Research and Development department has its own domain for security purposes, the network map may look like Figure 4.4.

Don't confuse the logical representation of your network with the actual physical entities. You could still have domain controllers from multiple forests within the same physical subnet, but the AD DS objects that define the resource can exist only within one forest.

FIGURE 4.3
Network map

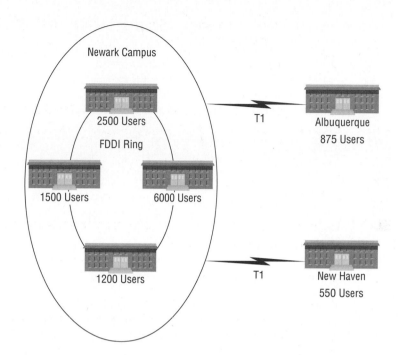

FIGURE 4.4
Multiple-domain
network map

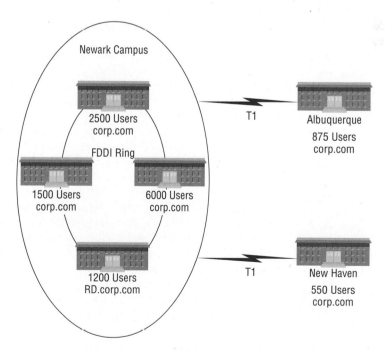

Setting Your Sites to Support the AD DS Design

Once you have created the network map, you can begin designing the required sites. Sites are collections of well-connected subnets that are used to control AD DS replication or to manage user and application access to domain controllers and global catalog servers. As with every other AD DS object, you should determine a naming strategy for sites and site links. *Site links* are objects that are created to connect sites so that replication can be controlled. Although a site is a logical representation of your network—and may not completely represent the physical layout of your network—the name for the site and site links should represent the physical location that the site represents. This is just a "friendly name" that is easier for you to administer. The location could represent a geographic location for organizations that have regional offices (the buildings within an organization's campus or distinct portions of a building). Once you have defined the naming strategy, make sure all the administrators who have the ability to create sites understand the strategy and follow it.

It is a good idea to create a document that details the sites that will be used within the design. This document should include the name of the site, the location that the site represents, the IP subnets that are members of the site, and the WAN links that connect the sites.

In Figure 4.4 the information that was gathered about the current infrastructure is shown in the network map. You need to use this information to create the site design, as shown in Figure 4.5. Notice that the primary locations are identified as sites within the design. Newark, New Haven, and Albuquerque are all identified as sites. Each of the IP subnets from the buildings at the Newark campus is shown as included within the Newark site, the IP subnets from the office in Albuquerque are included in the Albuquerque site, and the IP subnets from the office in New Haven are included in the New Haven site.

FIGURE 4.5
Site-design layout

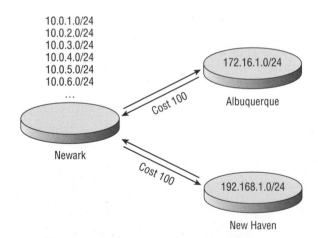

The WAN links that connect Albuquerque and New Haven to the Newark campus are shown on the site-design layout. But because the Newark campus is considered a single site, the FDDI connections between the buildings are not considered WAN links at this point. Later, when you address the replication needs, this may change.

You should also consider including information about the WAN links on the site layout. This information should include the locations that the WAN link connects, the speed of the link, the available bandwidth on the link during normal operation, and how reliable the link is. You may also want to consider including information concerning when the link is used the most, when the off-peak hours are, and whether the link is persistent or a dial-up connection. This information will help you determine the replication schedule.

Once the initial site choices are made based on the network requirements, determine whether you should create sites to support user and application requirements. Users sitting at workstations that are Active Directory–aware will authenticate to a domain controller from their domain if there is one within their site. If their site does not have a domain controller for their domain, they will authenticate with a domain controller within another site. All domain controllers determine when they are brought online whether any sites exist that do not contain domain controllers from their domain. If some sites match these criteria, the domain controller then determines whether it is located within a site logically near the site that has no domain controller. The domain controller determines this based on the cost of the site link or site-link bridges that connect the two sites. If it is determined that the domain controller is close to the site that is without a domain controller, it registers a service locator (SRV) record for the site. Microsoft refers to this as *automatic site coverage*. (For more information on how to configure domain controllers to register their services to other sites, see Knowledge Base articles 200498 and 306602.) Windows Server 2003 and 2008 servers use a Group Policy (more on Group Policy later in this chapter) setting that will allow you to configure whether domain controllers will participate in automatic site coverage.

AD DS replication can consume a considerable amount of network resources within a site. Replication traffic is not compressed between domain controllers that exist within the same site. If the available network bandwidth will not support the replication traffic you are anticipating, you may want to look into dividing up IP segments so that you can control the replication moving between the domain controllers. Once additional sites are created, site links can be configured. Replication traffic that passes across site links is compressed to conserve bandwidth if the data exceed 50 KB.

Another consideration is application support. Applications such as Exchange Server 2003 and 2007 require access to a global catalog server. If you want to control which global catalog server an Exchange server will use, create a site and place the two servers within the site to control the traffic between them. For example, within the `corp.com` domain, an Exchange Server 2007 server is located within Building 1 of the Newark campus. We have specified that a domain controller within Building 2 is to be used by the Exchange server when it sends queries to a global catalog server. To control the requests, we create another site that includes Building 1 and Building 2. Figure 4.6 represents the site design once the change has been made to support the decision.

FIGURE 4.6
Site design to support application requirements

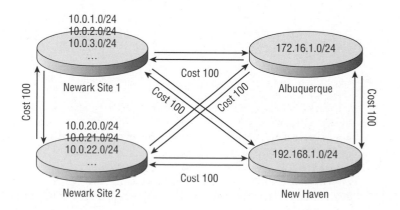

 **Real World Scenario**

AUTOMATIC SITE COVERAGE

Company G has two domains: corp.com and RD.corp.com. Five sites exist within their environment: A, B, C, D, and E. The graphic below shows the site layout and the site links that connect them. Within the sites are domain controllers for each of the domains. Note that Site C does not contain a domain controller for RD.corp.com. In this case, as domain controllers start up, they will check the configuration of the domain to determine whether a site exists without a domain controller from their own domain. When domain controllers from RD.corp.com start up, they will recognize that Site C does not have a domain controller. They will then determine whether they should register SRV records for the site based on whether they are in a site that is considered to be the nearest. Because Site B has the lowest cost value over the site link to Site C, RDDCB1.RD.corp.com will register SRV records on behalf of Site C. When users from the RD.corp.com domain authenticate from a computer in Site C, they will authenticate with the nearest domain controller, RDDCB1.RD.corp.com.

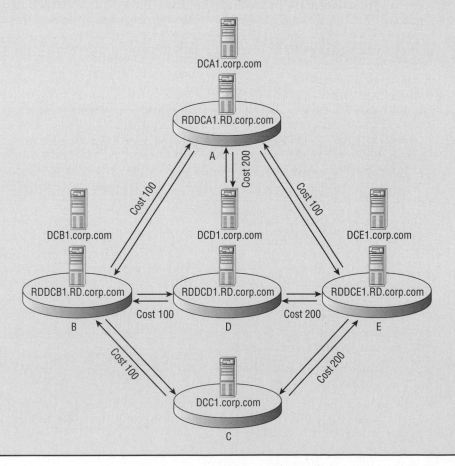

Designing Site Links and Site-Link Bridges

Because you have identified the WAN links that connect the sites within your design, you can decide easily on the site links needed to support the design at this point. You also need to address other considerations such as replication, logon authentication control, and application support.

Site-link bridges are collections of site links that allow replication traffic from domain controllers in one site to pass to domain controllers in another site when no explicit replication partners exist in the intermediary site that connects them.

In the following sections, we spend some time reviewing the options available for sites and site-link bridges.

Site Links

By default, one site link is created when the first domain controller is installed. This site link is called DEFAULTIPSITELINK, but it can be renamed to conform to your naming strategy. This site link uses remote procedure calls (RPCs) for replication. You could take advantage of using this site link for all the sites you have within your infrastructure if they all have the same replication requirements. For example, if all the sites are connected by WAN links that have approximately the same available bandwidth and they all use RPCs for replication, simply rename this site link to conform to your naming strategy and make sure all the sites are included.

You may also want to create additional site links to control when the replication can occur. You may have some sites that need to have objects updated at different schedules. Using site links, you can create a replication schedule between sites. However, you cannot define which physical connection a site link uses to control the replication traffic over specific network links. For instance, if you have a T1 connection and an integrated services digital network (ISDN) connection to a branch office, and the ISDN connection is used only as a backup communication link if the T1 goes down, you cannot create two site links with two different costs, one for each of the communication links.

When creating the site link, you can choose among the following options:

Protocol used for replication　Two protocols (IP and SMTP) can be used for replicating objects. When selecting IP, you are specifying that you want to use RPCs to deliver the replicated objects. You can select SMTP if the domain controllers between which you are replicating data are not within the same domain. If the domain controllers are within the same domain, the File Replication Service (FRS) has to use RPCs to replicate the SYSVOL data. Because FRS requires the same replication topology as the domain partition, you cannot use SMTP between the domain controllers within a domain. You can use SMTP if you want to control the replication between global catalog servers or domain controllers that are replicating the schema and configuration partition data between domain controllers.

Name of the site link　The name should follow your naming strategy and should define the sites that are connected using the link.

Connected sites　These are the sites that will explicitly replicate between bridgehead servers in each listed site.

Schedule　The schedule consists of the hours when replication can occur and the *interval*, or how often you want to allow replication to occur during the hours that replication data are allowed to pass between the bridgehead servers.

Cost of the connection　This value determines which link will be used. This cost, or priority, value is used to choose the most efficient site link. You will use the combination of site links with the lowest total cost to replicate data between any pair of sites.

Note the replication patterns when you are trying to determine the schedule. You could cause a good deal of latency to occur if the schedule is not compatible with other network traffic patterns or if other scheduled replication or synchronization is taking place. You may also have issues if the schedule you set does not match the schedule that is set for domain controllers at another site.

For example, a company may have a central office that acts as the hub for regional offices. The regional offices are responsible for replication to the branch offices in their regions. Figure 4.7 shows the schedule for the Atlanta central office, the Sydney and Chicago regional offices, and the Exmouth, Peoria, and Bloomington branch offices. Because all of the domestic U.S. links have approximately the same bandwidth availability, you could create a single site link that uses a 15-minute interval. You could then create a separate site link between Atlanta and Sydney for which the replication interval is set to every two hours so that replication does not adversely affect the WAN links. Between the Sydney and Exmouth sites, another site link uses a 1-hour interval to control traffic. Depending on the connection objects that are created by the KCC, the total propagation delay for an update in Chicago to reach Exmouth could be 3 or more hours—and that is only considering the replication interval. The schedule on the site link could be configured to allow replication traffic to flow only during select hours. If you have a schedule that is closed off for a portion of time, the propagation delay will increase even more. You need to make sure that this will be acceptable within your organization.

FIGURE 4.7
Replication schedules based on site links

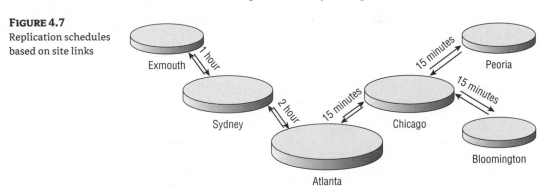

You should also plan the cost of site links carefully. The default site-link cost value is 100. If all of the communication links have the same available bandwidth, you could leave the default cost on all links. However, if different bandwidth constraints exist on any of the communication links, you will need to adjust the cost values. One method of determining a valid cost for site links is to divide 1,024 by the base-10 logarithm of the available bandwidth as measured in kilobits per second (Kbps). In doing so, you will find cost values that correspond to the entries in Table 4.1.

TABLE 4.1:   Example of Costs for Available Bandwidth

AVAILABLE BANDWIDTH IN KBPS	COST VALUE
4,096	283
2,048	309
1,024	340
512	378

TABLE 4.1:   Example of Costs for Available Bandwidth *(CONTINUED)*

AVAILABLE BANDWIDTH IN KBPS	COST VALUE
256	425
128	486
64	567
56	586
38.4	644
19.2	798
9.6	1,042

Site-Link Bridges

Site-link bridging is enabled for all site links by default in Active Directory if the Domain Controllers are Windows Server 2003 or later, making replication transitive throughout sites. In Figure 4.8, note that domain controllers are in all three sites from corp.com. Site B is the only site that does not have a domain controller from RD.corp.com. With site-link bridging enabled, replication from domain controllers for RD.corp.com in Site A will pass to RD.corp.com domain controllers in Site C.

FIGURE 4.8
Site-link bridge

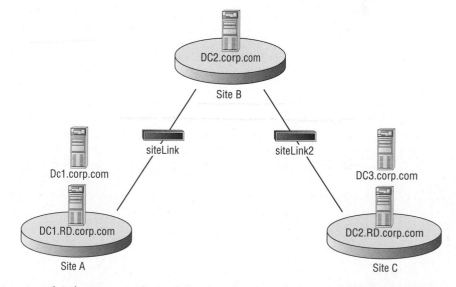

If you have a network infrastructure that is fully routed and all the locations can communicate directly with one another, you can leave this default setting turned on. However, if you have locations where not all the domain controllers are able to communicate directly with one another—for instance, if they are separated by firewalls—you may want to turn off the site-link bridging. You may also want to turn it off if you want to manually control where it is allowed. If you have a large, complex network, you could turn off the bridging and create your own site-link bridges by defining which site links will be included in a bridge.

Firewalls that exist within your organization's network infrastructure could also pose challenges. Rules could be in place that will allow only specific servers to communicate with internal resources. If you do have a firewall in place, you may need to turn off site-link bridging so you can control the site links that will pass replication traffic from site to site.

Remember that the site link does not define any physical network links. The physical connections are determined by how the domain controllers are connected to one another. A site link cannot detect if a physical link is down and, therefore, will not reroute the traffic immediately. When using bridging, determine your site link's costs based on the paths on which you would like replication to occur.

Organizational-Unit Design

Before we start looking at the organizational-unit (OU) design options, we should make one thing clear: the highest priority when designing OUs is the administrative control. OUs can be used for a myriad of purposes, but the basic design philosophy should be to ease the administrative burden. The rest of this chapter deals with designing for administrative control and how to enhance the administrative design with Group Policy.

When you are determining how the OU structure will be designed, you must understand how the organization is administered. If you do not, the OU structure you create might not be as efficient as it could be, and it might not remain effective over time. An unwieldy or faulty design could create more administrative problems than it helps alleviate.

Designing OUs for Administrative Control

To have complete control over an OU, you must first be delegated full-control permission. This delegation is provided by the domain owner and can be granted to users or groups. For efficiency's sake, create a group that will manage the OU, and delegate permissions to this group. You can then add user accounts that need to manage the objects, otherwise known as the OU *owners*, to the group with full-control permissions.

OU owners control all aspects of the OU over which they have been given authority, as well as over all the objects that reside within the OU tree. Like the domain owner, OU owners will not be isolated from outside influences, because the domain owner will have control if the need arises. However, this autonomy of control over the resources allows the OU owners to plan and implement the objects necessary to effectively administer their OU hierarchy. This includes delegating administrative control to those users who need to be OU administrators.

OU administrators are responsible for the specific objects within their OUs. Usually, they will not have the ability to create child OUs. Their control will more than likely be limited to working with a specific object type within an OU. For example, the OU owner could delegate permissions to the technical-support staff to create and delete computer objects. This would allow the technical-support staff to create and delete computer objects within the OU, but they would not be able to control or modify user objects within the OU. Controlling user objects could be delegated to a human-resources employee who is responsible for creating user objects when a person is hired, and for disabling and deleting objects when a person is discharged.

In the following sections, we look at some of the design options available when creating OUs. These include the choices that should be made so that changes within the organization will not adversely affect the OU structure.

Understanding the OU Design Options

The OU design should be predicated on the administrative structure of the organization, not the departmental organization as seen on the company's organization chart. Most companies do not base the administration of resources on the organization chart. Usually, the IT department is responsible for objects within the company no matter which department is using the resource.

Although this centralized approach is the most basic method of controlling the objects within AD DS, some organizations cannot utilize one single administrative group that has power over all the objects. Other organizations will not have a centralized administrative team; instead they will have decentralized control over objects. In such cases, design decisions will have to be made that will dictate where the objects will reside within the OU structure. Microsoft has identified five design options to use when developing the OU design: by location, organization, business function, location and then business function, or organization and then location.

OUs Based on Location

If an organization has resources that are centralized but the administrative staff is based at different geographic locations, the OU design should take on a location-based strategy. Using this strategy, the OU structure is very resistant to reorganizations, mergers, and acquisitions. Because all the objects are located beneath the top-level OU, which is based on company location, as seen in Figure 4.9, the lower-level OUs can be modified and the objects moved within the OUs to accommodate the changes. Consider the alternative: having domains that are used to host the objects. Moving objects between domains has many more implications because the security ID of the objects will have to change, as will the domain owners.

FIGURE 4.9
OU structure based
on location

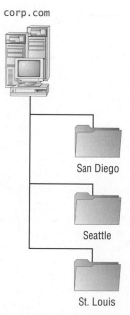

corp.com

San Diego

Seattle

St. Louis

However, some disadvantages to the location-based strategy exist. Unless the inheritance of permissions has been blocked, administrative groups that are granted authority at an upper-level OU will have the ability to affect objects in the lower-level OUs. This could create unwanted administrative control over objects as well as pose security concerns. You might want to prevent some administrative personnel from controlling some of your resources.

The location-based strategy works well within organizations that are using the departmental model but have geographically dispersed resources. In this manner, administrators located at the site where the resources are will have control over the objects that represent them in AD DS.

OUs Based on Organization

If a company has an administrative staff that reports to divisions and is responsible for the maintenance of the resources for that division, the OU structure can be designed to take advantage of the company's departmental makeup, as seen in Figure 4.10. Using this design strategy makes the OU structure much more vulnerable to change within the organization should a reorganization occur. However, it does allow departments to maintain autonomy over the objects they own.

FIGURE 4.10
OU structure based
on organization

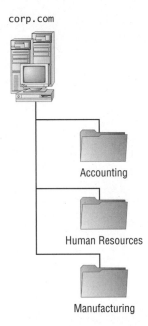

corp.com

Accounting

Human Resources

Manufacturing

This strategy is usually employed whenever business models based on cost center, product/service, or project are employed. This allows the resources to be grouped so that the cost centers are separate OU structures. The product, service, or project resources can likewise be isolated within an OU tree, and the administrators who are responsible for the resources can be delegated the ability to control the objects within AD DS.

OUs Based on Business Function

Smaller organizations that have an administrative staff that provides specific functions to the organization typically use an OU design strategy based on job functions, as seen in Figure 4.11. In these smaller organizations, the administrators will have several job responsibilities. Building the OU structure based on the job responsibilities allows the controlled objects to be grouped together based on the tasks that have to be administered. This type of OU deployment is resistant to company reorganizations, but because of the way the resources are organized, replication traffic may increase.

This strategy can be employed with any business model. Because it is usually implemented in smaller companies, a single administrative group such as IT is responsible for maintaining all the objects. The functions can be broken out based on the staff responsible for maintaining user objects, group objects, shared folders, databases, mail systems, and so on. Of course, the administrative staff will have to be trusted by all divisions if this model is employed, but this is usually not as much of an issue in smaller companies.

FIGURE 4.11
OU structure based
on business function

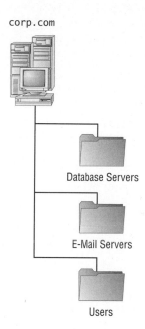

corp.com

Database Servers

E-Mail Servers

Users

OUs Based on Location and Organization

Two hybrid methods of organizing resources exist. Each one is based on a combination of the location of resources and the method the company uses to organize the objects.

OUs based on location then organization   When you use an OU design strategy that is based first on location and then on organization, the upper-level OUs are based on the location of the objects within the directory, and the lower-level OUs are broken out by the organization's departmental structure, as seen in Figure 4.12. This strategy allows the organization to grow if necessary, and it has distinct boundaries so that the objects' administration is based on local autonomy. Administrative staff will need to cooperate if administrative groups are responsible for the departments within the OU structure, because OU owners will have control over all the objects within the OU tree.

Large companies that employ the departmental business model might have several locations that have administrative staff controlling the resources. If this is the case, the OU owner for a given location can control all the accounts that are OU administrators for the individual departments within that location. This allows the OU owner to control users within the location for which they are responsible, while still maintaining control over their location. OU administrators would be able to affect only objects within their department at that location.

OUs based on organization then location With an OU design strategy that is based first on organization and then on location, the OU trees are based on the organization's departmental makeup, with the objects organized based on location, as seen in Figure 4.13. Using this strategy, the administrative control of objects can be delegated to administrative staff responsible for objects at each of the locations, whereas all the resources can be owned by a department's own administrative staff. This allows a strong level of autonomous administration and security; however, the OU structure is vulnerable to reorganization because the departmental design of the company could change.

Very large companies using the cost center–based, product/service-based, or project-based business models may create an OU tree that is based on the organizational makeup of the company and then have a decentralized administrative staff that is responsible for the resources within different geographic regions. This allows more efficient control of the resources while still allowing the OU owners to have a level of autonomy over the objects that represent their resources within the company.

FIGURE 4.12
OU structure based
on location then
organization

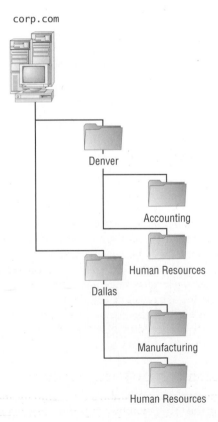

corp.com

Denver

Accounting

Human Resources

Dallas

Manufacturing

Human Resources

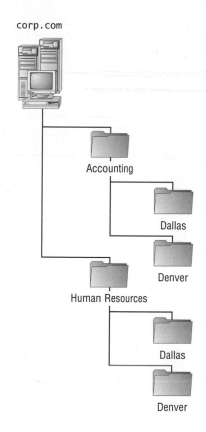

FIGURE 4.13
OU structure based on organization then location

corp.com

Accounting

Dallas

Denver

Human Resources

Dallas

Denver

CHOOSING THE BEST ADMINISTRATIVE OU DESIGN

Notice that each of the design options has its own unique set of advantages and disadvantages. To choose the best design for your company, weigh the pros and cons of each strategy so that you come up with the design that is the best fit for your environment. If your company is not going to undergo many reorganizations or mergers and acquisitions, you may want to choose a design that makes the delegation of control easiest for your current administrative model. Company reorganizations could force a reevaluation of the departmental makeup within the organization, therefore forcing the OU hierarchy to change. Projects that are completed or abandoned will also force the OU structure to change. You might not want to rework the OU structure every time management decides it wants to try running the business in a new fashion.

The adage "The only constant is change" will probably ring true no matter what strategy you employ, so try to employ the strategy that seems the least likely to change but that reflects the way the organization is administered.

Understanding OU Design Criteria

As you build your organization's OU hierarchy, make sure it uses the most efficient layout possible. Designing the OU hierarchy can prove very challenging. If you build too many OUs with several child OUs beneath them, you could create problems when trying to apply group policies. If you create too few, you may find that you have to perform special actions against the group policies so that you are not applying them to the wrong accounts.

OUs are built based on three criteria: autonomy over objects, control object visibility, and efficient group policy application. The following sections describe controlling the autonomy over and visibility of OUs. Later in the chapter we'll discuss designing with group policies in mind.

OPTIONS FOR DELEGATING CONTROL

Object autonomy should be the primary criterion by which most organizations design their OUs. Giving the OU owners the ability to control the objects for which they are accountable allows them to perform their job functions. At the same time, they will feel comfortable knowing those objects are not controlled by other OU owners or administrators from outside their OU structure, with the exception of the forest's and domain's service and data administrators. Once a group is identified as the OU owner, the members of that group can control the accounts to which administrative control within the OU tree can be granted.

Users do not usually have the ability to view OUs (and typically should not be given the ability, either). They use the global catalog to find objects that give them access to the resources within the network. OUs are designed to make administration easier for the administrative staff within the company. Keep this in mind when you are creating your OU structure. Build it with administration as the top priority; you can address other issues later.

Because so much power can be wielded when users are allowed to become OU owners, if you allow this, the users should be trained on the proper methods of delegation. This means that anyone who is allowed to delegate control to another user should understand the two methods of delegating permissions—object-based and task-based—as well as how inheritance affects the design. If OU owners are not properly trained on control delegation, the OU structure could be at a security risk if users have too much power or, at the opposite extreme, if users do not have the proper amount of authority to administer the objects they are supposed to control.

The OU owners are responsible for making sure that the appropriate users and groups have the ability to manage the objects for which they are responsible. In the following sections, we look at the options available to make sure those users and groups are properly configured for the access they need.

Understanding Delegation Methods

Object-based delegation grants a user control over an entire object type. Objects within AD DS comprise users, groups, computers, OUs, printers, and shared folders. If a user needs to have control over computer accounts, you can use the Delegation of Control Wizard to allow full-control permission over only computer objects within the OU. You might have another user who administers the user and group objects within the OU. This level of control can be delegated as well.

Task-based delegation grants a user the ability to perform specific functions against objects within the OU. Controlling objects at this level is more difficult to manage and maintain, but sometimes may be necessary. Take, for instance, a case in which a company has a help desk, and one of its job duties is to reset passwords for users. However, you don't want helpers to modify any of the user properties. If you delegate the ability to work with user objects, the help-desk personnel will have too much power. Instead, you can delegate the ability to reset passwords at the task level, thereby preventing the help-desk personnel from affecting the objects in any other way.

As mentioned earlier, however, it is much more difficult to manage the permissions granted at the task level than those at the object level. You will need to document the groups to which you are delegating permissions. Otherwise, you may find it problematic to track down where permissions are applied and troubleshoot access problems. As a best practice, design the OU structure so that you can take advantage of object-based delegation as much as possible.

Understanding Account and Resource OUs

In some Windows NT 4 directory service structures, the user accounts and resources are divided into their own domains, based on the administrative needs of the domain owners. Because the domain is the administrative boundary within NT 4, the user-account administrators have control over the account domain. Resource administrators have domains made up of the resources they are responsible for maintaining—usually systems that provide database, email, file, and print services, to name a few.

Depending on the administrative needs of the organization, delegation of the sublevel OUs should follow a couple of rules:

The OU owner will have full control. The OU owners will have the ability to work with any object within the OU tree for which they are the owners. Once the domain owner delegates full control to the top-level OU for the OU owner, the OU owner will be able to take ownership of any object within that OU tree.

The OU admins can control only objects for which they have been granted permissions. The OU owner should delegate only the ability to work with the object types that the OU owner needs to modify. If the OU administrator is an account administrator, then only user and/or group object permissions should be granted. If the administrator is a resource administrator, only the appropriate object type should be delegated. OU administrators should not have the ability to affect OUs, but only the objects within them.

Account OUs and resource OUs can provide the same functionality that account and resource domains provided under NT 4. Account OUs will hold the user and group accounts that are used when accessing the resources. Resource OUs will host the resources that users will need to access within the domain. These could be computer accounts, file shares, shared folders, and contacts. You can build an OU structure that allows the user, group, and resource objects to be separated based on the staff that needs to have administrative control over them.

Understanding Inheritance

Inheritance allows the permissions set at a parent level to be assigned automatically, or propagated, to each child level. The inheritance of object permissions from the parent object to the child object eases some of the administration headaches. Any object created within an OU will inherit the applicable permissions from the OU. With this being the case, whenever an account is granted permissions at the OU level, all of the child OUs and objects within those OUs inherit the settings. OU owners can control all the objects within their OU tree after the domain owner delegates the appropriate permissions to the top-level OU.

Occasionally the permissions set at higher levels within AD DS are not the permissions needed at a lower level. If this is the case, inheritance can be blocked, which means that permissions set at the parent level will no longer pass to the child objects. When blocking the inheritance of permissions, the administrator who is initiating the block can choose whether to copy the inherited permissions to the object or to remove them completely. You may want to copy the permissions if the majority of the permissions will stay the same, but you may only want to change one or two permissions. This will allow you to keep the majority of the permission entries and simply remove the permission entries you do not want instead of recreating the entire permission list. If the inherited permissions are removed from the object, only the permissions that are explicitly set at the object level will apply. This could restrict an upper-level OU owner, QU administrator, domain owner, or forest owner from being able to perform actions against the object. If this happens, the OU owner, OU administrator, domain owner, or forest owner can reset the inheritable permissions on the object or objects that were affected.

The blocking of inheritance could be problematic for users or groups who do not have the power to change the inheritable-permissions setting. If inheritance is blocked to objects that a group needs to have control over, they will not be able to effectively maintain those objects. At this point, the OU owner could step in and change the inheritance on the OU or object, or change the effective permissions on the objects that the group needs to control. Trying to troubleshoot inheritance issues can be time-consuming and difficult, so limit the amount of inheritance blocking you use within your design.

Creating an OU structure for a brand-new design can be challenging. Developing a design that allows the administrative functions to be performed easily is of the utmost priority. However, few organizations have the option of creating a brand-new design. An infrastructure probably exists already.

CONTROLLING VISIBILITY

You can use OUs to hide objects from users when they are searching within AD DS. By hiding the objects that users do not need to access, you add a level of security to those objects. If users do not have the list-contents permission to an OU, they will not be able to view any of the objects within the OU. In this manner, you can hide printers that users do not need to access, and shares that should not appear in search results. You can also hide user and group objects from other administrators.

When you design the OU structure, always start with designing for administrative control, and then consider visibility of objects. The primary goal of the OU design is to make administration of objects as efficient and easy as possible. Once you have completed the administrative design, you can address visibility requirements.

For example, take a company that has a printer whose access is restricted to a few authorized users printing to it. This printer is used to print accounts-payable and payroll checks. Only a few accounts-payable employees are allowed to send print jobs to this printer. Also, some shares on the accounts-payable server are for use exclusively by the accounts-payable staff. Because these resources need to be isolated from the rest of the organization, they should not show up when users from other departments perform searches within AD DS.

The accounts-payable department is part of the accounting division of the company. Because the company has all of the accounting resources located at the corporate office, the corporate IT department is responsible for maintaining the objects in AD DS. Other departments have staff located at other offices, and each of those offices has administrative staff responsible for maintaining the resources.

During the design phase, the design team decides to use the "location then organization" design approach. This allows them to assign control over all resources to the administrative groups that need to be owners of the OU hierarchy, and then to grant other levels of control at the departmental level for the administrators who control a subset of resources. The initial design looks like Figure 4.14.

The objects that need to be hidden from users should be placed within an OU that will not allow users to view its contents. For users to be able to see the objects within an OU, at the very least they will need the list-contents permission granted to them. If they do not have this permission, the objects contained within the OU will not show up in their searches. Because this permission is included in the standard read permission, accounts with read permission will be able to see the contents of the OU.

Because users need to view objects within the accounts-payable OU, the permissions to that OU cannot be changed. Instead, a child OU is created to control visibility of the objects. The users within the accounts-payable department who need to work with the objects will be able to see them when they access Active Directory tools or perform searches, but no one else will. It should be noted that the accounts-payable administrators need to be able to maintain the objects within the OU, so either their permissions will have to be added to the access control list or the existing permissions will need to be copied directly to the OU, with the unnecessary accounts and permissions removed. The final OU design for accounting will look like Figure 4.15.

As we have mentioned, the primary reason to create an OU structure is to have the ability to control administrative abilities and make resource administration more efficient. There is only one way to delegate administration of resources, yet there are many options to control group policies, as you will see in the next section. Remember, though, that the administrative design should take precedence.

FIGURE 4.14
OU design with
OUs created for ease
of administration

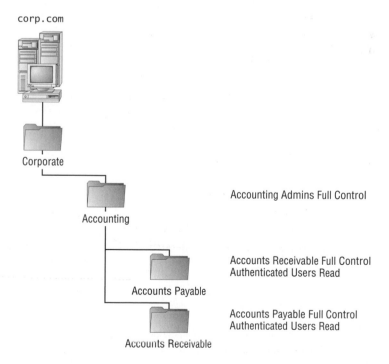

FIGURE 4.15
OU design with
the OU created to
control visibility

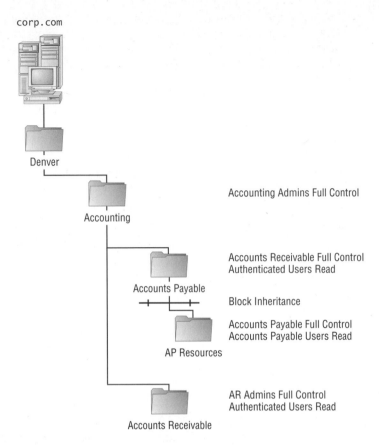

corp.com

Denver

Accounting — Accounting Admins Full Control

Accounts Payable — Accounts Receivable Full Control
Authenticated Users Read

Block Inheritance

AP Resources — Accounts Payable Full Control
Accounts Payable Users Read

Accounts Receivable — AR Admins Full Control
Authenticated Users Read

Designing OUs for Group Policy

Group Policy has proved to be one of the most widely used Active Directory technologies and, at the same time, one of the most misunderstood and misused. Many administrators who have taken advantage of Group Policy Objects (GPOs) to control the security of systems and to distribute software to users and computers do not fully understand the options available when using GPOs. Understanding the settings that can control security, restrict user sessions and desktops, deploy software, and configure the application environment should be given top priority when you are using GPOs. Options that affect how the GPOs are applied must be understood as well; some of the options we will discuss include blocking inheritance, enforcing settings, applying settings to specific users or systems, and filtering out the accounts that do not need to have settings applied to them.

To make your job much easier, Windows Server 2008 includes the Group Policy Management Console (GPMC). The GPMC is also available via download for Windows Server 2003. The GPMC simplifies the task of administering the GPOs used within your organization. From one location, all the GPOs from any domain in any forest of the organization can be controlled and maintained. As you can see in Figure 4.16, once this utility is installed on a system, the Group Policy tab on the property page of a site, domain, or OU will no longer show the GPOs linked at that object. Instead, a button to open the GPMC appears there. The GPMC also is added to the Administrative Tools menu. (For more information about the Group Policy Management Console and how to download your copy of this tool, go to www.microsoft.com/windowsserver2003/gpmc/default.mspx.)

The GPMC will function only on Windows XP, Windows Vista, Windows Server 2003, and Windows 2008 operating systems. Any administrators who need to use the GPMC will need a workstation running Windows XP or Vista, or they will need to work from a server where the GPMC has been added. (To run the Group Policy Management Console on a Windows XP–based system, you will need to load Windows XP Service Pack 1 and the .NET Framework 1.1 or later.) Figure 4.17 shows the GPMC. Notice how the group policies are all organized beneath the Group Policy Objects container. This allows you to go to the container and work with any of the GPOs that you are using in Active Directory. Also note that the domain and all the sites and OUs are organized within the console so you can see at which level GPOs are linked.

FIGURE 4.16
The Group Policy tab after the Group Policy Management Console is added

FIGURE 4.17
Group Policy Objects within the GPMC

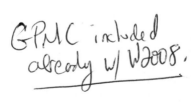

GPMC included already w/ W2008.

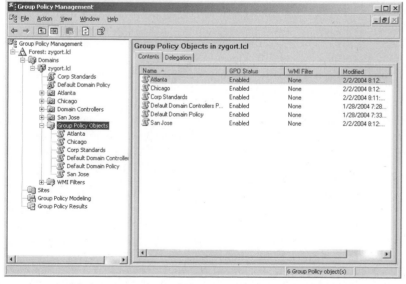

Of course, the real power of the GPMC is the ability to run scenarios and to determine which GPOs are being applied to a user or computer. As you design the GPOs that will be used within your organization, take the time to test the effects the GPO will have on users and computers when applied in conjunction with other GPOs. Figure 4.18 shows an example of the GPMC's Group Policy Modeling section. For more information on Group Policies and the GPMC, see Chapter 8, "Managing Group Policy."

In the following sections, we look at company uses for GPOs. These uses will include the security needs, software installation options, and restrictions for controlling the user's environment.

FIGURE 4.18
Group Policy
Modeling

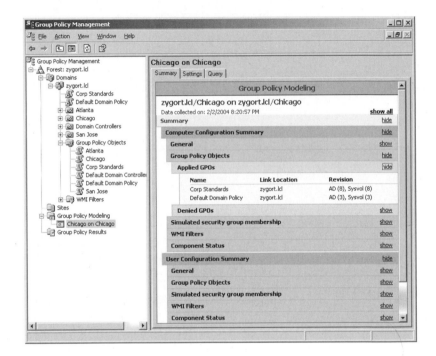

Understanding Company Objectives

Before designing the OUs that you will use for implementing GPOs, you need to understand the organization's needs. Although every AD DS rollout will have password requirements, lockout restrictions, and Kerberos policies applied, that is usually where similarities between organizations end. The first thing you should do is document your organization's administrative structure. This will give you a better understanding of how resources are administered within the organization.

Base your group policy design on this administrative design as much as possible. Most organizations find that if they create their OU structure based on the administrative functions, the group policy requirements follow along pretty well. Although you may still have to build OUs for special purposes (such as special software that a subset of users from a department needs to use, or restrictions on the systems that temporary employees will have), the basic design should be in place already.

A good group policy design starts with defining exactly what actions GPOs will perform for your organization. Because a GPOs is primarily an administrative tool, you can ease the administrative staff's load and allow the system to control users' environments. Some of the areas that can be controlled are security, software installation, and user restrictions.

IDENTIFYING SECURITY NEEDS

The security settings that will be enforced for users and the systems to which they connect are the first types of settings to determine. When Windows Server 2003 or 2008 is configured as a domain controller, the security policy for the domain requires users to use *strong passwords*. Microsoft has identified strong passwords as those that follow these guidelines:

◆ They are at least seven characters long.

◆ They do not contain your username, real name, or company name.

◆ They do not contain a complete dictionary word.

◆ They are significantly different from previous passwords. Passwords that increment (*Password1*, *Password2*, *Password3*, and so on) are not strong.

◆ They contain characters from at least three of the following four groups:

   ◆ Uppercase letters, such as *A*, *B*, and *C*

   ◆ Lowercase letters, such as *a*, *b*, and *c*

   ◆ Numerals, such as *0*, *1*, *2*, and *3*

   ◆ Symbols found on the keyboard (all keyboard characters not defined as letters or numerals), including the following:` ~ ! @ # $ % ^ & * ( ) _ + - = { } | [ ] \ : " ; ' < > ? , . /.

Training users on the proper methods of creating and employing passwords can prove to be diffi-cult. For instance, turning on the complexity requirements that force a user to have strong passwords usually ends up with the user writing their password down and placing it close to their computer. You should implement corporate standards that identify how passwords should be protected and the ram-ifications of not following the policy. Of course, training the users and explaining the reason pass-words are a vital defense mechanism can aid in the acceptance of the password policy.

Account lockout is another defense mechanism that should be used. Any time a brute-force attack is made against an account, the account-lockout policy prevents the attackers from being able to make too many attempts at discovering the password. Most companies have this setting configured to allow three to five attempts before the account is locked. Once it is locked, the person cannot try any additional passwords for the account until the account is unlocked. This brings us to the second part of account-lockout restrictions: you should always leave the accounts locked until an administrator unlocks it. Although this increases the administrative load to some extent, and more times than not the lockout is due to the user forgetting their password or having the Caps Lock key turned on, at least the administrator is notified of a possible attack. To make sure that you are not allowing an unauthorized user access to another user's account, put procedures in place that will help you identify the user who needs their account unlocked. This is especially true if they call to have their account unlocked and they mention that they cannot remember their password. Before changing the password, authenticate the identity of the user.

Aside setting account policies, you must identify other requirements. For instance, you may have users who need access to servers that hold confidential information. If users need to use an encrypted connection when accessing the data, you can use GPOs to specify the Internet Protocol Security (IPSec) policies that will be enforced. For example, if a user within the payroll department needs to modify the salary and bonus structure for an employee, and the employee data is hosted on a server that you want to make sure is accessed only when IPSec communication is used, you can create an OU—called IPSec Servers—for the payroll department's server and any other servers that require IPSec communication. You can then create a group policy for the IPSec Servers OU that enforces the Secure Server IPSec policy and apply it to all servers in the IPSec Servers OU. Another OU—Payroll Clients—can be created for the workstations within the payroll department. The group policy that is defined for the Payroll Clients OU could have the Client IPSec policy assigned to it, which would turn on IPSec communication whenever connecting to the payroll servers.

IPSEC

For more information about IPSec, IPSec policies, and using IPSec to secure domain controller to domain controller traffic, visit `http://support.microsoft.com/kb/254949`.

IDENTIFYING SOFTWARE-INSTALLATION NEEDS

Using GPOs to roll out software can drastically reduce the administrative efforts required to install and maintain software within the organization. At the same time, it can increase the load on the network to a point that is not acceptable. You need to determine whether the benefits gained from having automated installation of software outweigh the network overhead required. Of course, no matter how much you may want to use GPOs to push software to client machines, in some instances the network infrastructure will not allow it. This is especially true if you use WAN links between locations and the software distribution point is located on a server on the other end of the slow link.

A service-level agreement (SLA) could affect the rollout of software. SLAs are contractual obligations that dictate the amount of service availability that is required for servers or workstations. For instance, in some cases software can take several minutes to install. If SLAs that are in place restrict the amount of time that it takes to install an application, you may be forced to install the application manually for a user during times when they are not using the system. Another alternative is to link the GPO that contains the application after hours and have the software installation assigned to the computer. Because the Software Installation client-side extension is not included in the periodic refresh of GPOs, any changes you make to the software-installation options within a GPO are not processed on the client. Using remote-access tools, you could then restart the user's computer, which would initiate the installation of the software.

If you determine that you are going to assign or publish applications to users or computers, identify the required applications. Most applications written by commercial software vendors within the last few years take advantage of Microsoft's IntelliMirror technology and are supported by group policy. IntelliMirror is a technology that allows certain user-specific settings to follow the user, no matter where they are on the network. Part of this technology includes software installation and maintenance. IntelliMirror, combined with Group Policy software deployment is a powerful tool for application assignment and provisioning.

Make sure the software in question is stamped with Microsoft's seal of approval. If Microsoft has certified the software to run on Windows Server 2003 or 2008, the application will support IntelliMirror.

Work with all departments within the organization to determine their software requirements. This helps you identify the software packages that need to be rolled out through a GPO. You may need to make some trade-offs. If every user within the organization needs to have a specific application such as antivirus software, it may be easiest to create a system image that includes that operating system and the software. Using a third-party disk-imaging utility, you can create a generic image of a system that includes all the software and the appropriate system settings for the organization. Whenever the tech staff builds a new client system, the image is placed on the hard drive of the new computer, and when the computer is rebooted, it is configured with the default settings and software. This is a very quick and usually painless method of getting systems online in short order. However, you will encounter some drawbacks.

If devices on the new hardware were not supported at the time the image was originally created, the new hardware may not start up correctly and you will be left trying to install the correct drivers. As new software packages become necessary for the organization, you may have to rebuild the image to support the software, which brings us back to the advantages of group policy software deployment. Although operating systems cannot be deployed through a group policy—that is, through a function of Remote Installation Services (RIS)—new and updated software can be. Of course, Microsoft System Center Configuration Manager will also roll out software to client machines, and will do so with more efficient management options. One of the benefits of Configuration Manager that Group Policy has yet to implement is the ability to push the software package out at a predetermined time.

After determining the deployment options you are going to use, determine the software packages to be rolled out with Group Policy and how you will accomplish this.

IDENTIFYING USER RESTRICTIONS

User restrictions limit what actions users can perform on their workstations, or control the applications that are allowed to run. For some companies, not many settings are required. The users have control over their workstations and the administrators may only control the security policies that are put into effect with the default domain policy, which is where the password requirements, account-lockout settings, and Kerberos policy settings are configured. Other companies take full advantage of using GPOs to restrict their users from being able to access any of the operating-system configuration options. Some companies even force all the systems to have the corporate logo as a background image on the desktop.

As extreme as it may sound, the fewer configuration options a user is allowed to access, the less the user can affect and possibly change for the worse. Desktop restrictions can remove the icons for My Computer and My Network Places, or they can change what the user sees from the context menu when the user right-clicks these icons. The Display properties can be locked out so that the user cannot choose a monitor refresh rate or screen resolution that is not supported by the video subsystem. Start-menu items can be restricted so that the user does not have the ability to open the Control Panel and modify settings within the operating system.

For more information about Group Policy and the settings that you can use to control a user's environment, see the Group Policy section within the Windows Server 2003: Technical Reference on the Microsoft website, `www.microsoft.com/resources/documentation/WindowsServ/2003/all/techref/en-us/default.asp`.

Identify the operating-system configuration settings that users within the organization need to work with, and how much power they need to wield over their workstations. It may take you a little longer to plan out the group policy settings that should be applied to groups of users, but avoiding the administrative headaches alleviated by these restrictions is worth the trouble. As you design the group policy settings that will be used to control and assist the administrative structure, remember the designer's golden rule: keep it simple.

Creating a Simple Design

The underlying group policy design goal, aside from supporting the organization's objectives, should be simplicity. A simple design will allow more-efficient troubleshooting and processing of group policy settings. The fewer group policy settings that need to be applied to a computer or user, the faster the computer will start up and the quicker the users will be able to log on to their systems; because a small GPO can be 1.5 MB in size, network traffic will also be reduced. If problems arise due to group policy conflicts or inappropriate settings, it is easier for an administrator to troubleshoot the problem if the design is simple.

When determining the best and most efficient use of GPOs, review the requirements of the users who will be affected, and then consolidate settings into the fewest GPOs possible. Make sure you are taking advantage of the natural inheritance of AD DS and are not using too many options that change the inheritance state.

IDENTIFYING USER REQUIREMENTS

Determine what you need to provide for the users and their computers. Every company's requirements will be different. Understanding how employees function on a day-to-day basis and what they need to perform these functions will aid you in determining the group policy settings you need to enforce. Determine the settings that need to be applied based on employees' job functions and job requirements, and identify the corporate standards that should be put in place.

Corporate Standards

Corporate standards are usually the easiest settings to figure out. These are the settings that should be set across the board for every employee and computer. Corporate standards are settings that you define to control the environment so that no employee is allowed to perform actions that are prohibited. Settings that make up these standards include the password policy, account-lockout policy, software restrictions, Internet Explorer Security Zone settings, and warning messages that appear when someone attempts to log on.

Corporate standards are settings that should be applied as high in the group policy hierarchy as possible. The group policy hierarchy consists of the three levels at which a GPO can be linked: site, domain, and OU. Because the GPO settings are inherited from each of these levels, by linking the GPO at the highest level within the hierarchy where it applies, you will be able to enforce the settings over a large number of objects with the fewest GPOs.

Most designs apply the corporate standards at the domain level so that every user logging on and every computer starting up will have the policy applied to it. To ensure that these settings are imposed on every user and system, enable the Enforced setting on the GPO that represents the corporate standards. This way, if another administrator configures a GPO with settings that conflict with the corporate standards and links the new GPO to an OU, the corporate standards will take precedence.

Don't modify the default domain policy to include the settings for the corporate standards. Although this may seem like a logical place to enforce the settings because the default domain policy affects all users and computers within the domain, the Default Group Policy Restore Command utility (dcgpofix.exe) found in Windows Server 2003 and 2008 will not retain the settings that have been modified since the domain was created. (For more information about dcgpofix.exe, see the section "Options for Linking Group Policies" later in this chapter.)

If multiple domains exist within the organization, chances are the corporate standards also will apply to them. The GPMC will allow you to copy a GPO from one domain to another. Using this functionality, you can create a duplicate GPO that can be linked to a domain. This will alleviate having to link a single GPO to multiple domains. This is not an issue when in a given site you have domain controllers that host the GPOs, but if you have to pull the GPO from across a WAN link, you could increase the user's logon time considerably.

Job Function

Employees provide specific functions for the company. An employee within the human-resources department provides different functions than does a temporary employee providing data entry for the marketing department. Identify what the employees require to perform their jobs. Document your findings and determine what is the same among all employees within an OU and what is different. You may be able to create a single GPO for a department that applies to all the users and computers, and then link it at the parent OU for the department. Settings that are specific to a subset of users or computers can then be added to a GPO that is linked to the child OU where the user or computer accounts are located.

Organize all the settings required by employees within a department and create a GPO named after the department. You can then link that GPO to the department. Other settings that are specific to a subset of the users within that department can either be linked to the OU and configured so that only those users receive the settings, or linked to a child OU if the users and computers are distributed for administrative purposes.

Job Requirements

Sometimes users or computers must meet specific job requirements that are different even though the job functions may be very similar. Whereas all members of the human-resources department will need to access the training materials and benefits documents so that they can assist employees when necessary, a subset of human-resources personnel may have access to the employee database. If this database resides on a server that requires IPSec-encrypted communication, only the allowed human-resources personnel should fall under the control of the GPO that provides the appropriate IPSec policy settings. The human-resources personnel will communicate securely with the servers by using a two-step IPSec configuration policy. First, configure a GPO that enforces the servers to require IPSec for communication and link it to the server's OU. Next, create another GPO that uses the IPSec client policy and link it to the human resource department's client OU.

System requirements may be different for users, depending on their job requirements. Some users may need to use modems to connect to remote systems. Other users may need access to administrative tools. If a user has restrictions applied at the domain or parent OU, exceptions may have to be set to override these restrictions. . Make sure you document the special needs of every user.

MINIMIZING THE NUMBER OF GROUP POLICY OBJECTS

If you use as few GPOs as possible, it'll be easier to troubleshoot problems that arise than it would be if several GPOs could affect users and computers. Policy settings that are related—such as software restrictions that affect a large group of users—should be added to a single GPO. By adding settings to a single GPO instead of using multiple GPOs to enforce the settings, you reduce the GPO processing time.

SLAs are becoming more widespread. As systems become more vital to company operations, having these systems online becomes mandatory. Although we think of SLAs controlling servers and server maintenance, SLAs that affect workstations are also being put into place. Some of these dictate the amount of time that a user will have to spend for applications to load and the amount of time spent waiting for logon to complete. This may sound picky, but some financial institutions, brokerage firms, and other organizations require their workstations to be available at all times so that they can perform their duties.

If your organization falls under an SLA, determine how long it takes to process the GPOs you are planning. By combining settings into a single GPO, you decrease the amount of time required to process the settings. If the settings are spread among several GPOs, all of the settings for each of the policies will have to be processed.

Determine whether you can condense the settings into a single policy; if you cannot, condense to the fewest policies possible. Of course, this is a practice that you should follow whether or not you are working under an SLA. Users do not like to wait to access their systems. The faster they are able to see their logon screen and access their desktops, the happier they are. The happier the users are, the better your day will be.

Another method of making your GPOs more efficient is to disable part of GPO from processing. Each of the two sections in which you can configure settings—computer and user—can be disabled. When you disable these, you are essentially telling the system to ignore any of the settings in that section. Because the client-side extensions do not have to parse through the GPO to determine what needs to be enforced or disabled, the GPO will process faster, thereby reducing the time it takes for the computer to reach the logon screen or the users to log on to their systems.

IDENTIFYING INTEROPERABILITY ISSUES

Windows Vista, Windows XP, and Windows Server 2003 and 2008 are the only operating systems that can take full advantage of the new group policy settings in a Windows Server 2003 or higher Active Directory environment. Windows Vista and XP Professional can take advantage of all the new client-specific settings, whereas Windows Server 2003 and 2008 can take advantage of all the new server-based settings. For users running Windows 2000 Professional or servers running Windows 2000 Server, more than 200 possible settings will not be processed. When you edit the settings for a GPO, make sure each setting specifies to which operating-system platform it will apply.

Windows Management Instrumentation (WMI) filters provide additional functionality to a group policy application. By specifying operating-system or system options, you can control to which computers a GPO will apply. For instance, if you want to make sure that a system has enough free space on a partition or volume to install software, you can specify that the free space must exceed the minimum requirement for the application. Figure 4.19 is an example of a WMI filter that is used to control the installation of software to partitions or volumes with enough free space. If the requirement is not met, the application-installation setting is ignored. Again, Windows Vista, Windows XP, and Windows Server 2003 and 2008 can take advantage of WMI filters, but Windows 2000 cannot. If a WMI filter that controls whether a GPO is applied is present, and the computer is running Windows 2000, the WMI filter is ignored and the settings are applied.

Other operating systems, such as Windows NT 4, Windows 95, and Windows 98, will not process GPOs. To control computers running these operating systems, you have to use System Policy Editor. This means that you have to support two different technologies when trying to set user restrictions. Another drawback is that only a small subset of settings is supported by system policies. To efficiently control the systems and users within your environment, determine an upgrade path for the older operating systems.

DESIGNING FOR INHERITANCE

Just as permissions are inherited by the child OU from a parent OU, group policy settings will pass down through the hierarchy. Taking advantage of *inheritance*, you will be able to create a group policy hierarchy that allows you to efficiently apply GPOs to your organization and make it easy for your staff to troubleshoot issues arising from GPOs. You have several options when you are using inheritance. Implement best practices that will allow inheritance to work as it should, and then use the options that change the default behavior only when necessary. The more the options for enforcing (referred to as No Override if you are not using the GPMC), blocking, and filtering you use, the harder it is to troubleshoot the design.

Organizing OUs

Use the OU structure based on the administrative requirements as much as possible. Create additional OUs only if it makes the application of group policy easier to maintain and troubleshoot. For instance, in Figure 4.20, an OU structure has been created that allows the engineering department's administration to be broken out into two departments: graphic design and model shop. Each department has a different internal administrative staff responsible for maintaining the user and computer accounts. Within the model shop, some employees work with the research and development (R&D) department to build prototypes. For users to access the plans from the R&D servers, which are placed in an OU that has the required IPSec policy applied, they need to use IPSec-encrypted communication. The GPO that allows the IPSec client policy is applied to the R&D Model Shop OU, where the user accounts are located, giving them the ability to access the plans from which they need to build. The rest of the model shop employees' accounts are placed within the Users container.

FIGURE 4.19
WMI filter for detecting adequate drive space

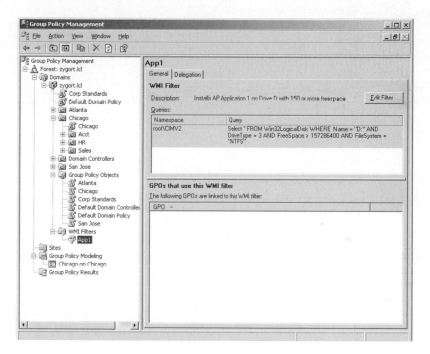

FIGURE 4.20
OU structure enhanced for Group Policy application

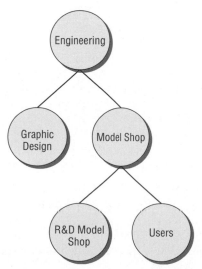

Defining Corporate Standards

Once the settings for corporate standards have been identified and configured within a GPO, they should be linked high within the hierarchy, preferably at the domain level. Once linked, the Enforced option should be set so that lower-level GPOs do not override any of the standards. Figure 4.21 shows a domain with the default domain policy and the corporate standards policy. Notice that the Corp Standards GPO has the Enforced option turned on. Figure 4.22 shows the inheritance of GPOs at the Accounting OU. Notice that the Corp Standards GPO is the GPO with the highest priority within the list because of its Enforced setting.

FIGURE 4.21
Corp Standards
GPO enforced at
the domain level

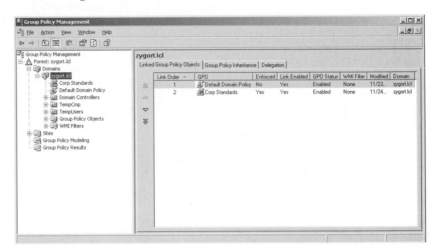

FIGURE 4.22
Corp Standards
affecting the
Accounting OU

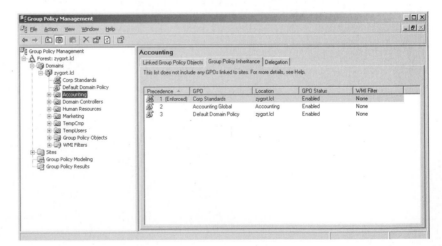

Using Blocking and Filtering Sparingly

The Block Inheritance option stops the natural inheritance of settings from GPOs higher in the hierarchy. When you use this option, you will block every GPO setting from any parent object with the exception of the domain account policies. Once blocked, the only way that a GPO's settings will override the Block Inheritance option is if you apply the Enforced option. The Enforced option takes precedence over any Block Inheritance option that it encounters, but it is applied only to an individual GPO. Set the Enforced option for every GPO that needs to override the blockage.

Filtering is the process of specifying to which accounts the GPOs will apply. By default, the Authenticated Users group will have the GPO applied to it at the location where the GPO is linked. This may work in some instances; for most applications, however, you will not want every account to be under the GPO's control. For instance, if the user account that has administrative rights to the OU is located within the OU, and the GPO restricts the use of administrative tools, administrative users will not have access to the tools they need to perform their job. Determine which accounts will need to have the GPOs applied to them, and create a group based on that need. Do not add the administrative users to the group for the user accounts; instead, create another group so that the administrators can be members of it. Configure the Security Filtering option to include the group to which the GPO will be applied.

If you are changing the permissions for a user or group so that the GPO is not applied to them, make sure you remove the Read permission if the accounts do not need to work with the GPO. If you simply remove the Apply Group Policy permission, the accounts will still process the GPO settings, resulting in longer logon delays.

Prioritizing

If more than one GPO is attached to a site, domain, or OU, determine the processing priority for each. As the GPOs are processed, the GPO with the lowest processing number (which is the highest priority) will override any of the other GPO's settings that are linked to the same location (with the exception of GPOs that have the Enforced options enabled). Compare Figure 4.20 to Figure 4.23. In Figure 4.23, the processing priorities of the three GPOs linked at the Accounting OU are set so that the Accounting Registry & File GPO has the lowest processing priority. Yet because the Enforced option is set, you can see in Figure 4.24 that the Group Policy Inheritance tab lists it with a higher priority than the other two GPOs.

FIGURE 4.23
Priorities for GPOs attached to the Accounting OU

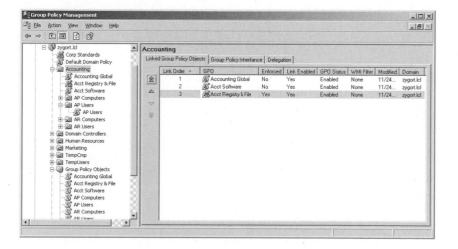

FIGURE 4.24
Processing order
for GPOs at the
Accounting OU

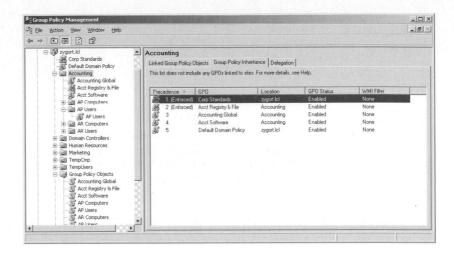

Enabling Loopback

Some computers within an organization should be used only for certain purposes. Kiosks will have access to public information, but because they are usually accessible to the general public, you may not want such computers to have access to sensitive corporate information. Some other computers may need to have user settings applied to the computer no matter which user is logged on. To enforce these settings, use the loopback feature. Once enabled, the settings from the User Configuration portion of the Group Policy Object that is applied to the computer's OU will take precedence instead of the User Configuration settings at the user's OU.

There are two methods of applying the settings once loopback processing has been enabled. The first, Merge, consolidates all the settings from the user's and computer's GPOs; if any settings conflict, the computer's setting will apply. When the second, Replace, is chosen, the user's settings are not processed. Instead, the computer's settings are applied, thereby restricting the user account to just the settings that are allowed by the computer's GPO settings.

OPTIONS FOR LINKING GROUP POLICIES

At this point, you should know that GPOs can be linked at the site, domain, or OU level. Although you might want to link at the site or domain level, doing so is usually not suggested. Linking at the OU level allows you to efficiently control the GPOs and how they are applied to users and computers, so usually linking at the OU level is best. Of course, there are always exceptions.

The primary exception is for the security settings that are applied at the domain level. You'll recall that the default domain policy is where the password requirements, account-lockout settings, and Kerberos policy settings are configured. These settings are then applied throughout the domain and cannot be overridden. This is the reason that a separate domain needs to be created if any settings within these options need to be different for different user accounts.

As a general rule, with the exception of setting the security-policy options, you should not make changes to the default domain policy. If any settings will define corporate standards other than the security-policy settings, and you want to apply them at the domain level, create a new policy for these settings. Although this goes against the recommendation that you use the fewest GPOs possible, it will allow you to have a central point to access the security policies for the domain and to separate any other policy settings that are applied. This also gives you the ability to re-create the default domain policy if it becomes damaged.

Included with Windows Server 2003 and 2008 is a utility called `dcgpofix.exe`. This command-line utility will re-create the default domain policy and the default domain controller policy if necessary. It will not create either policy with any modified settings; it will only re-create the policy with the initial default settings that are applied when the first domain controller in the domain is brought online. Keeping this in mind, make changes to only the security settings that are applied to either of these two policies, and make sure the settings are documented. After you run `dcgpofix.exe`, the settings that define the corporate security standards can be reset.

If you were to add settings to the default domain policy and then run `dcgpofix.exe`, the settings would be lost and you would have to re-create them. However, if you were to create a new group policy and add the settings to it instead, when the default domain policy is re-created, the new group policy would not be affected. The same rule holds true for the default domain controllers policy. Because some settings should be applied to domain controllers to ensure their security, do not edit the settings on this group policy. The `dcgpofix.exe` utility can be used to regenerate this policy as well.

For more information on `dcgpofix.exe` and how to regenerate the default domain policy and default domain controllers policy, consult Chapter 8.

As a rule of thumb, when you plan where the policies should be linked, if a policy applies to a large number of users, link it at the parent OU. If a policy applies to a specific subset of users, link the policy at the child OU. This should alleviate the need to have elaborate filtering and blocking schemes that will affect the natural inheritance of GPOs.

Creating the OU Structure

As stated previously, you should base your OU structure primarily on administrative needs. That point cannot be stressed enough. You should build the OU structure to make the administration of the domain as easy and efficient as possible. You can create GPOs to take advantage of the administrative structure of the OUs, and you can create additional OUs if the group policy requirements dictate it, but do so sparingly.

Two containers exist within AD DS: the Users container and the Computers container. If a user or computer account is created and an OU membership is not specified, then the user account is created in the Users container and the computer account is created in the Computers container. GPOs cannot be set on these containers. The only GPOs that will apply to these users are the settings applied at the site or domain level. If you are following the recommendation that GPOs be applied at the OU level as much as possible, these users and computers will not be under the jurisdiction of GPOs that would otherwise control what the accounts can do.

To avoid this scenario, Microsoft has included two utilities with Windows Server: `redirusr.exe` and `redircmp.exe`. As you can probably tell from their names, these utilities redirect the accounts to OUs that you specify instead of to the default containers. However, there is one caveat to using these utilities: the domain has to be, at a minimum, Windows 2003 functional level. If you can change your domain functional level to Windows 2003 or higher, you can create new OUs for controlling those new user and computer accounts. For more information about the `redirusr.exe` and `redircmp.exe` commands, see Chapter 6, "Managing Accounts: User, Group, and Computer."

IDENTIFYING OU STRUCTURAL REQUIREMENTS

After redirecting new accounts to the new OUs, you can identify the rest of the OU-structure needs. Most of the OU structure should already be designed because it is based on the administrative structure of the organization. In the first part of this chapter, we discussed creating the top-level OUs based on a static aspect of the organization. This holds true for group policy design. If the top-level OUs are based on either locations or functions, the structure is resistant to change. The child OUs can then reflect the administrative requirements. This allows for the administrative staff to have efficient control of the objects they need to manage.

GPOs will use this structure, but you may have to create other OUs to further enhance the group policy requirements. Be careful when you create additional OUs to implement group policy. The more layers in the hierarchy, the harder it is to manage the objects within. Remember: the key to the OU structure is to make administrative tasks easier. Investigate all the possible options when you are determining how to apply GPOs.

New OUs should be added to the OU structure only if they enhance the application of GPOs and make the assignment of settings and restrictions to a group of users or computers easier than if they were linked at an existing OU. Use the Group Policy Modeling Wizard within the GPMC to determine if the application of policies is going to work as you expect it to. Experiment with the linkage of GPOs at the OUs that you already have defined. View the results and see which accounts are adversely affected before you determine that an additional OU is required. You may find that filtering the GPO to a new group that you create allows you to assign settings to users within that group while keeping the users within the OU instead of creating a new OU to host them.

Users who have to create and link the OUs will need the appropriate rights delegated to them. You should also identify how you are going to maintain the GPOs and monitor how the GPOs are administered. Once the OU structure has been identified for applying group policy, the staff who will be responsible for the creation and maintenance of the GPOs will need rights delegated to them and training provided. If you are delegating the ability to perform specific functions to users who are working with GPOs, you can give them the ability to create, edit, and link GPOs. One user could have the ability to perform all three functions, or you could separate the functions so that only certain users can perform an individual task. The following section describes how you can design your GPO management for delegated administration.

IDENTIFYING ADMINISTRATIVE REQUIREMENTS

In smaller organizations, the same administrator who creates user accounts will maintain the servers and work with the GPOs. Such an administrator (also known as the Jack-of-All-Trades administrator) does it all. For this type of administration, identifying who is going to perform the tasks is simple. That administrator has to make sure that she or he is trained to perform the tasks at hand. In larger environments, however, one administrator cannot do it all. Usually specific tasks are assigned to users, and they are each responsible for their own little piece of the organization. In this case, the users who are delegated the tasks of maintaining GPOs have to be trained on the proper methods of maintaining the Group Policy infrastructure.

Training Users

You can assign different users to create GPOs than you assign to link the GPOs. In larger organizations where specialized job functions are assigned to employees, or in organizations that use delegated administration, users who are in charge of corporate standards can be allowed to create unlinked GPOs and modify GPOs with the settings determined by the corporate administration. The domain and OU owners are then responsible for linking the appropriate GPOs to their OUs or domains.

When you delegate the permission to perform actions on GPOs to users other than administrators who already have that ability, make sure that you are giving the users permission to do so only for the portion of AD DS for which they are responsible. Within the GPMC, you can delegate the ability to link GPOs at the site, domain, or OU level. By changing permissions within the discretionary access control list for the GPO, you can control who is able to edit the GPO. When you grant someone the Read and Write permissions, that user could modify settings within the GPO. Figure 4.25 shows the Delegation tab within the GPMC for an OU.

FIGURE 4.25
Delegation tab
for an OU

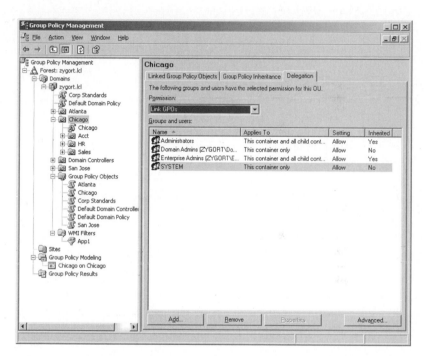

A special group exists to simplify delegating the creation of GPOs: the Group Policy Creator Owners group. When users are added to this group, they will be able to modify any GPO that they create, but they will not be able to link the GPO anywhere within AD DS unless they have been delegated the right to do so at a site, domain, or OU.

When employees are granted the ability to create, modify, or link GPOs, they should be trained on the proper methods of handling their responsibilities. Guidelines for the functions that can be performed should be explained to the OU owners, domain owners, and forest owners. Without a basic set of guidelines, users could inadvertently make changes or create GPOs that will not function properly within your environment. Document the guidelines you want to use and make sure everyone involved understands them.

The Group Policy administration training methodology should include best practices for the following topics:

- Creating GPOs

- Importing settings

- Editing settings

- Linking GPOs

◆ Setting exceptions for inheritance

◆ Filtering accounts

◆ Using the Group Policy Modeling Wizard

◆ Using the Group Policy Results Wizard

◆ Backing up and restoring GPOs

◆ Learning which settings apply to specific operating systems

◆ Using WMI filters

◆ Handling security templates

If users understand how each of these works, they will have a better understanding of why GPOs should be implemented the way they are; as a result, the troubleshooting required to determine problems should ease. The more training and understanding that goes on before the users are allowed to create and maintain GPOs, the less time you'll spend troubleshooting later in the life cycle of AD DS.

Identifying Required Permissions

For the most part, GPOs should be linked at the OU level. This allows you to use the most versatile method of controlling how the settings are applied. Sometimes, however, the best method of applying policies is to have the policy linked at the site or domain level. As mentioned previously, the account policies are always set at the domain level. You may also find a reason to link them at the site level (such as when all computers at the site need to have an IPSec policy applied to them).

In order for a GPO to be linked at the site level, the administrator who is performing the linking has to have enterprise-level permissions or have the permission to link to the site delegated to him or her. Adding an account to the Domain Admins global group, the Administrators domain local group at the root domain, or the Enterprise Admins universal group is not recommended unless that administrative account is the forest owner.

Administrative staff responsible for linking at the domain level will need to be members of the Domain Admins global group, or they will need to have the Manage Group Policy Links permission delegated to them. Members of the Domain Admins global group will also be able to use the GPMC and edit any GPOs for their domain. To have access to GPOs for any other domain, they need permissions delegated to them for the objects within the other domains, or they must be members of the Enterprise Admins universal group.

Policies linked at the OU level require the administrative staff to be members of the Domain Admins global group for the domain or to have the proper permissions delegated to them to work with GPOs.

Coming Up Next

Certain functions within AD DS are so important you will only have a single domain control running them. These are known as the Flexible Single Master Operations (FSMO) roles. As you will learn in the next chapter, understanding what these roles do for you as well as understanding where you should place these roles will help you when designing your domain-controller placement.

The Bottom Line

In this chapter we discussed proper planning and design related to the physical and logical aspects of AD DS. A proper design is crucial to the success of your implementation.

Design an efficient AD DS replication infrastructure   Designing your AD DS environment can often prove challenging. There is a delicate balance between designing an efficient replication topology and keeping the design easy to administer.

> **Master It**   You have a centralized data center and five remote branch offices: New York, Chicago, Atlanta, Peoria, and Bloomington. New York, Chicago, and Atlanta are connected to the data center via T3 connections. Two of the branch offices (Peoria and Bloomington) are connected to the Chicago branch office through a fractional T1 line, connecting at 512 Kb. The Peoria and Bloomington offices need to authenticate to AD DS, but all applications run local to the workstations. You must create a site topology that meets the authentication requirements while keeping down hardware costs and administrative overhead.

Design an organizational unit (OU) structure that fits your environment   There are many different ways to design an OU structure. Through proper assessment and planning you can develop a plan that fits your business model and has a logical administrative model.

> **Master It**   You are designing an OU structure for your company. Your company employs junior administrators that are responsible for different remote sites. Two administrators are assigned to each remote site. You send out software updates to different departments via Group Policy. You must determine the best plan for an OU structure based on these requirements and business practices.

Chapter 5

Flexible Single Master Operations Design

Certain tasks should be carried out by only a single entity. When adding chemicals to a pool, for example, you should make sure that only one person is measuring and dumping them in. You don't want more than one person doing the work, because one of them could throw off the chemical balance by making changes the others didn't know about.

And so it is with Active Directory Domain Services (AD DS). For the most part, AD DS has fail-safes in place that allow changes to be made on any domain controller. However, certain functions should be provided by only one domain controller at a time; otherwise, instability could be introduced into the AD DS infrastructure. These functions are collectively known as the Flexible Single Master Operations (FSMO).

Even though this may be the shortest chapter in this book, the information is still highly relevant to the successful functioning of your AD DS domain. In Chapter 13, "Managing the Flexible Single Master Operations Roles," we will take a look at some of the troubleshooting methodology that you will put into place when you have problems with one of these roles or with the domain controller that hosts them. Right now, however, I'll concentrate on introducing the roles and discussing what you need to consider when designing their placement.

In this chapter, you will learn how to

◆ Identify the five FSMO roles and explain each role's function

◆ Design FSMO placement according to AD DS's best practices and business requirements

What Are the FSMO Roles?

As mentioned, the FSMO roles are specialized services within AD DS that should be performed only by a single domain controller. In this context, the word *flexible* pertains to the ability to transfer the FSMO role to another domain controller, despite the fact that only one domain controller can host a FSMO role at a time. Because of this flexibility, you not only have the option of transferring the role to another domain controller if the original role holder goes down, but also the ability to plan which domain controller will hold the role, thus optimizing your network.

Five roles make up the FSMO: Schema Master, Domain Naming Master, Infrastructure Master, Relative Identifier (RID) Master, and Primary Domain Controller (PDC) Emulator. All five of these roles can coexist on one domain controller, or you can move them so that they all run on their own independent domain controller. Before transferring a role, you should consider the interaction between some of the roles, as well as how they interact with other AD DS services.

Schema Master

As discussed earlier in this book, all of the domain controllers within the domain allow administrators to create and make changes to the objects contained within the domain. As an administrator creates an object (e.g., a computer or user account), the schema controls how the object is built. Because all the domain controllers within the forest share the same schema, every object that is created from an object class contains the same attributes. Domain controllers work as peers to one another; as changes are made to attributes within the objects, the changes are replicated to other domain controllers. The only problem with this model is that two administrators can make changes at the same time and cause a replication problem.

The designers of AD DS, when presented with the challenge of making all the domain controllers members in the multimaster replication model, realized that allowing two or more administrators to change schema information could render objects, and possibly the entire domain or forest, completely useless.

To protect the schema from the corruption that could be caused by more than one administrator attempting to make changes to the schema on multiple domain controllers, the Schema Master was introduced. The Schema Master is the one domain controller within the forest that is allowed to access and modify the portion of the AD DS database that holds the schema. The schema partition, sometimes known as the schema naming context, resides on every domain controller within the forest, but can be modified only on one domain controller: the Schema Master. The schema partition can be accessed through an LDAP call to LDAP://cn=schema,cn-configuration,dc=*domainname*,dc=*TLD*, where TLD stands for Top-Level Domain.

For more information on issuing LDAP commands and what you can do when you access an LDAP-based directory, see the Scripting section (section 5) at the end of this book.

By default, the Schema Master is the first domain controller that is promoted within the forest. As a matter of fact, all five of the FSMO roles are held on this system until you transfer them. For most installations, the first domain controller can continue to participate as the Schema Master until you decide to decommission the system at the end of the hardware or system life cycle. Because the Schema Master is not heavily used, it does not have large resource requirements.

Besides being the central location for changes to the schema, the Schema Master is required to be online when the forest functional level is raised. Keep this in mind as you are in the process of adding Active Directory–based applications such as Exchange, System Center Configuration Manager, Microsoft Operations Manager, and others or when you are in the process of decommissioning the Windows NT 4 and Windows 2000–based domain controllers. If the Schema Master is not online, you will not be able to perform certain necessary functions.

For more information on transferring and seizing the Schema Master role, consult Chapter 13, "Managing the Flexible Single Master Operations Roles."

Domain Naming Master

As is true of the Schema Master, there is only one Domain Naming Master within the forest. The Domain Naming Master is the system that is responsible for making sure that domain names are unique and available when you're adding or removing domains from your forest. Typically this is not a FSMO role that is used very often once the organization's forest structure has been built and stabilized.

Because there is only one Domain Naming Master, it is important that the role be available as domains are created and removed, yet it does not consume very much in the way of resources on the system where it resides. And, just as you can with the Schema Master, you can leave this FSMO role on the first domain controller within the forest for as long as necessary. Once you deem it necessary to decommission the server running this role, determine which server will be responsible for hosting the Domain Naming Master role.

Because this is another role that is not used very often once your forest structure has become stabilized, if the domain controller that is holding this role fails, you can usually go without the role until you can bring the domain controller online again. If you do need to create a new domain or decommission an existing domain, you can seize this role on another system.

For more information on transferring and seizing the Domain Naming Master role, consult Chapter 13.

Infrastructure Master

Whereas the Schema Master and the Domain Naming Master can reside on only one domain controller within the entire forest, the Infrastructure Master, Relative ID Master, and PDC Emulator roles can be found within every domain in the forest. When you install the first domain controller for the forest, these roles are installed. When you add additional domains to your forest, each one will have these roles installed on the first domain controller within each domain.

The Infrastructure Master is an interesting role. Its job is to check other domains in the forest for changes to objects. If it finds a change to an object in another domain, it will update the attributes for any instances of that object, and then the changes will be replicated to other domain controllers from its domain. You are probably asking, "Why would the object be contained in more than one domain?" If an object is used within an access control list or as a member of a group, changes to the object within the other domain will not replicate to any other domains by default. The global catalog will pick up the change due to the intradomain replication that global catalogs participate in, but the non–global catalog domain controllers will not receive any domain partition updates.

If Infrastructure Master were to fail, you might not miss it for several days, depending on the size of your environment. If you were making several changes to objects within your forest on a daily basis, you might miss this function because the changes would not propagate immediately. Environments that do not implement many changes might not notice the failure of this role instantly, however.

For more information on transferring and seizing the Infrastructure Master role, consult Chapter 13.

RID Master

The RID Master, as mentioned earlier, is one of the roles that is available in each domain. It is responsible for making sure that each security principal within the domain has a unique identifier. This identifier is actually a number that is incremented for each object that can be created within the domain. Because each object takes on the security identifier (SID) of the domain for identification purposes, the relative identifier (RID) uniquely identifies the security principal within the domain.

It is important to note that the RID Master is not contacted for each RID that is handed out when an account is created. Instead, domain controllers contact the RID Master when they are promoted, and the RID Master allocates a large block of RIDs to the domain controller. When the domain controller is close to depleting the RIDs it has been allocated, the domain controller contacts the RID Master again to replenish its RID pool.

With the original implementation of Active Directory in Windows 2000, the RID pool allocation was 500 RIDs per domain controller, and the domain controllers would contact the RID Master when twenty percent of their RID pool remained. There were implementations in which this scenario caused problems. If an import utility such as `csvde` or `ldifde` were in use or if the Active Directory Migration Tool were used, the RID pool could potentially become depleted before the domain controller received a new allocation of RIDs. To solve this problem, Windows 2000 Service

Pack 4 changed the allocation-request limit to fifty percent. Windows Server 2003 and later versions all adhere to the same criteria.

Availability of the RID Master is important. Domain controllers responsible for creating accounts need to obtain their allocation of RIDs from the RID Master as their RID pool becomes depleted. If the RID Master is not available, the domain controllers will not be able to get any new RIDs.

For more information on transferring and seizing the RID Master role, as well as changing the default RID allocation amount, consult Chapter 13.

PDC Emulator

The final FSMO role that we'll cover is another role that is available in each domain within a forest: the Primary Domain Controller (PDC) Emulator. The name of this role is a little misleading because there are several other functions that this role provides besides acting as the PDC for Windows NT 4 domain controllers; time synchronization and password changes are also controlled here.

Whenever a domain is in mixed mode and Windows NT 4 Backup Domain Controllers (BDCs) exist within the domain, the PDC Emulator is responsible for keeping the Windows NT 4 BDCs and all other Windows 2000, 2003, and 2008 domain controllers updated. The PDC Emulator is also responsible for accepting password-change requests from pre–Active Directory clients. If the domain is placed in Windows 2000–native mode or the Windows Server 2003 functional level, the PDC Emulator becomes the clearinghouse for password changes within the domain. Any time another domain controller receives a password change from a client, the PDC Emulator is passed the change so that the other domain controllers can be notified of the change. If a user has entered a bad password, the authentication request is passed to the PDC Emulator to validate that the user's password was not changed on another domain controller prior to the authentication attempt.

By default the PDC Emulator is the domain controller that is responsible for making updates to group policies and is the master replication point when changes are made. Group Policy Objects (GPOs) consist of two parts: the Group Policy Container, which is an object that exists within AD DS, and the Group Policy Template, which is the configuration data for the GPO that resides within the Sysvol directory. As changes are made by an administrator, the changes are effected on the PDC Emulator, and then they are replicated to the PDC Emulator's replication partners. At any time, an administrator can choose another domain controller to work with GPOs, but you should have a good reason to do so.

For more information on working with GPOs, see Chapter 8, "Managing Group Policy."

Another important function of the PDC Emulator is time synchronization. All members of the domain—whether they are running Windows 2000, XP, Vista, Windows Server 2003, or Windows Server 2008 as their operating system—synchronize their clocks according to the time on the PDC Emulator and use the timestamp to authenticate clients. This timestamp is then used with the Kerberos service to authenticate clients. If the timestamp is off by more than five minutes, the Kerberos service will reject the authentication attempt.

The PDC Emulator is the one service whose functionality relies on having decent hardware resources. Without the PDC Emulator in place, you could have serious issues arise within your domain. For instance, without the PDC Emulator, Windows NT 4 domain controllers will not receive updates to accounts, Windows NT and Windows 98 systems will not be allowed to authenticate, time synchronization will not work, and accounts could be locked out because password changes are not being replicated in time.

For more information on transferring and seizing the PDC Emulator role, consult Chapter 13.

> ### Real World Scenario
>
> #### STANDBY SERVERS
>
> For any of the FSMO roles, you should consider which domain controllers will act as a standby system if the original role holder fails for any reason. There are no configuration settings on a domain controller that say, "I am a standby server for a FSMO role." Instead, just make sure that all administrative personnel are aware of your preference to use a specific server as the standby in case the first fails. Then, if a failure of the first server does occur, you can quickly seize the master operations on the second server. Make sure that the two systems are located close to one another and connected via a high-speed connection. You could even create connection objects between the two systems so that they replicate directly to one another, ensuring that their directories are as identical as possible.

Choosing FSMO Placement

Because of the importance of the FSMO roles, you should carefully choose where the domain controllers holding each of these roles are placed. Certain functions don't play well together; when placing the FSMO roles, consider the functional level of the domain and forest. The following sections discuss the guidelines to take into consideration.

Operations Masters in a Single-Domain Forest

Within a single-domain forest, the Infrastructure Master does not play a very important role. As a matter of fact, its services are not used at all. Because you don't have any remote domains to which the infrastructure master can compare domain information, it doesn't matter whether the domain controller is a global catalog server. In fact, in a single-domain environment, all domain controllers could be enabled as global catalog servers because there will be no additional replication costs. By default, the first domain controller within the domain will hold all the FSMO roles and will also be a global catalog server. You should designate another domain controller as a standby server. You do not have to configure anything special on this second domain controller.

Operations Master Site Placement in a Multiple-Domain Forest

The five FSMO roles will have to be placed on domain controllers where they will be the most effective. You should take certain criteria into consideration when you are deciding on which site these domain controllers will be placed.

FORESTWIDE ROLES

The two forestwide roles don't have a lot to do after the forest is stabilized, so they don't really require the "horsepower" that some of the other roles require, nor do they need to be highly available.

Schema Master

The Schema Master role is not used very often. Typically, the only time the Schema Master needs to be online after the initial installation of AD DS is when you are making changes to the schema or when the functional level of the forest is raised. You should place the Schema Master in a site where the schema administrators have easy access to it. You want to make sure that the changes made to the schema are done on a domain controller that is accessible within the same LAN-based infrastructure as the administrator making the change. Doing so makes sense from administrative and security standpoints. For security reasons, you don't want the schema changes that you are making traveling across a potentially vulnerable network connection. Any information that attackers can glean from information that you are working on could give up vital information about your AD DS infrastructure.

Also, consider the replication that will be incurred when a change is made. For this reason alone, you may want to place the Schema Master within a site that has the most domain controllers within the forest. As replication is initiated due to schema changes, if you have the Schema Master located close to a majority of the domain controllers within the domain, you incur the replication cost on the LAN segments (an acceptable cost in this instance) and reduce the amount of traffic that needs to be sent across the WAN links. Of course, you need to weigh the replication costs against the administrative requirements. If security is the highest concern, you may want to design your placement so that the domain controllers are close to the administrator, even though it may mean that you incur additional replication costs across the WAN links.

Domain Naming Master

Like the Schema Master, the Domain Naming Master is not used very often. Its role is to guarantee the uniqueness of domain names within the forest. It is also used when removing domains from the forest. For the Domain Naming Master to perform its function, it must be able to check in with a global catalog server. The global catalog server holds information from every domain within the forest, and when a new domain is added to the forest or a domain is decommissioned, the Domain Naming Master is responsible for identifying the domain information, making sure it is unique, and then updating the configuration information.

If the domain controller holding the Domain Naming Master role is a Windows 2000–based server, you should locate it on a global catalog server. Microsoft made changes to Windows Server 2003–based domain controllers to allow them to contact a global catalog server instead of having the Domain Naming Master reside on a global catalog server. This is the case with Windows Server 2008 as well.

The Domain Naming Master can be located on the same domain controller as the Schema Master because neither of the roles impacts the way the domain controller functions. As with the Schema Master, the Domain Naming Master should be located close to where the administrative staff has access, even though this role does not incur the replication costs that the Schema Master does.

DOMAINWIDE ROLES

The domainwide roles tend to be used a little more often, and to require that the domain controller holding the roles be highly available. When planning the hardware that will be used for these domain controllers, make sure that it is highly reliable.

Infrastructure Master

The Infrastructure Master holds a very important role within a multiple-domain forest. If users from one domain are added to the membership of groups from a second domain, the Infrastructure Master is then responsible for maintaining any updates when changes occur within the remote domain.

For instance, if a user from Domain A is added to a group in Domain B, and the user's name changes because of marriage, the user's account name in Domain A will not match the entry within the group membership of Domain B. The Infrastructure Master is responsible for reviewing the information from Domain A and checking for discrepancies. If it finds that a change has been made, the Infrastructure Master updates the information in Domain B so that the new name information within the group can be replicated to all the domain controllers.

If the Infrastructure Master is located on a global catalog server, it checks for differences between Domain A and Domain B, but it won't notice any discrepancies because the global catalog server hosts information from Domain A. Other servers that are not global catalog servers in Domain B won't have the correct information for the group, and the Infrastructure Master won't update the other domain controllers. So, in a multiple-domain forest, move the Infrastructure Master to a domain controller that is not a global catalog server. Of course, if you make every domain controller a global catalog server, you don't have to worry about the Infrastructure Master placement because every domain controller hosts information from every domain and replicates changes whenever they are made.

When you are determining the placement of the Infrastructure Master, place it within a site that also contains domain controllers from most, if not all, of the other domains in the forest. This ensures that the queries and updates are performed on the local network infrastructure.

RID Master

The RID Master is responsible for generating and maintaining the RIDs used by the security principals within the domain. Each domain controller will contact the RID Master to obtain a group of RIDs to be used as the accounts are created. If your domain is in native mode or higher, you should place the RID Master in a site that has domain controllers where administrators are creating a majority of the accounts. This allows the RID Master to efficiently hand out allocations of RIDs to the domain controllers performing most of the account-creation work. If your domain is in mixed mode, consider placing the RID Master on the same server as the PDC emulator. The PDC emulator is the only domain controller that can create accounts within the domain when the domain is in mixed mode.

Because the RID Master is responsible for handing out the RIDs for all the accounts that are created within the domain, you should designate a standby server so that you can seize the role quickly if necessary. As mentioned earlier, the standby server should be a direct replication partner to the original RID Master so that any updates to the RID Master are known to the standby server.

PDC Emulator

The RID Master is a highly utilized FSMO role, but the PDC Emulator is the busiest role of all. The domain controller hosting this FSMO role should be highly available and definitely have a standby server available. When a PDC Emulator goes down, you want to make sure you can seize the role quickly so that you do not lose the functionality it provides.

If you are making several changes to group policies, position the role close to the administrators responsible for making the updates to GPOs. This keeps the updates local for the administrators. However, if you have a majority of your domain controllers at a site other than where the administrators are located, you have to decide whether the replication cost of GPO updates outweighs local administration.

Keep in mind that whenever a user changes her or his password, the PDC Emulator is immediately notified of the change. When a user's credentials are sent to a domain controller that has not been updated with the new password, the domain controller will check with the PDC Emulator before incrementing the account-lockout counter and potentially locking out the user. Because of this additional traffic, consider placing the PDC Emulator close to a majority of the user accounts within the domain.

Another placement factor is the time-synchronization function. In an attempt to keep the traffic generated from this function to a minimum within the domain, identify the site that contains the most computer accounts and determine whether the PDC Emulator should be positioned within that site. If that site also contains the domain controller that supports the most user authentication, you won't have anywhere else to look. However, if the domain controllers that provide the authentication are at a site other than where most of the computers are located, you have to test the traffic that each function generates to decide the best placement for this role.

Another consideration is domains in mixed mode. Some administrators like to move each FSMO role to its own domain controller. This way, if one domain controller fails, the other roles are not affected. When a domain is in mixed mode, you may not want to separate the RID Master and the PDC Emulator. As mentioned earlier, when a domain is still in mixed mode, where AD DS assumes that there are still Windows NT 4 backup domain controllers that it has to support, the only domain controller that creates security accounts is the domain controller holding the PDC Emulator role. All the RIDs from the RID Master are handed over to the PDC Emulator and no other domain controller. If these two functions are held on the same domain controller, the allocation is very simple and does not incur any additional network traffic.

Coming Up Next

After looking at the FSMO roles and the placement options for each one, we can move on to a subject that is at the heart of the RID Master role: user, group, and computer creation. We'll also take a look at managing these accounts within an Active Directory–based environment. This moves us out of the planning phase of the book and into the management section.

The Bottom Line

In this chapter we discussed the AD DS Flexible Single Master Operations (FSMO) roles and what tasks they perform. Special care must be taken when designing an AD DS environment, because these roles do not have redundancy built in.

Identify the five FSMO roles and explain each role's function Designing your AD DS environment can often prove to be challenging. There is a delicate balance between designing an efficient replication topology and keeping the design easy to administer.

Master It There are five FSMO roles in any AD DS environment. Learn what each role is, what its function is, and where it is located on the network.

Design FSMO placement according to AD DS best practices and business requirements Proper FSMO design and server placement are important to your AD DS design for service availability and performance.

Master It You are designing the FSMO role placement in your AD DS environment. You have one forest and two domains. DomainA is a root domain that is used to protect certain resources from the main domain (DomainB). DomainA consists of two domain controllers: ServerA-1 and ServerA-2. DomainB consists of three domain controllers: ServerB-1, ServerB-2, and ServerB-3. ServerB-1 and ServerB-2 are also global catalog servers. All user accounts are located in DomainB except for administrative and service accounts.

Part 2

Active Directory Object Management

In this part:

Chapter 6

Managing Accounts: User, Group, and Computer

One of the most common administrative duties is working with User, Group, and Computer accounts. On any given day you will find that user accounts need to have their passwords reset, have attributes or names changed, or have additions and deletions performed. Group accounts will need to have users added and deleted. Computer accounts will need to be reset from time to time or added as new workstations and servers are introduced to the network.

You can choose from several methods when you are working with these accounts. Depending on your comfort level with the scripting options available, you could automate some of your tasks instead of having to manipulate the accounts manually. You can usually perform your administrative tasks faster when using a script, but many administrators find the learning curve of using scripts to be a drawback. One of our goals in this chapter is to make you feel more at ease with scripting.

First we'll look over the different accounts that are available within Active Directory, and then we will discuss the methods of management and maintenance.

In this chapter, you will learn how to:

- ◆ Create different account types and edit properties associated with them

- ◆ Use built-in and downloadable utilities to manage User, Group, and Computer accounts

Account Types

You will need to create accounts to differentiate each of your users on the network and to grant the appropriate permissions so those users can access the resources they need to perform their jobs. You will also need to create accounts for the computers that are going to act as members of your domain. Finally, you'll need to create accounts for users and computers within your domain that require the same rights and permissions.

Of course, you will also have accounts that will not need any rights or permissions, but you may have to represent them within your domain. For each of these accounts, you can create the account and use it within your domain, but then not have to worry about the account being used as a security principal within the domain.

Each account that needs access to resources must be assigned a unique security identifier (SID). The domain controller that is responsible for creating the account will build the SID from its Relative Identifier (RID) pool. If you have looked over Chapter 5, "Flexible Single Master Operations Design," you know that the RID Master is responsible for allocating the RIDs to each domain controller. These RIDs, combined with the SID from the domain, make up the account's SID. An account's SID identifies the domain in which the account resides and uniquely identifies the account within the domain.

(For more information on the RID Master and how it allocates RIDs to domain controllers, see Chapter 5 and Chapter 13, "Managing the Flexible Single Master Operations Roles.")

So why do we need to have RIDs? Why not just use the account's name? In short, names change. If we want an identifier that can be used for the lifetime of the account, we need to make sure that the identifier will not change. Having an identifier that changes makes more work for the administrator. If you were to change a user's name from Angela Jones to Angela Smith, and the account's permissions and rights were associated with the account's name, you would have to go into all the resources with which the account was associated and make the change. By using the account's SID (which should never change), you avoid this hassle.

Several accounts are already created within a domain, and they have SIDs that are considered well-known. Table 6.1 lists some of these well-known SIDs and the security principals with which they are associated. These are the SIDs that are used in every domain and are controlled by the operating system.

Table 6.2 shows the well-known security principals that are created for each domain. These are accounts that your users will employ when logging on to the domain or accounts your computers will use when authenticating to domain resources. Note that each SID of these security principals includes the domain identifier. Because these accounts could have access to resources within other domains, there has to be a way to identify them uniquely.

(These tables are not comprehensive lists of well-known SIDs. For more information about well-known SIDs, see Knowledge Base article 243330 at `http://support.microsoft.com`.)

In the following sections, we discuss the accounts you can create that will allow you to assign rights and permissions to the users and computers within your domain. The three accounts we start off with—Users, Computers, and Groups—are all known as security principals. The other two accounts that we examine—Contact and Distribution Group—are not security principals, but they provide other functionality within the forest.

TABLE 6.1:   Well-Known System-Controlled SIDs

SID	ACCOUNT
S-1-1-0	Everyone
S-1-3-0	Creator Owner
S-1-5-1	Dialup
S-1-5-2	Network
S-1-5-3	Batch
S-1-5-4	Interactive
S-1-5-7	Anonymous
S-1-5-9	Enterprise Domain Controllers
S-1-5-11	Authenticated Users
S-1-5-13	Terminal Server Users

TABLE 6.2: Well-Known Administrator-Controlled SIDs

SID	ACCOUNT
S-1-5-{Domain}-500	Administrator
S-1-5-{Domain}-501	Guest
S-1-5-{Domain}-512	Domain Admins
S-1-5-{Domain}-513	Domain Users
S-1-5-{Domain}-514	Guests
S-1-5-{Domain}-515	Domain Computers
S-1-5-{Domain}-516	Domain Controllers
S-1-5-{Domain}-518	Schema Admins
S-1-5-{Domain}-519	Enterprise Admins
S-1-5-{Domain}-544	Administrators
S-1-5-{Domain}-545	Users

Security Principal Accounts

In this section we will discuss three *security principal* accounts. A security principal is an account that has a SID associated with it; it can be assigned access to resources and can also be granted the ability to perform special functions within the forest.

USER-BASED ACCOUNTS

Two account types can represent a person who needs access to resources within your network infrastructure: the User account and the InetOrgPerson account. Both of these account types will grant users access to resources, but the InetOrgPerson account is an industry-standard Lightweight Directory Access Protocol (LDAP) account type that is interoperable with other X.500 directory services.

User Account

User accounts can be created for each of the users that you have within your organization—that is necessary to uniquely identify the user. Once created, user accounts can be used to grant resource access to the individuals they represent. You can also use these accounts to represent your users by populating the attributes on each account to further identify the person.

For instance, if you have a user who is a member of the Human Resources department, and her or his manager is Tom Avery, you could put this information within the user's properties and then use it to locate or group the user in the future. Figure 6.1 shows that there are several property pages ready for you to populate with information. The information that you supply will go a long way toward identifying the user within your domain. The more data you supply, the better off you will be when you are setting up and issuing queries.

FIGURE 6.1
User properties

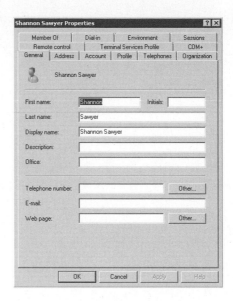

Informational Property Pages   All of these property pages are used to either configure the user's account or to aid in identifying the user within the directory. Although most of the property pages let you configure how the user account will be used within the directory, or the options that define the account, some are simply informational. Figure 6.2 shows the Address property page with several attributes that can be populated, but none of the information on this property page is required. The Telephones and Organization property pages work the same way; the fields don't have to be populated to affect the account's access to resources; however, all of the fields can be populated and, once populated, can be targets of a query.

FIGURE 6.2
Address property page
for user accounts

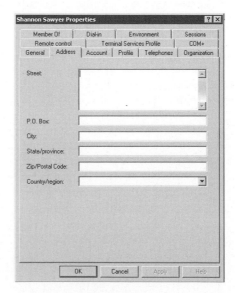

FIGURE 6.3

Account
property page

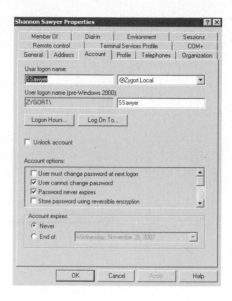

Account Property Page   The rest of the property pages all contain fields that affect access to resources within the domain. The first property page, and one of the most important, is the Account property page seen in Figure 6.3. This is a very busy tab because there are several options that control the account itself, including password information.

Although a user's account has a specific "personality," it is known under a few different names. On the Account property page, you will find these names listed near the top. The first name is the user logon name. You will notice that this name is broken up into two parts: the user account's alias (SSawyer) and the user principle name, or UPN, (@Zygort.Local). When the account is created, you have to specify what the user's alias will be. Once created, it can be changed here. The UPN, by default, takes on the domain name of the forest root domain. You can create other UPNs to match the naming conventions for your user accounts.

The second name that is used is the user logon name (pre–Windows 2000). This name is used for backward compatibility with operating systems that still rely on NetBIOS. When your domain is in Windows 2000 mixed mode, you will need to authenticate using this name. You can still log on to the domain using this method when you are in the Windows 2000 native mode or higher, but you do gain an advantage when you use the UPN version instead. In Figure 6.4, notice the typical logon screen as it appears when you are using the pre–Windows 2000 logon; you have to enter your username and password and pull down the domain name that you wish to authenticate. Once you click OK, the authentication request will be sent to a domain controller for the domain you specified. This is the same no matter which functional level your domain is in.

In Figure 6.5, notice that once you specify the UPN, the domain pull-down list is no longer accessible. When you click OK at this point, and your domain is in the Windows 2000 native mode or higher, the authentication request is passed to the nearest global catalog server for processing. The global catalog server locates the user account based on its UPN, processes the authentication request, and enumerates the account's universal group membership.

FIGURE 6.4
Logging on using a
pre–Windows 2000
logon name

FIGURE 6.5
Logging on using
a UPN

To change the UPN to fit your organization's naming conventions, right-click the Active Directory Domains and Trusts label within the snap-in of the same name and select Properties. You will find a property page that looks like the one shown in Figure 6.6. Entering additional name suffixes in the page will allow you to associate a user with a suffix. This comes in especially handy when you want to create a shorter UPN for domains that have a long namespace. For instance, you could create a UPN suffix `atl.int` and use that for the user's UPN instead of `hr.atlanta.na.zygort.lcl`.

Next on the Account property page are the two buttons that help you define when and where the user account can log on. The Logon Hours button leads you to a dialog box like the one in Figure 6.7. You can define the hours that a user is allowed to log on with this account by clicking in the boxes to select them and clicking the Logon Permitted radio button. For those hours you want to restrict the user from having the ability to log on, you simply select the boxes that represent the appropriate times and click the Logon Denied radio button.

The Log On To button will lead you to a dialog box, shown in Figure 6.8, that gives you the ability to define which workstations the user is allowed to use when logging on to the domain. Note that when you take advantage of this option, you must still have NetBIOS running within your infrastructure. Each workstation will also need to have NetBIOS enabled if you want to control the accounts that can log on to that system.

Back on the Accounts property page, notice that there are several options within a scroll box. Most of these options are for password control. Let's look at each one:

User Must Change Password at Next Logon Selecting the User Must Change Password at Next Logon check box forces the user to change the password the next time they log on to their account. This is a good option to enable when you first create an account or when an authorized individual changes a user's password. This way, the user can be certain that the administrator who set their password no longer knows what the user's password is.

FIGURE 6.6
Defining new UPNs

FIGURE 6.7
Logon hours

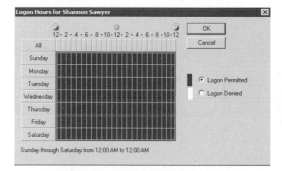

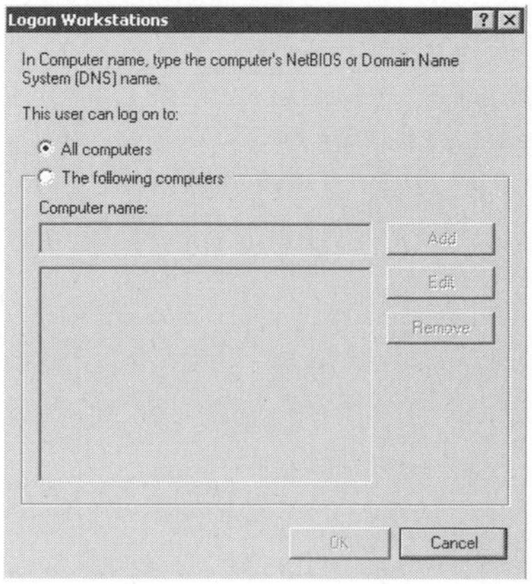

FIGURE 6.8
The Logon
Workstations
dialog box

User Cannot Change Password In some cases, such as service accounts, users are not in control of their passwords, and only administrative personnel have the ability to change the passwords.

Password Never Expires If you are trying to maintain secure passwords, do not select this option. This check box essentially overrides the Maximum Password Age setting within the effective domain group policy.

Store Password Using Reversible Encryption If you are using Digest authentication, enable this option so that Active Directory can store a version of the user's password that can be used for authentication purposes.

Account Is Disabled Once this option is selected, the account cannot be used. This is a good alternative to deleting the account when it is no longer needed in cases where you may want to keep the SID associated with the account, or where the account will be used sometime in the future.

Smart Card Is Required for Interactive Logon Selecting this option guarantees that the user will authenticate using a smart card instead of the traditional authentication that uses a username and password.

Account Is Trusted for Delegation This option appears only in a Windows 2000 native-mode domain; it will not appear in a Windows 2003 or higher functional-mode domain.

Account Is Sensitive and Cannot Be Delegated When an account has a high level of access to resources, you may want to select this option so that the account cannot be misused when compromised. Usually, delegated access is used by services and applications that need to be impersonated so that another system can act on behalf of the user. If you have accounts that have a high level of access to resources, consider selecting this option so that the account cannot be impersonated by another system; instead it can be used directly only by the account itself.

Use DES Encryption Types for This Account Select this option if you need the account to use one of the Data Encryption Standard (DES) security protocols.

Do Not Use Kerberos Preauthentication If the account is using another Kerberos implementation—such as one of the versions supplied with Unix—ticket-granting tickets may not be used during the authentication process. If they are not used, the time-synchronization check may not allow the authentication of the user unless this check box is selected.

Profile Property Page The Profile property page allows an administrator to define information that is used when the user's profile is created on a computer. This property page, shown in Figure 6.9, is divided into two sections: User Profile and Home Folder. The first line of the User Profile section displays the Profile Path, where the user's roaming profile is stored. User profiles come in a couple of flavors: standard and roaming. The standard profile is created and stored on the local computer. Whenever a user logs on for the first time and no entry is listed in the Profile Path box, the user's profile is generated from the Default User profile that is stored on the local computer. If an entry is listed in the Profile Path box, the profile is downloaded from the location specified.

The Logon Script option defines the logon script name that will be processed when the user logs on. When you specify a script on this line, you need to enter only the name of the script. It is assumed that the script will be run from the NETLOGON share, which is located in `%systemroot%\SYSVOL\sysvol\`*`domain_name`*`\scripts`, where `%systemroot%` is the location where the system files were loaded during setup and *`domain_name`* is the name of the domain for which the domain controller functions.

FIGURE 6.9

Profile property page

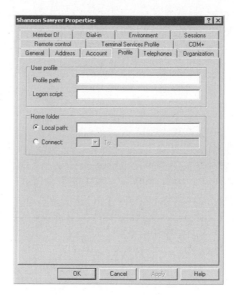

A home folder is a directory that is used to store data files with which the user works. Usually this is a folder on a network file server in your domain, but it doesn't have to be. In the Home Folder section, you can identify where the user's home folder will be located: either on a server within the network or on the local computer. If you want to define a path on the user's local system, you simply click the Local Path radio button and type the path that will be used on the computer where the user is logged on. As we mentioned earlier, the home folder is usually a network location. If you are using a file server, click the Connect radio button and then type the UNC path to the folder that will host the user's files.

There is a neat little function that is built into Windows domain-based operating systems. If you create a shared folder on a file server and assign the Users group Full Control permissions to the folder, you can automate the creation of each user's home folder. When you enter the path to the home folder for the user in the format \\server\share\%username%, the user's home folder is created in the share and the user's account is granted Full Control permissions to the folder.

COM+ Property Page   COM+ partition sets can be used to group applications within Active Directory and then to control which users have access to the applications. You can use COM+ partition sets to add another level of security to your applications by defining which users are allowed to use an application or set of applications. For more information on COM+ partition sets, see Chapter 10, "Managing Access with Active Directory Services."

Published Certificates Property Page   When a certificate is issued to a user account, whether the certificate is used for authentication purposes or for encrypting files, the certificate will appear on the Published Certificates property page for the user, as shown in Figure 6.10. This property page, which is available only in Advanced mode, can then be used to see which certificates are associated with the user.

FIGURE 6.10
Published Certificates
property page

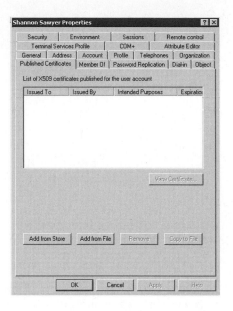

Member Of Property Page All of the groups of which the user is a member are displayed on the Member Of property page, shown in Figure 6.11. From here you can add and remove the user from groups. If you are going to add the user to several groups, you'll want to take advantage of this property page. If, on the other hand, you want to add several users to a single group, you would be better served to go to the group's properties and use the Members property page.

FIGURE 6.11
Member Of
property page

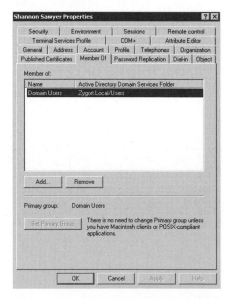

Dial-in Property Page The Dial-in property page, shown in Figure 6.12, allows you to define the options that control whether a user is allowed to dial into a Network Policy Server (NPS), and if so, the options that control the access to the NPS server.

Starting at the top of this property page, notice that there are three options that let you control whether the user can dial into the NPS server. The first two options explicitly control the level of access for the user. As you can probably tell, Allow Access and Deny Access will either grant you access or stop you from being able to connect. The third option is a little less clear, however. When you select the Control Access through NPS Network Policy radio button, you are removing control of the dial-up permissions from the user's account to a policy that is stored on the RAS server. While the domain remains in Windows 2000 mixed mode, the Control Access through Remote Access Policy option is not available because Windows NT 4 domain controllers could be authenticating the user. Windows NT 4 domain controllers do not know how to process NPS policies, so you will have to use the user account permissions.

When a user account is created, the default option selected for the user depends on the functional level of the domain. In Windows 2000 mixed mode, the Deny Access radio button is selected. In Windows 2000 native mode or higher, the Control Access through Remote Access Policy option is selected.

Many organizations like to control access to their Remote Access Server (RAS) infrastructure by using some type of RAS server-based preauthentication. Usually this means designating a phone number that is associated with the user who is allowed to dial in. The Verify Caller-ID option sets a phone number that the user has to call from when connecting to the RAS server. Once you select the check box and enter a phone number, the account can be used for dial-in purposes only if the user is calling from that one specific phone number.

FIGURE 6.12

Dial-in property page

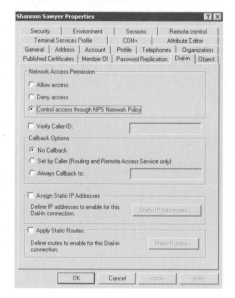

The Callback Options section also allows phone number–level control. The default option for this section is No Callback, which means that the user will dial into the RAS server, and the RAS server will accept the connection. The other two options in this section control how the RAS server will handle the initial connection by the user. When the user dials in to the RAS server, the RAS server will prompt the user for her or his credentials. After the user enters the credentials, the server will disconnect the session and then call the user back. If the Set by Caller (Routing and Remote Access Service Only) option is set, the phone number that is specified in the user's telephony entries within the user's profile is used. If the Always Callback To option is selected, the phone number that is entered in the text box will call the user back.

The Always Callback To option is used as a security mechanism, allowing only the predetermined phone number to be used when accessing the RAS server. This helps safeguard the system in case someone has compromised a user's account; the compromiser will not be able to connect to the RAS server unless he or she is using the predetermined phone number to dial in. The Set by Caller option comes in handy when you have users who travel from location to location and need to connect to the organization's resources, but you do not want them to incur hefty long-distance charges. The system will dial back on the designated number, putting the bulk of the long-distance charges on the company's accounts.

The last two options allow you to control how the user's system interacts with the RAS server and the network beyond it. Microsoft's Routing and Remote Access Service (RRAS) allows you to choose how the user's system will obtain its IP address. If the server is set to allow the user's computer to choose its own IP address, you will need to select the Assign Static IP Addresses check box and enter the address the user's computer will use.

The Apply Static Routes check box should be selected if you need to create a special routing table for the user's computer when it connects to the RAS server. Once you select this option, you can click the Static Routes button and enter routes that you want the system to use. This may come in handy if you want to control how the user's computer accesses resources on the organization's network, or if you have a specific route that you want to restrict the system to take advantage of while connected.

For more information about controlling user account dial-in access and how to configure RRAS, see our sister publication *Mastering Windows Server 2008*.

Environment Property Page   The last four property pages that we are going to discuss all pertain to Terminal Services and remote desktop connections. Any time a user connects to another system and starts a Terminal Services session, settings that control those sessions should be configured. Microsoft has taken care to make sure that the default settings will work in most environments; however, if yours is like many organizations, you will need to tweak some of the user accounts to work optimally and correctly.

The Environment property page, shown in Figure 6.13, specifies the available resources when the session is started. In the Starting Program section you have the option of specifying a program that will start when the session initializes. Usually this option is selected if you have a special application that the user needs to use during the session and the user will run no other programs. Once specified, when the user starts the session the application will start, and when the user closes the application, the session ends.

In the Client Devices section, you can specify which of the user's local devices are accessible within the terminal session. If you select the check box beside each one, the device setting will be applied. Connect Client Drives at Logon will allow the user's local drives to be accessible from the terminal session. This allows the clients to use and save files on their local hard drives as though they were located on the server where their session is running. The same goes for the Connect Client Printers at Logon option. Each printer that is configured in the user's profile becomes part of the session profile. And finally, the Default to Main Client Printer option sets the user's default printer to the same printer in their session as in their local profile.

FIGURE 6.13
Environment
property page

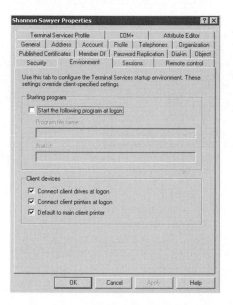

Sessions Property Page The Sessions property page controls how the user's session runs on the server. As seen in Figure 6.14, you have options to control how the user's session is handled if it has not been active, and what to do when the user tries to reconnect to the session. The first option, End a Disconnected Session, gives you the ability to set a time limit for a disconnected session to remain running on the server. Disconnected sessions are sessions during which the user's client software is no longer accessing the session but the session is still running on the server. The pull-down list for this option, seen in Figure 6.15, allows a wide range of timeout values to be chosen.

The next section controls how long sessions can remain active and what happens when timeouts occur. The Active Session Limit setting allows you to control how long a user's session is allowed to remain running. This option comes in very handy if you have several users who need to use a terminal session and you do not want them to remain connected to the terminal server for long periods of time, denying others the opportunity to connect. The Idle Session Limit setting specifies how long a session can remain inactive. For both of these options, the same timeout values that appeared for the End a Disconnected Session pull-down list apply.

The two radio buttons beneath the session limits control how the session is handled when the timeout value is reached. The first option, Disconnect from Session, will disconnect the client from the session, but it will not close out the session. The End Session option will end the session entirely.

The last section on the Sessions property page is Allow Reconnection. You can see two radio buttons here: From Any Client and From Originating Client Only. When a session is disconnected, the session itself remains running on the server, but there is no interaction with any client. When the user starts the client and authenticates, by default the user is reconnected to her or his existing session. If the From Any Client option is selected, the user could move to another computer and start up the Terminal Services client software and reconnect to the existing session. If the From Originating Client Only option is selected, the user can connect to their session only from the same computer where the session was initiated. For this option to work, NetBIOS needs to be running on the client and the server.

FIGURE 6.14
Sessions
property page

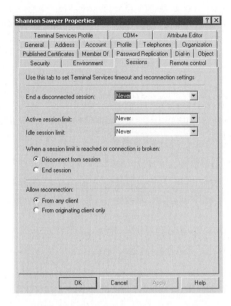

FIGURE 6.15
Timeout values for
ending a disconnected
session

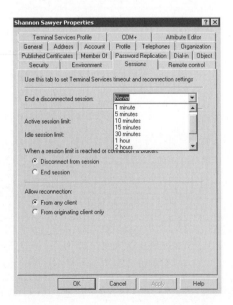

Remote Control Property Page   Whenever a user is running a terminal services session, the session can be viewed, and sometimes controlled, by anyone who has permissions to do so. The level of remote control can be configured using a Group Policy setting, or you can set each user individually on the Remote Control property page, shown in Figure 6.16. Selecting the Enable Remote Control option allows the user's session to be managed or viewed, depending on the other options set on this page.

Require User's Permission, when selected, sets the user's session to warn the user that someone wants to interact with the session, either by just viewing it or by controlling it. The user then has the power to deny the interaction or allow it. Before you deselect this check box, make sure that company policies, current legislation, and union rules allow you to connect to a session without the user's knowledge.

The Level of Control section allows you to specify how much control you have over the session. View the User's Session allows the session itself to be watched and monitored by another user or an administrator, but the user who has connected to the session will not be able to take over the session and control the mouse and keyboard. The Interact with the Session option gives the user who has connected to the session full access to control the session. Note that if you are trying to work with the session and the user who is logged on to the session is also trying to perform actions, you will fight over the mouse movement and both users' keystrokes will be entered in the session.

FIGURE 6.16

Remote Control
property page

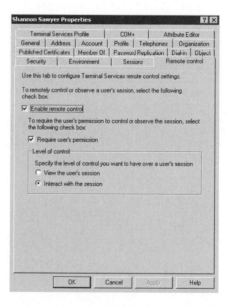

Terminal Services Profile Property Page   The Terminal Services Profile property page, shown in Figure 6.17, allows you to set alternate profile settings to be used during a terminal session rather than what the user typically uses when logging on to a computer. The options on this page work the same way that the Profile options work for a user's local login. Note that if a Profile Path option is not set for a roaming profile, the user's Terminal Services profile will be generated initially from the default profile on the server running Terminal Services.

The only option on this property page that is not available from the Profile property page is the check box Deny This User Permissions to Log on to Terminal Server. Selecting this check box does exactly what it says it does. If you have a user that you don't want to use Terminal Services at all, select this option.

FIGURE 6.17
Terminal Services
property page

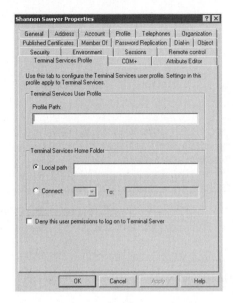

Password Replication Property Page   The Password Replication tab defines which read-only domain controller (RODC) servers hold a cached copy of the user's password. By default, all writable domain controllers contain a copy of the password.

You have the option of creating a password-replication policy if you install an RODC by using the advanced-mode installation. When a user authenticates to an RODC, the logon request is passed to a writable domain controller. If a password-replication policy is in place and the policy allows it, the credentials are cached on the RODC and available for future logon attempts. The servers that store a cached copy of the user's password will be listed in the box displayed in Figure 6.18.

More detail about read-only domain controllers and the Password Replication Policy is provided in Chapter 9, "Managing Active Directory Security."

Attribute Editor Property Page   On Windows 2008 Server domain controllers, a new tab, Attribute Editor, has been added to the User property page. Figure 6.19 shows the Attribute Editor tab. This property page allows you to access and edit the users Active Directory object information. This is information that was previously available only by using LDP.exe or ADSIedit.msc, and is a welcome change.

Windows 2000 and 2003 required the installation of a separate program to retrieve and edit this information. ADSIedit is still available, but now you can perform the same tasks from one tool instead of launching another program.

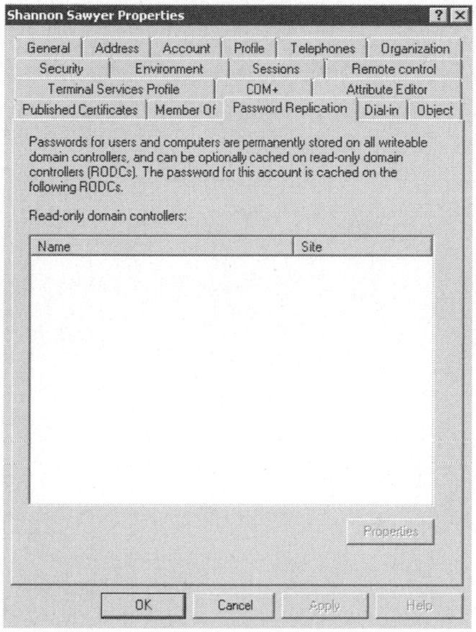

FIGURE 6.18
Password Replication
property page

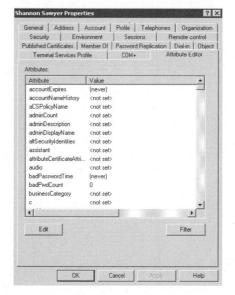

FIGURE 6.19
Attribute Editor
property page

InetOrgPerson Account

The InetOrgPerson account can take the place of a user account within Active Directory. The biggest advantage to using an InetOrgPerson account over a user account is that InetOrgPerson gives you interoperability with other directory services. Other directory services, such as Novell's eDirectory, include the InetOrgPerson account type as well. Any time you need to have an account that will easily interoperate with other LDAP-based directory services, you should consider creating the user's account by using the InetOrgPerson account type. (If you are able to run your AD DS environment at Windows Server 2003 forest functionality level or higher, you can convert a user account to an InetOrgPerson account at any time, and vice versa.)

The property pages that are available from the InetOrgPerson account contain several options that are very similar to those for the User account type. Figure 6.20 displays the Object property page that shows that the account is an InetOrgPerson account.

FIGURE 6.20
InetOrgPerson
account Object
property page

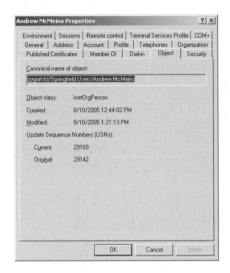

SECURITY GROUP

Security groups are used to organize accounts that need to have the same level of access to resources. Each security group has its own security identifier (SID) that is included with the user's SID when the user's access token is generated. After the access token is generated, the user will have the same level of access to resources as the other members of the group. Because the user's access token is generated only when the user logs on, whenever a user is added or removed from a security group, the user will have to log off and log back on for the new group membership to take effect.

General Property Page

Security groups have several property pages that you can configure. As you can see in Figure 6.21, just like any other account type that we have discussed, groups have names that help identify them when administrators are managing an environment. The name that you can alter here is the pre–Windows 2000 name or the NetBIOS name that is used with older operating systems such as Windows 98 and Windows NT. Other options on this property page include the Group Type and Group Scope options. You are able to change the group type at any time. Note, however, that when you change a security group to a distribution group, the group will lose its SID and will no longer have the rights and permissions that were assigned to the group. If you are going to change the group to a distribution group, check to make sure that none of the users who are members of the group need access to the resources, and that they no longer need to perform the functions granted to them through the group. If they do need to have their rights and permissions preserved, reconsider changing the group type.

FIGURE 6.21
General property page
of a security group

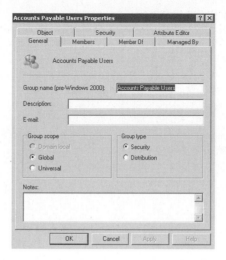

There are specific rules about the types of accounts that can populate each of the group scopes, and the rules change depending on the domain's functional level. Table 6.3 defines the group membership rules.

The group scope can be changed, but you will need to understand the limitations of changing the scope. The functional level the domain is in will determine what changes you can make. For instance, if your domain is still in the Windows 2000 mixed mode, you will not be able to change a global group to a domain-local group if the global group is a member of any domain-local groups. This is because a domain-local group cannot be nested within another domain-local group in mixed mode. Once you raise the functional level of the domain to Windows 2000 native mode or higher, you will be able to perform this change because domain-local groups are allowed to be nested within other domain-local groups.

Universal groups cannot be changed to any other group scope if the universal group contains another universal group as a member. If you need to change the scope of a universal group, make sure that you have removed any nested universal groups from the membership list. That is the only restriction imposed by the universal group.

TABLE 6.3: Group Membership Rules

GROUP SCOPE	WINDOWS 2000 MIXED	WINDOWS 2000 NATIVE/ 2003/2008
Domain local	User accounts and global groups from any domain in the forest	Universal groups; user accounts and global groups from any domain in the forest; domain-local groups from the same domain
Global groups	User accounts from the same domain	User accounts and global groups from the same domain
Universal groups	Do not exist within Windows 2000 mixed mode	Universal groups; user accounts and global groups from any domain in the forest

As mentioned earlier, a global group can be converted to a domain-local group as long as the global group is not a member of any other domain-local groups, unless the domain functional level is in Windows 2000 native mode or Windows Server 2003 or 2008 functional level. There is another limitation to global groups, however. If the global group is nested within another global group, you will not be able to convert the global group to a universal group. This is because a universal group cannot be a member of a global group.

Domain-local groups can be converted to either a global group or a universal group. The only caveat is that the domain-local group cannot have another domain-local group as a member.

Members Property Page

The second tab, Members, allows you to view the accounts that are members of the group. As you can see in Figure 6.22, there isn't a lot you can do from this tab except add and remove accounts. A handy feature is built in to this property page: if you double-click on any groups that are members of this group, it will take you to the group membership of the included group. You can do the same thing with user accounts and have the user-account properties appear.

FIGURE 6.22
Members
property page

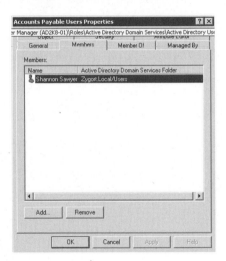

Member Of Property Page

The Member Of property page, shown in Figure 6.23, displays the group nesting that has been configured. As mentioned previously, you can nest groups based on the functional level of the domain. Just like the Members property page, it looks like the only thing you can do from the Member Of property page is add or remove accounts, but you can double-click on a member group and trace all the group memberships back to the first group in the group nesting line.

Managed By Property Page

The Managed By property page, shown in Figure 6.24, allows you to define who is responsible for maintaining the group. This property page contains four options: the Change, Properties, and Clear buttons and the Manager Can Update Membership List check box. When you want to define the manager of the group, you can click the Change button, which brings up a dialog box that allows you to define the manager. Once you have defined the manager, click the Properties button to view and change the account's properties, much like you could do if you right-clicked on the user's account. You will notice that some fields from the manager's properties appear on this property page. They are populated from the information that has been added to the user's properties. To change them, click the Properties button and make the changes. To remove the manager, click the Clear button.

The Manager Can Update Membership List check box allows you to delegate some administrative control over the membership of the group. When you define the manager, you can select the check box to grant the manager the ability to modify the accounts on the Members property page. You will find this the most useful, however, when you have distribution groups that have been mail-enabled for use with Exchange Server.

FIGURE 6.23
Member Of
property page

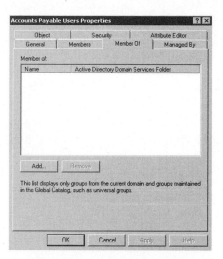

FIGURE 6.24
Managed By
property page

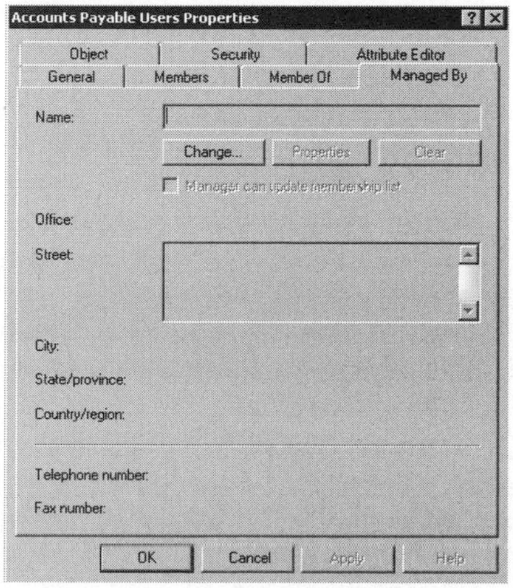

COMPUTER

Computers that become members of your domain need Computer accounts within Active Directory. These Computer accounts are then used for the computer to have access to resources. Each Computer account will be known by two different names: the host name and the NetBIOS name, sometimes referred to as the pre–Windows 2000 name.

The tabs that are available from the computer properties give you several options to work with. Figure 6.25 shows the General properties page, which has the computer names listed along with the domain controller type, if it happens to be a domain controller.

The Operating System property page, shown in Figure 6.26, shows the operating-system name, the version of the operating system that is installed, and the service pack that is currently installed.

FIGURE 6.25
General property
page for a computer
account

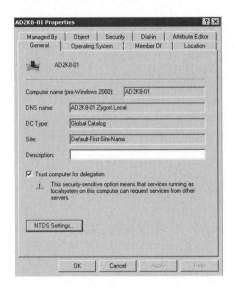

FIGURE 6.26
Operating System
property page

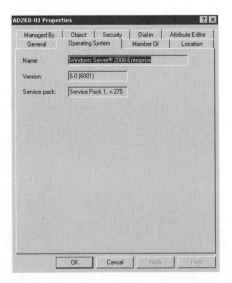

To view the groups that the computer is currently a member of, select the Member Of property page, shown in Figure 6.27. It allows you to add and remove the computer account to and from groups just as you would a user account.

You can define the Active Directory location for a computer within the Location property page shown in Figure 6.28. This allows you to specify where within Active Directory the computer account is located and acts as the default location specifier for any printers that are installed on the computer.

The Managed By property page simply identifies who is responsible for maintaining the computer account. Some organizations use this property page, shown in Figure 6.29, to identify the user who "owns," or is responsible for maintaining, the computer itself, not the account in Active Directory.

FIGURE 6.27
Member Of
property page

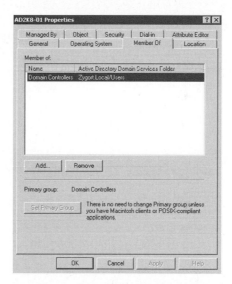

FIGURE 6.28
Location
property page

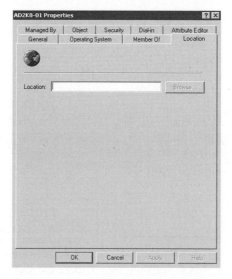

FIGURE 6.29
Managed By
property page

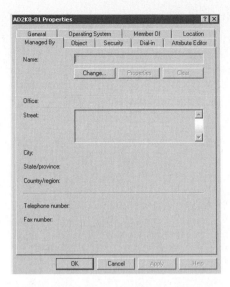

FIGURE 6.30
Dial-in property page

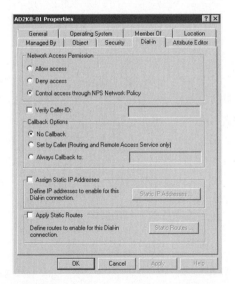

Finally, the Dial-in property page, shown in Figure 6.30, controls the computer account's ability to gain access using a remote-access session. The computer account can be used to authenticate to a RAS server in the same manner that a user account can. The settings on this property page work the same way as those shown on a user account.

Non–Security Principal Accounts

Sometimes you will want to represent people and groups within Active Directory even though they do not need access to any of your resources. You can create two types of accounts that are not considered security principals: Contact and Distribution Group. Both of these accounts are used primarily with the Microsoft Exchange Server email server.

CONTACT

A Contact account does not have access to resources in your domain, but is instead used as an identifier for accounts that you want to catalog information on within Active Directory. The most common use for a Contact account is email. When Exchange is used within your Active Directory infrastructure, you can mail-enable contacts. Doing so will assign several new attributes to the account and allow the account to be shown in the global address list and any other address lists that you have configured. By mail-enabling a contact, you allow your Exchange users to easily choose from their contacts the account that they want to email instead of having to type in the desired email address each time.

As mentioned, the Contact accounts will not have access to any of your domain resources. If you want to give a person access to domain resources, you will have to configure a user account. However, if all you want is an object that will identify a person and it is not necessary for that individual to use any of the resources that you administer, you can create the Contact account and populate the attributes.

The General property page, shown in Figure 6.31, contains attributes that are similar to those on the user account's General property page. In fact, all of the property pages of a Contact object look surprisingly similar to those of a user account. As with a user account, the information on the Address, Telephones, and Organization property pages is used primarily to further identify a Contact account.

The Member Of property page is the only one that seems to be a little out of place. As we mentioned, a contact does not have the ability to access resources because of the lack of a SID. So why would you need to add a contact to a group if the contact cannot be used to grant someone access to resources? Within an Active Directory environment, groups can be used as distribution lists. Any contact that has been mail-enabled can be added to a group and can therefore become a member of an email distribution list.

FIGURE 6.31

General property page
for a contact object

DISTRIBUTION GROUP

Like contact accounts, Distribution Groups are used primarily with Exchange email servers. Because Distribution Groups are not security principals, they do not have to be evaluated during a user's logon. If you are creating a group solely to use it as a distribution list for email, you should create a Distribution Group instead of a security group. The property pages for a Distribution Group are the same as for a security group.

Utilities

Instead of restricting administrators to one tool, Microsoft offers several methods you can use to create and manipulate accounts. As far as graphical tools are concerned, the Active Directory Users and Computers snap-in is installed on domain controllers when they are promoted, by installing the Admin Pack or by registering the dsa.dll dynamic link library The command-line utilities are also added to a domain controller when it is promoted, but can be included on a workstation by installing the Admin Pack. To install the Admin Pack, run the adminpak.msi file from the Windows Server CD or from a network share. You can find this file in the I386 directory.

Active Directory Users and Computers

Active Directory Users and Computers (ADUC) is the tool of choice for most administrators when they want to work with domain-based accounts. ADUC is a Microsoft Management Console (MMC) snap-in that can be added to any Windows 2000/XP/Vista/2003/2008 system as long as the appropriate libraries are installed and registered. During the promotion to a domain controller, the ADUC link is added to the domain controller's Administrative Tools menu, and you can also install it by running the adminpak.msi file that is found in the I386 directory of the Windows Server installation CD. Once it's added to the system, you will find that the link beneath the Administrative Tools menu will bring up the stand-alone version of ADUC, but you can also add ADUC to any MMC that you create. So if you want to have your own customized administrative console that holds several different snap-ins that you use on a regular basis, you can add it to your collection of tools.

When you open ADUC, you will see a view that looks much like Figure 6.32. Your domain will be listed within the containers pane along with a container called Saved Queries. You can double-click the domain to view the containers and organizational units (OUs). Figure 6.33 shows the view once you have expanded the domain to show these additional containers. For the most part, this is the view that you will probably use throughout your administrative lifetime, but there is more to this tool than meets the eye. If you click the View menu at the top of the MMC, you have the option to control how the ADUC snap-in looks and works. The Advanced Mode option allows you to see all the containers that are part of ADUC; the Users and Computers as Containers option allows you to view the additional objects that are part of the object but are not normally considered to be containers.

ADVANCED MODE

Advanced mode gives you a little more information about the objects that appear within ADUC. Figure 6.34 shows the ADUC containers that become available once you select this option. By comparing Figure 6.35, which displays the normal view of user-account properties, to Figure 6.36, you'll notice that additional property pages are available in Advanced mode.

Notice in Figure 6.34 that a container named LostAndFound is available when you use Advanced mode. This container holds objects that were orphaned when their container was deleted while they are being created or moved into the container. How does that happen? Remember that Active Directory is a multimaster replication model. Two administrators can perform administrative duties, each on a different domain controller. If one administrator were to delete an OU on DC1 while another administrator is creating an account on DC2, when replication occurs between the two systems, the

OU will be deleted, and since the user account has nowhere to be created during replication, the account is created in LostAndFound. You may want to check this container periodically to make sure that there are no orphaned accounts lying around.

FIGURE 6.32
Default view of Active Directory Users and Computers

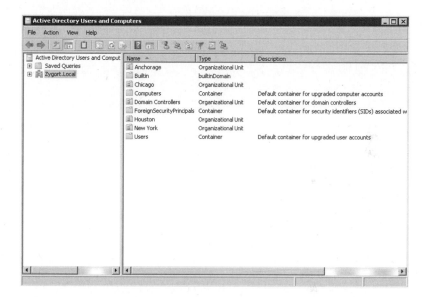

FIGURE 6.33
Expanded view of Active Directory Users and Computers

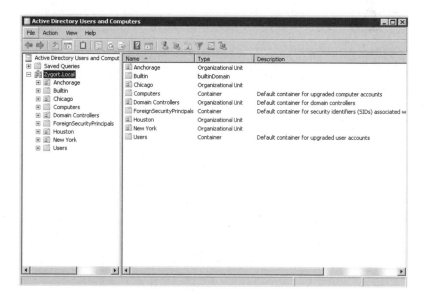

FIGURE 6.34
Additional containers become available in Advanced mode.

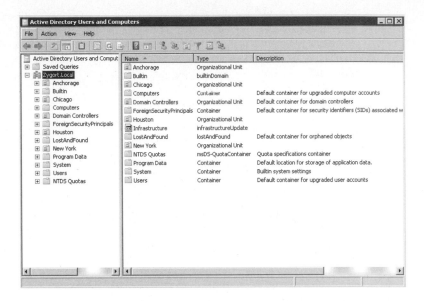

FIGURE 6.35
Normal view of a user account

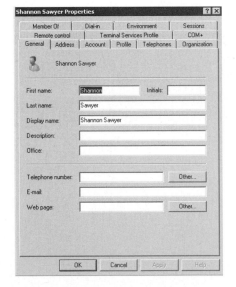

USERS, GROUPS AND COMPUTERS AS CONTAINERS

At times you may want to see the objects that are associated with accounts. One example would be the printer objects that are associated with computer accounts. From the normal view of ADUC these objects do not show up, so you will have to use another method to view the information.

Under the View menu in ADUC, you will find the menu item Users, Groups and Computers as Containers. Selecting this menu item will alter the information that is displayed so that each of the account types will show the objects associated with it. Normally, if you were to click on an OU you would see each of the objects contained within that OU appear in the details pane on the left side of the MMC console. If you select Users, Groups and Computers as Containers, each account object appears in the navigation pane in the MMC, and the objects that are associated with them appear in the details pane. Figure 6.37 shows the appearance of the accounts once Users, Computers and Groups as Containers is selected.

FIGURE 6.36
Advanced view of a
user account

FIGURE 6.37
Users, Computers and
Groups as Containers

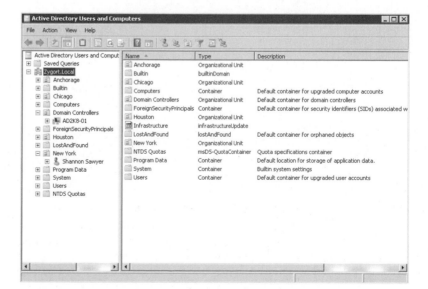

QUERIES

In small organizations, you can usually open ADUC, take a look at the accounts, and find exactly what you need to work with without too much trouble. Medium-sized and large organizations are another matter. Finding a user account in the directory can be a time-consuming chore. Finding accounts that meet specific requirements can seem nearly impossible.

Microsoft has added a handy Queries node to the ADUC interface. This node allows you to create queries that you issue commonly. It also saves queries that will help you cut down on some of your administrative chores. For instance, let's say that you wanted to find out how many of your user accounts were configured so that their passwords will not expire. You could create a simple query that would return the results to you within the ADUC snap-in. When you first open the Queries node, you will notice that there are no predefined queries. Most queries are very easy to create, and you can even create some very complex queries once you become more familiar with LDAP syntax.

To create a query, start by right-clicking the Queries node and selecting New Query. This presents you with the New Query creation utility, shown in Figure 6.38. This utility allows you to create some common queries as well as generate some very complex queries. Some of the easiest queries to create are to find accounts based on the account name or description or the attributes that are defined. Once you define the query name, you can click the Define Query button to open the Find Common Queries dialog box.

Figure 6.39 shows the options on the Users tab of the query utility when the Common Query option is used. Two check boxes allow you to quickly create a query that will display disabled accounts and accounts that have passwords that don't expire. Figure 6.40 shows the query that is generated from selecting the Non-Expiring Passwords check box.

If you select the Computers tab or the Groups tab, you will see options identical to those on the Users tab, except that the Non-Expiring Passwords check box is not available on either of these two tabs and the Disabled Accounts check box does not appear on the Groups tab.

In the Find query-types pull-down, you will see that other options are available if you don't like the limitations set in the Common Queries. If you select the Users, Computers and Groups option, you can create a query that can search based on any of the attributes within the accounts. You can make these queries as simple or as complex as necessary to fit your needs. If you want to create a query that shows you every user who is a member of the Accounts Payable department, you can select the Advanced tab and click the Field button to view the options, as shown in Figure 6.41.

FIGURE 6.38
New Query creation
utility

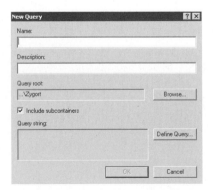

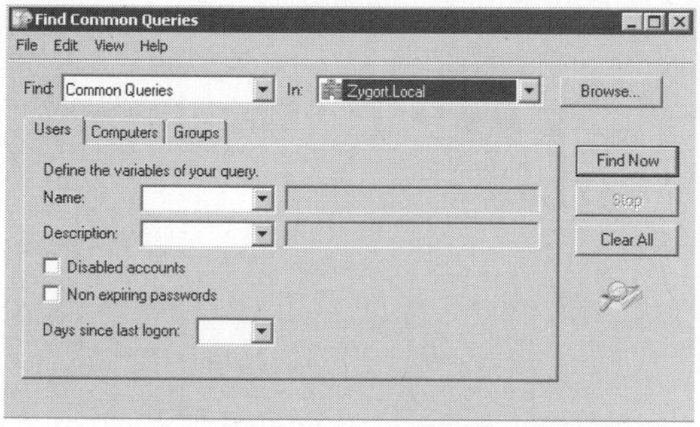

FIGURE 6.39
Common Query
options

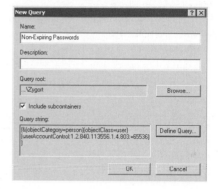

FIGURE 6.40
Query definition

When you hover the mouse over the account type—such as User—a menu appears with all the available attributes that you can include in your query. This menu scrolls so that you can review the entire list to see all the attributes available. If you select Department, you can define how you want to search. The next pull-down list, shown in Figure 6.42, allows you to set the conditions for the query. Six options are normally available:

Starts With   Choosing Starts With allows you to define the initial characters of a string that you want to search for. If you wanted to include all the users from the Accounts Payable and Accounts Receivable departments, you could enter **Accounts,** and both departments would be included in the results.

Ends With   The Ends With option is just the opposite of Starts With. You enter the characters at the end of the string so that you can search for specific information. If you wanted to include only the users who have *Payable* as the last part of the field, you'd choose Ends With and then type **Payable** in the box.

Is (Exactly)   The Is (Exactly) option allows you to completely define the string that you want to base the query on. For example, you can enter **Accounts Payable** in the text box after selecting the Is (Exactly) option, and only accounts that have the exact phrase entered will be returned in the results.

FIGURE 6.41
Account types for
which you can
define queries

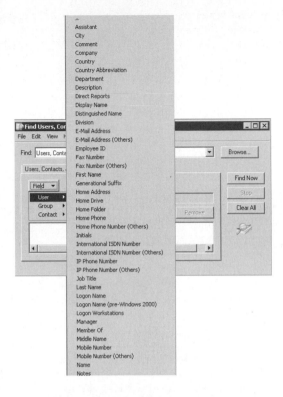

FIGURE 6.42
Conditions for the
query

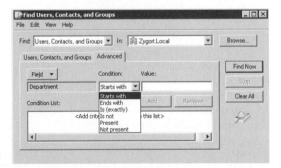

Is Not   This is pretty much the opposite of the Is (Exactly) option. When using the Is Not option, you enter the exact word or phrase that you do *not* want results returned for. For this option, if you want to find all the accounts that are not part of the Marketing department, you choose User ➢ Department, pull down the option for Is Not, and then type **Marketing**. The query returns all the user accounts that are not members of the Marketing department.

Present   When you use the Present option, you are specifying that you do not care what is populated in the field you have chosen, and that you want results returned only for accounts that have data entered in the attribute. You may use this option to check for accounts that have data entered into attributes. For example, you may want to know which accounts have data entered into the Custom Attribute 10 field. When building the query, if you choose User ➤ Custom Attribute 10 and then select Present from the pull-down list, all the appropriate accounts appear when you run the query.

Not Present   The most popular reason for using the Not Present option is to discover the accounts that do not have data in attributes that you normally populate. Remember, Active Directory searches and queries are only as good as the data that is populated in the accounts. If accounts are created and the attributes are not populated according to your standards and practices, you can find accounts that are missing critical information by using this query option. For example, if you want to find all the users that do not have their Manager attribute populated, you would select User ➤ Manager and then pull down the option for Not Present. Once you run this query, you see all the user accounts with missing Manager attribute information.

You are allowed to enter as many query options as you would like. If you want to create a query that displays all the user accounts that are members of the Accounts Payable department and whose manager is Tom Timmons, you would perform the following steps. From the Edit Query window click on the button labeled Define Query, select Users, Contacts, and Groups from the Find pull-down menu. From the Advanced tab, select the button labeled Field and select Department from the menu. Under Condition, select Is (Exactly) and type in the name Accounts Payable and click Add. To add the second criterion, select the Field button again and select Manager from the menu. Choose Is (Exactly) from the Condition pull-down and type in the name Tom Timmons in the Value window. At this point your custom query is defined, as shown in Figure 6.43.

There is a limitation to this, however. All the criteria that you add are considered a logical And operator. You do not have the option to select a Not or an Or operator. If you want to define a query that allows you to specify that the results be returned based on one set of criteria or another (rather than both criteria), you have to write your own query to do so.

To write your own query statement, select Custom Search from the Find query-types pull-down list. Of course, at this point you do not have the luxury of simply choosing a few options and filling in a few fields to generate a query—you will need to know LDAP syntax. You can begin by creating a query using the New Query wizard, and then copy and paste the query statement into the Custom Query dialog box. As shown in Figure 6.44, each query that you create will appear in the Query String dialog box for the query. You can highlight the query, right-click it, and then click Copy. Then open the Custom Search option from the query types pull-down list and paste in the query. You then have the ability to make changes to the query. Note that if you make a mistake in the query, it will not process or return results to you.

FIGURE 6.43

Multiple query options

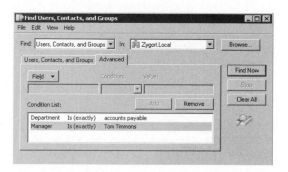

FIGURE 6.44
Query string

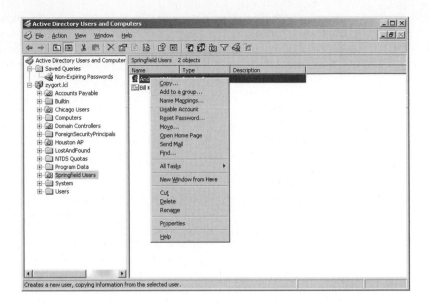

MANAGING ACCOUNTS

When it comes to time-consuming administrative tasks, managing accounts is at the top of the list. And most administrators will tell you that they tire of the administrative overhead that is involved with this task. But, as one administrator said, "Users are the bane of my existence, but if it weren't for users, I wouldn't have this job." During an account's lifetime, you will almost certainly make some changes to it.

So what is involved with account administration? The list includes creating and deleting accounts, adding accounts to groups, modifying account properties, unlocking locked accounts, resetting account passwords, and much more. In the following sections we look at ways to manage user, group, and computer accounts.

Managing Users

Most administrators and users who have been delegated administrative control over user accounts will use Active Directory Users and Computers to manage and manipulate accounts. Others swear by the command-line utilities, but the graphical utilities found in the Administrative Tools folder in the Start menu have become a natural extension to the Windows interface.

Before others can access resources in your organization, they need to have user accounts created for them. The user account is responsible for controlling access to resources and granting rights to perform tasks in the organization. Once you determine that you want to create a user account for someone, you have a couple of options. Most administrators use Active Directory Users and Computers to create the account, but you could just as easily write a script that will allow you to create the account from outside the built-in Active Directory administrative tools.

Whenever you are preparing to create an account, you should consider in which Active Directory container you will create the account. Right-click on the desired container and select New➢ User from the context menu. This brings up the dialog box where you can enter the user's identifying information, as shown in Figure 6.45. As you enter the user's first name, middle initial, and last name, the display name is generated for you. You need to provide the user logon name according to your organization's naming conventions.

Notice that the user logon name is just part of the user principle name (UPN). If you take the default options, the UPN consists of the username and the forest root name in what appears to be an email address. If you wanted to, you could have the user's email address and their UPN use the same format, but then you would run the risk of making your user's logon available to anyone who knows their email address. This is a security risk.

So what are all the options that you have when managing a user account? As you probably have deduced, a user account has several attributes with which you can work to help identify the person the account represents. Everything from the user's name to the cell phone used to the person's manager can be entered in the account properties. As we move forward in this section, we'll look at the properties available in the user account, and discuss ways to manipulate those properties. Along the way, we'll also point out the command-line options that are available for managing user accounts. (Everything we mention in this section is also accessible using various scripting methods. For more information on scripting access to Active Directory, check out the last three chapters of this book; they concentrate on managing Active Directory through scripting.)

First look at the options available from the context menu when you right-click on a user account in Active Directory Users and Computers. Figure 6.46 shows the menu that appears when you do not have any other applications (such as the Exchange System Manager snap-in) altering the default options. When the Exchange System Manager snap-in is added, the Exchange Tasks menu item becomes available, which allows you to manipulate the user's Exchange configuration. Let's start with the options that you will use the most.

The Copy option lets you copy the current user-object settings to a new user object. Not all the object properties will copy over, but those that are not specific to an individual user will. For instance, the username and password will not copy over to the new account, but the group membership will.

If you right-click on an active account, you will see an option called Disable Account. (If the account is disabled, you see an option for enabling the account.) This is a fast and easy way to either enable or disable an account without going into the account properties and selecting or deselecting the check box on the Account property page.

You'll use Reset Password frequently, and it does exactly what the name says: it allows an administrator to change the password on an account. As you can see in Figure 6.47, not only do you have the choice of changing the user's password, but you can also specify whether the user needs to change their password after successfully logging on after your password reset.

FIGURE 6.45
New Object - User
dialog box

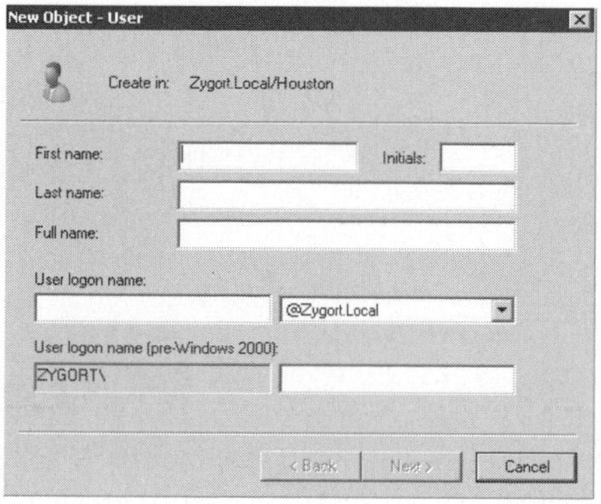

Another option on the context menu is Move. If you come from a Windows 2000 Active Directory environment, this is the only option you have to move an account from one OU to another. Figure 6.48 shows the dialog box that appears when you choose this option. To move the account, simply select the OU or container in which you want to place the account, and click OK. For any Windows 2003 or later domain environment, you can simply drag and drop the account to any OU or container you want.

FIGURE 6.46
The default
context menu

FIGURE 6.47
Reset Password
dialog box

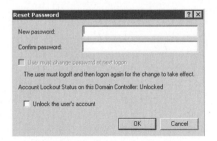

FIGURE 6.48
Move dialog box

You can move accounts into only OUs or containers within the same domain using this option. If you need to move an account to a location in another domain, you need to use another utility, such as the Active Directory Migration Tool (ADMT).

The final two options we'll cover that appear in the top portion of the context menu are Open Home Page and Send Mail. These perform their actions depending on whether the account has a default web page or email address associated with it.

If you hover the mouse pointer over the All Tasks menu item, you will see the same options that appear at the top of the context menu, but two other options are available here as well: Group Policy Modeling and Group Policy Results. If you have been granted the ability to run these two wizards (which is granted either from the Group Policy Management Console or the object's Security property page), you can check to see what Group Policy Objects (GPOs) were applied to the user or the user's computer the last time the user logged in, or you can see what GPOs will be applied to a user if you move that user to another location within Active Directory. (For more information on using the Group Policy wizards, see Chapter 8, "Managing Group Policy.")

Managing Groups

As shown in Figure 6.49, you don't get many options to work with when you right-click a group. Send Mail is the only option that appears at the top of the context menu. If the group has been assigned an email address, you will be able to open your default email application from here and compose a message to be sent to the members of the group. Of course, members will receive the email only if they are mail-enabled.

FIGURE 6.49
Group context menu

Managing Computers

Computer accounts act in a manner similar to user accounts. They are necessary to authenticate the computer account in the domain and to allow access to resources in that domain. The context menu for a computer account does not have as many options as a user account does, but there are still some important and useful options. Figure 6.50 shows the available options.

The first option we will look at is Reset Account. If you select this option, the account's password is reset and you will need to add the computer account back into the domain for a new password to be generated between the computer and Active Directory.

The next option is Move, which works the same way as the Move option under a user object's context menu. And just as with a user account, the drag-and-drop functionality that has been added to Active Directory Users and Computers is easy and intuitive to use.

The next option is Manage. This is a very handy option to have available to an administrator. Once you locate the computer that you want to work with, you can choose Manage from the context menu and the Computer Management console will appear. Although you could do the same thing by opening the Computer Management console directly and then choosing the computer you would like to manage, if you are already within Active Directory Users and Computers or if you cannot remember the full name of the computer that you want to manage, you can start the management console from here.

FIGURE 6.50
Computer
context menu

CREATING TASKPADS (WINDOWS 2000 AND 2003)

As you will see in Chapter 9, "Managing Active Directory Security," you can delegate rights and permissions to users so that they can perform actions in Active Directory even if they are not members of any of the default administrative groups. This makes it easy for the domain owners and domain administrators to delegate administrative control to other users without giving those users too much power in the domain. For example, if you want to give help-desk employees the ability to change passwords for users but you do not want them to have the ability to change other user properties, such as group membership or address and phone attributes, you can give them just that amount of power.

Even if you do give a user some level of administrative control, that user needs to have an interface in which to perform the functions. You can give a user access to the snap-in required for the taskpad by copying the `dsadmin.dll` file from a domain controller or extracting the file from the `adminpak.msi` file on the Windows Server CD into the `system32` directory on the user's computer.

You could register the dynamic link library (DLL) that is used for Active Directory Users and Computers by entering **regsvr32 dsadmin.dll** at a command prompt and then add the snap-in to an MMC, but then you would need to train each of the users on performing functions in the ADUC interface and you would probably have to explain why they cannot use many of the functions that they find in the interface.

Instead, you can create a taskpad that can be used for specific tasks. A taskpad is a Web-based interface that allows you to perform the same tasks that you can in a full version of a snap-in, but you can tailor it to your own needs, having it display only the functions you want to use. In our example of the help-desk employee who needs to have the ability to change users' passwords, you could create a taskpad that gives the employee that ability but nothing else from the ADUC snap-in.

You still need to register the DLL on the computer where the user will be performing his or her duties. Other than that, you don't have to do anything to the user's computer. You do need to create the taskpad, however. The process is very simple (but you can get sophisticated with taskpads if you want). First you must add the snap-in that is normally used to perform the administrative task that is going to be performed in the taskpad. Note that the default utilities that appear in the Administrative Tools menu will not allow you to create taskpads from them.

Once you've added the snap-in, navigate to the node where you would normally perform the function. For our example, you navigate to an OU that contains user accounts. Choosing Create Taskpad View from the menu brings you to a wizard for creating the taskpad. When the wizard starts, you will define how the taskpad will be identified and used. On the last page of this wizard is a prompt to launch another wizard that allows you to define the tasks that can be performed in the taskpad.

This second wizard starts by asking for the task you are defining. You have the options Menu Command, Script, or Navigation. A menu command is any command that is available from the context menu of an object. If you select the Script option, you can define a command or script that will run when you select the option in the taskpad. Selecting the Navigation option allows you to create a navigation link so that you can allow that user of the taskpad to jump to a predefined node.

For our example, we will create a simple taskpad that allows us to change passwords for users. The help-desk personnel will have the ability to change passwords for users in two different OUs: Chicago Users and Springfield Users. We define the taskpad appearance by following the wizard, as shown in Figures 6.51 through 6.55.

FIGURE 6.51
Start of the New
Taskpad View Wizard

FIGURE 6.52
Choosing the look
of the taskpad

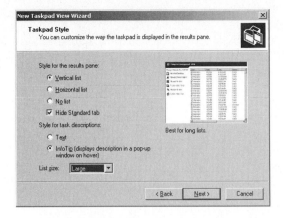

FIGURE 6.53
Selecting the scope
of the taskpad

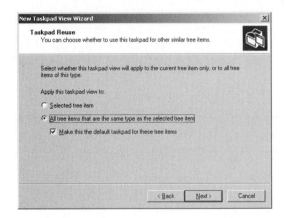

FIGURE 6.54
Naming the taskpad

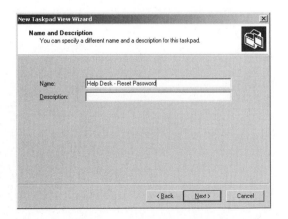

FIGURE 6.55
Choosing to add
new tasks using the
tasks wizard

When you reach the final page of the wizard, you can start the New Task Wizard to create the individual tasks. The first task we will create uses the Navigation option. Selecting the Navigation radio button (see Figure 6.56) and clicking Next takes you to the wizard page shown in Figure 6.57. When creating a navigation link, make sure that you have added the OUs or containers that you will reference to the Favorites list of the MMC. The wizard prompts you for the Favorites link you want to use, as shown in Figure 6.57. You also have the opportunity to choose an icon to appear next to the link, as shown in Figure 6.58. For each task you add, you have the option to add another task, as shown in Figure 6.59.

After the Navigation task is finished, you define the change password task. This will be a menu command, so select that radio button from the list. Figure 6.60 displays the available menu options. You can work with two different menu sets: the container options or the details options. If you choose the container options, you will see all the menu items.

Choosing the Reset Password option and clicking Next takes you to a screen that allows you to name the task. As with the Navigation tasks you added, you are presented with a screen that allows you to add an icon to the task link. Once you've added tasks to the taskpad, you will have a nice-looking administrative view that allows you to limit the functions that a user can perform. Figure 6.61 shows the taskpad. On the left side of the taskpad, notice the task links for navigation and resetting passwords.

FIGURE 6.56
Selecting the
Navigation option

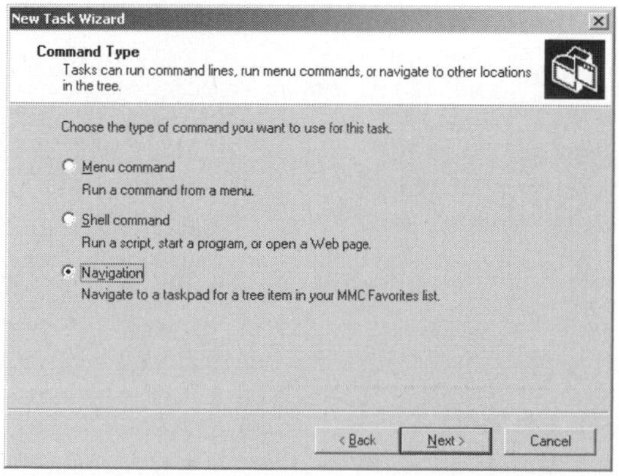

FIGURE 6.57
Selecting a favorite
to link to

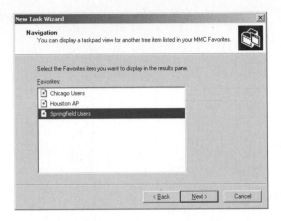

FIGURE 6.58
Choosing an icon

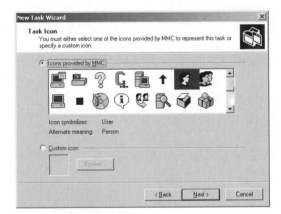

FIGURE 6.59
Choosing to create
another task

FIGURE 6.60
Menu Command
options

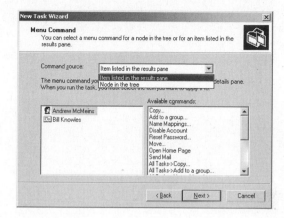

FIGURE 6.61
Navigating the
taskpad

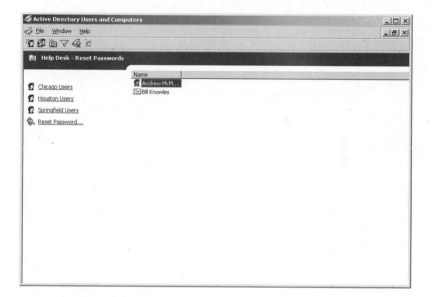

Command-Line Utilities

In case you like typing your commands or if you would like to script the administrative control of accounts, you can use command-line utilities to manipulate Active Directory–based accounts. There are limitations to the Active Directory Users and Computers interface. If you want to create several accounts, you have to right-click on the container or OU where you wish to create the account; as shown in the "Active Directory Users and Computers" section of this chapter, you can only enter the user's authentication information in the wizard that appears. You then have to find the account you just created, right-click the account, choose Properties, and then add any additional attributes for the account.

Another benefit to these utilities is that they can be used in a batch file or script. The batch file can then be altered for new accounts, and scripts can be written to allow for a prompt to appear. The administrator running the script could then enter the data when prompted.

Whether you are typing commands at the command line or including them in a script, you must have the appropriate rights to create the account. By default, any person who logs in with an Administrators, Domain Admins, Enterprise Admins, or Account Admins account or who logs on using the Administrator account will be able to use any of these utilities. You can also delegate the right to create object types in Active Directory. If the account with which you are logged in has been delegated the ability to create an account, you could use these utilities to create an Administrators, Domain Admins, Enterprise Admins, or Account Admins account.

For more information on delegating administrative access to nonadministrator accounts, see Chapter 7, "Managing Organizational Units."

DSAdd

The DSAdd utility lets you create accounts in Active Directory. When using DSAdd, you have the option to populate any of the attributes that are available from the account's properties when using Active Directory Users and Computers. The advantage to using DSAdd is that you can populate the attributes when the account is being created instead of modifying the account after it already exists in the directory service.

Any account type can be created when using DSAdd. If you take a look at the syntax of the command in Figure 6.62, you will notice the account options you have if you enter **dsadd /?** at the command prompt. If you want to further drill down and look at the options for any of the account types, such as a user account, you can enter **dsadd -user /?** at the command prompt and receive the results shown in Figure 6.63.

Notice in Figure 6.63 that you have a long list of attributes you can take advantage of when using DSAdd. This means that as you create the user account, you can populate the account attributes immediately instead of having to go back later and enter them.

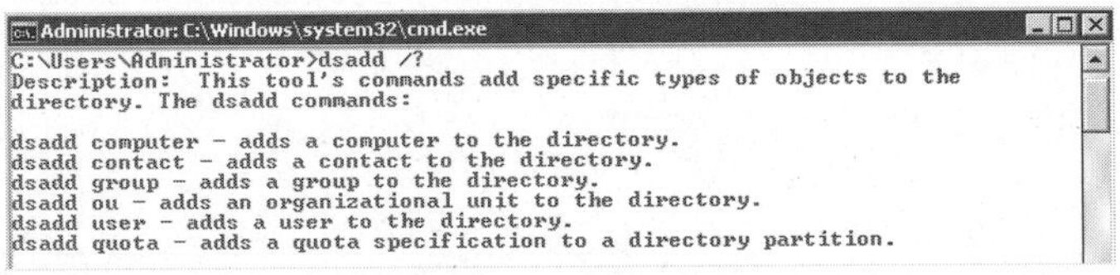

FIGURE 6.62
Syntax for the DSAdd utility

```
Administrator: C:\Windows\system32\cmd.exe

C:\Users\Administrator>dsadd /?
Description:  This tool's commands add specific types of objects to the
directory. The dsadd commands:

dsadd computer - adds a computer to the directory.
dsadd contact - adds a contact to the directory.
dsadd group - adds a group to the directory.
dsadd ou - adds an organizational unit to the directory.
dsadd user - adds a user to the directory.
dsadd quota - adds a quota specification to a directory partition.
```

DSMod

If you already have an account created, you can use the DSMod utility to modify the account's attributes. This is an easy way to make changes to several accounts at once. For example, let's say a company has relocated some of its employees to another office building. When they move to the new location, you could assign someone to open all of the affected accounts using Active Directory Users and Computers and change the address attributes, or you could write a quick batch file that reads a list of user-account names and then modifies the address attributes on those accounts. Writing a batch file might take a few minutes, but you could save a lot of time and reduce the number of typographical errors compared to changing the accounts manually. Figure 6.64 shows the syntax of the DSMod command when you enter **dsmod /?** at the command prompt.

FIGURE 6.63

Syntax when using
DSAdd to create a
user account

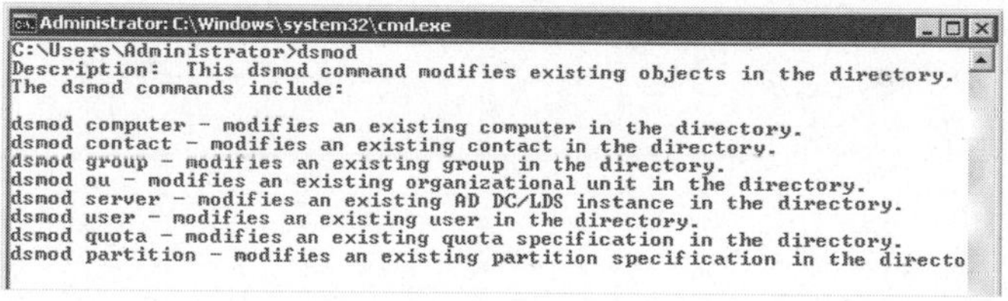

FIGURE 6.64

DSMod syntax

DSQUERY

Just as the name suggests, DSQuery allows you to locate accounts as well as other object types in Active Directory by issuing a command. Figure 6.65 shows the object types that you can search for using DSQuery. You can then find the syntax of each object type by retrieving the help information listing on each object type; for example, type **dsquery user /?** to find the query options for a user account.

When you use DSQuery, the results will be returned to you based on the query parameters. If you want to find all the users who have the name Angelo, you can issue the command **dsquery user -name Angelo***. With the asterisk acting as a wildcard, all of the user accounts who have the first name Angelo will appear. If you want to create a file from the results, you could enter **dsquery user -name Angelo*** > *d:\queryresultspath\queryfile.txt* where *d:* is the drive where you want to place the results, *queryresultspath* is the folder path, and *queryfile.txt* is the filename you want to use.

DSGET

DSGet will return attribute information when you specify an account as the target of the command. When issuing this command, you will need to know which attributes you want returned in the results. Figure 6.66 shows the syntax of the DSGet command used to display the user information.

DSRM

If you wish to remove accounts, you can use the DSRm command. Figure 6.67 shows this command; note that there are few parameters for this command, but a couple do come in handy. The -noprompt switch puts the command in silent mode, deleting the objects without prompting first. The -subtree switch deletes the entire tree structure, including the tree level you specified in the command. If you want to leave the tree level that you included in the command but delete the subtrees, you would use the -exclude switch.

FIGURE 6.65
Syntax for the
DSQuery command

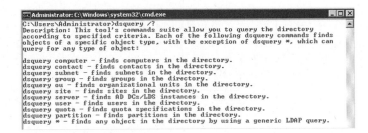

FIGURE 6.66
Syntax of the DSGet
command

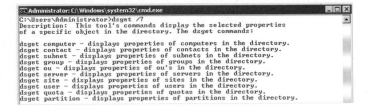

FIGURE 6.67
Syntax of the DSRm
command

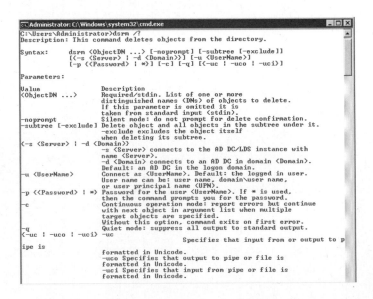

DSMove

To change the location in Active Directory, you can use the DSMove command and specify the new location for an existing object. Figure 6.68 shows the syntax of this command. Note that during the move from one Active Directory location to another, you can also specify a new name for the object. This comes in especially handy when you already have an object with the same relative distinguished name in that directory location.

One of the benefits of the directory service command-line utilities is its ability to send the results of command to one of the other utilities for processing. When you add the pipe symbol (|) between two commands, the results from the first command will be used as input arguments for the second command. For example, let's assume you are trying to move several users to an OU. You can create the OU either manually or by issuing the DSAdd command, and then use DSQuery to move the users to the new OU instead of moving them manually or using the DSMove command alone. For this example, let's move all of the users from the Accounts Payable OU to the new Houston AP OU that we have created. To do so, you simply issue the following command:

```
dsquery -user "ou=Accounts Payable,dc=zygort,dc=lcl" | dsmove
-newparent "ou=Houston AP,dc=zygort,dc=lcl"
```

FIGURE 6.68
Syntax of the DSMove command

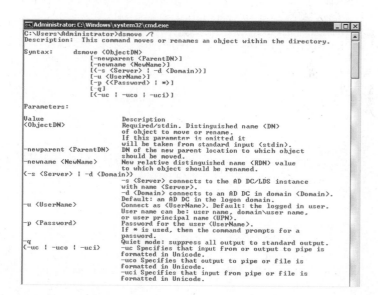

LDAP Utilities

You can access Active Directory by using LDAP commands, and by using utilities that use LDAP-based access. Two utilities have been available since the first version of Active Directory. With the arrival of the directory service utilities that were introduced with Windows Server 2003, the two LDAP utilities seem to have lost popularity, but some organizations still use them to some extent.

CSVDE

CSVDE is used to populate Active Directory from a comma-separated value file. If you already have a file that contains information about the user, group, or computer accounts that you want to use when populating Active Directory, you can quickly modify the file to fit the needs of CSVDE and then import the data quickly. CSVDE is most commonly used when a company is importing account information from an existing Exchange 5.5 implementation.

Each file that you want to import must be formatted correctly. For CSVDE, you need to make sure that the import file has all of the attributes separated by commas. You also need to make sure that the first line of the file is the header line, which defines each of the attributes that you are importing into the new accounts. Each account will have a separate line in the import file, and when imported, the Active Directory location and all of the attributes defined in the file will be used to create and define the account. (For more information on the attributes available for use in the CSVDE import file, see Knowledge Base article 281563.)

Once you've created the file and saved it to a location where it can be accessed by the user who has permissions to create accounts in the Active Directory locations specified in the import file, to run the tool you simply open a command line and enter **csvde -i -f file_location**.

When you specify the -i option, you are specifying that you are performing an import function. The -f specifies that the filename is the next item in the command line. One other option is available, -k, which informs CSVDE that it needs to ignore errors that are generated from the import file and continue with remaining entries in the file.

The limitation of CSVDE is that it cannot be used to modify existing accounts. The only options available are exporting existing accounts to a file or importing new accounts from a file. If you want to modify existing accounts, you will need to use a tool like LDIFDE.

LDIFDE

As does CSVDE, LDIFDE allows you to populate Active Directory with account information included in a file. The advantage to using LDIFDE rather than CSVDE is the ability to modify and delete entries in Active Directory. Also, the file format is a little different: CSVDE uses commas to separate the attributes; LDIFDE uses line breaks to separate the attributes.

Default Folder Redirectors

When you initially install Active Directory, two containers are used to hold user and computer accounts. If you open Active Directory Users and Computers, you will see these two containers (Users and Computers) directly beneath the domain node, as shown in Figure 6.69. You can tell immediately that these are containers instead of OUs by the icon used to represent them. An icon that has the directory symbol in the center of a folder indicates an OU, whereas containers are simply shown as folders.

These two containers are used primarily for interoperability with Windows NT 4–based domains. When you upgrade Windows NT 4 domains, you upgrade the Primary Domain Controller first, and in doing so, the dcpromo utility moves all of the user and group accounts in the domain to the Users container, and the computer accounts are moved to the Computers container. Although initially this doesn't look like a problem, you must remember that these are containers and not OUs.

Because containers are used for interoperability with Windows NT 4 domains, they cannot utilize group policies. OUs, on the other hand, were designed to be used with group policies. That means that the only GPOs that can be applied to users or computers in Active Directory are those that are applied at the domain or site levels. In Chapter 9 we will look at some of the reasons you want to link GPOs to OUs instead of linking them at the domain or site level. You will be very limited if you have only the options of linking at the domain or site level. OUs give you better control over how you apply the GPOs to users and computers.

FIGURE 6.69

Default containers in Active Directory Users and Computers

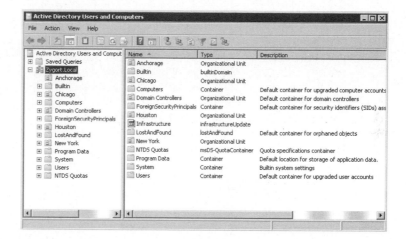

If you have created a new OU and named it Users, and the system files are installed in the WINNT folder on the D: drive and the domain name is zygort.lcl, your command would look like the following:

```
d:\winnt\system32\redirusr ou=users,dc=zygort,dc=lcl
```

REDIRCMP

By default, the Computers container is the default location for computer accounts, with the exception of domain controllers. To create a new OU that will take over as the default location, you need to use the redircmp utility. If the new OU will also be called Computers, you should first rename the Computers container to something that fits the naming standards for your Active Directory implementation. You can then create a new OU named Computers. Once you have the new OU created, you can redirect the creation of new accounts by opening a command prompt and using the following syntax:

```
%systemroot%\system32\redircmp container_distinguished_name
```

If you have created a new OU and named it Computers in the zygort.lcl domain, and the system files are installed in the WINNT folder on the D: drive, your command would look like the following:

```
d:\winnt\system32\redircmp ou=computers,dc=zygort,dc=lcl
```

Coming Up Next

Next we are going to discuss the options for managing access to Active Directory resources. There are different authentication mechanisms to help secure your Active Directory infrastructure, and you will need to know which methods to use depending on how users connect to your environment.

The Bottom Line

Create different account types and edit properties associated with them   There are two different account types: security principal accounts and non–security principal accounts. Security principal accounts comprise user, security group, and computer accounts. Non–security principal accounts comprise contacts and distribution groups.

Master It   Your company is preparing a new marketing campaign. The Marketing group currently consists of five employees. Marketing has just hired three new internal employees and four external employees that will be working on a contract basis.

You need to create the new accounts and create a mailing list so all of the users can communicate. The external users should not have access to any network resources.

Use built-in and downloadable utilities to manage user, group, and computer accounts
AD DS includes many tools and utilities to manage and configure user, group, and computer accounts. There are also many Microsoft utilities and third-party tools you can download and use in your environment to help manage these accounts.

Master It   You have just received a request to add 100 new users to your domain. When you create these users, you must populate the account with information such as department, phone number, manager, and location.

Chapter 7

Maintaining Organizational Units

Active Directory (AD) functions as a central repository of objects. These objects represent users, groups, computers, printers, and other items. You can control who has access to these objects, and the scope of operations that may be performed upon the objects once that access is allowed. One special object type within Active Directory was designed to make an administrator's life a little easier: organizational units, or OUs. By using OUs, you can organize other objects and control administrative access to those objects. This chapter will help you control and manage the resources you choose to put within OUs.

In this chapter you will learn how to:

◆ Manage access to objects within your organizational units

◆ Manage administrative control of the objects within your organizational units

◆ Monitor the activity of the objects within your organizational units

Understanding Organizational Units

OUs have specific purposes within Active Directory. First and foremost, they are used for managing administrative control of resources. If you look back at Chapter 3, "Active Directory Domain Services Forest and Domain Design," you will find a lengthy discussion about creation of OUs and the criteria to consider when designing your OU structure. You should not create OUs to conform to a company's organizational chart. Instead, you should create them in such a way that they answer the question, "Who manages what?" Once you have determined who is responsible for the objects within Active Directory, you will have a much easier time planning your OU structure.

The other OU design criterion is the efficient implementation of group policies. Once you have designed the administrative structure of OUs, you should enhance the design so that you can use group policies to control user environments and manage security settings. Taking both administrative control and group policies into account when designing your OU infrastructure can be a daunting task, but once you have successfully deployed your OU structure, the administrative overhead will be reduced.

Components of Resources

OUs organize resources. That plain and simple statement gets right to the point. Once we have the OU structure in place, we can add the Active Directory resources to their respective OUs. Some of the more common resources you can create in Active Directory and place within OUs are computer, group, organizational unit, printer, shared folder, or user objects. Depending on how you manage your resources, you could have an OU that is dedicated to printer objects, and then the users who are responsible for maintaining those printers could be granted the permissions required to do their jobs.

Before we can take advantage of using OUs, we need to create the OU structure. Creating OUs works in much the same way as creating the accounts we worked with in Chapter 6, "Managing Accounts: User, Group, and Computer." To create OUs, you can use Active Directory Users and Computers, you can use the command-line utility DSAdd, or you can write a script. The method you are most comfortable with is the method you should use. Do seriously consider the scripting solutions, however, because they are very powerful. (For more information on creating administrative scripts, see Part 5: "Streamlining Management with Scripts," which covers scripting and managing Active Directory using scripts.)

Once created, the OUs can be populated with objects. We covered user, contact, InetOrgPerson, and computer accounts in Chapter 6. The other two object types commonly grouped within OUs are printer and shared folder objects.

PRINTER OBJECTS

A printer becomes a printer object when you publish the printer in Active Directory. When you install and share a printer on a server running Windows 2000 or higher, it is automatically published in Active Directory. There is an option to remove a printer from Active Directory by going to the properties of the printer and clearing the List in the Directory check box shown in Figure 7.1.

The property fields of a printer are populated when the printer is created and published in Active Directory. This allows users to search for printers by name, capabilities, or other criteria. A user can also search for printers by printer location. If you have Printer Tracking Location enabled and properly configured, a user can find a printer based on location and not have to hunt for the closest printer. We will discuss this feature further in the section "Printer Location Tracking." Users typically search for printers by using the Find Printer option in the Start menu or by performing a search in Active Directory.

You will not find a printer if you are searching the Active Directory console itself. Printers that are published are not directly visible because they appear beneath their computer objects, and computer objects themselves are not usually treated as containers. If you want to view a printer, you have to change the view of the Active Directory and Users console to Users, Contacts, Groups, and Computers as Containers. Once you do this, you can view printers (see Figure 7.2).

FIGURE 7.1
Property for listing the printer in Active Directory

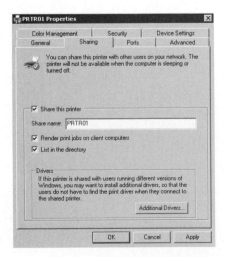

FIGURE 7.2

Enabling the View Users, Contacts, Groups, and Computers as Containers option

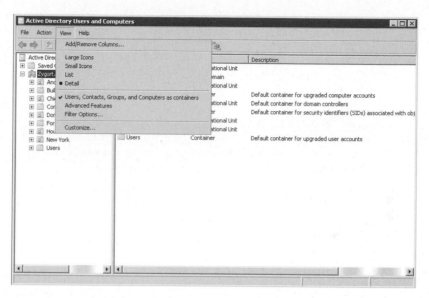

You should control access to your printers for security, cost, and departmental requirements. Some printers simply cost more than others to operate, and you may want to limit which users have access to these printers, and when. Three permission levels are available (besides Special Permissions): Print, Manage Documents, and Manage Printers, as you can see in Figure 7.3. When you install a printer on the network, the default permission of Print is assigned. As with other areas of your network, you will want to plan what permissions are assigned to users and groups. Spending some time doing this will help you maintain greater control over your printers and will help limit costs. You assign permissions to a printer the same way you do to any other resource—through the Security tab on the properties sheet. Let's use the newly installed printer object Office Printer and assign our manager, John Doe, the Manage Documents permission for our new printer.

FIGURE 7.3

Printer permissions

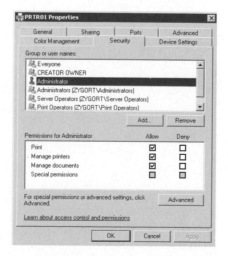

One thing to keep in mind when multiple permissions are applied to a group of users is that the effective permissions for a given printer will be the least restrictive of all assigned permissions. This does not hold true with the Deny permission; Deny takes precedence over all other assigned permissions.

We have determined the permissions we are going to assign the printer, and we have applied them. Now we need to look at the Advanced tab on the properties sheet for a printer. Through the settings in the Advanced tab you can specify the hours a printer will be available, and you can control how a printer is accessed based on printer priorities. You can also specify how printer spooling will be handled, if and how separator pages will be used, and other options. In Figure 7.4, we have specified the printer is only available from 7 AM to 6 PM. So along with the normal permissions applied, the printer also has limited availability.

FIGURE 7.4
Advanced settings for printers

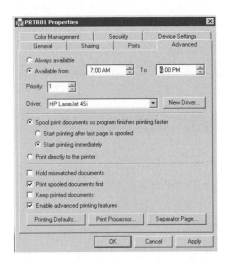

Printers and Group Policy

Group Policy is a powerful tool that you as an administrator can use to secure and control your network. This holds true with your printers and printing as well. You can use Group Policy to manage and control access to your printers once you have published your printers in Active Directory. (As you'll recall, a printer is published in Active Directory once it is created and shared.) The Group Policy Management Editor contains a number of policies that you can use to streamline printing and facilitate control in your network, as you can see in Figure 7.5. Printer policies are in the `Computer Configuration/ Administrative Templates/Printers` section of the Group Policy Management Editor. We will take a closer look at these policies and implement methods for including web-based printing and printer location tracking in an Active Directory environment.

Printing Policies for Accessing and Controlling Printers

Two policies we will look at more closely are Automatically Publish New Printers in Active Directory and Allow Printers To Be Published. These two policies are mutually exclusive because Allow Printers To Be Published takes precedence over Automatically Publish New Printers in Active Directory.

Thus, if you disable the Allow Printers To Be Published policy, users will not be able to use Active Directory to find printers. If you disable the Automatically Publish New Printers in Active Directory policy, users will have to add printers manually.

FIGURE 7.5
Group Policy settings for printers

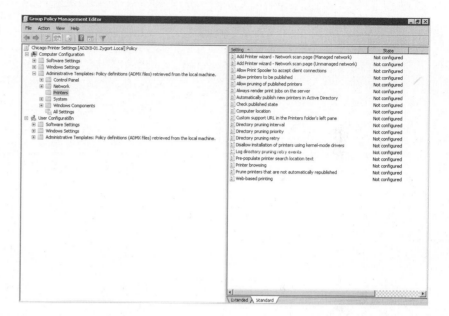

Web-Based Printing

This feature allows users to connect to a printer via an HTTP connection, such as `http://printerservername/printers`. Some configuration on your part is required for this to function properly—namely, setting up Internet Information Services (IIS) to accommodate web-based printing. Web-based printing uses the Internet Printing Protocol (IPP) within HTTP to allow printing. You can control access to web-based printing through the directory security on the IIS server for the web-based printer website.

Note: For more information on web-based printing and a white paper that goes into more detail on IPP, see `www.microsoft.com/windowsserver2003/techinfo/overview/internetprint.mspx`.

Printer Location Tracking

This new feature allows a user to find printers based on the user's location in the network, by implementing a systematic naming convention for the logical sites in your network. You then use this naming convention from your logical sites in the Location field in the properties sheet of the printer. You also need to create subnet objects in Active Directory Sites and Services for each site location. After establishing a naming convention and creating the requisite objects in Active Directory Sites and Services, you need to enable the Pre-populate Printer Search Location Text policy in the `Computer Configuration/Administrative Templates/Printers` settings in the Group Policy Management Editor for the container, as shown in Figure 7.6.

FIGURE 7.6
Enabling printer
location tracking

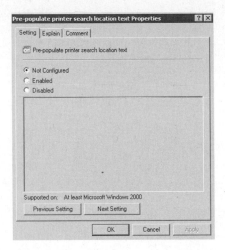

SHARED FOLDER OBJECTS

The last AD object we are going to discuss is shared folder objects that have been published in Active Directory. A folder that has been published in Active Directory is accessible to all users with the appropriate permissions. The advantage for your users is that once a folder has been published, users can search AD for the object; users don't have to know where the folder is stored or its share name, and they can use a Universal Naming Convention (UNC) format (*server**share*).

You must first decide which container will host your newly created shared folder. Once you have decided on the container, follow the steps you used earlier for creating users and groups, except choose Shared Folder instead. You must specify a correct UNC for the location of the share in the form *server_name**share_name*. The two remaining fields are optional, and the information contained there only helps facilitate users' searches of Active Directory for these shared folders. You can enter a description of the shared folder and also use keywords by clicking the Keywords tab and typing what is needed.

When working with shared folders, remember that if users have mapped a drive to the shared folder and you move the share to another server, users will have to re-create the mapped drives based on the new location for the shared folders.

You will not be able to see the Security or the Object tab in the default view settings for the shared folder. To view these tabs, go to the View tab in Active Directory Users and Computers and click the Advanced Features tab.

Granting Administrative Control

Security principals access objects in Active Directory. A security principal can be a computer, group, service, or user. Every security principal is automatically assigned a security identifier (SID), which uniquely identifies the specific security principal in Active Directory and is specific to a domain. Every object you create in Active Directory has an associated security descriptor. In fact, any object you create or store on an NT File System (NTFS) partition has an associated security descriptor. An object's security descriptor states who owns the object, who is allowed to access it and to what degree, and what—if any—auditing is enabled for the object. (For more on security descriptors, see the "Security Descriptors" section later in this chapter.) The accessibility level of an object is controlled by the discretionary access control list (DACL), which is itself composed of an access control list and access control entries. Auditing for Active Directory objects is handled by the system access control list (SACL).

User Rights and Permissions when Accessing Resources

It is common for people to use the terms *rights* and *permissions* interchangeably, but they do have their own specific meanings and applications. Rights, or user rights, are privileges that you assign to users or groups. Permissions are used to control access to objects.

How do AD and NTFS work together using rights and permissions to ensure only authorized individuals gain access to approved resources? This is accomplished through the use of security descriptors, security principals, DACLs, SIDs, and access tokens.

User Rights

A right, also called a user right, is a privilege that allows the designee to perform certain tasks. Rights can be assigned to users and groups. Rights can be very specific and detailed or can be broad in scope. You can employ user rights to deny actions as well as to permit actions. Rights can implicitly deny actions (for example, if you don't grant rights to a group, that group cannot perform a task), as well as explicitly deny rights by categorically denying someone permission. Rights can have a very broad or very narrow scope. Some rights could affect multiple domains. For example, imagine having a site with multiple domains and you applied an action to that site. If you had users or computers from two different domains in the same site, when the policy is applied to the site, the users or computers would have to get their policies from both domains.

Security Descriptors

Every object you create in Active Directory or on an NTFS partition that can be secured has a security descriptor that is created when the object itself is created. A security descriptor is used to control access to the object and is composed of several parts: the DACL, the SACL, and information about the object's owner.

COMPONENTS OF A SECURITY DESCRIPTOR

An object's security descriptor states who owns the object, who is allowed to access the object, and what auditing is enabled for the object (and if it is, to what degree it is enabled). The DACL controls an object's accessibility level, and the SACL handles auditing of any accessed objects. A user's access token is compared with the requested action, and if a match is found within the DACL, the user is granted access. The DACL contains five fields that are used together, as shown in Table 7.1.

TABLE 7.1:   Structure of a Security Descriptor

FIELD	ENTRIES
Header	Identity information
Owner	Owner's SID
Group	Group's SID
DACL	Access-control entries for rights or access permissions
SACL	Access-control entries for auditing

Access to resources in Active Directory is set at the object level and is determined by the different permissions or levels of access. You can set the security for an object when it is created. If you don't make any security settings at the time you create an object, the object inherits settings from the parent object. The parent object can be the OU, folder, hard drive, or other container in which the object was created. If the parent object doesn't have security set, the object will use the default levels.

Security Principals

As we mentioned earlier, security principals are accounts that have permissions applied to them that allow them to access objects. When you create a security principal in Active Directory, that account or security group, once properly authenticated by a domain, will have access to resources contained in the domain. But what permits or denies a security principal access to resources? This is accomplished through a unique security identifier, which is generated at the same time you create a security principal. We track security principals by name, whereas Active Directory tracks them by their SIDs. A security principal's SID is unique for a domain; no two security principals will ever have the same SID in a domain. We will spend more time with SIDs later in this chapter.

We know that security principals can consist of computer, group, or user objects; user and group objects are typically the ones you will spend the most time administering because companies and their corresponding networks are dynamic. Employees come and go, have name changes, are promoted, change offices, and so forth. Groups usually don't require as much time administering as users do, except for changes in membership.

Discretionary Access Control List

As mentioned earlier in the chapter, the security descriptor is the basis for access to objects within Active Directory. Part of the security descriptor is the access control list (ACL). Access to objects is determined by the access token of the security principal accessing the object, and the object's ACL.

The ACL comprises four parts: an ACL size, an ACL revision number, an access control entry (ACE) count, and the ACEs themselves. The ACL size is the amount of memory, in bytes, that the ACL will occupy. An ACL can accommodate about 1,820 ACEs, based on maximum memory usage. The ACEs themselves are stored in the ACL in the order in which they were added, following a canonical pattern. The canonical order is listed as Explicit Deny, Explicit Allow, Inherit Deny, and Inherit Allow. This ensures that if there is an Explicit Deny, it will take precedence over an Explicit Allow. An ACL Revision number is given to every object in Active Directory. This is the number of the ACL's data structure. Active Directory objects are given a revision number of 4, while most other objects receive a revision number of 2.

When an object is accessed, the object checks to see if a DACL is present. If a DACL is not present, access is granted automatically. If a DACL is present, the ACEs are examined to see if any are applicable for the security principal accessing the object. If an Access Denied ACE is found first, access is denied to the object requesting access.

System Access Control List

You use a system access control list (SACL) to log any attempts to access an object that has been configured. When you configure auditing, events that are enabled will be written to the security log as successes or failures. When configuring the SACL, you specify the accounts upon which you want to perform auditing and the rights and permissions that you wish to audit. For example, if you wanted to audit who changes permissions on a printer, you would add the Everyone group and specify that you want to audit the Success and Failure options on the Change permission.

An SACL generates entries in the log on only the domain controller where the actual access attempt occurred, not on every replicating domain controller. This is a situation in which using Microsoft Audit Collection System (MACS) in Microsoft Operations Manager would be beneficial, as it collects these entries into a single location for ease of viewing.

Security Identifier

A security identifier (SID) is a unique identifier assigned to every security principal or security group upon its creation. Every SID is composed of two parts: a relative identifier (RID) and the SID of the domain. Thus, each SID in any domain in your enterprise network is unique and never repeated. The SID of a domain account is stored as part of the domain user or group account attributes, and is used as part of the authentication and authorization processes when generating an access token.

As part of the object-creation process, a globally unique identifier (GUID) is generated at the same time the SID is created, and that GUID is one of an object's attributes published in the global catalog. AD uses the GUID to locate and identify objects, not just users and groups.

SID HISTORY

A SID is unique within a domain, but what happens to an object if it is moved to a new domain? If a user account is moved to a new domain, a new SID is generated. The value of a SID will change when it is moved. The losing domain (the domain the object is being moved from) will store the SID in the SIDHistory attribute of the user object, and the gaining domain will create a new SID for the object. When a user logs on to the network and an access token is generated for the user, the current SID and all SIDs in the SID history are placed in the access token. Thus, a user object maintains a listing or history of the SIDS if the domain functional level is set at Windows 2000 native or to higher.

So, what happens to the GUID if the SID changes for an object? Nothing; the object's GUID remains the same throughout the object's lifetime, as long as that object is moved *within* the forest. The GUID will change if the object is moved to another forest.

A script is available to clear the SID history on an object. See "How to Use Visual Basic Script to Clear SidHistory" at `http://support.microsoft.com/default.aspx?scid=kb;en-us;295758` for more information.

SID FILTERING

Because Microsoft gives us the ability to move user objects across domains and even forests, there is the potential to misuse this capability and gain unauthorized access to resources. To help control this, you can use SID filtering. SID filtering is mainly used with external domain trusts and trusts between forests. It prevents SIDs from outside the forest from gaining access to any resource within the forest. You can allow users outside the forest to access resources within the forest by including the users' SIDs in the permission list on the resource. You can use the `Ldp.exe` utility in the Windows Server Support Tools to perform actions on SIDs.

You can use the `Ldp.exe` utility available in the Support Tools to view information about Active Directory objects, including SID data. More information on LDP is available at `http://support.microsoft.com/kb/224543`.

Access Token

An access token is generated when a user logs on to the domain and is authenticated by a domain controller. The access token has a listing of all SIDs contained in the user's SID History field (see the previous sections "SID History" and "SID Filtering") and SIDs for all the groups to which the user belongs.

When a user attempts to access a securable object, the user's SID is verified against the DACL to ensure the user is authorized to have access. This is where the ACL and ACEs we talked about earlier are used.

If a user is made a member of a new group, the user does not inherit any of the permissions from that group until the user logs off and then back on again; during the login process, the user's access token is updated with new group-membership access.

Permissions

Objects in Active Directory and on NTFS partitions have permissions assigned to them, either through inheritance from a parent container or directly applied by the owner of the object or by another user who has been granted or delegated permissions. Access to the object is controlled through the object's DACL, which shows what users or groups have access to the object and what they are allowed to do with the object.

You assign permissions to control access to resources in your network. In some situations you will grant limited access, in others you might grant full control, and in a few situations you might explicitly deny access to resources. If you want to change permissions on an object, you must be the owner of the object or the object's owner must have granted you the right to change permissions.

Implicit and Explicit Permissions

Assigning permissions is one of the first steps in granting or denying someone access to resources. You can grant someone permissions, deny them access, or not grant them permissions at all. If you grant someone access, they get the access level granted, plus any that they might inherit (more on that later). If you do not grant someone access, you have *implicitly denied* them access. If you select the Deny box for a permission, then you have *explicitly denied* access, as shown in Figure 7.7. The Deny permission has the potential to cause problems with shares, so it is generally best to just not grant access (implicit denial), rather than to deny access explicitly.

FIGURE 7.7
Explicitly denying permissions for an object

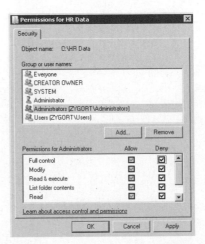

You are the owner of an object because you created the object, were given ownership, or clicked the Take Ownership button. As the object's owner, you can grant permissions to others to access your object. Generally, explicit permissions will take precedence over inherited permissions—for example, if an object inherits a Deny permission from a parent object, it will not prevent access to an object if there is an explicit Allow permission assigned to that object.

Permissions Inheritance

When you assign permissions to a container, those permissions by default will affect that container and any objects in that container. Known as *permissions inheritance,* this is a very useful tool for ensuring that permissions are applied systematically to all objects; it also helps to reduce administrator error when assigning permissions, and is more efficient than assigning permissions manually.

Inheritance is enabled by default, but can be changed according to your administrative or security requirements. In some situations, you want to ensure that corporate-approved permissions are applied but you also need to change the permissions that are applied at lower levels. To see if a specific permission is inherited, check the Security Properties sheet for the object; if the Allow or Deny box is grayed out, that specific permission is inherited from the parent container, as you can see in Figure 7.8. A parent container holds the object in question; this can be another folder or even the domain itself.

To change the permissions inheritance of an object, you must go to the properties sheet of the object, click the Security tab, and then click the Advanced button. To change permissions inheritance, you must deselect the option Include Inheritable Permissions from This Object's Parent, as shown in Figure 7.9. To do this, you must click the Edit button. At the Edit screen, uncheck the box labeled Include Inheritable Permissions from This Object's Parent. When you deselect that box, another dialog box (Figure 7.10) asks you how you want to handle the current inherited permissions, which were displayed in the window:

◆ Specify that permissions be copied to all child objects.

◆ Specify that inherited permissions be removed from all child objects and later explicitly define what permissions will be applied.

◆ Click the Cancel button.

FIGURE 7.8
Changing permissions inheritance

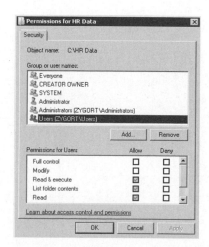

FIGURE 7.9
Changing inherited
permissions

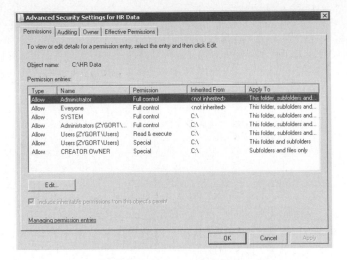

FIGURE 7.10
Permissions inherit-
ance from a parent
container

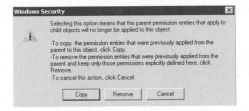

Special Permissions

You can apply special access permissions to files or folders to provide more-granular control over or access to objects to meet security or corporate concerns. These special permissions are a further refinement of the basic permissions found in the Security Properties page.

You assign special permissions through the Advanced tab on the Security Properties sheet. Click the user or group to which you need to assign special permissions, and click Edit. This will open the Permission entry box for the object (Figure 7.11), where you can specify to which objects the permissions will be applied: This Folder, Subfolders and Files, or one of six other options, from the This Folder Only option to the Files Only option. When you've finished and clicked the OK button, the Permissions entry for the user or group will change to Special under the Permission tab.

Effective Permissions

As you can see, permissions can be assigned to a user directly (although you usually want to avoid this option) or to a group, or they can be inherited from parent containers. Trying to ascertain what permissions a user or group has applied or inherited can be daunting. Recall John Doe, our user from our earlier example. He has permissions assigned to him directly; he is also a member of a group that has permissions applied to it and inherits permissions from another container. What are John Doe's overall permissions? This can be determined using the Effective Permissions feature.

Effective Permissions is a new feature that allows an administrator to quickly determine what the overall permissions are for a user or group on an object. To access Effective Permissions, select the Advanced tab in the Security Settings dialog box for the object. Click the Effective Permissions tab and select the user or group you want to check. The effective permissions for the selected entity will be displayed, as shown in Figure 7.12.

FIGURE 7.11

Special permissions

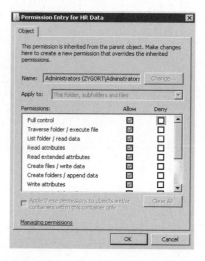

FIGURE 7.12

Viewing effective permissions for a user

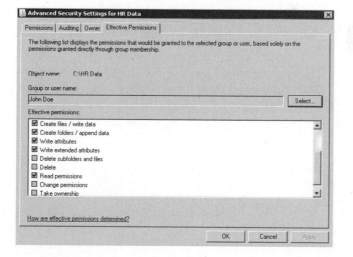

Taking Ownership

In some instances an object (such as a printer or a shared folder) was created by an employee who is no longer with the company, and immediate access is required. How do you go about rectifying this situation? A nice feature is available that allows an administrator or someone who has been granted permission through a Group Policy Object (GPO) to take ownership of the object. However, this feature is available only in Windows 2003 and 2008 (not in Windows 2000).

Every object that is created has an owner—somebody created that object, either on an NTFS partition or in Active Directory. The object's owner has the ability to set permissions on the object to include the Take Ownership right. If an object's owner assigns this permission to another user, that user can either take ownership of the object for himself or herself, or assign ownership rights to other groups of which the user is a member, as shown in Figure 7.13.

By default, administrators are granted the Take Ownership of Files or Other Objects right.

FIGURE 7.13
Granting of Take
ownership rights

Delegation of Control

One feature in AD DS that enhances our ability to administer networks is *delegation of control*. This means Windows 2003 and 2008 administrators can now delegate administrative tasks to specific non-administrator users or groups, as well as limit the functionality of other administrators. We can delegate control to practically all levels in our network: sites, domains, or OUs. Because we have this granularity of delegation capability, we can assign or delegate what are normally considered administrative tasks without giving up complete administrative authority for our network. No longer is it necessary to give someone administrative privileges or make that person a member of an administrators group just to enable them to change user properties or reset passwords. We will now discuss creating a delegation strategy and the mechanics of delegating administrative control.

The DSREVOKE tool enables you to view or revoke the permissions on a user or group in Active Directory. You can download the tool and find more information at the following URL:

```
www.microsoft.com/downloads/details.aspx?FamilyID=77744807-c403-4bda-b0e4-
c2093b8d6383&DisplayLang=en
```

Designing Delegation of Control

As with any other aspect of network design, you should plan your delegation-of-control policies carefully before implementing them on the network. This is especially true when talking about granting administrative or partial administrative access to and control over parts of your network to other people. You are, in effect, giving the keys to the network to those to whom you delegate permissions. As part of your delegation strategy, you should incorporate auditing—which we will talk more about later—to ensure you have a record of what others are doing on your network.

There are several factors to consider when designing your strategy for delegation of control. First you need to determine what task or tasks are going to be delegated. Then you need to decide to whom you are going to delegate them. Is there a group already created, or do you need to create one? What users will be members of the group? Having decided on what is delegated and to whom, you need to determine how the permissions will be assigned and whether these permissions will be generic or property-specific. Included in this is whether the delegated group will be allowed to create and delete any child objects. One of the final things to decide is at what level you are going to assign control. Is this something you are going to allow for the entire domain, or just for a site or an OU? Are you going to create an OU just for control purposes?

As we discussed earlier with groups, you want to avoid, as much as possible, assigning permissions directly to a user. This also applies to delegated permissions. By assigning permissions to a group instead of directly to a user, you limit potential administrative problems and security holes. You can always add a user to a group and have the user log off and log on to receive the effective permissions of the group. There is the potential to forget that you assigned permissions directly to a user and, if the user is reassigned elsewhere, the permissions will follow the user.

You have identified the group to which you are going to delegate; now you have to decide on the level of delegation. This is critical. Permission assignments can assist the administration of your network or become a security nightmare. Careful planning, coordination, and design sessions need to take place to ensure that the delegation will occur according to design, that corporate objectives are met, and that security is maintained.

The level of delegation for an object can run the gamut from full control of an OU to the granting of only one specific, limiting task. The following scenarios are typically employed in an organization for delegation:

◆ You can delegate permission to modify only one specific property in an OU. This would be applicable in a help-desk scenario or for a new administrator in a controlled OU environment.

◆ You might delegate partial control of an OU to a group that might administer parts of an OU. It could be an OU that is remote to the rest of your organization, and the administrators require greater control than the help desk can provide (such as creating or deleting child objects, or adding or removing users to or from groups).

◆ In some cases you might assign full control of an OU to a group. This might be because of legal, political, or corporate concerns.

Another aspect of designing a delegation-of-control strategy is to decide if you need to create OUs for optimizing management and administration of your network—that is, creating OUs only for administration or management. This requirement could be the result of management wishes for delegation, or to give control over OUs to specific administrators based on corporate policies or governmental regulations, or because of the acquisition of other companies.

Implementing Delegation of Control

Once you have decided on the level of control and who is going to receive the delegation, the next task is to actually delegate control. You do this through the Delegation of Control Wizard.

USING THE DELEGATION OF CONTROL WIZARD

To delegate control of an OU, go through Active Directory Users and Computers and right-click the OU you want to delegate; then click Delegate Control. There are four steps in the delegation process:

1. Choosing which users or groups are going to receive delegated permissions

2. Designating the actual tasks to delegate, and whether you're:

- Using a common task
- Creating a custom task

3. Specifying the Active Directory object type

4. Specifying permissions:

- General
- Property-specific
- Creation or deletion of specific child objects

In the first step, you choose the users or groups that are going to have permissions delegated to them. This should follow some sort of coherent design strategy to ensure that another group could not be used and that the group would constitute a security risk.

You must next decide whether to select Delegate the Following Common Tasks or Create a Custom Task to Delegate, as shown in Figure 7.14. If you choose a common task, you are finished. If you choose to create a custom task to delegate, you must complete a few extra steps. On the next screen you will choose between two options: This Folder, Existing Objects in This Folder, and Creation of New Objects in This Folder, or Only the Following Objects in the Folder; Figure 7.15 shows these two options. Also on this screen, you will specify whether these are applicable for creating or deleting selected objects in this folder.

In the last step, you must choose what permissions you wish to delegate and at what level, as Figure 7.16 shows.

FIGURE 7.14
Delegation of tasks

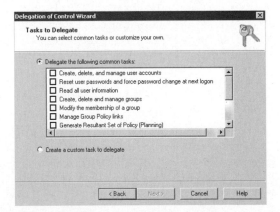

Also in this last step, you can see just how far you can delegate and to what granularity of control you can delegate. After deciding who will receive the delegation, you must decide what will be delegated. Some tasks that are commonly delegated include the following:

- Create user accounts
- Delete user accounts
- Manage user accounts

♦   Reset passwords on user accounts

♦   Read all user information

♦   Create, delete, and manage groups

♦   Modify the membership of a group

♦   Manage Group Policy links

In the next section we will look at some best practices for implementing and employing delegation of permissions in a networked environment.

FIGURE 7.15
Scope of delegation

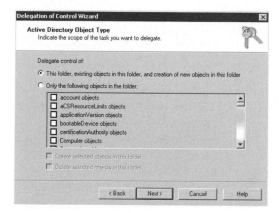

FIGURE 7.16
Delegation of permissions

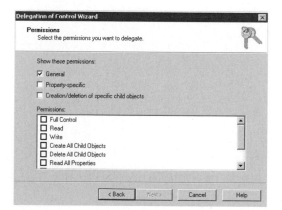

Auditing

So far we have talked about enabling and controlling access to Active Directory objects and resources. Another important aspect of controlling access and improving security is auditing. This section will not cover all aspects of auditing—only those areas relevant to object access and Active Directory access.

As with delegation, you want to spend some time planning your audit strategy. Auditing involves deciding which server and what actions will be recorded. Yes, you can audit every server for every listed action, but that would result in too much information to sort through in an organized manner, especially in a large network. Not all objects or machines require auditing for both success and failure of the listed actions. If you suspect one of your administrators or delegated users of misusing their permissions, you should audit the container the administrator has been delegated permissions to control.

 **Real World Scenario**

BEST PRACTICES FOR DELEGATION

Delegation is a powerful tool for administering your network. If it is used carefully, it will prove quite helpful. So far in this section we have mentioned a few good practices to use when delegating; now let us expand on these and explore more examples:

Create groups and OUs that will have delegation applied to them.　This facilitates security as well as administration.

Avoid assigning permissions directly to a user.　Create a group (see our earlier discussion) and place the user in that group. Creating a group to house one user is not as burdensome as it might seem initially; in fact, it will make your administrative life much easier than trying to track down why this one individual can still perform actions that she or he shouldn't.

Least is most: Assign the *least* amount of permissions to users and groups.　This will help make your network *most* secure. Users might think they are entitled to full control for everything, but they rarely, if ever, require it.

Use full control sparingly!　Full control can backfire on you when users or groups start taking advantage of your largesse. Full control gives the user an opportunity to work with an object's permissions. That means the users could give themselves greater permissions than the administrator intended. In addition, if someone gains control of this account, then that person could cause more mayhem than they would otherwise.

To further enforce security and enhance good administration techniques, delegate object creation and object management to different groups.　This is known as TPI: *two-person integrity.* If you split the responsibility between two individuals or groups, there is less likelihood of mismanagement by either. Think of this as splitting the create-backup and restore permissions between two groups.

Create Taskpad views.　Taskpad views are great when you want to delegate tasks to help-desk personnel or other groups that require some permissions but you don't want them to have access to the full console. This technique can help train new administrators before you give them the keys to the domain.

You can delegate at levels higher than an OU, but avoid doing this as a rule.　If you delegate permissions to a user or group at the domain level, that user or group could have a potentially far greater impact on your network than you anticipated.

Once you have set up and are using an audit policy, you need to review the events that are recorded. Audit events are recorded in the security log found in the Event Viewer. Of all the logs in the Event Viewer, the security log has the tightest controls limiting access. By default, only administrators have access to this log, and you might consider limiting even that access to only a few individuals. The security log lists all successful and failed events that you have configured auditing to monitor. Some of the people you are monitoring might have access to the security log and could remove evidence of their actions. Thus, you want to limit access to this log.

A consideration to keep in mind is that event logs are server-specific: actions that occur on server A440 are listed only on server A440 and are not replicated throughout the network. This means you will have to check the logs and filter events on each server. Another option is to use Microsoft Operations Manager 2007, which includes Microsoft Audit Collection System (MACS). MACS collects the security event logs from your servers and stores them in a centralized SQL database.

Although there are 10 audit-event categories, we are mainly concerned with the six that pertain to accessing objects in Active Directory: Audit Account Logon events, Audit Account Management events, Audit Directory Service Access events, Audit Logon events, Audit Privilege Use events, and Audit Object Access events. Of these, only Auditing Object Access is done at the object level; the rest are handled through Group Policy.

Auditing of Security Events

Having decided what events you want to audit, configure your group policies in support of that auditing. Configuring an audit policy is done through the Group Policy Management Editor Microsoft Management Console (MMC) snap-in on the specific object level (site, domain, or OU). For our example in Figure 7.17, we will use the Personnel OU in our bloomco domain. The audit-policy configuration settings are located in the Computer Configuration ➤ Windows Settings ➤ Security Settings ➤ Local Policies tab in the Group Policy Management Editor.

FIGURE 7.17
Configuring an audit policy

AUDITING ACCOUNT LOGON EVENTS

This policy tracks when users log on to the domain and when the logon is validated by a specific domain controller. The log is updated at the domain controller that authenticated the user. This is very useful for verifying and recording when a user actually logs on to the network, or fails to do so.

AUDITING ACCOUNT MANAGEMENT EVENTS

Account management is concerned with tracking actions that affect user accounts, groups, and computer accounts. Any time a user account is created, deleted, disabled, enabled, or modified, the log is updated. Any time groups are created or deleted, or the membership changes, an entry is made in the log. If passwords are reset or changes are made to security policies, these actions will be recorded in the event log.

AUDITING DIRECTORY SERVICE ACCESS

Directory service access occurs any time an object is accessed or changed in Active Directory. Use this policy to track when objects are accessed or if someone tries to access an object.

AUDIT PRIVILEGE USE

This is logged every time a user tries to exercise almost any right. Enable this for failure to detect possible network permissions problems or when someone is trying to gain access to resources that are not granted to them. This is typically seen when someone tries to take ownership of a resource. If set for success auditing, your log will grow very quickly.

AUDIT OBJECT ACCESS

Object access is the only auditing event we are going to discuss that is not handled through the object editor in Group Policy This auditing is handled on a per-object basis and is configured in the Advanced Security Settings properties sheet of the object you wish to audit.

To enable auditing on a folder or any other object, open the properties sheet for that object, click the Security tab, and click the Advanced button in the Security Properties window. In the Advanced Security Settings window for the object, click the Auditing tab, as shown in Figure 7.18. In the Auditing window you will specify which users and/or groups you want to audit by clicking the Add button and choosing whether you want to audit Successful, Failed, or both in the Auditing Entries window, as shown in Figure 7.19. Other options you have available in this window are to specify at what level you are going to apply auditing (that is, whether it will apply to This Folder, Subfolders and Files, or one of six other settings depending on your auditing needs).

We've only discussed applying auditing to a folder, although you can apply it to other Active Directory objects in the same way. Auditing can be enabled for objects in Active Directory by going through Active Directory Users and Computers. Before you can view the Security tab for objects in the Active Directory Users and Computers MMC snap-in, you need to enable them for viewing. By default, you cannot view the Security tab on Active Directory objects; you enable this by clicking the View button and then selecting the Users, Contacts, Groups and Computers as Containers or Advanced Features listing in the View drop-down box. This also applies to any printers you might have listed in Active Directory. They will not be visible unless you also select the Users, Contacts, Groups and Computers as containers tab. Now that you are able to view the Security tab, you can make changes to the permissions, as shown in Figure 7.19.

FIGURE 7.18
Enabling auditing of
an object

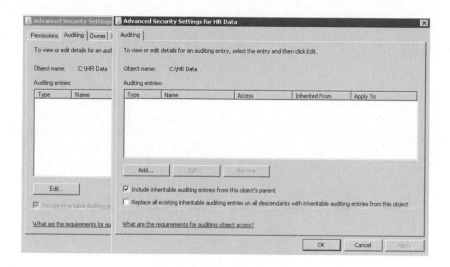

FIGURE 7.19
Configuring auditing
of an object

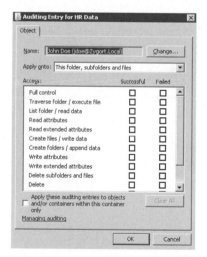

Auditing Printers and Printing

As with other objects, Audit Printer access should be audited to see who has been printing or is trying to print to the new high-resolution color printer or high-speed duplex printer. Our first step is to determine who has access; we can do this through Effective Permissions. We talked before about Effective Permissions, but not with respect to printers. We will use the same interface for printers as we did for objects. To access Effective Permissions, right-click the printer in the Printers and Faxes tab, select Properties, and select the Security tab. Then click the Advanced tab and select the Effective Permissions tab. At this point you can choose the users or groups you want to check for permissions, as shown in Figure 7.20. This will tell you who has the potential access but not who is accessing the printer. To determine who is accessing the printer and when, you will use auditing.

You enable auditing on a printer in the same way as you do for other objects. You can access the Auditing window through the Advanced tab under Security Settings. Select the users or groups you want to audit; then specify what events to audit for and whether to audit for Successful, Failed, or both, as shown in Figure 7.21.

FIGURE 7.20
Viewing effective permissions on a printer

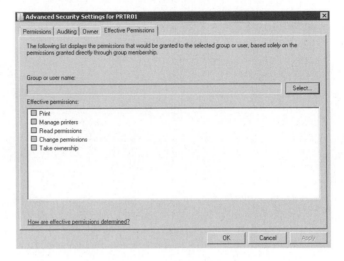

FIGURE 7.21
Viewing audit permissions of a printer

Moving Objects in Active Directory

Certain assumptions were made about the growth and structure of the network in the initial design of an Active Directory network. A network is rarely static; it will grow and contract. You may add child domains or create new trees or even add forests. Within the domains, you may add or remove OUs to facilitate administration, and you will definitely move users, computers, printers, and other objects. This is especially true if you are taking over a network from someone else and need to reorganize. If you need to move objects between domains or between forests, you will have to use tools other than Active Directory Users and Computers. If you need move object between domains, you can use the movetree command-line utility or the Active Directory Migration Tool. If, however, you need to move objects between forests, you can again use the Active Directory Migration Tool (ADMT) or, if you are moving just security principals, the clonepr tool. We will discuss all of these tools later in this section.

Moving Objects within the Domain

Several methods are available for moving objects in Active Directory. You can use a script to move large numbers of objects. The dsadd command mentioned earlier is always available, but you must be careful when using dsadd because of typos and syntax errors. When you are moving objects, you're most likely to use the Active Directory Users and Computers console. When using it, you can either drag and drop an object to a new container or use the move command. Either approach will accomplish the same thing.

The drag-and-drop feature is quite handy for moving computer objects. Just click and hold the computer object you want to move, and drag it to its new container. When using this method, a dialog box will appear telling you that ""Moving objects in Active Directory can prevent your existing system from working the way it was designed," and ask, "Are you sure you want to move this object?" as shown in Figure 7.22.

FIGURE 7.22

Moving an object within a domain

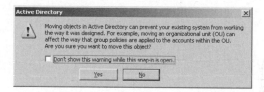

If you plan to use the move command, right-click the object, click the Move tab, and specify the new container in which you want to place the object, then click the OK button. You will not receive the warning you did when using the drag-and-drop method.

Moving of objects is not confined to computers. You can move printers, users, and shared folders using the same methods as we used with computers. If you are moving a printer to a new container you will need to connect it so it can be used. You connect a printer by right-clicking the printer and selecting Connect.

Moving Objects between Domains

You cannot move objects directly between domains as readily as you can within a domain. If you need to move objects between domains, use the movetree command-line utility included in the Support Tools on the Windows Server CD.

MOVETREE

The movetree command-line utility allows you to move Active Directory objects, organizational units, computers, user accounts, and other objects to other domains *within the same forest*. That is the caveat for using movetree—all movement must be within the same forest. Some requirements must be met before you can successfully use movetree; the destination domain must have a domain functional level of Windows 2000 native or higher; you must have proper permissions on both source and destination computers; and there must be proper DNS name resolution with source and destination domains.

What Contents Are Moved?

What is moved and what is not? Computer accounts are moved, but not valid; if you need to have valid computer accounts, use the `netdom` command-line utility, which we will discuss next. Users and OUs are moved completely. Users' passwords will be moved with the user accounts. Groups, however, are a special case. Universal groups and their members can be moved to a new domain without any problem. Domain local and global groups can be moved to the new domain only if the groups are empty. You will have to re-create all the group memberships in the new domain.

If you are planning to move any OUs, be aware that all associated Group Policy Object links will remain intact from the original (source) domain. These links will remain in effect and continue to be applied and updated to the OU across your WAN links. This cross-domain linkage of Group Policy Objects could have a detrimental impact on your network performance, especially for slower WAN links. In this scenario, it is more effective to create new Group Policy Objects in the destination domain.

Syntax

The syntax of `movetree` is:

```
Movetree /[/start | /continue | /check | /startnocheck] /s /d /sdn /ddn
```

The options are as follows:

- `/start` initiates the move and includes the `/check` by default. The command will continue until it is finished or there is an interrupt.

- `/startnocheck` initiates the move but excludes the `/check`. The command will continue until it is finished or there is an interrupt.

- `/continue` will resume the move if there is an interrupt.

- `/check` will conduct a practice run without moving any objects—great for testing a move first.

- `/s` is the fully qualified primary DNS name of the server in the source domain.

- `/d` is the fully qualified primary DNS name of the server in the destination domain.

- `/sdn` is the distinguished name of the source subtree.

- `/ddn` is the distinguished name of the destination subtree.

Remember that the distinguished name is the complete LDAP name for the object or tree you wish to move. If you want to move the Managers OU in the Operations child domain of AcmeEnterprises.com, the complete distinguished name (DN) would be ou=managers, dc=operations, dc=acmeenterprises, dc=com.

Let us move our Managers OU from before to a new domain, planning. What would it look like?

```
Movetree /start /s opserver1 /d planserver1 /sdn
ou=managers,dc=operations,dc=acme enterprise,dc=com ➡
/ddn ou=managers,dc=planning,dc=acme enterprise,dc=com
```

For more information on `movetree`, see http://support.microsoft.com/default.aspx?scid= kb;en-us;238394.

NETDOM

As we mentioned earlier, if you want to move a computer account to a different domain, you will have to use the `netdom` command-line utility. This powerful tool has many purposes beyond just moving a computer account. You can use it to create one-way and two-way trusts between domains; query the domain for trust information; add, join, and remove computers to/from the domain; reset secure connections between a workstation and a computer; and many other tasks. The `netdom` utility is in the `Support\Tools` folder on the Windows Server CD and can be installed with the `suptools.msi` command.

If you wanted to join the `ws053` computer to the `AcmeEnterprises` domain in the planning OU, the syntax would look something like this:

```
Netdom join /d:acmeenterprises.com ws053 /ou:ou=planning, dc=acmeenterprises, dc=com
```

For more information on `netdom`, see `http://technet2.microsoft.com/windowsserver/en/library/460e3705-9e5d-4f9b-a139-44341090cfd41033.mspx?mfr=true`.

Moving Objects between Forests

As your network grows, sometimes you may need to reorganize and create new domains in a new forest or maybe migrate older domains to a new Windows Server 2008 forest. In either case, you can use the Active Directory Migration Tool to copy users, groups, and computers between two forests. To copy only security principals, you would use the `clonepr` tool.

ACTIVE DIRECTORY MIGRATION TOOL

The Active Directory Migration Tool (ADMT) is used to move users, groups, and computers between forests and within forests. If you use ADMT to migrate objects within the forest, it will move the objects to the new domain; this is a destructive process.

There are more options available for configuring the domains when using ADMT than when using the other methods we have talked about. To install ADMT, double-click the `admigration.msi` file in the `i386\admt` folder on your Windows Server CD. ADMT is installed in your Administrative Tools by default. Once it's installed, you can begin the process of configuring permissions, migration groups, and computers for migration.

How you set up ADMT depends on whether you will use it for migrating objects within a forest or between forests. If you are going to migrate objects within a forest, you should create account-migration groups and resource-migration groups (if applicable) in both the source and destination domains. Within each of these groups, create the migration accounts necessary.

If you are planning on using ADMT to migrate objects to a different domain, you will need Administrator rights in the source domain and on every computer you want to migrate. You will also have to configure the source domain to trust the target domain. You must ensure that the computer on which you have installed ADMT is a member of either the target or the source domain.

The actual process of moving is simplified using the wizards in ADMT. Open the ADMT console in your Administrative Tools and click the Actions tab at the top of the console. Then click the appropriate Migration wizard, as shown in Figure 7.23. Once you have opened the wizard, choose whether you want to migrate now or test the migration. On the next screen you will specify the source and destination domains involved in the migration. Next you will specify the user and the group computer you are going to migrate, and then the target OU that will receive the migrated object. The last two screens contain the user and naming-conflicts options you can configure.

FIGURE 7.23

Accessing a migration wizard

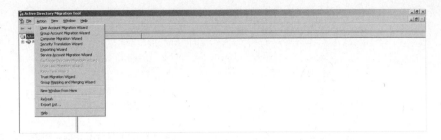

The latest version and more information on ADMT can be found here: `http://www.microsoft.com/downloads/details.aspx?familyid=D99EF770-3BBB-4B9E-A8BC-01E9F7EF7342&displaylang=en`.

To download ADMT version 2, go to `www.microsoft.com/downloads/details.aspx?FamilyID=788975b1-5849-4707-9817-8c9773c25c6c&DisplayLang=en`.

CLONEPRINCIPAL OR CLONEPR

The `clonepr` and `movetree` tools are similar in function: they both can be used to migrate users from one domain to another. However, `movetree` can be used only inside a forest for moves, whereas `clonepr` can migrate users to different forests. Another major difference is that `clonepr` copies the users to the new domain without their passwords, maintaining the integrity of the source domain. On the other hand, `movetree` moves the users to the new domain, maintaining their passwords and thus removing those objects from the source domain.

Coming Up Next

In this chapter, as well as in Chapter 3, we have discussed how you should build your OU design to accommodate administrative control and group policies. In the next chapter ("Managing Group Policy"), we will delve into the world of group policies. Within this world you will find the tools that allow you to control your users' environments and maintain the security levels of your systems. We will also cover the utilities that are used to maintain the myriad Group Policy settings as well as keep track of all of the group policies that you may implement.

The Bottom Line

In this chapter we discussed effective ways to access, control, and monitor objects in your organizational units. There are many different tools that you can use to define, control, and monitor activity.

Manage access to objects within your organizational units There are two ways to control access to Active Directory objects in an OU: rights and permissions.

Rights define a task that a person or group is allowed to perform; permissions define the access a user or group has to a particular object.

Master It You have created a new folder named `BlueprintArchive` under a share named `Blueprints`. Administrators and members of the BPEngineering group are the only users that should have access to the BluePrints share. John Kaminski requires access to the BlueprintArchive folder but making him a member of the BPEngineering group will give him too much access.

You explicitly grant John Kaminski the Read permission at the BlueprintArchive folder. You notice that John Kaminski is able to remove files from the folder, as well as create new folders. Using the tools you learned about in this chapter, you need to determine how John Kaminski is able to perform these tasks and lock the folder down so John Kaminski only has read access to this particular folder.

Manage administrative control of the objects within your organizational units Administrators can define the other administrators (such as branch administrators or junior administrators) who have access to manage the OUs or objects within the OUs. This can be accomplished by delegating control over certain OUs to these administrative users.

> **Master It** Your company has just hired a new administrator who is assigned to the Berwick, Illinois branch. Previously, all resources from this office were part of the Galesburg OU. The new administrator will take over the management of users and computers for the Berwick branch.

Monitor the activity of the objects within your organizational units As you are creating your OU structure, creating AD DS objects, assigning rights and permissions, and delegating control over these OUs to other administrators, it is a good idea to keep tabs on what is going on by creating or modifying audit settings on the objects that reside in those OUs.

> **Master It** Expanding on our preceding example, now that you have delegated control to the Berwick OU to the Berwick admin, you want to audit activity to the OU.

Chapter 8

Managing Group Policy

As an administrator, one of my pet peeves is walking to a user's workstation to make a settings change. I am busy enough with my daily activities that I don't really want to take the time to visit the user's cubicle to administer a system. And when there are several systems that all need the same modification, it becomes even more bothersome. Although there aren't as many servers to manage, I feel the same way about them. Incorporating a change across multiple servers takes time. What I really like is having a means of managing all of the systems from one central location. That is where Group Policy comes in.

Group Policy allows you to manage settings on several systems by configuring the settings and choosing which systems will be affected. You can have a single group policy that controls all of the systems within your organization; you can have multiple group policies controlling all of your systems; or you can have multiple group policies that are targeted at managing different groups of systems. You can design a group policy infrastructure that is as granular as you need it to be so that you can manage your systems. And if you are a control freak, you will be glad to know that the policies that you implement are continually re-evaluated and reinforced.

In this chapter you will learn how to:

- ◆ Identify the different group policy types

- ◆ Use the Group Policy Management Editor (GPME)

- ◆ Use the Group Policy Management Console (GPMC)

Group Policy Primer

Before we go any further in this chapter, there is one thing I want to set straight: this chapter is not going to be a comprehensive run-down of Group Policy. That would consume more space than I have been allotted for this book. Bookstores and Internet booksellers offer books written on Group Policy. Look at what is considered to be the holy grail of group policy books, Jeremy Moskowitz's *Group Policy: Management, Troubleshooting, and Security: For Windows Vista, Windows 2003, Windows XP, and Windows 2000.* You will find it is nearly 800 pages on its own. So this chapter is intended only to familiarize you with Group Policy and detail some of the new features made available with Windows Server 2008.

What Makes Up a Group Policy Object?

Two parts make up a Group Policy Object (GPO): the Group Policy container and Group Policy template. Even though the two parts of the GPO are stored in different locations, both must be available for group policy processing to work. The Group Policy container is a construct of Active Directory. The container is used to control permissions for the GPO and to store attributes that allow us to identify the GPO. The permissions that we can set control who can manage the GPO, as well as the systems and users that will have the GPO applied to them. Whenever we look at the properties of a GPO, we are actually looking at the Group Policy container object within Active Directory. Figure 8.1 shows some of the information stored within the container object.

GROUP POLICY CONTAINER ATTRIBUTES

You can view the attributes for a GPO in a couple of different ways. The easiest is to open the Group Policy Management Console (GPMC) and select a group policy. Figure 8.1 displays what you will see when you expand the forest, domain, and Group Policy Objects levels, select a group policy, and then click the Details tab. It is here that you will find not only the domain and owner, but also some other information that might come in handy. Two date and time fields let you know when the policy was created and the last time that it was modified. You can also see how many changes the user and computer settings have gone through. The nicest thing about the version numbers is that you can see if the container and template are at the same revision level. The first number for either the user version or computer version is the container, denoted by the (AD) suffix, and the second number is the template, denoted by the (sysvol) suffix.

FIGURE 8.1
Attributes for a GPO

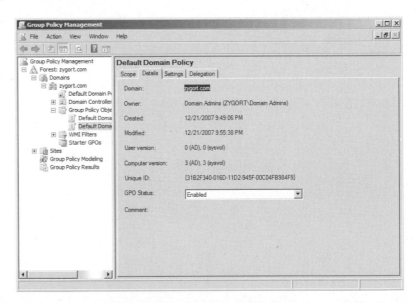

The Unique ID field displays the globally unique identifier (GUID) of the policy. While this may seem like just a nice bit of information to have when you are documenting the group policy, it is actually a very useful piece of information. As you can tell, working with the Group Policy container is not very hard; you can simply open the GPMC and view the information. Finding the actual template within the file system is, however, a little more difficult. The template is identified only by the group policy's GUID. Figure 8.2 shows the policy that we have been looking at in the GPMC, highlighted in the `%systemroot%\SYSVOL\sysvol\domain_name\Policies` directory.

The GPO Status drop-down, seen expanded in Figure 8.3, allows you to control how the group policy will function. The first of the four settings, All Settings Disabled, allows you to completely stop the group policy from taking effect. Once selected, it will no longer be applied against any of the systems where it is linked. This is a very handy setting to have if you want to temporarily stop a group policy from being applied within the domain but you do not want to remove any of the links that you have already configured. You may want to enable the group policy later on, and you don't want to have to remember where the group policies were linked.

That brings us to the third option in the list, Enabled. This is probably the most common setting you will find. As it sounds, when this setting is selected, the group policy is enabled and will be applied where applicable. Being the polar opposite of All Settings Disabled, Enabled is used to have the group policy turned on and working.

The other two settings leave part of the group policy settings enabled while turning others parts off. Computer Configuration Settings Disabled will keep the user setting enabled while not allowing the computer settings to be applied. User Configuration Settings Disabled does just the opposite. You may be asking, "Why would you want to turn off part of a group policy?" The simple explanation is, to make the group policy more efficient. Whenever a group policy is applied, every setting within the group policy is evaluated to determine what affect it has against the user or system. In an environment where several group policies are applied, there could be so many group policies being evaluated that the system startup or user logon could take a long time.

When you are creating group policy and you are not configuring any user-configuration settings, you can use the User Configuration Settings Disabled option to alleviate a little of the processing burden. When the computer starts up, it will not evaluate any of the user settings. The same goes for the computer side. If there are not any computer settings within the group policy, use the Computer Configuration Settings Disabled option, and the computer settings will not be evaluated.

FIGURE 8.2
Group Policy template shown in the sysvol folder

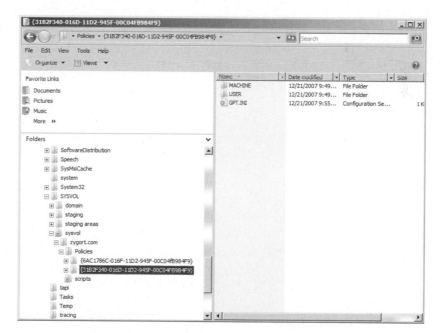

FIGURE 8.3
GPO Status settings

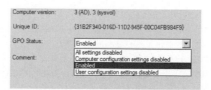

You probably noticed that the Comment area is blank in Figure 8.1. Not only that, but it doesn't appear as though there is any way to enter any information into the Comments section; there is, however, and it can come in handy to have some information in this field. Many administrators use this field to enter change information. You can put in information that lets another administrator know what the group policy is used for and some of the changes that have been made it.

To enter information, right-click the group policy and select Edit. This will open the GPME. From here, you can right-click the name of the group policy and select Properties. You can then use the Comment tab, seen in Figure 8.4, to enter any text that you wish to have displayed within the Comments section of the group policy details. Figure 8.5 shows the Comment section after a change has been made.

FIGURE 8.4
Comment tab
of Group Policy
properties

FIGURE 8.5
Comment on the
Details tab

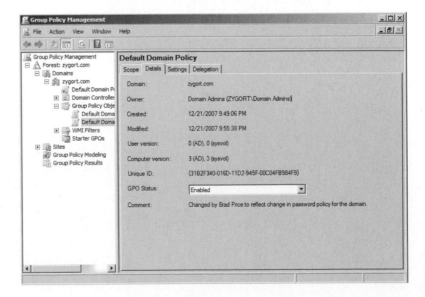

More of the container information can be seen on the Scope tab. This is where you can see where the group policy is linked and the accounts that will be affected by the group policy settings. However, before we go too far into the information that you find on this tab, we need to discuss some of the terminology and configuration options to help you understand how group policies are applied.

Link

When you create a group policy, you can configure it so that its settings do not affect any systems or users. When you *do* want your settings to affect them, you need to link the GPO to the domain, site, or organizational unit (OU) where the systems or users are located. When the link is enabled, the GPO is evaluated and the settings are enforced. In Figure 8.6, the link for Default Domain Policy is highlighted within the GPMC.

FIGURE 8.6

Default Domain Policy link

It is easy to confuse the link with the actual GPO that is found in the Group Policy Objects container—they are named the same, and you will see many of the same functions when you select or right-click either them. However, there are differences between the two objects. Right-clicking the link will not display any options for backing up and restoring the group policy. Right-clicking the GPO will not display the options for enabling and enforcing the link. Note the difference between the icons for the link and the actual GPO: the link has the small arrow on it.

Looking at the context menu, you will find four options to work with a link: Edit, Enforced, Link Enabled, and Save Report. If you select Edit, you are taken to the GPME, where you can make changes to the settings within the GPO.

The Enforced option configures the GPO to have superhuman powers. Actually, the Enforced option configures the GPO to have the highest priority over any other GPO when there is a conflicting setting. It also allows the GPO settings to remain in effect when a Block Inheritance setting is configured beneath it in the OU structure. In other words, if you configure a GPO with the Enforced option, the enforced GPO's settings will always take precedence over every other GPO in the hierarchy and the settings cannot be blocked.

Link Enabled allows you to control whether the GPO is configured to affect the systems or users within the location where it is linked. For instance, if you have a GPO linked to an OU, the computers and users that are placed within that OU would be affected, by default, by the settings within the GPO. If you clear the Link Enabled setting, the GPO would no longer apply at the OU. If it were linked at other OUs, the GPO would still be applied in those OUs. This is different from disabling the GPO within the GPO settings. When you disable the GPO, it is disabled wherever it is linked. Using the context menu to turn off the link allows you more granular control over where the group policy is applied.

Finally, the Save Report option allows you to generate an HTML-based report of the settings that are configured.

Order of Precedence

You can link multiple GPOs at once to a domain, site, or OU. So how do you know which group policy will actually affect the computer or user? We need to discuss the order of precedence when evaluating group policies. To start off, you need to understand where a group policy can be linked. Group policies are evaluated in the following order:

1. OU

2. Site

3. Domain

If you have a policy linked at the domain level and another linked at the site level, the site GPO settings will take precedence. The same holds true for group policies linked at an OU; conflicting entries from the OU's GPO will take precedence over those set at the domain and site levels.

When we say *conflicting entries*, we mean a setting that is configured at each level. For instance, look at Figure 8.7; if you configure folder redirection at the domain level so that all users in the domain have their My Documents folders redirected to a central file server in the corporate office, and you have another group policy that is linked to an OU so that users in a branch office will have their My Documents folders redirected to the file server at the branch office, the GPO linked at the OU will take effect for all users that are placed in that OU. They will not use the settings configured in the GPO linked to the domain. So, in Figure 8.7 the Boston Folder Redirection GPO will take precedence over the Domain Folder Redirection GPO.

When you link more than one GPO to the same object, let's say an OU, you need to set the order of precedence yourself. This is an easy configuration task, but planning which policies will take precedence over others may not be as easy. Once you have decided the processing order for your GPOs, open the GPMC, create and link the required GPOs, and then select the object where they are linked. Figure 8.8 shows three GPOs that are linked at the Toronto OU. When you select one of the GPOs from the Linked Group Policy Objects tab in the details pane, you will be able to change the link order, or processing order, by clicking the arrow to move them up or down.

FIGURE 8.7
GPOs linked to objects
in the domain

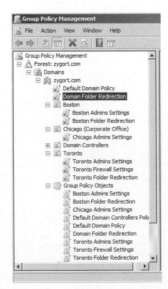

FIGURE 8.8
Setting the link order

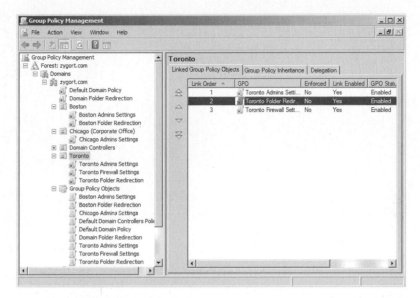

So there you have it—GPOs linked to the domain are processed in link order from highest to lowest, with the lower link orders taking precedence when there is a conflict. Then the GPOs linked to the site are processed, again with the lower link number taking precedence over any conflicts within the site and with GPOs linked to the domain. Finally, GPOs linked at the OUs are evaluated the same way, with the lower-number GPOs taking precedence over any linked GPOs at the site and domain objects when there are conflicts.

Of course, we need to take this one step further. As you know, you can nest OUs to create a nice organized administrative structure. GPOs that are linked at OUs within the hierarchy take precedence over those that are linked at the parent OUs. Setting the order of precedence is easy, but planning out the GPOs that you will need, linking them at the correct object, and making sure they have the correct link order can take a lot of work.

Overriding the Default Order of Precedence

There are a few ways to alter the default GPO-processing order. Do note that if you do override the default processing order, troubleshooting may become a little more difficult. There are more steps you have to take to determine if a policy is being applied, and which policy settings are being applied. You have three options to work with when changing the default behavior: Block Inheritance, Enforced, and Security Filtering.

Block Inheritance Blocking inheritance negates any of the settings that should be applied at an upper level from being applied to the object where the inheritance is blocked. For instance, in Figure 8.9 the Chicago (Corporate Office) OU has been configured to block the inheritance of any GPOs from the domain or site level. The exclamation mark on the OU object denotes the blocked setting. At this point, only the GPO set at the OU level would be applied to the computers and users within the Chicago (Corporate Office) OU, with the exception of the account policies that are configured for the domain. You can see in Figure 8.10 the blocking of the other policies by that would occur if you selected the OU and then selected the Group Policy Inheritance tab.

FIGURE 8.9
Blocked Inheritance
set at an OU

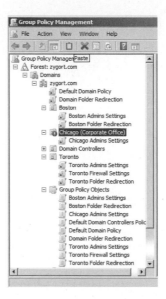

FIGURE 8.10
Viewing inheritance

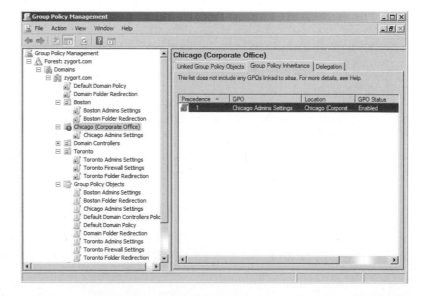

Enforced When you set the Enforced option, the GPO on which you configure the setting becomes king of the hill. Essentially, you are saying that no other GPO that is processed after this GPO will take precedence when a conflict in settings occurs. The enforced GPO will also ignore any blocked inheritance settings. You are creating a GPO that will break through the blockade and become the champion over any other GPO. In Figure 8.11 you can see that the Domain Folder Redirection GPO has been configured with the Enforced option, and the inheritance settings on the Chicago (Corporate Office) OU reflect the setting. The Domain Folder Redirection GPO icon now shows a lock symbol, and the GPO is given a precedence of 1 in the inheritance list.

FIGURE 8.11

Enforcing a GPO

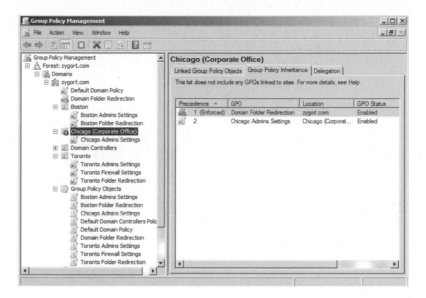

Security Filtering By default, all of the computers and users within the location where the GPO is linked will have the GPO applied to them. But what happens if you have a user that needs to be in an OU, but you do not want the GPO to apply? In this case, you need to configure the filtering option. Security filtering can be applied in a couple of ways. If you select a GPO, you can manipulate the accounts that appear within the Security Filtering pane as seen in Figure 8.12. You'll notice the default setting of Authenticated Users. Any user that is placed within the OU (using the Add button) is a member of the Authenticated Users group, and you cannot change that membership. You can remove the Authenticated Users group from this list and reconfigure the settings as needed, though, using the Remove button.

In Figure 8.13 the security filtering has been reconfigured to include only the group membership to which we want to apply the GPO. We have removed the Authenticated Users group and added the Boston Admins group. Now if someone inadvertently adds a user who is not a member of the Boston Admins group to the OU, the GPO will not be applied to them.

But what if you have a user who is a member of the group that you have listed within the Security Filtering pane, but you don't want the GPO to apply? To get even more granular with your security, you need to open the access control list for the GPO and manage the permissions. To do so, click the Delegation tab when you have a GPO selected, then click the Advanced button at the bottom of the window. You will be presented with an access control list that looks like the one in Figure 8.14. Notice that Rebecca Price has been added into the list and the Read and Apply Group Policy settings have been set to Deny. Now she will not have the GPO applied to her when she logs on.

Be careful when using the access control list to manage the GPO. When you set a Deny permission, you are overriding any Allow. If the user or group of users on which you are setting the permission needs to be able to read the GPO for administrative purposes, you will need to make sure they have the Read permission set to Allow. In our example, we were assuming the Rebecca was not allowed to administer the GPO, so we denied the Read permission. This works out as a twofold benefit; Rebecca can manipulate the GPO and the GPO will not be evaluated when she logs on. If she did need to be able to manipulate the GPO, leaving the Read permission at Allow would let her make changes and manage the GPO if necessary. However, the GPO would still be read and evaluated even though it could not be applied to her account because of the Deny setting on the Apply Group Policy permission. Be aware that when you configure the settings within the access control list, you will not see those entries reflected within the Security Filtering pane, which could make troubleshooting a little more troublesome.

FIGURE 8.12
Security Filtering
defaults

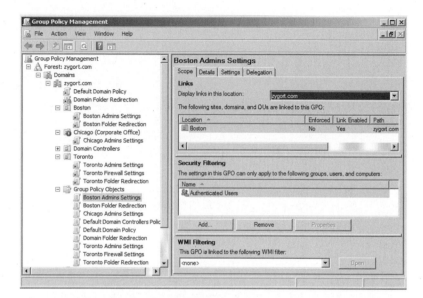

FIGURE 8.13
Filtering to just the
Boston Admins group

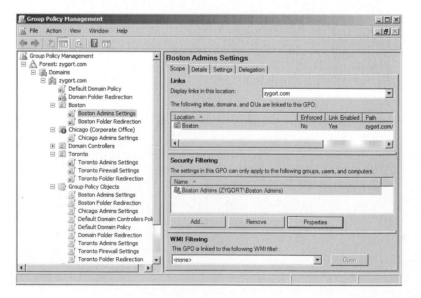

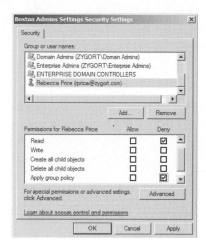

Delegation

While we are talking about the Delegation tab of the GPO, let's take a look at what delegation does. If you select a GPO and then select the Delegation tab, up comes a list of users and groups, the permissions they are assigned, and the inheritance status of the permission. Whenever a user, computer, or group is added to the Security Filtering section, it is automatically added to the Delegation tab. Other accounts can be added and permissions can be applied so that those accounts can manage the GPO.

As shown in Figure 8.15, you can control the settings to allow just the right amount of access to manage the GPO. Anyone who needs to be able to read the GPO, whether for managing or to have the GPO applied to them, will appear with the Read permission. Read permission comes in two varieties: Read (from Security Filtering) and Read. As you may surmise, when the account is added to the Security Filtering section of the Scope tab, the Read (from Security Filtering) permission is applied automatically. The other option, Read, has to be defined explicitly.

The Edit Settings permission allows anyone who has been granted that permission to make changes to the settings within the GPO by using the GPME. The Edit Settings permission does not allow the account to make changes to the permissions on the GPO or to delete the GPO.

The final setting that you can use is the Edit Settings, Delete, Modify Security option. As it sounds, anyone who has been granted this permission can change any of the settings, modify the security on the GPO, and get rid of the GPO. Make sure the users who have this permission are well-versed in all things Group Policy before you let them loose to make drastic changes to your network.

GROUP POLICY TEMPLATE SETTINGS

The actual settings that are applied to accounts are stored in the SYSVOL container within the Group Policy template. The easiest way to view all of the settings is to open the group policy within the GPME. Figure 8.16 shows a group policy that has been expanded to display some of the settings. Notice that there are two major sections to the group policy: Computer Configuration and User Configuration. Settings within each section control how the computer and user are managed when they start up or log on.

FIGURE 8.15
Delegation
permissions

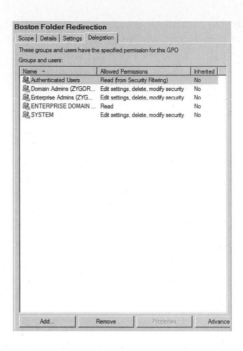

FIGURE 8.16
Group Policy settings

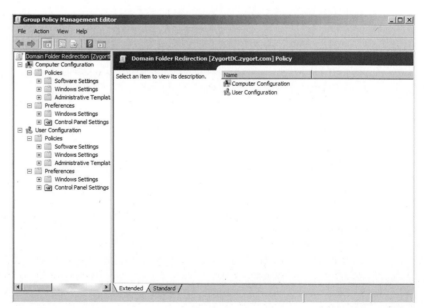

Computer Configuration

When the computer starts up, the settings that are configured within the Computer Configuration section are applied. The settings in this section typically are targeted toward the settings for manipulating the operating system and toward applications that are specific to the computer. For instance, the Software Settings section allows you to install software on systems, making the software available to anyone who uses the system. The Computer Configuration section of a GPO manages most of the security settings that control the way the computer and the user can access the network as well as the local system.

When you expand the Computer Configuration section of a group policy, you will find two top-level containers: Policies and Preferences. One side note about Preferences—they will not be found in Windows 2000 or Windows Server 2003–based Active Directory environments. They were introduced with Windows Server 2008. You can add them into a Windows Server 2003 environment as long as you have access to the Microsoft Desktop Optimization Pack for Software Assurance.

Policies are used to control the system and maintain the settings so that an administrator can be assured that the computer is configured according to the organization's standards. When you configure policy settings, you are, for the most part, locking down those settings so that a user cannot make changes to the settings, thus altering the way the system functions.

Preferences are configuration settings that the user can change. When using preferences, you want to configure a baseline of settings that the system will use; once changed by the user, however, the preference from the GPO will no longer be applied to the system. This allows you to configure the systems with default settings that are used when they are deployed initially, but still allow the users to have control over how they work with their computers.

User Configuration

As you might have guessed, the User Configuration section of a group policy is processed when the user logs on to the system. Settings that are found in this section typically affect only the user's session, not settings for the system. Just as in the Computer Configuration section, there is a Software Settings container; but the settings that are applied on the User Configuration settings apply to only the current user. If you were to assign software to a user in this manner, only the user who had the GPO applied against them would receive the software; other users that use the system would not have the software available to them.

When you expand the User Configuration section you will find the same two top-level containers as in the Computer Configuration section: Policies and Preferences. You can use the policies to control the systems, and use preferences to set the user-configured settings to an initial value.

PROCESSING OF GPOS

We have already discussed how GPOs are processed when there are multiple GPOs linked at the domain, site, and OU levels. We also need to discuss how the processing of GPOs occurs when the computer starts and the user logs on. Typically, the computer settings from the GPOs apply to the computer as it starts, and the user settings apply to the user's profile when the user logs on. The processing of settings works remarkably well when the user and the computer are in the same OU. The same hierarchy of GPOs exists for both user and computer.

But what happens when the user's account is not in the same OU as the computer account to which the user is logging on (which is typically the case)? As the computer starts, the computer settings in the GPOs are evaluated from the GPOs that make up the hierarchy to the OU where the computer resides. When the user logs on to the computer, the user settings within all of the GPOs in the hierarchy leading to the user's OU are evaluated. Neither user settings for the computer nor computer settings for the user are evaluated. Earlier we mentioned that the computer user settings could be disabled. This would be a good time to start thinking about disabling the user settings for all of the GPOs that affect only the computer, and disabling the computer settings for GPOs that affect only the user.

But it's not always be as simple as that. What if you want to control a user setting on a computer so that you can restrict a profile option for anyone who may log onto that system? Take for instance a computer that is used as a kiosk system. You want that system to be completely locked down so that none of the configuration options can be seen and only a specific program can run. No one should be able to perform any actions on the system except running that one program. The settings that control the profile for the user settings are stored in the user section of the GPO. If a user were to log on to the kiosk, that user's settings would apply to his or her profile, which you don't want to happen.

In the Computer Configuration options there is a setting for *loopback processing*. Loopback processing is used to force the user settings from the computer's GPOs to take precedence over the user settings from the user's GPOs. To do this, the computer's computer settings are applied at startup and the user's user settings are applied when the user logs on, but the computer's user settings are applied before the user is presented with a profile.

There are two settings available for loopback processing: Merge and Replace. When Merge is used, the settings are merged between the user and computer GPOs. When there is a conflict between the user's user settings and the computer's user settings, the computer's user settings will take precedence. When Replace is used, the user's user settings are completely ignored in favor of all of the settings within the computer's user settings.

PERIODIC PROCESSING

Periodic processing is one of the nicest capabilities of group policies. We know that a GPO is applied to a computer when it starts and to a user when the user logs on. But that is not the last time the GPO is applied. To make sure that the computer settings and the user profile have the latest settings and that the settings remain enforced, GPOs are processed and applied periodically. This reevaluation is called the *refresh interval*. By default, the refresh interval is 90 minutes plus a random value that can be as much as 30 minutes. Thus one computer could have a refresh interval of 98 minutes, and another could have a refresh interval of 112 minutes. This random offset frees the network and domain controller from having all of the systems and users refreshing their GPOs at the same time. As with nearly anything else within group policies, the refresh interval can be configured to meet your needs.

Editing Group Policies

Group Policy templates are the parts of the GPO that are stored within the SYSVOL container of domain controllers, and the parts of the GPO that the GPME can manipulate. When you are editing group policies, make sure you plan how and when you will make the changes. Any change that you make to a GPO goes into effect immediately. Of course, chances are that you will not see the change affect a system as soon as you make it, but the change will be available the next time the periodic processing cycle runs. Many of the settings that we discussed in the previous section can be manipulated with the GPME.

In versions of Active Directory prior to Windows Server 2008, the Group Policy Object Editor was the only mechanism to work with group policies unless you installed the GPMC. Therefore, most of the settings for the container as well as for the template were exposed from this console. There are a few exceptions, however, such as the filtering options. To work with the links for the GPO, you had to use either Active Directory Users and Computers or Active Directory Sites and Services. The GPMC allowed you to work with all aspects of GPOs and made them easier to manage.

In Windows Server 2008, the GPMC is included with the base installation and does not have to be installed as a separate product. The Group Policy Object Editor has been replaced by the GPME, although most of the functionality is the same in both products.

Using the Group Policy Management Editor

The Group Policy Management Editor allows you to directly edit a group policy and configure the settings that will affect computers and users. You can open up the GPME by right-clicking any of the group policies within the GPMC and selecting Edit. The group policy that you selected will appear within a new window. Figure 8.17 shows a group policy open and ready to be edited. We have already talked about the sections you can work with—Computer Configuration and User Configuration—so we will move on to some of the settings that you can manipulate.

FIGURE 8.17
GPO open for editing

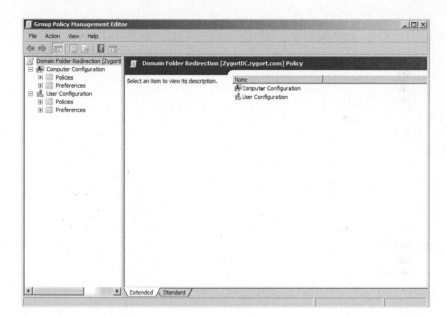

MANAGING SETTINGS

The settings you can manipulate come in a few flavors. Depending on what a setting does, you will be presented with different configuration options. The most basic of the settings simply enable or disable an option. More advanced settings allow you to configure the values that will be used. Figure 8.18 shows a simple policy item that can be either enabled or disabled. Figure 8.19 displays a setting that has more information that you can enter when enforcing a policy.

ADDING ADMINISTRATIVE TEMPLATES

Every time the GPO is evaluated, all of the settings within the GPO are evaluated to determine how they affect the user or computer. As you can probably imagine, the more settings there are to evaluate, the longer it takes for the computer to start and the user to receive the logon dialog. That is why Microsoft made the decision to not add all of the available administrative templates into the group policy architecture. Instead, you can add only the administrative templates you need within your environment.

By right-clicking on the Administrative Templates node, you can add an administrative template by selecting the Add/Remove Templates option. Once the Add/Remove Templates window appears, you can click the Add button and navigate to the location of the template. Templates can usually be downloaded from the provider of the software you are trying to manage. Additionally, Microsoft provides several templates to control its operating-system features and applications. Once you have added a template, you will see the new settings appear within the Administrative Templates container.

FIGURE 8.18
Simple enable and
disable settings

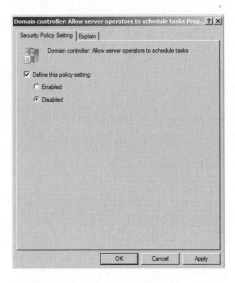

FIGURE 8.19
Setting with more
options to configure

FILTERING ADMINISTRATIVE TEMPLATES

Those who have worked with group policies know that one of the hardest things to do is find the correct group policy setting to use when managing systems. Because there are hundreds of configurable settings, it can be overwhelming to find the one setting you need to configure. Microsoft has always offered the Group Policy Settings Reference, which is a spreadsheet you can use to find the settings you want to work with. The spreadsheet was configured with easy search options that allow you to filter out any nonmatching options. But this required you to leave the Group Policy Object Editor and open up the spreadsheet to find the setting, then go back to the Group Policy Object Editor and follow the path to the setting. Included in the GPME is an administrative template filter. You can essentially hide any of the settings that do not meet the filter criteria, making it easier to find settings directly within the editor.

Right-clicking any of the containers within Administrative Templates under either Computer Configuration or User Configuration displays two options on the context menu: Filter On and Filter Options, as seen in Figure 8.20. Selecting Filter On applies the current filter settings to the administrative templates. Clearing Filter On returns the view to the default, which displays all of the administrative template settings. Figure 8.21 shows that the Administrative Templates container has been filtered, and only a subset of the available options appears.

To configure the filter to meet your requirements, you need to select Filter Options from the context menu. You will see a window that looks like Figure 8.22. The three sections help you create the filter that you will use to view the configuration settings. The first section allows you to search for settings that meet just basic criteria: Managed, Configured, and/or Commented. Managed settings make changes to registry settings. Configured settings are those that are set to either Enabled or Disabled. Commented settings are those that have entries within the Comments section.

The second section allows you to search for keywords within the settings. Once you enable this section, you can type in keywords to search for and the search parameters. You can select to search in the title, in the explain text, and/or in the Comment sections of the settings. Using keyword filters, you can perform a very powerful search through the settings.

The final section allows you to limit the operating-system and application criteria through which you are searching. If you are looking for settings that apply to only Windows XP systems, you can simply select the Microsoft Windows XP Family option, and settings that apply to any version of Windows XP will appear. The drop-down menu shown in Figure 8.23 allows you to control whether to display settings that apply to *any* of the operating systems that you select from the list, or if the setting has to apply to *all* of the selections that you have made.

 Real World Scenario

DON'T OVERDO IT

Administrative templates are a great way to extend your control over the applications and services within your network. Just make sure that you don't add unnecessary ones. As you add administrative templates, you are creating more settings that need to be reviewed every time a computer or user account evaluates the group policy.

Case in point: an organization that had implemented Active Directory became caught up in its quest to manage the organization. Staff found several administrative templates they thought looked interesting, and imported each of the ADM files into every one of their group policies. They theorized that they needed to give all of their group policies standardized settings.

The problem with this theory is that when you add administrative templates, you are increasing the number of settings that have to be checked. Whenever a computer started up or a user logged on, the additional settings were evaluated, whether the template applied or not. The organization found that its users were not happy with the new startup and logon times. After being informed of what was happening, the staff reviewed the requirements for each of the GPOs they had, and removed the unnecessary administrative templates.

FIGURE 8.20
Filter options

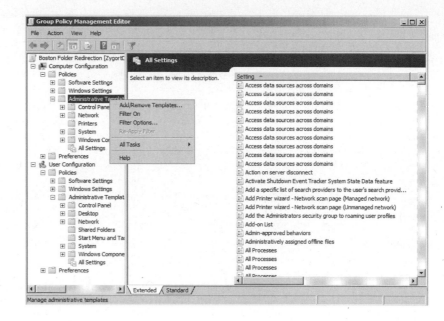

FIGURE 8.21
Administrative
Templates container
filtered

In Figure 8.24 we are creating a filter that will display only the settings that have a keyword of *offline* and apply to Windows Server 2003 or Windows XP systems. After we configure the filter, we have turned on the filter setting, and as you can see in Figure 8.25, the policy settings that meet our requirements are shown. In contrast, if we remove the operating-system requirement in the filter, the list changes to what is seen in Figure 8.26. Because there are several more options available in Windows Vista and Windows Server 2008, you will see more settings appear when you remove the operating system criteria from the filter.

Having the filter functionality built into the Group Policy Management Editor lets you search through all of the administrative templates, whether they were provided by Microsoft or another company. When using the Group Policy Settings Reference that Microsoft provides, you have only the settings that apply to Microsoft products.

The drawback to the filter is that it applies only to administrative templates. The settings in all other areas of group policy are not affected and cannot be filtered. However, those settings do not get updated and changed as frequently as the administrative templates.

POLICIES AND PREFERENCES

Earlier we discussed the fact that an administrative template is made up of policies and preferences. Policies have always been available in Active Directory. Preferences were originally added through a product called PolicyMaker, which Microsoft acquired. You can now manage preferences natively within the Group Policy Management Console included with Windows Server 2008, or the with Remote Server Administration Tools. Using both of these constructs allows you to manage your organization's resources better than if you had only the policies in place.

The main difference between policies and preferences is the way that they are applied. Policies are mandated settings that users are not allowed to change. This is accomplished by writing the settings for the policy in the Policy branches of the registry. These branches are protected by permissions that do not allow standard users to access them. Once the settings are applied in the registry, applications that are group policy–aware will review the Policy branches of the registry for enforcement settings. If a given setting is not configured by a GPO, the application will look to the standard registry branches for application-specific settings.

Preferences are not written to the Policy branches, however. Policy settings are written to the same registry locations that the applications and operating system use. Because these branches are not locked down by permissions, users can make changes to the settings through the operating-system management tools, through the applications themselves, or even through some registry tweaks. As an added bonus, applications do not have to be group policy–aware to take advantage of preferences, because they don't need to understand how to access the Policy branches of the registry.

FIGURE 8.22

Filter configuration settings

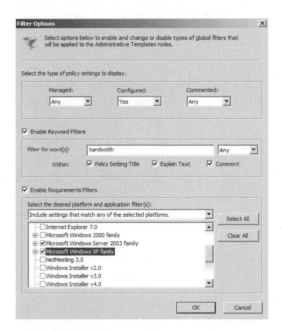

FIGURE 8.23

Specifying the matching-operating-system criteria

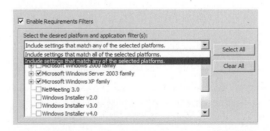

FIGURE 8.24
Configuring a filter

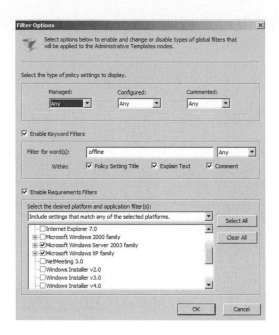

FIGURE 8.25
Viewing the results
of the filter

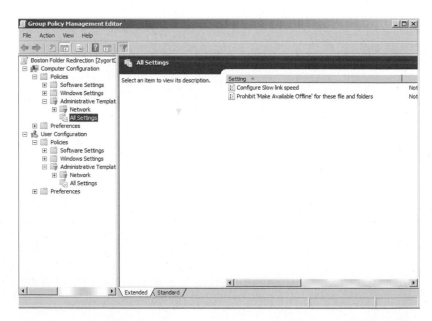

Both policy and preference settings are refreshed according to the refresh interval, but you have the ability to specify that a preference setting will not refresh. This way you can allow users to make changes to their systems, and the settings will not be overwritten when the refresh occurs. If you look at Figure 8.27, you will see the setting for Apply Once and Do Not Reapply that can be configured within the Common tab.

FIGURE 8.26
Viewing the filter
without operating-
system limitations

FIGURE 8.27
Setting a preference so
that it is not reapplied

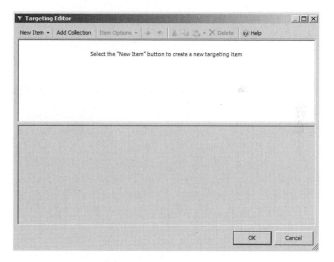

As shown in Figure 8.27, there is also a check box labeled Item-Level Targeting. When you select this option, the Targeting button becomes available. Clicking the button will activate a window, seen in Figure 8.28, that allows you to create a filter. This filter is used to identify the computer account or user account to which the preference will apply. This is quite different from policies. Windows Management Instrumentation (WMI) filters can be created for policies, but the WMI filter specifies whether the entire GPO is applied against a computer or user. You don't have the ability to create a different WMI filter for each policy item. With preferences, each preference item you create can have a different filter.

As seen in Figure 8.29, you can specify exactly which object type the filter will be evaluated against. Choosing one of the objects will create the targeting item options as seen in Figure 8.30. You can select the options that you want to use, and add additional target items as necessary. In Figure 8.31, you can see that a target query has been created that determines if the notebook computer is docked and, if it is, that it has a battery present, that the CPU is at least a 1GHz processor, and that it is running any version of Windows XP.

FIGURE 8.28
Creating a target filter

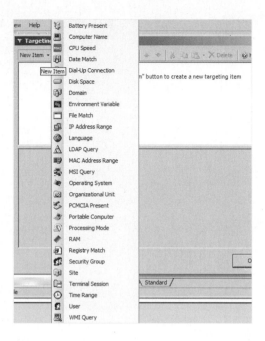

FIGURE 8.29
Objects for which you
can create a filter

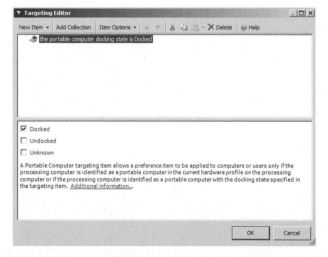

In Figure 8.32, the Item Options drop-down displays the options that you can use when defining the logical evaluation of the query items. The And option evaluates two options to be true; the Or option evaluates whether at least one of the options is true; the Is option sets a comparison between items to evaluate to True; Is Not sets a comparison between items so that at least one item is False. And using the Label option, you can create friendly text for one of the query items so that it is easier to understand how the options are evaluated.

FIGURE 8.30
Entering an object
query item

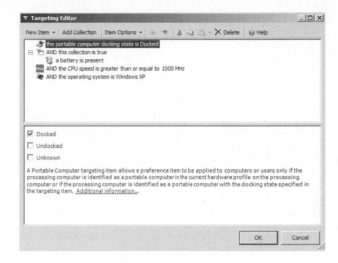

FIGURE 8.31
Query to be applied
to systems

FIGURE 8.32
Logical evaluators

The other options on the Common tab include the following:

Stop Processing Items In This Extension If an Error Occurs   Selecting this option allows you to stop the processing of all of the preferences within the container so that you do not inject several errors into the event log and cause the system to attempt to apply the settings when the client-side extension may have a processing problem.

Run in Logged-On User's Security Context (User Policy Option)   When a preference is configured within the User Configuration settings, the user's credentials will be used to process the preference.

Remove This Item when It Is No Longer Applied   When the preference item is deleted from the GPO, the Preferences settings will be removed from the registry settings.

As you can see in Figure 8.33, you can configure several containers within the Preferences container. The best way to get to understand them all is to start working with them. The following is a brief summary of what each container is used for:

FIGURE 8.33

Preferences
containers

Windows Settings   The following settings can be found within the Windows Settings container. Some are available on the Computer Configuration settings, some are available in the User Configuration settings, and some are in both.

Applications   User Configuration option used to configure settings for applications that include a preference plug-in.

Drive Maps   User Configuration option used to create, replace, update, or delete mapped drives on a system. Can also be used to show or hide mapped drives on the system.

Environment   Computer Configuration and User Configuration option used to create, replace, update, or delete environment variables on systems.

Files   Computer Configuration and User Configuration option that can be used to create, replace, update, or delete files on systems.

Folders   Computer Configuration and User Configuration option that can be used to create, replace, update, or delete folders on systems.

Ini Files   Computer Configuration and User Configuration option that can be used to create, replace, update, or delete configuration .ini files on systems.

Registry   Computer Configuration and User Configuration option that can be used to create, replace, update, or delete registry values on systems.

Network Shares   Computer Configuration option that can be used to create, replace, update or delete shares on systems.

Shortcuts   Computer Configuration and User Configuration option that can be used to create, replace, update, or delete shortcuts on systems.

Control Panel Settings   The following settings can be found within the Control Panel Settings container. Some are available on the Computer Configuration settings, some are available in the User Configuration settings, and some are in both.

Data Sources   Computer Configuration and User Configuration option that can be used to create, replace, update, or delete database data source name (DSN) values on systems.

Devices   Computer Configuration and User Configuration option that can be used to enable or disable devices on systems.

Folder Options   Computer Configuration and User Configuration option that can be used to create, replace, update, or set file associations on systems, as well as to manage how the folder information is displayed to the user.

Internet Settings   User Configuration option that can be used to manage Internet Explorer configuration settings.

Local Users and Groups   Computer Configuration and User Configuration option that can be used to create, replace, update, or delete local user and group accounts on systems.

Network Options   Computer Configuration and User Configuration options that can be used to create, replace, update, or delete virtual private network or dial-up networking settings.

Power Options   Computer Configuration and User Configuration options that can be used to manage the power configuration settings on systems.

Printers   Computer Configuration and User Configuration options that can be used to create, replace, update, or delete printer settings on systems.

Regional Options   User Configuration option that can be used to manage the formatting that is used for currency, numbers, date, and time for the user.

Scheduled Tasks   Computer Configuration and User Configuration options that can be used to create, replace, update, or delete scheduled tasks on a system.

Services   Computer Configuration option that can be used to manage how services start and how they function on a system.

Start Menu   User Configuration option that can be used to manage how the Start Menu appears in a user's profile.

Backing Up and Restoring Group Policies

As you do with anything else within your infrastructure, you need to safeguard all of the group policy settings you have put into place. This means you need to back up the group policies and have the backup available to restore if needed. Any good backup program will back up the container as part of the Active Directory backup, and the template will be backed up when the SYSVOL is backed up. Having these two components stored in different locations makes for a slightly more difficult restore. Both components need to exist for the GPO to work properly.

The GPMC has its own backup component that will allow you to back up both parts of the GPO and restore them when necessary. Using the backup option from within the GPMC allows you to back up GPOs and store them in a convenient location. When you need to restore the GPO, you don't have to worry about finding the correct backup set from the backup utility your organization uses, you can simply go to the network location where you keep your GPO backups.

You can back up GPOs in two ways: all GPOs at once, or individually. If you right-click on the Group Policy Objects container within the GPMC, you will see the option Back Up All.

Differences between Group Policy Versions

When Windows Vista was developed, a different format for group policies was introduced. Instead of using a proprietary format for displaying the settings that make up a GPO, standards-based XML files are used. On a day-to-day basis most administrators will not notice a difference. However, if you need to modify the administrative templates or create your own, working with XML could prove to be much easier than learning another markup language just to create an administrative template.

Administrative templates that are used with Windows 2000, Window XP, or Windows Server 2003 use the `.adm` extension, whereas Windows Vista and Windows Server 2008 administrative templates use the `.admx` extension. Only the definition of the template settings that are actually formatted as such. When the group policy is applied, it doesn't matter which format is used; the settings sent to the computer are in the form of commands that are executed on the computer, so it doesn't matter if you are managing the group policies from a Windows Vista system and those settings apply to a Windows XP system—they will be applied.

Managing Your Environment

When you expand a domain within the GPMC, you will find that only OUs appear within the list. You won't find any of the containers that appear within Active Directory Users and Computers, such as Users and Computers. This is because you cannot link a GPO to a container. Only those constructs that are used within the group policy infrastructure are represented in the GPMC.

A nice feature of the GPMC is that you don't have to leave it to create OUs. If you have permissions to create OUs within Active Directory, you can use the GPMC and create your hierarchy of OUs. At the domain or at a parent OU, you can right-click and select New Organizational Unit. A dialog like the one in Figure 8.34 appears, allowing you to name the OU. Unfortunately, you cannot do the same for sites. However, a menu option will let you open Active Directory Sites and Services easily when you need it.

Once you have your OU structure created and the GPOs linked, you can view the GPOs easily for each of the levels within the hierarchy. This makes for easy management of the GPOs. However, quickly determining what might happen when you link a new GPO or checking to see what happens when a user logs on to a specific computer might not be as clear-cut. That is where a couple of tools within the GPMC come in handy. We will look at them in the next section.

Planning and Monitoring Group Policies

Being able to determine what might happen when you link a GPO to a domain, site, or OU might not sound difficult, but what if you are in an environment where you have several hundred GPOs and hundreds of users and computers spread out through many OUs? As your environment grows and becomes more complex, you may have a difficult time documenting all the settings for the GPOs and figuring out the correct processing order, depending on where the user and the computer are located.

If you have the ability to create GPO "templates," you can save yourself a lot of time and headaches. In Windows Server 2008, you can use the new Starter GPOs to create these template files. Essentially you are configuring settings that will be applied to other GPOs when they are created so that you don't have to invest additional time in recreating settings that should be applied to other GPOs that you are creating.

At the bottom of the GPMC are two nodes: Group Policy Modeling and Group Policy Results. Using these two tools, you can determine not only what happened the last time a user logged onto a computer, but also the effects of changes you've made to your organization. Group Policy Modeling allows you to evaluate changes before you make them. Group Policy Results will display the settings that were applied the last time the computer started and the user logged on.

STARTER GPOS

Starter GPOs were introduced with Windows Server 2008. The basis of Starter GPOs is that you may have a baseline you want to start with for GPOs you create. So instead of having to enter the same information in every GPO you create, you can enter the common information into a starter GPO and then use it as the template for others. And you are not restricted to having a single starter GPO; you can create as many as you need within your environment.

As you can see in Figure 8.35, when you first select the Starter GPOs container, the button labeled Create Starter GPOs Folder appears. You have to create a folder to host the starter GPOs. After you click the button, the Starter GPOs container shows the starter GPOs that you create, as well as the delegations that you configure. Delegations indicate which users have the ability to manipulate the starter GPOs. Figure 8.36 shows the Starter GPO for Boston.

FIGURE 8.34

Creating an OU from the GPMC

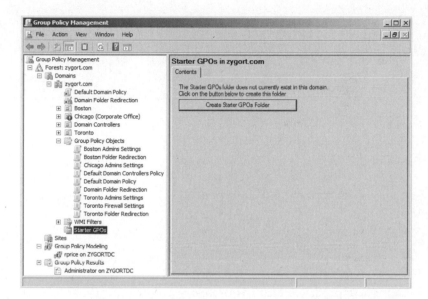

FIGURE 8.35

Creating the Starter GPOs folder

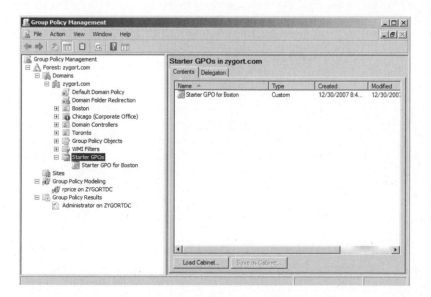

FIGURE 8.36
Starter GPOs for a
domain

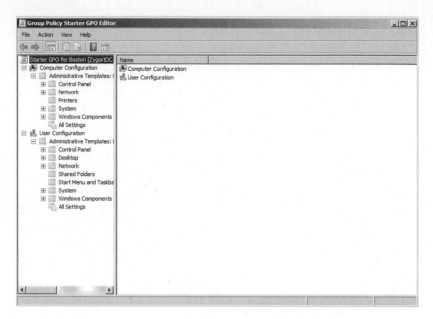

FIGURE 8.36
Starter GPOs for a
domain

When you right-click a starter GPO and choose the Edit option, you are presented with a Group Policy Management Editor, just as if you were editing a GPO. However, there are not many settings you can manage from starter GPOs. As a matter of fact, you can edit only the Administrative Templates settings, as seen in Figure 8.37.

Once you have the starter GPO created, you can use it as the basis for GPOs that you use within your environment. Figure 8.38 shows the dialog that appears when you create a new GPO. Notice that you can specify a starter GPO that you will use for the initial settings included in the new GPO.

The Starter GPOs container becomes powerful in the export and import area. If you create a set of starter GPOs that you want to use in multiple domains or forests, you can use the Save As Cabinet button to export the starter GPO. Once you have saved the starter GPO, you can import it by using the Load Cabinet button. This way, you don't have to re-create the starter GPO in each domain and forest in your environment.

Make sure you back up the starter GPOs. When you back up the GPOs within your environment by using the backup options in the Group Policy Objects container, the starter GPOs are *not* backed up. You will find the same backup options within the Starter GPOs container, but those options will back up only the starter GPOs, not your production GPOs.

FIGURE 8.37
Starter GPO open for
editing

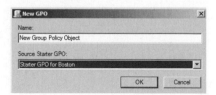

FIGURE 8.38

Creating a new GPO
from a starter GPO

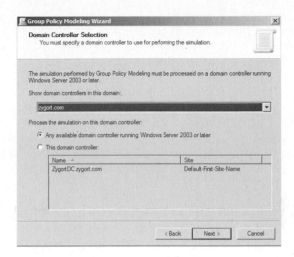

GROUP POLICY MODELING

If you have ever wondered whether moving a user or computer to a different OU would cause some unforeseen problems, you find out by testing changes without actually introducing them. The Group Policy Modeling tool can be used to evaluate changes you want to make. The results can then be reviewed so you can determine whether your changes will work or if they need to be modified.

Right-clicking the Group Policy Modeling container and selecting Group Policy Modeling Wizard will present you with a wizard that will step you through defining the change you want to make. After you click Next to go past the splash screen, you will see the first page of the wizard, as shown in Figure 8.39. Here you can specify the domain controller you want to use when you are running the model. By default, the Any Available Domain Controller Running Windows Server 2003 or Later option is specified. If you use this option, a domain controller within the site in which your system is located will be used to evaluate the model. You can choose another domain controller by selecting the This Domain Controller option and then selecting from the list the domain controller you want to use.

FIGURE 8.39

Choosing the domain
controller

On the next page you'll select where the user and computer are located within the domain. You can select a container to evaluate what would be applied for any member of the container, or you can select a specific user and/or computer to evaluate. If you leave the option set to Container, you can browse to an OU or container where the account is located by clicking the Browse button and navigating to the correct location, as seen in Figure 8.40.

If you want to specify an account, you can select the User or Computer option and then locate the appropriate account by using the Browse button that appears. When looking for the account, you will be presented with a standard Select User or Select Computer dialog, as shown in Figure 8.41. When you select a specific account instead of using a container, you are presented with an additional page in the wizard. This page allow you to model what would happen if you moved the account to a location other than the one in which it currently resides.

You have probably noticed the handy check box at the bottom of the screen. If you check it, you can immediately move to the end of the wizard without specifying any additional options. This check box appears on every page of the wizard, allowing you to quickly finish the model if there are not any more settings you want to configure.

The next page, Advanced Simulation Options, seen in Figure 8.42, allows you to configure special settings that might be configured for a GPO. The first, Slow Network Connection, will show the processing applied when a slow network connection is detected. Within your group policy settings, you can specify the connection speed that is considered slow, as well as the processing options that will be ignored when the slow connection is detected. If you want to see what would be applied and what would be ignored, select this check box.

FIGURE 8.40
Choosing the container

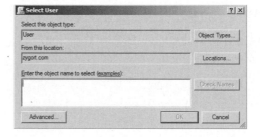

FIGURE 8.41
Selecting a user or computer to evaluate

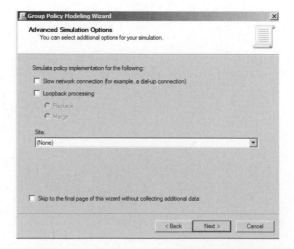

FIGURE 8.42
Advanced Simulation
Options

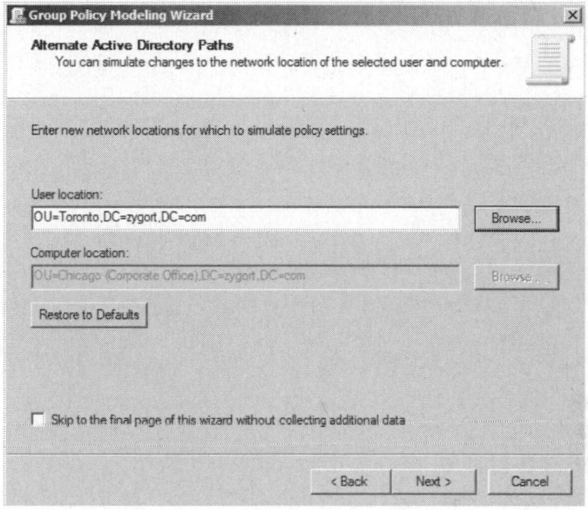

The second setting allows you to evaluate what would happen if loopback processing were turned on. The radio buttons that appear allow you to configure the loopback processing simulation for replace or merge. The final setting allows you to determine what would happen if you placed the computer within a specific site. The drop-down contains all of the sites available within the forest.

The next page, Alternate Active Directory Paths, shown in Figure 8.43, is the page you will use to simulate moving a user to a new container. If you want to see what would happen if you moved a user from the Users container to an OU, click the Browse button and select the OU into which you want to move the user. If you change your mind, you always have the handy Restore to Defaults button that will reenter the account's current location.

The next two pages allow you to change the group membership for accounts. The first of the two pages (seen in Figure 8.44), User Security Groups, can be used to add the user's account to a group as well as remove the user from existing group membership. The page that follows allows you to do the same for the computer account. You can use the Add and Remove buttons to modify the simulated group membership and the Restore Defaults button to return the account membership to the original settings.

FIGURE 8.43
Choosing alternate
directory location

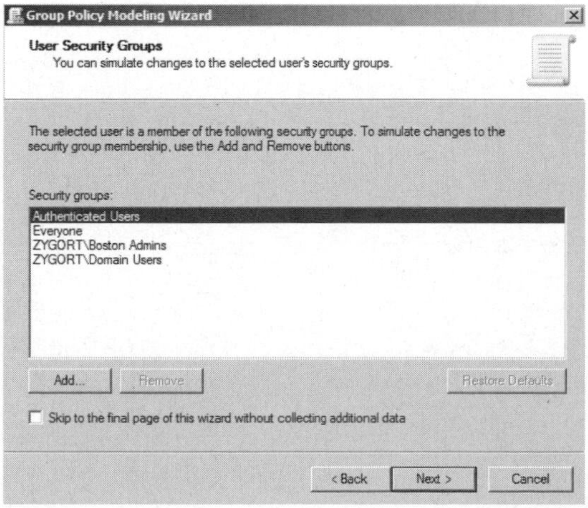

FIGURE 8.44

Selecting group
membership

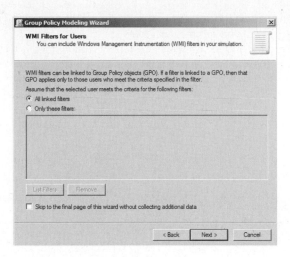

The WMI Filters for Users page that appears next, shown in Figure 8.45, allows you to specify WMI filters that are linked to the users in the selected container or to the user you have selected. The next page does the same thing for computer accounts. WMI filters allow you to specify the criteria the account has to match to have the GPO apply. A simple example of this is a WMI filter that determines if the computer has enough free space to install an application. If the account does not meet the criteria specified on the WMI filter, the GPO will not be evaluated or applied to the account.

FIGURE 8.45

Choosing WMI filters

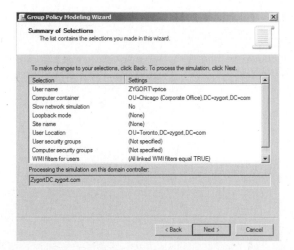

The final page of the wizard, seen in Figure 8.46, presents a summary of the settings that you had just configured. You can review this information to determine if you made the correct changes to the settings. If you are done, you can click Next to run the simulation and generate a report. After clicking Finish to end the wizard, the report—an example of which can be seen in Figure 8.47—will give you insight about what would happen when the accounts are moved to different containers or an account is created within a container. The Summary tab displays the settings that were used to generate the modeling report. You can view the information from this page by clicking the Show link for a specific component (versus the Show All link, which expands them all). Doing so will expand that summary section so you can see if everything processed according to your plan. If there are any settings that were not applied as you thought they should be, it is here that you can investigate why that might have happened. Keep in mind the Group Policy Objects section, seen expanded in Figure 8.48. Two subsections beneath it will show you which GPOs were applied and which were not. The handy Denied GPOs section will show you the reason why a given GPO was denied.

FIGURE 8.46

Summary screen

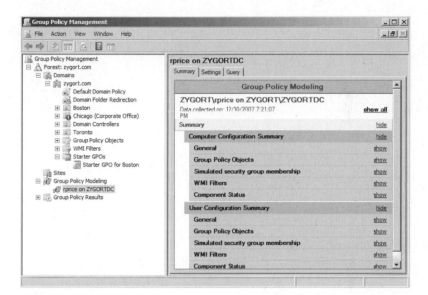

FIGURE 8.47

Modeling report

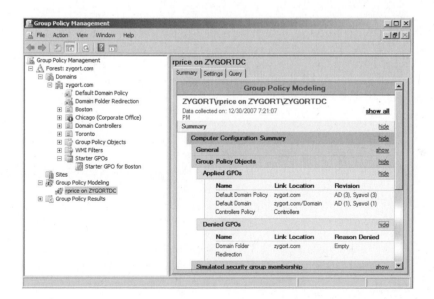

FIGURE 8.48
Summary showing applied and denied GPOs

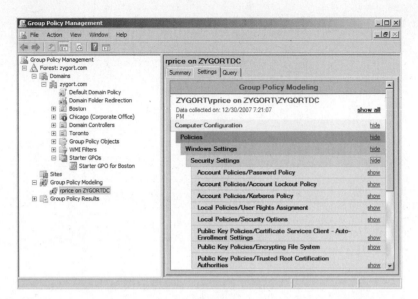

The Query tab displays the settings that you chose when you were creating the model by stepping through the Group Policy Modeling Wizard. If the results you find from the modeling do not match what you think should appear, you can double-check the query that was run to make sure you set everything correctly.

The Settings tab displays all of the effective settings that would be applied if the change you are modeling were to take place. It is on the Settings tab that you can determine what would happen when the computer starts and the user logs on. Just as on the Summary tab, clicking the Show link will expand the settings so that you can review the information found there. Figure 8.49 shows a Settings page that was generated when the model was simulated.

Once you have your model report generated, you can save a copy of it by right-clicking on the report itself and choosing Save Report. A dialog will appear, as shown in Figure 8.50, that will allow you to name the report and to save the file in either HTML or XML format.

If you like the way a model is configured and you want to create another one that has like settings, you can right-click the model and choose the Create New Query from This One option. The Group Policy Modeling Wizard will start again, but will already be populated with the settings from the original model. All you have to do is make the changes that you want to test, and another report will be generated for you.

FIGURE 8.49
Settings page

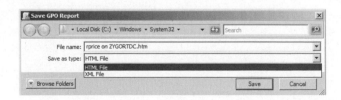

FIGURE 8.50
Saving the modeling
report

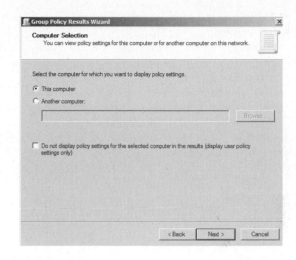

GROUP POLICY RESULTS

If you right-click on the Group Policy Results container and select Group Policy Results Wizard, you will be presented with a wizard that allows you to specify a user and/or computer and then to view the settings that were applied the last time the computer started and the user logged on. After clicking the Next button on the wizard's welcome page, you are presented with a page that allows you to specify the computer you are going to evaluate, as shown in Figure 8.51. You can choose the computer you're currently logged on to, or you can specify another computer within the domain. Notice that you can click the check box for Do Not Display Policy Settings for the Selected Computer in the Results. Selecting this option will bypass evaluating the settings that were applied to the computer. You may want to select this option if you are concerned only with reviewing the settings that were applied to a user.

FIGURE 8.51
Selecting a computer
to query

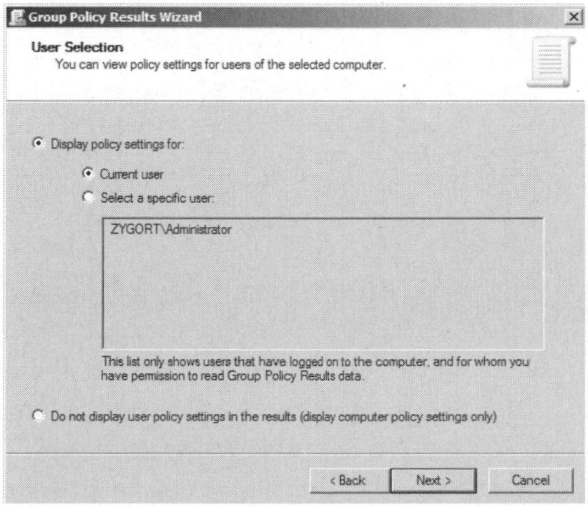

The next page, seen in Figure 8.52, is the User Selection page. This page is used to choose the user account on which you want to check the settings. You can select the current user account in the results query or select a user from the list. Notice that the list includes only users that have logged onto the computer. This is because the Group Policy Results wizard needs to evaluate the settings that were applied to the user's profile when she or he logged on. If a user has not logged onto the computer before, that user will not have any information to query.

Once you've chosen the accounts, a summary page is displayed. After you click the Next button, the computer is queried and the user's profile is reviewed. The results are then displayed in a report that you can review just as you did with Group Policy Modeling.

FIGURE 8.52
Selecting a user
profile to query

Coming Up Next

In the next chapter we are going to look at the security that goes into protecting Active Directory and making sure the accounts are safeguarded. There is a lot of information stored in Active Directory—everything from account information to configuration data for applications and services. Without the security that has been integrated within Active Directory, the sensitive information that is stored in the directory service could be attacked and taken advantage of.

The Bottom Line

Identify the different group policy types   Microsoft has changed the format of group policy templates so that they are easier to manage. Instead of using a proprietary format, the new group policy templates that are used with Vista and Windows Server 2008 are based on XML.

Master It   Administrative templates are formatted using two different markup languages. What formats are they created in and which operating systems support the group policies that are configured with each?

Use the Group Policy Management Editor   The Group Policy Management Editor allows you to configure settings that will be used to manage systems when they initially start. The settings that are initially used are not enforced, so the user that logs onto the system can make configuration changes.

Master It   When working with the Group Policy Management Editor, you want to set initial settings for client systems, but you also want to allow the user to be able to make changes to the settings. What section of the GPO would you use to configure these settings?

Use the Group Policy Management Console   The Group Policy Management Console makes managing group policies much easier than using just the Group Policy Object Editor and Active Directory Users and Computers. The tools that are included in the GPMC include a Group Policy Results wizard that allows you to determine how the GPOs applied to a user or computer, the Group Policy Modeling wizard, which allows you to determine how GPO will affect a user or computer, and the ability to create Starter GPOs.

Master It   You have identified settings within your group policies that you want to include in all GPOs. These settings are primarily comments you want to make sure are included when other administrators edit the GPOs, but they also contain configuration settings you want to make sure are included in each GPO. How would you go about creating an easy way to apply these settings?

Chapter 9

Managing Active Directory Security

The final chapter in this section deals with the management of Active Directory objects. We will start by introducing the basics of the Active Directory Domain Services (AD DS) security, and follow with steps you can take to secure your AD DS objects. Finally, we will highlight new features in Windows Server 2008 that you can use in your AD DS environment to enhance security.

In this chapter you will learn the following:

◆ The basics of AD DS security

◆ How to secure AD DS objects

AD DS Security Basics

As you design security in your environment, it is important to understand the "building blocks" of AD DS security. Once you understand the how these items work together, you can start to form a foundation that you can use to build your security infrastructure. AD DS security starts with security principals, access control lists, access tokens, and authentication.

Security Principals

A security principal is any AD DS object that can be authenticated to Active Directory. This includes user accounts, computer accounts, or any process that runs as a user or computer account. Security principals are the only objects in AD DS that can be assigned permissions to access resources.

When a security principal is created, it is assigned a security identifier (SID). The SID is unique to the object; two objects cannot possess the same SID in your environment. When you grant permissions to a user, group, service, or computer, you are granting permissions to the "friendly name" of the SID.

Take for instance the user Sonja Souza. The "friendly name" for the user is Sonja Souza, and that is what you see when you are managing that user account. Behind the scenes, however, Windows and AD DS are using the SID that is associated with that user to manage permissions and access control. This allows you to change user's name without adverse affects on permissions and access control throughout the network.

The SID is made up of two parts: the domain identifier and the relative identifier (RID). The domain identifier is the same for all security principals in the domain. The RID is unique to each security principal in the AD DS domain.

Access Control Lists

As stated earlier, permissions are granted to security principals so they can access resources on the network. Controlling the access to those resources is the job of the access control lists (ACLs).

ACLs are defined for objects in AD DS; they define the access the security principal has to that object. These objects could be a printer object, an organizational unit (OU), or a file on a network share. The level of access is defined by the permissions that have been assigned to the security principal. These permissions are listed in the ACL on the object.

Each ACL actually contains two different kinds of ACLs: a discretionary access control list (DACL) and a system access control list (SACL). The DACL displays the security principals that have been assigned (or denied) permissions to an object. The DACL will also list the level of access assigned to the security principal; this list is made up of access control entries (ACEs). An ACE lists one SID and defines the access that SID has to the object.

The SACL is a list of security principals that have auditing rules applied to them. Like the DACL, the SACL also has a list of ACEs that define whose access is to be audited and at what level.

Access Tokens

Now we have security principals that have permissions assigned to them, and we have ACLs that control the access that security principals have to objects. Now we must link the security principal to the ACL. This is done with an access token.

Upon login to AD DS, the security principal is assigned an access token. The access token consists of the user's SID, the SIDs for any groups to which the user belongs, and the user's rights and privileges. When the user attempts to gain access to a network resource that has an ACL assigned to it, the security subsystem will compare the information from the access token to the recource's ACL and determine if the security principal is allowed access. The SIDs from the access token are compared to the ACEs in the ACL; if there is a match, the SID is checked for the level of permission, and that level is then given to the security principal.

Authentication

Authentication is the process that ensures that the people who are trying to access the network are who they say they are. Once a user has authenticated to AD DS and received an access token, the SIDs and ACLs can do their job.

When a user logs in from a network computer, the Winlogon service on that computer loads the `msgina.dll`. The user enters his or her password, and the `msgina.dll` passes the logon information back to the Winlogon process. The Winlogon service then passes that information to the Local Security Authority (LSA). The user's clear-text password is hashed and the clear-text copy of the password is deleted. The username and hashed password are passed along to the Security Support Provider (SSP). In Windows 2000 and later, Kerberos is used as the SSP. The SSP then sends the username and hashed password to the domain controller for authentication.

If this entire procedure is successful, the user is considered authenticated and is granted access to the network.

Authorization

After the user has been authenticated to the network, he or she must gain access to network resources. This is known as authorization. Think of authentication as showing your identification at the door of a club. Your identification shows that you are allowed to be there because you are of age. You get in to the club, but your hand is stamped with a red stamp instead of a green stamp. The red stamp means that you can be in the club, but cannot drink alcohol. Authorization comes into play when you walk up to the bar to order a drink. Because you have a red stamp, you are not authorized to buy a drink; that is reserved for people with green stamps.

It's the same process when accessing the network. During authentication, you have proved your right to be on the network. After you are authenticated, authorization takes over and checks you wherever you try to go. If you try to access some files on a file server and you have the correct permissions (think green stamp), you are allowed access to the files. You are authorized to use those files. If you try to access a printer object on a print server, authorization checks your permissions again to see if you can use that printer object. If not (red stamp), you are denied access.

Securing the Base Operating System

One of the most important steps to ensure the stability of your domain is often overlooked. Most administrators will take steps to secure AD DS, but most fail to take the extra steps to secure their domain controllers. A security breach of a domain controller means a breach of your entire Active Directory infrastructure, including all user accounts, domain information, and possibly Active Directory Certificate Services.

People can gain physical or remote access to your domain controllers; however, there are preventative measures you can take to guard against this. You can also take steps to ensure you can track information on the attacks to see who is attempting the attack or who was successful.

Physical Security for Domain Controllers

Probably the most overlooked area in security is physical access to the domain controllers. I have worked on teams that engage in "social engineering" to try to find weaknesses in clients' networks. Social engineering is the act of manipulating people to get information about a computer system or network instead of trying to breach the computer systems themselves. We were hired by the company's executives to try to gain access to the network.

Of all the processes that we tried, I was very surprised to find that the physical-access test was more successful than I had originally anticipated. While this test does not have a very high success rate, it is higher than I had thought it would be.

Later in the chapter we will discuss read-only domain controllers (RODCs). You can use an RODC in areas where physical security to the domain controller cannot be guaranteed.

The steps you can take to deny physical access to a server include more than just putting a lock on the server-room door. Every layer of security adds time to an intrusion attempt and possibly adds to the frustration level of the person making the attempt. If someone gains access to your server room, you shouldn't have your entire bounty laying there waiting to be taken. Even Indiana Jones had to go through many tests to obtain his treasure. Even after success, he still had to deal with that big boulder chasing him.

Locking the server-room door is great, and a lot of people do that, but many other layers are often missed. Put all of your servers in racks that lock. To prevent someone from booting your domain controller into an alternative operating system, you can also remove the floppy and CD-ROM or CD-RW drives from the server. You should also disable external ports (serial, SCSI, USB, etc.) that are not being used. Plug and Play technology makes it very easy for external drives to be connected and to be configured easily without a reboot. Many USB "thumb drives" can hold 8 GB or more of information. If someone gains physical access to these machines, a wealth of information could walk out the door in someone's pocket.

If you enable Syskey (discussed later in this chapter), you may need to keep a floppy drive located on the domain controller, depending on the level of Syskey you decide to use.

READ-ONLY DOMAIN CONTROLLERS

A new feature in Windows Server 2008 directly addresses the issues that some companies have with physical security. The RODC was introduced specifically for implementations where a domain controller was needed but physical security could not be guaranteed.

The perfect scenario for this would be a remote branch or remote office that requires a domain controller. Often physical security is an issue, because there is typically not an area for the server that is as safe and secure as the data center where all of the other servers reside.

The RODC hosts a read-only copy of the AD DS database. It contains the same objects and attributes as a writable domain controller, but changes cannot be made directly on the RODC. Changes to the AD DS database are made on a writeable domain controller and replicated to the RODC. This helps contain issues that may arise from an attack on a remote domain controller that would typically replicate changes from the branch throughout the organization.

The RODC holds a copy of all of the AD DS objects and attributes that a writable domain controller does, except for account passwords (unless otherwise configured). When a user authenticates against an RODC, the RODC forwards the request to a writable domain controller. If the writable domain controller responds favorably, the user is allowed to log in. The RODC also requests a copy of the appropriate credentials to store locally in its cache so the next logon does not have to traverse the network back to the hub site again.

If the writable domain controller receives the request from an RODC, it will check the Password Replication Policy for that particular RODC to see if it is allowed to replicate the credentials to the RODC. If the Password Replication Policy states that the RODC can keep a local copy of the credentials, then they are sent and the RODC stores them in its cache. Figure 9.1 displays the Password Replication Policy tab that is viewable by opening the properties of a domain controller in ADUC.

FIGURE 9.1
Password Replication
Policy

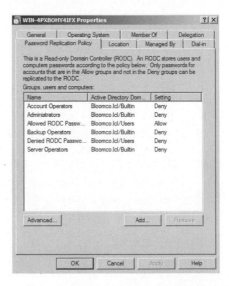

Another advantage of the RODC is the ability to give a non-administrative user at a remote site the ability to administer applications that may be running on the server. Often, the domain controller at a remote site also performs another role, such as that of a print server or an application server. A user would require administrative credentials in order to administer these applications. While this is an easy fix on a member server (make the user a local admin), it is much more difficult on a domain controller. If you give the remote user access to a domain controller, you give access to your AD DS environment as well.

You can give a user administrative rights over an RODC without making the user a member of the Domain Admins group, thus keeping the user from having the ability to manage other domain controllers.

SERVER CORE AS A DOMAIN CONTROLLER

Windows Server Core is new in Windows 2008. It takes up about five times less disk space than a standard Windows Server install. The theory is that with fewer moving parts, there are fewer attack surfaces. Server Core is basically a GUI-less Windows 2008 server.

Server Core can run as a domain controller. You will not, however, be able to simply run `dcpromo` and walk through the screens. You must launch `dcpromo` from a command line with an unattended install file as a command-line option.

Because Server Core does not have a GUI, administration is a little more cumbersome than traditional Windows servers for the admin that is not comfortable using the command line. The tradeoff on this is that because it is harder to administer, it is also harder to manipulate and harder to move around if someone were to gain access to the console.

In Chapters 18 and 19 ("ADSI Primer" and "Active Directory Scripts") we go into great detail on scripting. If you would like to take advantage of Server Core, pay close attention to those chapters. One issue I have with Server Core is that you cannot run PowerShell on it. When you look at the reason why, however, it makes sense and shows you just how much Microsoft has stripped out of this product. PowerShell requires .NET Framework on the server. You cannot install .NET Framework on Server Core. Chances are, you will have at least one non–Server Core domain controller in your environment, and PowerShell works on those servers just fine.

Guarding against Remote-Access Attacks

You can take many steps to prevent remote-access attacks. You can secure and/or delete certain built-in accounts, secure your password information with the Syskey utility, relocate the AD DS database files, and even block ports with Internet Protocol Security (IPSec) so that communication between domain controllers is encrypted. We will look at each one of these settings individually.

DOMAIN CONTROLLER AUDIT-POLICY SETTINGS

Figure 9.2 shows the recommended settings for the audit policy for a domain controller in a Windows 2008 domain functional level domain. There are two conditions you can audit: success or failure. If you configure auditing settings for Success, each time an object successfully completes the monitor action, an event is created. The Failure setting is the opposite; if an object is unsuccessful when attempting to perform an action, a Failure event will be recorded.

FIGURE 9.2
Auditing options for
domain controllers

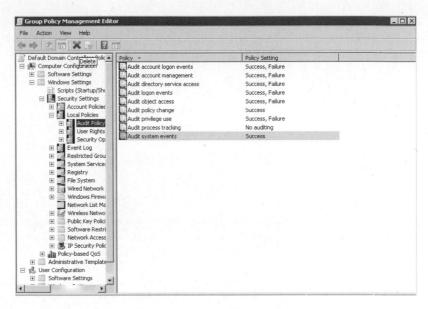

Audit Account Logon Events   This setting should be configured to Success,Failure. An event will be logged each time a user attempts to log on to a domain controller.

Audit Account Management   This setting should be configured to Success,Failure. Events are created when security-principal accounts are created, deleted, or modified. Events are also created if an attempt to create, delete, or modify account management is unsuccessful.

Audit Directory Service Access   This setting should be configured to Success,Failure. When an AD DS object with a system access control list (SACL) is accessed, an event will be generated.

Audit Logon Events   This setting should be configured to Success,Failure. Events are recorded when a user attempts to interactively log on to a domain controller, or authenticates to a domain controller to retrieve a logon script or policy.

Audit Object Access   This setting should be configured to Success,Failure. An event will be created each time an attempt is made to access objects such as files, folders, and registry keys.

Audit Policy Change   This setting should be configured to Success. Changes to user-rights assignment policies, audit policies, or trust policies will generate a policy-change event.

Audit Privilege Use   This setting should be configured to Success,Failure. An event will be created for each instance of a user exercising a user right.

Audit Process Tracking   This should be set to No Auditing.

Audit System Events   This setting should be configured to Success. System events—such as a restart or shutdown of the domain controller—and security events will be recorded in the event log.

CONFIGURING USER-RIGHTS ASSIGNMENTS

By default, user-rights assignments are defined at the domain controllers organizational unit (OU) and are defined by the Default Domain Controllers Policy. Certain items that are required to be in the Default Domain Controllers Policy can be tightened. Editing the default policy is not recommended, however, because you may want to recover the Default Domain Controllers Policy at some point. Restoring it would remove any policy changes that you have made.

You can, however, create a new policy and link it to the domain controller's OU. This policy is known as the Domain Controller Baseline Policy (DCBP), and it takes precedence over the Default Domain Controllers Policy.

Microsoft has included three `.inf` files to be used for the DCBP:

♦ Legacy client domain: `controller.inf`

♦ Enterprise client domain: `controller.inf`

♦ High-security domain: `controller.inf`

When configuring the security for domain controllers, not all settings will have to be enforced on member servers. The setting Network Security: Do Not Store LAN Manager Hash Value on Next Password Change should be enabled on your domain controllers. Member servers will typically have this setting for all three security environments. The DCBP disables this policy for the legacy client, but leaves it enabled for the enterprise client and high-security client. If you have any legacy clients, such as Windows 9x or Windows NT, they would not be able to log on after a password change if this policy setting were enabled.

The following services are also defined in the DCBP. Defining the service startup mode in Group Policy prevents the service from being configured by anyone besides an administrator. It also prevents users, even administrators, from accidentally disabling the service. All of the following services are defined to start automatically in the baseline policy for the legacy client, enterprise client, and high-security client:

♦ Distributed File System Services

♦ DNS Server Service

♦ File Replication Service

♦ Intersite Messaging Service

♦ Kerberos Key Distribution Center Service

♦ Remote Procedure Call (RPC) Locator Service

DOMAIN CONTROLLER SECURITY OPTIONS

Following is a list of the recommended settings for the Domain Controller Security Options Policy. The section of the policy titled Security Options determines behavior with AD DS, network, file system, and user logon security.

Some of the settings are shown in Figure 9.3. Each setting differs depending on whether the forest is in Windows 2000 mixed mode, Windows 2003 native mode, or Windows 2008 native mode. Each setting in the Windows 2008 native mode is a recommended change for Windows 2000 mixed or Windows 2003 native modes.

The security options relevant to securing your domain controllers, along with their recommended settings, are discussed in the following text.

Audit: Audit the Access of Global System Objects   Disable this setting to prevent the creation of default SACL on system objects such as events, semaphores, and MS-DOS devices.

Audit: Audit the Use of Backup and Restore Privilege   Disable this setting to disable auditing for the use of user privileges, including backup and restore operations.

Audit: Shut Down System Immediately If Unable to Log Security Events   Disable this setting so your domain controllers will not shut down if they cannot record an event log.

FIGURE 9.3
Security options for
domain controllers

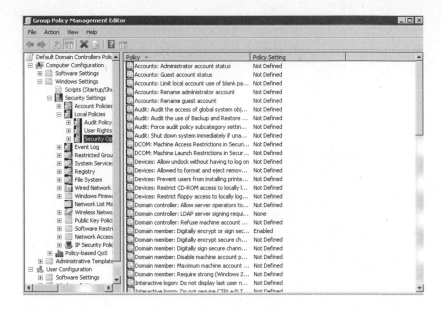

Devices: Allow Undock without Having to Log In   Disable this setting because it is very unlikely your domain controller is a mobile computer.

Devices: Allowed to Format and Eject Removable Media   This setting should be configured for administrative users only. It will allow administrative users to accomplish this task while keeping others from stealing important information.

Devices: Prevent Users from Installing Printer Drivers   This setting should be set to enabled so only users in the Administrators and Server Operators groups can install printer drivers. Malicious users can perform disk-space attacks by submitting large print jobs.

Devices: Restrict CD-ROM Access to Locally Logged-On User Only   This setting will keep the CD-ROM from being accessed over the network. Only interactive sessions can access the CD-ROM.

Devices: Restrict Floppy Access to Locally Logged-On User Only   This setting will keep the floppy drive from being accessed over the network. Only interactive sessions will have access to the floppy drive.

Domain Controller: Allow Server Operators to Schedule Tasks   Set this to Disabled to restrict the number of users who can schedule tasks, because tasks usually run at an elevated level.

Domain Controller: Refuse Machine Account Password Changes   This setting should be changed to Disabled because it is much more secure to have machine accounts change their passwords on a regular basis.

Domain Member: Digitally Encrypt or Sign Secure Channel Data (Always)   Change this setting to Enabled to ensure that all domain controllers are at least Windows NT 4 SP 6a. Make sure that all security fixes have been made.

Domain Member: Disable Machine Account Password Changes   Change this setting to Disabled so machine accounts can regularly change their passwords.

Domain Member: Maximum Machine Account Password Age   Configure this setting for 30 days. A best practice is to have machine accounts reset their passwords on a regular basis.

Domain Member: Require Strong (Windows 2000 or Later) Session Key   This setting should be set to Enabled to eliminate negotiated key strength and to require a 128-bit encrypted secure channel so that the most secure connection is always used.

Interactive Logon: Do Not Display Last User Name   This should be set to Enabled. As I mentioned earlier in the chapter, you shouldn't give away part of the puzzle to a would-be attacker. If this setting is enabled, users will be required to enter both a username and a password to access the domain controller.

Interactive Logon: Do Not Require Ctrl+Alt+Del   This should be set to Disabled to ensure that users have a secure logon.

Interactive Logon: Number of Previous Logons to Cache (in Case Domain Controller Is Not Available)   This should be set to 0 logons, thus preventing the domain controller from caching any previous logons, and requiring authentication at each logon.

Interactive Logon: Prompt User to Change Password Before Expiration   Change this setting to 14 days. This will notify administrators logging into the domain controllers that their passwords are about to expire, and they can come up with another strong password in that time.

Interactive Logon: Require Domain Controller Authentication to Unlock Workstation   Set this to Enabled so changes made to an account are enforced immediately. If cached credentials are used to unlock the console, changes to the account are not enforced.

Interactive Logon: Require Smart Card   If you have a Public Key Infrastructure (PKI) infrastructure in place, you can set this to Enabled to take advantage of this level of security.

Interactive Logon: Smart Card Removal Behavior   Set this to Force Logoff to prevent administrators from walking off and keeping their session open on the server. A domain controller should never be left alone when logged into the network with administrator credentials.

Microsoft Network Client: Send Unencrypted Password to Third-Party SMB Servers   Changing this setting to Disabled prohibits the Server Message Block (SMB) redirector from sending plaintext passwords to servers that do not support password encryption.

Network Access: Do Not Allow Storage of Credentials or .NET Passports for Network Authentication   Change this setting to Enabled. If someone accesses a logged-in session on a domain controller, this can keep that user from accessing any information or websites that may be stored with the administrator's credentials.

Network Access: Restrict Anonymous Access to Named Pipes and Shares   Change this setting to Enabled. Administrators can define which named pipes and shares can be accessed by changing the following settings: Network Access: Named Pipes that Can Be Accessed Anonymously; and Network Access: Shares that Can Be Accessed Anonymously.

Network Security: LDAP Client Signing Requirements   Set this to Require Signing if all of your domain controllers are at Windows 2000 SP3 or higher.

Recovery Console: Allow Automatic Administrative Logon   Change this to Disabled. By doing so, an administrator must submit username and password to gain access to the domain controller.

Recovery Console: Allow Floppy Copy and Access to All Drives and Folders   This should be set to Disabled to prevent unauthorized users from manipulating the Active Directory database and other files on the domain controller.

Shutdown: Allow System to Be Shut Down without Having to Log On Set this to Disabled. Domain controllers should be shut down only by an authenticated administrative user or an authenticated service account.

Shutdown: Clear Virtual Memory Pagefile Change this setting to Enabled to prevent memory data from going into the pagefile on shutdown should a user gain access to the pagefile.

System Objects: Strengthen Default Permissions of Internal System Objects (e.g., Symbolic Links) Change this setting to Enabled to allow users who are not administrators to read shared objects. The users will not be able to modify the shared objects.

System Settings: Optional Subsystems The Posix subsystem is the only subsystem that is enabled by default. If you do not need Posix, you can change this policy and remove Posix so that your list will be empty.

System Settings: Use Certificate Rules on Windows Executables for Software Restrictions Policies If you are using PKI in your environment, you can enable this setting to check certificate-revocation lists to verify the software certificate and the signature.

Protecting Systems during Installation

Most administrators dread the thought of installing the operating system on a new system and will instead take measures to automate the installation. The most popular methods of automating the installation include creating an image, using an automated installation file, or using Microsoft's Windows Deployment Services (WDS). There are pros and cons to each of the installation types, but all of them are far more efficient than installing manually.

USE OPERATING-SYSTEM BEST PRACTICES

A domain controller's base operating system should be as secure as possible so that you do not risk it being susceptible to common attacks. Follow these guidelines to make sure you have your bases covered.

Format the drives with NTFS. The NT File System (NTFS) is the only file system that protects files locally as well as across the network.

Load only TCP/IP. TCP/IP should be the only protocol loaded onto the domain controller. You should not have any applications that require any other protocols to be loaded on the domain controllers, and your clients should use only TCP/IP when connecting using the domain controller's services. Additional protocols invite additional methods of access and potentially additional attack approaches.

Apply service packs and security rollups. Apply current service packs and security rollups before you promote a domain controller. This adds an additional level of security by closing up the known security holes before the operating system is in production.

Secure DNS. Make sure DNS is already configured and set up securely before promoting your domain controller. We will discuss DNS security later in the chapter.

Do not install IIS. Domain controllers do not require Internet Information Server (IIS) to function. Windows Server 2003 and 2008 do not install this service by default as part of the operating system as Windows 2000 did. If you are installing Windows 2003 or 2008, make sure IIS is not installed before promoting a server to a domain controller.

SECURE INSTALLATION LOCATION

As you build domain controllers, make sure you are working in a secure location where the automated installation files and media can be protected. Unattended installation files and automated promotion files used in dcpromo can include passwords for the administrator account used to promote the domain controller, or sensitive information about the system.

If you are using the advanced version of DCPromo, you should make sure that you destroy the media that includes the system state of the original domain controller after you finish promoting the domain controller. The system state is valid only for the tombstone lifetime, and DCPromo will not use a system state that is out of date.

DISABLE 8.3 AUTO NAME GENERATION

Typically, when a file is created with a long filename, the system will automatically generate an associated 8.3 version of the filename so that the file can be used by 16-bit programs. Several viruses have been written as 16-bit applications that take advantage of the 8.3 version of the filename. Because domain controllers do not typically have additional programs running on them, you can safely turn off the auto name generation by editing the registry and changing the value of HKEY_LOCAL_MACHINE\ SYSTEM\CurrentControlSet\Control\FileSystem\NtfsDisable8dot3NameCreation to a decimal 1.

Securing Well-Known User Accounts

When malicious users attempt remote access to a server, they often use a brute-force password attack. The first accounts they attempt to use are the built-in Administrator and Guest accounts. These accounts cannot be deleted, but they can be renamed. If these accounts are not renamed, you have done 50 percent of the work for the would-be hackers; they will only need to determine the password for these accounts.

The built-in account Guest is disabled by default. Make sure this account is still disabled, and I strongly recommend that you do not enable it for any reason.

The built-in Administrator account should be changed immediately upon configuration of the server. In addition to renaming the account, you should modify the description of the account. You can easily rename the Administrator account to jsomebody, but if you leave the description field as "Built-in account to administer the domain," anyone who has viewing rights to Active Directory Users and Computers (ADUC) will be able to see which account is the Administrator account.

An added step in securing your Administrator accounts is to create a new account that has all of the same rights, and then disable the built-in Administrator account. Many programs available on the Internet will scan for an administrator's SID on the system. As you learned in an earlier chapter, you can rename the account, but the SID will always stay the same. The built-in Administrator SID always ends in 500, and these programs will find those SIDs.

SECURING SERVICE ACCOUNTS

Domain account passwords are stored in the Local Security Authority (LSA) secrets. If a domain controller is physically compromised, these LSA secrets can be dumped and all domain account passwords can be obtained easily. This is the number-one reason that services should never bet set to run under the security context of a domain account.

USING THE SYSKEY UTILITY TO SECURE PASSWORD INFORMATION

All domain passwords are stored in the AD DS database. As you read previously, these passwords can be obtained easily if the domain controller is physically compromised. You can encrypt the passwords on a system by using a utility called Syskey. The system key is used to encrypt the password data in the database on the domain controller. Syskey can operate at three different levels:

Level 1 is enabled on all Windows 2003 and 2008 servers by default. A system key is randomly generated, and an encrypted key is stored locally on that server.

Level 2 operates in the same manner as Level 1, but the administrator selects an additional password to enter into the system when the computer is starting up. Unlike Level 1, this password is not stored locally.

Level 3 requires much more administrator interaction. The computer randomly generates a key and stores it on a floppy disk. The computer will not start unless the administrator has the floppy disk to put into the system during bootup.

Level 2 and Level 3 are suggested for areas where the domain controller is subject to physical attack (for example, in an unlocked room). Keep in mind that with Level 2 or Level 3, administrator interaction onsite is required for the server to boot properly. Losing the floppy disk or forgetting the password will render a domain controller useless. There is no way to recover the domain controller; it will have to be rebuilt.

You can run Syskey from a command prompt or from the Run dialog box. Simply type **Syskey** and click OK. Select Encryption Enabled, and then click Update. Click on the desired option, and then click OK.

Defining Domain Controller Communication with IPSec Filters

Defining the IPSec filters is an added level of security that is recommended only for very high-security environments. Microsoft recommends that you create the IPSec filters found in table 9.1 on all domain controllers in high-security environments.

TABLE 9.1:   High-Security IPSec Filters for Domain Controllers

SERVICE	PROTOCOL	SOURCE PORT	DESTINA- TION PORT	SOURCE ADDRESS	DESTINA- TION ADDRESS	ACTION	MIRROR
CIFS/SMB server	TCP	Any	445	Any	DC	Allow	Yes
	UDP	Any	445	Any	DC	Allow	Yes
RPC server	TCP	Any	135	Any	DC	Allow	Yes
	UDP	Any	135	Any	DC	Allow	Yes
NetBIOS server	TCP	Any	137	Any	DC	Allow	Yes
	UDP	Any	137	Any	DC	Allow	Yes

TABLE 9.1: High-Security IPSec Filters for Domain Controllers *(CONTINUED)*

Service	Protocol	Source Port	Destination Port	Source Address	Destination Address	Action	Mirror
	UDP	Any	138	Any	DC	Allow	Yes
	TCP	Any	139	Any	DC	Allow	Yes
Monitoring client	Any	Any	Any	DC	MOM server	Allow	Yes
Terminal Services server	TCP	Any	3389	Any	DC	Allow	Yes
Global catalog server	TCP	Any	3268	Any	DC	Allow	Yes
	TCP	Any	3269	Any	DC	Allow	Yes
DNS server	TCP	Any	53	Any	DC	Allow	Yes
	UDP	Any	53	Any	DC	Allow	Yes
Kerberos server	TCP	Any	88	Any	DC	Allow	Yes
	UDP Any 88	Any	DC	Allow	Yes		
LDAP server	TCP	Any	389	Any	DC	Allow	Yes
	UDP	Any	389	Any	DC	Allow	Yes
	TCP	Any	636	Any	DC	Allow	Yes
	UDP	Any	636	Any	DC	Allow	Yes
NTP server	TCP	Any	123	Any	DC	Allow	Yes
	UDP	Any	123	Any	DC	Allow	Yes
Predefined RPC Range	TCP	Any	57901-57950	Any	DC	Allow	Yes
Domain Controller Communication	Any	Any	Any	DC	DC	Allow	Yes

TABLE 9.1:   High-Security IPSec Filters for Domain Controllers *(CONTINUED)*

SERVICE	PROTOCOL	SOURCE PORT	DESTINA-TION PORT	SOURCE ADDRESS	DESTINA-TION ADDRESS	ACTION	MIRROR
ICMP	ICMP	Any	Any	DC	Any	Allow	Yes
All inbound traffic	Any	Any	Any	Any	DC	Block	Yes

Modifying the Default Services

Most domain controllers will not need to have all the default services enabled. These services do not provide any additional functionality on most domain controllers, and they become an additional attack point. Consider disabling unused services or, at the very least, configuring them to start manually in case another service depends on that service. Keep in mind, however, that your domain controller may need some of the items presented in Table 9.2; every environment is different. The DNS server service is a perfect example. Table 9.2 recommends setting the service to Disabled or Manual, but some domain controllers may also be DNS servers, and in that case you would definitely want to skip that option. The bottom line is, as you look through the list, plan carefully and assess every domain controller in your environment to ensure the changes you may make will not adversely affect the environment.

Table 9.2 shows the services you should consider disabling or setting to start manually.

TABLE 9.2:   Potentially Unnecessary Services

SERVICE	2000 SETTING	2003 SETTING	2008 SETTING	RECOMMENDED SETTING
Application Management	Manual	Manual	Manual	Consider setting to Disabled or Manual
Automatic Updates	Automatic	Automatic	Automatic	Consider setting to Disabled or Manual
Background Intelligent Transfer Service	Manual	Manual	Automatic	Consider setting to Disabled or Manual
Computer browser	Automatic	Automatic	Disabled	Consider setting to Disabled or Manual
DHCP client	Automatic	Automatic	Automatic	Consider setting to Disabled or Manual
Distributed Link Tracking Client	Automatic	Manual	Manual	Disabled

TABLE 9.2:   Potentially Unnecessary Services *(CONTINUED)*

SERVICE	2000 SETTING	2003 SETTING	2008 SETTING	RECOMMENDED SETTING
Distributed Link Tracking Server	Automatic	Disabled	N/A	Disabled
DNS server	Automatic	Automatic	Automatic	Consider setting to Disabled or Manual
Error Reporting Service	Automatic	Automatic	N/A	Consider setting to Disabled or Manual
Fax	Automatic	Automatic	N/A	Consider setting to Disabled or Manual
IIS Admin Service	Automatic	Automatic	N/A	Consider setting to Disabled or Manual
Indexing Service	Manual	Disabled	N/A	Consider setting to Disabled or Manual
Internet Connection Sharing	Manual	Disabled	Disabled	Consider setting to Disabled or Manual
License Logging	Automatic	Disabled	N/A	Disabled
Microsoft Software Shadow Copy Provider	Manual	Manual	Manual	Consider setting to Disabled
NetMeeting Remote Desktop Sharing	Manual	Disabled	N/A	Disabled
Performance Logs and Alerts	Manual	Manual	Manual	Consider setting to Disabled
Print Spooler	Automatic	Automatic	Automatic	Consider setting to Disabled or Manual
Remote Access Auto Connection Manager	Manual	Manual	Manual	Consider setting to Disabled
Remote Access Connection Manager	Manual	Manual	Manual	Consider setting to Disabled
Remote Procedure Call (RPC) Locator	Manual	Manual	Manual	Consider setting to Disabled
Removable Storage	Automatic	Manual	N/A	Consider setting to Disabled or Manual

TABLE 9.2: Potentially Unnecessary Services *(CONTINUED)*

SERVICE	2000 SETTING	2003 SETTING	2008 SETTING	RECOMMENDED SETTING
Shell Hardware Detection	Automatic	Automatic	Automatic	Disabled
Special Administrator Console Helper	Manual	Manual	Manual	Disabled
Telephony	Manual	Manual	Manual	Consider setting to Disabled
Telnet	Manual	Disabled	N/A	Consider setting to Disabled or Manual
Terminal Services	Manual	Manual	Automatic	Consider setting to Disabled or Manual
Uninterruptible Power Supply	Manual	Manual	N/A	Consider setting to Disabled
Upload Manager	Manual	Manual	N/A	Disabled
Utility Manager	Manual	Manual	N/A	Disabled
Volume Shadow Copy	Manual	Manual	Manual	Consider setting to Disabled
Windows Audio	Automatic	Automatic	Manual	Disabled
Wireless Configuration	Automatic	Automatic	N/A	Consider setting to Disabled or Manual

Securing AD DS

Securing the operating system and physically securing your domain controllers, as we've discussed in the preceding sections, are good first steps in the security process; however, there are still some steps you should take with the AD DS database itself to make sure all your bases are covered.

Throughout this section, we will present some of the options you have to maintain the integrity of your AD DS infrastructure. Many of the tools you have to work with were covered in previous chapters of this book.

Placement of the Active Directory Database File

The Active Directory database contains information about directory data, user logon processes, authentication, and directory searches. This information is stored in three files: `ntds.dit`, `edb*.log`, and `temp.edb`. I strongly recommend moving these files from their default location when you promote the domain controller. You should also consider moving these files on existing domain controllers if the files still reside in their default location. A malicious user will be very aware of where these files are located and will search that location first when looking for the files. Also, because the default location is the system partition of the domain controller, an attacker will have access to your directory-service database if an attack successfully accesses the system drive.

You should also resize the active directory event-log files. By default, the directory-service and file-replication event log files are set to a maximum size of 512 KB. For proper auditing, the maximum size of these log files should be increased to a Microsoft-recommended 16 MB.

 Real World Scenario

GUARANTEEING DATABASE SPACE

Two reserve log files are used in case the partition that holds the log files fills to capacity. These reserve log files are 10 MB each and will move along with the Active Directory log files when you move them. You should not rely on these log files to be adequate if there is an attack on your system. 10 MB is not going to be enough space in case of an emergency or if you come under a denial-of-service (DoS) attack.

Consider creating a dummy file that will take up space on the partition where you have placed your directory database files. Create this reserve file so it takes up at least 250 MB of the partition. On large partitions you can create the reserve file to be at least 1 percent of the partition size, but the minimum size should not be smaller than 250 MB.

Creating reserve files becomes a good practice by guaranteeing that an attack on the database partition, or poor planning by the administrator, does not allow the database partition to become too full to recover efficiently.

To create the reserve file, you need to log on to a Windows XP, Vista, Server 2003, or Server 2008 system with an account that has Domain Administrator rights. Connect to the partition on the domain controller on which you want to create the reserve file. For instance, if you placed the directory database on the E: partition on the domain controller `rosebud.zygort.lcl`, you would open a command prompt and type `net use x: \\rosebud.zygort.lcl\e$`.

Once you have mapped the drive, you can open a command prompt, change to the mapped drive, and issue the command `fsutil file createnew ReserveFileName ReserveFileSize`. The Reserve-FileSize must be entered in bytes. If you want to reserve 250MB on your partition and name the file `ReserveFile`, enter the command `fsutil file createnew ReserveFile 256000`.

After you create the file, make sure you set the permission on the file so any administrative user who is responsible for the domain controller has the ability to remove the file if they need the additional room on the partition.

Maintaining the Service Account Administrators

Another step you can take to help protect your AD DS infrastructure is to ensure that you are protecting your Service Account Admin accounts by controlling membership in the Enterprise Admins, Domain Admins, and Administrators groups. These groups have a high level of authority within the forest/domain and should be monitored closely. Remember that any account that is a member of the Domain Admins group from the forest root will be able to add themselves into the Enterprise Admins and Schema Admins groups. For this reason alone, many companies have implemented empty forest root domains so they do not have to worry about these forestwide administrative accounts.

Turn on auditing for account management so you can track when changes to group membership occur. To do this, modify an audit policy within the domain or OU where you want to monitor the group. Using the Group Policy Object Editor, open the Audit Policy container and check the Success and Failure boxes of Audit Account Management Policy, as shown in Figure 9.4.

To monitor the changes, open the security log within Event Viewer and look for event ID 641, which denotes a change in a security group. You can then search for event ID 632, which is reported when a user is added to a security group, or 633, which is reported when a user is removed from a security group.

FIGURE 9.4
Audit account
management

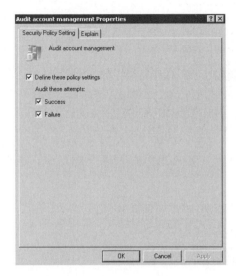

Creating a Baseline

Just as when you are preparing for performance monitoring, you should create an Active Directory baseline that includes all of the settings you have made during the configuration of your domain controller. You should document all your settings so that you can pull out the documentation whenever you want to review the settings.

Make sure you double-check the auditing settings as well as all directory service permissions and service-account administrator-group memberships. Documenting these items will give you a starting point when you are trying to determine what has changed within your environment.

Updating the documentation after you make a change to the system is just as important as creating a baseline for your systems. If you don't update the documentation, you might think a change is a problem instead of part of the solution.

Using Secure Administrative Methods

You can take measures to enhance the security of your systems. Some of these tips employ tools that are built into the operating system; others are practices you should consider implementing to keep special functions locked away from attackers or rogue administrators.

SECONDARY LOGON

All of your domain controllers are important systems, as are the member servers you have in your Active Directory environment. To perform some of the administrative tasks on these servers, you must log in to an account that has special rights and permissions. Many administrative users find it convenient to add their account to groups that have administrative privileges so they can perform these tasks very quickly. Doing so, however, could introduce problems within your network. If you are logged on with an administrative account and a virus finds its way past your defenses, it could attack your systems with administrative-level privileges. For this reason, Windows 2000 and higher servers and Windows XP and higher workstations allow the use of a secondary logon.

Whenever you log on to your workstation, you should authenticate as a standard user account that does not have special system privileges. You can then use the `runas` command to launch your administrative tools. This allows you to authenticate as another account for the purpose of using that utility, but the operating system will still use the typical user account for all other applications.

With Windows Server 2003 and 2008, you can use a smart card with the `runas` command. The secondary logon protects the operating system from attacks, and the administrative functions can be limited to users who use smart cards to authenticate. Just make sure you have not disabled the secondary-logon services when you were trying to harden your servers.

TWO-PERSON AUTHENTICATION

This practice is used by high-security installations when they want to make sure it takes two people to perform a specific task. You have probably seen movies in which it takes two people, each with her or his own key, to open a safety deposit box, or two people to activate a missile that is going to rain destruction on an enemy.

The same theory applies here. You could use an account to change the schema for your organization, and you can associate that account with a smart card. Don't give the card holder the PIN used to authenticate. Give the PIN for the smart card to another administrator, but don't give that person the smart card. Under this scenario, both users are required to authenticate the account so that the schema can be modified.

You do not have to limit this type of two-person authentication to schema changes; you can use it whenever you want to restrict enterprise-level administrative management. Do consider, however, what steps to take if one of the users is not available when a change needs to be made.

Coming Up Next

After looking at the ways to secure your Active Directory infrastructure, we are going to take a step forward and discuss the options that are available to you for managing access to Active Directory resources. There are different authentication mechanisms in place to help secure your Active Directory infrastructure, but you will need to know which methods to use depending on how users connect to your environment.

The Bottom Line

In this chapter we discussed Active Directory security, from the basics of AD security to securing AD objects to new tools introduced in Windows Server 2008 that can aid in your security plans.

The Basics of Active Directory security   Understanding the key terms and security processes is key to planning security in your environment.

Master It   Define the five following terms and give examples of how they all work together:

◆ Security principals

◆ Access control lists

◆ Access tokens

◆ Authentication

◆ Authorization

How to Secure AD DS objects There are many tools you can use to help secure your AD DS objects. Threats can come at you from internal or external users, and you must be prepared for any threat.

Master It List steps you can take to protect your AD DS objects from accidental harm and malicious users, including steps you can take to track down what happened and who could have done the damage.

Part 3

Active Directory Service Management

In this part:

Chapter 10

Managing Access with Active Directory Services

Creating an Active Directory–based infrastructure is a good first step in controlling user access to resources within your organization. Having Active Directory in place, however, doesn't mean that gaining access to those resources will be easy for all of your users. Once you have planned out how you are going to implement Active Directory for your organization's users, you may need to enable other user accounts to access your resources.

A good case in point is when you are working with another organization, as a business partner or possibly in a manufacturer-supplier relationship. In both cases, the Active Directory environment may be composed of two or more Active Directory forests. Active Directory forests are the security boundary for the entire Active Directory infrastructure. Prior to Windows Server 2003, if you wanted to allow resource access to accounts that resided within another Active Directory forest, you had to create an explicit trust relationship, known as an *external trust*, between the domains where the account and the resources resided. Windows Server 2003 changed the rules by including a forest-trust relationship, thereby granting resource access to accounts within any domain of the neighboring forest. With the release of Windows Server 2003 R2, a new feature known as Active Directory Federation Services (AD FS) is available to grant an application-level trust. Using AD FS, you can specify which applications users have available to them when they access your forest, and you can enable a single sign-on (SSO) environment for them. Windows Server 2008 includes AD FS and enhances the management tools to make it easier to implement.

In this chapter we look at the new features that are included with Windows Server 2008. First, we are going to present AD FS, which has piqued several administrators' curiosity because it allows you to control access to resources on a user-by-user basis if desired, but also allows control based on criteria such as group membership. Following AD FS, we will delve into Active Directory Lightweight Directory Services (AD LDS) and see how you can use an LDAP-based directory service for applications and to enhance Active Directory Domain Services (AD DS).

In this chapter you will learn how to:

◆ Install and manage Active Directory Federation Services

◆ Install and manage Active Directory Lightweight Directory Services

◆ Use DSDBUtil to manage Active Directory Lightweight Directory Services

Active Directory Federation Services

As just mentioned, there are traditional methods of allowing access to resources between forests. Servers based on Windows 2000 and later will let you create a trust relationship, known as an external trust, with domains that are outside your Active Directory forest. These domains can be in another

Active Directory forest, a Windows NT 4.0 domain, or a Unix Kerberos realm. The drawback to using an external trust is that the trust relationship is restricted to the two domains that are linked with the trust. The nontransitive nature of the external trust makes it difficult when trying to grant resource access to a user account that resides in a domain in one forest but the resources reside in several domains in another forest. When that is the case, you need to create an external trust relationship between every domain where the resources reside and the domain where the account resides.

Windows Server 2003 made things a little easier by providing a forest trust. The forest trust creates a transitive trust between two forests, allowing any account in any domain in one forest to have resource access to any domain in the other forest. Having only one trust relationship to manage made it much easier for administrators to allow two Active Directory forests to interoperate. Once the forest trust is created, the enterprise administrators for each forest can control how access is granted within their forests. They have the option to allow all users to authenticate to all of the servers within their forest, or they can limit the authentication to specific servers, thus controlling object access to a finer degree. (For more information about external and forest trust relationships, see Chapter 3, "Active Directory Domain Services Forest and Domain Design.")

Although these options allow administrators to have control over their resources while allowing another organization to control their user accounts, there are some drawbacks to using trust relationships between forests. First, a trust relationship assumes that the two Active Directory infrastructures are going to interoperate. Usually when a trust relationship is created, the two divisions of an organization, or the two organizations that are involved, will have a distinct business need for the two directory services to be linked. If we're talking about two divisions within the same organization, they usually need to have separation of administrative control and maintain a security boundary between the two directory services. If the trust relationship interconnects two separate organizations, it is usually because of a business merger or acquisition, although trusts between business partners are not uncommon.

Maintaining trust relationships between two organizations can be troublesome. When the trust relationships are created, the proper communication channels have to be created to allow both organizations to pass the appropriate directory-service information so users can gain access to the resources they need to perform their duties. Some organizations have very specific rules about the type of traffic they will allow outside their organization, and are leery of allowing sensitive directory-service information to be accessible outside their own network infrastructure.

As companies start partnering with other organizations to form business relationships, one of the greatest concerns is the security and reliability of their data. They need to make sure that they are allowing access to the right data so that their business partners can do their jobs, while making sure that they restrict access to the sensitive data to which the business partners should not have access. Although trust relationships have made progress in allowing access to resources, many organizations do not allow the trust relationships because of organizational standards or limitations in technology, or they would rather create an application-level trust that allows access to specific applications and application features.

Usually an organization's development staff creates application-level trusts so they can allow external users to access applications and view, and possibly even manipulate, data. A typical example of this is a company that creates a web-based frontend to a database. They make the interface available on their web servers, but to gain access to it, the external users have to authenticate. Once authenticated, the external user can access the data, and the organization has control over what data is viewed. Controlling the user accounts then becomes tricky for the administrator. If the administrator is responsible for maintaining the accounts, the administrator has to remain in constant contact with the business partners to make sure the user accounts are still valid. Otherwise, if an external user leaves the business partner's organization, she or he may still have access to data

external trusts (restricted to the *domains linked to twty*)
forest trust is transitive ⟹ any action
any domain in one forest to have resource access to any domain in the other forest.

ACTIVE DIRECTORY FEDERATION SERVICES | **269**

within the administrator's organization. The external users are also inconvenienced. When they gain access to the data that they need from the business partner, they are more than likely going to have to maintain another user account that will probably have a different password and possibly a different naming convention from their internal user account. The two companies could agree on a method of controlling user access, such as certificate mapping, which allows a user to be authenticated based on the user certificate associated with the user's account. The only drawback to this method of authentication is that it becomes difficult to control which users have access to which set of data.

Microsoft and IBM, along with other organizations, have been developing another method of access control between organizations. Known as the Web Services (WS-*) architecture, its goal is to allow the secure exchange of data between organizations while maintaining a simple method of data access for users. Ideally, the users should be able to access data from the partner organization using their existing Windows-based account, and the administrators should be able to map the accounts to the level of application access that the users need. Specifically, AD FS falls under the WS-Federation (WS-F) subheading beneath the WS-* specifications.

Once the AD FS trust is created, the administrator of the data will not have to be as concerned about the user accounts, because when a user leaves the partner organization, his or her account should be disabled or removed by the administrators at the partner organization. Users should be able to access the resources or applications from the partner organization using their existing accounts without having to provide authentication credentials.

How AD FS Works

AD FS creates trust relationships between entities through a web-based interface. Let's say we have two companies, Zygort and BloomCo. When the two companies work out a business relationship, the Information Technology group from each will determine the resources that must be made available to the other company. Using AD FS and other web technologies, each company could create a web interface for the users to access; based on users' account attributes, they will have access to just the data they need to work. All of this can be provided by using an SSO solution so the users will not have to authenticate again once they have accessed the partner's website.

Once the web applications are built, you can use AD FS to provide access to the applications and control the sign-on capabilities. Both organizations have to support AD FS to make this work seamlessly, but once it is implemented, the level of administrative support is greatly reduced because you will no longer have to control access on a user-by-user basis. Future partnerships are also easier to establish once an AD FS solution is implemented, because you can add the new partnership rules into AD FS instead of building an entirely new solution for the new business partner.

For a high-level overview of AD FS, let's consider the two companies from our earlier example. Zygort is a manufacturing company, and BloomCo provides preassembled parts for Zygort's products. BloomCo needs to be able to view the production schedule that Zygort has planned, as well as the specifications of the parts that they need to provide. All of this data is contained within the Zygort internal network utilizing several servers and databases. Zygort, on the other hand, wants to view the current inventory levels and the production schedules that BloomCo has planned.

Once the business arrangement was finalized, the two companies set about deciding the best method of sharing information. Traditionally, a trust relationship or a custom application would be created to allow the two companies to interact. If a forest-level trust is created between the two organizations, the trust and a method of communication need to be maintained. Usually some type of virtual private network (VPN) connection is created between the two organizations so they can share their information.

But what if one of the companies is not using Active Directory within its environment? Or what if there are company standards in place that will not allow the appropriate firewall ports to be open

Web Services (WS*)
AOFS (WS-F)

to maintain the trust relationship? And if those ports are not open, what are you going to do if one of the companies has a policy in place that will not allow the clients from another organization to access their internal network? The solution might be to create an application that is run through a web page. The web server to which the user connects can reside within the company's perimeter network, safely seated behind an external firewall yet sitting on the outside of the company's internal network; the perimeter network and the internal network are also separated by a firewall.

The firewall that sits between the internal network and the perimeter network will have rules in place that allow the web server to access data within the internal network. The firewall that sits between the web server and the external clients will allow just the standard web ports. Applications can then be written that will allow an external client to have access to the necessary data, but to nothing else. So when users from BloomCo connect to the Zygort website, they are presented with an authentication dialog box. The users authenticate and are then presented with the applications necessary to view the production schedule and schematics for the parts they are producing.

So what is wrong with that scenario? Granted, it does get the job done. The user from BloomCo can get the data necessary for BloomCo's production needs. But what if a user leaves BloomCo? A Zygort administrator is responsible for removing or disabling the user's account. If the Zygort administrator is not notified of the employee departure, the account could remain active—a security breach. Also, the users from each company will need to remember not only the username and password they use for their own company's resources, but also another username and password to gain access to the business partner's resources. With AD FS, the administrators of each company maintain their employees' accounts that are used to gain access to the resources in either forest. Thus, when a user leaves BloomCo, the administrator of the BloomCo accounts either disables or deletes the user's account. Using a method of mapping accounts between forests, the user's account does not have to be duplicated in each forest, and the user does not need to know a different user account and password when accessing the resources from the other forest.

When you start thinking about deploying AD FS, you must identify which organization needs to access web resources from its partner. Once you have determined the user accounts that will need to access those resources, from one organization or possibly both, you can start making choices about how you need to create the federation trust. The organization responsible for maintaining the web resources is known as the *resource partner*. The organization that hosts the user accounts that need to use those resources is known as the *account partner*.

In comparison, if you create a trust within Active Directory, you need to make the same design decisions. If you create an external trust or a forest trust, you need to decide where the user accounts are located in relation to the resources they need to access. You can build the trust relationship such that users in only one forest have access to resources in another, or you could allow users from both forests to access resources in both. The trust relationship, once created, controls access to the resources based on the trust settings. (For more information on Active Directory external and forest trusts, see Chapter 3.)

AD FS trust relationships are not Active Directory constructs, however. Whereas Active Directory trust relationships are hard-coded, based on the trust properties, AD FS trusts can be modified quickly. Essentially, you are designing rules and settings that control how the company's websites and the applications within those websites are accessed.

AD FS Components

To get all this working, you need to be using an Active Directory or WS-F infrastructure in both organizations, and your servers taking on the federation server roles must be Windows Server 2003 R2– or Windows Server 2008–based. Because any Active Directory environment can be used, even

Windows 2000, you do not have to upgrade your existing infrastructure to take advantage of AD FS. You do, however, need to decide how you are going to implement your AD FS solution. Because there are different uses for AD FS, you need to make sure you have the appropriate services installed so that your solution will work yet also meet your security requirements. Let's look at the services that are part of an AD FS solution.

FEDERATION SERVICE

The Federation Service, the primary component of AD FS, is responsible for retrieving account information from an account store and building access tokens based on the rules created for the federated trust. In a typical solution, each entity within the federated trust, which we will refer to as the business partners, will create a Federation Service system. When a Federation Service is responsible for contacting the user store, in this case Active Directory, it is known as the *account-side* Federation Service, or FS-A. A Federation Service responsible for building the access token used to grant access to a resource is known as the *resource-side* Federation Service, or FS-R. The FS-A is responsible for accessing the user's account from the account store and determining what claims are to be used within the token that is passed to the FS-R.

Claims

Claims are assertions used to determine a user's level of access to an application. A claim can be as simple as a user's account name or as complex as the groups of which the user is a member, and Active Directory attributes you can populate for the account. For instance, Jim's user account is named jimc and the user principle name (UPN) for the account is `jimc@bloomco.lcl`. When Jim logs on using his UPN and then accesses Zygort's partner web page, his UPN is the claim that is used to identify him. Jim's level of access to the applications available from the web page depends on the access that has been granted to his UPN. Zygort's administrative staff can also specify that the applications be available based on the user's group membership. Someone within the HR Administrators group can be granted access to more functionality than can users who are members of the HR Users group.

Claims have to be agreed on before either partner can configure its trust policies for claims. A map of outgoing claims from the account partner has to be configured for the incoming claims at the resource partner. Once the claims have been mapped between partners, they can be entered into the trust policy so the users can be granted the appropriate level of access to the web applications. Claims come in three flavors: identity claims, group claims, and custom claims.

Identity claims The identity claim type allows you to identify an account based on information that should uniquely identify the user account. The information used within the claim can take the following forms:

UPN Each user account within an Active Directory forest will have a UPN assigned to it. The UPN uniquely identifies the user within the forest, regardless of the domain in which the user's account is created.

E-mail Email addresses are assumed to be unique. When you assign an email address to a user account, the address should be unique on the Internet as well as unique to the account and resource partners.

Common name Common name is not usually seen as a unique name type. Several objects could contain the same common-name data. When using the Common Name option, make sure you are also identifying the accounts by another means.

Group claims Group claims are seen as a means of identifying a user's group membership. However, the groups that are used on each side of the AD FS trust do not have to be identical. You can create rules that allow you to define which groups are analogous to one another on each side of the trust.

Custom claims Custom claims allow you to make account assertions that do not fit into the other two claim types. You can use a custom claim to expose attributes from the account side of the trust to the resource side, or to extract attribute information from an account, such as department, manager, and description, and then pass that data to the resource side.

Tokens

Claims are included within a token that is passed to the resource side of the trust relationship and is used to grant access to the applications. Tokens are encrypted so their contents cannot be viewed when intercepted, and are signed so that their authenticity can be proved. If they are intercepted and manipulated before arriving at the resource side, the FS-R will invalidate them. When the token is received on the resource side, the FS-R reviews the claims and then passes the token to the Federation Web Component, the website used with AD FS, which in turn creates the view that is appropriate to the user from the account side.

FEDERATION SERVER PROXY

The Federation Service Proxy (FSP) is used as an intermediary pass-through system so you do not have to place your Federation Service system within the company's perimeter network. As with the Federation Service, there are account- and resource-side FSPs, known as the FSP-A and FSP-R, respectively. Unlike the FS-A and FS-R, however, the FSP is an optional service. A system configured as a Federation Service can perform its own account and resource duties without the FSP; if, however, you want to have another level of security, place the FSP in the company's perimeter network where it can intercept AD FS requests and pass them to the appropriate FS-A or FS-R.

SSO AGENT

The single sign-on (SSO) agent is an Internet Server application program interface (ISAPI) extension you can install and enable on an Internet Information Services (IIS) web server. This agent is responsible for accepting access tokens and managing the authentication cookies. The SSO agent on the account side of the trust is responsible for building and delivering cookies to the user accounts so they can access all web resources on the resource side without having to authenticate again. On the resource side, the SSO agent is responsible for building and delivering cookies to the user account so the user account does not have to return to the FS-A every time it accesses an AD FS–enabled site.

ACTIVE DIRECTORY ACCOUNT STORE

Within a Windows Server 2003 or 2008 environment, Active Directory or Active Directory Lightweight Directory Services (AD LDS) can be used as the account store. When a user attempts to access an application on the resource side, the Federation Service extracts the user's account information from Active Directory. The Federation Service then compiles the user's account information into a token, which includes only the user-account attributes that have been converted to claims.

Federated Web Single Sign-On

In our ongoing saga, the decision has been made to allow users from BloomCo access to resources within your domain (Zygort). However, you do not want to set up a VPN connection because the BloomCo users do not need to have access to very much of your data. Instead, you have decided to

Ofederation pervr
IS
asp.net
com+
microsoft
.NET framework 2.0

allow them to access your website and use web applications. These applications will be configured to give the BloomCo users access to the data that they need to manufacture the subcomponents.

Once the decision is made to create the website for BloomCo users, you determine that applications should be created that will give users access to the production schedule and the schematics for the subcomponents they will be manufacturing. Because the two web applications are going to be used by different groups of users at BloomCo, you determine that you will need to have different access permissions so the users will be able to view only the information that they need.

Prepare Your Infrastructure

The first step is to make sure that your current infrastructure meets the requirements for AD FS. At this point you are concerned only with your infrastructure and not with the partner's infrastructure. Because AD FS can interoperate with other WS-F–compliant systems, your partner's organization could be running another operating system entirely. You need to make sure that your organization has Active Directory deployed before you can take advantage of AD FS. Other services will also be needed:

Active Directory   Active Directory or Active Directory Lightweight Directory Services can be used as your account store. Because either of these account stores holds user-account authentication mechanisms, they provide the federation server with authentication information that can be used as claims to populate the tokens sent to the resource partner.

DNS   Any time you are using web-based applications, you must have a mechanism in place that allows you to find the servers that host those applications. AD FS is no different; it relies on DNS for name resolution to find the web servers that are used in the federation trust.

Certificate services   For your AD FS solution to function, you need to obtain certificates that allow you to secure your website and the AD FS tokens that you will be passing to your partner's organization. On the resource side, you will secure your website so that all access to the website uses Secure Sockets Layer (SSL). This will guarantee that the data passing from your site to the users on the account side are secure. On the account side, tokens will be generated to include the claims that will be used to authenticate the user to resources. These tokens need to be signed so that the resource partner can validate the authenticity of the tokens.

Federation Server Prerequisites

Before you install the federation server, make sure you have all of the required services and software installed on your Windows Server 2008 system. IIS 7.0 is required for the federation server; for this reason alone, it is recommended that the federation server not reside on a domain controller. Domain controllers should have as few services as possible running on them so they do not have a very large attack footprint for hackers.

IIS   IIS needs to be installed with some of the most common options for a web server, but you also need to add in a few options you may not enable on any of your web servers. To install IIS, open Add/Remove Programs and click the Add/Remove Windows Components icon. In the Add/Remove Windows Components dialog box, select Application Server and click the Details button. This brings up the options for the application-server services, of which IIS is a part. Select the IIS check box along with the ASP.NET and COM+ check boxes.

Microsoft .NET Framework 2.0   The .NET Framework 2.0 can be selected from the Add/Remove Windows Components dialog box at the same time you add IIS. You can also install either one separately; no matter which approach you choose, however, both need to be installed before you install the federation server.

Certificates   During the installation of the federation server, you will be required to provide token-signing certificates for the federation to use when it generates a token to be passed to the partner's forest. These token-signing certificates are used to validate the security tokens that contain the claims used for authentication in the remote forest. For testing purposes, you can use certificates generated by programs such as SelfSSL (which comes with the IIS 6.0 Resource Kit) or other third-party programs. These types of certificates should not be used in production, however; you should implement some type of public key infrastructure (PKI). (For more information on how to create certificates for use in web-page SSL and token signing, see the Microsoft website: www.microsoft.com/windowsserver2003/technologies/pki/default.mspx.)

COMMON FEDERATION-SERVER INSTALLATION OPTIONS

Once the prerequisites are met, you will be able to install the federation server within each of the partner forests. In this section we are going to look at the installation requirements that are the same for both forests. In the sections that follow, we will look at the installation options and requirements that are unique to the resource and account forests.

The steps that start the installation of the federation server are the same for the two forests. As long as all of the prerequisites have been met, you can install the Federation Service by opening the Add Roles Wizard and selecting Active Directory Federation Services. The Role Services page shown in Figure 10.1 displays the options available.

One of the nice things about the new Add Roles Wizard is that it will display the services required when adding a role. You can choose if you want to allow the wizard to add the roles with default values, or you can cancel the install and add the roles on your own. Clicking the Add Required Role Services button queues the appropriate installation configuration settings for the required services and presents you with the next page of the wizard.

FIGURE 10.1
Active Directory
Federation Service's
Role Services

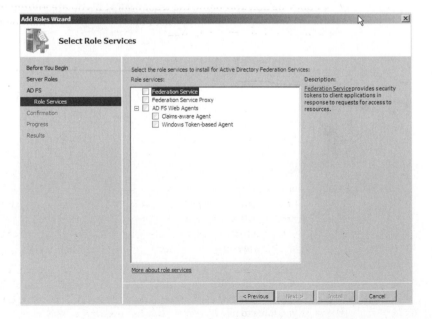

The Server Authentication Certificate for SSL Encryption page appears next, requesting a certificate that will be used when communicating between the account and resource entities. You essentially have three options at this point: you can create a certificate that is signed by your company's root certification authority, you can create a certificate that is signed by a third-party certification authority, or you can use a self-signed certificate.

The wizard page that follows, Choose a Token-Signing Certificate, is used to identify the certificate that will be used to prove the authenticity of the tokens as they are passed from one organization to another. Although you can create a certificate that can be used for both the encryption and authentication, you may want to use two different certificates so that you can revoke one and not have to worry about both functions.

The Select Trust Policy page allows you to define the trust policy you will use for the AD FS trust relationship. Choosing Create a New Trust Policy allows you to define where your trust policy will be stored and what its name is. Choosing Select an Existing Trust Policy gives you the chance to define the trust policy you want to use from those that have already been created.

If you did not have IIS installed already, the Web Server IIS page and the Role Services page that follow will allow you to define the IIS functionality that will be enabled for your server. You can add additional roles if you need them, but be sure not to add any roles that are not required. The more roles you enable on your server, the greater the possibility that you open up your system for attack.

Once the Confirmation page appears, you can review the settings you want to use. Clicking Install will use the settings as they appear within the summary pane. The installation will take a few minutes, but once it is complete you will see the results displayed just as you did the summary information.

The Federation Service page shown in Figure 10.2 will appear, requesting the token-signing certificate. Specify the location of the certificate, either explicitly or by browsing for it. In the lower portion of this page, specify whether this is the first federation server that is installed, or if it is another federation server within an existing federation server farm. If it is the first, select the Create a New Trust Policy option and name the trust policy. If you are joining this server to an existing server farm, select the Use an Existing Trust Policy option. After making your selections, click the Next button, then click the Finish button.

USING CERTIFICATES

Using a self-signed certificate is usually not a viable option. You will have to configure the certificate manually within the client systems. The other drawback is that you have to deliver the certificate to the other organization, and that organization has to import it into their systems. By default, the self-signed certificate is trusted only by the entity that created the certificate. About the only time a self-signed certificate should be used is in a test environment.

When you use a certificate that is signed by a certification authority (CA), you can use the root certificate from the CA to validate your certificates. If you use a certificate that has been signed by an organization's own root CA, you will have to distribute the root CA's root certificate to any partner organizations with which you want to work. They will have to make sure that your root certificate is imported into any of the systems that are going to interoperate with your organization.

Using a third-party trusted root certificate allows you to start working with certificates quickly, without having to make sure the other organizations trust your organization. It is much easier to start working with partner organizations if you use a trusted third party; however, the cost of using certificates goes up because you have to pay the third party for its services.

FIGURE 10.2
Federation Service
token-signing certificate request page

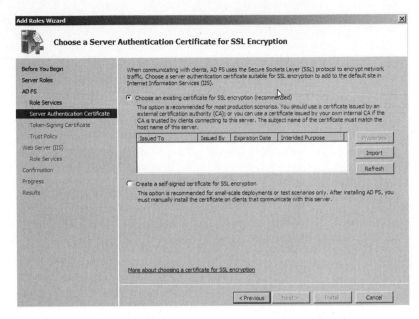

Once the Federation Service has been installed successfully, you need to define the trust policy that all of the Federation servers within the server farm will use. The trust policy contains the information required to locate the federation's organization name as well as the URL required to locate the federation servers.

To edit the information used within the trust policy, open the Active Directory Federation Services snap-in from Administrative Tools or your own custom Microsoft Management Console (MMC). Double-clicking the Federation Service node will allow you to gain access to the Trust Policy node shown in Figure 10.3. Right-click on Trust Policy and select Properties. Figure 10.4 shows the properties pages available for the trust policy. If you are using a Windows Server 2003 R2 system, you will have to modify settings on the General tab; you will need to replace the generic entries with identifying information for your side of the federation.

In the Federation Service URI (Uniform Resource Identifier) line, insert the name of your domain. In the Federation Service Endpoint URL line, the computer name that you specified when installing the Federation Service will appear. Notice that the name is not fully qualified. For the Federation Service to work correctly, you will need to supply the fully qualified domain name of the server. In our example, you would replace `https://fs/adfs/ls/` with `https://ZygortDC.zygort.lcl/adfs/ls/`.

FIGURE 10.3
Trust Policy node

FIGURE 10.4
Trust-policy
properties

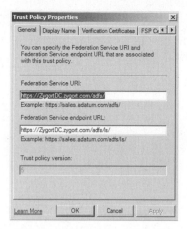

In a test environment, if your Federation Service is running on a domain controller, you should change the AD FS application-pool identity to run as the Local System account. This is not necessary on a member server. As a best practice, do not install the Federation Service on a domain controller in a production environment.

CONFIGURING THE ACCOUNT FEDERATION SERVER

The account forest side of the federation is responsible for maintaining the user accounts that will have access to the web pages on the resource side of the trust. Because the account partner is sending tokens to the resource partner, the federation server is not restricted to only Active Directory as the account store. Active Directory Application Mode (ADAM) can also be used as an account store, but you will not be able to use Kerberos as the authentication mechanism.

To add an account store, open the Active Directory Federation Services snap-in from the Administrative Tools or from your own custom MMC. Expand Federation Service ➢ Trust Policy ➢ My Organization to see the view shown in Figure 10.5. Right-click on Account Stores and select New ➢ Account Store from the context menu. The Add Account Store Wizard will appear. Click Next, and you will be presented with the options Active Directory and Active Directory Application Mode (ADAM). Selecting Active Directory and clicking Next will take you to a page that has a check box that allows you to enable the account store for use by the Federation Service. If you do not select the check box, the account store will be added but not used for authentication purposes. Clicking Next will take you to the final screen, the Completing the Add Account Store Wizard page, on which you can click Finish to see your account store appear in the snap-in.

For each Active Directory group you want to map to claims that are sent to the resource partner, you need to create an organization claim. Expanding Federation Service ➢ Trust Policy ➢ My Organization and then right-clicking on Organization Claims will bring up a context menu from which you can choose New ➢ Organization Claim.

FIGURE 10.5
Account stores in the
Federation Service

The dialog box that appears, shown in Figure 10.6, allows you to type in a claim name and specify whether it is a group claim or custom claim. Choose Group Claim to map an Active Directory group, and Custom Claim to map user attributes.

The claims then need to be associated with user account information. The FS-A can determine the group memberships of user accounts and discover Active Directory attributes from the user accounts, but until those groups and attributes are mapped to claims, the claims will not be usable. To perform the claim mapping of Active Directory accounts, identify the properties that are associated with the claim. To do so, expand Federation Server ➤ Trust Policy ➤ My Organization ➤ Account Stores, and then right-click on the account store. From the context menu, select New ➤ Group Claim Extraction or New ➤ Custom Claim Extraction.

Figure 10.7 shows the Create a New Group Claim Extraction dialog box. To map a group, click Add and select the group from the Select Users or Groups dialog box. Once you've selected the group, use the Map to This Organization Claim pull-down menu to associate the group with the appropriate claim.

The custom-claim mapping works similarly to the group mapping. In the Create a New Custom Claim Extraction dialog box, type in the attribute you want to map to a claim, and then use the Map to This Organization Claim pull-down menu to associate the attribute to the appropriate claim.

Once you've created the organization claims and configured the Active Directory mappings, you need to add the resource partner that will be part of this trust relationship. Expanding Federation Service ➤ Trust Policy ➤ Partner Organization, right-clicking on Resource Partner, and selecting New ➤ Resource Partner from the context menu will present you with the Welcome to the Add Resource Partner Wizard. Click Next to start the wizard at the Import Policy File page.

If the resource partner has provided you with a policy file, you can click Yes and enter the path to the policy file; if not, select No and click Next to enter the information manually. On the Resource Partner Details page, enter the URI and URL for the FS-R as shown in Figure 10.8.

FIGURE 10.6
The Create a New
Organization Claim
dialog box

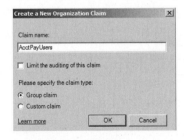

FIGURE 10.7
Extracting account
information

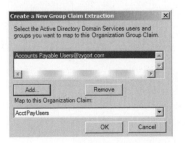

FIGURE 10.8

Resource Partner
Details page

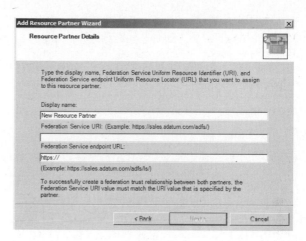

After clicking Next, you are presented with the Resource Partner Verification Certificate page. This is where you need to make sure you have obtained the token-signing certificate from the partner. Without the token-signing certificate, you will not be able to move forward and add the account partner to the trust policy, and you will not be able to create a trust relationship with the account partner. Either enter the path or browse for the certificate, and click Next.

The final step is to configure the outgoing claims that will be sent to the FS-R. Expand Federation Service ➤ Trust Policy ➤ Partner Organizations ➤ Resource Partners and right-click the resource partner. From the context menu, select New and then choose either Outgoing Group Claim Mapping or Outgoing Custom Claim Mapping. If you are mapping a user's group membership to a group claim, you can use the Outgoing Group Claim Mapping; if you are mapping any type of attribute associated with the user's account, you have to use the Outgoing Custom Claim Mapping option.

When you select the Outgoing Group Claim Mapping option, you will be presented with a dialog box, as shown in Figure 10.9. Type in the group-name claim that will be generated from the FS-A. Make sure you type this information correctly; if the claim is misspelled, the mapping will fail and the user will lose access to the resources. Once you have typed in the group name, you can select the organization-claim name from the pull-down menu. If you do not see the correct entry in the pull-down menu, the organization claim has not yet been created.

Before moving on to configuring the Resource federation server, you should export the FS-A server authentication certificate to a file that can be used when the FS-R's trust policy is created. Have an administrator who is responsible for your public key infrastructure (PKI) export the certificate and then send the certificate file to the administrative staff responsible for creating the trust policy at the FS-R.

FIGURE 10.9

Outgoing-claim
mapping

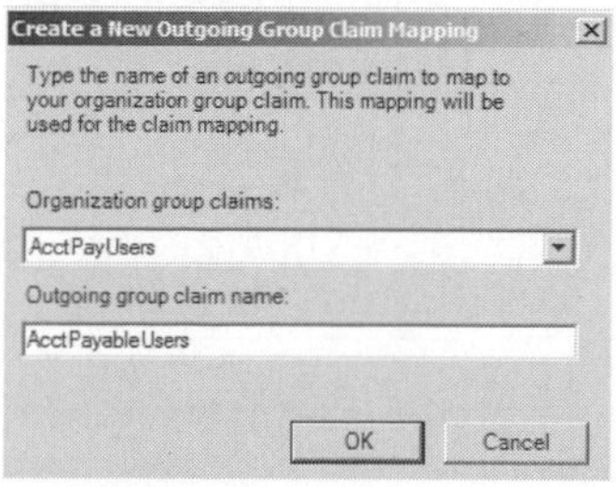

CONFIGURING THE ACCOUNT FEDERATION SERVER PROXY

When the users access your web server to gain access to their partner website, the resource AD FS systems will request authentication of the user account. If your federation server is to be protected in your internal network and you do not want it sitting in the perimeter network, you will need to configure a server to appear as the federation server to the partner organization, otherwise known as the *Federation Server Proxy*. This service is not required for an AD FS solution; you could have your users access the federation server directly, but that decreases the security level of your AD FS infrastructure. As with any solution, the smaller the attack vector you have available, the better off you are.

You can add the Federation Server Proxy role by using Server Manager, but you must have the prerequisites in place before you can add the role. You need to have IIS installed, and you must have configured SSL for the default website. If you have not done so, you will not be allowed to install the Federation Server Proxy.

In much the same way that you added the federation server, you add the Federation Server Proxy. From the Active Directory Federation Services option in Server Manager, select to add the Federation Server Proxy. Note that you cannot install this role on a server that is already configured as a federation server. The federation server will accept requests that are sent to it directly; it does not need to have a Federation Server Proxy in place. But if you decide to place the federation server within the internal network so that external users cannot access it, you will have to make sure the Federation Server Proxy is available in the perimeter network instead.

CONFIGURING THE RESOURCE FEDERATION SERVER

You create the federation server on the resource side in much the same way you did on the account side. There are some specific differences, however. The FS-R cannot use AD LDS for an account store; it is restricted to using Active Directory.

Add Applications

You must need to add any claims-aware or traditional Windows applications to the FS-R so the FS-R knows what applications are available and how the claims are to be used. Using Windows SharePoint Services, you can control access to the traditional Windows applications. For more information on using SharePoint with AD FS, see http://technet.microsoft.com/en-us/library/cc288259.aspx.

When adding claims-aware applications, you have the option to enable claim types so that the claim can be extracted from the tokens sent by the FS-A used to authenticate the user to the application. The application's logic will determine what tasks the user is allowed to perform at that time. You can configure the applications to allow specific levels of access to users based on the claims that are presented.

Add an Account Partner

The account partner information must be entered into the FS-R so the trust can be built. You must perform two steps to enable the account partner to be trusted by the resource partner: obtain the account partner's token-signing certificate, and add the account partner using the Trust Policy node.

There are several methods of obtaining the account partner's token-signing certificate: you could have an administrator from the account partner organization email it to you; you could have it sent on digital media through a courier; or you could even connect to a secure website and download it. No matter which method you choose, you should make sure that any transmission method you use is secure.

Once you've obtained the certificate, you can add the account partner to the trust policy. In the Active Directory Federation Services node of Server Manager, open Federation Service ➤ Trust Policy ➤ Partner Organization. Right-click on the Account Partners node and select New ➤ Account

Partner from the context menu. The Add Account Partner Wizard will start; click Next to continue. On the Import Policy File page shown in Figure 10.10, you can provide the path to the policy file provided by the account partner, or you can click No and enter the information manually. If you select No and then click Next, you will be prompted for the account-partner details. On the Account Partner Details page, shown in Figure 10.11, enter the display name as well as the URI and URL of the account partner's federation server.

After clicking Next, you are presented with the Account Partner Verification Certificate page. This is where you will need to make sure that you have obtained the token-signing certificate from the account partner. Without the certificate, you will not be able to move forward and add the account partner to the trust policy, and you will not be able to create a trust relationship with the account partner. Either enter the path or browse for the certificate, and then click Next.

As shown in Figure 10.12, the Federation Scenario options include Federated Web SSO and Federated Web SSO with Forest Trust. If you have configured a forest trust between the resource and account partners, you can select the second option, but most companies will use the first option. Partner organizations that are taking advantage of AD FS typically will not have Active Directory trust relationships built; they will be relying on AD FS for access to the web apps instead.

FIGURE 10.10
Import Policy
File page

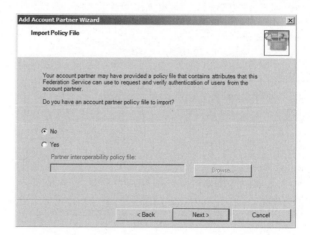

FIGURE 10.11
Account Partner
Details page

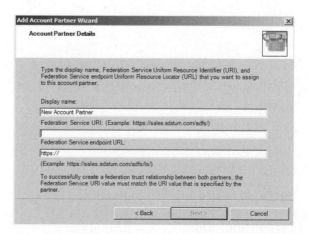

FIGURE 10.12
Federation
Scenario page

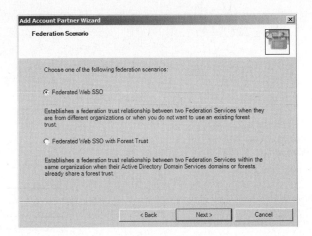

With that said, you could have a scenario in which your organization hosts both the resource-partner and account-partner sides of the trust relationship. This could be due to your having a perimeter network that has an Active Directory infrastructure separate from your internal network. To allow users to access web applications, you could configure AD FS to use the existing trust relationships for authentication purposes.

To continue our example, select Federated Web SSO and click Next. The Account Partner Identity Claims page appears, as shown in Figure 10.13. On this page you can specify which claim types you are going to enable for the account partner. As described earlier, the claim types of UPN, E-mail, and Common Name are available from this page. If you choose either the UPN or E-mail claim types, you will be presented with Accepted UPN Suffixes or Accepted E-mail Suffixes, respectively, and you must enter the suffixes you want to allow. If you selected Common Name, you will be presented with the Enable This Account Partner page. The Enable This Account Partner check box is selected by default. Deselect it if you are not ready to enable the trust between the partners.

After you click Finish on the final page of the wizard, you will see the account partner beneath the Account Partners node in the Active Directory Federation Services snap-in. The claim types that you have enabled, in this case UPN and E-mail, appears in color; the claims that you did not enable are grayed out.

FIGURE 10.13
Account Partner
Identity Claims page

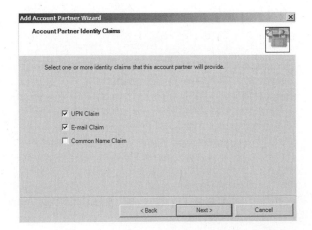

Add Additional Token-Signing Certificates

If you are configuring only one federation server, you can move on to creating claims; if, however, you have additional federation servers within the server farm, you should add the token-signing certificates from each one to the Verification Certificates tab on the account partner's properties sheet. To do so, right-click on the account partner within the account partner's node and select Properties. Once the properties sheet appears, select Verification Certificates, as shown in Figure 10.14. Then click Add and enter the path to the token-signing certificate.

FIGURE 10.14
Verification
Certificates tab

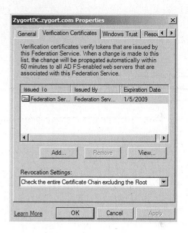

Configure Claims

Claims need to be configured so that the access entries within the claims-aware applications have the correct entries passed to them from the account partner. When we configured the initial trust-policy settings, we selected to enable the UPN claim and entered a UPN suffix. This was assuming that the application used UPN criteria to grant access to an application. Other claims can be added so that when a user attempts to access a website, the claims that are passed on behalf of the user account can be processed and the appropriate application access can be granted.

To configure a claim, open the trust policy within your Active Directory Federation Services snap-in and right-click on Organization Claims. From the context menu select New ➤ Organization Claim. The Create a New Organization Claim dialog box appears, which allows you to name the claim and select the type of claim, either group or custom. At this point make sure that you are coordinating your efforts with the application-development team so you know what claims they have used within the application. For each claim you want to use, create it as either a group or custom claim type. If you no longer need a claim, you can delete it from the list, but the original three claims—UPN, E-mail, and common name—cannot be removed.

Once all of the claims have been created, they need to be mapped to the claims that will be arriving within the tokens sent from the account partner. To configure this mapping between the account partner's claims and the resource partner organization's claims, right-click on the account partner's entry in the Account Partners node in the trust policy and select either Incoming Group Claim Mapping or Incoming Custom Claim Mapping under the New menu item. If you are mapping a user's group membership to a group claim, you can use the Incoming Group Claim Mapping option, but if you are mapping any type of attribute that is associated with the user's account, you have to select Incoming Custom Claim Mapping.

When you choose the Incoming Group Claim Mapping option, you are presented with the dialog box shown in Figure 10.15. Here you can type the group-name claim that will be generated from the FS-A. Make sure you type this information correctly; if the claim is misspelled, the mapping will fail and the user will lose access to the resources. Once you have typed the group name, you can select the resource partner organization's claim name from the pull-down menu. If you do not see the correct entry in the menu, the organization claim has not yet been created.

After the claims have been configured, you can select the application from within the Applications node and view the claims that are available. Right-clicking any of these claims presents a context menu that allows you to enable the claim for use with the application. If at any time you wish to limit a claim's access, you can disable it.

The FS-R server-authentication certificate should be exported to a file that can be imported into the Trusted Root Certification Authorities store on the web server. Have an administrator who is responsible for your PKI export the certificate and send the certificate file to the administrative staff responsible for managing the web server.

FIGURE 10.15

Incoming group claim mapping

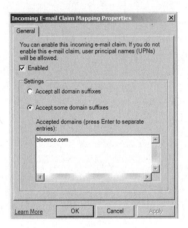

CONFIGURE THE WEB SERVER

Web servers that are going to be responsible for hosting the AD FS-enabled applications will need to understand how AD FS is incorporated into the AD FS solution. To make them AD FS-aware, you must add AD FS web agents that will be used to interpret the claims and allow access to the web applications. Two agents are available to install: the claims-aware agent and the Windows NT token-based applications agent. Depending on the application types you are using, you may have to install one or both of the agents on your web servers.

Claims-aware applications can take advantage of using Authorization Manager's (AzMan's) built-in role-based authorization. Windows NT token-based applications are used with Windows SharePoint Services, which control the access to the applications based on a security token generated from Active Directory. If you are using traditional web applications and want to control the level of access users have, you can use SharePoint's role-based control, limiting users to specific levels of control over the website.

For more information about using AzMan, see the MSDN website at `http://msdn2.microsoft .com/en-us/library/aa375758.aspx`. For more information about using Windows SharePoint Services, see the Microsoft website at `http://technet.microsoft.com/en-us/windowsserver/ sharepoint/default.aspx`.

examples of claims - aware applications

AD FS Web Agents

The AD FS web agents can be installed from Active Directory Federation Services ➤ Federation Service ➤ AD FS Web Age_____ _____ Server Manager. Selecting the check box for the application type that you will be us____

When you install th____

Framework 2.0, COM+____

Website SSL

The website you will be____

the PKI team to obtain a____

net Information Service____

tory Security tab and th____

The wizard that app____

ing on how your PKI i____

authority, or you will s____

enabled, you may be a____

certificates that they is____

For testing purpos____

signed SSL certificate____

use these certificates____

As you step throu____

tificate request file w____

and then have your____

generated, you can ____

for use. Start by click____

ing Request and Ins____

For more informa____

.com/windowsserve____

Claims-Aware Appl____

Windows Server 20____ The

primary purpose o____ e the

primary authorizat____ ten to

take advantage of ____ laims

presented and ther____ roles.

If you determin____ your

development team____ ou can

find information o____ rary/

bb897402.aspx, t____

Outlook — only log on
open

Windows SharePoint
Point Server 3.0

[only great old
for Sit Misen]

Poppins Austen 13

SharePoint Services Access

SharePoint can control the level of access a user has when accessing a traditional web application. Windows SharePoint Services must be installed; once it is, you can add applications and configure the level of access users have to the application. The access you grant through SharePoint Services is based on the Active Directory accounts you create. The accounts are then tied to incoming claims sent from the FS-A.

Microsoft has provided more information about how to manage SharePoint Services at the MSDN website, http://technet.microsoft.com/en-us/library/cc262696.aspx.

Configuring the web.config File

You need to edit the website's web.config file to include the location of the FS-R. Once you've done this, requests sent to the website will use the web.config file and pass the data contained in the token to the FS-R. You must add the following code to your web.config file:

```
<compilation defaultLanguage=""c#"" debug=""true"">

<assemblies>

<add assembly=""System.Web.Security.SingleSignOn, Version=1.0.0.0,
Culture=neutral, PublicKeyToken=31bf3856ad364e35, Custom=null"" />
<add assembly=""System.Web.Security.SingleSignOn.ClaimTransforms,
Version=1.0.0.0, Culture=neutral, PublicKeyToken=31bf3856ad364e35, Custom=null""
/>
</assemblies>

</compilation>

<customErrors mode=""Off"" />

<authentication mode=""None"" />

<httpModules>
<add name=""Identity Federation Services Application Authentication Module""
type=""System.Web.Security.SingleSignOn.WebSsoAuthenticationModule,
System.Web.Security.SingleSignOn, Version=1.0.0.0, Culture=neutral,
PublicKeyToken=31bf3856ad364e35, Custom=null"" />
</httpModules>

<websso>

<urls>
<returnurl>https://apppath </returnurl>
</urls>

<cookies writecookies=""true"">
<path>/ apppath </path>
<lifetime>240</lifetime>
</cookies>

<fs>https://federationservername /adfs/fs/federationserverservice.asmx</fs>

<authenticationrequired>
</authenticationrequired>

<loghttpevent>1</loghttpevent>

<auditlevel>255</auditlevel>
```

```
<tokenCacheSize>1</tokenCacheSize>

<tokenCacheEntryLifetime>5</tokenCacheEntryLifetime>

<tokenCacheScavengePeriod>5</tokenCacheScavengePeriod>

</websso>

</system.web>
```

In the preceding example, the entries for the path to the application and the Federation Service need to reflect your environment. For example, if your domain name is `zygort.lcl`, the application you are using is called `researchapp`, and it is hosted on the web server `fsweb`, you would replace the line `<returnurl>https://apppath </returnurl>` with `<returnurl>https://fsweb.zygort.lcl/researchapp </returnurl>`.

If your Federation server is named `fs`, the line `<fs>https://federationservername /adfs/fs/federationserverservice.asmx</fs>` will need to show `<fs>https://fs.zygort.lcl /adfs/fs/federationserverservice.asmx</fs>`.

Configuring Clients

Each client that will access the website must use a secure channel. After the website has been configured to use SSL, the client will have to use an HTTPS call through the web browser to make the connection. The client may also have to connect to a specific port number to make the connection if host headers are not used. Consider the following options for providing the user with a positive experience when using the partner's website.

Installing SSL Certificates on Clients

Each client system that will operate within the federation will need to trust the certificates used by both the FS-A and the FS-R. The easiest method of configuring the client to trust the federation servers is to install the root certificate for both into the Trusted Root Store. To do so, you could use a group policy that contains the root certificates that need to be installed on the client. When the clients log into the computer, the certificates will already be installed, and the clients will then be able to connect to the federation servers without being prompted to trust the certificates.

To use a group policy to install the certificates, open the Group Policy Management Console, navigate to the Group Policy container in your domain, right-click the group policy you want to modify, and select Edit. Once the Group Policy Object Editor opens, navigate to Computer Configuration ➢ Windows Components ➢ Security Policy ➢ Public Key Policies. Right-click Trusted Root Certification Authorities and select Import. Once the wizard starts, enter the path to the certificate you wish to import and choose Place All Certificates in the Following Store. When the wizard is complete, the group policy will install the certificates on the clients as the computer is started or the refresh interval for the computer is reached. (If you want to install the certificates immediately after the group policy has been modified, run `gpupdate /force` from a command prompt at the client computer.

If the client's computer is not a member of your domain, group policies will not apply. In that case, you can instruct the users to open a web page that prompts them to install the root certificate for the company. If you are using a third party for your trusted root certificate, direct the users to install the root certificate from the third party by accessing the third-party website that hosts the root certificate.

Configuring Internet Explorer

Once you have the certificates installed, you can configure Internet Explorer to trust the FS-A and the FS-R. To do so, open the Internet Options dialog box and select the Security tab. From the Security tab, select the Trusted Sites icon and click the Sites button. Each of the federation server's URLs should be entered in this dialog box. If the users access the FS-A and the FS-R directly, the URL to the federation servers should be entered here, but if you are using a Federation Server Proxy, the URL to the proxy should be entered here. In any case, the URL that is used within the trust policy to identify the federation server to the clients should be the one you have entered into the trusted sites.

Once the entire configuration is complete, users who need to access resources managed by administrators on the other side of the federation will be able to do so, and they won't have to enter their usernames and passwords when connecting. The advantage for the administrators is that they won't have to manage individual accounts for each user who needs to access the website. It becomes a win-win situation and helps make the user's experience a pleasant one. And as we all know, the happier users are, the more real work we administrators can perform.

Active Directory Lightweight Directory Services

If you have worked with previous versions of Windows Server or have been a developer who is interested in using an LDAP-based directory service for your application, you have probably heard of Active Directory Application Mode (ADAM). In Windows Server 2008, ADAM has been given a new moniker: Active Directory Lightweight Directory Services (AD LDS).

AD LDS is used as a storage location for configuration information and application data, just like Active Directory Domain Services. The primary reason for using AD LDS is to reduce the number of changes to Active Directory. After all, you won't find very many administrators willing to make changes to their Active Directory implementation just because a developer or another administrator wants to use it for an application.

There are other benefits of using AD LDS instead of AD DS besides just substituting it for a data storage location. AD LDS allows you to configure which systems will host a copy of AD LDS. AD LDS is not limited to running on a domain controller; you can place a copy on any server that needs to host the directory service. As a matter of fact, you don't even need a domain in place to use AD LDS, although in many cases it does come in handy.

Installing AD LDS

As we have done so many times in this chapter, we are going to open up Server Manager. Right-clicking on Roles and selecting Add Roles will allow you to prestage the installation of AD LDS. Select the Active Director Lightweight Directory Services check box, and then complete the wizard to start the installation. The summary page will let you know if everything completed correctly.

To actually create an AD LDS instance, you use the AD LDS Setup Wizard. Find this tool by selecting the Active Directory Lightweight Directory Services node in Server Manager, and click the AD LDS Setup Wizard link in the Advanced Tools section. The wizard presents a series of options, the first of which allows you to specify if you are creating a new AD LDS instance or a replica of an existing instance. In other words, are you creating a new directory service partition, or are you configuring replication of a partition that already exists?

If you choose to create a new instance, the wizard pages that follow allow you to specify the name for the instance, the port that will be used to access the instance, whether an application directory partition should be created, the location of the data files, the service and administrator accounts, and the LDIF files used to define the objects within the instance.

Real World Scenario

WORKING WITH DEVELOPERS

Many developers will request access to Active Directory when developing their applications that use AD DS as the configuration store. The main problem with this scenario is that the developer could make a mistake and cause serious problems with the existing AD DS environment. Bill ran into a scenario such as this when he started working as a company's senior systems administrator.

When Bill started reviewing the systems within the organization, he discovered that everyone was a domain administrator within the company's forest root. As he dug deeper into the system configurations, he found that several developers had extended the AD DS schema for projects that they had worked on over the past few years. Instead of using AD LDS for development purposes, the company's production network served as the test network also.

As Bill uncovered this information, he also discovered that two projects had been scrapped because the applications that were being tested would not install correctly. As it turned out, some of the schema modifications that the developers had made conflicted with the applications that they were testing. If the developers had used a separate AD LDS store for their applications, they might have avoided the issues that they ran into when testing other applications.

As you come up with a naming convention, make sure you use only supported characters. For AD LDS, you can use only the characters *A* through *Z* and *a* through *z*, numbers 0 through 9, and the hyphen (-) character. If you try to use any other character, you will find yourself staring at the warning seen in Figure 10.16.

FIGURE 10.16
Warning for using the wrong characters

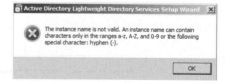

The ports you use to access the directory services should be unique on the system. The default ports, seen in Figure 10.17, are 50000 and 50001. You can change these to any ports you would like to use as long as no other service is already using them. As a best practice, use port numbers that are greater than 1024, because anything between 1 and 1024 is considered a standard port. Take special care not to use ports 389 and 636. These two ports are used with Active Directory Domain Services. If both AD DS and AD LDS are running on the system, you will have to avoid those two ports.

AD LDS requires an application directory partition to host the data that the service uses. When choosing whether to create an application directory partition, determine if the application that will be using AD LDS creates its own partition. As you may have guessed, if you have an application that does not create its own application directory partition, it will be up to you to create one. It is likely that the application's developer has included an installation script that creates the application directory partition instead of relying on an administrator to create it. If you choose the option Yes, Create an Application Directory Partition, as in Figure 10.18, you must supply the fully qualified LDAP name.

FIGURE 10.17

Specifying ports to use

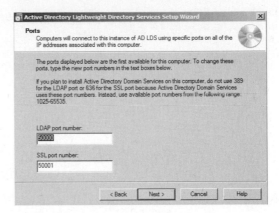

FIGURE 10.18

Specifying the application directory partition name

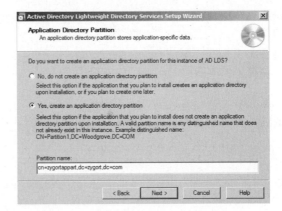

After specifying what you will use for an application directory partition, you have the option to specify where the data files for AD LDS will be stored. This is the same data-file technology as in Exchange Server, SQL Server, and Active Directory databases. As you can see in Figure 10.19, the Data Files text box lets you specify where the database data file will be located, and the Data Recovery Files text box is used to specify where the transaction logs are stored.

Figure 10.20 shows the Service Account Selection page, where you can choose the account under which the AD LDS instance will run. Take care to identify an account that has only the permissions and rights that are absolutely required for the service. Make sure that the account has enough power to perform the required operations. The default account is the network service account. Using this account, the service account is restricted from having too much access to resources. If you have requirements that the network service account will not provide, choose the This Account option and specify an account to use instead.

The next page that appears, AD LDS Administrators, seen in Figure 10.21, is used to identify the account that will manage this instance of AD LDS. As a best practice, use the This Account option and specify a group that will be used as an administrative group. This way you can add any account into the group that needs to manage this instance.

FIGURE 10.19
Specifying the
data-file locations

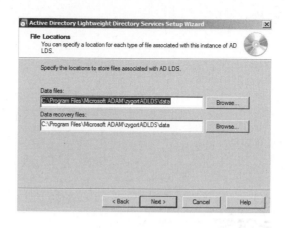

FIGURE 10.20
Specifying the
service account

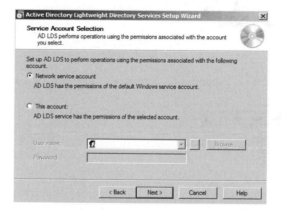

FIGURE 10.21
Specifying the
administrative group

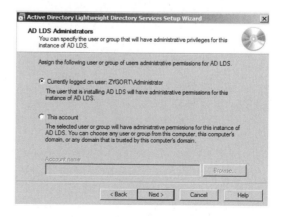

The final configuration page of the wizard allows you to define the schema that will be used for the partition. Selecting one or more of the LDIF files listed will import the classes used within that LDIF file. For instance, if you select the options seen in Figure 10.22, you will import the two classes that are used to identify users: User and InetOrgPerson. You can add additional LDIF files to this list by copying them to the %systemroot%\ADAM directory.

FIGURE 10.22
Choosing schema
classes to import

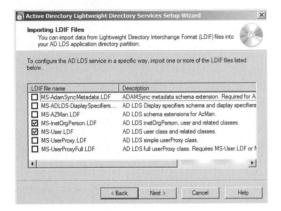

Configuration Options for AD LDS

The nice thing about using AD LDS to store information for applications and services is that it can be managed using the same tools as for AD DS. In Server Manager, you will find Active Directory Lightweight Directory Services within the Roles node. When you select this option, the details pane will appear with sections that you can use to determine how well AD LDS is functioning, and with tools that you can use to manage AD LDS.

Figure 10.23 shows these sections: Summary, Advanced Tools, and Resources and Support. Expanding the Summary tab displays the Events list and the System Services view, both of which show only the items related to AD LDS, as shown in Figure 10.24. This is a handy feature to have so you are not required to use Event Viewer and the Services Control Panel applet to see the information.

In the Events section, you can filter the events to show only the AD LDS event types you would like to see, and the properties for each of those events. If you would like to see the other events that occurred on the system, you can quickly go to the Event Viewer by selecting Go to Event Viewer.

FIGURE 10.23
The sections of
the AD LDS role-
management view

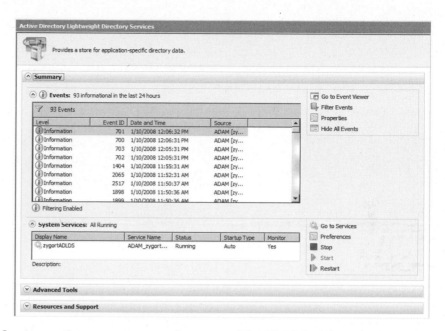

In the System Services section, you can start and stop any of the AD LDS instances and manage the properties of each one. In case you want to work with other services, there is also a handy Go to Services link that will open the Services Control Panel applet for you.

The Advanced Tools section gives you access to other utilities you need for managing AD LDS. The links that are included here, seen in Figure 10.25, allow you to quickly jump to those tools instead of having to leave this console to find them. The first link, AD LDS Setup Wizard, presents you with the same wizard that we used in the section "Installing AD LDS."

The second and third options launch ADSI Edit and `Ldp.exe`, respectively. ADSI Edit is the graphical tool you can use to manage the classes and attributes within the partition. Figure 10.26 displays a view of the partition we just created. ADSI Edit functions the same way as in Chapter 4, "Organizing the Physical and Logical Aspects of AD DS."

FIGURE 10.25
Advanced Tools
section

Active Directory Lightweight Directory Services	
Provides a store for application-specific directory data.	
Summary	
Advanced Tools	
Create a new AD LDS instance	AD LDS Setup Wizard
Query, view, and edit objects and attributes in the directory	ADSI Edit
Perform LDAP operations against the directory such as connect, bind, search, modify, add, and delete	Ldp.exe
Resources and Support	

FIGURE 10.26
Viewing ADSI Edit

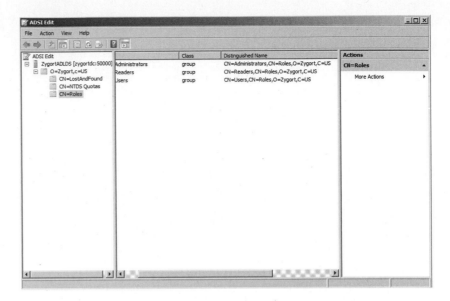

DSDBUtil

Just as you can use NTDSUtil for performing advanced management tasks for AD DS, you can use DSDBUtil to manage AD LDS. Figure 10.27 shows the help-information screen displaying the major commands that can be used. Before you can start managing any of the partitions, you need to activate the instance within the utility. The first command shown in the figure allows you to do just that. However, what if you are not sure of the name of the partition with which you want to work? You can use the List Instances command to find the name of the instances, where they are installed, the port numbers used to access them, and their state, whether running or stopped.

FIGURE 10.27
Help information
screen for DSDBUtil

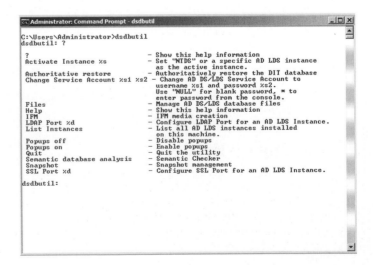

Once you activate an instance, you can perform several functions. Probably the most impressive is the IFM option. IFM stand for *install from media*. Using this option, you can create an installation file using the partition you have already created. For developers who are creating AD LDS instances for use with their applications, this is an easy way for them to use existing partition information to create an installation file when they distribute their software. Figure 10.28 shows the options that are available when using IFM. You can also use this option when you want to create an Active Directory domain controller partition.

FIGURE 10.28

IFM options

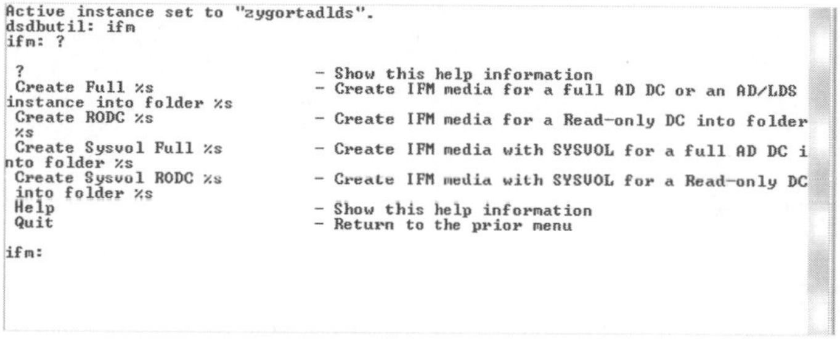

```
Active instance set to "zygortadlds".
dsdbutil: ifm
ifm: ?

 ?                            - Show this help information
 Create Full %s              - Create IFM media for a full AD DC or an AD/LDS
instance into folder %s
 Create RODC %s              - Create IFM media for a Read-only DC into folder
%s
 Create Sysvol Full %s       - Create IFM media with SYSVOL for a full AD DC i
nto folder %s
 Create Sysvol RODC %s       - Create IFM media with SYSVOL for a Read-only DC
 into folder %s
 Help                        - Show this help information
 Quit                        - Return to the prior menu

ifm:
```

The other options that are included within DSDBUtil are the following:

◆ Change Service Account %s1 %s2—Changes the service account for the AD LDS instance from the original account, %s1, to a new account, %s2.

◆ Files—Used to manage the database files. When you enter this option, you are able to manage the database and log-file locations, check the database integrity, configure the backup directory path, and perform recovery on the database.

◆ LDAP Port %d—Used to configure the port number that will be used for LDAP-based communication.

◆ List Instances—Used to list all of the AD LDS instances on the system.

◆ Popups On/Popups Off—Used to control whether popup messages will appear.

◆ Semantic Database Analysis—Used to check whether the database is healthy.

◆ Snapshot—Used to manage snapshots. When this option is entered, you can manage the snapshots by creating, mounting, or dismounting snapshots.

◆ SSL Port %d—Used to configure the port number that will be used for secure LDAP-based communication.

Coming Up Next

Now that we have configured the interoperability options and methods of access to resources using the new Active Directory services, we need to make sure that all of the resources are accessible to the appropriate clients. In the next chapter, we will look at how to control access to objects when they are within our organization and when they leave our network. Controlling the rights others have to our resources allows us to make sure the content is not manipulated in ways we do not intend.

The Bottom Line

Install and manage Active Directory Federation Services Active Directory Federation Services allows you to control access to resources within your organization. When using AD FS, you do not have to create the traditional trust relationships between your forest and an external organization's forest; you can use web-based access rights to manage who is allowed to access the resources. Both organizations have to create the federated access, but once it's in place, it is much easier to maintain than the traditional methods.

Master It Jamie is configuring the resource-partner side of the AD FS installation. The partner organization is going to be responsible for the account-partner side of the solution. Jamie is trying to decide which of the Certificate Services options she would like to use. Should she create her own certificate using her own root certification authority, use a certificate signed by a third-party root certification authority (CA), or use a self-signed certificate?

Install and manage Active Directory Lightweight Directory Services Applications and services can use Active Directory Domain Services as a storage location for configuration information and data. However, to do so usually entails extending the Active Directory schema. Instead, you can use Active Directory Lightweight Directory Services to create a new directory-service container to use for application and service storage. As a bonus, the AD LDS container can be replicated to only the systems that need to host it instead of being hosted on all of the domain controllers.

Master It Nick needs a configuration database for an application he is developing. He wants a local copy of the database on system where the application is installed. What criteria should he consider when determining whether he will use AD DS or AD LDS for his application?

Use DSDBUtil to manage Active Directory Lightweight Directory Services AD DS has the NTDSUtil utility for managing the database. To manage the AD LDS database, you use the DSDBUtil utility.

Master It DeAnn needs to change the SSL port used when accessing an AD LDS instance so that it meets the company's new communication standards. How would she make the change so that SSL communications uses port 58445?

Chapter 11

Managing Active Directory Rights Management Services

All organizations must secure and safeguard their intellectual property and confidential data. Microsoft offers Active Directory Rights Management Services (AD RMS) to protect proprietary information by restricting access to rights-protected content without risking losses in productivity. AD RMS allows policies and permissions to remain with content so policy is recognized and implemented wherever the content travels. AD RMS allows authors (and publishers) a great amount of flexibility by securing sensitive documents through encryption and usage policies, which would remain with the content, so that content will be decrypted only by intended people and groups under certain conditions and during certain periods of time. An AD RMS Server transparently manages applications, users, and policies for content and information, exclusions, policy expiration settings, and other settings relevant to enforce content permissions.

AD RMS services are designed in Extensible Rights Markup Language, are based on client-server architecture, and work in conjunction with AD RMS–aware applications. At this point, Microsoft is working with several independent software vendors and partners to make third party applications RMS-enabled. Once RMS-enabled, an application can control and track any content, no matter where it resides, who accesses it, or how it is accessed. AD RMS provides the licensing, certification, and publishing services for RMS-enabled applications and clients.

In this chapter, you'll learn to:

◆ Understand rights-management servers

◆ Understand certificates

◆ Troubleshoot decryption of contents

◆ Know the importance of RMA in an AD RMS infrastructure

Understanding Active Directory Rights Management Services

Loss of confidential information and increase in computer-related crimes are causing significant damage to organizations. More and more organizations require sharing digital information between partners, customers, and retailers, which increases the risk of information leaks. All digital information—which may include email messages, Microsoft Office documents, financial reports, contacts, employees' performance reviews, project-related documents, customer data, business intelligence, planning and vision documents, product research, personal records, and other sensitive data—is susceptible to attack.

Who Are Publishers, Authors, and Consumers?

In this chapter, we'll use these definitions:

Publisher and author   We'll use these terms to refer to someone who creates rights-protected content such as an email message, a web page, or a document created in Office 2003 or Office 2007.

Consumer   We'll use this term to refer to someone who needs to access rights-protected content.

In addition to the threats of misusing information and theft of confidential documents, the government, healthcare, and legal sectors are challenged to comply with emerging legislative standards to protect their valuable digital information against malicious use. For example, many organizations must comply with at least one of the following government regulations:

◆ United States: Sarbanes-Oxley Act of 2002 (SOX), Health Insurance Portability and Accountability Act of 1996 (HIPPA), USA Patriot Act, Gramm-Leach-Bliley Act

◆ Canada: The Personal Information Protection and Electronic Documents Act

◆ Europe: European Union Data Protection Directive (EUDPD)

◆ Japan: Japan's Personal Information Protection Act

Securing your digital information is not an easy task. The growing use of DVD drives, USB keys, USB hard drives, and the introduction of "connect from anywhere to any device" connectivity through the Internet have made protecting corporate information an essential security consideration. Typically, organizations use a variety of methods to secure digital information, including traditional access-control mechanisms such as Mandatory Access Control (MAC), Discretionary Access Control (DAC), and role-based access control to restrict users access to files and information. Some organizations may use variety of third-party solutions to encrypt documents and secure in-transit emails; however, these third-party tools, software, and utilities have certain limitations. After receiving a document, the recipients can still edit the content or distribute it to other people without your permission. This introduces another kind of risk into an organization's security model because a recipient can forward the information to people who may have malicious intentions toward you or your organization.

Organizations of all sizes have started using the Rights Management Services (RMS) to safeguard digital information from unauthorized and malicious use. RMS is a Microsoft technology that has been developed in response to the previously mentioned problems and to help create reliable solutions to protect and safeguard your private, sensitive, and valuable information. Microsoft Active Directory Rights Management Services (AD RMS) is a convenient, easy-to-use document-protection service that provides policy-based encryption from sender to recipient.

RMS was first introduced in Windows Server 2003. These services are now integrated with Windows Server 2008 Active Directory Domain Services and referred to as Active Directory Rights Management Services supporting Windows Vista, Windows XP, Windows Server 2003, and Windows 2008 clients.

AD RMS is based on proved security technologies, including encryption, digital certificates, authentication, and Extensible Rights Markup Language (XrML). Together, these allow users to protect their contents online and offline—inside and outside the perimeter network. This means that the RMS policy expressions will remain within files, thus allowing you to force usage policies even when rights-managed content leaves the network. AD RMS allows the owner of a document to define policies to control who can access rights-protected documents and control operations such as copying, editing, modifying, printing, deleting, and forwarding the rights-protected content. RMS-protected content contains an embedded usage policy, which defines the rights (View, Save, Print, Edit, Add, Allow Macros, Forward, Reply, and Reply All) that each trusted entity (user or group) has to the

🌐 Real World Scenario

PROTECTING CONTENT

Steve is the IT manager for a manufacturing firm that is responsible for building automotive parts used in several of the automotive industry's vehicles. One of the projects for which he is responsible over the next six months involves developing a way to manage and protect the blueprints and documents used when designing the parts his firm builds. They have several parts that are in a research and development cycle that they do not want a competitor to see.

To protect their assets, the firm has decided to implement some type of digital rights management. Doing so will allow them to specify exactly who can access their files and to be able to limit each user's rights. Most of the files that the research and development department uses are standard Microsoft Office files that can be protected without any problems; however, the CAD program that is used to create the blueprints is not RMS–enabled.

After investigating how he is going to protect the blueprints, Steve starts a dialog with the application provider, trying to determine how they can WRM-enable the application. He also decides that by using Internet Explorer to view the blueprints, he can limit access to the files until the CAD program is WRM-enabled. Although using Internet Explorer is not a perfect solution, it does allow him to protect the intellectual property until a better solution is found.

content. Establishing time-based expiration rules will cause the permissions to expire at a specific point in time, forcing recipients to obtain a new license. These policies reside in a published license issued by the AD RMS server. When a user opens any rights-protected document, the RMS-aware application contacts the AD RMS server to check the user permissions and to obtain a use license, which the application then uses to access the document and, which enforces the usage rights for that user. AD RMS addresses many security problems inherent in discretionary access control list (DACL), access control list (ACL), and role-based access control solutions. It is important to understand that these traditional security-control solutions are associated with the container in which the content is stored. In AD RMS, usage-rights policies are associated with the protected content. The email messages and documents protected with AD RMS technologies remain protected whether they are copied on a CD-ROM or USB drive, are forwarded as an email attachment, or are uploaded to a website. This is a big improvement over traditional security methods.

To access and to create any rights-protected document, you need a Rights Management Server that issues RMS licenses (typically, this server is hosted on Windows Server 2008 or on Windows Server 2003), an RMS client, and an RMS-aware application. In all RMS deployments, you need at least one RMS root server in your environment. A single RMS server, which is a single point of failure, does not provide any redundancy; therefore, we highly recommended the inclusion of additional RMS servers in the RMS cluster, not only to provide failover capabilities, but also to improve RMS performance. When restricting any document, a trusted entity encrypts a random Advanced Encryption Standard (AES) key with a Rivest, Shamir, and Adelman (RSA) public key (RMS uses 2,048-bit keys for the RMS server and 1,024-bit keys for the machine and user). RMS Server issues XrML certificates intended to represent users, and a policy expression to define permissions on content. RMS uses the AES key to encrypt the document. When a user accesses any protected content, the RMS client authenticates the user to the RMS Server using the XrML license. Users must obtain a valid XrML Rights Management Account Certificate (RAC) from an RMS certification server before getting a use license. If your users don't have RACs, the RMS-aware application will run the wizard and walk the user through the process of obtaining them. The RMS server then issues a use license (which is used to enforce policies and content permissions) to the RMS client so that the client will be able to decrypt and view the protected document.

Components of AD RMS

Now that you have a basic understanding about AD RMS, let's quickly discuss different components of the AD RMS in your AD RMS infrastructure.

AD RMS CLUSTER

Every AD RMS deployment, whether it is a single or multiple server deployment, is referred to as an *RMS cluster*. In a typical RMS deployment scenario, the RMS cluster consists of multiple RMS servers, which could be load-balanced by using either Microsoft Network Load Balancing or a hardware-based load balancer. All servers in an RMS cluster share a common back-end SQL database. The first server in an RMS cluster is referred to as the *Primary Root server*. All additional RMS servers in the RMS cluster are referred to as *Joined RMS servers*. There can be only one RMS root cluster per Active Directory forest.

AD RMS SERVER

An AD RMS server is a server component that issues RMS certificates and licenses, enrolls servers and users, performs administrative functions, and manages licensing of rights-protected information.

There are two types of RMS servers:

Root Certification server   The Root Certification server is the first RMS server, and it is a trusted entity responsible for issuing licenses to Windows RMS clients in your organization; it also enrolls other RMS certificate servers. All the certificate providers and the ultimate user must trust the destination. This is known as the "root of trust." The Root Certification server should be installed and configured in a cluster to provide fault tolerance and load balancing.

License Cluster server   This server issues and delegates control of RMS publish and use licenses to individual departments so the departments can have more control of their publish and use licenses. The License Cluster server should be installed and configured in a cluster to provide fault tolerance and load balancing.

In a nutshell, Microsoft AD RMS server protects private, sensitive, and valuable information by doing the following:

◆ Enabling authors to protect sensitive contents by issuing XrML certificates called *publish licenses*

◆ Enabling users to open RMS-protected contents by issuing XrML certificates called *use licenses*

◆ Managing the computers and users that can employ AD RMS to protect or open RMS-protected contents

◆ Providing the tools to administer an RMS environment

AD RMS CLIENT

An AD RMS client is a client component that can be used by RMS-enabled applications to publish and to access RMS–protected contents. Each client computer in your AD RMS infrastructure must have this component installed. At the time of writing of this book, the AD RMS client component is available for Windows 98 SE, Windows Me, Windows XP, Windows 2000, Windows 2003, Windows 2008, and Windows Vista platforms. The client component works as an application program interface (API) and interacts with the RMS-enabled application.

RMS-ENABLED APPLICATIONS

RMS-enabled applications allow content authors to use published licenses to protect digital data, which may includes email messages, Microsoft Office documents, financial reports, contacts, employees' performance reviews, project-related documents, customer data, business intelligence, planning and vision documents, product research, personal records, and other sensitive data. RMS-enabled applications also allow a user to view RMS-protected contents by using a valid use license.

Microsoft Office 2003 and 2007 (Enterprise Edition) are RMS-enabled applications. If your application is not RMS-aware or if there is no native RMS functionality available for your application, you may have to use add-ons to make your application RMS-enabled. One significant feature of the RMS system is that it allows users to view a document in Microsoft Internet Explorer when an intended application is not available; however, anyone attempting to view the data must download and install the Rights Management Add-on (RMA) for Internet Explorer. For example, if your users don't have Microsoft Word 2003 or Microsoft Excel 2003 installed on their machines and they are unable to open the content, the RMA for Internet Explorer allows users to view, but not modify, rights-protected documents. RMA is an RMS-based technology, and any application built to support AD RMS technology can take an advantage of RMA. Microsoft also offers the Windows RMS software-development kit (SDK), which can be used to RMS-enable other applications.

SERVER LICENSOR CERTIFICATE

A server licensor certificate (SLC) grants permission to an RMS server to issue certificates and licenses to users, computers, and other RMS servers. In earlier versions of RMS, the RMS server needed to have an Internet connection to receive the SLC from the Microsoft Enrollment Service. This requirement has been removed from AD RMS. The AD RMS included with Windows Server 2008 installs a server self-enrollment certificate and a private key on the AD RMS server, The server self-enrollment certificate is then used to create an SLC for AD RMS. The SLC is valid for your server's lifetime and is chained into the certificate hierarchy.

CLIENT LICENSOR CERTIFICATE

A client licensor certificate (CLC) is useful for mobile users who need to publish RMS-protected content without being connected to the corporate network. To receive a CLC, an author initiates a request from a client computer to the licensing server or to the root certification server, which will then return a CLC to the client computer. The CLC uses the CLC filename prefix and is stored in a user's profile under:

```
%USERPROFILE%\Local Settings\Application Data\Microsoft\DRM
```

For Microsoft Vista clients, the location is:

```
%USERPROFILE%\AppData\Local\Microsoft\DRM
```

RIGHTS ACCOUNT CERTIFICATE

Rights account certificates (RACs) are issued by an RMS server to associate a user's account with specific computers. If a user logged on to multiple computers—for example, office desktop, laptop, home desktop, and kiosk machine—the user would receive an RMS RAC on every computer to which they log on. The RAC identifies users by either a Windows security identifier (SID) or a Passport Unique ID (PUID). The RAC is used to tie a machine certificate to an issuance license, and must be included with the request for client licensor certificate (a CLC is required to publish RMS-protected content) and for use licenses (use licenses allow access to RMS-protected contents). The RMS server automatically issues the RAC to authenticated users when those users try to protect or access any RMS-protected content. Each RAC includes a user's public key in plain text and the user's private key in an encrypted format. Those keys are used to encrypt and decrypt data that is intended for that user. As explained later, the RAC ties a specific user to a specific machine certificate, which means that the RAC private key is encrypted by the user's computer's public key, so that you won't be able to transfer an RAC to another computer and expect it to work. When you acquire an RAC from an AD RMS service, the service stores the user's key pair (user's public and private key), so that if the user loses their certificate or needs a new certificate on another machine, the new RAC will contain the old key pair, thus allowing the user to share encrypted content to the same end-user license across multiple computers.

Your computer might be holding several RACs, for the following reasons:

◆ For different users

◆ For the same user using different authentication types

◆ For the same user, but obtained from different service points

An AD RMS service will issue an RAC only if the following conditions are met:

◆ User ID (Windows SID or PUID) is valid.

◆ The given user is allowed to be activated by the group identity policy.

◆ The client's computer is activated, as an activation service needs the computer certificate to tie up with the user certificate.

There are two types of RACs: *standard* and *temporary*. By default, standard certificates are valid for 365 days, whereas temporary certificates are valid for only 15 minutes. Moreover, standard certificates include the user's SID, whereas temporary certificates don't. The validity period for both certificates can be specified; however, we recommend that you use the default. Consider the pros and cons of your decision. For example, in case of temporary certificates we recommend the validation period of 15 minutes because users might be accessing content from a kiosk machine, airport terminal, public library, or Internet café. Changing the temporary validity period may impact your entire information-security infrastructure. The RAC uses a Group Identity Certificate (GIC) filename prefix, and is stored in a user's profile under:

```
%USERPROFILE%\Local Settings\Application Data\Microsoft\DRM
```

as `GIC-<userid@domain.com>`. For Microsoft Vista clients, the location is

```
%USERPROFILE%\AppData\Local\Microsoft\DRM
```

RMS MACHINE CERTIFICATE

RMS machine certificates are issued by an RMS server to a computer or device that the RMS server trusts. The RMS machine certificate is the last certificate on the certificate chain. This certificate contains the machine public key and is signed by the trusted root certificate. When a user uses the computer to protect or access the RMS-protected content, the RMS server will issue the RMS machine certificate.

There are no requirements for computers or devices to be members of an Active Directory domain. The machine certificate uses the CERT filename prefix, and is stored in the user's profile under:

```
%USERPROFILE%\Local Settings\Application Data\Microsoft\DRM
```

as `CERT-Machine.drm`. For Microsoft Vista clients, the location is:

```
%USERPROFILE%\AppData\Local\Microsoft\DRM
```

MACHINE AND USER ACTIVATION

Both a computer and a user (or group) need to be activated to work in the AD RMS environment. There are two types of activation: *machine activation* and *user activation*. Machine activation (also called machine certification) is the process of obtaining an RMS machine certificate; user activation (also called user certification) is the process of obtaining an RAC that ties a specific user, identified by their Windows logon ID or their Passport, to a specific machine certificate.

RIGHTS POLICY TEMPLATES

Administrators can create templates to enable organizations to define global RMS-usage policies for their staff, partners, vendors, and customers. Templates provide a manageable way to assign usage policies. They can be used to protect a company's proprietary data, financial reports, project-related documents, customer data, business intelligence, business-partner information, product research, personal records, and other sensitive data. For example, an organization may want to create several rights policy templates for their employees to assign different usage rights and conditions for different type of data.

PUBLISH AND USE LICENSES

AD RMS Server issues a *publish license* (also known as an *issuance license*). A publish license is created when a document is first protected. It defines usage policies on the content, which includes usage rights and the list of authorized users who can request a use license. Every document you protect gets its own publish license, which is signed by the private key of the RMS server that issued the publish license, ensuring that it cannot be opened with a license from another RMS server.

AD RMS Server issues a *use license,* also known as an *end-user license (EUL),* and is required to decrypt the content, enforce policies, and control content permissions. The use license guarantees that only the intended clients will be able to decrypt and view the protected document. Every document you protect requires its own use license. Depending on the rights policies, use licenses can be stored on the client's machine and reused to open a protected document. With Outlook 2003 and 2007, the use license is stored on the user's computer. When the end user opens a rights-protected email for the first time, a dialog box will appear, prompting the user to store the licenses locally. Depending on your environment, you can enable this behavior or disable it permanently. This use license will be issued from the same RMS server that issued the corresponding publish license. RMS Server will use its private key to sign the use license, ensuring its authenticity. The license will be issued only if the user is listed in the content's publish license. The use license uses the EUL filename prefix, and is stored in a user's profile under:

```
%USERPROFILE%\Local Settings\Application Data\Microsoft\DRM
```

For Microsoft Vista clients, the location is:

```
%USERPROFILE%\AppData\Local\Microsoft\DRM
```

Types of AD RMS Rights

AD RMS–enabled applications—such as MS Office 2003 and MS Office 2007—offer a variety of rights (read, print, copy, modify, save, and forward) to control rights-protected content access. User rights also can be set to expire on a specific date. As an author, you can choose (a) to apply default read rights to all consumers, (b) to use customized templates to create a predefined set of rights for specific individuals or groups, or (c) to use customized permissions to expand rights offered and assigned to each specified individual or group of consumers.

Table 11.1 shows the default AD RMS rights.

TABLE 11.1:   Default AD RMS Rights

RIGHTS	DESCRIPTION
Full control	This right is used to transfer ownership of protected content by providing the consumer with the same abilities given to the publisher.
View	This right enables the consumer to read protected content, but not edit, save, export (save as), print, forward, reply, reply all, extract, allow macros, or view rights.
Edit	This right enables the consumer to read, edit, and save changes to protected content, but not print or perform other tasks.
Save	This right enables the consumer to save changes to protected content.
Export (Save as)	This right enables the consumer to save changes to protected content, and saves as a different filename.
Print	This right enables the consumer to read and print protected content.
Forward	This right enables the consumer to read and forward protected content (emails).
Reply	This right enables the consumer to read and reply to protected content (emails).
Reply all	This right enables the consumer to read and reply to all users of protected content (emails).
Extract	This right enables the consumer to read and extract protected content.
Allow macros	This right enables the consumer to read and execute macros in protected content.
View rights	This right enables the consumer to view rights of protected content.

As publisher, you can further enhance the security of the rights-protected document by defining the expiration policy for the content in the rights policy templates. You can choose one of the following options:

Content Never Expires   This is the default option, and it enables the consumer to access the content as long as the content is available.

Content Expires On   This option enables the publisher to specify a specific date on which the content expires, which means that the use license will expire on the date specified and the user won't be able to acquire another use license.

Content License Expires *n* Days after Publishing Date   This option enables the publisher to specify the number of days after which the consumer will not be able to acquire another use license.

Use Licenses for Content Must Be Renewed Every *n* Days   This option enables the publisher to force the consumers to renew their license after any given period of time.

AD RMS Publishing and Consumption Work Flow

Before installing and configuring Active Directory Rights Management Services, it is important to understand the publishing and consumption work flow. The following high-level work flow is presented by Microsoft in its online documentation, but it is reworded and reorganized here for clarity.

1. A publisher receives a client licensor certificate (CLC) from the RMS server. This is a one-time step, and it is useful for users who need to publish RMS-protected content without being connected to the corporate network. If the publisher has not published and secured any content before, it means a CLC has not been installed on that user's machine. As soon as the publisher secures his or her first content, the publishing computer will request a CLC from the AD RMS server. The AD RMS Server generates a CLC and grants the publishing computer to publish secure content offline. The CLC is unique to each publishing computer, as it is generated with an RMS server public key and a random symmetric key. Once you have the CLC installed on your machine, the publisher doesn't need to access the RMS server to protect any content.

2. A publisher creates a file and defines usage policies on the content by using the installed CLC to generate and sign the document's publish license (also known as an issuance license).

3. AD RMS then encrypts the document file with the random symmetric key and binds the publish license to the document file. The random symmetric key used to encrypt the protected file is joined with the rights policy assigned to the encrypted object and encrypted with the public key of the AD RMS server. By using the public key of the AD RMS server, only the AD RMS server that originally issued the CLC to the publisher can issue licenses to decrypt and open the symmetric key–encrypted content. The publish license contains the (URL) of the RMS server. As per Microsoft, if the publisher is using an RMS-enabled application that performs online file publishing, a CLC is never created; nor is one used as part of the publication process. Instead, the application generates a symmetric key and sends a request for a publish license directly to the RMS server. The request includes the symmetric key and the usage policies. The RMS server generates a publish license, encrypts a random symmetric key with the server public key, and returns the publish license to the application. Online publishing requires this process for each document published.

4. The publisher distributes the content to the consumer through a regular distribution channel, such as email, a network share, a SharePoint website, or removable disk storage media.

5. A consumer opens a file, either with an RMS-enabled application or via Internet Explorer with the RMA.

6. To validate the user and get a use license, the RMS-aware application sends a request to the RMS server that issued the CLC used to protect the content. The request includes the consumer's RAC, which contains the consumer's public key, the publishing license that contains the encrypted symmetric key that encrypted the file, and the rights policy information.

7. Once the AD RMS server receives the request from RMS-aware application, it validates the consumer and creates a use license. During this process, the server decrypts the symmetric key by using the server's private key, re-encrypts it by using the consumer's public key, and adds it to the use license, which contains the rights specified in the rights policy information of the use-license request. This step ensures that only the intended consumer can decrypt the symmetric key and thus decrypt the protected file.

8. Once the validation is complete, the AD RMS server returns the use license to the consumer's client computer.

9. The application renders the use-license file and enforces the user rights defined in the use license. The user rights policy information includes any relevant conditions to the use license, such as the expiration, an application exclusion, or an operating-system exclusion.

Installing and Configuring AD RMS

Now that you've got a basic understanding about AD RMS, it's time to begin installing and configuring it in your organization. The following is a step-by-step guide to build RMS solution in your environment.

1. Ensure that the server meets the hardware and software requirements and recommendations.

2. Create an AD RMS service account.

3. Create an AD RMS installation account.

4. Review the considerations for installing AD RMS.

5. Assign an email address to AD RMS users and groups.

6. Raise the domain functional level.

7. Install SQL Server 2005 on the member server.

8. Install AD RMS.

9. Configure AD RMS Cluster Settings.

10. Verify AD RMS functionality.

The following sections describe these steps in detail.

Step 1: Ensure that the Server Meets the Hardware and Software Requirements and Recommendations

The first step in the process is to make sure that the server meets the minimum hardware and software requirements. Table 11.2 shows the minimum hardware requirements for AD RMS; Table 11.3 shows the minimum software requirements to install it.

TABLE 11.2:   Hardware Requirements for AD RMS

ITEM	MINIMUM CONFIGURATIONS	RECOMMENDED CONFIGURATIONS
Processor	One Pentium 4.3 GHz processor or higher	Two Pentium 4.3 GHz processors or higher
Hard disk	40 GB of available disk space	80 GB of available disk space
Memory	2 GB	4 GB

TABLE 11.3:   Software Requirements for AD RMS

ITEM	RECOMMENDATIONS
Operating system	Microsoft Windows Server 2008
Messaging	Message Queuing (also known as MSMQ) for logging and AD integration
Web services	Internet Information Services (IIS); ASP.NET
Domain	Active Directory domain with domain controllers running Windows 2000 Server with Service Pack 3 (SP3) or above, Windows Server 2003, and/or Windows Server 2008
Database server	SQL Server 2005
Email properties	All users and groups who use AD RMS to acquire licenses and publish content must have an email address configured in Active Directory.
Deployment server	Software-deployment solution such as SMS
Client software	Windows RMS client software: Supported client operating systems are Windows 2000 SP3 or above, Windows 98 SE, Windows Server 2003, Windows XP, Windows Vista, and Windows Server 2008.
RMS-enabled applications	Microsoft Office 2003 or above; Internet Explorer RMS plug-in

Step 2: Create an AD RMS Service Account

The second step in the process is to create a domain user account that will be used as the AD RMS service account. This account will not need any additional permissions or rights associated with it. During the installation, this account will be made a member of the AD RMS service group and will be granted the permissions defined for that group.

To create an AD RMS service account, do the following:

1. Log on to the domain controller.

2. Click Start ➤ All Programs ➤ Administrative Tools ➤ Active Directory Users and Computers. In the console tree, expand *domainname*.

3. Right-click Users ➢ New and then click User.

4. In the New Object – User dialog box, type **ADRMSSRVC** in the Full Name and User Logon Name boxes, as shown in Figure 11.1. Then click Next.

5. Type a password of your choice in the Password and Confirm Password boxes. Uncheck the User Must Change Password at Next Logon check box (Figure 11.2).

6. Click Next and then click Finish.

7. Close the Active Directory Users and Computers console.

FIGURE 11.1
Creating a new user

FIGURE 11.2
Setting password conditions

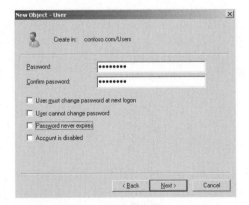

Step 3: Create an AD RMS Installation Account

The third step in the process is to create an installation account for AD RMS installation services, which will also be used to administer AD RMS services. This account will be made a member of the Domain Admins and Enterprise Admins groups. Later on, you'll add this account as a member of the Local Administrators group on the SQL server and the AD RMS Server.

Complete the following steps to create AD RMS installation account:

1. Log on to the domain controller.

2. Click Start ➤ All Programs ➤ Administrative Tools ➤ Active Directory Users and Computers. In the console tree, expand *domainname*.

3. Create a new user account by following steps 3–6 in the previous section, but for Full Name and User Logon Name enter **ADRMSADMIN**.

4. In the Active Directory Users and Computers console, click Users, and then double-click Enterprise Admins.

5. Click Members, and then click Add.

6. Type **ADRMSADMIN**, click Check Names, and then click OK.

7. Repeat steps 4–6 to add ADRMSADMIN to the Domain Admins group.

8. Close the Active Directory Users and Computers console.

Step 4: Review the Considerations for Installing AD RMS

The fourth step in the process is to review the following considerations before installing AD RMS in your environment. These considerations are presented by Microsoft in its online documentation, but they are reworded here for clarity.

♦ Use a dedicated database server to host the AD RMS database.

♦ Avoid using the Windows Internal Database in a production deployment; Windows Internal Database is intended to use only for a test environment, and does not support remote connections, which means that you will not be able to add another server to the AD RMS cluster.

♦ For the AD RMS cluster, use an SSL certificate from a trusted root certificate authority (such as VeriSign). For test and lab environments, you can use self-signed certificates or certificates from your IIS server.

♦ You must have an SSL certificate present on the new member server of the cluster before the AD RMS installation starts.

♦ AD RMS does not support using the name localhost as the cluster URL.

♦ To avoid publishing all rights-protected files, it is recommended that you create a separate DNS alias (CNAME) record for the AD RMS cluster URL and for the computer hosting the AD RMS configuration database.

♦ For the AD RMS cluster, reserve a URL that will be available throughout the lifetime of the AD RMS installation.

♦ Make sure that the user account you use for installing AD RMS is different from the service account. The account you use must have permissions on the database server to create new databases. Microsoft recommends that if you are registering the AD RMS service connection point (SCP) during installation, the user account installing AD RMS must be a member of the AD DS Enterprise Admins group. The user account must have permissions to query the AD DS domain.

♦ If the AD RMS service connection point (SCP), the object in Active Directory that defines the services, already exists in the Active Directory forest, ensure that the cluster URL in the SCP is the same as the cluster URL for the new installation. If the URLs are not the same, you should not register the SCP during AD RMS installation.

Step 5: Assign an Email Address to AD RMS Users and Groups

The fifth step in the process is to ensure that you have an email address defined in the properties for each user and group account that you want to configure with AD RMS.

Do the following to add an email address to a user account:

1. Log on to the domain controller.

2. Click Start ➤ All Programs ➤ Administrative Tools ➤ Active Directory Users and Computers. In the console tree, expand *domainname*.

3. In the Active Directory Users and Computers console, select Users, right-click the user account, select Properties and then type in **userlogonid@domain.com** in the E-mail box, as shown in Figure 11.3. Click OK.

4. Repeat step 3 for all users and groups that will use AD RMS service in your environment.

5. Close the Active Directory Users and Computers console.

FIGURE 11.3
Assigning an email
address

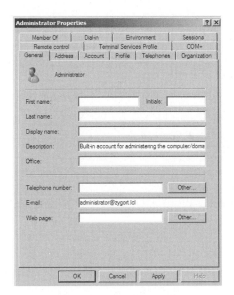

Step 6: Raise the Domain Functional Level

Although you can perform this step before any of the previous steps, you need to raise the Active Directory domain functional level to Windows Server 2003 native or higher for all Active Directory domains where you will be installing AD RMS. Doing so will allow universal groups to be used. If you are running only Windows 2008 servers, this step is unnecessary.

To raise the domain functional level, complete the following steps:

1. Click Start ➤ All Programs ➤ Administrative Tools ➤ Active Directory Users and Computers.

2. Right-click your Active Directory domain and choose Raise Domain Functional Level in the context menu.

3. In the Select an Available Domain Functional Level box, select Windows Server 2003 ➢ Raise.

4. You will see a warning box that reads, "This change affects the entire domain. After you raise the domain functional level, it cannot be reversed." Click OK to continue.

5. The information message will appear indicating that the domain functional level has been raised. Click OK.

6. Close the Active Directory Users and Computers console.

Step 7: Install SQL Server 2005 on a Member Server

The next step in the process is to install SQL Server 2005 on a member server in the AD DS domain:

1. Log on to the server on which you want to install SQL Server 2005.

2. Insert the SQL Server 2005 installation media into the DVD drive. As soon as you insert the SQL Server 2005 media into the DVD drive, setup will start automatically and begin initializing.

3. Read the license agreement. Click the I Accept the Licensing Terms and Conditions check box on the License Agreement page, and then click Next.

4. On the Installing Prerequisites page, click Install.

5. Click Next.

6. On the Welcome to the Microsoft SQL Server Installation Wizard page, click Next, and then click Next again.

7. In the Name box, type your name. In the Company box, type the name of your organization, and then type in the appropriate product key. Click Next.

8. Select SQL Server Database Services. Additionally, you can select the Workstation components, Books Online, and Development Tools check boxes if you want to install those components on your server, and then click Next.

9. Select the Default Instance option, and then click Next.

10. Select Use the Built-in System account, and then click Next.

11. Click Windows Authentication Mode, and then click Next.

12. Click Next, accepting the default collation settings, and then click Next again.

13. Click Install. Setup will then install SQL Server 2005 on the computer, copy SQL files from the source (DVD-ROM) to the destination path on your hard drive, and install the SQL server. When the status of all the selected components is finished, click Next.

14. Click Finish.

Once you finish installing SQL Server 2005, you should add the AD RMS installation account (created under "Step 3: Create an AD RMS Installation Account" as the ADRMSADMIN Domain Admin user account) to the local Administrators group on the SQL server. This account needs administrative permissions in order to create an AD RMS database. After the AD RMS installation, you can remove the AD RMS installation account from this group.

Step 8: Install AD RMS

The eighth step in the process is to install AD RMS in your environment. Make sure that the Windows Server 2008 member server is a part of your Active Directory domain. Ensure that you have a public or domain certificate for the AD RMS server before you proceed with the following instructions. We are assuming that you have a public certificate from a trusted source such as VeriSign for your AD RMS server. Alternatively, you can obtain a domain certificate if users will be using a domain certificate to access AD RMS.

Do the following to obtain a domain certificate for your AD RMS server:

1. Log on to the server on which you want to install AD RMS.

2. Click Start ➢ All Programs ➢ Administrative Tools ➢ Internet Information Service (IIS) Manager.

3. In the console tree, expand ADRMSServer.

4. In the details pane, double-click Server Certificates (Figure 11.4).

5. In the Actions pane, click Create Domain Certificate.

6. In the Create Certificate dialog box, for Common Name enter **ADRMSServer**, and for Organization Unit enter **DC**. Fill in the other fields with your organization's name and location.

7. Click Next.

8. On the Online Certification Authority page, click Select. Click Online Certificate Authority, and then click OK.

9. Type **ADRMSServer** in the Friendly Name field, and then click Finish.

10. Close the Internet Information Services (IIS) Manager window.

FIGURE 11.4
Open the Server Certificates window.

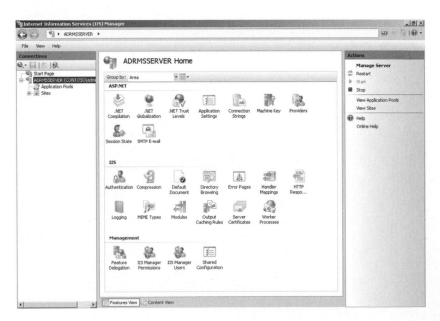

ADDING AN AD RMS INSTALLATION ACCOUNT TO THE LOCAL ADMINISTRATORS ACCOUNT

Before you install AD RMS, you should add the AD RMS installation account (created under "Step 3: Create an AD RMS Installation Account" as the ADRMSADMIN Domain Admin user account) to the local Administrators group on the AD RMS Server. This account needs administrative permissions on the local machine in order to install AD RMS services.

AD RMS ROLES PREREQUISITES

The AD RMS server role requires Internet Information Services (IIS) 7.0, Message Queuing, and Windows Internal Database. Installing the AD RMS role will automatically select and install the prerequisite components.

Do the following to install AD RMS:

1. Log on to the server on which you want to install AD RMS.

2. Click Start ➤ All Programs ➤ Administrative Tools ➤ Server Manager.

3. In the Roles Summary box, click Add Roles. The Add Roles Wizard opens.

4. Read the Before You Begin section, and then click Next.

5. On the Select Server Roles page (Figure 11.5), select Active Directory Rights Management Services and click Install.

6. The Add Roles Wizard page appears (Figure 11.6), informing you of the AD RMS–dependent role services and features. Make sure that Web Server (IIS) and Windows Process Activation Service are listed. Click Add Required Role Services, and then click Next.

7. Read the Introduction to Active Directory Rights Management Services page, and then click Next.

FIGURE 11.5
Choosing server roles

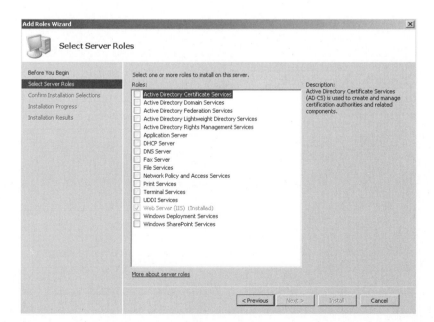

FIGURE 11.6
The wizard alerts
you about prerequi-
site elements.

8. On the Active Directory Rights Management Role Services page, verify that the Active Directory Rights Management Server check box is selected, and then click Next.

9. On the Specify Setup Type page (Figure 11.7), make sure Use This Server To Create a New AD RMS Cluster is selected, and then click Next.

10. On the Set Up Configuration Database page, choose Use the Database Engine Built into Windows, and then click Next. (Note: If you are planning to use a dedicated SQL server in your environment, then select Specify an Existing Database Server to type in the server name and SQL Server instance information.)

11. On the Specify Service Account page, choose Domain User Account and then click Select User. Type in **ADRMSSRVC** as the user name and enter the password in the Windows Security dialog box, and then click OK to continue. Click Next.

12. On the Set Up Key Management page (Figure 11.8), click Use AD RMS Encryption Mechanism, and click Next.

FIGURE 11.7
Set up a cluster.

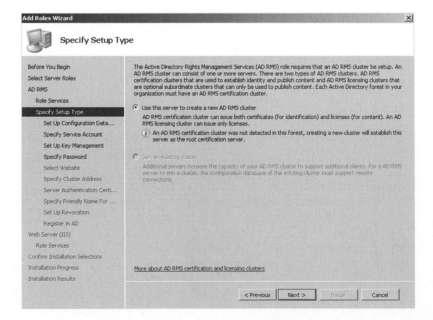

FIGURE 11.8
Choose an encryption
method.

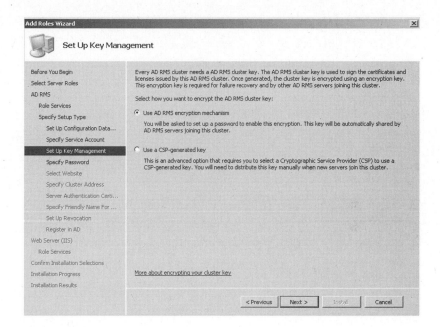

13. On the Specify Password for AD RMS Encryption page, in the Password and Confirm Password fields, type a strong password, and then click Next.

14. On the Select Website page, choose the website where AD RMS will be installed, and then click Next. (Note: In an installation that uses default settings, the name of the only available website should be Default Web Site.)

15. On the Specify Cluster Address page (Figure 11.9), select the Use a Secure (https://) Cluster Address option, and then click Validate. Click Next.

16. On the Choose a Server Authentication Certificate for SSL Encryption page (Figure 11.10), ensure that Choose an Existing Certificate for SSL Encryption (Recommended) is selected, and then select your server. (Note: This is the certificate that has been imported for this AD RMS cluster.) Click Next.

17. On the Specify a Friendly Name for the Licensor Certificate page, type a name that will help you identify the AD RMS cluster in the Friendly Name box, and then click Next.

18. On the Set Up Revocation page, click Next.

19. On the Register This AD RMS Server in Active Directory page (Figure 11.11), choose Register Later if you are planning to install additional AD RMS servers before your clients can utilize licenses and certificates issued by this server. Choose the Register Now option if you want to register the AD RMS service connection point in Active Directory during installation, so that AD RMS will be available to clients immediately after this installation. Click Next.

20. On the Web Server (IIS) page, read the Introduction to Web Server (IIS) information, and then click Next.

21. On the Select Role Services page (Figure 11.12), keep the Web Server default check-box selections and then click Next.

FIGURE 11.9
Choose a cluster
address type.

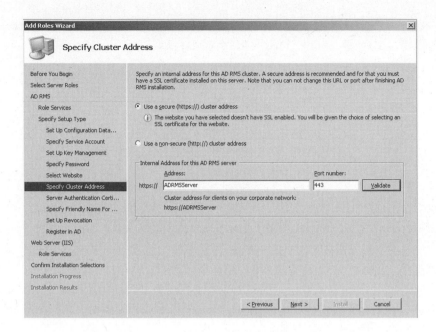

FIGURE 11.10
Select a certificate.

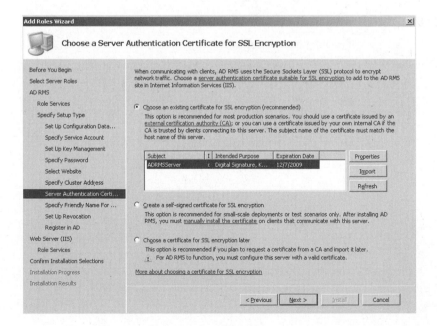

FIGURE 11.11

Are you ready to register?

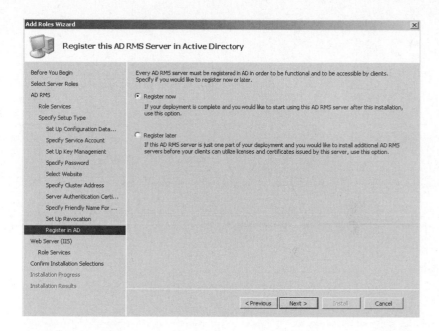

FIGURE 11.12

Leave these options at their default.

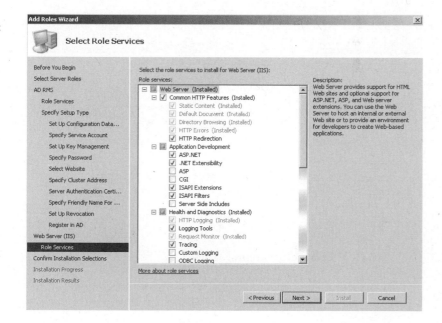

22. On the Confirm Installation Selections page, click Install. It can take up to 30 minutes to complete the installation.

23. On the Installation Results page, click Close.

24. Log off of the computer, and then log back on with an ADRMS Installation account. This is important, as you need to get a new security token of the logged-on user account before you proceed with the AD RMS administration. The user account that is used to install AD RMS is automatically made a member of the local AD RMS Enterprise Administrators group.

Step 9: Configure AD RMS Cluster Settings

The ninth step in the process is to configure AD RMS cluster settings:

1. Log on to the AD RMS server.

2. Click Start ➤ All Programs ➤ Administrative Tools, and then click Active Directory Rights Management Services.

3. In the console tree, click ADRMSServer (Local).

4. In the Actions pane, click Properties.

5. On the ADRMSServer (Local) Properties dialog box, click the SCP tab. Click Change SCP, make sure Set SCP to Current Certification Cluster is selected, and then click OK.

6. Click Yes on the Active Directory Rights Management Services dialog box to register the SCP in Active Directory Domain Services.

7. In the console tree, right-click the ADRMSServer (Local), and then click Refresh to refresh the screen.

8. Close the Active Directory Rights Management console window.

Step 10: Verify AD RMS Functionality

The last step in the process is to verify AD RMS functionality. Do the following to accomplish this:

1. Log on to the Windows Vista workstation as DOMAIN\User1.

2. Open Internet Explorer.

3. Click Tools ➤ Internet Options and then click the Security tab.

4. Select Local Intranet ➤ Sites (Figure 11.13) and then click the Advanced button.

5. Type **https://adrmsserver** and then click Add (Figure 11.14).

FIGURE 11.13
Click Advanced to add
a server.

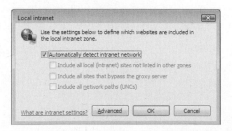

FIGURE 11.14
We've added the
AD RMS server.

6. Click Close. Click OK twice.

7. In Internet Explorer, enter this URL to make sure that you are able to acquire RMS licenses (Figure 11.15): `https://adrmsserver/_wmcs/licensing/license.asmx`.

8. In Internet Explorer, enter this URL to make sure that you are able to access the certification website (Figure 11.16): `https://adrmsserver/_wmcs/certification/certification.asmx`.

9. Launch Microsoft Word 2007.

10. Click OK on the User Name dialog box.

11. Type in few lines of text.

12. Click the Microsoft Office button ➤ Prepare ➤ Restrict Permission ➤ Restricted Access.

13. Click Restrict Permission to This Document.

14. In the Read field, type **user1@domain.com**, and then click OK.

FIGURE 11.15
Checking license
acquisition

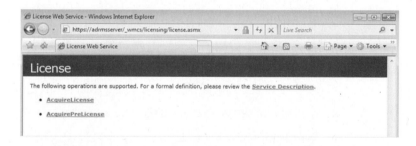

FIGURE 11.16
Checking certification

15. Click the Microsoft Office button and then click Save As ➤ Word Document.

16. In the Save As dialog box, locate the network share and, in the File Name field, type in **adrmstest.doc** and then click Save.

17. Close Microsoft Word and log off as DOMAIN\User1.

18. Log on to the Windows Vista workstation as DOMSIN\User2.

19. Locate the network share, and then double-click `adrmstest.doc`.

20. Click OK on the User Name dialog box.

21. The following message appears: "Permission to this document is currently restricted. Microsoft Office must connect to http://ADRMSSERVER:443/_wmcs/licensing to verify your credentials and download your permission." Click OK.

22. The following message appears: "Verifying your credentials for opening content with restricted permissions . . . ." When the document opens, click the Microsoft Office button. You will notice that the Print option is not available. Click View Permission in the message bar. You should see that `User2@domain.com` has been restricted to only viewing the document.

23. Click OK to close the My Permissions dialog box, and then close Microsoft Word 2007.

AD RMS Application Template

Now that you've installed and tested AD RMS, it's time to create and deploy AD RMS policy templates, which describe rights that can apply to information, and the context in which those rights exist. AD RMS templates enable organizations to define global RMS policies for their staff, partners, vendors, and customers for confidential data and information. Templates can be used to protect company proprietary data, financial reports, project-related documents, customer data, business intelligence, business-partner information, product research, personal records, and other sensitive data. Initially no rights policies exist, so you'll need to create your own.

The following step-by-step guide will help you create a rights policy template, deploy this template to a client computer, and verify that the client computer can use the newly created rights policy template to secure content and information.

Here is a high-level overview to deploy an AD RMS application template:

1. Create a shared folder on the AD RMS cluster to store application templates.

2. Create an AD RMS application template.

3. Configure an AD RMS client to allow access to the rights policy templates.

4. Verify the AD RMS functionality.

Step 1: Create a Shared Folder on the AD RMS Cluster to Store Application Templates

The first step in the process of deploying AD RMS application templates is to create a shared folder on the AD RMS cluster to store AD RMS rights policy templates. This shared folder will serve as a central repository of rights policy templates. In order for the rights policy template

---

TEMPLATE USAGE

Administrators can create templates to enable organizations to define global RMS usage policies. Each template in the AD RMS environment has a name defined, users' rights, a revocation policy, and an expiration policy. We recommend you create multiple templates for users in your organization and outside of your organization and establish usage policies for such things as Confidential, Read-Only, Read-Only but Allow Forwarding and Printing, confidential for Internal Full-Time Employees, and so on. Here is an example:

Organization Confidential   The intended audience of this template is organization staff, not including any vendors, partners, or distributors. Any person outside of the organization will not be able to open the content.

Organization Confidential Read-Only   The template modifies the previous template with application of restrictive read-only rights.

Organization Full-Time Employee Confidential   The intended audience of this template is organization full-time staff. Any person outside of the full-time employee scope (such as part-time employees, contractors, outside vendors, partners, and distributors) will not be able to open the content.

Organization Full-Time Employee Confidential Read-Only   The template modifies the previous template with application of restrictive read-only rights.

Organization Part-Time Employee Confidential   The intended audience of this template is organization part-time staff. Any person outside of the part-time employee scope (for instance, full-time employees, contractors, outside vendors, partners, and distributors) will not be able to open the content.

Organization Part-Time Employee Confidential Read-Only   The template modifies the previous template with application of restrictive read-only rights.

Organization Public Read-Only   The intended audience of this template is the organization's public, including organization staff, contractors, outside vendors, partners, and distributors; however, they will be able to only read the document, not print the content.

---

export function to work correctly, make sure that the AD RMS service account has access to this central repository.

Perform the following steps to create the AD RMS rights policy template shared folder:

1. Log on to the AD RMS server.

2. Click Start ➢ Computer, and then double-click the local disk (C:) drive.

3. Click Organize ➢ New Folder, type the name **Templates**, and then press Enter.

4. Right-click the Templates folder ➢ Properties ➢ Sharing.

5. Click Advanced Sharing and then click Share this Folder.

6. Click Permissions ➢ Add, and type **ADRMSSRVC** in the box for Enter the Object Names to Select. Click Check Names, and then click OK.

7. Click ADRMSSRVC (ADRMSSRVC@yourdomain.com) in the Group or User Names box, and then assign change permissions by clicking the Change check box in the Allow column. Click OK twice.

8. Click the Security tab, and then click Edit.

9. Click Add, type **ADRMSSRVC** in the box for Enter the Object Names to Select. Click Check Names, and then click OK.

10. Click ADRMSSRVC (ADRMSSRVC@yourdomain.com) in the Group or User Names box, and then assign Modify permissions by selecting the Modify check box in the Allow column, and then click OK.

11. Repeat steps 6–10 for all users and groups who would be using the AD RMS service.

12. Close Windows Explorer.

Step 2: Create an AD RMS Application Template

The second step in the process is to create Active Directory Rights Management Services templates and store them on the shared folder/repository on the AD RMS cluster.

COPYING TEMPLATES TO CLIENT MACHINES

After you create AD RMS rights policy templates, you must export them to a central shared repository so that they can be copied to the AD RMS clients. To access these templates, your internal users must have read access to this central repository. For traveling users with a laptop or other mobile device, you can either manually copy these templates to the client computers or distribute these templates using distribution methods like Active Directory Group Policies or System Center Configuration Manager 2007.

Do the following to create the AD RMS rights policy template:

1. Log on to the AD RMS server.

2. Click Start ≻ All Programs ≻ Administrative Tools ≻ Active Directory Rights Management Services.

3. In the console tree, click ADRMSServer (Local).

4. In the Results pane, click Manage Rights Policy Templates. To enable exporting of the AD RMS rights policy templates, click Properties in the Actions pane (Figure 11.17).

5. Select the Enable Export check box (Figure 11.18), type **\\adrmsserver\templates** in the Specify Templates File Location (UNC) box, and then click OK.

6. In the Actions pane, click Create Distributed Rights Policy Template to start the Create Distributed Rights Policy Template Wizard. Click the Add button.

7. In the Add New Template Identification Information dialog (Figure 11.19), choose the appropriate language for the rights policy template. Type *Yourdomain.com* **CC** in the Name box, and type **Company Confidential Documents** in the Description box.

8. Click Add, and then click Next (Figure 11.20) to continue.

9. Click the Add button on the Add User Rights screen (Figure 11.21).

FIGURE 11.17
Click Properties to
enable exporting.

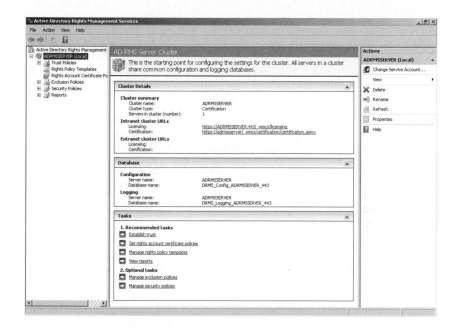

FIGURE 11.18
Enable
exporting here.

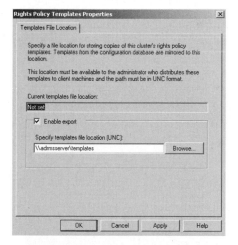

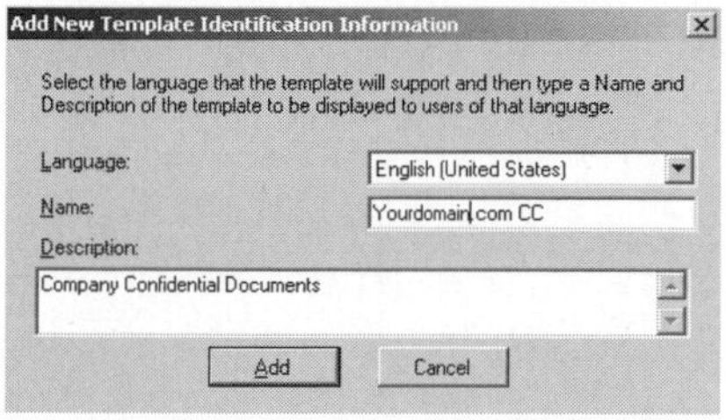

FIGURE 11.19
Set up the new
template.

FIGURE 11.20
The new template

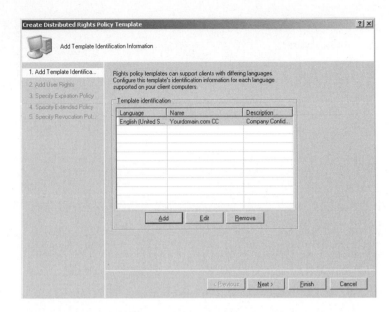

FIGURE 11.21
Adding user rights to
the template

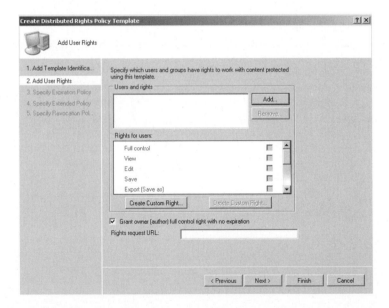

10. Type *username@yourdomain.com* in the E-mail Address of a User or Group box. Click OK.

11. Repeat steps 9 and 10 to add multiple users and groups who will be using this template (Figure 11.22). (Note: To give the owner (author) full-control rights with no expiration, make sure Grant Owner (Author) Full Control Right with No Expiration is selected.)

12. Click Finish.

FIGURE 11.22
Users granted rights to
the template

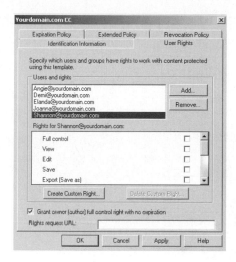

Step 3: Configure an AD RMS Client to Allow Access to the Rights Policy Templates

The third step in the process is to configure the AD RMS client to access the AD RMS rights policy templates. To achieve this, you must copy the AD RMS rights policy templates to the client computer and then create a registry entry that points to the central repository of the rights policy templates.

Perform the following steps to configure the AD RMS clients to access the AD RMS rights policy templates:

1. Log on to the Windows Vista workstation as Local Administrator.

2. Click Start ➤ Computer and then double-click the local disk (C:) drive.

3. Click Organize ➤ New Folder, and then type **ADRMSDocs**.

4. Right-click the ADRMSDocs folder, and then click Properties.

5. Click the Security tab, and then click Edit.

6. Click Users and in the Permissions for Users box, select the Modify check box in the Allow column.

7. Click OK twice.

If your clients are traveling users and they need to locate the templates offline, you must complete the following steps before rights-protecting a document:

1. Log on to the Windows Vista workstation as a user.

2. Click Start ➤ Run, and type **cmd.exe.** Then press Enter or click OK.

3. Type **Regedit**.

4. Navigate to:

    HKEY_CURRENT_USER\Software\Microsoft\Office\12.0\Common\DRM

Select DRM ➤ Edit ➤ New ➤ Expandable String Value, and then type **AdminTemplatePath**.

5. Double-click the AdminTemplatePath registry value and type **%UserProfile%\AppData\Microsoft\DRM\Templates** as the Value data, and then click OK.

6. Close Registry Editor.

7. Verify that the path C:\Users*UserName*\AppData\Microsoft\DRM\Templates\ is valid. If it is not, create the appropriate folders.

8. Click Start, type **ADRMSServer\Templates** in the Start Search box, and then press Enter.

9. Copy the exported AD RMS rights policy templates from \\ADRMSServer\Templates to C:\Users*UserName*\AppData\Microsoft\DRM\Templates.

10. Close Windows Explorer.

Step 4: Verify the AD RMS Functionality

The last step in the process is to verify AD RMS functionality to make sure that the AD RMS rights policy templates are working properly. To achieve this, you log on as User1 and then use the policy template created in the previous step to restrict permissions on a Microsoft Word 2007 document. This policy template will allow certain users to read the document but not to modify, edit, delete, print, or copy it. All other people in your organization will have no access to the document.

Do the following to verify the functionality of the AD RMS rights policy templates:

1. Log on to the Windows Vista workstation (user1@yourcompany.com).

2. Launch Microsoft Word 2007.

3. Click OK on the User Name dialog box.

4. Type in few lines of text.

5. Click the Microsoft Office button ➤ Prepare ➤ Restrict Permission, and then click Restricted Access.

6. Click Restrict Permission to This Document As, select user1@yourcompany.com in the Select User dialog box, and then click OK.

7. Save the file as \\ADRMSServer\data\ADRMSTest.docx.

8. Log off.

The next step is to log on as another user and open the document ADRMSTest.docx. To view a protected document, do the following:

1. Log on to the Windows Vista workstation as another user (user2@yourcompany.com).

2. Launch Microsoft Word 2007.

3. Navigate to \\ADRMSServer\data and open ADRMSTest.docx.

4. The following message appears: "Permission to this document is currently restricted. Microsoft Office must connect to http://ADRMSSERVER:443/_wmcs/licensing to verify your credentials and download your permission." Click OK.

5. The following message appears: "Verifying your credentials for opening content with restricted permissions…." When the document opens, click the Microsoft Office button. You will notice that the Print option is not available. Click View Permission in the message bar. You should see that your AD RMS rights policy template has been applied to the document.

6. Click OK to close the My Permissions dialog box, and then close Microsoft Word 2007.

AD RMS Auditing

Active Directory Rights Management Services (AD RMS) allows you to enable logging to track user activities, including their successful and failed attempts to access data. It's helpful to audit this data during any forensic investigation. The AD RMS cluster records all activities to a log file that is stored in a database. The AD RMS logging services uses Microsoft Message Queuing (MSMQ) to send log messages from the cluster to the logging database. If a connection to the database is not present, MSMQ stores the logging information in the cache, and once the connection is restored, all the information from the cache will be replicated to the database. Though this logging and auditing is an optional feature, we recommend enabling it.

Do the following to enable and disable the logging:

1. Log on to the AD RMS server.

2. Click Start ➢ All Programs ➢ Administrative Tools ➢ Active Directory Rights Management Services.

3. In the console tree, click ADRMSServer (Local).

4. In the Actions pane, click Properties.

5. On the ADRMSServer (Local) Properties dialog box, click the Logging tab, and then select or clear the Enable Logging check box.

6. Click OK.

Repeat these steps for each server in the AD RMS cluster.

The Bottom Line

Understanding rights-management servers   The AD RMS Server is a server component that will issue RMS certificates and licenses, enroll servers and users, perform administrative functions, and manage licensing of rights-protected information.

Master It   Shannon is the administrator of a large nationwide distribution company. She is implementing AD RMS servers for different departments in different geographical regions. She has installed the Root Certification server, but the consultant, Jami, said Shannon needs to install one more server in each geographical region before she can distribute license roles geographically. What server should Shannon install to distribute publish and use licenses geographically?

Understanding certificates   Understanding certificates and their uses is important in an AD RMS environment. The certificates that clients use are stored in the users' profile; however, you must understand the certificates' usage if you have to troubleshoot AD RMS licensing issues.

Master It   Juan works as an AD RMS administrator for a medium-size bank in Toronto. While installing a new AD RMS server on the domain, Juan found there are multiple certificates installed on each client's machine. He is unable to identify RACs. How can he identify them?

Troubleshoot decryption of contents   Understanding licenses and their uses is important in an Active Directory Rights Management Services (AD RMS) environment. Licenses are required for encrypting and decrypting message contents.

Master It   Spiros is the administrator of a large manufacturing company in Greece. His company is often the target of hackers that are interested in trade secrets and intellectual property. To address these issues, Spiros has implemented AD RMS in his organization. After he installed it, he began receiving a lot of help desk calls complaining that users are unable to get the use license. He has to explain the term *use license* to his manager, Demi. How should he explain it?

Know the importance of RMA in an AD RMS infrastructure   Understanding RMS-aware applications is important in an AD RMS environment. Although other AD RMS components (such the AD RMS cluster, Root Certification server, license cluster, server licensor certificate (SLC), client licensor certificate (CLC), and so on) are equally important to understand and implement, understanding AD RMS–aware applications is important to troubleshooting and open RMS-protected application.

Master It   Elanda is planning to use AD RMS for remote users. She is responsible for identifying tools, utilities, and implementation strategies to enable RMS for remote users who do not have RMS-aware applications installed on their machines. Which applications can she use to view documents in Microsoft Internet Explorer when an intended application is not available?

Chapter 12

Managing Active Directory Certificate Services

With the rise in malicious attacks on companies from within and without, it is important to have a good mechanism in place to verify the identity of users, computers, applications, and network devices. Additionally, many organizations must now comply with stiffer U.S. government requirements for data security. Certificate Services encompasses many different features and services that enable both large and small organizations to meet their security needs.

The process of securing information has been around for centuries and is called cryptography. Julius Caesar used a simple substitution cipher (replacing the letter A with a D, B with an E, and so on) to encrypt messages sent to his generals. The word *cryptography* is derived from a Greek word for "hidden writing."

Primarily, cryptography is concerned with safeguarding either the storage or the transmission of information. To achieve this, cryptography must fulfill five security objectives:

◆ Cryptography must protect the confidentiality of the information; only authorized users should be able to access the information.

◆ Cryptography must provide for authentication of the sender; the message recipient should know who the sender is.

◆ Cryptography must ensure the integrity of the information; the message recipient will know that the message has not been modified during transmission.

◆ Cryptography must enforce nonrepudiation, meaning the sender can't deny having sent the message, and the recipient can't deny having received the message.

◆ Cryptography must be available for system-access control. Computer networks often use tokens, as in Kerberos-based systems, to control access to encrypted data stored on a disk drive.

Certificate Services meets all of these requirements, as do the digital certificates that it creates. In this chapter, you will learn:

◆ What Certificate Services is

◆ How Microsoft implements Certificate Services

◆ What's new in the Windows Server 2008 implementation of Certificate Services

◆ How to configure and manage the components of Active Directory Certificate Services (AD CS)

What Is Certificate Services?

Microsoft's Certificate Services enables organizations to enhance their overall security via the distribution and use of certificates. Certificate Services enables organizations to issue and manage digital certificates. In Windows Server 2008, you use the Server Manager Add Roles Wizard to add Certificate Services and create a certification authority (CA). The CA will then receive requests for digital certificates, verify the information provided by the requester, issue the certificate if the request is approved, revoke certificates when necessary, and publish a certificate-revocation list (CRL).

To understand how Microsoft implements Certificate Services, it is important to understand what digital certificates are, how they are created, and where they are used. The next section provides a concise overview of digital certificates.

X.509—Digital Certificates

X.509 is an international standard—defined by the International Telecommunication Union (ITU), which defines the format for digital certificates—that is the most widely used certificate format for public key infrastructure (PKI). X.509 also includes standards for certificate-revocation list implementations—an often neglected aspect of PKI systems. The following protocols support X.509:

◆ Secure Sockets Layers/Transport Layer Security (SSL/TLS)

◆ IP Security (IPSec)

◆ Secure Multipurpose Internet Mail Extensions (S/MIME)

◆ Smart cards

◆ Secure Shell (SSH)

◆ Hypertext Transfer Protocol over Secure Socket Layer (HTTPS)

◆ Lightweight Directory Access Protocol (LDAP), Version 3

◆ Extensible Authentication Protocol (EAP)

◆ Trusted Computing Group Trusted Network Connect (TCG TNC)

◆ Web Services Security (WS-Security)

The X.509 specification was developed in 1988 in association with the X.500 directory standard. It is a vastly different format than the one used by Pretty Good Privacy (PGP), which uses a process called *web of trust*. Essentially, web of trust works this way: A trusts B, B trusts C, and therefore A trusts C. X.509 instead uses a strict hierarchical system of certification authorities (CAs) that issue the digital certificates. Over the years, new and enhanced versions have added more fields, support for directory access control, and support for other topologies. A full definition of X.509 would take several chapters; however, those wishing to learn more can review the following specifications: RFC 3280: www.ietf.org/rfc/rfc3280.txt, RFC 4325: www.ietf.org/rfc/rfc4325.txt, and RFC 4630: www.ietf.org/rfc/rfc4630.txt.

The heart of the X.509 system is the CA who issues a certificate that binds a public key either to a name (as defined by X.500), a Domain Name Service (DNS) entry, or an email address. This certificate is authenticated by a certification authority that is supported by a root certificate.

CERTIFICATE KEYS

The electronic keys that a certificate creates are much like a set of car keys. Most new cars come with two types of keys: a master set that opens everything, and a valet set that only opens the door and starts the engine. Certificate keys come in two types as well: a private set used only by the certificate holder to encrypt documents, and a public set that can be shared with anyone who needs to read those encrypted documents.

Excellent examples of root certificates are the ones installed in your web browser. Most browsers have several well-known CAs configured by default so the user does not need to figure out how to contact the CA and go through the processes of verifying other users' certificates. It is all taken care of in the background processing of the web browser. Figure 12.1 shows such a preinstalled root certificate. Root certificates are trusted absolutely.

The CA can be internal to an organization. Most server operating systems (for example, Windows Server) offer the ability to install and configure a CA service. An organization can also install more than one CA server. The first server is usually referred to as the *root CA*. CAs below the root are referred to as *intermediate*, *subordinate*, or *issuing CAs*. When a company uses its own CA, administrators can configure how authentication will take place, how to maintain the certificates, and how to recall certificates when necessary.

Other types of CAs are organizations dedicated to this type of service and, for a fee, individuals and companies subscribe to their service. VeriSign, Comodo, GoDaddy, and Equifax Secure are all examples of popular commercial CAs. CAs that publicly issue digital certificates usually require that the requesters provide identifying documents, such as driver's licenses, passports, or various corporate documentation.

FIGURE 12.1
Browser-installed
root certificate

You can think of a digital certificate as an electronic identification card, much like a driver's license or employee badge, that validates your identity when doing business or other transactions over the Internet. A digital certificate can be presented to prove identity or to grant the right to access information or other services online. When used in conjunction with encryption, a digital certificate provides improved security by ensuring the identities of all the parties involved in a transaction. Digital certificates can also be used to identify items other than humans, such as servers, routers, and software applications.

Unlike most forms of identification that you carry, say a driver's license or passport, it is completely safe to exchange digital certificates with someone else; they do not contain any confidential information nor a copy of the certificate holder's private key. Further, it is not possible to modify a digital certificate without the changes being detected.

Typically a digital certificate contains the following information that both describes the certificate and limits the scope of its use:

◆ Certificate holder's public key

◆ Information about the individual, computer, or organization to which the certificate was issued

◆ Information about the CA or organization that issued the certificate

◆ Date that the certificate was issued and its expiration date

◆ Serial number and version number of the certificate

◆ Algorithm ID information

In addition to those items, a digital certificate may contain information about the certificate's intended use. This would allow an application, for example, to verify a user's credentials to determine what that user is permitted to do. Applications can also verify the validity of the certificate and find out if the certificate has been revoked. Digital certificates are often kept in registries so that authenticating users can look up other users' public keys.

Life Cycle of a Digital Certificate

No digital certificate should live forever. Employees leave, old computer hardware is removed and new hardware is installed, applications are updated, and cryptographic standards evolve continually. Each of these changes affects the usefulness of a digital certificate. The life cycle of a certificate is generally divided into four parts: creation, revocation, expiration, and suspension.

DIGITAL-CERTIFICATE CREATION

During this stage, the certificate is created and issued to the user. Issuing or receiving a certificate can be done in a number of ways. The most basic method is for users to create certificates themselves. One self-issuing method uses the Microsoft software Digital Certificate for VBA Projects. When a user runs this program, he or she is presented with the screen shown in Figure 12.2.

Unfortunately, self-issuing certificates are not considered to be trusted because there is no CA to vouch for the user's identity. The preferred method requires that the users be positively identified before the digital certificates can be created for them. The type of certificate requested and any existing security policies will determine how the user's identity must be confirmed. Generally an email digital certificate may require no more than an email message sent from a user, whereas a digital certificate for performing transactions at a financial institution may require much more.

FIGURE 12.2
VBA digital-certificate creation

Once the user's identification has been verified, the request for a digital certificate is sent to the CA. If the request is approved, the CA then applies the appropriate signing key to the certificate, effectively signing the public key. The CA then updates the relevant fields, and the certificate is forwarded to the registration authority (RA) server (if one is being used) or to the user. The CA may also keep a local copy of the certificate it generated. A certificate, once issued, may also be published to a public directory if needed.

DIGITAL-CERTIFICATE REVOCATION

When a certificate has reached its expiration date it is revoked, and the certificate is no longer valid. When a digital certificate is revoked, the CA updates its internal records and any relevant CRLs with the required certificate information and timestamp. The CA signs the CRL and places it in a public repository where other applications using certificates can access it to determine the status of a certificate. The CRL is a critical element that provides a PKI's security and integrity. In some situations, a certificate may be revoked before its normal expiration date—for instance, when a user's private key is lost or compromised. Either the user or the CA can initiate a revocation process.

DIGITAL-CERTIFICATE EXPIRATION

Every certificate issued by a CA must have an expiration date. Once the certificate has expired, the certificate may not be used any longer for any type of authentication. The issuing CA or RA may remind the user of the upcoming expiration of a certificate. The user will be required to follow a renewal process. If this process is successful, the user will be issued a new certificate with a new expiration date. Generally the renewal of a digital certificate does not require the generation of a new pair of public and private keys.

DIGITAL-CERTIFICATE SUSPENSION

Suspension of a certificate can occur on and off throughout the life of any digital certificate. At this stage, the certificate's validity is suspended temporarily. One example of when suspension might occur is when an employee is gone on a leave of absence. It may be important that the user's digital certificate not be used until the user's return. When the user returns, either the suspension can be withdrawn or the certificate can be revoked.

Where Digital Certificates Are Used Today

Most people will encounter digital certificates on the Web, specifically on any site with an "https" designation. Whether you are making online purchases or using an electronic bill-payer system, you want to be sure the information that you are sending will be secure. Because so many of us today use electronic banking, let's look at how digital certificates play a role in your transactions. The process works like this:

1. Using your web browser you connect to your bank's secured site. Internet Explorer will show a locked icon in the Security Status bar; other browsers will use different methods to indicate the presence of a secure site. At the very least, verify that the web address starts with https.

2. A digital certificate is sent from the web server at your bank to your web browser.

3. When your browser receives the certificate, it checks the certificate store on your computer. If the CA that issued the bank's certificate is trusted, the transaction is allowed to continue. A copy of the digital certificate from your bank is stored in your browser's certification store for future use.

4. To ensure that the information transmitted between you and your bank is encrypted, your web browser creates a unique session key. Your browser uses the bank's certificate to encrypt the session key so that only your bank's web server can read the messages sent from your browser.

5. At this point the secure session has been established, and information can be securely passed from you to your bank.

Other places where digital certificates are used include the following:

◆ Encrypted email messages—The sender encrypts the message with his or her private key and shares his or her public key with the message recipient. The recipient uses the sender's public key to read the secure message.

◆ Remote VPN connections to servers—Digital certificates are used to ensure the identity of both the user connecting to the server, and the server to which the user has connected.

◆ Business-to-business transactions and communications—Many organizations order supplies and materials directly from other companies over the Internet. Digital certificates are used to ensure the identity of both parties.

◆ Simplified identification—a user can authenticate to a computer by logging on with a smart card. The digital certificate provides part of the authentication process.

Microsoft's Implementation of Certificate Services

Now that we have discussed what digital certificates are, we will take a look at how Microsoft implements Certificate Services.

Microsoft Certificate Services enables organizations to create customizable services for issuing and managing digital certificates for use in software security systems requiring PKI technologies.

Certificate Services Components

With Microsoft Certificate Services you can create a private CA that will receive certificate requests from users, verify that all necessary information has been provided, verify the identity of the requester, issue approved certificates to requesters, renew or revoke certificates, and create and publish a CRL.

Trust in a CA hierarchy is created when a copy of the root CA certificate is located in the trusted root certification authority store. In addition, none of the certificates in the certification path can be revoked or have its validity period expire. With Microsoft the certification path includes every certificate issued to every CA, from the top root CA down to the lowest subordinate CA. Subordinate CAs require two certificates: their own and the root CA's. Organizations employing Active Directory will have their trust in the CA established automatically.

The process of inheritance works for certificates in the same way that it works in a folder hierarchy. For example, if you install a root CA certificate in a computer's trusted root certification authority store, any user of that computer will see that certificate in the user trusted root certification authority store. If the computer trusts the CA, any user of that computer will trust the CA. This process, however, does not work the other way around. If a user has a root CA certificate in her or his user trusted root certification authority store, the computer will not trust that CA unless a copy of it is installed in the computer's trusted root certification authority store.

There are two types of CAs available through Microsoft: enterprise and stand-alone.

ENTERPRISE CERTIFICATE AUTHORITY

Microsoft enterprise CAs can be used to issue certificates for secure email using S/MIME, digital signatures, secure authentication to web services, and authentication to a Windows Server domain with a smart card. After the service is installed, it uses Group Policy to transmit its certificate to the trusted root CA certificate store for access by all users and computers in the domain.

A number of requirements must be met when setting up an enterprise certification authority:

◆ Active Directory must be installed on the domain, and the host computer must be a member of that domain.

◆ Active Server Pages must be enabled through Internet Information Services (IIS). This is required for the web interface for the CA.

◆ If IIS is running on the host computer, you will be prompted to stop the service before the installation can continue. IIS will be restarted after installation occurs.

◆ The name of the CA cannot be changed once the setup is completed.

◆ The administrator performing the installation must have Write permission to Active Directory. In most cases the user would be logged in as an enterprise admin.

An enterprise CA uses many different types of certificates, most of which can be based on a certificate template. Active Directory is used to verify a requester's identity and can provide some of the information needed to complete the certificate request. The requesters' security permissions will determine the types of certificates that can be issued to them. If the server on which the CA is installed is a member of the Cert Publishers group, both the user certificates and the CRL can be published in Active Directory.

A user can request a certificate either through the CA web page or by using the Certificate Request Wizard in the Certificates MMC.

STAND-ALONE CERTIFICATE AUTHORITY

Stand-alone CAs do not require AD Domain Services (AD DS), are less automated, and will require more input from the users than will an enterprise CA. However, they are able to use Active Directory, if it is accessible, for publishing user certificates and the CRL. Generally, stand-alone CAs are used as a trusted offline root CA in a large CA hierarchy or where organizations are using an extranet and the Internet.

Stand-alone CAs issue certificates for digital signatures, to secure email using S/MIME, and to provide authentication to a secure web server. A stand-alone CA cannot issue certificates for authentication to a domain using smart cards.

By default, users can request a certificate only through the CA's web page. Certificate templates are not used with stand-alone CAs. All stand-alone CAs flag the status of certificate requests to *Pending* until the administrator is able to verify the identity of the requester and approve the request. This is because stand-alone CAs are unable to verify the certificate requester's credentials. The administrator has to explicitly distribute the stand-alone CA's certificate to the domain user's trusted root store, or the user must perform that task.

Certificate Services Policies

Certificate Services policies are a set of rules or instructions used when processing requests for certificates; when certificates are issued, revoked, renewed; and when publishing CRLs. These rules consist of a combination of administrative policies and configuration settings established on the CA itself and can be summarized as described next.

Administrative policies are generally used to define how certificate requests must be received and the requirements for granting such requests.

A default set of configuration rules and settings are created when you install Certificate Services. These cover the CA's own certificate, default issuance behavior, and recovery agents. Depending on the type of CA you install, you also have the option to install a number of preconfigured certificate templates, which control the information on a certificate request, and how that request is processed.

If administrators want to place restrictions on the certificate-request process to control what certificates are issued and how the issuance process is implemented, they will create *enrollment policies*. Some of the requirements you might find in enrollment policies include multiple authorized-signature requirements, certificate manager approval, and whether application and issuance policies should be implemented for a certificate.

Application policies define what the different types of certificates issued by the CA can be used for. This eliminates concerns that certificates may be misused or used in unintended ways. Application policies are represented in the object identifier (OID) defined at the CA. The OID is included in all issued certificates. These policies are sometimes called *extended* or *enhanced key-usage policies*.

The administrative rules implemented when certificates are issued are called issuance policies. These policies are also included in the OID. When a user presents a certificate, the target examines the certificate to determine if the requested action can be performed.

Certificate Services Processing

Microsoft provides a number of ways to create digital certificates for users:

◆ Use a web interface or the Certificates Microsoft Management Console (MMC) snap-in, or use a process called auto-enrollment.

◆ Digital certificate templates can be used to simplify the choices a certificate requester has to make, depending on the policy set at the enterprise CA.

◆ AD DS can be used to publish trusted root certificates, issued certificates, and CRLs.

When the request for a certificate is made, the information in that request gets passed from the requesting program to the CryptoAPI, the source code interface provided by Microsoft for creating secured applications. The CryptoAPI in turn passes the data to a program known as the *cryptographic service provider* (CSP) installed on the user's computer. Software-based CSPs will generate a private-and-public key pair for the user. Hardware-based CSPs—such as those found in smart cards—will instruct the hardware to generate the key pair. The user's public key is then sent along with the user's identifying information to the CA. If the certificate request is granted, the CA generates the certificate, which is either sent to the user automatically or retrieved manually and stored locally on the user's computer.

Security Considerations

Because digital certificates provide such a vital service for an organization, the CAs should be provided with the highest degree of protection. While a full listing of appropriate security actions would take several chapters, provisions that should be considered include physical protection for the CA server, private-key management, and a restoration plan.

PHYSICAL PROTECTION

Once an organization's root CA has been set up and one or more subordinate CAs have been installed, the root CA should be taken offline and have its signing key backed up to a secure location, and the server itself should be placed in a facility accessible only to security administrators. Microsoft recommends that the root CA server be a stand-alone server with IIS installed and running.

In addition, organizations should not use the root CA to issue certificates. A minimum of a two-level CA hierarchy should be deployed, which allows the lower-level issuer CAs to issue the actual certificates. This separation not only provides flexibility, but protects the root CA from malicious compromise.

KEY MANAGEMENT

Because they provide the basis for trust in the certification process, a CA's most valuable assets are its private keys. Microsoft Server software includes software-based cryptographic service providers (CSPs) that enable administrators to make backups of the keys, which should then be placed in highly secure storage facilities. A number of hardware-based CSPs compatible with Microsoft Certificate Services provide tamper-resistant key-storage solutions and isolate the cryptographic operations from other software services that might be running on the CA server. It is the administrator's responsibility to ensure compatibility before installing a hardware-based CSP.

All certificates issued by a CA should have a lifetime (valid period) that is less then or equal to the remaining lifetime on the CA's own certificate. This will ensure that users do not encounter problems with their certificates and that they are able to renew them. To avoid the unplanned expiration of certificates, the CA administrator must ensure that the CA's own certificate is renewed before any issued certificates come up for renewal.

RESTORATION

Ensuring that there are adequate backups of the CA database, the CA certificate, and the CA keys is integral to any restoration plan. How frequently the CA should be backed up depends on how frequently certificates are issued. The more frequently you issue certificates, the more frequently you should back up the CA. Microsoft recommends performing full backups to ensure the fastest recovery time and the most reliable data redundancy.

What's New for Certificate Services in Windows Server 2008

In Windows Server 2008, AD CS provides a variety of customizable services that can be employed to create and manage certificates for use in software security systems that employ PKI technologies. With AD CS, organizations are able to enhance security by binding the identity of a person, device, or service to a private key. Also included with AD CS are a number of features that allow administrators to manage the certificate life cycle from enrollment through revocation in a variety of environments.

AD CS supports a number of applications, including the following:

◆ Secure wireless networks

◆ Virtual private networks (VPN)

◆ Secure/Multipurpose Internet Mail Extensions (S/MIME)

◆ IP Security (IPsec)

◆ Smart-card logons (enterprise CAs only)

◆ Encrypted File System (EFS)

◆ Digital signatures

◆ Secure Socket Layer/Transport Layer Security (SSL/TLS)

New Features

Microsoft has made a number of changes to AD CS components included in earlier server software and has added some new features, including the following:

◆ Improved enrollment capabilities that enable delegated enrollment agents to be assigned on a per-template basis

◆ Integrated Simple Certificate Enrollment Protocol (SCEP) enrollment services, which allows routers and other network devices that do not have domain accounts to obtain certificates

◆ Scalable, high-speed revocation-status response services combining CRLs and integrated Online Responder services

Now let's take a detailed look at some other new features.

CRYPTOGRAPHY NEXT GENERATION

Cryptography Next Generation (CNG) is the long-term replacement for CryptoAPI and was first introduced with Windows Vista. CNG is extensible at many levels, thus enabling administrators to create, update, and use custom cryptography algorithms in AD CS, SSL, and IPsec.

One important feature of CNG is that it implements the U.S. government's Suite B cryptographic algorithms, including algorithms for encryption, digital signatures, key exchange, and hashing. In 2005, the U.S. National Security Agency (NSA) announced a coordinated set of symmetric encryption, asymmetric secret agreement (also known as key exchange), digital signature, and hash functions for future U.S. government use called *Suite B*. Suite B is used for the protection of information designated as Top Secret and Secret and for private information that previously was designated Sensitive-but-Unclassified.

The APIs in CNG can be used to do the following:

◆ Create hashes and encrypt and decrypt data.

◆ Create, store, and retrieve cryptographic keys.

◆ Install and utilize additional cryptographic providers.

Among its many features, CNG has the following capabilities:

◆ The ability for organizations to use their own cryptographic algorithms or implementations of standard cryptographic algorithms, or to add new algorithms

◆ Support for cryptography in the kernel mode for use by boot processes, SSL/TLS, and IPsec. CNG uses the same API in kernel and user mode for fully supported cryptographic features. According to Microsoft, not all CNG functions can be called from kernel mode.

◆ Compliance with Common Criteria (CC) requirements by utilizing and storing long-lived keys in a secure process

◆ Support for CryptoAPI 1.0 algorithms

◆ Support for elliptic curve cryptography (ECC) algorithms required by the U.S. government's Suite B

◆ Support for Trusted Platform Module (TPM) computers which provide key isolation and key storage in TPM

◆ Support for algorithms currently supported by CryptoAPI

◆ The ability to replace the default random-number generator (RNG) by specifying a particular RNG to use within selected calls

---

CNG OPERATING-SYSTEM LIMITATIONS

For organizations to make use of the new cryptographic algorithms, installed applications must be able to handle certificate chain validation and use the keys generated with Suite B algorithms. Currently only Windows Vista and Windows Server 2008 are able to support Suite B algorithms such as ECC. It is not possible to use the new certificate types with earlier Windows desktop or server operating systems. However, classic algorithms such as Rivest, Shamir, and Adleman (RSA) can be used even if the keys have been generated with a CNG key provider. Both Windows Vista and Windows Server 2008 are able to use either CryptoAPI 1.0 or the new CNG API because they can run concurrently. Existing implementations of applications such as SSL, S/MIME, IPsec, and Kerberos will have to be updated to use Suite B algorithms.

Preparing for CNG

Microsoft recommends that organizations do not deploy certificates with Suite B algorithms before those organizations meet the following requirements:

◆ Verify that existing CAs and operating systems are able to support ECC algorithms before issuing any certificates.

◆ Verify that any existing PKI-enabled applications can use certificates that rely on CNG cryptographic providers.

◆ Verify that smart-card logon devices can handle the CNG algorithms.

Organizations that currently do not have a PKI structure implemented can install a Windows Server 2008 CA once they ensure that all existing applications can support Suite B algorithms.

Organizations utilizing PKI with CAs on earlier Windows Server operating systems should add a subordinate CA on a Windows Server 2008 computer. However, they must continue using classic algorithms until their existing CAs have been upgraded. One option is to add a second PKI and perform cross-certification between the two CA hierarchies.

RESTRICTED ENROLLMENT AGENT

Users designated as enrollment agents can enroll smart-card certificates on behalf of other uses. The restricted enrollment agent enables limiting those permissions. The enrollment agent is authorized to use one or more certificate templates. Administrators can select which users or security groups the enrollment agent can enroll on behalf of. With this feature, organizations will be better able to control the delegation of trust and the inherent risks that come with granting trust.

LIMITATIONS

Active Directory organizational units (OUs) or other containers cannot be used to constrain an enrollment agent. In addition, the Restricted Enrollment Agent option is not available on Windows Server 2008 stand-alone CAs.

Organizations should consider the following when planning to deploy a restricted enrollment agent:

◆ CA performance will be affected when using restricted enrollment agents. You can optimize performance by minimizing the number of accounts listed as enrollment agents. Microsoft also recommends that the number of accounts in the permissions list for the enrollment agent be kept to a minimum, depending on the server hardware and other factors. As always, Microsoft recommends the use of group accounts for both lists as opposed to individual user accounts.

◆ Because Windows Server 2008 uses the new version 3 certificate templates introduced with Windows Vista, you can only use Windows Vista or Server 2008 operating systems to open or modify these templates.

◆ When using the Certificate Templates snap-in while the CA dialog box is open, new certificate templates may not appear in the list of available certificates. Simply close and reopen the dialog box to view new templates in the available-certificates list.

WEB ENROLLMENT

Certificate web enrollment has been available since the Windows 2000 operating system. However, Microsoft is replacing the earlier enrollment control XEnroll.dll with CertEnroll.dll in both the Windows Vista and Server 2008 operating systems. CertEnroll.dll is more secure, easier to use, and easier to update than XEnroll.dll. The biggest compatibility issues may arise when users running Windows Vista or Windows Server 2008 attempt to request a certificate by using web enrollment pages installed on earlier versions of Windows.

Organizations running the new Windows Server 2008–based CAs will be able to support web enrollment requests from users and computers running earlier versions of Windows operating systems because the web enrollment pages are designed to detect the user's operating system and switch to using the XEnroll.dll installed locally on the client computer.

NETWORK DEVICE ENROLLMENT SERVICE

The Network Device Enrollment Service (NDES) is the Microsoft implementation of the Simple Certificate Enrollment Protocol (SCEP) that was developed by Cisco Systems as an extension to HTTP, Public-Key Cryptography Standards (PKCS) #10, PKCS #7, RFC 2459, and other standards to enable network devices—such as routers and switches as well as applications—to request certificate enrollment with CAs. In Windows Server 2003, Microsoft SCEP (MSCEP) was available only as a Resource Kit add-on that could only be installed on the same computer as the CA. With this new version, MSCEP has been renamed NDES and is now part of the operating system. In addition, NDES may be installed on a different computer from the CA.

NDES performs the following functions:

◆ Retrieves pending requests from the CA

◆ Receives and processes SCEP enrollment requests on behalf of software running on network devices

◆ Generates and provides one-time enrollment passwords to administrators

Some of the biggest changes from MSCEP to NDES are in the extension to the IIS registry keys used to store configuration settings. All settings are now stored under the following registry key: HKEY_LOCAL_ROOT\Software\Microsoft\Cryptography\MSCEP. The cryptography registry keys are listed in Table 12.1.

TABLE 12.1:   Cryptography Registry Keys

SETTING NAME	OPTIONAL?	DEFAULT VALUE	POSSIBLE VALUES
Refresh	No	7	Number of days pending requests are kept in the NDES database.
EnforcePassword	No	1	0 = password not required 1 = password required
PasswordMax	No	5	Maximum number of passwords that can be cached. (Previously the default was 1,000.)
PasswordValidity	No	60	Number of minutes a password is valid.
PasswordVDir	Yes	n/a	When set, this is the name of the virtual directory that can be used for password requests. When this is left empty or not configured, password requests are accepted from any virtual directory.

TABLE 12.1:   Cryptography Registry Keys *(CONTINUED)*

SETTING NAME	OPTIONAL?	DEFAULT VALUE	POSSIBLE VALUES
CacheRequest	No	20	Number of minutes that issued certificates are kept in the SCEP database.
CAType	No	Based on setup	0 = stand-alone CA 1 = enterprise CA
SigningTemplate	Yes	Not set	When set, NDES uses this value as the certificate-template name when clients enroll for a signing certificate.
EncryptionTemplate	Yes	Not set	When set, NDES uses this value as the certificate-template name when clients enroll for an encryption certificate.
SigningAndEncryptionTemplate	Yes	Not set	When set, NDES uses the value as the certificate-template name when clients enroll for a signing and encryption certificate, or when the request does not include any extended key usage.

Organizations must make a number of decisions before deciding to deploy NDES, including the following:

- The name of the NDES registration authority (RA), and what country/region to use: any certificates issued will include this information.

- Whether to use the existing Network Service account or to create a dedicated user account for the service

- The cryptographic service provider (CSP) to employ for the signature key used to encrypt communication between the CA and the RA

- The CSP to employ for the encryption key used to encrypt communication between the RA and the network device

- The key length for each of these keys

- How to configure the certificate templates that will be used with the NDES for requesting certificates

Implementing NDES with Existing RAs

When NDES is installed, it creates a new RA and deletes any pre-existing RA certificates installed on that computer. For that reason, when installing NDES on a computer where another RA has been configured, any pending certificate requests should be processed and any unclaimed certificates should be claimed before installing NDES.

ONLINE CERTIFICATE STATUS PROTOCOL SUPPORT

A major part of the life cycle of a digital certificate is certificate revocation. Commonly, certificate status is distributed by issuing certificate-revocation lists (CRLs). In Windows Server 2008, the older PKI revocation process service, which uses conventional CRLs, has been replaced with the Online Certificate Status Protocol (OCSP), which is used to manage and distribute revocation status information.

Traditionally, CRLs are distributed periodically and contain information about all certificates that have been revoked or suspended. As you can imagine, this process can contain an extensive amount of information. However, OCSP Online Responder receives and responds only to clients' requests for information about the status of an individual certificate. This newer process means that the amount of data retrieved per request remains constant no matter how many revoked or suspended certificates there might be.

Windows Server 2008 OCSP Online Responder includes the following features:

- ◆ Web proxy caching for the Online Responder service that is implemented as an Internet Server API (ISAPI) extension hosted by IIS

- ◆ Prevention of replay attacks to Online Responder responces with the inclusion of configuration options for nonce and no-nonce requests

- ◆ Ability to configure Online Responder for both ECC and SHA-256 cryptography for cryptographic operations

- ◆ Simplified deployment by using an OCSP Response Signing certificate template

- ◆ Ability to process Online Responder requests and responses along with Kerberos password authentication for prompt validation of server certificates at logon

- ◆ Compliance with RFC 2560 for OCSP: it is because of this compliance that Online Responder certificate status responses are sometimes called OCSP responses.

- ◆ Ability to create responder arrays by linking multiple computers hosting Online Responders and processing certificate-status requests

---

NONCE AND NO-NONCE

In computer-security terminology, a nonce is a number that is used only once. It is often a randomly generated number used by an authentication protocol to ensure that old communications cannot be reused in replay attacks. A nonce can also be used as a time stamp or a counter on a web page.

A no-nonce is just the opposite: a number that is used more than once. While no-nonces can be used for verification purposes, they are seldom used with computer security technology.

Online Responder

Essentially an online responder is any computer running the Online Responder service. While you can configure a CA as an online responder, Microsoft recommends that you place the CA and the online Responder on separate computers. A single online responder can provide revocation-status information for certificates issued by either a single CA or multiple CAs. CA revocation can also be distributed by using multiple online responders.

You should install online responders on the network after the CAs are installed but before any client certificates are issued. The service can retrieve certificate-revocation data from a published CRL from both Microsoft and non-Microsoft CAs.

The following must be present before you configure a CA to support the Online Responder service:

◆ IIS must already be installed on the target computer. The correct configuration of IIS for the online responder is installed automatically when you install an online responder.

◆ An OCSP Response Signing certificate template must be configured on the CA with autoenrollment used to issue an OCSP Response Signing certificate to the target computer.

◆ The URL of the online responder must be included in the authority information access (AIA) extension of certificates issued by the CA. The Online Responder client uses this URL to validate certificate status.

Once you have installed the online responder, you will need to create a revocation configuration for each CA and CA certificate that the online responder serves.

Hardware and Software Considerations

AD CS will run on any computer hardware capable of supporting Windows Server 2008 and AD DS. Specific requirements for additional memory and hard-drive storage will depend upon the types of services and applications that computer is supporting.

AD CS is available for most Windows Server 2008 versions. Table 12.2 shows on which Server 2008 versions AD CS components will run.

TABLE 12.2:   AD CS Components and the Windows Server 2008 Versions that support them

AD CS COMPONENT	WINDOWS SERVER 2008 VERSIONS			
	WEB	STANDARD	ENTERPRISE	DATACENTER
CA	No	Yes	Yes	Yes
NDES	No	No	Yes	Yes
Online Responder	No	No	Yes	Yes

On a Windows Server 2008 computer that has been configured as a CA, some server-version restrictions apply to AD CS features, as shown in Table 12.3.

TABLE 12.3:   AD CS Features and the Windows Server 2008 Version that Support Them

AD CS FEATURE	WINDOWS SERVER 2008 VERSIONS			
	WEB	**STANDARD**	**ENTERPRISE**	**DATACENTER**
Version 2 and 3 certificate templates	No	No	Yes	Yes
Key archiving	No	No	Yes	Yes
Role separation	No	No	Yes	Yes
Certificate Manager restrictions	No	No	Yes	Yes
Delegated Enrollment Agent restrictions	No	No	Yes	Yes

SERVER-CORE LIMITATION

Because there is a limited set of server roles available for Server Core in Windows Server 2008, AD CS cannot be installed on a Server Core installation of Windows Server 2008. Although you can deploy AD CS on a single server, most organizations will need to configure one or more servers as CAs, with additional servers configured as online responders, and others as web enrollment portals.

Installing Certificate Services

The new Server Manager tool in Windows Server 2008 gives administrators a single source for managing, configuring, and identifying problems on a server. The Add Roles Wizard is used to install AD CS on a server. However, before you can begin installation, you must do the following:

- Ensure that the computer's name will not need to be changed. Once you complete the AD CS setup, changing the computer's name would invalidate all of the certificates issued by the CA installed on that computer.

- Ensure that the computer's domain status has been finalized. Depending upon the type of CA that you install, the computer may need to be a domain controller. You will not be able to change the computer's domain membership once the installation is complete. However, if you rename the domain all you have to do is reconfigure the CA to support the name change.

- Ensure that you are running the correct version of Windows Server 2008 for the type of CA that you wish to configure. Refer to the "Hardware and Software Considerations" section for more information.

- Establish a CA naming convention. This name will become the common name of the CA and is reflected in every certificate issued by that CA. To eliminate potential security vulnerabilities Microsoft recommends against using the fully qualified domain name as the common name of the CA. The CA name cannot be longer than 64 characters.

- For security purposes, ensure that you have an NTFS partition or volume available to install the CA database on. The default location of the database is *systemroot*\system32\certlog. The actual name of the database file is based on the name of the CA and has an .edb extension.

Your next big decision will be to determine the type of CA that you want, or need, to install. There are two types: enterprise and stand-alone. While both types perform similar functions, there are some differences below that you should keep in mind.

Enterprise CA

◆ AD DS is required.

◆ Group Policy is used to propagate the certificate to the Trusted Root CA certificate store for all domain users and computers.

◆ Both user certificates and the CRL are published in AD DS. Because of this, the CA server must be a member of the Certificate Publishers group.

Stand-Alone CA

◆ AD DS is not required. Generally a stand-alone CA is used as a trusted offline root CA in a CA hierarchy, or when issuing certificates to users over an extranet or the Internet.

◆ Because Active Directory is not being utilized, users will have to provide identifying information to the CA when requesting certificates. All certificate requests should be set to Pending until reviewed by the administrator.

◆ Certificate templates cannot be used.

◆ Certificates cannot be issued to log on to a Windows Server 2008 domain using smart cards.

◆ Certificates must be explicitly distributed by the administrator or users must complete the process themselves.

Installing the Certificate Authority

Your first step when configuring a CA is to install a root CA. The root CA will provide the foundation and establish the basic rules that control the issuing, use, and revocation of all certificates in the PKI.

1. Log on to the server as an administrator. You will need to log on as a domain administrator if you are planning on configuring an enterprise CA.

2. Click Start, point to Administrative Tools, and then click Server Manager.

3. In the Roles Summary section, click Add Roles.

4. On the Select Server Roles page, select the Active Directory Certificate Services check box. The dialog box shown in Figure 12.3 will be displayed. Read the information carefully, especially the Things to Note section, and click Next when ready to proceed.

5. On the Select Role Services page, select the Certification Authority check box, as shown in Figure 12.4, and then click Next.

6. On the Specify Setup Type page, click Stand-Alone or Enterprise, and then click Next. (You must have a network connection to a domain controller to install an enterprise CA.)

7. On the Specify CA Type page, click Root CA, and then click Next.

FIGURE 12.3
Active Directory
Certification Services
(AD CS) installation
dialog box

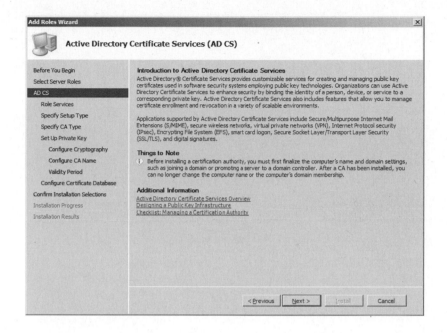

FIGURE 12.4
AD CS Select Role
Services dialog box

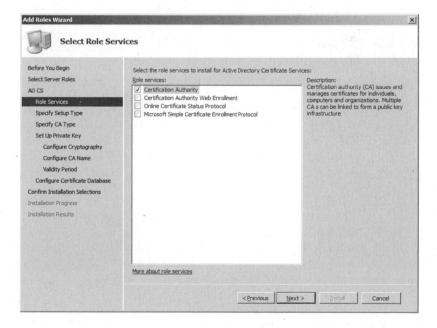

8. On the Set Up Private Key and Configure Cryptography for CA pages, you can configure optional configuration settings, including cryptographic service providers. Click Next.

9. In the Common name for This CA box, type the common name of the CA, **RootCA1**, and then click Next.

10. On the Set the Certificate Validity Period page, accept the default validity duration for the root CA, and then click Next.

11. On the Configure Certificate Database page, accept the default values or specify other storage locations for the certificate database and the certificate database log, as shown in Figure 12.5, and then click Next.

12. After verifying the information on the Confirm Installation Options page, click Install.

13. Review the information on the confirmation screen to verify that the installation was successful.

FIGURE 12.5
AD CS Configure
Certificate Database
dialog box

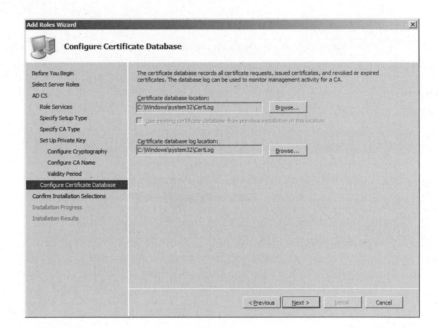

Installing the Online Responder

You can install an online responder on either a Windows Server 2008 Enterprise or Datacenter server. The Online Responder can receive revocation data from a variety of CAs: Windows Server 2008, Windows Server 2003, or even a non-Microsoft CA.

Ensure that IIS is installed on the target computer before beginning the installation process.

1. Log on to the server as a domain administrator.

2. Click Start, point to Administrative Tools, and then click Server Manager.

3. Click Manage Roles. In the Active Directory Certificate Services section, as shown in Figure 12.6, click Add Role Services.

4. On the Select Role Services page, select the Online Responder check box. You are prompted to install IIS and Windows Activation Service, if they are not already installed.

FIGURE 12.6
AD CS Add Role
Services dialog box

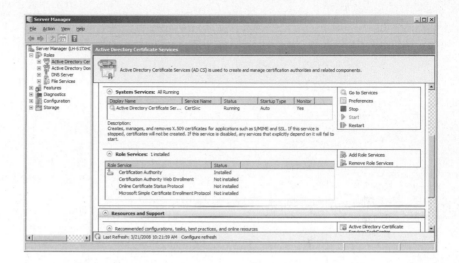

5. Click Add Required Role Services, and then click Next three times.

6. On the Confirm Installation Options page, click Install.

7. When the installation is complete, review the status page to verify that the installation was successful.

Installing the Certificate Authority Snap-in

The easiest way to administer your new CA is with the CA snap-in, shown in Figure 12.7. With this tool you can administer a CA on the existing computer or on another computer. To complete this process you must be logged on as a CA administrator.

Following are the steps necessary to install the snap-in to configure a CA on the existing computer:

1. Click Start, click Run, and then type **mmc**.

2. On the File menu, click Add/Remove Snap-in.

3. Add the Certification Authority snap-in to the list on the right.

FIGURE 12.7
Certification
Authority Snap-in

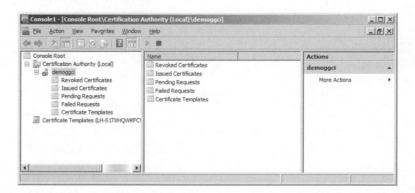

4. Click OK when asked whether you want to use the snap-in to administer the CA on this computer or a different computer.

5. Click OK.

Follow these steps if you want to administer a CA on a different computer:

1. Open the Certification Authority snap-in.

2. On the Action menu, click Retarget Certification Authority.

3. Click Another Computer, and type the name of the computer.

A handy feature of the CA snap-in is the ability to use display filters to restrict the items displayed in the details pane to meet a set of criteria that you desire. For example, you may want to view only certificates issued after a specific date.

Although you do not need to be logged on as a CA administrator to complete this process, you must have permissions to perform administrative tasks on the CA to complete the following steps:

1. Open the Certification Authority snap-in.

2. Click any of the displayed folders except Certificate Templates.

3. On the View menu, click Filter. The dialog box shown in Figure 12.8 will appear.

4. For each of the selection criteria, do the following:

    1. Click Add.

    2. In Field, click the field on which to filter.

    3. In Operation, click the operation to qualify the filter value for this field.

    4. In Value, type the qualification value.

FIGURE 12.8
Filter Restrictions
dialog box

Configuring the CA for OCSP Response Signing Certificates

Part of configuring a CA for supporting Online Responder services includes configuring certificate templates and issuance properties for OCSP Response Signing certificates.

1. Log on to the server as a CA administrator.

2. Open the Certificate Templates snap-in.

3. Right-click the OCSP Response Signing template, and then click Duplicate Template.

4. You will see the dialog box shown in Figure 12.9. Select the Windows Server version that your organization will need to support.

5. In the Properties of New Template dialog box, as shown in Figure 12.10, type a new name for the duplicated template.

6. Click the Security tab. Under Group or User Names, as shown in Figure 12.11, click Add, and then type the name or browse to select the computer that will host the Online Responder service.

7. Click the computer name and, in the Permissions dialog box, select the Read and Autoenroll check boxes.

8. While you have the Certificate Templates snap-in open, you can configure certificate templates for users and computers by substituting the desired templates in step 3, and repeating steps 4 through 7 to configure additional permissions for the server and your user accounts.

FIGURE 12.9
OCSP Response
Signing certificate
Duplicate Template
dialog box

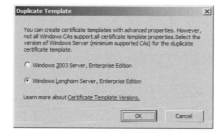

FIGURE 12.10
New Template
General properties

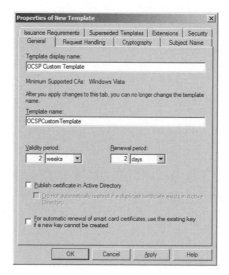

FIGURE 12.11
New Template
Security properties

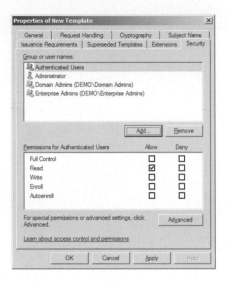

Next you need to configure a CA to support the Online Responder service:

1. Open the Certification Authority snap-in.

2. In the console tree, click the name of the CA.

3. On the Action menu, click Properties.

4. Click the Extensions tab, the dialog box shown in Figure 12.12 will appear. In the Select Extension list, click Authority Information Access (AIA).

5. Select the Include in the AIA Extension of Issue Certificates and Include in the Online Certificate Status Protocol (OCSP) Extension check boxes.

6. Specify the locations from which users can obtain certificate-revocation data, and click OK. When prompted to restart the AD CS service, click Yes.

7. In the console tree of the Certification Authority snap-in, right-click Certificate Templates, and then click New Certificate Templates to Issue.

8. In Enable Certificate Templates, as shown in Figure 12.13, select the OCSP Response Signing template and any other certificate templates that you configured previously, and then click OK.

9. Open Certificate Templates, and verify that the modified certificate templates appear in the list.

Configuring a Revocation Configuration

A revocation configuration contains all the settings needed to respond to status requests on certificates issued using a specific CA key. Included in these settings are the CA certificate, the signing certificate for the online responder, and the locations where clients should send their status requests.

Before setting up the revocation configuration, you must ensure that certificate enrollment has taken place and that a signing certificate exists on the target computer, and adjust the permissions on the signing certificate to allow use by the online responder.

FIGURE 12.12

Online Responder
Properties dialog box

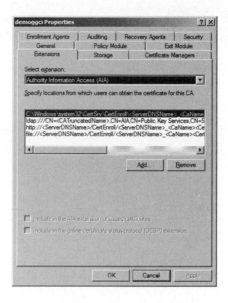

FIGURE 12.13

Enable Certificate
Templates dialog box

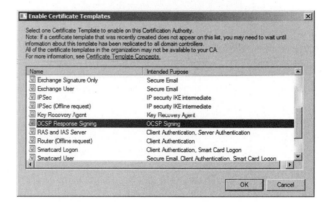

Follow these steps to verify that the signing certificate is properly configured:

1. Start or restart the target CA to enroll for certificates.

2. Log on as a CA administrator.

3. Open the Certificates snap-in for the computer account. Open the Personal certificate store for the computer, and verify that it contains a certificate titled OCSP Response Signing.

4. Right-click this certificate, and then click Manage Private Keys.

5. Click the Security tab. The dialog box shown in Figure 12.14 will appear. In the User Group or User Names box, click Add, enter Network Service to the Group or User Names list, and then click OK.

6. Click Network Service, and in the Permissions dialog box, select the Full Control check box.

7. Click OK twice.

FIGURE 12.14
Signing certificate
security permissions
dialog box

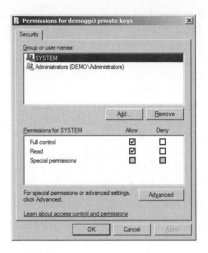

Follow these steps to configure a revocation configuration:

1. Open the Online Responder snap-in.

2. In the Actions pane, click Add Revocation Configuration to start the Add Revocation Configuration Wizard, and then click Next.

3. Select the appropriate CA certificate location, as shown in Figure 12.15, and then click Next.

4. On the Name the Revocation Configuration page, type a name for the revocation configuration, and then click Next.

5. On the Select CA Certificate Location page, click Select a Certificate from an Existing Enterprise CA, and then click Next.

6. On the following page, the name of the CA should appear in the Browse CA Certificates Published in Active Directory box.

    1. If it appears, click the name of the CA that you want to associate with your revocation configuration, and then click Next.

    2. If it does not appear, click Browse for CA Computer and type the name of the computer, or click Browse to locate this computer. When you have located the computer, click Next.

    3. You might also be able to link to the CA certificate from the local certificate store or by importing it from removable media in step 3.

7. View the certificate and copy the CRL distribution point for the parent root CA:

    1. Open the Certificate Services snap-in. Select an issued certificate.

    2. Double-click the certificate, and then click the Details tab.

    3. Scroll down and select the CRL Distribution Points field.

    4. Select and copy the URL for the CRL distribution point that you want to use.

    5. Click OK.

8. On the Select Signing Certificate page, accept the default option, Automatically Select a Signing Certificate, as shown in Figure 12.16, and then click Next.

9. On the Revocation Provider page, click Provider.

10. On the Revocation Provider Properties page, as shown in Figure 12.17, click Add, paste the URL of the CRL distribution point, and then click OK.

11. Click Finish.

12. Using the Online Responder snap-in, select the revocation configuration, and then examine the status information to verify that it is functioning properly. You should also be able to examine the properties of the signing certificate to verify that the online responder is configured properly.

FIGURE 12.15
Select CA Certificate Location dialog box

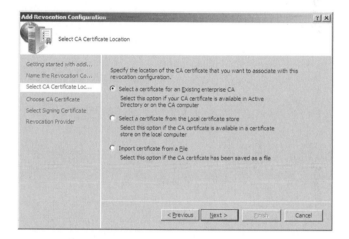

FIGURE 12.16
Select Signing Certificate dialog box

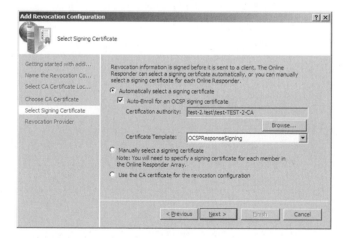

FIGURE 12.17
Revocation Provider
Properties dialog box

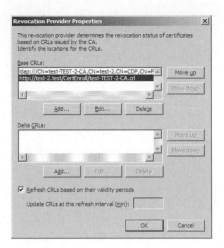

Configuring Network Device Enrollment Service

In Windows Server 2008, NDES is the replacement to Windows Server 2003 Microsoft SCEP (MSCEP). It enables software on routers (and other types of network devices that do not have domain credentials) to obtain certificates.

Before configuring NDES, you should create a user account for NDES and add the user to the IIS user group. Next you will need to use the Certificate Templates snap-in to configure both Read and Enroll permissions for the NDES user on the IPsec (Offline Request) certificate template.

1. Log on to the target server as an enterprise administrator.

2. Start the Add Roles Wizard. On the Select Server Roles page, select the Active Directory Certificate Services check box, and then click Next two times.

3. On the Select Role Services page, clear the Certification Authority check box, and then select Network Device Enrollment Service. (On some Windows Server 2008 versions this may be called Microsoft Simple Certificate Enrollment Protocol.)

   You will be prompted to install IIS and Windows Activation Service, if they are not already installed.

4. Click Add Required Role Services, as shown in Figure 12.18, and then click Next.

5. On the Specify User Account page, as shown in Figure 12.19, click Select User, and type a user name that is a member of the local machines IIS_IUSRS group. This account will be used to authorize certificate requests. Click OK, and then click Next.

6. On the Specify CA page, select either the CA Name or Computer Name check box, click Browse to locate the CA that will issue the Network Device Enrollment Service certificates, and then click Next.

7. On the Specify Registry Authority Information page, type the name of the RA server in the RA name box. Under Country/Region, select the check box for the country/region you are in, and then click Next.

8. On the Configure Cryptography page, accept the default values for the signature and encryption keys, and then click Next.

9. Review the summary of configuration options, and then click Install.

10. When the installation is complete, review the status page to verify that the installation was successful.

11. If this is a new installation and there are no pending SCEP certificate requests, click Replace Existing Registration Authority (RA) Certificates, and then click Next.

When the Network Device Enrollment Service is installed on a computer where a registration authority already exists, the existing registration authority and any pending certificate requests are deleted.

FIGURE 12.18
Add Required Role Services

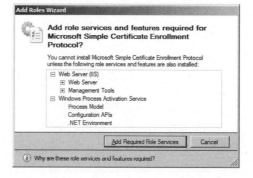

FIGURE 12.19
Specify User Account dialog box

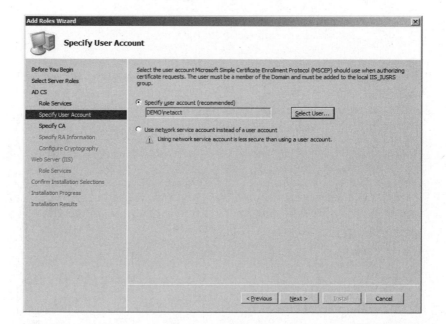

Managing AD CS

Administrators need to perform two types of management tasks on a CA:

- Recurring tasks that are part of the daily operations of the CA—for example, issuing certificates, revoking certificates, and publishing CRLs. Such tasks are performed either daily or weekly.

- Infrequent tasks such as key archival and recovery, deploying templates, and managing policy

Recurring Tasks

The CA administrator has a number of tasks to perform when managing certificate enrollment, such as the following:

- Using AD CS to configure certificate enrollment and autoenrollment options

- Configuring default certificate-request handling options for the CA

- Determining whether to allow certificates to be published to the file system

- Approving or denying pending certificate requests

- Managing the certificate revocation process for all issued certificates

The following sections explore these topics in more detail.

CONFIGURING CERTIFICATE AUTOENROLLMENT

The easiest way to issue certificates to users, computers, and services is to have it happen automatically without the user even being aware that the process is taking place. The first step is to configure a certificate template with Autoenrollment permissions. Then follow the steps below to configure the autoenrollment options in Group Policy:

1. On a domain controller running Windows Server 2008, click Start, point to Administrative Tools, and then click Group Policy Management.

2. In the console tree, double-click Group Policy Objects in the forest and domain containing the Default Domain Policy Group Policy Object (GPO) that you want to edit.

3. Right-click the Default Domain Policy GPO, and then click Edit.

4. In the Group Policy Management Console (GPMC), go to User Configuration ➢ Windows Settings ➢ Security Settings ➢ Public Key Policies.

5. Double-click Certificate Services Client—Auto-Enrollment.

6. Select the Enroll Certificates Automatically check box to enable autoenrollment. If you want to block autoenrollment from occurring, select the Do Not Enroll Certificates Automatically check box.

7. If you are enabling certificate autoenrollment, you can select the following check boxes:

   - Renew expired certificates, update pending certificates, and remove revoked certificates

   - Update certificates that use certificate templates

8. Click OK to accept your changes.

CONFIGURING DEFAULT ACTION FOR CERTIFICATE REQUESTS

While you can configure incoming certificate requests on an enterprise CA to be issued automatically, for security purposes Microsoft recommends that all incoming certificate requests on a standalone CA be marked as pending. Because enterprise CAs utilize AD DS for requester verification it is generally not a security issue and you can configure the option to have the certificates issued automatically.

1. Open the Certification Authority snap-in.

2. In the console tree, click the name of the CA.

3. On the Action menu, click Properties.

4. On the Policy Module tab, click Properties.

5. Click the option you want:

    ◆ To have the CA administrator review every certificate request before issuing a certificate, click Set the Certificate Request Status to Pending.

    ◆ To have the CA issue certificates based on the configuration of the certificate template, click Follow the Settings in the Certificate Template, if Applicable. Otherwise, select Automatically Issue the Certificate.

6. Stop and restart the CA.

Impact When Changing These Settings

Changing this setting from Set the Certificate Request Status to Pending to Follow the Settings in the Certificate Template, if Applicable, will affect only certificate requests that the CA receives after the change takes effect. Otherwise, Automatically Issue the Certificate will apply only to certificate requests that the CA receives after the default action has been changed. Existing pending requests will remain pending until the CA administrator either approves or denies the request.

PUBLISHING CERTIFICATES TO A FILE SYSTEM

A certificate will be published only if the request includes the file-system location where the certificate should be published. When requesting a certificate to be published to a file system, the request must include a `certfile:true` attribute. Once the certificate is issued, it is copied to *FileName*`.cer`, where *FileName* is the request ID of the certificate request. This file is copied to the `CertEnroll` folder on the CA.

1. Open the Certification Authority snap-in.

2. In the console tree, click the name of the CA.

3. On the Action menu, click Properties.

4. On the Exit Module tab, click Properties.

5. On the Publication Settings tab, select the Allow Certificates to Be Published to the File System check box, and then click OK.

6. Stop and restart the CA.

REVIEWING PENDING CERTIFICATE REQUESTS

CA administrators will spend the greatest part of their time approving and revoking certificates, especially if they are administering a stand-alone CA.

1. Open the Certification Authority snap-in.

2. In the console tree, click Pending Requests.

3. In the details pane, examine each certificate request by noting the values for requester name, requester email address, and any other critical information for issuing the certificate.

MANAGING CERTIFICATE REVOCATION

There are a number of reasons that an administrator might need to revoke a certificate, including the following:

◆ The user no longer requires the certificate.

◆ The certificate has been replaced by another certificate.

◆ The certificate key has been compromised.

◆ The CA that issued the certificate has been compromised.

Follow these steps to revoke a certificate:

1. Open the Certification Authority snap-in.

2. In the console tree, click Issued Certificates.

3. In the details pane, click the certificate you want to revoke.

4. On the Action menu, point to All Tasks, and click Revoke Certificate.

5. Select the reason for revoking the certificate, adjust the time of the revocation, if necessary, and then click Yes. Available reason codes are as follows:

   ◆ Unspecified

   ◆ Key Compromise

   ◆ CA Compromise

   ◆ Change of Affiliation

   ◆ Superseded

   ◆ Cease of Operation

   ◆ Certificate Hold: this is the only reason code that can be used when you might want to reissue the certificate in the future.

Infrequent Tasks

Generally infrequent tasks are needed only when you're initially deploying a CA, or when you must make major changes to the CA. Infrequent tasks include the following:

◆ Providing for Active Directory Certificate Services security

- ◆ Managing key archival and recovery

- ◆ Deploying certificate templates

- ◆ Managing CA policy and exit modules

We will take a closer look at infrequent tasks next.

CONFIGURE ACTIVE DIRECTORY CERTIFICATE SERVICES SECURITY

One of the most important tasks when implementing AD CS is to ensure the security of your CA infrastructure. In order to ensure that no one person can compromise the infrastructure, Microsoft recommends that management roles for the CA infrastructure be distributed across multiple individuals within an organization.

Role-based administration utilizes predefined CA roles that have unique tasks assigned to them. Each role member is able to perform a specific set of tasks but is unable to access tasks assigned to different roles. Table 12.4 provides a description of these roles.

TABLE 12.4:   AD CS Role-Based Security Administration

ROLES AND GROUPS	SECURITY PERMISSION	DESCRIPTION
CA Administrator	Manage CA	Configure and maintain the CA: this is a CA role and includes the ability to assign all other CA roles and renew the CA certificate. These permissions are assigned by using the CA snap-in.
Certificate Manager	Issue and Manage Certificates	Approve certificate enrollment and revocation requests: this is a CA role. This role is sometimes referred to as CA officer. These permissions are assigned by using the CA snap-in
Backup Operator	Back up files and directories	
Restore files and directories	Perform system backup and recovery. Backup is an operating system feature.	
Auditor	Manage auditing and security log	Configure, view, and maintain audit logs: auditing is an operating system feature. Auditor is an operating system role.
Enrollees	Read	
Enroll	Enrollees are clients who are authorized to request certificates from a CA. This is not a CA role.	

Use the steps below to configure the CA administrator and certificate manager security permissions:

1. Open the CA snap-in.

2. In the console tree, click the name of the CA.

3. On the Action menu, click Properties.

4. Click the Security tab, and specify the desired security permissions.

MANAGING KEY ARCHIVAL AND RECOVERY

No matter how much software and hardware changes, users will continue to lose things, including their private keys. However, a good administrator will be prepared by ensuring that keys are archived. Archived keys are encrypted and stored by the CA.

The process of key archival and recovery is not enabled by default because of possible security issues. Organizations need to decide which certificates should be covered by key archival and recovery, as well as who will be authorized to perform the recovery process.

To recover a private key, an administrator has to retrieve the encrypted certificate and the corresponding private key, and then use a key-recovery agent to decrypt them. Upon receipt of a correctly signed key-recovery request, the user's private key and certificate are issued to the requester.

The basic steps for configuring a CA for key archival are as follows:

1. Create a key-recovery agent account or designate an existing user to serve as the key-recovery agent.

2. Configure the Key Recovery Agent certificate template and enroll the key-recovery agent for a key recovery agent certificate.

3. Register the new key-recovery agent with the CA.

4. Configure a certificate template, such as Basic EFS, for key archival, and enroll users for the new certificate. If users already have EFS certificates, ensure that the new certificate will supersede the certificate that does not include key archival.

5. Enroll users for encryption certificates based on the new certificate template.

Users are not protected by key archival until they have enrolled for a certificate that has key recovery enabled. If they have certificates that were issued before key recovery was enabled, data encrypted with these certificates will not be covered by key archival.

DEPLOYING TEMPLATES

Certificate templates can be used with only enterprise CAs. These templates are stored in AD DS, where they can be made available to all enterprise CAs in the forest. This makes managing security and upgrading the CA server much easier. It is important that the root domain Domain Admins group be granted Full Control permissions to all certificate templates or that this permission be delegated to another group.

The process of replicating the certificate templates throughout the domain will take approximately eight hours to complete. Plan accordingly when preparing to deploy certificate templates.

Follow the steps below to add a certificate template to a CA:

1. Open the Certification Authority snap-in, and double-click the name of the CA.

2. Right-click the Certificate Templates container, click New, and then click Certificate Template to Issue.

3. Select the certificate template and click OK.

MANAGING POLICY

AD CS comes with two default modules: a policy module, `Certpdef.dll`, and an exit module, `Certxds.dll`. The policy module determines what happens to a certificate request: approve, deny, or mark as pending. The exit module determines what happens to a certificate after it is issued.

The CA administrator can use the existing modules or replace them with custom policy and exit modules. Microsoft also supports policy and exit modules from other vendors.

Follow these steps to select a different module:

1. Open the Certification Authority snap-in.

2. In the console tree, click the name of the CA.

3. On the Action menu, click Properties.

4. On either the Policy Module or Exit Module tab, click Select.

5. Click the new module, and then click OK.

6. If the module has its own configuration interface, configure it by clicking Properties.

7. Stop and restart the CA.

 Real World Scenario

DOING BUSINESS ON THE INTERNET

Terry is the system administrator at a pool-supply company that is planning on selling its products over the Internet. To accomplish this he first contacts a commercial CA so that the company can get a certificate for their website. This certificate will assure customers that they have reached the correct company, and will be used when customers connect to the secured, online web pages.

After verifying that the company's servers meet the hardware requirements for Windows Server 2008, Terry determines the type of CA that they need to install. Because the company will be utilizing the Internet to sell their products, Terry will install a stand-alone CA.

Once the root CA has been deployed he creates the policies for issuing, utilizing, and revoking the certificates. He also creates the root signing key and ensures that it is backed up to a secure location.

To provide fault tolerance, Terry creates two subordinate CAs that will be used as issuing CAs. After distributing the root signing key to these subordinate CAs, Terry takes the root CA offline and places it in a secured location.

The pool-supply company's customers will now be able to log on to the company website securely and conduct their business in a secured environment.

Coming Up Next

Now that you have a pretty good understanding of Windows Server 2008 Active Directory Certificate Services, how it works, and how to manage the services, we can look at how to manage the different Flexible Single Master Operations (FSMO) roles in your environment.

The Bottom Line

In this chapter we looked at Active Directory Certificate Services, what's new in Windows Server 2008, and how to configure and manage AD CS.

Because AD CS services are integral to an organization's security configuration, it is important to understand the differences between enterprise and stand-alone CAs, how to implement a CA, and how to properly manage a CA.

Identify the differences between a stand-alone CA and an enterprise CA and know their uses Before you can install AD CS you must have a thorough understanding of the types of CAs that are available in Windows Server 2008 so that you can select the right one.

> **Master It** Two types of CAs are available in Windows Server 2008. Learn what they are, the prerequisites for installing them, and the differences between the services they provide.

Install your first CA Before implementing Certificate Services, most organizations will need to install a number of different CAs. It is important to know which is the starting CA.

> **Master It** When tasked with setting up Certificate Services for her company, Mary needs to select the correct type of CA to start with.

Understanding CA management procedures Installing Certificate Services is only part of the story. Most administrators' duties involve the care and feeding of the CA servers. For a CA administrator, it is important to understand the types of tasks that need to be performed.

> **Master It** Understanding the types of maintenance tasks that must be performed on CA servers is critical to keeping those servers functioning properly.

Chapter 13

Managing the Flexible Single Master Operations Roles

As you saw in Chapter 5 ("Flexible Single Master Operations Design"), the Flexible Single Master Operations (FSMO) roles play an important part of the Active Directory infrastructure. Because those roles can be held by only one domain controller at a time, the placement planning that you performed during the design and planning phases is important. If you do not place these roles where they can be used effectively and efficiently, you could cause your Active Directory infrastructure to perform slowly, or you could introduce unnecessary network traffic.

At this point we are going to assume that you have taken our recommendations and have already configured your FSMO role holders. So what happens if you lose the domain controller that holds one, some, or all of your FSMO roles? And what are your options if you want to take offline the domain controller holding those roles or if you want move the roles to another system? This chapter answers these questions.

Let's start by discussing how you can locate each of the five roles. Then we can look at how and why you would transfer each of the roles to another domain controller, and the options available if you have lost the role-holding domain controller.

In this chapter you will learn how to:

♦ Determine which servers hold the FSMO roles

♦ Transfer FSMO roles between servers

♦ Seize FSMO roles

Identifying the Role Holders

As with many things in the Windows environment, there are several ways to find out which domain controller holds a FSMO role. Some ways are easier than others; it depends on your familiarity with the built-in utilities that ship with Windows Server and with the support tools.

One of the easiest ways to find out which domain controller is hosting a FSMO role is to use the built-in Active Directory utilities. Most of the Active Directory utilities are easy to find and work with, but one of them is hidden from view. Let's look at what each utility has to offer.

Active Directory Users and Computers

You can use the Active Directory Users and Computers utility to find the domain controllers that hold domain-specific roles. As discussed in Chapter 5, each domain has an Infrastructure Master, a RID Master, and a PDC Emulator. So it only makes sense that to find the role holders of these FSMO roles, you consult a utility that helps you maintain aspects of your domain.

When you open Active Directory Users and Computers, it is not immediately obvious that the FSMO role holders can be found there. However, if you right-click on the domain node, you see the option Operations Masters in the context menu, as shown in Figure 13.1. Clicking this option presents you with the Operations Masters dialog box shown in Figure 13.2.

Notice the tabs at the top of this dialog box, one for each of the domain-based roles: RID, PDC, and Infrastructure. As you select each of these tabs, two domain controllers appear in the window. If you target the Active Directory Users and Computers snap-in on the domain controller that is holding the FSMO role, you will see that domain controller listed in both spots. If you are not focused on the role holder, you will see the current role holder listed first in the Operations Master field, and the domain controller you are focused on listed in the transfer field.

FIGURE 13.1
Domain node
context menu

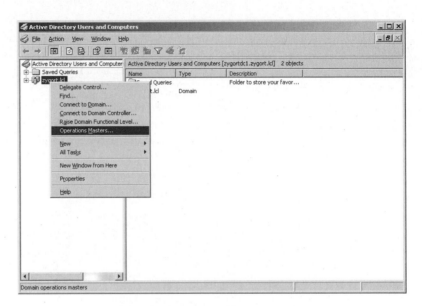

FIGURE 13.2
Operations Masters
dialog box

To transfer roles, you must target the Active Directory Users and Computers snap-in on the domain controller that you want to take over the role. When you have decided to which domain controller you want to transfer the role, all you have to do is open Active Directory Users and Computers, right-click on the domain, and select Connect to Domain Controller, as shown in Figure 13.3. Once the dialog box appears, as shown in Figure 13.4, you can enter the name of the domain controller you want to host the role.

FIGURE 13.3
Context menu that lets you choose a domain controller

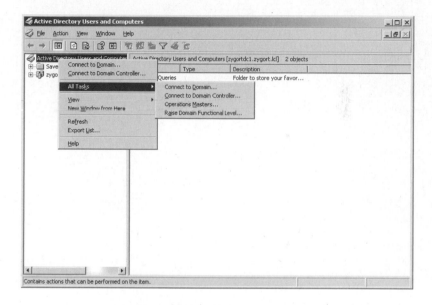

FIGURE 13.4
Changing the domain controller

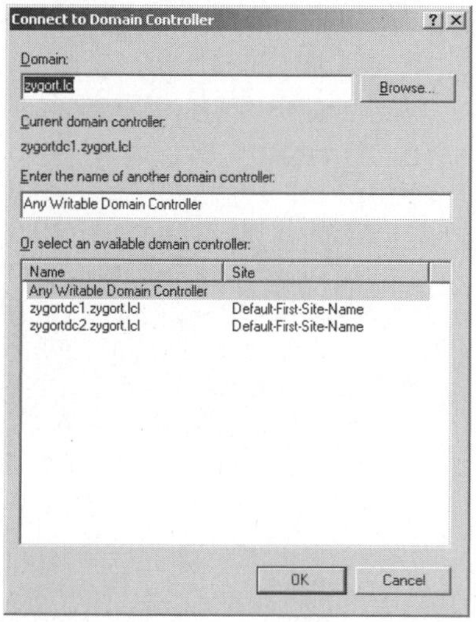

Active Directory Domains and Trusts

The first of the two forest-based roles is easy to locate using the Active Directory Domains and Trusts snap-in. You can find the Domain Naming Master role by using the same method as is used to find the domain-based roles. Right-click on the domain node in the Active Directory Domains and Trusts snap-in and select Operations Master. The dialog box that appears, shown in Figure 13.5, displays the current role holder and the domain controller that you want to become the role holder. Just as with Active Directory Users and Computers, you can choose which domain controller will take over the role by selecting it from the context menu that appears when you right-click the domain node in the snap-in.

FIGURE 13.5
Change Operations
Master window

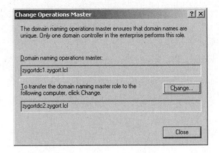

Active Directory Schema

This is the one snap-in that is not available to administrators unless they choose to register the dynamic link library (DLL) necessary for it to be displayed and used. The designers of Active Directory did this intentionally because they did not believe the tool should be available to every administrator within the forest. Instead, Microsoft forces anyone who wants to use this tool to research how to get to the schema. Because the schema should not be altered unless there is a valid business case for doing so, this snap-in would not be used very often anyway. To gain access to the Active Directory Schema snap-in, you will need to register it using the command line `regsvr32 schmmgmt.dll`.

Command-Line Options

Some command-line utilities allow you to identify the role holders. Although these utilities may not be as intuitive as the snap-ins we have been discussing, they can come in very handy when you are already at a command prompt. The first, `ReplMon`, allows you to view role holders and query against them. `Netdom` shows you all the role holders at the same time, while `dsquery` allows you to find individual roles when you ask for them. The `DCDiag` utility shows you all the roles. The final utility, `dumpfsmos.cmd`, displays the FSMO roles that the domain controller knows about. You can find this utility in the Windows Server Resource Kit.

REPLMON

The Active Directory Replication Monitor utility (`ReplMon`) included with the support tools on the Windows Server CD can identify the current FSMO role holders as well as send a query against them to see if they are up and running. To start `ReplMon`, type **ReplMon** at the support tools command line. When the tool opens, you will need to add a domain controller to the console. Right-click the Monitored Servers node, and then select Add Monitored Server from the context menu, as shown in Figure 13.6.

The resulting dialog box allows you to type the domain controller's name, or you can search Active Directory for the domain controller you want to use. Figure 13.7 displays the dialog box that you use to choose the monitored server, and Figure 13.8 shows the methods you can use to search for the domain controller's name.

Once you have added the domain controller to the monitored servers list, by right-clicking on the server and selecting Properties, you can look at the properties of the domain controller to learn which domain controllers hold the FSMO roles. After opening the properties, you can click the FSMO Roles tab to view the current role holders, as Figure 13.9 shows. Notice the Query button next to each role. Clicking this button causes Replication Monitor to check the current role holder to see if it is online. If it is online, the message shown in Figure 13.10 appears. If the role holder cannot be contacted, you see the message shown in Figure 13.11.

FIGURE 13.6

Choosing to monitor a server in Replication Monitor

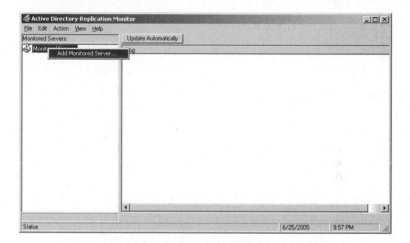

FIGURE 13.7

Choosing the monitored server

FIGURE 13.8
Searching for
the domain
controller's name

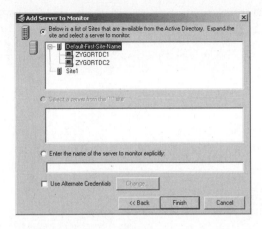

FIGURE 13.9
Server Properties
FSMO Roles tab

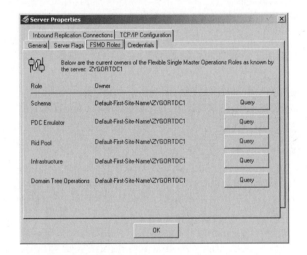

FIGURE 13.10
Positive result from
FSMO query

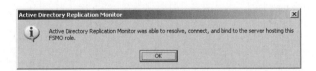

FIGURE 13.11
Negative result from
FSMO query

NETDOM

The `netdom` command syntax that reports the role holders is as follows:

```
netdom query fsmo /domain:zygort.lcl
```

Of course, you replace `zygort.lcl` with your domain name. This returns a list of all the role holders. The results appear in the command-prompt window, as shown in Figure 13.12.

DSQUERY

To find individual role holders with the `dsquery` command, use the following commands:

◆ To find the Schema Master:

```
dsquery server -hasfsmo schema
```

◆ To find the Domain Naming Master:

```
dsquery server -hasfsmo name
```

◆ To find the Infrastructure Master:

```
dsquery server -hasfsmo infr
```

◆ To find the RID Master:

```
dsquery server -hasfsmo rid
```

◆ To find the PDC Emulator:

```
dsquery server -hasfsmo pdc
```

This command-line utility also presents the results in the command-prompt window. Figure 13.13 shows an example of what you receive when you issue one of the commands.

FIGURE 13.12
The netdom command lists the FSMO roles.

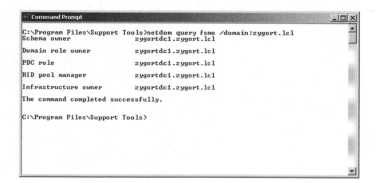

FIGURE 13.13

dsquery results for the Schema Master

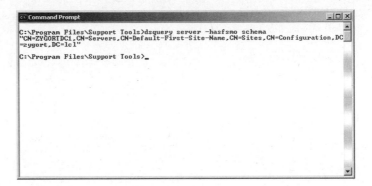

DCDIAG

The DCDiag utility is used as follows:

```
dcdiag /test:knowsofroleholders /v
```

Because we included the verbose switch (/v), this command returns the role holders and provides information on each. Figure 13.14 displays a portion of the information you receive when you issue this command at a command prompt.

DUMPFSMOS.CMD

The dumpfsmos.cmd utility from the resource kit is a small script that starts NTDSUTIL and issues the appropriate commands to return a list of the role holders. The syntax for this command is as follows:

```
dumpfsmos.cmd zygort.lcl
```

Of course, you replace zygort.lcl with the name of the domain you are querying against. Figure 13.15 shows the information returned when you issue this command at the command prompt.

Maintaining the Role Holders

There are reasons to move a role from one domain controller to another. Many organizations need to move at least one role because they have more than one domain in their forest. The Infrastructure Master cannot work effectively on a global catalog server when there are two or more domains. Other reasons to make changes to the location of your FSMO roles are addressed in the following sections.

Depending on your situation, you can transfer the role to another domain controller if the original role holder is still online, or you can seize, which means forcibly taking the role, if the original role holder has failed. Transferring the role is the preferred method because it performs a controlled switch-over from one domain controller to the next. You should consider seizing a role only if the original role holder cannot be brought back online. Of course, safeguards are in place to protect the forest or domain from data corruption should the original role holder come back online, but you shouldn't take a chance. If the original role holder has failed and you have seized the role on another domain controller, do not attempt to bring the original role holder back online until you can remove that role from the server.

FIGURE 13.14
DCDiag results

FIGURE 13.15
dumpfsmos.cmd
results

TRANSFERRING THE ROLE TO ANOTHER DOMAIN CONTROLLER

If you are demoting a role holder, make sure that you transfer the role to another domain controller, preferably the domain controller you have designated as the standby role holder. Doing so guarantees that you are transferring the role to the appropriate domain controller instead of allowing dcpromo to choose another domain controller on its own. Remember: it is always better to have control over these things than to allow chance to control your organization.

SEIZING THE ROLE ON THE STANDBY DOMAIN CONTROLLER

You should have already designated another domain controller as the standby server in case a role holder becomes unavailable. If you have configured the original role holder and the standby as replication partners, there is a very good chance that they are completely synchronized with one another. If the original role holder becomes unavailable and you deem it necessary to have the standby server become the role holder, you can seize the role on the standby server. Again, this is a drastic measure and should be performed only if you are certain the original role holder is not going to be reintroduced on the network.

(If you are taking a domain controller offline permanently, whether or not it is a role holder, you should demote it so the references to the domain controller are removed from Active Directory.)

In the following sections, we cover each of the roles and the steps necessary to transfer or seize each role. We start with the two forest-level roles and then discuss the domain-level roles. We also cover the ramifications of not moving a role to another domain controller when the original domain controller is offline.

Maintaining the Schema Master

The Schema Master role is not one that you will have to worry about if the domain controller holding it goes offline. The Schema Master is used whenever you have to make a change to the forest's schema and when the forest functional level is raised. Otherwise, the Schema Master just waits for changes to be made by a member of the Schema Admins group or an administrator who is responsible for raising the forest functional level. Obviously, neither of these options is performed very often. The forest functional level can be raised only one time and cannot revert to its previous level; thus, schema changes should be kept to a minimum.

You might want to move the Schema Master to another system for a couple of reasons. A controlled move, or transfer, may be necessary if you are planning on decommissioning the domain controller that holds the Schema Master role. If this is the case, it is much easier to transfer the role to the domain controller that is taking over the Schema Master responsibility than to seize it later on.

Another reason to transfer the role lies in how companies maintain their FSMO roles. Many companies prefer to have all of the roles held on one domain controller. This way, they know which domain controller is performing these functions, they can control the services that are operating on the domain controller, and they can isolate the domain controller for security purposes.

TRANSFERRING THE SCHEMA MASTER ROLE

The Schema Master is not readily transferable using the standard administrative tools. As a matter of fact, Microsoft intentionally hid the Active Directory Schema snap-in so that people would not have easy access to it. To make it accessible, you must register the DLL that it uses on the system where you will administer the changes. To register the DLL, open a command prompt, or at the Run line type **regsvr32 schmmgmt.dll**.

Using the Active Directory Schema Snap-In

Once you have registered the snap-in, you can open it by creating your own Microsoft Management Console (MMC) and adding the snap-in to it. With the snap-in, you can connect to the domain controlle whose role responsibility you want to take over, by right-clicking on the Active Directory Schema node and selecting Change Domain Controller. Notice that for the Schema Master the dialog box for connecting to another domain controller (Figure 13.16) is different than the one for the other snap-ins. Once you are focused on another domain controller, you can change the Operations Master by right-clicking the same node and choosing Operations Master.

The current role holder appears in the top text box, and the domain controller on which you are focused appears in the lower section, as shown in Figure 13.17. When you click the Change button, the entry in the upper text box reflects the change, and will then match the name of the domain controller in the lower section.

That's all there is to it. The transfer of the role is usually a very quick process. One domain controller is told to take the token that identifies it as the one that can perform schema updates, and the other has the token taken from it. If the original role holder is not available, it may take a minute or two for a dialog box to appear that states the original role holder could not be contacted. If the original role holder has failed, you have to seize the role on the new domain controller. Otherwise, if it is still up and running, you must troubleshoot to learn why the original role holder could not be contacted by the potential role holder.

FIGURE 13.16
Connecting to the
Schema Master

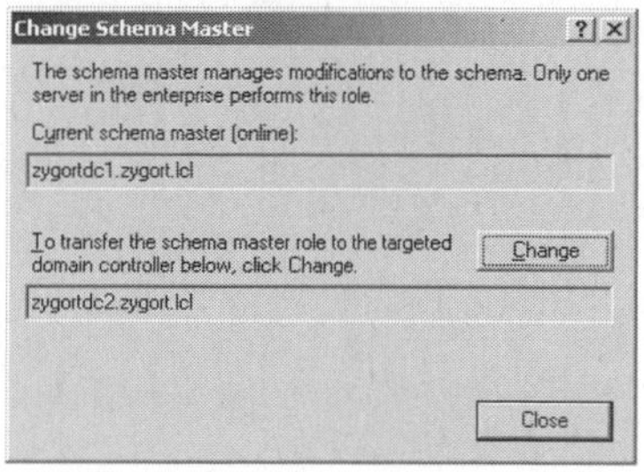

FIGURE 13.17
Schema Master
Operations Master

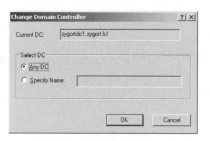

Using NTDSUtil

You can also transfer the role by using NTDSUtil. This command-line utility allows you to perform many functions in Active Directory, including transferring and seizing the FSMO roles if necessary. After you open a command prompt and type **NTDSUtil**, perform these steps to transfer the Schema Master:

1. At the ntdsutil: prompt, type **roles** to enter fsmo maintenance.

2. At the fsmo maintenance: prompt, type **connections** to enter server connections.

3. At the server connections: prompt, type **connect to server *domain_controller***, where *domain_controller* is the name of the domain controller to which you are going to transfer the role.

4. At the server connections: prompt, type **quit** to enter fsmo maintenance.

5. At the fsmo maintenance: prompt, type **transfer schema master**.

After you have transferred the role, type **quit** twice to exit NTDSUtil. You can then use one of the utilities listed earlier to verify that the role was transferred to the appropriate domain controller.

SEIZING THE SCHEMA MASTER ROLE

If you have lost the original Schema Master and you want to designate another domain controller as the Schema Master, you must use NTDSUtil. This allows you to force the new domain controller to take on the responsibility. Open a command prompt and enter **NTDSUtil**; then follow these steps:

1. At the ntdsutil: prompt, type **roles** to enter fsmo maintenance.

2. At the fsmo maintenance: prompt, type **connections** to enter server connections.

3. At the server connections: prompt, type **connect to server *domain_controller***, where *domain_controller* is the name of the domain controller to which you are going to transfer the role.

4. At the server connections: prompt, type **quit** to enter fsmo maintenance.

5. At the fsmo maintenance: prompt, type **seize schema master**.

After you have transferred the role, type **quit** twice to exit NTDSUtil. You can then use one of the utilities listed earlier to verify that the role was transferred to the appropriate domain controller.

Maintaining the Domain Naming Master

The Domain Naming Master role is used just slightly more than its forest-level brethren, the Schema Master. Whenever a domain is created or removed from the forest, the Domain Naming Master is queried to make sure everything is valid in the request. If a domain exists that has the same name as the domain being created, the Domain Naming Master halts the creation of the new domain. If an attempt is made to remove a domain, and the Domain Naming Master finds anything about the request that is not valid, it will stop the removal of the domain.

As with the Schema Master, you don't have to worry about the resource requirements for the Domain Naming Master. It can continue to run on the original domain controller for the remainder of that server's lifetime. If you lose the server or if you want to decommission it, you can move the role to another machine by either transferring or seizing the role.

TRANSFERRING THE DOMAIN NAMING MASTER ROLE

Transferring the Domain Naming Master role using a graphical interface requires fewer steps than does transferring the Schema Master. The interface you use to transfer it is available on domain controllers and is one of the snap-ins made available when you load the administrative tools onto your workstation. The snap-in that you will be using for this procedure is Active Directory Domains and Trusts.

Using Active Directory Domains and Trusts

To perform the transfer you must be a member of the Enterprise Admins group. Once you open the snap-in in an MMC, you need to connect to the domain controller to which you are going to transfer the role. To do so, right-click the domain node and select Connect to Domain Controller, as shown in Figure 13.18.

Once you have targeted the snap-in on the domain controller that will be taking over the Domain Naming Master role, you can right-click the domain once again and select the Operations Masters option. This takes you to a screen that displays the current role holder in the top pane and the domain controller you are transferring the role to in the bottom, just like in Figure 13.19.

FIGURE 13.18
Selecting the domain controller

FIGURE 13.19
Transferring the role

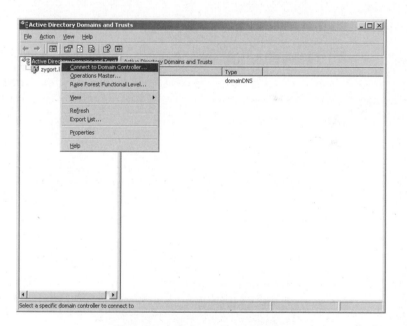

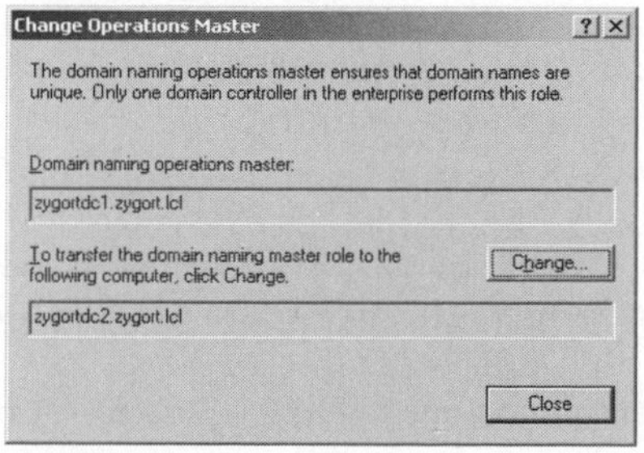

Using NTDSUtil

You can also transfer the role by using the NTDSUtil command-line utility. Open a command prompt and type **NTDSUtil**. When the NTDSUtil interface appears, issue the following commands to transfer the role to the desired domain controller:

1. At the `ntdsutil:` prompt, type **roles** to enter `fsmo maintenance`.

2. At the `fsmo maintenance:` prompt, type **connections** to enter `server connections`.

3. At the `server connections:` prompt, type **connect to server** *`domain_controller`*, where *`domain_controller`* is the name of the domain controller to which you are going to transfer the role.

4. At the `server connections:` prompt, type **quit** to enter `fsmo maintenance`.

5. At the `fsmo maintenance:` prompt, type **transfer domain naming master**.

After you have transferred the role, type **quit** twice to exit NTDSUtil. You can then use one of the utilities mentioned earlier to verify that the role was transferred to the appropriate domain controller.

SEIZING THE DOMAIN NAMING MASTER ROLE

The Domain Naming Master can remain offline for quite some time before you will be required to bring it back online. Because its main role is to check and approve domain additions and deletions, you will not need it online unless you are making a critical change to your forest. If you do want to seize the role, either because of needing the Domain Naming Master online or determining that the original role holder is not going to be restored, you can follow these instructions:

1. At the `ntdsutil:` prompt, type **roles** to enter `fsmo maintenance`.

2. At the `fsmo maintenance:` prompt, type **connections** to enter `server connections`.

3. At the `server connections:` prompt, type **connect to server** *`domain_controller`*, where *`domain_controller`* is the name of the domain controller to which you are going to transfer the role.

4. At the `server connections:` prompt, type **quit** to enter `fsmo maintenance`.

5. At the `fsmo maintenance:` prompt, type **seize domain naming master**.

After you have transferred the role, type **quit** twice to exit NTDSUtil. You can then use one of the utilities mentioned earlier to verify that the role was transferred to the appropriate domain controller.

Maintaining the Infrastructure Master

If you are working in a multiple-domain environment, the Infrastructure Master can be your best friend or your worst enemy. It is the Infrastructure Master's job to make sure that accounts from other domains that are members of a group are kept up-to-date. You do not want an account to have access to resources that it is not supposed to, and if changes are made to users and groups in other domains, you need to make sure that the same changes are reflected in your domain. For instance, let's say the administrator of `bloomco.lcl` has just added two accounts to a global group and removed one from the group. Within the `bloomco.lcl` domain, the changes are replicated throughout. In your domain, there is a domain local group that contains the global group. Because the changes are not replicated to domain controllers in your domain, the user who was removed from the group might still have access to resources in your domain and the two new accounts might not.

The Infrastructure Master needs to be able to maintain the differences between domains so that the correct group membership can be applied at all domain controllers. This is why the Infrastructure Master should not be on a domain controller that is acting as a global catalog. The Infrastructure Master will contact a global catalog and compare the member attributes for the groups with the attributes that are contained in the Infrastrucutre Master's domain. If there is a difference, the Infrastructure Master updates the attributes to keep everything synchronized. If you want to change the default scanning interval for the Infrastructure Master, set the following Registry value from two days to whatever value works best in your environment:

```
HKEY_LOCAL_MACHINE\System\CurrentControlSet\Services\
NTDS\Parameters\Days per database phantom scan
```

(For more information on the Infrastructure Master and how to control the scanning interval, see Knowledge Base article 248047 at `http://support.microsoft.com/default.aspx?scid=kb;EN-US;248047`.)

Loss of the Infrastructure Master is a little more severe than would be the loss of the previous two Operations Master roles. If the Infrastructure Master is offline for an extended period of time, the data cannot be synchronized and users could have access (or be denied access) to the wrong objects. If you cannot resolve the problem with the Infrastructure Master, you may want to seize the role on the standby server.

TRANSFERRING THE INFRASTRUCTURE MASTER ROLE

As with all of the domain-level Operations Masters, you can transfer the Infrastructure Master role to another domain controller by using the Active Directory Users and Computers snap-in. This snap-in is available when you promote a domain controller and when you add the administrative tools to another system, such as your workstation.

Using Active Directory Users and Computers

To initiate the transfer, open Active Directory Users and Computers; then connect to the domain controller that will become the Infrastructure Master by right-clicking on the domain name and choosing Connect to Domain Controller. Of course, this assumes that you are working with domain controllers from the domain in which your user account resides. You could very easily be an administrator for another domain within your forest and need to perform a transfer of a role in another domain. If that is the case, choose the Connect to Domain option from the context menu, and then select Connect to Domain Controller to connect to the domain controller that will become the Infrastructure Master.

Remember that the Infrastructure Master should not reside on a global catalog server unless you are in a single-domain environment or all of your domain controllers are also global catalog servers. Then, to transfer the role you will again right-click on the domain and choose Operations Masters. The dialog box that appears, shown in Figure 13.20, has three tabs representing the domain-level FSMO roles. Click Infrastructure; you should see the current Infrastructure Master listed at the top and the domain controller you are focused on at the bottom. Clicking the Change button transfers the role to the new role holder.

FIGURE 13.20
Operations Masters
transfer dialog box

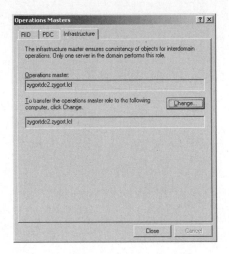

Using NTDSUtil

You can also transfer the role by using the NTDSUtil command-line utility. Open a command prompt and type **NTDSUtil**. When the NTDSUtil interface appears, issue the following commands to transfer the role to the desired domain controller:

1. At the `ntdsutil:` prompt, type **roles** to enter `fsmo maintenance`.

2. At the `fsmo maintenance:` prompt, type **connections** to enter `server connections`.

3. At the `server connections:` prompt, type **connect to server** *`domain_controller`*, where *`domain_controller`* is the name of the domain controller to which you are going to transfer the role.

4. At the `server connections:` prompt, type **quit** to enter `fsmo maintenance`.

5. At the `fsmo maintenance:` prompt, type **transfer infrastructure master**.

After you have transferred the role, type **quit** twice to exit NTDSUtil. You can then use one of the utilities mentioned earlier to verify that the role was transferred to the appropriate domain controller.

SEIZING THE INFRASTRUCTURE MASTER ROLE

The infrastructure Master is not as critical to the functionality of the domain as other roles are, so you will probably not have to seize the role. However, if you deem that the original Infrastructure Master is not going to be brought back online, or if there are changes going on in other domains, you can seize the role using the following instructions.

1. At the `ntdsutil:` prompt, type **roles** to enter `fsmo maintenance`.

2. At the `fsmo maintenance:` prompt, type **connections** to enter `server connections`.

3. At the `server connections:` prompt, type **connect to server** *`domain_controller`*, where *`domain_controller`* is the name of the domain controller to which you are going to transfer the role.

4. At the `server connections:` prompt, type **quit** to enter `fsmo maintenance`.

5. At the `fsmo maintenance:` prompt, type **seize infrastructure master**.

After you have transferred the role, type **quit** twice to exit NTDSUtil. You can then use one of the utilities mentioned earlier to verify that the role was transferred to the appropriate domain controller.

Maintaining the RID Master

Whenever a security principal—such as a user, group, or computer account—is created within a domain, it has an associated security identifier (SID). An account's SID consists of the domain's SID and a relative identifier (RID) unique to the security principal. Allocating and keeping track of all of the RIDs for the domain is the RID Master's responsibility. Having the RID Master online allows you to sleep better at night knowing that a duplicate SID will not be generated within the domain. Even if the security principal associated with a RID is deleted, the RID will still not be regenerated and used again.

If you look at a SID, you will notice that it is an alphanumeric combination that is not easy to understand. There is logic behind the madness, however. Looking at the SID or a user account, you will see something like this:

```
S-1-5-21-1068514962-2513648523-685232148-1005
```

Broken down, the sections that make up the RID fall into these categories:

S The initial character *S* identifies the series of digits that follow as a SID.

1 This is the revision level. Every SID that is generated within a Windows environment has a revision of 1.

5 This third character is the issuing-authority identifier. Most SIDs will have the Windows NT issuing-authority number of 5, but some well-known built-in accounts will have other values.

21 The fourth character set represents the subauthority. The subauthority identifies the service type that generated the SID. SIDs that are generated from domain controllers will contain the character set 21, while built-in accounts may have other character sets, such as 32.

1068514962-2513648523-685232148 This long string of characters is the unique part of the SID for a domain. If you are working with local accounts, it represents the unique SID for the computer.

1005 The last set of characters represents the RID for the account. The RID Master starts at 1000 and increments by 1 for every RID it allocates to the domain controllers.

Because any domain controller within a native-mode domain can generate a RID to an account, you must make sure that only one domain controller is allocating and controlling the RIDs. For this reason, make sure that you do not seize the RID role on a domain controller when the original role holder is only temporarily unavailable. You could create a nightmare of trying to troubleshoot permission problems.

You're likely to miss the RID Master role sooner than you'd miss some of the others if you lost them. The RID Master allocates blocks of RIDs to the domain controllers within the domain. If a domain controller uses up its last RID while creating a security principal, it will no longer be able to create security principals. Another drawback to losing the RID Master is that you cannot promote another domain controller without having the RID Master online. For these reasons, you should attempt to recover the original RID Master role holder as quickly as possible; otherwise you will have to seize the role on the standby server as the RID pools on the domain controllers start to deplete.

TRANSFERRING THE RID MASTER ROLE

Transferring the RID Master role to the standby server is another very easy task. When you deem it necessary to move the role to another domain controller, you can use the Operations Masters dialog box from Active Directory Users and Computers, or NTDSUtil. Your utility of choice should be determined by the method you are most comfortable using.

Using Active Directory Users and Computers

The RID Master is another domain-level role that you can find within Active Directory Users and Computers. When you select the Operations Masters menu item and select the RID tab, click the Change button to move the role to another domain controller, just as you did with the Infrastructure Master.

Using NTDSUtil

You can also transfer the role by using the NTDSUtil command-line utility. Open a command prompt and type **NTDSUtil**. When the NTDSUtil interface appears, issue the following commands to transfer the role to the desired domain controller:

1. At the `ntdsutil:` prompt, type **roles** to enter `fsmo maintenance`.

2. At the `fsmo maintenance:` prompt, type **connections** to enter `server connections`.

3. At the `server connections:` prompt, type **connect to server** *domain_controller*, where *domain_controller* is the name of the domain controller to which you are going to transfer the role.

4. At the `server connections:` prompt, type **quit** to enter `fsmo maintenance`.

5. At the `fsmo maintenance:` prompt, type **transfer RID master**.

After you have transferred the role, type **quit** twice to exit NTDSUtil. You can then use one of the utilities mentioned earlier to verify that the role was transferred to the appropriate domain controller.

SEIZING THE RID MASTER ROLE

You can get by without the RID Master role for a short period of time. The amount of time it can remain down depends on the number of accounts you are creating. Because each domain controller receives an initial allotment of 500 RIDs, you can probably get by for some time before you run out of RIDs.

If your domain is still in Windows 2000 mixed mode, however, you may have a shorter time frame for your RID Master's absence. The PDC Emulator is the only domain controller that can create accounts in mixed mode. Therefore, you do not have the option to connect to another domain controller to create an account. To seize the role, follow these steps:

1. At the `ntdsutil:` prompt, type **roles** to enter `fsmo maintenance`.

2. At the `fsmo maintenance:` prompt, type **connections** to enter `server connections`.

3. At the `server connections:` prompt, type **connect to server** *domain_controller*, where *domain_controller* is the name of the domain controller to which you are going to transfer the role.

4. At the `server connections:` prompt, type **quit** to enter `fsmo maintenance`.

5. At the `fsmo maintenance:` prompt, type **seize RID master**.

After you have transferred the role, type **quit** twice to exit NTDSUtil. You can then use one of the utilities mentioned earlier to verify that the role was transferred to the appropriate domain controller.

Maintaining the PDC Emulator

The PDC Emulator is probably the busiest of the master operations, and yet it is the only one that is not known by the name "master." This is also the role that confuses new administrators, because they think that the role is needed only until all of the NT 4 Backup Domain Controllers (BDCs) are taken offline. This is far from the truth. Microsoft should consider changing the name of this master operation to reflect the other functions it provides.

First off, the PDC Emulator allows for replication of directory information to Windows NT 4 BDCs while the domain is still in mixed mode. Because it has to act like a Windows NT 4 Primary Domain Controller (PDC), this is the only domain controller that will create security principals while the domain is in mixed mode. Make sure you place this role holder in a location that will create the most accounts.

This is also the only domain controller allowed to change passwords for legacy operating systems such as Windows 98 and Windows NT. They will look for the PDC of the domain, and the PDC Emulator fulfills that roll. This role holder also has the final say when there is a password change. When an account's password is changed, the PDC Emulator is notified immediately. After a user types in her or his password for authentication, and before notifying the user that they typed in the wrong password, the domain controller attempting to authenticate the user will check with the PDC Emulator to make sure the user's password has not been changed.

Two other functions—time synchronization and global policy centralization—are functions of the PDC Emulator. All the other domain controllers within the domain will look to this role holder as the official timekeeper in the domain. You should set the PDC Emulator to synchronize with an external time source so that all the other domain controllers will have the correct time.

This is also the domain controller that is used as the default location for changing group policies. Making one domain controller the default Group Policy Object (GPO) holder allows you to control policy changes and to minimize conflicting changes within the domain. (In a multiple-domain forest, the PDC Emulator for the forest root becomes the Time Master for all PDCs within the forest.)

Because of the number of responsibilities the PDC Emulator has, it will probably be the Operations Master that you will miss the most if it fails. When it fails, you should immediately assess how long it will take to recover the domain controller that holds the PDC Emulator role. If it looks as if the domain controller is going to be offline for an extended period of time—let's say more than a couple of hours—you should seize the role on the standby server. Although losing other FSMO roles may cause problems for administrators, users will be affected by a loss of the PDC Emulator, and they will let you know that they see something wrong!

TRANSFERRING THE PDC EMULATOR ROLE

This is yet another of the domain-level roles. As with the Infrastructure Master and RID Master roles, the Active Directory Users and Computer snap-in is the tool to use to transfer the PDC Emulator. This, as does NTDSUtil, allows you to connect to the domain controller that you want to become the PDC Emulator, and to transfer the role.

Using Active Directory Users and Computers

Following the same steps that were outlined in the "Transferring the Infrastructure Master Role" section, you can take the change token away from the existing PDC Emulator and allow another domain controller to take its place as the role holder.

Using NTDSUtil

You can also transfer the role by using the NTDSUtil command-line utility. Open a command prompt and type **NTDSUtil**. When the NTDSUtil interface appears, issue the following commands to transfer the role to the desired domain controller:

1. At the `ntdsutil:` prompt, type **roles** to enter `fsmo maintenance`.

2. At the `fsmo maintenance:` prompt, type **connections** to enter `server connections`.

3. At the `server connections:` prompt, type **connect to server** *domain_controller*, where *domain_controller* is the name of the domain controller to which you are going to transfer the role.

4. At the `server connections:` prompt, type **quit** to enter `fsmo maintenance`.

5. At the `fsmo maintenance:` prompt, type **transfer PDC**.

After you have transferred the role, type **quit** twice to exit NTDSUtil. You can then use one of the utilities mentioned earlier to verify that the role was transferred to the appropriate domain controller.

SEIZING THE PDC EMULATOR ROLE

This is the one role that you may need to seize very quickly after the original role holder has failed. You may be able to go for a short period without it; however, all of the password changes, account-lockout information, time synchronization, and group policy updates are made on this system. With that in mind, and considering that the process of seizing this role is less disruptive to the domain than is seizing other roles, you will likely want to seize this role on the standby system almost immediately after the original role holder has failed.

If you are working in a Windows 2000 mixed mode domain, the PDC Emulator is the only domain controller that is allowed to create user accounts. To create accounts after the PDC Emulator has gone offline, you need to seize the role on another machine by following these steps:

1. At the `ntdsutil:` prompt, type **roles** to enter `fsmo maintenance`.

2. At the `fsmo maintenance:` prompt, type **connections** to enter `server connections`.

3. At the `server connections:` prompt, type **connect to server** *domain_controller*, where *domain_controller* is the name of the domain controller to which you are going to transfer the role.

4. At the `server connections:` prompt, type **quit** to enter `fsmo maintenance`.

5. At the `fsmo maintenance:` prompt, type **seize PDC**.

After you have transferred the role, type **quit** twice to exit NTDSUtil. You can then use one of the utilities mentioned earlier to verify that the role was transferred to the appropriate domain controller.

 Real World Scenario

BE PREPARED

Nicholas is the administrator of an AD DS domain that consists of five domain controllers. He has implemented a proactive monitoring solution in his network. Nicholas has found that the process of transferring and seizing roles in his network, although not frequent, is time-consuming because of the manual process of typing in all of the commands in the NTDSUtil menus. Nicholas would like to automate this process to reduce time and possibility of human error.

The NTDSUtil program allows Nicholas to enter numerous commands in a single command line, with a space between commands. Nicholas can now create batch file (.bat) scripts that will allow him to transfer and seize roles from one server to another simply by running the batch file.

To transfer the PDC Emulator role from Server1 to Server2, the syntax of the batch file would be as follows:

```
ntdsutil roles "connections" "connect to server Server2" quit "transfer PDC" quit quit
```

Failed Role Holders

When a role holder fails, you need to seize the role using NTDSUtil because transferring the role won't be possible. You will realize this when you are first attempting to open the Operations Masters dialog box for any of the roles. The initial connection takes a considerable amount of time, and then the dialog box appears with the word *ERROR* in the Operations Master section. Figure 13.21 shows the dialog box with the error message that you receive. Figure 13.22 shows the error message that appears if you attempt to transfer the role while the original role holder is not online.

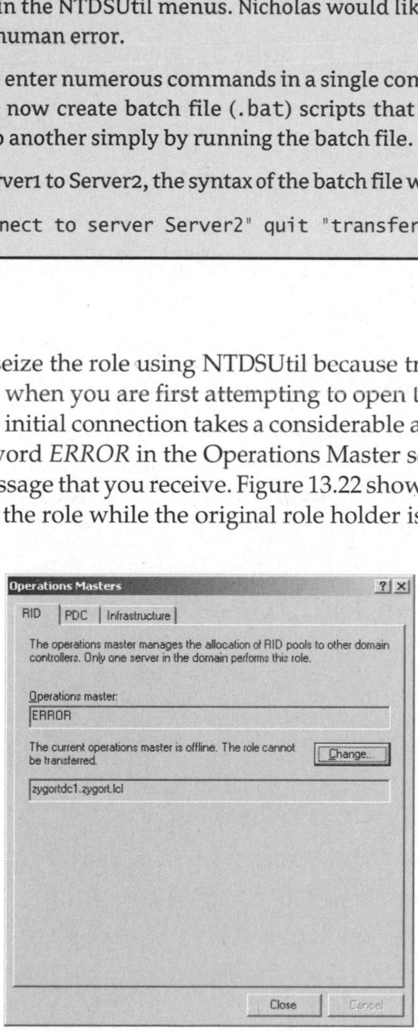

FIGURE 13.21
Operations Master dialog box showing original role holder problem

FIGURE 13.22
Error message when
attempting to transfer
the role

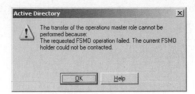

Coming Up Next

Although Microsoft has done a very commendable job of developing a stable directory service, things happen with any type of file, service, or database that can cause problems and, ultimately, corruption. In the next chapter, we investigate the troubleshooting steps and tools that help you assess and repair your directory service.

The Bottom Line

FSMO roles by their nature are special domain controllers that contain roles that can be a single point of failure for that particular role. Special planning and steps are necessary to ensure these roles can be moved or brought back up in a meaningful time frame.

Determine which servers hold the FSMO roles   The first step in FSMO planning and management is determining which domain controllers hold which FSMO roles. You can do this by checking the built-in AD DS tools or by using downloadable tools from Microsoft.

Master It   Determine which domain controllers in the environment hold FSMO roles.

Transfer FSMO roles between servers   There will be times when you must transfer FSMO roles from one server to another—usually when you want to demote a server, to bring a server offline for a period of time, or to spread out the roles among servers if one server has multiple roles.

Master It   Use the built-in AD DS tools to transfer roles from one server to another.

Seize FSMO roles   If a domain controller that holds a FSMO role is down or unresponsive, you may need to seize a FSMO role.

Master It   You must be able to seize each FSMO role in case a role resides on a server that has crashed or is unresponsive.

Chapter 14

Maintaining the Active Directory Database

The term *database* has many interpretations. The most common is "a collection of persistent data." Currently, Microsoft leverages an object-oriented database to store Active Directory (AD) data. There is little doubt Microsoft will leverage relational-database technology in future versions of Active Directory. This often leads to the following questions: what is the difference, and why should you care? Let's start with how they differ.

The object-oriented database paradigm is simply the extension of object-oriented programming languages to support a persistent state of the transient data found in executing code. The process of storing and using data in the same format has been employed since the dawn of computing and is still in wide use today. Object-oriented databases are nothing more than large, structured files linked by indexes that are themselves structured files.

Relational database management systems (RDBMSs) are based on E.F. Codd's relational database theory, which is founded on relational algebra and calculus. The greatest deviation from earlier storage models—such as object-oriented—is the concept of tables or entities and their relationships to each other. Each record in a table represents a unique instance of the entity described. An RDBMS uses matching values in multiple tables to relate the data in one table to that in other tables. Gone is the concept of storing data as methods use it. Data structure is now defined by the business rules that govern it and the interdependence of the entities stored.

Consider for a moment a file cabinet full of various human-resources forms. The object-oriented model is concerned only with storing the forms. As data are manipulated and persisted, forms are created or altered and placed in the file cabinet. The same file cabinet is used for all forms: hirings, promotions, and terminations.

In a relational model, the data elements of a given form are reorganized into tables or entities and stored. A single record in a table, or on a piece of paper in a folder, describes one instance of the entity defined by the table. Following our example, all three form types contain attributes of employees, the job they are fulfilling, and their current employment status; thus employee, job, and employment-status tables might be created in a relational model, each storing an employee ID so the data set could be reconstructed when needed.

Why should you care? Relational databases are easier to understand. This opens the door for administrators, programmers, and business users to leverage the corporate data assets embedded within Active Directory.

In this chapter you will learn how to:

- Defragment the Active Directory Domain Services (AD DS) database
- Use NTDSUtil to manage the AD DS database
- Implement best practices for optimizing the AD DS database

The Active Directory Database

Active Directory stores its data in a file named `ntds.dit`. By default, this file is located in the `%systemroot%/NTDS` folder. In addition to using the database file, Active Directory uses log files that store information prior to committing it to the database.

For the most part, the system is self-maintained, but there are a few reasons that you may need to maintain the database:

◆ Low disk space

◆ Hardware failure

◆ Need to recover disk space

During day-to-day operation, objects will get deleted from Active Directory on a somewhat regular basis. As your Active Directory environment grows, the database grows as needed. The reverse is not true, however. As you delete objects from Active Directory, the database will not automatically shrink itself.

This process creates "white space" (or unused space) in your database. Think of it like this: you have a row of pop cans (or soda cans, if you prefer) on a table. If you have a row of 20 cans of pop in a single-file line, and you put another anywhere in the line, the line grows. If you take a few pop cans out of the middle, the line is still just as long as it was before, but now you have some empty spaces in there.

You can add cans back to the empty space (or white space). On a regular basis, Active Directory will defragment the database to reorganize the data. This is done through the Garbage Collection Agent. The garbage-collection process runs every 12 hours and will defrag the white space to help with performance, but it does not do anything for the unused space that could be returned to the disk partition where the database resides. Performing an online defragmentation, enhances your performance, but you do not actually reclaim any drive space. To reclaim the unused white space, you must perform an offline defragmentation.

Defragmenting the Active Directory Database

You may experience a great amount of white space if you performed a bulk deletion or if the size of your system-state backup is significantly increased because of the white space. Often, removing the Global Catalog role from a domain controller will result in large amounts of white space.

You can determine how much space is recoverable by changing the logging level of the Garbage Collection Agent. Two levels of logging are available:

◆ 0—Only critical events or error events are logged in the directory service log.

◆ 1—High-level events are logged. Event ID 700 is recorded when defragmentation begins, and event ID 701 is recorded when defragmentation ends. Event ID 1646 reports the amount of free space (white space) in the database and the total amount of allocated space.

If you find from this process that you can recover a significant amount of space, you may want to perform an offline defragmentation of the Active Directory database file. To do so, follow these steps:

CHANGING THE GARBAGE COLLECTION LOGGING VALUE

1. Click Start, click Run, type **regedit**, and then press Enter.

2. In Registry Editor, navigate to Garbage Collection in HKEY_LOCAL_MACHINE\SYSTEM\ CurrentControlSet\Services\NTDS\Diagnostics.

3. Double-click Garbage Collection; for Base, click Decimal.

4. In the Value data box, type **1**, and then click OK.

BACKING UP THE SYSTEM STATE

1. Click Start ➤ Run ➤ Programs ➤ Accessories ➤ System Tools ➤ Backup.

2. On the Welcome to the Backup or Restore Wizard page, click Next.

3. Select Back Up Files and Settings, and then click Next.

4. Select Let Me Choose What to Back Up, and then click Next.

5. In the Items to Back Up window, double-click My Computer.

6. In the expanded list below My Computer, click the box labeled System State, and then click Next.

7. Select a location to store the backup.

8. Type a name for this backup, and then click Next.

9. On the last page of the wizard, click Advanced.

10. Keep the default settings for in the Type of Backup screen. Normal should be selected, and the check box should remain cleared for Backup Migrated Remote Storage Data. Click Next.

11. Select Verify Data after Backup, and then click Next.

12. In the Backup Options dialog box, select a backup option, and then click Next.

13. If you are replacing the existing backups, select the option to allow only the owner and administrator access to the backup data and to any backups that are appended to this medium, and then click Next.

14. In the When to Back Up box, select the appropriate option for your needs, and then click Next.

15. Click Finish to perform the backup operation according to your selected schedule.

TAKING THE DOMAIN CONTROLLER OFFLINE

1. Restart the domain controller.

2. When the screen for selecting an operating system appears, press F8.

3. From the Windows Advanced Options menu, select Directory Services Restore Mode.

4. When prompted, log on as the local administrator.

PERFORMING AN OFFLINE DEFRAGMENTATION

In Directory Services Restore mode, compact the database file to a local directory or remote shared folder, as follows:

1. For a local directory:

   ◆ At the command prompt, enter **ntdsutil** and press Enter.

◆ At the `ntdsutil:` prompt, type **files** and press Enter.

◆ At the `file maintenance:` prompt, type **compact to *drive:\LocalPath*,** where ***drive:\LocalPath*** is the path to a location on the local computer—for example, e:\NTDS.

2. For a remote directory:

You must map a drive to the shared folder to which you are copying the files. Because you are logged on as a local administrator, you will probably not have permissions to your remote share. To map the drive and authenticate, you must supply domain administrator credentials when mapping the drive:

◆ Open a command prompt.

◆ Type the command **net use *drive:* *server**share*** /user:*DomainName\Username*, where ***drive:*** is the drive letter you would like to use for the mapping, ***server*** is the remote server name, ***share*** is the name of the shared folder, ***DomainName*** is the name of your domain, and ***Username*** is the name of a user who has rights to that folder.

◆ Type the password for \\\\server\share that corresponds to the username defined in the command line.

◆ At the command prompt, enter **ntdsutil** and press Enter.

◆ At the `ntdsutil:` prompt, type **files** and press Enter.

◆ At the `file maintenance:` prompt, type **compact to *drive:\MappedDrive*** where ***drive:\MappedDrive*** is the path that was created in the steps listed previously—for example, p:\NTDS.

Figure 14.1 shows a screenshot of defragging the Active Directory database.

FIGURE 14.1
Defragging the Active
Directory database

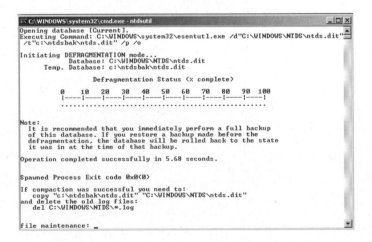

WHAT COULD GO WRONG?

If errors appear when you restart the domain controller, do the following:

1. Restart the domain controller in Directory Services Restore mode.

2. Check the errors in Event Viewer.

   You may find Event ID 1046 or 1168 in the Event Viewer. If you find these events, you should respond to them accordingly, as follows:

   Event ID 1046 "The Active Directory database engine caused an exception with the following parameters." You cannot recover from this error, and you must restore from backup media.

   Event ID 1168 "Internal error: An Active Directory error has occurred." If you see this error message, Active Directory is missing information in the registry and you must restore from backup media.

3. Check database integrity and then proceed as follows:

   If the integrity check fails, copy the original version of the Ntds.dit file that you preserved to the original database location and repeat the offline defragmentation procedure.

   If the integrity check succeeds, perform semantic database analysis with fixup.

4. If semantic database analysis with fixup succeeds, quit Ntdsutil.exe and restart the domain controller normally.

5. If semantic database analysis with fixup fails, contact Microsoft Product Support Services.

If the database integrity check fails, perform semantic database analysis with fixup.

When you run semantic database analysis with the Go Fixup command instead of the Go command, errors are written into Dsdit.dmp.xx log files. A progress indicator reports the status of the check.

TO PERFORM SEMANTIC DATABASE ANALYSIS WITH FIXUP

Figure 14.2 shows semantic database analysis with fixup.

1. Open a command prompt.

2. Type the command ntdsutil: and then press Enter.

3. At the ntdsutil: prompt, type **semantic database analysis** and then press Enter.

FIGURE 14.2
Semantic database
analysis with fixup

4. At the `semantic checker:` prompt, type **verbose on** and then press Enter.

5. At the `semantic checker:` prompt, type **go fixup** and then press Enter.

If errors are reported during the semantic database analysis with `fixup`, perform a directory database recovery. (The `recover` and `repair` commands are not to be confused. Never use the `repair` command in NTDSUtil, because forestwide data loss can occur.)

If semantic database analysis with `fixup` is successful, close `Ntdsutil.exe`, and then restart the domain controller normally.

Using NTDSUtil for Active Directory Database Troubleshooting and Repair

The Active Directory database is the same type of database that is used within applications such as Microsoft Exchange Server. If you are familiar with the utilities used with an Exchange server, you should be familiar with some of the utilities used with Active Directory. A benefit of using NTDSUtil is that the cryptic commands needed to manage the Exchange databases are encapsulated into easier-to-understand commands.

Upcoming chapters will introduce some of the other utilities, such as `dsastat` and `dcdiag`; however, for now let's concentrate on the tool that is used to manage the consistency of the Active Directory database—NTDSUtil. Using this tool, you can perform the following actions:

◆ Check database integrity

◆ Recover the database

◆ Compact the database

◆ Move the database

◆ Move the log files

◆ Remove orphaned objects

◆ Maintain security accounts

In the following sections, we detail the steps required to perform each of these actions. Although you'll rarely have to perform most of these actions, you should understand when and how to use NTDSUtil to perform each one.

The NTDSUtil utility is included on Windows domain controllers. There are very few differences between the versions of NTDSUtil that ship with Windows Server (2000, 2003, and 2008), so most of what is presented within this chapter applies to any of your domain controllers. We will point out the differences as we go along.

COMMITTING TRANSACTIONS TO THE DATABASE

Because of the nature of the Extensible Storage Engine (ESE) database, all the transactions are processed in memory and written to log files before they are committed to the database on the hard drive. If the server were to fail, the transaction logs would still contain all the information necessary to bring the database back to a consistent state.

Before performing most of the actions detailed here, commit the transactions to the database; this is also known as performing a recovery procedure. Just follow these steps:

1. When starting the computer, press F8 to enter the Startup Selection screen.

2. Select Directory Services Restore Mode.

3. Once you log on with the Directory Services Restore Mode Administrator account, open a command prompt.

4. At the command prompt, type **ntdsutil** and press Enter.

5. From the ntdsutil: prompt, type **Files** and press Enter.

6. From the file maintenance: prompt, type **Recover** and press Enter.

As shown in Figure 14.3, the screen will display information about what is taking place as the recovery is running. After the recovery is complete, the database will be consistent and you will be able to run other utilities as necessary.

FIGURE 14.3
NTDSUtil is used to commit the transactions to the database.

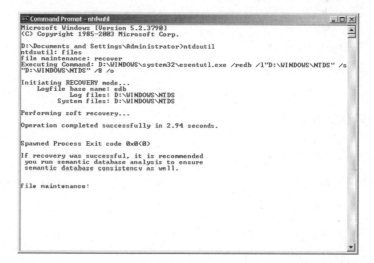

If errors crop up while you're running the recovery on a Windows 2000–based domain controller, and the recovery option does not repair them, you may need to repair the database. Exercise caution before you run this command against your database, because you could lose data in the process.

Make sure you have a good backup of your domain controller. You might want to contact Microsoft Product Support Services to make sure that you have covered all your bases; they may have another option for you to try before you run a repair.

Once you are committed to running the repair process, follow these steps:

1. When starting the computer, press F8 to enter the Startup Selection screen.

2. Select Directory Services Restore Mode.

3. Once you log on with the Directory Services Restore Mode Administrator account, open a command prompt.

4. At the command prompt, type **ntdsutil** and press Enter.

5. From the ntdsutil: prompt, type **Files** and press Enter.

6. From the file maintenance: prompt, type **Repair** and press Enter.

CHECKING DATABASE INTEGRITY

When you are checking the integrity of the database, every single byte of data within the database is analyzed for corruption. This procedure can take a great deal of time if your database is large. This is not something you should do just because you want to see what happens. Before starting an integrity check, make sure you have performed the recovery procedure as detailed previously. The steps to perform an integrity check are as follows:

1. When starting the computer, press F8 to enter the Startup Selection screen.

2. Select Directory Services Restore Mode.

3. Once you log on with the Directory Services Restore Mode Administrator account, open a command prompt.

4. At the command prompt, type **ntdsutil** and press Enter.

5. From the ntdsutil: prompt, type **Files** and press Enter.

6. From the file maintenance: prompt, type **integrity** and press Enter.

As you can see in Figure 14.4, the utility will perform the check against the database. If any errors are reported, contact Microsoft Product Support Services to determine how you should proceed.

FIGURE 14.4
NTDSUtil integrity
check

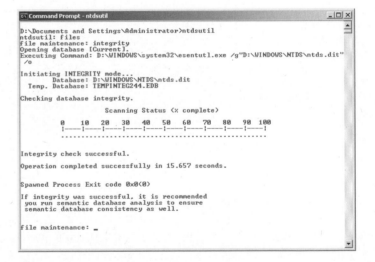

COMPACTING THE DATABASE

During normal operations, the Active Directory database will not need to be compacted. Every domain controller will perform its own garbage collection every 12 hours by default. During this garbage collection, the database will be defragmented, but the database size will not be reduced. This usually does not present a problem, because databases tend to grow over time to take up the additional free space.

With that being said, there are times when you may want to recover disk space with an offline defragmentation and compaction. If you have just deleted a large number of objects from Active Directory, have removed the Global Catalog role from a domain controller, or have just moved several accounts to another domain, you may want to reduce the size of your database.

To log an event to the Directory Services event log that will tell you the amount of space that you can free up during an offline defragmentation, you can change the registry entry at HKEY_LOCAL_MACHINE\SYSTEM\CurrentControlSet\Services\NTDS\Diagnostics\Garbage Collection to a value of 1.

To compact your database, follow these steps:

1. When starting the computer, press F8 to enter the Startup Selection screen.

2. Select Directory Services Restore Mode.

3. Once you log on with the Directory Services Restore Mode Administrator account, create an empty directory to store the new compacted database.

4. Open a command prompt.

5. At the command prompt, type **ntdsutil** and press Enter.

6. From the ntdsutil: prompt, type **Files** and press Enter.

7. From the file maintenance: prompt, type **compact** and press Enter.

After the compact command finishes, copy the new compacted database file, ntds.dit, to the location of the original database file. The utility will let you know where to copy the database if you are unsure, as seen in Figure 14.5.

You should also delete the old log files that were associated with the original bloated database file. Again, if you are unsure of the location of the log files, the compact utility will let you know where they are located.

FIGURE 14.5
NTDSUtil after moving the database

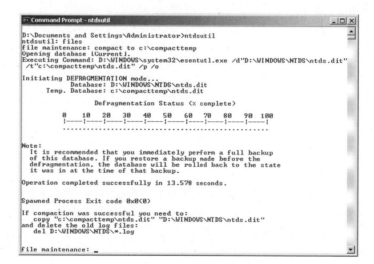

MOVING THE DATABASE

As databases age, they tend to grow. Even with our best intentions and attempts to create partitions and volumes large enough to hold databases, sometimes they grow too large. There are also times when you may want to take a database off a spindle that shows signs of having problems. Being proactive and moving the database to another drive may save you headaches later on.

To move the database, follow these steps:

1. When starting the computer, press F8 to enter the Startup Selection screen.

2. Select Directory Services Restore Mode.

3. Once you log on with the Directory Services Restore Mode Administrator account, open a command prompt.

4. At the command prompt, type **ntdsutil** and press Enter.

5. At the `ntdsutil:` prompt, type **Files** and press Enter.

6. At the `file maintenance:` prompt, type **move DB to *\<directory\>*** and press Enter. The ***\<directory\>*** can be any location on a partition or volume that has enough space to hold the database and that, preferably, has room for the database to continue growing. If the directory to which you are moving the database does not already exist, the utility will create it for you.

The utility will also configure the system to use the new location so that you do not have to perform any other steps to tell the operating system where to locate the database. However, you should perform a backup of the domain controller after moving the database so that your backup files reflect the new location of the database.

MOVING THE LOG FILES

The same issues hold true for the transaction log files that affect the database. You may not have enough room on a partition or volume to hold the logs; more than likely, however, you either will have a failing drive or you will simply want to separate the transaction log files and the database. As a matter of fact, I recommend that you move the transaction logs off the physical disk where the database files are. Place them on their own physical disk so that they do not have to compete for disk time with any other service. Once you do so, the system will perform better.

The steps to move the transaction logs are basically the same as those to move the database:

1. When starting the computer, press F8 to enter the Startup Selection screen.

2. Select Directory Services Restore Mode.

3. Once you log on with the Directory Services Restore Mode Administrator account, open a command prompt.

4. At the command prompt, type **ntdsutil** and press Enter.

5. At the `ntdsutil:` prompt, type **Files** and press Enter.

6. At the `file maintenance:` prompt, type **move logs to *\<directory\>*** and press Enter.

Again, ***\<directory\>*** does not have to exist before you take these steps; the system will create the directory for you. You should back up the system after performing the move so that the files can be restored if necessary.

REMOVING ORPHANED OBJECTS

Typically, when you decommission a domain controller the entries for the domain controller are removed from the database. The same holds true when you remove the last domain controller from a domain. If you select the check box that identifies the domain controller as the last one for the domain, all of the metadata for the domain will be removed from all the other domain controllers within the forest.

Removing Orphaned Domain Metadata

In a perfect world, you would not have to concern yourself with the metadata stored in the database—but as we know, nothing is perfect. You may encounter instances when the metadata for domain controllers or domains is not removed from the database correctly. This could be because a domain controller was demoted unsuccessfully or because a domain controller failed and you cannot restore it. In such an instance, services might try to connect to domain controllers that they think still exist. This can cause problems with replication as well as with the Knowledge Consistency Checker (KCC).

To remove a domain's orphaned metadata, follow these steps:

1. Log on to the domain using an account that is a member of the Enterprise Admins group.

2. Make sure that all the domain controllers have been demoted or taken offline. Also, verify that all of the remaining domain controllers within the forest have replicated successfully.

3. Identify the domain controller that holds the Domain Naming Master Operations role. You can do this by opening Active Directory Domains and Trusts, right-clicking on the root node, and selecting Operations Master. You will find the Domain Naming Master domain controller within the Current Operations Master box.

4. Open a command prompt, type **ntdsutil**, and press Enter.

5. At the ntdsutil: prompt, type **metadata cleanup** and press Enter.

6. At the metadata cleanup: prompt, type **connections** and press Enter.

7. Type **connect to server *servername*** where ***servername*** is the name of the domain controller holding the Domain Naming Master Operations role.

(If you have not logged on using an account that is a member of the Enterprise Admins group, you can set your credentials at this point by typing **set creds** *domainname username password* and then pressing Enter.)

8. Once you have received confirmation that the connection has been made, type **quit** and press Enter.

9. Type **select operation target** and press Enter.

10. Type **list domains** and press Enter.

11. From the list of domains that appears, locate the domain from which you want to remove the metadata, and the number with which that domain is associated.

12. Type **select domain number** and press Enter.

13. Type **quit** and press Enter.

14. Type **remove selected domain** and press Enter.

15. Once you receive confirmation that the domain metadata have been removed, type **quit** and press Enter.

16. Once you receive confirmation that the connection to the Domain Naming Master has been disconnected, type **quit** and press Enter.

Removing Orphaned Domain Controller Metadata

To remove Domain Controller metadata, you begin by using the same method you used to remove the domain; however, you need to remove additional data with other utilities to complete the removal. After running NTDSUtil, you have to remove the computer account, the File Replication Service (FRS) member, and the trustDomain object using ADSI Edit. The DNS entries using the DNS snap-in and the domain controller object within Active Directory Sites and Services will also need to be removed. The steps for all these procedures are given in the following sections.

We will start with Metadata Cleanup. To remove domain controller metadata, follow these steps from the NTDSUtil command-line utility:

1. Log on to the domain using an account that is a member of the Enterprise Admins group.

2. Verify that all the domain controllers within the forest have replicated successfully.

3. Open a command prompt, type **ntdsutil**, and press Enter.

4. At the ntdsutil: prompt, type **metadata cleanup** and press Enter.

5. At the metadata cleanup: prompt, type **connections** and press Enter.

6. Type **connect to server *servername***, where ***servername*** is the name of the domain controller holding the Domain Naming Master Operations role.

(If you have not logged on using an account that is a member of the Enterprise Admins group, you can set your credentials at this point by typing **set creds *domainname username password*** and then pressing Enter.)

7. Once you have received confirmation that the connection has been made, type **quit** and press Enter.

8. Type **select operation target** and press Enter.

9. Type **list domains** and press Enter.

10. From the list of domains that appears, locate the domain of which the domain controller is a member, and note the number associated with the domain.

11. Type **select domain number** and press Enter.

12. Type **list sites** and press Enter.

13. From the list of sites that appears, locate the site of which the domain controller is a member and note the number associated with the site.

14. Type **select site number** and press Enter.

15. Type **list servers in site** and press Enter.

16. From the list of domain controllers that appears, locate the domain controller and note the number associated with it.

17. Type **select server number** and press Enter.

18. Type **quit** and press Enter.

19. Type **remove selected server** and press Enter.

20. Once you receive confirmation that the domain metadata have been removed, type **quit** and press Enter.

21. Once you receive confirmation that the connection has been disconnected, type **quit** and press Enter.

MAINTAIN SECURITY ACCOUNTS

You can use the `security account management` option in NTDSUtil to perform tasks against security accounts. The tasks you can perform include checking for duplicate security identifiers (SIDs) or cleaning up duplicate SIDs.

To check for duplicate SIDs on the domain, follow these steps from the NTDSUtil command-line utility:

1. Log on to the domain using an account that is a member of the Enterprise Admins group.

2. Verify that all the domain controllers within the forest have replicated successfully.

3. Open a command prompt, type **ntdsutil**, and press Enter.

4. At the `ntdsutil:` prompt, type **security account management** and press Enter.

5. At the `security account maintenance:` prompt, type **connect to server** *ServerName* and press Enter.

6. Type **check duplicate sid**.

Using ADSI Edit to View Directory Service Partitions

ADSI Edit is a utility that is part of the support tools. Once you add the support tools, ADSI Edit is available from the Start menu ➤ Programs ➤ Support Tools. The Windows Server 2003 version is an MMC snap-in. With Windows Server 2008, when you view the advanced properties of an object, you will see a new Attribute Editor tab. From this tab, you can edit the settings that are available in ADSI Edit. You can perform the same tasks here that you can perform in ADSIEdit, but instead of having access to all objects and attributes in your AD DS environment, you are limited to just the object selected. With either version, you can connect to domain controllers and view the Directory Service partitions.

Figure 14.6 shows the dialog box that appears when you choose the Connect To option from the ADSI Edit context menu. From here, you can name the connection you are making to anything that will help you identify the naming context you are accessing. In the Connection Point text boxes, you can enter the fully qualified name of the naming context to which you are connecting, or you can choose one of the four well-known naming contexts. If you are connecting to one of the new application partitions, identify it by its fully qualified name.

In the Computer section, choose a domain controller to connect to, or default to the domain controller you're logged in to if you are running ADSI Edit from a domain controller.

Once you choose the naming contexts and the server to which you are connecting, you see them reflected within the ADSI Edit window, as shown in Figure 14.7. You can now expand the appropriate naming context to locate the objects you need to manipulate. Later in this chapter, and in other chapters in the book, we show how to use ADSI Edit to perform administrative troubleshooting.

FIGURE 14.6
ADSl Edit Connection
Settings dialog box

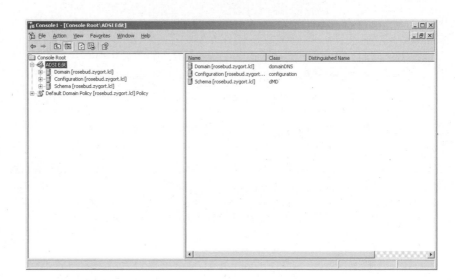

FIGURE 14.7
ADSl Edit with
naming contexts
added

USING ADSl EDIT TO REMOVE A COMPUTER ACCOUNT

If you are unsuccessful removing a computer account by using Active Directory Users and Computers, you can use this method:

1. Open ADSI Edit.

2. Expand Domain NC.

3. Expand DC=domain,DC=tld.

4. Expand OU=Domain Controllers.

5. Right-click CN=domain controller and click Delete.

Figure 14.8 displays the Domain Controllers node within ADSI Edit and the menu items you can choose.

FIGURE 14.8

ADSI Edit dialog box

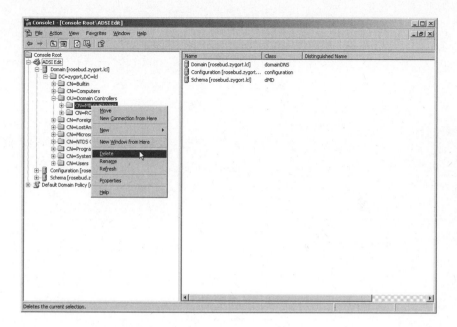

USING ADSI EDIT TO REMOVE THE FILE REPLICATION SERVICE MEMBER

To remove a File Replication Service (FRS) member, use these steps:

1. Open ADSI Edit.

2. Expand Domain NC.

3. Expand DC=domain,DC=tld.

4. Expand CN=System.

5. Expand CN=File Replication Service.

6. Expand CN=Domain System Volume.

7. Right-click the FRS member you are removing, and click Delete.

USING ADSI EDIT TO REMOVE THE TRUST DOMAIN OBJECT

If you need to remove a trust because of a failure of the GUI utilities to perform the operation, use these steps:

1. Open ADSI Edit.

2. Expand Domain NC.

3. Expand DC=domain,DC=tld.

4. Expand CN=System.

5. Right-click the Trust Domain object and click Delete.

Use the DNS Snap-in to Remove DNS Records

DNS records may need to be removed manually. If so, follow these steps:

1. Locate the A record within the zone, right-click the A record, and click Delete.

2. Expand the _msdcs container, locate the CNAME record, right-click the CNAME record, and click Delete.

3. If the server was a DNS server, right-click the zone, choose Properties, and then remove the server's IP address from the Name Servers tab of the resulting dialog box.

Using Active Directory Sites and Services to Remove the Domain-Controller Object

After you have removed the domain-controller references, you may have to remove the replication object from Active Directory Sites and Services:

1. Open Active Directory Sites and Services.

2. Expand Sites.

3. Expand the server's site.

4. Expand the Servers node.

5. Right-click the domain controller and click Delete.

Maintaining Security Accounts

For all of the safeguards that Microsoft has provided to ensure that identical security identifiers (SIDs) are not introduced into a domain, two accounts could still have the same SID if an administrator seizes the Relative Identifier (RID) Master role while the original RID Master is offline but still operational. If the original RID Master did not have an opportunity to receive updated replication information and is brought online, it could generate identical RIDs and allow them to be used within the domain. Any time you seize the RID Master role, you should run a check.

To check for accounts that may be using identical SIDs, follow these steps:

1. Open a command prompt.

2. Type **ntdsutil** and press Enter.

3. Type **security account management** and press Enter.

4. Type **check duplicate SID** and press Enter.

The log file that is created from this check is placed within the directory path where you started NTDSUtil. If you changed directories to the root of the D: partition and then started NTDSUtil, you will find the dupsid.log residing there. If you are lucky, you will not have any entries within the files. If there are entries, note them and delete the duplicates.

To delete a duplicate SID, follow these steps:

1. Open a command prompt.

2. Type **ntdsutil** and press Enter.

3. Type **security account management** and press Enter.

4. Type **cleanup duplicate SID** and press Enter.

The object with the newer globally unique identifier (GUID) is removed from the database. You will then need to re-create the account that was removed during this process.

BEST PRACTICES FOR OPTIMIZING ACTIVE DIRECTORY

Active Directory is the heart of your organization's infrastructure, and you need to make sure that is it performing optimally. You should be familiar with some of the tools for troubleshooting and treating any problems you may have:

♦ When troubleshooting Directory Services, increase the logging level gradually to isolate the problem if the problem isn't apparent.

♦ Always use the Recover option in NTDSUtil to commit all transactions to the database prior to running any other utilities.

♦ Don't run an offline defragmentation on the database unless you have deleted a large number of objects or you are planning to move the database and want to reduce its size.

♦ If any domain controller fails during demotion, make sure you remove the associated metadata from the database and remove all of the object information using ADSI Edit.

♦ If the last domain controller for a domain fails during demotion, make sure you remove the associated metadata from the database.

♦ Move the transaction log files to their own drive to increase the domain controller's efficiency.

♦ If the RID Master role is inadvertently seized while the original is still functioning but offline, check for duplicate SIDs when the original is returned to the network.

The Active Directory Schema

The Active Directory database is made up of attributes and object classes that form the Active Directory schema. Some of the object classes are users, groups, computers, domains, organizational units, and security policies.

You can modify the schema by defining new object types and attributes associated with them or by adding new attributes to existing objects. This is accomplished by using the ADSI Edit MMC snap-in.

This may sound very confusing. Here is a brief description of each schema component:

Object classes Define the objects that can appear in the Active Directory. Classes are collections of attributes. These attributes store the actual information stored in the directory.

Class derivations Define a method for building new object classes out of existing object classes.

Object attributes Define the available attributes. This includes extended attributes that govern actions that can be taken on object classes. Attributes are the pieces of information that an object can hold.

Structure rules Determine possible tree arrangements.

Syntax rules Determine the type of value, such as date or integer format, for an attribute that can be associated with a given class. For example, you can define an attribute named "office number" and state that the syntax will only allow an integer as a value.

Content rules Determine the attributes that can be associated with a given class.

Extensible schema Additions can be made to the list of available classes and attributes.

Dynamic class assignments Certain classes can be assigned dynamically to a specific object rather than to an entire class of objects.

To keep the database clean and in order, rules must be established to keep the schema behaving properly. These rules fall into three categories:

Structure rules Each object class has certain classes that can be directly above it; these are called *possible superiors*. This structure rule is very important because classes inherit attributes from their parents. Structure rules prevent putting a User-class object under a totally unrelated container class (such as IPSEC-Base or NTDS Settings).

Content rules Every object class has certain attributes with values that cannot be left blank when an object is instantiated. These are called *must-contain* attributes. Other attributes are optional and are designated *may-contain* attributes.

Only attributes that have values are stored in the database. This greatly reduces the size and complexity of the database. Because attributes can be added after an object is created and then later removed if they are set to null, the database engine must pack and repack the data constantly. This is done by the garbage collection agent that runs every 12 hours.

Syntax rules Attributes store data. Data must have a data type to define the storage requirements. Real numbers have a different form from integers, which are different from long integers, which are different from character strings. An attribute can have only one data type. It cannot hold a string when associated with one object class and an integer when associated with another. The syntax rules in the schema define the permissible value types and ranges for the attributes.

For each class in Active Directory, there is a `classSchema`. For every object attribute in the database, there is an `attributeSchema` object.

The `attributeSchema` attributes provide information about attributes of another Active Directory object. The `attributeSchema` mandatory attributes are as follows:

attributeID Identifies the attribute with a unique value.

attributeSyntax Identifies the object that defines the attribute type.

cn Provides the Unicode string name of an attribute.

isSingleValued This attribute is set to either `true` or `false`. When it is set to `true`, it indicates that there is only one value for the attribute. When set to `false`, the attribute can have several values.

LDAPDisplayName Contains the LDAP Unicode name string used to identify the attribute.

NTSecurityDescriptor Contains the object security descriptor.

ObjectClass This attribute is always `attributeSchema`.

OMSyntax Identifies the object syntax specified by the open object model.

SchemaIDGUID Contains the GUID value of the attribute.

The `classSchema` attributes provide information about another Active Directory object. The `classSchema` mandatory attributes are the following:

Cn Contains the Unicode string name of the object.

DefaultObjectCategory Contains a distinguished name of where the object belongs.

GovernsID Contains a unique number identifying the class.

LDAPDisplayName   Contains the LDAP Unicode name string used to identify the object.

NTSecurityDescriptor   Contains the object security descriptor.

ObjectClass   This setting is always `classSchema`.

ObjectClassCategory   This setting is an integer that describes the object class type. The values that this attribute will hold are as follows:

◆ 0—Type 88 class: This class doesn't have a type, or it is a class type created before 1993, before class types were standardized in the X.500 format.

◆ 1—Structural class: This class can have objects created from it, and it is the class type that is contained as an object in the directory.

◆ 2—Abstract class: This is a class that cannot be an object, but is used to pass attributes down to subclasses.

◆ 3—Auxiliary class: This class provides structural or abstract classes with attributes.

SchemaIDGUID   Contains the unique GUID value of the class.

SubClassOf   Contains the identifier of the parent class.

Modifying the Schema

The schema should be modified only when absolutely necessary. Changes to the schema must be made from the domain controller that holds the Schema Operations Master Flexible Single Master Operations (FSMO) role. This server must be able to update the schema. Each schema object has permissions set through the Windows security model.

By default in Windows 2003 and later versions of AD DS, the schema is already enabled for updates. Nothing more must be done unless the registry has specifically been locked down to keep schema updates from occurring on the domain controller that hosts the Schema Master FSMO role.

To edit this registry setting, perform the following steps:

1. Navigate to Start ➢ Run.

2. In the Open dialog box, type **<regedit>** and press Enter.

3. Navigate to the following registry key: HKLM\SYSTEM\CurrentControlSet\Services\ NTDS\Parameters.

4. On the Edit menu, click New, then click DWORD Value.

5. Enter the following information:

   Value Name: Schema Update Allowed

   Data Type: REG_DWORD

   Base: Binary

   Value Data: Use a value of 1 to enable schema updates, 0 to disable schema updates.

6. Close the registry editor.

There are many ways to modify the schema:

◆ Application programming interfaces (APIs)

◆ Lightweight Directory Interface Format (LDIF) scripts.

◆ The LDIFDE bulk schema modification tool

◆ The CSVDE bulk schema update tool

When the schema is modified, Active Directory performs consistency and safety checks to ensure Active Directory database availability. Consistency is checked to verify that identifiers are unique and that mandatory attributes exist. The existence of superclasses in the schema is also checked. Safety checks ensure Active Directory functionality is not disrupted. Category1 and Category2 object types are checked.

Because both classes and attributes are represented in the directory as objects, you simply need to add a new `class-definition` or `attribute-definition` object with the necessary attributes. If instead you would like to modify a class or attribute, modify the `class-definition` or `attribute-definition` object.

Before you can modify the schema, you must add a value to the registry. Open the registry-editing program, navigate to `HKLM\System\CurrentControlSet\Services\NTDS\Parameters`, and add a registry value of Schema Update Allowed. Make it of type `REG_DWORD` and give it any nonzero positive integer value.

 Real World Scenario

PROTECTING THE AD DS SCHEMA

Jessie is an administrator of a large online shopping company. She recently created a new AD DS environment and performed a migration from another network operating system to AD DS. All of her domain controllers are Windows 2008.

By default, the administrative account used for installing AD DS is a member of the Domain Admins, Enterprise Admins, and Schema Admins groups. Jessie followed best practices and renamed the Administrator account used for the install, delegated certain administrative functions to other Administrator accounts, and only logs into the network with the renamed administrative account when she needs to perform work that requires administrative access.

Recently Jessie went through all of her AD DS configurations and settings and decided to tighten the security around the very important Schema Admins group.

To do so, she created a new administrative user specifically for functions that required the Schema Admins group. She then took the renamed Enterprise Admin user out of the Schema Admins group. This left the Schema Admins group empty.

This configuration allows Jessie to log in as the renamed Enterprise Admin account to perform functions that require that level of access, but it also keeps that renamed Enterprise Admin account from having access to modify or edit the AD DS schema.

When Jessie needs to modify or edit the AD DS schema, she simply logs on as the renamed Enterprise Admin account and adds the newly created Schema Admin user to the Schema Admins group. Jessie can then log in and modify the schema as needed. When she is done, Jessie logs in as the renamed Enterprise Admin and removes the Schema Admin from the Schema Admins group, once again leaving it empty to keep it protected from accidental modification.

Coming Up Next

The next section of the book (Section 4, "Active Directory Best Practices and Troubleshooting") deals with troubleshooting. We start with a discussion about overall troubleshooting methodology, and then advance into more-detailed discussions about tools, utilities, and troubleshooting techniques for network infrastructure, resources, and the Active Directory database.

The Bottom Line

Keeping the AD DS database in good health is essential to keeping your environment running its best. You may have to manage the AD DS database manually to perform certain tasks.

Defragment the AD DS database The AD DS database performs certain maintenance tasks automatically on a regular basis. One thing it cannot do is rid itself of the "white space" that occurs as you delete items from the database.

Master It Chris is the administrator of a large AD environment that contains user accounts for 1,000 temporary employees that work as seasonal help every year. When the seasonal work is done for these users, the user accounts are disabled and then eventually deleted. How can Chris determine how much white space is contained in his database and then reclaim that space?

Use NTDSUtil to manage the AD DS database The main tool you will use to manage the AD DS database manually is the NTDSUtil command-line utility.

Master It There are many functions of the NTDSUtil command-line utility. Name the functions that relate directly to managing the AD DS database.

Implement best practices for optimizing the AD DS database Taking a proactive approach with the AD DS database is key to maintaining the database in good health. Following best practices may help eliminate the need for the troubleshooting and recovery options that we discussed earlier.

Master It When working with the AD DS database, what are the best practices you should follow to help alleviate downtime and poor performance?

Part 4

Active Directory Best Practices and Troubleshooting

In this part:

Chapter 15

Microsoft's Troubleshooting Methodology for Active Directory

Microsoft employs a standard troubleshooting practice with every problem it diagnoses. This standard methodology, which we'll examine in this chapter, helps find the answer to problems in a structured way.

In this chapter, you will learn

◆ The six essential steps of the troubleshooting methodology

◆ Proactive steps to take to help circumvent problems

High-Level Methodology

Figure 15.1 illustrates the six-step plan Microsoft Product Support Services engineers use as a basis for all troubleshooting situations.

You can follow this method to help track down your problem and find a solution. By using this strategy, you'll cut your troubleshooting time because you're using a structured approach to your troubleshooting efforts.

Discover and Document the Problem

This step is often reactive as opposed to proactive. Usually you discover a problem with Active Directory by receiving a phone call to alert you of a problem, by viewing messages in Event Viewer, or by identifying a problem with some performance counters you are monitoring.

Document as much information as you can so you can reproduce the problem at will. Gather information about symptoms, the rate of occurrence, the servers involved, the sites involved, the communication mechanisms between computers or sites, and so forth.

Documentation is an important part of your troubleshooting plan. Not only can documenting all your changes reduce misunderstandings, but it can also provide an accurate history you can reference if Microsoft technical-support personnel have to get involved. You will reference and update this documentation as you follow the next steps in the troubleshooting process.

Typically, a problem is reported to the help desk by a user. A Microsoft best practice for Active Directory is to use a monitoring system to monitor services related to Active Directory's health.

FIGURE 15.1
Microsoft
troubleshooting
methodology

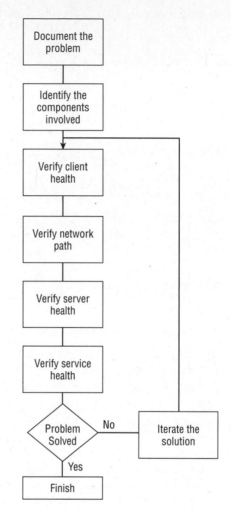

Information about the problem collected from a user or from the monitoring system should include the following:

◆ Date and time of occurrence

◆ Error message number and text

◆ Client information:

   ◆ Computer name of the client's workstation

   ◆ User ID being used when the problem occurred

   ◆ TCP/IP configuration

- List of DNS servers the client is configured to use
- Operating-system version, service pack, and any hotfixes

- Server information:
  - Computer name for the server the client is trying to access
  - TCP/IP configuration
  - Operating-system version, service pack, and any hotfixes

- Network information:
  - Domain name of the client
  - Domain name of the server
  - Application name and related settings
  - The service involved in the problem—e.g., network BIOS (NetBIOS), DNS, Server Message Block (SMB), or Lightweight Directory Access Protocol (LDAP)

In addition, identify if any of the following are true:

- The problem is repeatable. If so, include the steps taken to reproduce the problem.
- Others are having the same problem.
- The help desk is able to duplicate and verify the issue. Include any troubleshooting steps already taken by the help desk, such as using Ping to verify network connectivity to the client or server.

Often the source of a problem is related to some aspect of the system configuration, such as an outdated software component, a service that has not been properly tested, or an incompatible hardware component. Recording the details of the system configuration is an important part of gathering information about the conditions surrounding the occurrence of a problem.

You can create a text file that contains important system-configuration information. This text file can be created by a GUI utility or by a command-line utility.

To create the system-configuration file by using a GUI utility, do the following:

1. Click Start ➢ Run.

2. Type **msinfo32** in the Run box and click OK.

3. Open the File menu and select Save.

4. Enter a name for the file and click Save.

You can now use the System Information tool to view the NFO file that is created by this process. The file is in XML format.

To create the system-configuration file by using a command-line utility, do the following:

1. Click Start ➢ Run.

2. Type **cmd** and click OK.

3. Execute these commands:

```
systeminfo > c:\folder\filename.txt
tasklist > c:\folder\filename.txt
openfiles > c:\folder\filename.txt
```

Explore the Conditions and Identify the Components Involved

If you have ever worked the help desk at a company, during your first week of work you probably learned two key phrases: "Have you tried rebooting?" and "What changed?" While you may be asking yourself the first question, we're going to explore the second question in this section.

Review the affected system's (or systems') event logs, error logs, and history to determine what configuration changes (if any) took place since the affected system(s) last worked correctly. Have new hardware, software, service packs, hotfixes, or other updates been installed on the affected system(s) or supporting infrastructure?

Except for hardware failures, you can usually narrow down this list to service packs, hotfixes, or security updates that were recently applied. A stable system will remain stable as long as it is untouched, except for a hardware failure. Unfortunately, you cannot get a server to a stable point, lock it in a cabinet, and never touch it again. In today's world you have to deal with updates, which come out frequently.

Start your search with recent updates to the system. Check your documentation to see what was changed and when, and then determine what effect the update may have had on your system. Many problems are caused by recently installed software, especially unsigned drivers or beta applications. Unsigned drivers have not been approved by Microsoft and can cause instability issues.

Some common Active Directory events that appear in the event logs are listed in Table 15.1.

Identify the specific components that are involved in the problem, including the clients, network paths, and services. This can quickly narrow down where your problem is and with what service you are having a problem.

TABLE 15.1: Common Active Directory Events Recorded in the Event Viewer

EVENT SOURCE	EVENT ID	REFERENCE
FRS	13508, 13509, 13512, 13522, 13567, 13568	Chapter 16, "Troubleshooting Problems Related to Network Infrastructure"
Netlogon	5774, 5775, 5781, 5783, 5805	Chapter 16
NTDS	1083, 1265, 1388, 1645	Chapter 17, "Troubleshooting Problems Related to the Active Directory Database"
UserEnv	1085	Chapter 17
W32Time	13, 14, 52-56, 60-64	Chapter 16

Verify Client Health

Start with the client defined in the previous step. Because all client-server communication begins with the client, start the troubleshooting process there. Verify the health of your client computer by checking to see if it is configured correctly, is connected to the network, and is communicating properly. Some tests you can perform to check client health include the following:

◆ Verify network connections. Make sure the client is actually connected to the network by checking network cables, link-status indicators on your card and hub and or switch, or connection status in your wireless network card settings.

◆ Use Performance Monitor to ensure that the client's CPU usage is not too high.

◆ Verify network configuration for the client. Verify that the client's IP configuration settings are correct. This includes the IP address, subnet mask, default gateway, and any DNS or WINS settings that may be defined.

Verify Network Path

Verify that the network path between the client and server is working properly. If the server health check turns out okay, the problem may lie at either the client or the path between the client and the server. If you then perform a client health check and it also turns out okay, you may want to run Network Monitor (`NetMon`) to perform traces at both the client and the server.

Verify Server Health

To verify server health, start by following the same troubleshooting pattern as with the client health check. More often than not, the client has received its settings from a Dynamic Host Configuration Protocol (DHCP) server, while the server is often assigned with static information. When a server has static settings, the chance for human error always exists. As I was typing that last sentence I hit the Backspace key at least three times.

Human error can cause any number of problems with static mappings. An administrator can "fat-finger" or transpose numbers in any one of the IP settings on the client. A server on a class-C subnet with a subnet mask of 192.168.1.0 is going to have a hard time talking to other servers on the subnet defined as 192.186.1.0.

Verify Service Health

To verify the health of the service, follow these steps:

◆ Verify that the service is installed properly on the server.

◆ Verify that the service is running.

◆ Verify that the user has permissions to make the request.

Regularly review the application event log. The log is where services usually record their events and indicate whether they are error, warning, or informational events. If you find a warning or error event in the event log, determine the source and search knowledge-base information (internal or external to your company) for that particular error, event ID, and event source.

Explore Possible Problems via Microsoft System Center Operations Manager

Microsoft System Center Operations Manager with the Active Directory Management Pack (ADMP) provides you with a comprehensive overview for a proactive approach of monitoring your network for possible problems.

Operations Manager has built-in monitoring alerts that give you an idea of problems that may occur in your network. This will give you a proactive approach for troubleshooting your network.

The following monitoring alerts are included in the Active Directory Management Pack for Operation Manager 2007. Monitor the following events daily:

A domain controller has received a significant number of new replication partners. This can happen when a server is in the process of becoming a global catalog server or bridgehead server. It can also happen when new domains or domain controllers are added to the network. Site link problems or replication problems can cause this alert to trigger.

Active Directory Essential Services has detected [message]. This is a high-priority alert that indicates that the domain controller is unusable for the reason specified in the message. This can sometimes indicate that a service is not running on the server. Sysvol (the shared directory that stores domain information and is replicated throughout the domain) problems may indicate problems with the File Replication Service (FRS), and problems with a domain controller not advertising may indicate problems with the Domain Name System (DNS).

Active Directory global catalog search failed. This high-priority alert warns you that a global catalog server cannot be reached.

Active Directory—lost objects warning. This alert warns you of a high number of objects in the LostAndFound directory.

Active Directory replication is occurring slowly. This indicates that replication times have exceeded set time thresholds.

Failed to ping or bind to the <operations master> role holder. This alert indicates that there may be network connectivity problems with the Flexible Single Master Operations (FSMO) role holder in the error message.

High CPU alert. This alert indicates that an application or server is consuming a large amount of CPU processing time.

Replication is not occurring, all AD replication partners failed to synchronize. This alert may be triggered occasionally, but extended failures indicate a problem. Investigate problems that occur for more than a few hours.

Time skew detected. The system time on the server indicated in the alert is not synchronized.

Identify Possible Approaches to a Solution

After you have gathered as much information about the problem as you can, the next step is to determine a possible plan of attack. This is the research portion of the plan. Your findings in this stage will determine the approach you will take to implement your fix.

At this stage, Microsoft recommends you take the following direction for resolving the problem:

1. Submit an error report, if prompted, and study the analysis.

2. Review problem-tracking databases internal to your organization.

3. Read the relevant Microsoft Knowledge Base articles.

4. Escalate the problem to Microsoft technical support.

This is great in a perfect world—or if you work for Microsoft. Not many organizations have an up-to-date problem-tracking database. I've seen many companies that have an internal knowledge base, and almost as many companies with administrators who laugh when you suggest looking up the error in their own database first. In the real world, the search for a fix goes a little something like this:

1. Help and Support Center: Okay, all of you old-schoolers can stop chuckling now. I will admit that I would have laughed at this statement three or four years ago. The online help guides (for the most part) are a very good starting point now. The Help and Support Center not only provides information and links about Windows Server, but it also includes troubleshooting tools and wizards that can come in very handy.

2. Microsoft's Knowledge Base articles: Microsoft has a wealth of information on its website. You can use keywords to locate all the types of information you gathered in the previous step. For example, you can search for event IDs, exact error messages, and so forth. To become familiar with how to get the best results from your search, read Knowledge Base article 242450, "How to Query the Microsoft Knowledge Base by using Keywords and Query Words" (`http://support.microsoft.com/kb/242450`).

3. Internet newsgroups: Well-known or favorite newsgroups are often a "first check" for many administrators. Newsgroups offer very technical discussions on subjects that are similar to your problem. There are many Active Directory newsgroups, including Microsoft public newsgroups that many Microsoft employees and Microsoft Most Valuable Professionals (MVPs) visit on a daily basis to discuss problems and answer questions.

4. Google and other websites: Intuitive search engines and web-based forums are quickly becoming more popular than newsgroups. You will find the same type of interaction as with newsgroups, often with a friendlier interface. One of the more popular forums is Experts Exchange (`www.experts-exchange.com`).

5. Microsoft technical support: If all else fails, you can escalate the problem to Microsoft's tech support.

Of course, everyone is different and each situation is different. I usually follow the path just outlined, but I have also skipped steps 1 and 3, and a few times I have gone directly to step 4.

Attempt a Solution

By this time, you should have many possible approaches that could resolve the problem. Determine the items from your list that are most likely to fix the problem. For example, say you recently upgraded the Network Interface Card (NIC) driver on a server in a remote site. Using the troubleshooting steps listed earlier, you first find that information in Active Directory is not being replicated to one remote site. You then find that the server at that remote site, which is a replication partner for your main site, is not working correctly. You perform a diagnosis of that server, and discover that it is not communicating properly. Once you realize that the NIC driver was updated recently, you decide to roll back the driver to a previous version.

Always back up your system-state data and other vital service files for that domain controller. Execute the plan that is most likely to resolve the problem, documenting all steps along the way. Real-world admins are kindly asked to refrain from snickering at this comment.

Check for Success

To determine whether your plan was successful, reproduce the conditions that caused the problem. If the error or problem continues to occur, return to the Web to search for a different approach.

If the steps listed earlier do not locate the problem for you, you must take additional measures to track down the problem. This could involve identifying the next client, server or the service that might be involved in the problem and verifying the health of each of those components until you reach the actual source of the problem.

Once the problem is fixed, you're done, right? You can walk away and simply forget about everything you've done to this point? If you stopped here, you would be missing out on a valuable opportunity to cut down troubleshooting time if similar problems should arise in the future.

Document Your Findings

This is where your documentation will come in handy. You're still documenting at this point, right? How many times, while troubleshooting, have you tried one approach only to find that you were going down the wrong road and your change or "fix" didn't change or fix anything? After the unsuccessful attempt, did you then roll back your changes so the system was in the same state it was in before you started your tests?

Documentation is very important; it gives you a clear path of what has been changed on a system in case a rollback procedure is required. It also provides you with a quick reference to view information about your systems that can come in handy when reviewing potential system changes or updates.

You can then turn this into detailed information about your current environment, modifying it as you change your systems. You can use the documents to reduce the chance of redundant work and can possibly avoid future problems by using the information in the document to take preventive action.

Periodically verify, update, and back up this documentation so you will not have to document everything again should you lose the information. Items to note in the documentation include the following:

- Changes made to the system

- Time and date of changes

- Reasons for the change

- Name and contact information of the administrator who made the change

- Positive and negative effects the change had on system stability and/or performance

- Information found through research to back up reasoning for making the change

- Your contact information (so you can be contacted with specific questions about the changes you made to the system or network)

- Screenshots of important configuration settings or changes. When making a change or adding software there is often a "review" screen before you actually install the software or make the change. This is a perfect opportunity to capture all of your settings or changes in one screenshot.

Real World Scenario

DOCUMENT! DOCUMENT! DOCUMENT!

Some of the discovery portions of the troubleshooting process can be eliminated if you create very detailed information about your environment and past troubleshooting results. Use this document as a starting point and compare notes from the custom troubleshooting guide against information you find during the discovery phase.

Keep the following information available to the personnel performing Active Directory troubleshooting:

◆ Active Directory configuration, including replication-related configuration information

◆ DNS, DHCP, and IP configurations

◆ Application and service documentation (such as Exchange)

◆ Administrative model

◆ Server placement and configurations

Personnel performing Active Directory troubleshooting should have a basic understanding of the following:

◆ Name resolution, including DNS and NetBIOS name resolution with broadcasts, LMHOSTS files, and WINS

◆ Replication

◆ Time synchronization

◆ Group Policy and FRS

◆ Core Active Directory concepts, including an understanding of the global catalog, domains, and forests

◆ Authentication (both Kerberos authentication and LAN Manager)

◆ Active Directory Microsoft Management Console (MMC) snap-ins and Active Directory-related tools

◆ Operations master roles: PDC emulator, relative identifier (RID) master, domain naming master, schema master, and infrastructure master

◆ Key Distribution Center (KDC)

◆ Knowledge Consistency Checker (KCC)

◆ Intersite topology generator (ISTG)

◆ Time reference server (TRS)

Because Active Directory interacts with so many external services and protocols, a broad range of knowledge is required for this type of troubleshooting. Ultimately determining the cause of a problem and applying a solution can become very complex.

If you do not already have baseline documentation for your servers, you can use this document to create a baseline. After you have created a baseline, keep track of all information listed here and add it to the baseline document.

When you have finished troubleshooting, you may want to document other findings that came as a result of the troubleshooting process. You should ask questions such as the following:

◆ What changes resulted in improvements?

◆ What changes made the problem worse?

◆ What downtime occurred while implementing the solution, and how did it affect users?

◆ Was system performance restored to expected levels?

◆ What actions were redundant or unnecessary?

◆ How effectively were technical-support resources used?

◆ What tools or information not used might have helped?

◆ What unresolved issues require further testing?

Be Proactive

The best time to take care of problems is when they are still considered "potential" problems. There are a lot of things you can do to prevent outages:

◆ Consistently back up system-state data and configuration settings. Regular backups of the system state will give you a good restore point in case you need to restore to a previous state. It is also a good idea to back up the system state or configuration settings if you think that changes you make while implementing a possible solution may have an adverse effect on your system, or if you are unsure of the results.

◆ Periodically test troubleshooting and recovery plans. Recovery plans are great if you know that they have been tested and are known to work. Many companies back up the system state on a regular basis because it is a best practice. But ask them how to restore system state if it's lost completely or ask them if they would feel comfortable actually performing the steps themselves, and you may get some blank looks. If someone told me I could safely land a plane by pressing a series of 10 buttons in a certain order, I would feel pretty safe and think it would be pretty easy to do. If the plane started going down, however, I wouldn't feel quite as comfortable unless I had actually performed the task and felt comfortable about the process and seen success in the past.

◆ Rapidly evaluate and deploy updates. To ensure updates are deployed in a relatively timely manner, implement a process to test and deploy updates in your environment. In an ideal world, the testing portion would be done in a lab environment. (We discuss this later in the list.) After the update has been tested, it must be quickly and efficiently deployed to all the affected servers in your network. This could prove to be a time-consuming process. Microsoft has helped this process with the introduction of Windows Server Update Services (WSUS).

◆ Use antivirus software. Antivirus software has traditionally been viewed as a requirement for client computers and application and data servers on networks. As malicious software becomes more prevalent, smarter, and more damaging, it is just as important to protect your domain controllers as well as all other devices. Use an antivirus package that is Windows Server–compatible.

◆ Improve the computing environment. Servers are happy in nice, clean, cool, quiet rooms. When I say "quiet," I'm not talking about sound volume; I'm talking about traffic volume. The more traffic, the better the chances of some type of impact damage. Make these checks periodically in your server room:

   ◆ Test uninterruptible power supply (UPS) batteries.

   ◆ Check room temperature, humidity, and air circulation.

   ◆ Check server fans and system boards for a buildup of dust.

◆ Monitor performance and event logs. Often, warnings in the Event Viewer will notify you of impending doom. Check the event logs first thing in the morning, throughout the day when possible, and before you leave for the day, looking for warnings and errors that do not seem familiar. It's odd to think that there may be warnings or errors that do look familiar, but some warning messages that may appear on a daily basis might have no effect on your system's health. Use the Performance console (`perfmon.msc`) to compare current settings and results to the baseline you created when the server was running at optimal health.

◆ Document hardware and software changes. Along with recording system changes, you should record information regarding the computer operation, such as Group Policy and network infrastructure changes.

◆ Plan for hardware and software upgrades. As "beefy" as your system is when you purchase it, at some point in its life cycle a piece of hardware or software on the system will require an update. This could be due to an increased demand for computing resources or discontinued support for a device or software.

◆ Test changes in a lab environment before implementing them on production systems. As mentioned earlier, in a perfect world all testing would be done in a lab environment that mimics your live environment. Change your lab environment as you change your live environment so the lab will remain mirrored.

◆ Use compatible and tested hardware.

◆ Use compatible software.

◆ Reduce the use of legacy software to eliminate conflicts and increase fault tolerance.

Become Comfortable with Active Directory Tools

The following list of tools will help you in your troubleshooting methodology. Become familiar with the tools to make your troubleshooting efforts easier.

Tool	Function	Covered in Chapter
Active Directory Domains and Trusts	Administer domain trusts, add user principle name suffixes, and change the domain mode.	16, 17

Tool	Function	Covered in Chapter
Active Directory Sites and Services	Administer the replication of directory data.	16, 17
Active Directory Users and Computers	Administer and publish information in the directory.	16
ADSI Edit	View, modify, and set access control lists (ACLs) on objects in the directory.	17
Backup Wizard	Back up and restore data.	16
Control Panel	View and modify computer, application, and network settings.	16
`Dcdiag.exe`	Analyze the state of the domain controllers in a forest or enterprise.	16, 17
DNS snap-in	Manage DNS.	16
`Dsastat.exe`	Compare directory information on the domain controllers and detect differences.	16
Event Viewer	Monitor events recorded in event logs.	16
`Ipconfig.exe`	View and manage network configuration.	16
`Ldp.exe`	Perform Lightweight Directory Access Protocol (LDAP) operations against Active Directory.	16, 17
`Linkd.exe`	Create, delete, update, and view the links that are stored in junction points.	16
MMC	Create, save, and open administrative tools that manage hardware, software, and network components.	16, 17
`Netdiag.exe`	Check end-to-end network connectivity and distributed services functions.	16, 17

Tool	Function	Covered in Chapter
Netdom.exe	Allow batch management of trusts, joining computers to domains, and verifying trusts and secure channels.	16
Net use, start, stop, del, copy, time	Perform common tasks on network services, including stopping, starting, and connecting to network resources.	16
Nltest.exe	Verify that the locator and secure channel are functioning.	16
Ntdsutil.exe	Manage Active Directory, manage single master operations, and remove metadata.	16
Performance Monitor	View system-performance data and performance logs and alerts, and trace log files.	16
Pathping.exe	Trace a route from a source to a destination on a network, show the number of hops, and show packet loss.	16
Ping.exe	Verify network connectivity.	16
Regedit.exe	View and modify registry settings.	16
Repadmin.exe	Verify replication consistency between replication partners, monitor replication status, display replication metadata, and force replication events and topology recalculation.	16, 17
Secedit.exe	Manage Group Policy settings.	16

Tool	Function	Covered in Chapter
Services snap-in	Start, stop, pause, or resume system services on remote and local computers, and configure startup and recovery options for each service.	16
Setspn.exe	Manage service principal names.	16
Task Manager	View process and performance data.	16
Terminal Services	Access and manage computers remotely.	16
W32tm	Manage Windows Time service.	16
Windows Explorer	Access files, web pages, and network locations.	16

Coming Up Next

We have now discussed a general "road map" for your troubleshooting efforts. An understanding of the tools listed in this chapter will help with your troubleshooting efforts and reduce your troubleshooting time frame.

In the next chapter, we will discuss troubleshooting techniques relating to network infrastructure.

The Bottom Line

Having a good troubleshooting methodology will help you when problems related to Active Directory arise. Understanding the troubleshooting roadmap will save troubleshooting time.

The six essential steps of the troubleshooting methodology   Troubleshooting AD DS problems can be very time-consuming. Having a solid plan of action when problems arise can save you time and effort.

Master It   AD DS replication to all remote sites is failing. You must come up with a plan of action to determine where the problem lies.

Proactive steps to take to help circumvent problems   Proactive planning is always better than reactive troubleshooting. There are many proactive steps that you can take to help cut down on problems that may arise.

Master It   After a severe network outage, Nick decides to design a proactive plan for checking AD DS health and stability. What should Nick include in his network plan to help discover potential problems?

Chapter 16

Troubleshooting Problems Related to Network Infrastructure

Understanding how the various elements in your network function and how they work together is important when you're trying to diagnose network communications problems. This chapter will introduce you to various components of your network infrastructure, discuss some useful trouble-shooting tools, and cover ways you can troubleshoot problems with the network infrastructure.

In this chapter you will learn how to:

◆ Use tools to troubleshoot name-resolution problems

◆ Troubleshoot Dynamic Host Configuration Protocol (DHCP) issues

Components of Network Infrastructure

A generic computer network has two basic parts: software and hardware. The software runs on the hardware and, in some cases, controls how the hardware will run and communicate. The hardware provides the means of conveyance for the software to communicate—think of the seven layers of the Open System Interconnection (OSI) model. The network infrastructure falls into both the hardware and software categories. When we talk about our hardware network infrastructure, we mean the cables, routers and switches, servers, workstations, and other physical items. The software network infrastructure consists of the operating systems, services, and other applications that run and use the cables, routers, and switches. Here we are concerned with the services that run on the servers.

The types of services that form your infrastructure will vary somewhat; they depend on your own network configuration and any specific network requirements imposed by management. Typically, however, you are going to have an operating system (Windows Server in this case), some method of name resolution, a way to get a valid IP address, and some type of remote access mechanism.

Name resolution is handled by Domain Name System (DNS), Berkeley Internet Name Daemon (BIND), or WINS. Yes, WINS is mentioned because there are legacy computers and applications that require WINS.

In a typical TCP/IP-based network you need to have some address-issuance mechanism. Dynamic Host Configuration Protocol (DHCP) will automatically assign and manage IP-based network addresses.

Remote connectivity is typically handled by Routing and Remote Access (RRAS), Network Policy Server (NPS), or by a Virtual Private Network (VPN).

Name-Resolution Methods

Name resolution is the process that occurs when you're trying to find a device on the network by an address or a name. All computers, servers, printers, and other networking devices have names. These devices also have an address assigned to them. Name resolution ensures that you can find a device by either name or address when required. The two methods we are concerned with here are WINS and DNS.

Windows Internet Name Service (WINS)

WINS has been around for a long time, and there is now a method to allow you to finally decommission those old WINS servers. There are still valid requirements for continued use of single-name or NetBIOS resolution in your network. Some legacy clients, servers, and applications require WINS, and this requirement extends to Windows Server 2008, which uses WINS for Network Load Balancing (NLB), as discussed later in this chapter.

The WINS service provides a dynamic address registration service that is used to register clients and resolve NetBIOS names to IP addresses on your network, to enable clients to find other computers and resources. NetBIOS names were developed to provide a mechanism for applications and computers to communicate in a networked environment. Each NetBIOS name is composed of a 16-byte address. The first 15 bytes represent the name of the computer, and the 16th byte represents the service provided by the computer or application.

Windows Server 2008 introduces the GlobalNames Zone in DNS that allows administrators to configure a DNS zone that will resolve single-label names in the same way WINS currently does, possibly allowing you to move away from WINS.

INSTALLING WINS

As I said earlier, WINS can still be used with Windows Server 2008 for much the same reason as it was used in Windows 2000 Server and Windows Server 2003—for the resolution of NetBIOS names. You install WINS by opening Add/Remove Programs and then clicking Add/Remove Windows Components. When the Windows Components dialog box appears, select the Network Services option, click the Details button, and select Windows Internet Name Service. Once the installation is complete, open the WINS console from Administrative Tools and click on the name of the server; the green upward arrow appears, as you can see in Figure 16.1. In most cases, installing the WINS service and using the default settings with the installation will suffice in providing name resolution for your network.

You will need to add some static mappings to your WINS server for proper connection to servers and possibly to some clients. If you need to create a static mapping, right-click the Active Registrations tab, select the New Static Mapping tab, and fill in the information fields as shown in Figure 16.2. There is the potential for problems with static mappings, which we will cover in the section "Troubleshooting Tools and WINS."

CURRENT USES AND APPLICATIONS FOR WINS

The need for WINS still exists in Windows Server 2008, mainly for Network Load Balancing (NLB) because NLB uses NetBIOS names. NLB enables you to enhance the scale and availability of IP-based servers. Using NLB with several servers running the same program—for example, Active Directory Federation Services (AD FS)-enabled web servers in an NLB cluster—will provide a redundant environment for critical applications. The functionality of WINS can be met by using another NetBIOS Name Service (NBNS) or an LMHOSTS file.

FIGURE 16.1
Installation of WINS

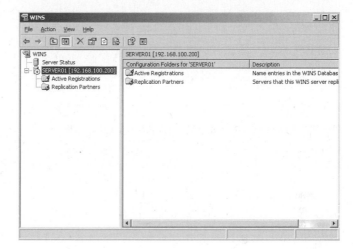

FIGURE 16.2
Creating a static
mapping in WINS

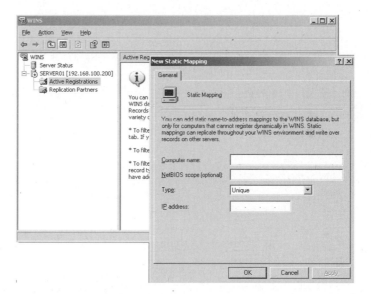

THE GLOBALNAMES ZONE TO HELP REPLACE WINS

While the GlobalNames Zone can resolve single-label names such as WINS, it may not be a complete replacement for WINS. WINS may still be required for single-label name resolution for records that are dynamically registered in WINS. These records are not typically managed by administrators, nor are they scalable for large enterprises with multiple domains or forests.

Domain Name System (DNS)

DNS is another name-resolution service that is used to find resources on a network. These resources are stored in a hierarchical database that lists all of the computers and other resources contained within a database. For Active Directory to function properly, you must have DNS configured and running properly. Once this is done, clients can find resources by querying the DNS database, and they can find a domain controller by searching the DNS database and other servers.

Active Directory requires a name-resolution method to function properly. You do not have to use a Windows DNS server to support Active Directory. You can use BIND as long as you are using version 8.1.2 or later and it supports service locator (SRV) records and dynamic updates.

 Real World Scenario

MOVING FROM WINS TO THE GLOBALNAMES ZONES

Mark wants to enable and configure the GlobalNames Zone so he can decommission his current WINS servers. His domain in a single-forest, single-domain AD DS environment.

Mark's first step is to enable GlobalNames Zone functionality. To do this, he must complete the following steps:

◆ From the command prompt, type **dnscmd /ServerName /config /Enableglobalnamessupport 1**. This allows you to enable the GlobalNames Zone functionality. Then you must create the Global-Names Zone.

◆ Open the DNS console and right-click a DNS server, and select New Zone from the menu. When the New Zone Wizard starts, create a new zone named GlobalNames.

Alternatively, Mark could perform the same task from the command line by typing in **dnscmd /ServerName /ZoneAdd GlobalNames /DsPrimary /DP /forest**.

CNAME (Alias) DNS records can now be added to the GlobalNames Zone to allow resolution to the single-label names.

INSTALLING DNS

The DNS service can be installed as part of the process of creating a domain controller, or separately from it. When you create a domain controller, the dcpromo process queries the network to hunt for a DNS server; if none is found, a dialog box will appear asking if you want the Active Directory Installation Wizard to create a DNS server for you (or fix the problem later), as you can see in Figure 16.3.

FIGURE 16.3
Installing DNS through the Active Directory Installation Wizard

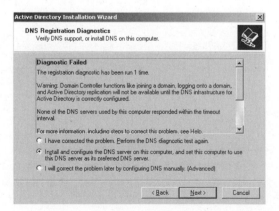

Installing DNS when you do not have Active Directory installed is straightforward. You install the DNS service through Add/Remove Programs and click on the DNS tab in Administrative Tools. This is different from installing DNS along with Active Directory in that you have the option of creating one of three types of zones: primary, secondary, or stub, as shown in Figure 16.4. Although you can create them at this point, you cannot yet store them in Active Directory.

FIGURE 16.4

Creating a zone in DNS

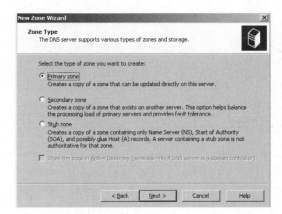

RESOURCE RECORDS

The DNS database is composed of one or more zone files. These zone files are made up of resource records, which contain the actual information used by the domain. Each resource record is a reference to specific computers, servers, and services in a domain. There are 25 types of resource records available in DNS; Table 16.1 lists the six most commonly used. (For more information about DNS records, see RFCs 1035, 1183, and 1886, 2052, and 2782 which can be found at www.faqs.org.)

TABLE 16.1: Common Resource-Record Types

RECORD	PURPOSE
Host (A)	Specifies the IP address of a computer to a specific host name.
Alias (CNAME)	Used to map another name to a specific host.
Mail Exchanger (MX)	The name of a server that is used for messaging.
Name Servers (NS)	Specifies the name servers for a specific domain.
Pointer (PTR)	Specifies the hostname of a specific computer given the IP address. This record is stored in the reverse-lookup zone.
Service (SRV)	Specifies the name of a computer and the service it provides, such as SRV records to locate a domain controller.

SERVICE LOCATOR RECORDS

One of the main purposes of DNS is to provide a service for clients to find resources. In the case of service locator (SRV) records, the resources referenced are domain controllers. The SRV record enables a client to find a domain controller on the network and can be viewed through the DNS console, as you can see in Figure 16.5.

FIGURE 16.5
Viewing an SRV record in the DNS console

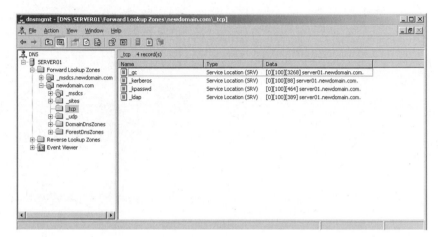

The actual SRV record informs a client of where a particular server can be found based on the domain name of the client. The format used by SRV resource records is described in detail in RFC 2782. The actual format for SRV records has 10 parts:

```
Service Protocol DomainName TTL Class SRV Priority Weight Port Target
```

Service Specifies the service that the server is running. For Active Directory, the service setting will be kerberos or ldap.

Protocol Specifies the protocol the client uses to connect to the service: UDP or TCP.

DomainName The fully qualified name of the domain where the domain controller is running.

TTL Time-to-live: the amount of time in seconds that the record can be cached on the client.

Class The class of the record, which in the case of SRV records is always the Internet class, IN.

SRV Identifies this record as a service locator record.

Priority Identifies the priority for this record. If the priority setting is a lower value than that of the other SRV records for the same service in the same domain, this will be the preferred record.

Weight When other records for the same service and domain have the same priority, the weight determines the preferred record. If multiple records have the same priority and weight, they are used equally by the clients.

Port The TCP or UDP port that is used by the service.

Target Identifies the domain controller's fully qualified domain name that is hosting the service.

When a domain controller named DC5 registers its SRV resource records, the Kerberos record would appear as:

```
_kerberos._tcp.zygort.lcl. 600 IN SRV 0 100 88 dc5.zygort.lcl
```

When you run `dcpromo` on a server to create a domain controller, a file called `Netlogon.dns` is created in the `%systemroot%\system32\config` folder. The `Netlogon.dns` file contains all the resource records that Active Directory needs, as shown in Figure 16.6.

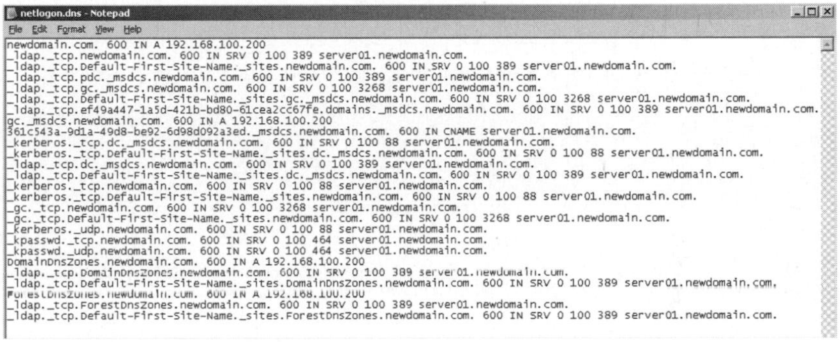
```
newdomain.com. 600 IN A 192.168.100.200
_ldap._tcp.newdomain.com. 600 IN SRV 0 100 389 server01.newdomain.com.
_ldap._tcp.Default-First-Site-Name._sites.newdomain.com. 600 IN SRV 0 100 389 server01.newdomain.com.
_ldap._tcp.pdc._msdcs.newdomain.com. 600 IN SRV 0 100 389 server01.newdomain.com.
_ldap._tcp.gc._msdcs.newdomain.com. 600 IN SRV 0 100 3268 server01.newdomain.com.
_ldap._tcp.Default-First-Site-Name._sites.gc._msdcs.newdomain.com. 600 IN SRV 0 100 3268 server01.newdomain.com.
_ldap._tcp.ef49a447-1a5d-421b-bd80-61cea2cc67fe.domains._msdcs.newdomain.com. 600 IN SRV 0 100 389 server01.newdomain.com.
gc._msdcs.newdomain.com. 600 IN A 192.168.100.200
361c543a-9d1a-49d8-be92-6d98d092a3ed._msdcs.newdomain.com. 600 IN CNAME server01.newdomain.com.
_kerberos._tcp.dc._msdcs.newdomain.com. 600 IN SRV 0 100 88 server01.newdomain.com.
_kerberos._tcp.Default-First-Site-Name._sites.dc._msdcs.newdomain.com. 600 IN SRV 0 100 88 server01.newdomain.com.
_ldap._tcp.dc._msdcs.newdomain.com. 600 IN SRV 0 100 389 server01.newdomain.com.
_ldap._tcp.Default-First-Site-Name._sites.dc._msdcs.newdomain.com. 600 IN SRV 0 100 389 server01.newdomain.com.
_kerberos._tcp.newdomain.com. 600 IN SRV 0 100 88 server01.newdomain.com.
_kerberos._tcp.Default-First-Site-Name._sites.newdomain.com. 600 IN SRV 0 100 88 server01.newdomain.com.
_gc._tcp.newdomain.com. 600 IN SRV 0 100 3268 server01.newdomain.com.
_gc._tcp.Default-First-Site-Name._sites.newdomain.com. 600 IN SRV 0 100 3268 server01.newdomain.com.
_kerberos._udp.newdomain.com. 600 IN SRV 0 100 88 server01.newdomain.com.
_kpasswd._tcp.newdomain.com. 600 IN SRV 0 100 464 server01.newdomain.com.
_kpasswd._udp.newdomain.com. 600 IN SRV 0 100 464 server01.newdomain.com.
DomainDnsZones.newdomain.com. 600 IN A 192.168.100.200
_ldap._tcp.DomainDnsZones.newdomain.com. 600 IN SRV 0 100 389 server01.newdomain.com.
_ldap._tcp.Default-First-Site-Name._sites.DomainDnsZones.newdomain.com. 600 IN SRV 0 100 389 server01.newdomain.com.
ForestDnsZones.newdomain.com. 600 IN A 192.168.100.200
_ldap._tcp.ForestDnsZones.newdomain.com. 600 IN SRV 0 100 389 server01.newdomain.com.
_ldap._tcp.Default-First-Site-Name._sites.ForestDnsZones.newdomain.com. 600 IN SRV 0 100 389 server01.newdomain.com.
```

FIGURE 16.6
Contents of the Netlogon.dns file

When you make changes to a DNS server, you might have to re-register SRV records. You can do this either through a command line or through the Services snap-in. To use a command line, open a command prompt and type **`net stop netlogon`** and then **`net start netlogon`**. If you are going to use the interface, open the services interface (either through Administrative Tools or by typing **`services.msc`** in the Start ➤ Run box) and right-click the Netlogon tab, and stop or start the service.

DNS Zones

When creating your DNS structure, you will have the option of creating different types of zones depending on the purpose of the zones. Normally you can create primary, secondary, or stub zones. If you create a primary or stub zone, you can store the zone in Active Directory. We will discuss these standard zones and their options in this section. We'll also cover Active Directory–integrated zones. We will point out the difference between Active Directory–integrated zones and standard zones, especially the benefits of each.

Primary Zones and Secondary Zones

When you create your DNS zone, you have the option of deciding what type of zone you will create. In this case, the primary zone represents the initial point where you will create and update all records for your domain and whether they are stored on only one domain. This makes for ease of use—you have only one server to work with—but it does not provide for any fault tolerance in case of server failures.

If you want to spread out the work of name resolution and provide fault tolerance with DNS, create a secondary server. A secondary server will receive updates from the primary server through zone transfer and will still respond to name queries of clients even if the primary server is offline. You will still need to create new records and manage updates from the primary server because it is the only copy of the zone file that can be modified. Any changes or modifications will automatically be replicated to the secondary servers.

There are drawbacks associated with a standard zone, namely replication and latency. To ensure effective name resolution and provide access to resources, you need to create a secondary zone that will replicate with the primary zone. What if there were a better way to accomplish this replication and provide better service for clients? This is accomplished by creating Active Directory–integrated zones.

Active Directory–Integrated Zones

It is now time to create an Active Directory–integrated zone in DNS. To begin, right-click the name of the DNS server, specify New Zone, and click Next. The next screen is where you will specify the type of zone and where the zone will be stored. At the bottom of the Zone Type screen is a box that reads Store the Zone in Active Directory (Available Only if DNS Server Is a Domain Controller), as you can see in Figure 16.7. Checking this box means that the zone file will be stored in Active Directory and will be replicated when Active Directory replicates to the domain controllers or DNS servers you specify. The next screen will determine how and where zone replication will occur. There are three choices here: To All DNS Servers in the Active Directory Forest *domain name*, To All DNS Servers in the Active Directory Domain *domain name*, and To All Domain Controllers in the Active Directory Domain *domain name*. The last choice is the default choice, as shown in Figure 16.8.

FIGURE 16.7
Storing zone
information in
Active Directory

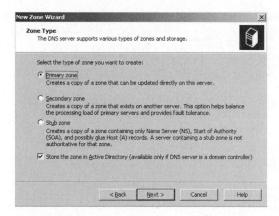

FIGURE 16.8
Choosing
replication
scope in Active
Directory

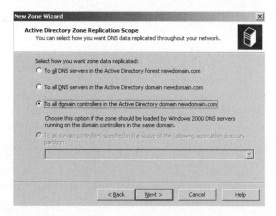

An Active Directory–integrated zone improves the whole replication process by removing zone replication from the primary and secondary zones to Active Directory. Moving the database and replication to Active Directory makes sense for a number of reasons, including security. The benefits for allowing Active Directory to handle replication include the following:

◆ It ensures timely updates to the zones because replication occurs through Active Directory rather than from a standard primary server to secondary servers.

◆ Because all domain controllers that have DNS installed are in effect primary DNS servers, there is increased replication.

◆ You can limit what is replicated—only changes are replicated, not the entire database.

◆ Updates are secure; you have greater control over which servers will receive updates.

Application Directory Partitions

A relatively new feature in Windows Server is application directory partitions. With application directories, you will replicate only to specific domain controllers, whereas with domain partitions you would replicate with all domain controllers. Application directories allow you to have more control over where replication will occur in your network.

When you initially create a domain controller, you have the chance to install DNS at the same time (if there isn't a DNS service available), as we covered in the "Installing DNS" section earlier. When you installed DNS, two new directory partitions are created: the DomainDnsZone and the ForestDnsZone, which are stored in Active Directory. These two directories enable you to specify where replication will occur: either to DNS servers in the domain or to DNS servers in the forest.

If you install DNS first and then promote a server to become a domain controller, the two directory partitions will not be created. You can create these later by right-clicking the DNS server name and choosing the Create Default Application Directory Partitions option.

Dynamic Host Configuration Protocol (DHCP)

The Dynamic Host Configuration Protocol is used to automatically assign IP addresses and other required networking information to DHCP-enabled hosts on your network from a central location. You configure and authorize a DHCP server in Active Directory to respond to requests from clients for configuration information. There is always the possibility of assigning duplicate addresses or incorrect addresses to clients if you configure them manually on your network. Because the assignment of these addresses is done automatically with DHCP, there is little chance for human error to affect your network. This also ensures that only the information you want the hosts to receive actually reaches them. Other benefits include the ability to quickly handle changes of IP addresses for hosts such as laptops, and the ability to use DHCP relay agents to pass along DHCP requests and assignments to network segments that do not have a DHCP server.

The DHCP server service can be installed on a domain controller, a domain member server, or a stand-alone server. Generally, you will install DHCP on a domain controller or a domain member server. Once you have the service installed, you will need to create a scope or a range of addresses. Included in a scope will be any options you wish to have assigned to hosts. These options can include subnet masks, DNS and WINS servers, default gateways, and domain names, as well as other services used within the TCP/IP protocol stack.

AUTHORIZING DHCP SERVERS

Each and every DHCP server is authorized in Active Directory to prevent unauthorized or rogue servers from either issuing new IP-address leases or renewing existing IP-address leases. This authorization will occur before any leases are issued or renewed. For a DHCP server to be authorized in Active Directory, it must either be configured as a domain controller or be a member server that is in the domain. The actual authorization process is done through the DHCP console. To authorize a server, right-click on the server name in the console and click on Authorize. An unauthorized DHCP server will appear with a red downward arrow beside the server name. Once the server has been authorized in Active Directory, this red arrow will disappear, and you'll see something like Figure 16.9. For the red arrow to change to a green upward arrow, you might have to refresh the console by pressing the F5 key or selecting the Refresh option after right-clicking the console. The green arrow indicates the DHCP server has been authorized.

FIGURE 16.9

Authorizing a
DHCP server in
Active Directory

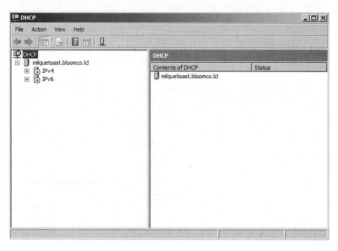

Most of the problems you will encounter with a DHCP server are related to authorization or network connectivity issues such as connectivity between segments rather than with the servers themselves. As stated earlier, a DHCP server must be authorized in Active Directory to issue addresses. If you have a server that is not responding to client requests for new or renewed addresses and there is connectivity to the server, check whether the server is authorized. If it is not authorized, use the steps outlined earlier and authorize the server.

Once you have your server authorized and you have created a scope, you must activate the scope for the server to issue addresses. Activating a scope enables the server to respond to requests from clients on the local network segment. To activate a scope, go to the DHCP console, right-click on the scope, and click Activate. The scope is successfully activated when the red downward arrow disappears, as you can see in Figure 16.10.

FIGURE 16.10

Activating a scope on a
DHCP server

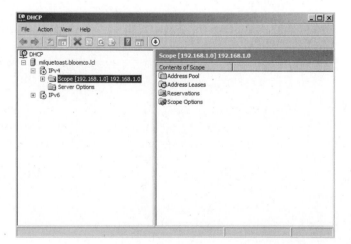

In some scenarios, you might have your DHCP server configured to support clients on multiple network segments. In that case, if clients on one segment are not receiving addresses, check the default bindings for the network connections. If your DHCP server is multihomed, the DHCP service will bind to the first IP address that is statically configured for each network connection. If the first network connection is configured dynamically, the connection is disabled in the server bindings. However, if the first connection is configured statically, then the connection is enabled in the server bindings.

There is a command line called dhcploc included in the support tools folder of the Windows Server CD or DVD that is useful for detecting any DHCP servers on a specific network segment and for discovering if there are any unauthorized servers. Usage for dhcploc is dhcploc -p *machine-ip-address*. The -p switch will preclude authorized DHCP servers from this query, and *machine-ip-address* specifies the machine from which the utility is run, as shown in Figure 16.11.

FIGURE 16.11
Using dhcploc

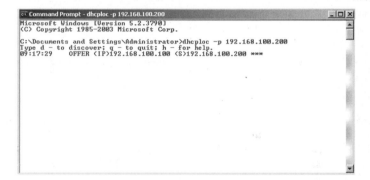

DHCP RELAY AGENT

Now that you have your DHCP server authorized, you must look at DHCP relay agents A DHCP relay agent requests a DHCP address on behalf of a client on network segments that do not have DHCP servers. DHCP relay agents are created in the Routing and Remote Access console (not through the DHCP interface), as Figure 16.12 shows. Once the agent is configured, it is transparent to users where the address comes from—all they know is that they have an address.

If you have a DHCP relay agent configured but clients on a segment are not receiving addresses, check the Routing and Remote Access server and ensure that the service and interfaces are running. You should also ensure that the Relay DHCP Packets box is checked on the interface in question.

DHCP DATABASE

You can back up the DHCP database in one of three ways: through a normally scheduled backup of the system using Windows Backup or your preferred backup solution, synchronously through automatic backups that occur every 60 minutes, or via asynchronous or manual backups through the DHCP console. If synchronous or manual backups have been performed, you can recover the database through the DHCP console by right-clicking the server name and clicking Backup, as you can see in Figure 16.13.

FIGURE 16.12

Configuring a DHCP relay agent

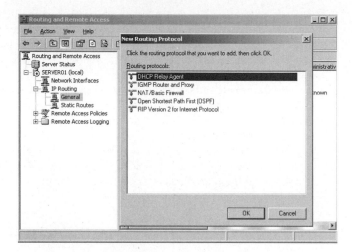

FIGURE 16.13

Backing up a DHCP database

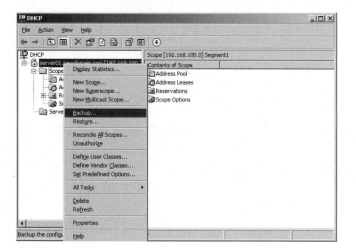

Network-Troubleshooting Methodologies

As an administrator, one of your most important tasks is to troubleshoot problems on your network. Troubleshooting is as much an art as a science, and is network-dependent. All networks have their own quirks and issues that affect performance and reliability. These can be related to environment, people (users), technology, or outside influences.

Numerous troubleshooting models and methodologies are available. Eventually you will find what works for you, your network, and your users. Most troubleshooting follows a systematic approach to isolating and repairing the problem, but on some occasions a more intuitive approach is required; sometimes you'll use a combination of the two. Experience will help you learn when to choose between a systematic and an intuitive approach. As you saw in Chapter 15, "Microsoft's Troubleshooting Methodology for Active Directory," the Microsoft methodology helps make troubleshooting less stressful.

As mentioned earlier, when troubleshooting you should try to isolate the problem. While you are trying to fix a network problem, do not make too many changes at once—preferably only one or two at a time. If you make too many changes, you might inflict more harm to your network while trying to fix the problem. Additionally, if you need to undo any or all of your previous actions, you might not remember what you did.

Consider taking screenshots of, or writing down, the changes you make to the network as you make them. This will help you remember what troubleshooting and repair actions you have performed on the network, and you can readily undo them if required. This will also serve as a roadmap for anybody who has to perform the same task in the future.

The last thing we need to discuss is priorities. The priority of your actions will be determined by a number of factors: how critical the problem is, who the problem affects, who has "interest" in the problem, and how long the outage will last. Any one of these factors can influence the order in which you will try to fix network outages.

Tools for Troubleshooting

Learning how to successfully and quickly troubleshoot is important, and knowing what tools to use in given situations will assist you immensely. Many tools can be used for basic troubleshooting of your network infrastructure, and we will cover some of the basic ones in this section.

IPCONFIG

The IPCONFIG command-line utility is used for displaying current TCP/IP configuration for a client, for troubleshooting DHCP issues with a client, and as a basic client-side DNS tool. One of the most common uses of IPCONFIG is the display of a client's basic IP-address information. When you type **ipconfig** at a command prompt, the IP address, subnet mask, and default gateway for a client will be displayed, as shown in Figure 16.14. The IPCONFIG command has a number of common switches that are used for gathering information used in troubleshooting.

When you use the basic ipconfig command and get an address returned in the 169.254.$x.x$ range, you know that for some reason the client cannot contact a DHCP server to receive or renew an IP address. You might try the /release and /renew switches to release the current address and then contact a DHCP server to get a new address, as shown in Figure 16.15.

Another switch you can use is /flushdns, which will clear and reset the DNS client resolver cache, as shown in Figure 16.16. This is useful when verifying proper DNS resolution for a client.

Two last switches we will talk about are /registerdns and /displaydns. The /registerdns switch is used to manually update dynamic DNS-name and IP-address registrations, as shown in Figure 16.17. This switch is extremely useful when verifying name resolution with a DNS server.

FIGURE 16.14

Display results
for IPCONFIG

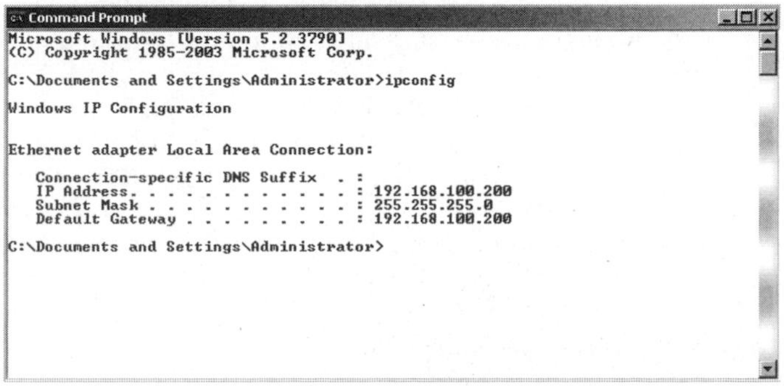

```
Command Prompt                                                    _ □ ×
Microsoft Windows [Version 5.2.3790]
(C) Copyright 1985-2003 Microsoft Corp.

C:\Documents and Settings\Administrator>ipconfig

Windows IP Configuration

Ethernet adapter Local Area Connection:

        Connection-specific DNS Suffix  . :
        IP Address. . . . . . . . . . . . : 192.168.100.200
        Subnet Mask . . . . . . . . . . . : 255.255.255.0
        Default Gateway . . . . . . . . . : 192.168.100.200

C:\Documents and Settings\Administrator>
```

The /displaydns switch will display the contents of the local clients' DNS resolver cache, including all preloaded entries from a local Hosts file and any entries newly added, as shown in Figure 16.18. This command is useful for seeing what has been resolved—especially when used in conjunction with the /registerdns command.

FIGURE 16.15
Releasing and
renewing an
IP address

FIGURE 16.16
Clearing and
resetting the
client resolver
cache

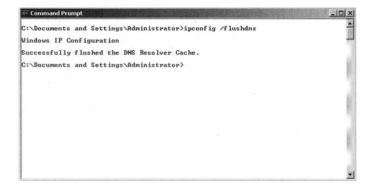

FIGURE 16.17
Using the
/registerdns
switch

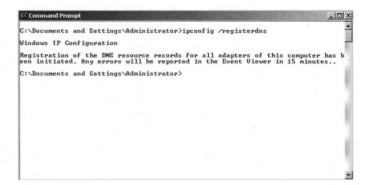

FIGURE 16.18

Verifying the contents of the client resolver cache

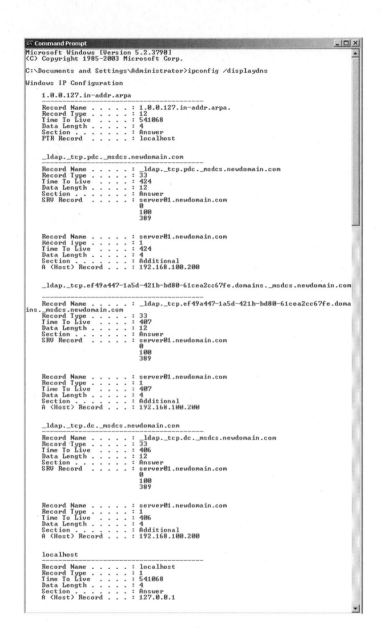

NSLOOKUP

This is a command we will discuss in much greater depth later in this chapter. It can be used for a variety of useful and powerful tasks. For our basic troubleshooting concerns at the moment, it can be used to diagnose DNS issues and to check for name resolution by querying a DNS server, as shown in Figure 16.19.

FIGURE 16.19

Using the basic
nslookup command

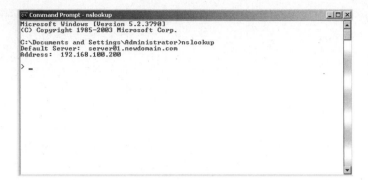

NETDIAG

This command-line tool can be used to help diagnose and isolate connectivity issues in your network. It does this by performing a number of tests on the system and displaying network and configuration information. The information that is generated, as shown in Figure 16.20, can be used to start troubleshooting connectivity issues.

FIGURE 16.20

Displaying the
results of Netdiag

PING

This command-line utility is used for testing connectivity between systems. Using ping in its basic form, you can determine whether you can "see" the target object you are trying to reach.

You use this command-line utility to test connectivity between two systems by using either the name or the IP address of the target system, as shown in Figure 16.21. In Windows Server 2003 and 2008 you can specify that IPv6 is used by ping to identify the name of target host. You do this by using the -6 switch in the command line. If you know the IP address but not the host name, you can use the -a switch in the command line to find the host name.

Figure 16.21

Testing connectivity with ping

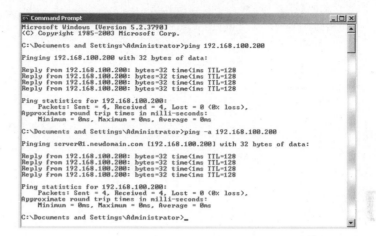

```
Command Prompt                                                    _ □ ×
Microsoft Windows [Version 5.2.3790]
<C> Copyright 1985-2003 Microsoft Corp.

C:\Documents and Settings\Administrator>ping 192.168.100.200

Pinging 192.168.100.200 with 32 bytes of data:

Reply from 192.168.100.200: bytes=32 time<1ms TTL=128
Reply from 192.168.100.200: bytes=32 time<1ms TTL=128
Reply from 192.168.100.200: bytes=32 time<1ms TTL=128
Reply from 192.168.100.200: bytes=32 time<1ms TTL=128

Ping statistics for 192.168.100.200:
    Packets: Sent = 4, Received = 4, Lost = 0 (0% loss),
Approximate round trip times in milli-seconds:
    Minimum = 0ms, Maximum = 0ms, Average = 0ms

C:\Documents and Settings\Administrator>ping -a 192.168.100.200

Pinging server01.newdomain.com [192.168.100.200] with 32 bytes of data:

Reply from 192.168.100.200: bytes=32 time<1ms TTL=128
Reply from 192.168.100.200: bytes=32 time<1ms TTL=128
Reply from 192.168.100.200: bytes=32 time<1ms TTL=128
Reply from 192.168.100.200: bytes=32 time<1ms TTL=128

Ping statistics for 192.168.100.200:
    Packets: Sent = 4, Received = 4, Lost = 0 (0% loss),
Approximate round trip times in milli-seconds:
    Minimum = 0ms, Maximum = 0ms, Average = 0ms

C:\Documents and Settings\Administrator>_
```

PATHPING

Knowing the path that data packets take in a network can help with troubleshooting communications problems. The `pathping` command-line utility is a very useful tool in finding the path that packets take in a network, as well as determining the latency involved with each intervening router, switch, and subnet.

The syntax for `pathping` is as follows:

```
pathping [-n] [-h MaximumHops] [-g HostList] [-p Period] [-q NumQueries]
Â[-w Timeout] [-T] [-R] [TargetName]
```

When you initiate the `pathping` command, it sends echo requests as ICMP packets out to each intervening hop that a data packet traverses, and displays the information it collects concerning the latency at each subsequent level. In this way you will have information that will help you identify the source of the bottleneck on the network. As part of the testing process, `pathping` tests each segment or hop, and as such, there can be a delay in the test completing, as shown in Figure 16.22. Because `pathping` uses ICMP, there is the potential for firewalls to block these packets and have incomplete data displayed for a specific segment.

TRACERT

This command-line utility functions in a manner similar to that of `pathping`, but with a few exceptions. `tracert`, like `pathping`, uses ICMP echo packets to display the path a packet takes from source to destination. But unlike `pathping`, `tracert` does not display the latency of communications, or of the packets as they traverse the network—it displays only the path it takes, as shown in Figure 16.23. Also like `pathping`, `tracert` will be affected by firewalls because it uses ICMP echo packets, and many firewalls block ICMP packets.

The syntax for `tracert` is as follows:

```
tracert [-d] [-h MaximumHops] [-j HostList] [-w Timeout] Â[-R] [-S SrcAddr]
[-4][-6] TargetName
```

There are two switches of interest in `tracert`. Like `ping`, `tracert` has the capability of using only IPv6 for testing purposes. If you use the `-6` switch, `tracert` will use only IPv6 for this test.

The -d switch is useful for improving performance; it will prevent tracert from resolving the names of intervening routers. By default tracert has a maximum hop count of 30, although you can change this by using the -h switch.

FIGURE 16.22
Switches available for pathping

```
C:\WINDOWS\system32\cmd.exe
C:\Documents and Settings\Administrator>pathping -n microsoft.com

Tracing route to microsoft.com [207.46.232.182]
over a maximum of 30 hops:
  0  192.168.1.200
  1  192.168.1.1
  2  216.166.242.65
  3  64.40.72.18
  4  204.9.126.253
  5  204.9.121.2
  6  144.232.249.45
  7  144.232.23.53
  8  144.232.20.109
  9  144.232.20.156
 10  144.232.6.10
 11  144.224.113.146
 12  207.46.44.1
 13  207.46.41.94
 14  207.46.35.138
 15     *        *        *
Computing statistics for 375 seconds...
            Source to Here   This Node/Link
Hop  RTT    Lost/Sent = Pct  Lost/Sent = Pct  Address
  0                                           192.168.1.200
                                0/ 100 =  0%   |
  1    1ms     0/ 100 =  0%     0/ 100 =  0%  192.168.1.1
                                0/ 100 =  0%   |
  2   33ms     1/ 100 =  1%     1/ 100 =  1%  216.166.242.65
                                0/ 100 =  0%   |
  3   34ms     0/ 100 =  0%     0/ 100 =  0%  64.40.72.18
                                0/ 100 =  0%   |
  4   44ms     0/ 100 =  0%     0/ 100 =  0%  204.9.126.253
                                0/ 100 =  0%   |
  5   48ms     0/ 100 =  0%     0/ 100 =  0%  204.9.121.2
                                0/ 100 =  0%   |
  6   44ms     0/ 100 =  0%     0/ 100 =  0%  144.232.249.45
                                0/ 100 =  0%   |
  7   44ms     0/ 100 =  0%     0/ 100 =  0%  144.232.23.53
                                0/ 100 =  0%   |
  8   55ms     0/ 100 =  0%     0/ 100 =  0%  144.232.20.109
                                0/ 100 =  0%   |
  9   99ms     0/ 100 =  0%     0/ 100 =  0%  144.232.20.156
                                0/ 100 =  0%   |
 10   99ms     0/ 100 =  0%     0/ 100 =  0%  144.232.6.10
                                0/ 100 =  0%   |
 11  108ms     0/ 100 =  0%     0/ 100 =  0%  144.224.113.146
                              100/ 100 =100%   |
 12  ---     100/ 100 =100%     0/ 100 =  0%  207.46.44.1
                                0/ 100 =  0%   |
 13  ---     100/ 100 =100%     0/ 100 =  0%  207.46.41.94
                                0/ 100 =  0%   |
 14  ---     100/ 100 =100%     0/ 100 =  0%  207.46.35.138
                                0/ 100 =  0%   |
 15  ---     100/ 100 =100%     0/ 100 =  0%  0.0.0.0

Trace complete.
```

FIGURE 16.23
Display results from tracert

```
Command Prompt

C:\Documents and Settings\Administrator>tracert -h 15 www.wiley.com

Tracing route to www.wiley.com [208.215.179.146]
over a maximum of 15 hops:

  1    15 ms     9 ms    25 ms  10.1.0.1
  2    36 ms    38 ms     9 ms  63-252-75-133.ip.mcleodusa.net [63.252.75.133]
  3    12 ms    14 ms    49 ms  209-254-131-41.ip.mcleodusa.net [209.254.131.41]
  4    14 ms    12 ms    13 ms  CHCGILWUH53JC01-SO2-1-0-0.mcleodusa.net [64.198.100.85]
  5    21 ms    18 ms    20 ms  CHCGILDTHBUJC01-SO0-3-0-0.mcleodusa.net [64.198.100.46]
  6    56 ms    82 ms    43 ms  sl-st20-chi-5-0.sprintlink.net [144.223.241.1]
  7    38 ms    38 ms    39 ms  sprint-gw.cgcil.ip.att.net [192.205.32.149]
  8    57 ms    83 ms    57 ms  tbr1-p014001.cgcil.ip.att.net [12.123.6.34]
  9    60 ms    69 ms    81 ms  tbr1-cl14.n54ny.ip.att.net [12.122.10.1]
 10    61 ms    57 ms    59 ms  gbr6-p30.n54ny.ip.att.net [12.122.11.14]
 11    56 ms    56 ms    58 ms  gar3-p370.n54ny.ip.att.net [12.123.1.189]
 12    65 ms    61 ms    68 ms  12.125.50.162
 13     *        *        *     Request timed out.
 14     *        *        *     Request timed out.
 15     *        *        *     Request timed out.

Trace complete.

C:\Documents and Settings\Administrator>_
```

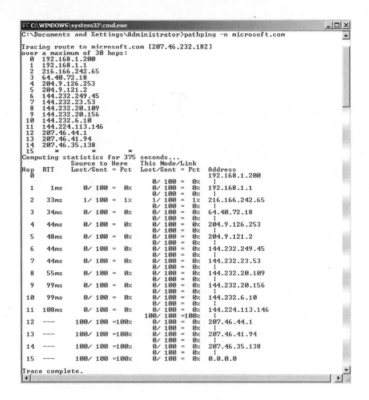

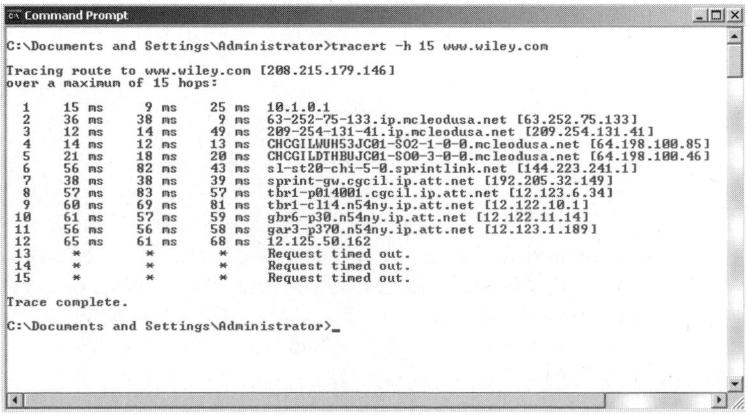

DNS Troubleshooting Tools

Knowing the tools that are in your troubleshooting arsenal is important when deciding how to tackle a problem with DNS. You can use several command-line utilities—such as the popular nslookup—to manage your DNS server with DNSCMD. We will discuss the most common tools in this section and give some examples of how you can use them for troubleshooting.

The first step in troubleshooting is to ensure that you have the proper permissions for using the tools (that is, you are a member of the Administrators group or you have been delegated permission to use the tools). If you are using a secondary logon, make sure you specify the proper account. Permissions tend to be overlooked initially when troubleshooting.

DEBUG LOGGING

One place you can look for information on the performance of your DNS server is the event logs, and if you have DNS debug logging enabled, you can use it as well. To enable DNS debug logging, right-click on the name of the server, click Properties, and click the Debug Logging tab. On that tab click the Log Packets for Debugging box, as shown in Figure 16.24. Once you are in the debug console window, you can specify logging for packet direction, transport protocol, packet contents, packet type, and other options. The actual log file is stored in the C:\Windows\System32\DNS folder, but you can change the location to suit your needs.

FIGURE 16.24
Enabling debug logging for DNS

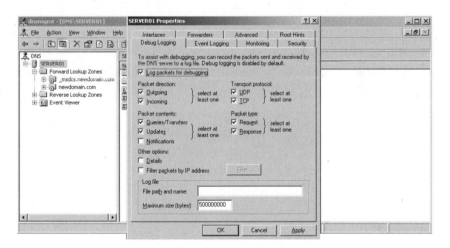

DOMAIN INFORMATION GROPER (DIG)

This command-line utility is derived from Unix. The query feature is what makes dig more powerful than nslookup. When you initiate a query in dig, you must specify what you want to query and any associated records or switches. dig can also be used to make zone transfers in the same way as nslookup. Dig is part of BIND, which you can download from www.isc.org/sw/bind/view?release=9.4.2.

DNSCMD

This command-line tool is found in the support tools folder of the Windows Server CD or DVD and enables you to create, modify, and delete resource records and zones. If you want to view the DNS information and statistics of a server, type **dnscmd <server name> /info** at a command prompt, as shown in Figure 16.25. By typing **dnscmd** at a command prompt, you will get a listing of all the commands you can use, as you can see in Figure 16.26. Keep in mind that this utility is usually run on one computer, but is used to act upon another system.

Other useful switches with DNSCMD are as follows:

/Zoneinfo   This will display information about the target zone.

/DirectoryPartitionInfo   This command will display the directory partition information for the target partition.

DNSLint

This is a command-line utility for Windows Server 2003 and higher and is located in the Support Tools folder of the Windows Server CD or DVD. It can be used to check for and verify DNS records and server functionality and to generate a report in HTML, as you can see in Figure 16.27. The syntax for DNSLint is as follows:

```
dnslint /d domain_name | /ad [LDAP_IP_address] | /ql input_file
[/c] Â[smtp,pop,imap]] [/no_open] [/r report_name] [/t] [/test_tcp]
Â[/s DNS_IP_address] [/v] [/y]
```

FIGURE 16.25

Information-display results for dnscmd

FIGURE 16.26
List of commands available for dnscmd

FIGURE 16.27
Running DNSLint with the /AD switch displayed in HTML format

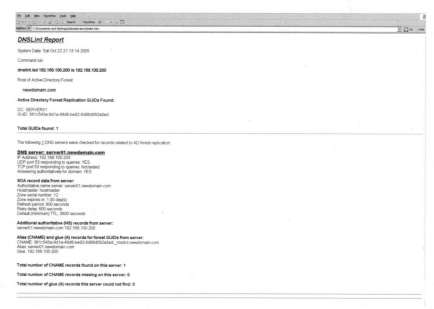

When using DNSLint, you must specify one of three switches—/d, /ql, or /ad—in the command line, as shown in Figure 16.28. Each switch is further explained here:

/d Diagnoses problems with "lame delegation." Lame delegation occurs when an NS record points to an invalid host. You cannot use the /ad switch with the /d switch, and you must specify a domain to test.

/ql Verifies a user-defined set of DNS records on multiple servers.

/ad Verifies DNS records specifically used for Active Directory replication. You must use the /s switch with the /ad switch. The /s switch specifies the IP address of a DNS server that is authoritative for the _msdcs zone in the Active Directory forest. When using the /ad switch, DNSLint will compare the domain controller's canonical name (CNAME) record that is registered within the domain's zone in DNS with the alias that is found as an attribute of the domain controller's computer object.

FIGURE 16.28
DNSLint
command line

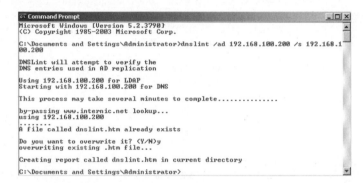

A switch that is commonly overlooked is /test_tcp. When running DNSLint tests, only UDP port 53 is tested. By using this switch, TCP port 53 will be tested to see if it is responding to queries. Another switch that is not usually utilized to its fullest is /s. When the /s switch is used with /d, it will not query the InterNIC whois lookup site. Using the /s switch by itself will query the InterNIC whois lookup site by default. This allows private networks to be tested, and for you to determine which DNS server is queried.

NSLOOKUP

This is, perhaps, the most important tool at your disposal for troubleshooting DNS issues. There are two modes available for nslookup: interactive and noninteractive. Which mode you will use depends on the location and the type of information you are seeking.

The noninteractive mode is used for searching for only one record or other specific information. To use nslookup in noninteractive mode, you type the following:

```
Nslookup [name or IP address of target] [name or IP address of a DNS server]
```

If you need to search for a number of different records, then you would use the interactive mode of nslookup. If you type only **nslookup** at a command prompt, you will get a result similar to what you see in Figure 16.29. In this case you see the FQDN and IP address for server01. This is the basic form of the interactive mode.

FIGURE 16.29

Display using
nslookup

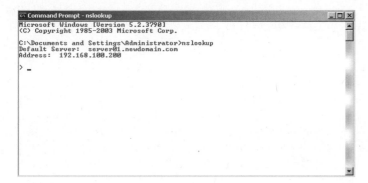

You can use nslookup to search for detailed records. If you need to search for a specific record type, you would specify through a set type=*resource_record_type* command what resource-record type you are looking for, as shown in Figure 16.30.

You can also use nslookup for zone transfer. You do this by using the ls command. The syntax for this command is:

Ls [-a | d | t type] domain [> filename]

-**a**   Displays all the aliases and canonical names.

-**d**   Displays all data from the target domain.

-**t**   Filters data by specific type.

FIGURE 16.30

Displaying a specific
record with nslookup

```
Microsoft Windows [Version 5.2.3790]
(C) Copyright 1985-2003 Microsoft Corp.

C:\Documents and Settings\Administrator>nslookup
Default Server:  server01.newdomain.com
Address:  192.168.100.200

> set type=ptr
> server01
Server:  server01.newdomain.com
Address:  192.168.100.200

newdomain.com
        primary name server = server01.newdomain.com
        responsible mail addr = hostmaster
        serial  = 21
        refresh = 900 (15 mins)
        retry   = 600 (10 mins)
        expire  = 86400 (1 day)
        default TTL = 3600 (1 hour)
>
```

WINS Troubleshooting Tools

The WINS server itself is fairly robust, but as with all servers, some problems might arise. We will go through some troublesome areas and discuss a few of the tools to use when troubleshooting. (Before performing too much work on the WINS database, you should back up the database by right-clicking the server, clicking the Backup Database option, and specifying the backup location.)

One of the most basic problems is a WINS server not giving out addresses. If this happens, ensure the WINS server is started and is on the proper subnet. If you need to start the WINS server, right-click the server name, select All Tasks, and then click the Start option.

Eventually you will need to use static mappings in WINS, but you should use them judiciously, because they can adversely affect your network if you have duplicate names. When a client connects, the client will attempt to register its name with an NBNS. The NBNS will check its database to see if the name is unused. If a client attempts to register a name and the requested name is in use, the NBNS server will query the first machine to see if the name is still being used. If it is still in use, the requesting machine will be sent a negative name-registration response. Otherwise, the NBNS will register the name for the client.

Another issue associated with static mappings is updating. If you have changed the network or if you have modified any servers (for example, a server name, address, or type) and have not updated your static mappings, clients or other servers may not be able to connect. You will need to devise a strategy to ensure you keep your static mappings current to avoid these pitfalls.

NETSH WINS

This tool is mainly used for configuring your WINS server from the command line, but can be used for viewing potential problems and for troubleshooting. By typing **netsh wins server \\<*servername*>**, you get the results shown in Figure 16.31. If you type only **netsh wins**, you will just get the help screen. From this console you perform many tasks against the options listed. You can check current settings, set options, or show information about the options that are listed. The information displayed can be used to start the diagnosis of your WINS server.

FIGURE 16.31

Showing the output of netsh wins server

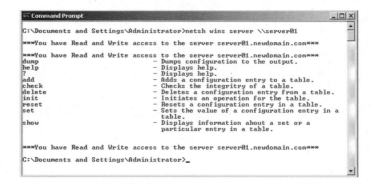

NBTSTAT

The nbtstat tool is used to display information about NetBIOS functions on your server. You can use it to display protocol statistics with NetBIOS over TCP/IP (NetBT), display or purge the NetBIOS name cache, and release and refresh the name of the local machine if it is registered with a WINS server.

Following is the syntax for nbtstat:

```
nbtstat [-a RemoteName] [-A IPAddress] [-c] [-n] [-r] [-R] Â[-RR] [-s] [-S]
[Interval]
```

You have many capabilities available with nbtstat, but in most cases you are going to use it to view, purge, and refresh the cache. To view the name cache, open a command prompt and type **nbtstat -c**, as shown in Figure 16.32. If you need to purge and reload the #PRE-tagged entries (the entries that are loaded first from the LMHOSTS file), use nbtstat -r, as shown in Figure 16.33. The -RR switch will clear and refresh the cache on the local computer from which it is run, as shown in Figure 16.34.

FIGURE 16.32
Displaying the NetBIOS name cache with nbtstat

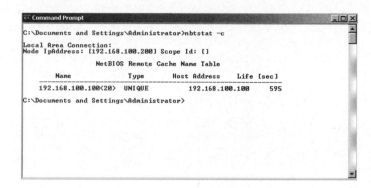

FIGURE 16.33
Purging and reloading the #PRE-tagged entries

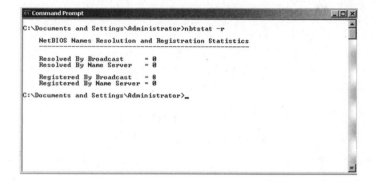

FIGURE 16.34
Clearing and refreshing the name cache with the -RR switch

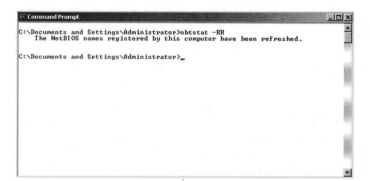

Coming Up Next

Now that you have learned about troubleshooting the network infrastructure and services that AD DS relies upon, it is time to move on to troubleshooting Active Directory itself. As with most of the Windows Server services, there are several tools for isolating problems related to Active Directory. We will introduce those tools and cover how they are used in the next chapter (Chapter 17, "Troubleshooting Problems Related to the Active Directory Database").

The Bottom Line

There are many tools available for troubleshooting issues related to network infrastructure. Most of these tools help you troubleshoot issues related to name resolution and DHCP.

Use tools to troubleshoot name-resolution problems   Problems related to name resolution can be difficult to troubleshoot. Where the issue lies—with DNS or with WINS—will determine which tools you will use.

Master It   You are having a problem with AD DS database replication. You need to determine why replication is failing between servers.

Troubleshoot WINS issues   Often, communication problems or name-resolution problems occur with computers that use WINS.

Master It   You are trying to communicate with a workstation that is named CAD01. The IP address of this workstation is 10.100.1.29. You ping the workstation by name and by IP address, but the ping command times out. Upon further inspection, you find that the IP address that is returned to you is 10.100.3.29. This is the IP address that CAD01 had before it was moved to the 10.100.1.0 subnet.

You check the WINS database, and the IP address associated with CAD01 is listed in the database as 10.100.1.29.

Chapter 17

Troubleshooting Problems Related to the Active Directory Database

The Active Directory database consists of database files and log files, and the overall health of these files is key to Active Directory's stability. In this chapter, we discuss problems related to these files, such as corrupted files or inconsistent data due to replication problems.

In this chapter you will learn how to troubleshoot:

◆ Database replication

◆ FSMO roles

◆ Logon failures

Active Directory Files

The key to a successful Active Directory backup is the system state. The Active Directory file system is built to handle full and complete restoration even when time has elapsed since the backup occurred. Following are the files that make up the system state:

◆ NTDS.DIT: This file is the Active Directory database file.

◆ EDB.LOG: This log file contains the transactions that have occurred since the last backup.

◆ EDB001.LOG, EDB002.LOG, etc.: These log files are similar to the EDB.LOG file; they are created when the EDB.LOG is full.

◆ EDB.CHK: This file contains an authoritative list of all transactions contained in the EDB files.

◆ RES*n*.LOG: These files are created when the EDB.LOG file creation fails. When the NTDS.DIT file is backed up, the current EDB.LOG file is deleted and a blank 10 MB EDB.LOG file is created. If there is not enough disk space for the new file creation, RES*n*.LOG (where *n* is a number, assigned in sequence to each file) files are created. One file is created per transaction. This allows more transactions to be recorded.

◆ *.PAT: These files are created when a transaction is split between log files. During a restore, these files are used to patch transactions that span more than one log file.

The Guts of NTDS.DIT

For the true database geeks out there, let's take a quick look inside the NTDS.DIT file. Earlier, we defined this file simply as the Active Directory database file. Well, there is a little more to it than that.

NTDS.DIT is the heart of Active Directory. It holds information about Active Directory, including user accounts, computer accounts, and so on. A deeper look into how this information is stored reveals the following tables:

◆ Schema table: This table contains data about the types of objects that can be created in Active Directory, the relationships between then, and the attributes (both mandatory and optional) that exist on each type of object. This table changes only when the Active Directory schema is altered.

◆ Link table: This table contains data about linked attributes, which contain values referring to other objects in Active Directory. A prime example of this is the MemberOf attribute on a user object. That attribute contains values that reference groups to which the user belongs.

◆ Data table: This is the largest table in the database. Users, groups, application-specific data, and any other data stored in Active Directory are contained in this table. Think of this table as having rows, where each row represents an instance of an object (such as a user), and columns, where each column represents an attribute in the schema (such as GivenName).

What Happened to NTDS.DIT?

In Chapter 14, "Maintaining the Active Directory Database," we talked about how to perform an offline defrag of the NTDS.DIT file. This is a great procedure you should run to reclaim "white space" from the database file.

What would happen if the file were corrupted, deleted, or missing? The restore process is the same for each of these instances. To restore NTDS.DIT from backup, perform the following steps:

1. Reboot the domain controller.

2. Press F8 at the appropriate time to display the Advanced Options menu.

3. Select Directory Services Restore Mode and press Enter.

4. Log on using the Administrator account and password you specified when you were installing Active Directory on the server.

5. When prompted, click OK at the warning screen that says you will be entering safe mode.

6. Click Start ➢ Programs ➢ Accessories ➢ System Tools ➢ Backup.

7. Select the Restore tab.

8. Click the + button to expand each of the following items:

   ◆ File

   ◆ Media Created

   ◆ System Drive (assuming default installation)

   ◆ Winnt

   ◆ NTDS

9. Click the NTDS folder to display the files in the folder.

10. Click the check box to select the NTDS.DIT file.

11. Leave the Restore Files To box set to Original Location. If you select to restore to an alternate location, you will have to copy the NTDS.DIT file to the location where it is supposed to exist.

12. Click Start Restore.

In some instances, you will want to move a database or log file. To perform this task, follow these steps:

1. Reboot the domain controller.

2. Press F8 at the appropriate time to display the Advanced Options menu.

3. Select Directory Services Restore Mode and press Enter.

4. Log on using the Administrator account and password you specified when you were installing Active Directory on the server.

5. Start a command prompt.

6. Type **ntdsutil.exe**.

7. At the ntdsutil: prompt, type **files**.

8. At the file maintenance: prompt, do the following:

   ◆ To move a database, type **move db to** %s, where %s is the drive and folder where you want the database moved.

   ◆ To move log files, type **move logs to** %s, where %s is the drive and folder where you want the log files moved.

   ◆ To view the log files and database, type **info**.

   ◆ To verify the integrity of the database at its new location, type **integrity**.

   ◆ Type **quit**.

   ◆ Type **quit** to return to a command prompt.

9. Restart the computer in Normal mode.

Circular Logging

This feature is turned off by default, and leaving it turned off follows best practices. Circular logging turns the EDB.LOG file into a first-in, first-out (FIFO) bucket. The data in the file are constantly up-to-date.

Sequential log files grow until they reach a specified size. After that, another log file is created, and so on until all transactions are committed to the database. Every 12 hours, the garbage-collection process deletes unnecessary log files. If your server cannot run for 12 hours between reboots, these files cannot be deleted, and will eventually consume valuable disk space. Enabling circular logging will help minimize the amount of logged data the physical disk must store.

Do we recommend this? No, definitely not! In very few instances—such as the one listed earlier—circular logging makes sense, but the negatives definitely outweigh the positives.

The main reason that circular logging is turned off is for disaster-recovery purposes. If a restore should become necessary, the system will restore the NTDS.DIT from tape and will look at the EDB.CHK file to get a list of all the transactions that occurred since the last backup. The system will then pull in the EDB log files to restore all the changes that occurred since the NTDS.DIT was last backed up. If circular logging is turned on and the Active Directory database hasn't been backed up in a while, transactions will be lost. Because we are working with a FIFO bucket, transactions can be overwritten before they have a chance to be backed up. The resulting changes defined in those transactions will be lost forever.

With storage costs falling and allowing most domain controllers to run with disks that are measured in the hundreds of gigabytes, concerns about saving disk space are not as prevalent as in years past.

Database Capacity Planning

You must consider many factors when planning an Active Directory implementation. One very important step is to plan for proper placement and sizing of the partition where your Active Directory database will reside.

On an Active Directory domain controller, database-file access will probably consume the most processes on that server. Keeping the database on a different partition than the system and boot files will help with performance. By default, the Active Directory database installs itself in the %systemroot%\ntds folder.

When planning your Active Directory implementation, use the ADSizer utility to plan for Active Directory's disk-space requirements. ADSizer will automatically estimate the size of the database for you, based on the following number estimates: each security principal (users, groups, and computers) will consume about 3,600 bytes, while other items, such as share files, may take only around 1,100 bytes each.

Figure 17.1 shows the ADSizer utility, which will lead you through a series of questions and give you recommendations based on your answers.

FIGURE 17.1

The ADSizer utility

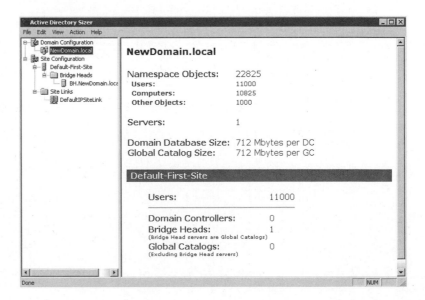

Troubleshooting Active Directory Replication

Nothing is more stressful than having domain controllers that are not sharing information. By their very nature, domain controllers are supposed to be multimaster replicas of one another, and you should have identical information on all domain controllers within a domain. However, some issues can rear their ugly heads and cause you to have a nightmarish day of troubleshooting.

Replication Overview

Understanding how something works is the first part of knowing how to troubleshoot a problem. Whereas having troubleshooting methodology will help you ascertain the problem, you will have a better "feel" for where to start looking for problems if you understand the way something works and behaves.

Active Directory replication is probably one of the most obscure things that you will have to learn. Most administrators know why they need replication, but they don't know how it gets the objects from one domain controller to another. A quick review of the process is in order before we move on to troubleshooting replication problems.

If your DNS infrastructure has issues, Active Directory replication may not work. Verify that your DNS infrastructure is stable and that name resolution is working correctly. Chapter 16, "Troubleshooting Problems Related to Network Infrastructure," covers some of the options you have when maintaining and troubleshooting your DNS infrastructure.

If DNS is working correctly, domain controllers will have a better chance of replicating the objects between one another. The first thing a domain controller does when replicating objects is examine the connection objects to other domain controllers. The domain controller will not be concerned about domain controllers other than those to which it has a connection.

Within the configuration partition, the domain controller will find the domain controllers to which it is connected. Active Directory will return the GUID that is associated with the domain controller defined on the connection object. Each domain controller registers the service locator (SRV) records for the Active Directory services it supports, and its GUID. If you open the _msdcs zone for the domain, you will find the domain controller GUID. Figure 17.2 shows the GUID for the domain controllers within the zygort.Local domain. The GUIDs appear as the last two lines within the details pane.

FIGURE 17.2
Domain controller GUIDs registered in DNS

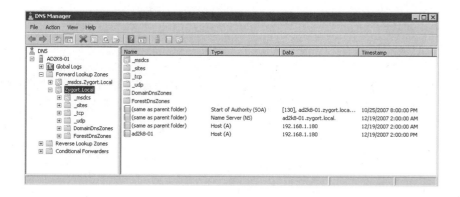

After the domain controller has obtained the GUID for the partner domain controller, it sends a query to DNS to locate the host name; then, using the host name, it queries for the IP address. Once the domain controller has the partner domain controller's IP address, it can initiate a Remote Procedure Call (RPC) connection to the partner and begin the replication process.

Determining DNS Problems

When domain controllers are brought online, they register records within the DNS server they are configured to use. This registration includes the GUIDs that are registered within the _msdcs zone. If the domain controller fails to update its GUID, other domain controllers will not be able to locate it to replicate Active Directory objects. To troubleshoot DNS issues, you can use the DNSLint command. (See Chapter 16 for more information on the additional uses of DNSLint.)

When using DNSLint to troubleshoot Active Directory issues, you need to use the /ad switch. This will force DNSLint to compare the GUIDs within the DNS server to the domain controllers for the domain. The command is issued at the command prompt in the form:

```
Dnslint /ad domain_controller_ip_address /s dns_server_ip_address
```

The /s switch informs DNSLint that you are not going to attempt name resolution to the Internet root domains; instead, you will work with specific DNS servers to validate the name resolution information. For instance, if your domain controller is using IP address 10.23.74.1 and the DNS server that you are testing against is using IP address 10.23.77.5, your command line would appear as:

```
Dnslint /ad 10.23.74.1 /s 10.23.77.5
```

Once issued, DNSLint will attempt to bind to the domain controller to retrieve the GUIDs for all of the domain controllers within the domain. If successful, it will then compare the GUIDs to those within DNS by issuing queries to the _msdcs zone looking for the CNAME records. At this point, the DNS server that you identified when using the /s parameter will need to be authoritative for the _msdcs zone. If it is not, the DNS server must have an entry listed within it that will allow DNSLint to locate a DNS server that is authoritative for the zone.

Once the DNS server is located and the GUIDs are queried, if a positive response is returned, DNSLint will attempt to locate the A record for the domain controller based on the host name that is returned from the CNAME record. If everything is successful, you will not receive any errors on the HTML output that DNSLint provides. Otherwise, you will notice errors and you'll have a starting point when trying to determine why replication is not working correctly. Figure 17.3 is an example of the first half of the HTML report that is generated; it shows the GUIDs that were found.

To check a domain controller that is also configured as a DNS server, you can issue the command DNSLint /ad /s localhost. Doing so will cause DNSLint to use 127.0.0.1 as the IP address of the domain controller, and the internal DNS server as the DNS starting point.

Verifying Replication

You may want to verify that objects have been completely replicated throughout the domain before you attempt to run applications or perform administrative management of the domain controllers. To do so, you can use the dsastat.exe utility from the Support Tools folder located on the Windows Server CD or DVD. This utility will allow you to compare the contents of the Active Directory database so that you can determine whether replication has completed. In its most basic form, you can issue the command and specify only the domain controllers you want to compare, separated by semicolons, such as:

```
Dsastat -s:domaincontroller1;domaincontroller2
```

FIGURE 17.3

DNSLint report showing GUIDs of domain controllers

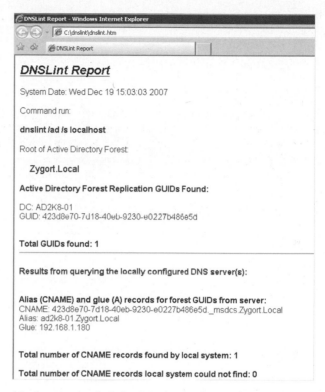

When issuing the command in the zygort.lcl domain for the domain controllers rosebud and milquetoast, the command line would look like this:

```
dsastat -s:rosebud;milquetoast
```

The utility will attempt to make LDAP connections to each of the domain controllers and query the partition information. It will compare both directory databases and return whether or not they are identical. Figure 17.4 shows the response that is returned if the databases are identical, and Figure 17.5 shows the response when replication has not completed.

The dsastat.exe utility can also be used to verify that specific portions of the Active Directory structure are synchronized. For more information on the switches available for use with dsastat.exe, enter **dsastat /?** at the command prompt.

Other tools are available that can provide information about your AD directory service and tell you whether the replicas are up-to-date. The first is the command-line tool RepAdmin, which can be found in the Support Tools. If you are more comfortable using the GUI-based tools, the ReplMon utility is available to perform the same functions. The final tool we will discuss is the DCDiag utility.

USING REPADMIN

The RepAdmin utility can assist you when you are trying to determine the cause of replication problems. Some of its most popular options include checking the status of the Knowledge Consistency Checker (KCC), viewing the replication partners for domain controllers, and viewing which domain controllers have not replicated. If you want to view the KCC status, enter this command:

```
repadmin /kcc
```

FIGURE 17.4

Response from
dsastat.exe if replica-
tion has completed

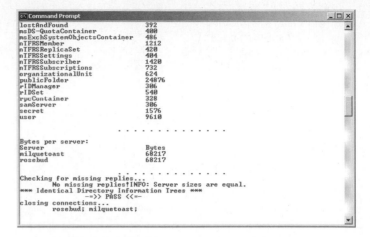

FIGURE 17.5

Response from
dsastat.exe if
replication has
not completed

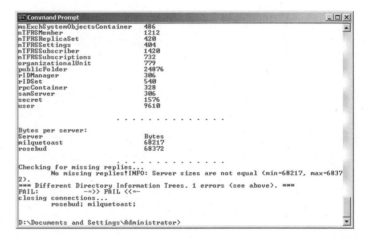

If you want to view the replication status of the last replication attempt from a domain controller's replication partners, enter this command:

```
repadmin /showreps
```

Windows 2000 Server and Windows Server 2003 both use the /showreps option, but the RepAdmin utility included with Windows Server 2003 R2 and Windows Server 2008 Support Tools can use the /showrepl switch to do the same thing. Windows Server 2003 and 2008 also use the /replsummary switch—sometimes abbreviated as /replsum—to allow you to view the failures and replicated objects. You should see a minimum of three connections per domain controller, one connection for each of the directory partitions. If the /showreps or /showrepl options do not display any connections to other domain controllers, you should run the KCC by using the ReplMon utility. If you are working within a Windows Server 2003 or 2008 environment, you can open Active Directory Sites and Services, right-click the NTDS Settings object, and select All Tasks ➢ Check Replication Topology. If you still receive errors because the KCC did not create the appropriate connection objects, manually create a connection object between the domain controllers. (If you use the Check Replication Topology option on the domain controller that is the Inter-Site Topology Generator (ISTG), you will recalculate the intersite and intrasite replication topology. If you run it from any other domain controller, you will recalculate the intrasite topology.)

You can force synchronization for any of the partitions with the RepAdmin tool by using the /sync switch. This will force replication for a specific partition from a replication partner that you use in the command. If you want to force replication between all domain controllers, you can use the option /syncall. By default, the Active Directory replication is *pull replication,* meaning that the domain controller will request the data from its partners. You can change that behavior by using the /P switch, which forces the domain controller to *push* its objects to its partner domain controllers. The command looks like this:

```
repadmin /syncall domain_controller_FQDN directory_partition /P
```

USING REPLMON

ReplMon is the graphical utility that allows you to view the connections between domain controllers and troubleshoot issues with Active Directory replication. It also enables you to view the update sequence number (USN) of the replication partners and the last successful replication time. ReplMon is not installed on Windows Server by default. It is included in the Windows Support Tools, located on the Windows Server CD at \Program Files\Support Tools\.

As shown in Figure 17.6, you can add the domain controllers you want to monitor within the contents pane of the utility and perform tests on them. Beneath the domain controller, all of the directory partitions are listed. When you expand the partition, you will see the replication partner and the replication results for the last replication attempt for that partition. In large environments, this can generate a lot of information for you to view.

The menu in Figure 17.7 shows the options that are available when working with a domain controller. You can perform the same functions from this menu that you can from the RepAdmin command-line utility.

FIGURE 17.6

ReplMon interface

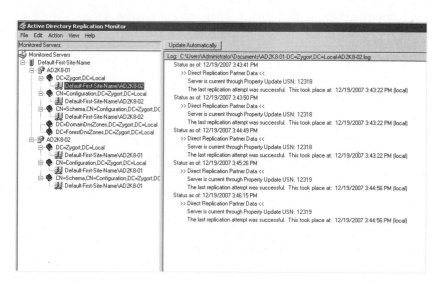

FIGURE 17.7
ReplMon menu
options

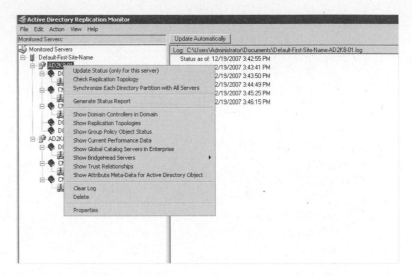

To push the changes from one domain controller to another, you need to enable push mode on the directory partition that you want to force to the partners. To do so, right-click on the partition you want to push, and select the Synchronize this Directory Partition with All Servers option. In the dialog box that appears, you can select the Push Mode option. The other options in this dialog box can also come in handy. The option Disable Transitive Replication will force replication to the partner domain controllers only, and will not cause them to send out notifications to their partners. The option Cross Site Boundaries will allow you to replicate the data to all domain controllers regardless of the site in which they are located.

USING DCDIAG

DCDiag is a command-line utility that will run diagnostic tests against the domain controller. It runs several tests, and the output can span many screens. If you want to perform specific tests against the domain controller, use the /test: switch. For instance, if you want to make sure that the replication topology is fully interconnected, issue the following command:

```
dcdiag /test:topology
```

To test that replication is functioning properly, issue the command:

```
dcdiag /test:replications
```

To view the status of global catalog replication, use the command:

```
dcdiag /v /s:domain_controller_name | find "%"
```

You may have to issue this command a few times from the command line to monitor the progress. As soon as DCDiag has no more output to show, the replication is complete.

Best Practices for Troubleshooting AD Replication

If your domain controllers are not replicating objects correctly, users will not be able to gain access to the objects they need, and may fail to log on at all. Keep the following tips in mind when troubleshooting replication issues:

Real World Scenario

CONTROLLING REPLICATION IN LARGE ORGANIZATIONS

Celeste is the administrator of a large manufacturing company. Lately she has noticed CPU and memory performance issues on the bridgehead servers as they attempt to compress data that need to be sent between sites. Celeste has determined that the problem lies with the KCC and ISTG functions. Currently they run at the default setting, every 15 minutes, to calculate and repair the replication topology. This adds additional load on the domain controller in this large environment.

Celeste decides to implement the Active Directory Load Balancing (ADLB) tool to perform advanced load-balancing tasks within the forest. This allows her to configure load balancing on her domain controllers and to set time staggering on her Windows 2003 and Windows 2008 servers.

Time staggering allows Celeste to stagger the replication schedule, allowing her to stagger the updates for the directory partitions so that they are not sent at the same time.

- ◆ Use the tool you are most familiar with when troubleshooting replication problems, but become familiar with the tools you are not used to using.

- ◆ Verify the replication topology to make sure all of the domain controllers from all sites are interconnected.

- ◆ Urgent replication—such as account lockouts—will occur within the site, but will not be replicated to other sites until the site link allows it to replicate. Use RepAdmin to force the change.

- ◆ Create connection objects between domain controllers that hold FSMO roles and the servers that will act as their backup if the FSMO role holder fails. Make sure replication is occurring between the two servers.

Troubleshooting FSMO Roles

In Chapter 5, "Flexible Single Master Operations Design," we discussed the Flexible Single Master Operations (FSMO) roles and where you should place each one. Because there can be only one domain controller holding each of the roles, you need to make sure you keep them operational. Of course, with some of these roles, getting them up and operational is more important than it is with others; however, you should still know what is required to get them into an operational state.

This section deals with making sure you know which FSMO roles you need to repair immediately and which ones you can probably leave offline for a while. It also covers how you can move the roles to other domain controllers and how you can have another domain controller take over roles in case of an emergency.

FSMO Roles and Their Importance

Each FSMO role is important within the forest. Without them, you will not have a means of identifying objects correctly, and data corruption can occur if two or more administrators make changes to objects within the forest. As we move through this section, we'll introduce each of the FSMO roles and how important it is to get each one back online immediately. If you are familiar with the FSMO roles, you may want to head directly to the "Transferring and Seizing FSMO Roles" section later in this chapter.

For efficiency's sake, you should identify (in advance—don't wait until the worst-case situation) another domain controller that could be used as the role holder if the original role holder were to fail. You have to do very little to configure another system to become the standby server. Realistically, you should have the role holder and the standby on the same network segment, and they should be configured as replication partners of one another. This will give you a higher probability that all of the data is replicated between the two systems in case the role holder fails.

SCHEMA MASTER

The Schema Master controls all the attributes and classes that are allowed to exist within Active Directory. Only one Schema Master can reside within the forest. The domain controller that holds the role of Schema Master is the only domain controller that can make changes to schema objects within the forest. Once changes are made to a schema object, the changes are replicated to all other domain controllers within the forest.

You should not be too concerned if the Schema Master goes offline. The only time that you will need the Schema Master is when you have to make changes to the schema, either manually or when installing an application that modifies the schema. The forest can exist and function for an extended period of time without the Schema Master being online. If you cannot repair the Schema Master and you need to make a change to the schema, you can seize the role on the standby domain controller.

DOMAIN NAMING MASTER

Like the Schema Master, there can be only one Domain Naming Master within the forest. This is the domain controller that is responsible for allowing the addition and deletion of domains within the forest. When dcpromo is executed and the creation of a new domain is specified, it is up to the Domain Naming Master to verify that the domain name is unique. The Domain Naming Master is also responsible for allowing deletions of domains. Again, as dcpromo is executed, the Domain Naming Master is contacted, and the domain being deleted will then be removed from the forest by the Domain Naming Master.

Losing the Domain Naming Master should not affect an organization's day-to-day operations. The only time the Domain Naming Master is required to be online is when a domain is added or removed from the forest. As with the Schema Master, you can allow the Domain Naming Master to remain offline as you try to recover the domain controller. If the Domain Naming Master is still offline when you need to add or remove a domain, or if the original role holder is not recoverable, you can seize the role on the domain controller that has been identified as the standby server.

INFRASTRUCTURE MASTER

If you are working in a multiple-domain environment, the Infrastructure Master can be your best friend or your worst enemy. It is the Infrastructure Master's job to make sure that accounts from other domains that are members of a group are kept up-to-date. You do not want an account to have access to resources that it is not supposed to, and if changes are made to users and groups in other domains, you will need to make sure that the same changes are reflected in your domain. For instance, suppose the administrator of bloomco.lcl has just added two accounts to a global group and removed one from the group. Within the bloomco.lcl domain, the changes are replicated throughout. Within your domain, there is a domain-local group that contains the global group. Because the changes are not replicated to domain controllers within your domain, the user who was removed from the group might still have access to resources within your domain, and the two new accounts might not.

The Infrastructure Master must be able to maintain the differences between domains so that the correct group membership can be applied at all domain controllers. This is why the Infrastructure

Master should not be on a domain controller that is acting as a global catalog. The Infrastructure Master will contact a global catalog and compare the member attributes for the groups with the attributes that are contained within its domain. If there is a difference, the Infrastructure Master updates the attributes to keep everything synchronized. If you want to change the default scanning interval for the Infrastructure Master, you can set the following registry value from two days to whatever value works best in your environment:

```
HKEY_LOCAL_MACHINE\System\CurrentControlSet\Services\
NTDS\Parameters\Days per database phantom scan
```

For more information on the Infrastructure Master and how to control the scanning interval, see Knowledge Base article 248047 at `http://support.microsoft.com/kb/248047/en-us`.

Loss of the Infrastructure Master is a little more severe than the loss of the previous two master operations roles. If the Infrastructure Master is offline for an extended period of time, the data cannot be synchronized and users could have access, or be denied access, to the wrong objects. If you cannot resolve the problem with the Infrastructure Master, you may want to seize the role on the standby server.

RELATIVE IDENTIFIER MASTER

Whenever a security principal, such as a User, Group, or Computer account, is created within Active Directory, it has an associated security identifier (SID). A SID consists of the domain's SID and a relative identifier (RID) that is unique to the security principal. Allocating and keeping track of all of the RIDs for the domain is the RID Master's responsibility. Having the RID Master allows you to sleep better at night knowing that a duplicate SID will not be generated within the domain. Even if the security principal associated with a RID is deleted, the RID will still not be regenerated and used again.

A SID is an alphanumeric combination that is not easy to understand. There is a logic behind the madness, however. A SID for a user account may look like this:

```
S-1-5-21-1068514962-2513648523-685232148-1005
```

Broken down, the sections that make up the SID fall into these categories:

S The initial character *S* identifies the series of digits that follow as a SID.

1 This is the revision level. Every SID that is generated within a Windows environment has a revision of 1.

5 This third character is the issuing-authority identifier. Most SIDs will have the Windows NT issuing-authority number of 5, but some of the well-known built-in accounts will have other values.

21 The fourth character set represents the subauthority. The subauthority identifies the service type that generated the SID. SIDs that are generated from domain controllers will contain the characters 21, while built-in accounts may have other characters, such as 32.

1068514962-2513648523-685232148 This long string of characters is the unique part of the SID for a domain. If you are working with local accounts, it represents the unique SID for the computer.

1005 The last set of characters represents the RID for the account. The RID Master starts at 1000 and increments by 1 for every RID it allocates to the domain controllers.

Because any domain controller within a native-mode domain can generate a RID to an account, you must make sure that only one domain controller is allocating and controlling the RIDs. For this reason, make sure that you do not seize the RID role on a domain controller when the original role holder is unavailable only temporarily. You could cause yourself a nightmare trying to trouble-shoot permission problems.

If the RID Master role were lost, you might miss it sooner than you would some of the others. The RID Master allocates blocks of RIDs to the domain controllers within the domain. If a domain controller uses up its last RID while creating a security principal, it will no longer be able to create security principals. Another drawback to losing the RID Master is that you cannot promote another domain controller without the RID Master online. For these reasons, you should attempt to recover the original RID Master role holder as quickly as possible or seize the role on the standby server.

PRIMARY DOMAIN CONTROLLER EMULATOR

The PDC Emulator was created to allow an Active Directory domain to work in mixed mode with Windows NT domains. The PDC Emulator allows for replication of directory information from Active Directory to Windows NT 4 Backup Domain Controllers (BDCs). Many administrators will get confused by this and think that this role is only needed until all NT4 BDCs are taken offline. This is far from true however, as the PDC Emulator is probably the busiest of the FSMO role servers.

The main task of the PDC Emulator is to allow for replication of directory information to Windows NT4 BDCs while the domain is still in mixed mode. This server is also the only domain controller that will create security principals while the domain is in mixed mode.

This server is also the only domain controller that is allowed to change passwords for legacy operating systems such as Windows 98 and Windows NT. By nature, these servers look for the PDC of the domain and the PDC emulator fulfills that role. Whenever an account changes its password, the domain controller that is making the change will check with the PDC Emulator to make sure the user's password has not been changed before it notifies the user that the wrong password was entered.

The PDC Emulator is also responsible for time synchronization and global policy centralization. All domain controllers within the domain look to this role holder as the official timekeeper within the domain. The PDC Emulator can bet set to synchronize its time with an external time source so all of the other domain controllers in the domain will have the correct time. In a multiple-domain forest, the PDC Emulator for the forest root becomes the Time Master for all PDCs within the forest.

Group policy changes are performed on the PDC Emulator by default. Making one domain controller the default Group Policy Object (GPO) holder allows you to control policy changes and to minimize conflicting changes within the domain.

Transferring and Seizing FSMO Roles

Transferring a FSMO role to another system is a rather painless process. Because all of the domain controllers within a domain have identical data within the Active Directory database, when you transfer a FSMO role, you are simply changing a flag that specifies that one domain controller can control the master operation and the other cannot.

Seizing a FSMO role has serious implications. If you are going to take this drastic step, you must commit yourself and make sure that the original role holder is never reintroduced onto the network. Reintroducing it could cause serious problems within your Active Directory infrastructure.

The following sections discuss the methods you can use to identify the systems that currently hold the master operations roles, and the methods you can use to make sure the domain controller identified as the standby server can take over a role.

IDENTIFYING THE CURRENT ROLE HOLDER

There are several ways to identify which domain controller is holding a FSMO role. With some of these options, you will be able to see all of the role holders at one time; with others, you are forced to view them separately.

Built-in Active Directory Tools

You can view which domain controllers host four of the five roles by using the Active Directory Users and Computers (ADUC) and Active Directory Domains and Trusts (ADDT) snap-ins. Using ADUC, you can identify the PDC Emulator, RID Master, and Infrastructure Master role holders. ADDT will allow you to identify the Domain Naming Master. To get to the screen shown in Figure 17.8, you need to open ADUC, right-click on the domain name, and select Operations Masters.

Figure 17.9 shows the Domain Naming Master when you choose the Operations Masters option from the context menu available when you right-click the Active Directory Domains and Trusts label within the ADDT snap-in.

FIGURE 17.8

FSMO roles listing in Active Directory Users and Computers

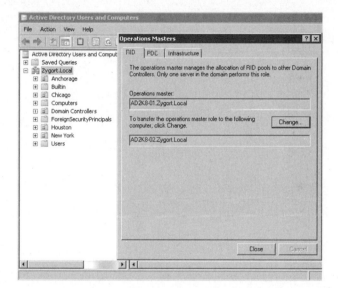

FIGURE 17.9

Domain Naming Master role as seen in Active Directory Domains and Trusts

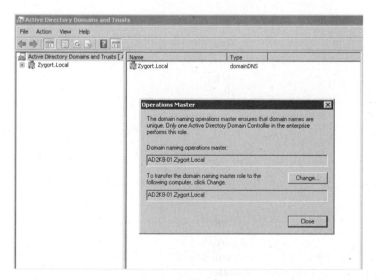

Active Directory Schema The Active Directory Schema snap-in is listed separately because it is not available by default. To access this snap-in, you must register its associated dynamic link library (DLL). To do so, type **regsvr32 schmmgmt.dll** at the run line or at a command prompt. After you receive a message stating that the DLL is registered, you can add the snap-in to a Microsoft Management Console (MMC). You can view the Schema Master role holder, as shown in Figure 17.10, by right-clicking the Active Directory Schema container within the MMC and selecting Operations Master.

ReplMon This tool was discussed in Chapter 15, "Microsoft's Troubleshooting Methodology for Active Directory." In addition to the benefits that we introduced in that chapter, Rep1Mon has the ability to view the role holders within the domain. When you add a monitored server to the console, you can view its properties by right-clicking on the server and choosing Properties. As shown in Figure 17.11, you can view all five of the role holders from the FSMO Roles tab. Note the naming convention for the RID Master (Rid Pool) and Domain Naming Master (Domain Tree Operations).

FIGURE 17.10
Schema Master role as seen in Active Directory Schema snap-in

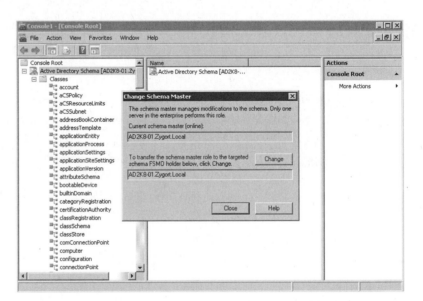

Command-Line Options

Some command-line utilities allow you to identify the role holders. The first, netdom, will show you all of the role holders at the same time. The second, dsquery, will allow you find individual roles when you ask for them. The DCDiag utility will show you all of the roles. The final utility is from the Windows Server resource kit, dumpfsmos.cmd.

netdom The netdom command syntax that will report the role holders is as follows:

```
netdom query fsmo /domain:zygort.1c1
```

Of course, you would replace *zygort.1c1* with your domain name. This will return a list of all of the role holders.

FIGURE 17.11
Identifying the roles using ReplMon

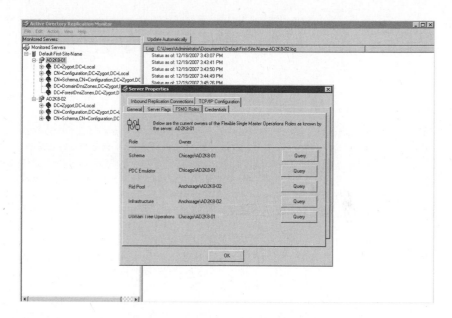

dsquery To find individual role holders with the dsquery command, use the following commands:

- ◆ To find the Schema Master:

```
dsquery server -hasfsmo schema
```

- ◆ To find the Domain Naming Master:

```
dsquery server -hasfsmo name
```

- ◆ To find the Infrastructure Master:

```
dsquery server -hasfsmo infr
```

- ◆ To find the RID Master:

```
dsquery server -hasfsmo rid
```

- ◆ To find the PDC Emulator:

```
dsquery server -hasfsmo pdc
```

DCDiag The DCDiag utility is used as follows:

```
dcdiag /test:knowsofroleholders /v
```

Because the verbose switch (/v) is used, this command will return the role holders and give you information on each.

dumpfsmos.cmd   The dumpfsmos.cmd utility from the Windows Server resource kit is a small script that actually starts NTDSUtil and issues the appropriate commands to return a list of the role holders. The syntax for this command is:

```
dumpfsmos.cmd zygort.lcl
```

Of course, you would want to replace *zygort.lcl* with the name of the domain you are querying against.

TRANSFERRING THE ROLE TO ANOTHER DOMAIN CONTROLLER

If you are demoting a role holder, be sure to transfer the role to another domain controller, preferably the domain controller you have designated as the standby role holder. Doing so will guarantee that you are transferring the role to the appropriate domain controller instead of allowing dcpromo to choose another domain controller on its own. Remember: it is always better to have control over these things than to allow chance to control your organization. (If you are taking a domain controller offline permanently, whether it is a role holder or not, you should demote it so that the references to the domain controller are removed from Active Directory.)

Transferring the role to another domain controller is a very simple process. Using the snap-ins that we discussed in the "Identifying the Current Role Holder" section, you can simply connect to the domain controller that you want to be the new role holder, choose the Operations Master option to view the role holder, and click Change. Look back at Figure 17.8 and note that the snap-in is currently connected to the domain controller rosebud.zygort.lcl. The RID Master role is currently held by milquetoast.zygort.lcl. When you click the Change button, the role will be transferred to milquetoast.zygort.lcl.

You can also use NTDSUtil to transfer the roles. To do so, start a command prompt and enter the ntdsutil command. Once the ntdsutil: prompt appears, enter the following commands:

1. At the ntdsutil: prompt, type **roles** to enter fsmo maintenance.

2. At the fsmo maintenance: prompt, type **connections** to enter server connections.

3. At the server connections: prompt, type **connect to** *server domain_controller*, where *domain_controller* is the name of the domain controller to which you are going to transfer the role.

4. At the server connections: prompt, type **quit** to enter fsmo maintenance.

5. At the fsmo maintenance: prompt, type one of the following to transfer the appropriate role:

   ◆ To transfer the Schema Master:

   ```
   transfer schema master
   ```

   ◆ To transfer the Domain Naming Master:

   ```
   transfer domain naming master
   ```

   ◆ To transfer the Infrastructure Master:

   ```
   transfer infrastructure master
   ```

- To transfer the RID Master:

```
transfer rid master
```

- To transfer the PDC Emulator:

```
transfer PDC
```

After you have transferred the role, type **quit** twice to exit NTDSUtil. You can then use one of the aforementioned utilities to verify that the role was transferred to the appropriate domain controller.

SEIZING THE ROLE ON THE STANDBY DOMAIN CONTROLLER

You should have already designated another domain controller as the standby server in case a role holder becomes unavailable. If you have configured the original role holder and the standby as replication partners, there is a very good chance they are completely synchronized with one another. If the original role holder becomes unavailable and you deem it necessary to have the standby server become the role holder, you can seize the role on the standby server. Again, this is a drastic measure and should be performed only if you are certain the original role holder is not going to be reintroduced on the network.

To seize a role, follow steps 1 through 4 as outlined in the preceding section, "Transferring the Role to Another Domain Controller." Once you have connected to the domain controller that will become the role holder, use one of the following commands from the NTDSUtil `fsmo maintenance:` prompt:

- To seize the Schema Master:

```
seize schema master
```

- To seize the Domain Naming Master:

```
seize domain naming master
```

- To seize the Infrastructure Master:

```
seize infrastructure master
```

- To seize the RID Master:

```
seize rid master
```

- To seize the PDC Emulator:

```
seize PDC
```

Now that the role has been seized, type **quit** twice to exit NTDSUtil. Verify that the role has been taken over by the new role holder. If the original system is repaired and could be used again, make sure you reformat the system and reinstall the operating system. This will guarantee that you will not introduce problems within Active Directory by having a rogue role holder in place.

The PDC Emulator and Infrastructure roles are designed for "graceful seizure." This means that the old role holders can be brought back online after a seizure with no ill effects. If a domain controller does go offline and you are not going to reintroduce it to the network, be sure to remove all references to the domain controller within Active Directory. See Chapter 14 for information on removing orphaned objects.

Best Practices for Troubleshooting FSMO Roles

Just a few pointers here, but they are good to remember:

◆ Do not seize a role unless you are positive you will never reintroduce the original role holder to the network.

◆ If demoting a role holder, transfer the role to another domain controller first.

◆ Keep documentation that identifies the role holders and the domain controllers that are designated as the standby servers.

Troubleshooting Logon Failures

Nothing is more frustrating for users than attempting to log on first thing on a Monday morning, only to receive an error. Immediately their workweek is off to a bad start. Troubleshooting is your realm, so it's up to you to determine what is causing the problem and to set things back on track. Within an Active Directory domain, several things could be at fault.

If you are using a Windows Server 2003– or Windows Server 2008–based domain, the default password policy uses complex passwords. Although this is a good policy to use from the standpoint of most of your security auditors, you will find that it can cause additional headaches. Complex passwords, while more secure, are also more difficult for users to remember. You will probably end up unlocking users' accounts and changing their passwords for them more often than you would with simpler passwords. You will also run into the problem of users writing down their passwords and leaving them close to their systems. Controlling passwords, monitoring authentication, and maintaining a sensible password and lockout policy will help you minimize logon problems, but you will still be forced into troubleshooting these issues.

Auditing for Logon Problems

As with any troubleshooting, you should start with checking out the event logs on the client system and the domain controllers within their sites. Although many administrators criticize the event logs, you can find out some interesting and useful information from them. If you have enabled auditing of account logon and logon events, you will receive events in the security log that pertain to accounts as they authenticate—or fail to authenticate. To watch for failures, you must audit the failure of authentication by using an audit policy. Once you do that, you can peruse the audit log for specific entries if users start having difficulty authenticating.

Figure 17.12 shows an example of a GPO that is being used to implement auditing for a domain. When you choose the options to audit and you want to see information concerning authentication, you should set the options shown in Table 17.1.

Setting Failure for Audit Account Logon Events will tell the system to send an event to the security log any time a domain user account fails to authenticate. Doing the same thing for Audit Logon Events will audit a local-account authentication failure. Successful changes to any account, whether it is a password reset or the unlocking of an account, will be registered by the Audit Account Management setting.

FIGURE 17.12
Audit Policy in a GPO

FIGURE 17.12
Audit Policy in a GPO

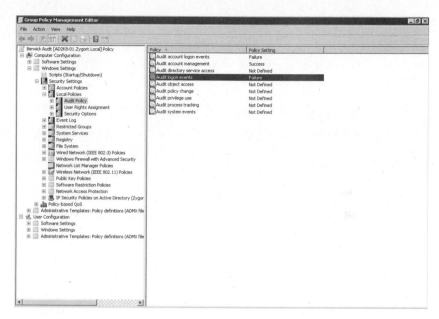

TABLE 17.1:   Audit Settings for Monitoring Domain Logon Problems

AUDIT OPTION	SETTING
Audit Account Logon Events	Failure
Audit Account Management	Success
Audit Logon Events	Failure

Once these settings are enacted, you will be able to view the security logs for common events. On domain controllers, you can look for information concerning account lockouts and changes to the accounts. Event ID 675 will show you the IP address of a client computer from which the bad password originated. If this IP address is not the computer from which the client normally authenticates, it may be an indication of an attack on the account. Event ID 644 will appear if the Audit Account Management auditing option is set for Success. This event is generated any time an account is locked out because of improper credentials.

You can also view the security logs on client systems and search for common Event IDs. Event 529 is recorded if the system does not have the user account that is attempting to log on. This could be due to the user accidentally pressing the wrong keys when they are logging on, but it could also be an indication of someone trying to hack into a system by guessing an account name. Event ID 531 indicates that the account that was attempting to authenticate is locked out or has been disabled by an administrator.

Table 17.2 lists the Event IDs you will encounter as you troubleshoot logon failures and account lockouts.

TABLE 17.2: Logon Event IDs

EVENT ID	DESCRIPTION
528	Successful interactive logon
529	Failed logon: Due to either unknown account or bad password.
530	Failed logon: Time restrictions prohibited authentication.
531	Failed logon: Account disabled.
532	Failed logon: Expired account.
533	Failed logon: Computer restrictions do not allow logging on to the chosen computer.
534	Failed logon: Disallowed logon type.
535	Failed logon: Expired password.
536	Failed logon: NetLogon is not available to accept authentication request.
537	Failed logon: The reason for the logon failure may not be known.
538	The logoff process was not completed.
539	Failed logon: Account locked out.
540	Successful network logon
541	The local computer and its partner completed the main mode Internet Key Exchange (IKE) authentication, or quick mode has established a data channel.
542	Data channel terminated.
543	Main mode was terminated.
544	Main mode authentication failed due to invalid certificate, or the signature was not validated.
545	Main mode authentication failed due to Kerberos failure or invalid password.
546	IKE security association establishment failed due to invalid proposal.
547	IKE handshake failure
548	Failed logon: The security identifier (SID) from a trusted domain does not match the client's account domain SID.
549	Failed logon: SIDFiltering filtered out all SIDs that correspond to untrusted namespaces during an authentication across forests.

TABLE 17.2:   Logon Event IDs *(CONTINUED)*

EVENT ID	DESCRIPTION
550	A denial-of-service (DoS) attack may have occurred.
551	User logged off.
552	A user successfully logged on to a computer using explicit credentials while logged on as a different user.
672	Kerberos successfully issued and validated an authentication service (AS) ticket.
673	Kerberos successfully granted a ticket-granting service (TGS) ticket.
674	An AS or TGS ticket was renewed.
675	Preauthentication failed. The key distribution center (KDC) generates this event if an incorrect password is entered.
676	Authentication ticket request failed. This event is not generated in Windows XP or in the Windows Server 2003 or higher family.
677	A TGS ticket was not granted. This event is not generated in Windows XP or in the Windows Server or higher family.
678	An account was successfully mapped to a domain account.
681	Failed logon: A domain account logon was attempted. This event is not generated in Windows XP or in the Windows Server 2003 or higher family.
682	A user has reconnected to a disconnected terminal server session.
683	A user disconnected a terminal server session without logging off.

Figure 17.13 shows an example of an event that was generated as a user attempted to log on to a system. Take note of the data within the event, especially the Logon Type entry. You can determine the kind of logon attempt that was attempted. Table 17.3 describes the logon types and the code that is entered into events.

acctinfo.dll

The acctinfo.dll file is actually part of the Account Lockout and Management Tools you can download from Microsoft, which we discuss later in the "Account-Lockout Problems" section. Once added into your system, acctinfo.dll includes an additional property page for the user-account properties. As Figure 17.14 shows, this additional property page will allow you to determine when the account's password was set, when the password expires, when the user last logged on or off the domain, as well as other lockout information.

FIGURE 17.13
Logon event

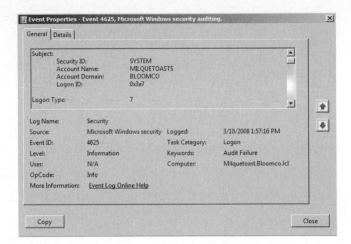

TABLE 17.3: Logon-Type Codes

TYPE	REASON RECORDED	CODE
Interactive Logon	User logged on directly on a computer.	2
Network Logon	User connected to the computer from a remote computer.	3
Batch	Account was authenticated when used from a batch queue.	4
Service	Account used by a service when the service was started by a service controller.	5
Unlock	Credentials entered to unlock a locked account.	7
NetworkClearText	Account was authenticated with a clear-text password.	8
NewCredentials	Account connected to the system after password was changed.	9
RemoteInteractive	Account authenticated from a remote system, but the account is used interactively through a Terminal Services session.	10
CachedInteractive	The user was logged onto the computer using cached credentials.	11

One of the best features of `acctinfo.dll` is that it allows you to change a user's password on a domain controller within the site where the account is used. This allows you to make the change on a domain controller close to the user so that you do not have to wait until replication passes the password change across the site links. Figure 17.15 shows the screen that appears once you have clicked the Change Password on a DC in the Users Site button. You'll still have the option to reset the password normally, but you will also have the additional site-level options.

FIGURE 17.14
acctinfo.dll
property page

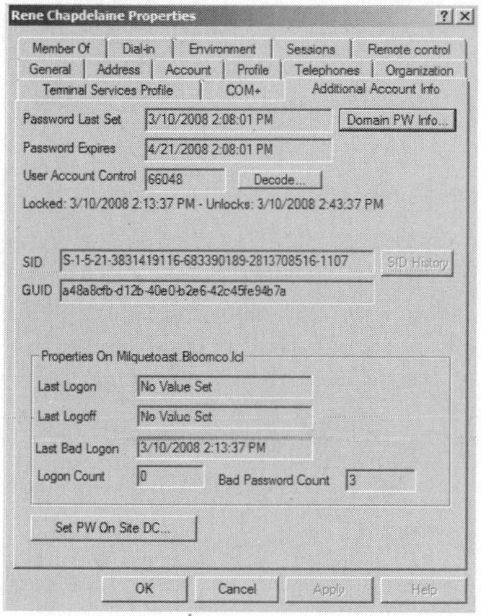

FIGURE 17.15
Set Password on a DC
in the Users Site

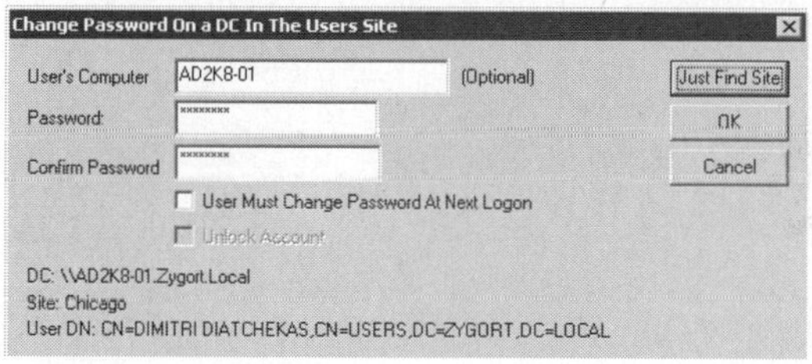

Kerberos Logging

You can have the system present more-detailed information concerning authentication by turning on Kerberos logging. To do so, you can either edit the registry manually or run a script provided within the Account Lockout and Management Tools (see the "Account-Lockout Problems" section for more information). If you plan to edit the registry on a domain controller to enable Kerberos logging, you will need to open `regedt32` and navigate to the following registry key:

```
HKLM\System\CurrentControlSet\Control\LSA\Kerberos\Parameters
```

You must add the REG_DWORD entry `LogLevel`. If you set the value of this entry to 1, you will be able to monitor the system event log for Event ID 4. If Event ID 4 appears in the log, it will indicate that a bad password was sent to the Kerberos service for authentication or that the account was locked out. If the error code within this event specifies `0x18 KDC_ERR_PREAUTH_FAILED`, the password was incorrect. An error code of `0x12 KDC_ERR_CLIENT_REVOKED` indicates that the account was locked out.

Native-Mode Logon Problems

Once you have switched your domain out of Windows 2000 mixed mode, you will be required to have global catalog servers available. Windows 2000 native, Windows Server 2003, and Windows

Server 2008 functional levels require that a global catalog server be available so that a user's universal group membership is checked prior to authentication. Universal security groups do not exist within a Windows 2000 mixed-mode domain. However, once you have changed your domain to support them, each user's universal group membership is checked to make sure that the user is not a member of a universal group that has been denied permission to a resource.

Problems occur when you have replication issues between domain controllers, and the universal group membership is not replicated to the local global catalog server. A user who is a member of a universal group could be denied access to a resource because the replicated information has not arrived at the domain controller to which the user is authenticating. The same is true about having access to resources to which the user should be explicitly denied access. If the global catalog has not received the new group membership, the user could access resources that you want to prevent them from accessing.

As important as it is to know which resources the user should be able to access, the requirement of having a global catalog server online can cause logon issues for some administrators. Take, for instance, an organization that has remote offices and, because of bandwidth restrictions, the administrative staff has decided not to use any of their domain controllers as global catalogs within those offices. Global-catalog queries are sent to a nearby site that has a global catalog. However, if the users attempt to log on and they cannot contact a global catalog in the nearby site, whether because of downed WAN links or unavailable global catalog servers, those users will not be able to log on to the domain.

Starting with Windows Server 2003, Microsoft addressed this limitation with a feature known as universal group membership caching. You enable this feature on a per-site basis, and any Windows Server 2003 or higher –based domain controller will start using it. As users authenticate, the domain controller servicing the request will query a global catalog server within another site for the user's universal group membership and then cache the details. (Global catalog caching will support a maximum of 500 users per site. Also, the cache is updated only once every eight hours. You should not consider this option if you have frequent group updates or many users.)

If your domain does not have any Windows Server 2003 or higher–based domain controllers, you will have to either configure a domain controller within the office as a global catalog server or turn off the universal group membership requirement. The latter is not a recommended solution, however, because the user could be allowed to access resources for which he or she should not have permissions. The inverse could also occur; the user could be denied access to resources that she or he needs to use. If you want to turn off group membership checking when global catalog servers are unavailable, navigate to the following registry entry:

```
HKEY_LOCAL_MACHINE\SYSTEM\CurrentControlSet\Services\NTDS\Parameters
```

From there, you will need to add a new key called `IgnoreGCFailures`. This will tell the domain controller to authenticate a user even though the universal group membership is not evaluated for the user's access token. Again, we stress that this is not a secure way to run your organization. However, if you are not using universal groups or if you are desperately seeking a way to allow your remote users to authenticate when WAN link failures occur, you can implement this fix.

Account-Lockout Problems

Having the ability to lock out accounts when they are being attacked is a great security feature; however, this policy can cause some headaches. If the settings are too restrictive, users will lock themselves out by mistyping their passwords. If they are not restrictive enough, you potentially open up a security hole that will allow accounts to be attacked. Another potential problem occurs if you have the settings too restrictive and you do not reset the bad-password count when users authenticate; they could become locked out of their accounts because of scripts that map drives because the scripts have the wrong password associated with them. The most common causes of account lockouts are discussed here:

Programs   Several programs store a user's credentials so that the program can access resources that it requires. If the user changes her or his password but the program still has the credentials cached, the user's account could become locked by the program trying to authenticate.

Reset Account Lockout Counter After setting   You should consider keeping this setting at the default level of 30 minutes or higher. If this setting is too low, you could cause a false lockout as programs attempt to access resources. Cached credentials or mapped drives that attempt to connect with invalid credentials could also cause lockouts if this setting is too low.

Domain controllers are instructed to deny the last two passwords that a user has used; if these two passwords are entered, they will not increment the bad-password count. Most of the common account-lockout problems can be resolved by installing the latest service pack from Microsoft.

Persistent drive mappings   If a user has a persistent drive mapping, and that mapping has an incorrect or old password, the account associated with the mapped drive could become locked as the user attempts to access it.

Outlook and Outlook Web Access   If you are using email clients to access mail stored on an Exchange server, and the client has cached the password for the account, the multiple attempts made to access the user's mail could result in a locked-out account.

Disconnected terminal-server sessions   Terminal-server sessions from which a user has disconnected will remain running on the server. If the user changes his or her password while the session is running, the session still uses the original password. If applications running within the session attempt to access resources, they could cause the account to become locked.

Microsoft addressed these issues with Windows 2000 Server SP4. Windows Server 2003 and later releases do not have this issue.

In case you still have issues with locked-out accounts, Microsoft has released a set of tools called the Account Lockout and Management Tools that you can use when troubleshooting account-lockout problems. The included tools are discussed in the following paragraphs. You can download them from the Microsoft website at the following location:

```
http://www.microsoft.com/downloads/details.aspx?FamilyId=7AF2E69C-91F3-4E63-
8629-B999ADDE0B9E&displaylang=en
```

LockoutStatus.exe   As shown in Figure 17.16, `LockoutStatus.exe` displays information concerning a locked-out account. Use this tool to determine which computers were involved in the lockout by the account and when the lockout occurred. You need to copy this tool to the same directory as `AcctInfo.dll` is on if you want to have access to it from the user-account properties. This tool is also available from the Windows Server Resource Kit.

FIGURE 17.16

LockoutStatus.exe showing information about a user account

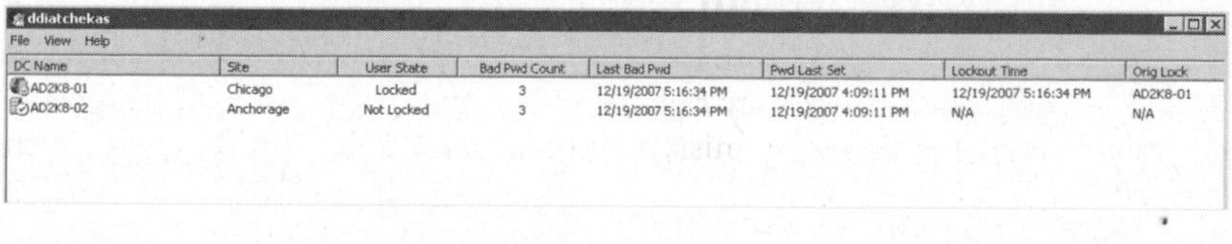

DC Name	Site	User State	Bad Pwd Count	Last Bad Pwd	Pwd Last Set	Lockout Time	Orig Lock
AD2K8-01	Chicago	Locked	3	12/19/2007 5:16:34 PM	12/19/2007 4:09:11 PM	12/19/2007 5:16:34 PM	AD2K8-01
AD2K8-02	Anchorage	Not Locked	3	12/19/2007 5:16:34 PM	12/19/2007 4:09:11 PM	N/A	N/A

ALockout.dll   This tool, when configured on a system, will monitor the account-authentication attempts and deliver the results to a file named `ALockout.txt` that is stored in the `winnt\debug` directory. To use this tool, copy the `ALockout.dll` and `appinit.reg` files, which are included in the Account Lockout and Management Tools, to the `systemroot\system32` folder. Once they are copied, double-click on the `appinit.reg` file to embed the registry entries into the computer's local registry and reboot the system to activate the changes.

ALoInfo.exe   If you want to view all of the accounts and the associated password ages, you can run this command at the command line. This will allow you to view the accounts that are about to have their passwords expire so that you can anticipate the flood of calls that will occur right after the new passwords go into effect.

AcctInfo.dll   As mentioned previously, `AcctInfo.dll` will add another property page to the user's account properties within Active Directory. Figure 17.17 shows the Additional Account Info tab that is available from the user's property page. Once you click on this tab, you can click the Domain PW Info button to display the Domain Password Policy window seen in Figure 17.18. To install `AcctInfo.dll`, type **regsvr32 acctinfo.dll** at a command prompt or from the run line. You will need to close and reopen Active Directory Users and Computers for the change to take effect. You should also have `LockoutStatus.exe` loaded to get lockout information available from this new property page.

EventCombMT.exe   This tool will search through the event logs on several systems looking for events you have specified. The default events for which the tool will search are 529, 644, 675, 676, and 681. You can add additional event IDs if you know which events you want to search. You can also control how many threads are used during the search so that you do not consume too many resources within the domain. The fewer threads you specify, the longer the search will take.

EnableKerbLog.vbs   This is a script that changes the registry to enable Kerberos logging. Once it has been run, additional events are sent to the event log so you can monitor what the Kerberos service is doing during account authentication.

NLParse.exe   NLParse is used to find `NetLogon` status codes that have been dumped to the `netlogon.log` file when `NetLogon` logging has been enabled. It will dump the data that it finds into a comma-separated value file that you can pull into a spreadsheet or database. Several codes can be searched on, but 0X0000006A and 0x0000234 are the default options.

Any time you are troubleshooting logon and account-lockout problems, start by enabling `NetLogon` logging and then view the logs to determine which domain controllers may be involved. `NetLogon` logging has been available since Windows NT 4, and it was used to check the PDC within the domain. You can still use this tool to view the interaction between the domain controllers and the PDC Emulator. To enable `NetLogon` logging, open a command prompt and enter the command **nltest /dbflag:0x2080ffff**. This will create a log file called `netlogon.log` within the *systemroot\Debug* directory. (After running the `nltest` command to enable `NetLogon` logging, if the `netlogon.log` file does not exist, stop and restart the `NetLogon` service.)

When you view the `netlogon.log` file on the PDC Emulator, you can look for instances of event 0xC000006A for authentication requests that have been passed to the PDC Emulator from other domain controllers. To differentiate between authentication requests that are sent directly to the PDC Emulator and those that are passed to it from other domain controllers, note the reference within the entries that shows transitive network logons and the domain controller that passed the request. In the log file, any line that shows the entry "via" displays the computer on which the user was attempting the logon and the domain controller that the user was authenticating against. If the password is not valid on the domain controller, the user's credentials are sent to the PDC Emulator to verify that the user's password has not been changed recently, but the password is not yet replicated to the domain controller. (Because of the additional overhead consumed when you are logging the NetLogon service, you should turn off the logging when you have finished troubleshooting. To do so, run the command **nltest /dbflag:0x0**.)

FIGURE 17.17
Domain Password
Policy screen

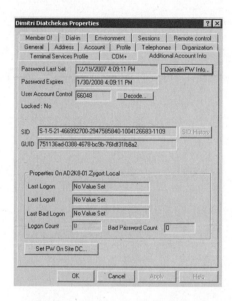

FIGURE 17.18
Property page added
by acctinfo.dll

Because the netlogon.log files can be as much as 10 MB in size, you may want to use the NLParse utility to ease your searching woes. With NLParse, you can select the codes for which you want to search, and have the utility load the results into a comma-separated value (.csv) so that you can view the results in a spreadsheet. You have several options to choose from, but you should start by taking the default options of searching for status codes 0xC000006A and 0xC0000234. These two codes will reveal the authentication attempts and the domain controller that locked out the account. Using the resulting .csv file will help you determine whether the lockout was due to a program or service, because the user would send several attempts within a matter of a second or two. If the attempts came from a user account, there would be a few seconds between attempts. Table 17.4 details the status codes that you will find in a netlogon.log file and that you can search for with NLParse.

TABLE 17.4: NLParse Status Codes

STATUS CODE	DESCRIPTION
0x0	Successful logon
0xC0000064	User does not exist.
0xC000006A	Incorrect password
0xC000006C	Password policy not met.
0xC000006D	Bad username
0xC000006E	User account restriction prevented successful logon.
0xC000006F	Time restrictions prevented user from logging on.
0xC0000070	Workstation restrictions prevented user from logging on.
0xC0000071	Password has expired.
0xC0000072	The user account is currently disabled.
0xC000009A	Insufficient system resources
0xC0000193	User's account has expired.
0xC0000224	User must change password before the first logon.
0xC0000234	The user account has been locked.

Remote-Access Issues

If you are using the Routing and Remote Access Service (RRAS) as a remote-access server, you need to make sure that the remote-access policies are configured correctly. Several layers of control are associated with these policies, and a user could be stopped from authenticating even before she or he connects to the network.

Remote-access policies are not stored within Active Directory; they are configured on a per-server basis. With this in mind, you should make sure that all of the RRAS servers to which a user will connect have the same policy parameters. Otherwise, the user's connection attempts could be erratic.

The only way to guarantee that the RRAS servers are using the same policy is to configure an Internet Authentication Service (IAS) server with a policy and make each RRAS server a client of the IAS server. This still does not store a copy of the policy within Active Directory, but you will have a central repository for the remote-access policies.

Are You Being Attacked?

Account-lockout policies are not simply for administrators to test the patience of their users; they are used to protect an organization's resources against attack. Companies that are very cautious or that have very sensitive data can set the lockout count to between 3 and 5, but most companies I'm familiar with have a policy setting between 5 and 7. This should be sufficient when your users mistype their passwords, and it should protect the network sufficiently.

If you are not sure whether you are under attack or if you have a user problem, look through the `NetLogon` log files on your domain controllers to determine the extent of the problem. Your PDC Emulator will be a central location for the events to be recorded. Any time a bad password is entered, the PDC Emulator is checked to validate the attempt. If you see several accounts with bad passwords, and there are 15 to 20 attempts on each account, chances are that an attack is occurring, either internally from a virus or Trojan program, or from an external source attempting to hack an account.

Check the computer that appears in the status code to determine if a rogue program is attempting to authenticate. If the computer that is listed within the status code is a remote-access server, an external account could be attempting to attack the network.

Controlling WAN Communication

Typically, a user will log on within the same site most of the time. Within a site, when a user changes a password, he or she does not have to worry the password change replicating to other domain controllers throughout the organization. If this is the case, you can reduce the replication traffic sent between remote sites and the site where the PDC Emulator is located.

To do so you need to add the `AvoidPdcOnWan` value under the `HKEY_LOCAL_MACHINE\System\CurrentControlSet\Services\Netlogon\Parameters` registry key. If you set the value to 1, the domain controller will ignore sending password updates as a critical update when the PDC Emulator is located in another site. A setting of 0 restores normal operation.

When you turn this value on (set the value to 1), the PDC Emulator receives the password change during the normal replication cycle. Note that if the user does travel to another site prior to the replication of the password change, that user may be denied access to the network if her or she is trying to use the new password.

Best Practices for Logon and Account-Lockout Troubleshooting

Nothing frustrates administrators and users alike more than logon issues. The calls that flood in right after a mandatory password change can be frustrating, but if you follow the information in this chapter, and especially the following tips, you may be able to reduce the resulting headache.

- Only enable universal group membership caching if you want to reduce the replication across a WAN link and you have a small number of users who will be affected.

- Only turn off universal group membership enumeration for a native-mode domain unless you are not using universal security groups.

- Turn on auditing for account logon and account management so that you can identify logon failures and can determine the causes.

- Take advantage of the new Account Lockout and Management Tools to aid in troubleshooting account lockout.

- Monitor the PDC Emulator for authentication attempts. All attempts with a bad password are forwarded to the PDC Emulator.

- Turn off logging when it is not necessary so it does not consume additional resources.

Coming Up Next

The next part of the book (Part 5, "Streamlining Management with Scripts") discusses scripting techniques you can use in your AD DS environment. Throughout the next four chapters, you will learn time-saving techniques that will allow you to manage your AD DS environment more efficiently.

The Bottom Line

Problems with the AD DS database can cause a multitude of issues in your environment. Determining what is causing a problem with the database can be difficult. Being prepared with a wide array of tools will help you narrow down the issues and come to a quick resolution.

Troubleshoot database replication   Keeping information current and in sync is very important to the health of your AD DS database. Replication is the technology that keeps all domain controllers up-to-date with changes from other domain controllers.

> **Master It**   Marcus is the administrator of a large nationwide distribution company. He receives a call that states that Joe Davis from the sales department has been fired and that his account must be disabled as soon as possible.
>
> Marcus disables the account, but because Joe is a traveling employee, he could log in from anywhere on the domain. Instead of waiting for replication to occur at its regularly scheduled time, what should Marcus do to trigger replication to ensure the change propagates through the network immediately?

Troubleshoot FSMO roles   FSMO roles are unique in an Active Directory environment because they are the only domain controllers that are not fault-tolerant. The roles that these domain controllers host could be lost if a domain controller were to fail. You must plan specifically to ensure you can recover these special roles quickly.

> **Master It**   Low is the Active Directory administrator of a medium-size bank. While installing a new server on the domain, The dcpromo task fails when Low tries to promote it to a domain controller. After some investigation, Low finds that the domain controller that holds the RID Master FSMO role is down and it cannot be recovered. What should he do next?

Troubleshoot logon failures   FSMO roles are unique in an Active Directory environment because they are the only domain controllers that are not fault-tolerant. The roles that these domain controllers host could be lost if a domain controller were to fail. You must plan specifically to ensure you can recover these special roles quickly.

> **Master It**   Ginger is the administrator of a large robotics-manufacturing company. Her company is often the target of hackers who are interested in trade secrets and intellectual property.
>
> Ginger starts receiving a lot of help-desk tickets for locked-out accounts. She determines that someone is trying to log into the network using known usernames. She must determine where the login attempts are coming from.

Part 5

Streamlining Management with Scripts

In this part:

Chapter 18

ADSI Primer

By this point in the book, you should have a good understanding of Active Directory—what it is and what it can do. You've been working with AD from the outside, using the tools supplied by Microsoft. Now we're going to start working with AD from the inside, where we're going to write the tools. To accomplish this, we need a way to communicate with the directory service itself, and that's where Active Directory Services Interface (ADSI) comes in.

In this chapter, you'll learn to:

◆ Connect to Active Directory using the ADSI provider

◆ Understand how the schema affects the objects stored in Active Directory

◆ Read and write the properties available in Active Directory, objects such as Users, Groups, and Organizational Units

◆ Develop a Lightweight Directory Access Protocol (LDAP) query to retrieve objects from Active Directory

◆ Use a common, consistent approach to writing scripts that manipulate Active Directory

What Is ADSI?

ADSI stands for Active Directory Services Interface, but that name is not entirely accurate. The name implies that it is just an interface for working with Active Directory, when in fact it can work with a number of directory service providers, including Novell's NetWare Directory Services (NDS) and Bindery Services for NetWare 3.12 and below.

ADSI vs. Active Directory

It is not uncommon for administrators to confuse ADSI with Active Directory. Active Directory is the Microsoft directory service provider of choice for Windows domains. It holds the objects that define your domain, including sites, subnets, users, computers, printers, and so on. You can consider it a database of sorts and treat it as such. When you create a new user or other object, Active Directory's job is to house it. The task of creating that user, however, falls on the shoulders of ADSI.

ADSI is an object-oriented programming interface, but it is not a language. Rather, it is a toolset for directory services that is used by the programming language. You can think of it as a set of properties and routines focused on doing one job: manipulating a directory service. ADSI is built on Component Object Model (COM) technology, which allows it to work with any programming language that supports COM (and it's tough finding one that doesn't anymore!). The examples in this book and the downloadable samples are in VBScript, but if you choose to use another language, you are more than welcome to!

COM Interfaces

COM technology gives programming languages the ability to communicate and work with programming objects. You can think of COM as a set of windows that you can look through and open to get access to an object. These sets of windows are called *interfaces*. Each object implements at least one interface for access to the object, and it is not uncommon for Active Directory objects to implement more than one. The individual interfaces themselves are beyond the scope of this book; however, you can find more information on them if you research ADSI objects further.

By defining a valid set of operations for an object, COM interfaces act like a programming contract. A contract spells out what you can and sometimes what you cannot do. If we try to do something outside the bounds of that contract, we are very likely going to get errors. Most Active Directory objects implement a standard set of interfaces, allowing you to access the same properties and operations on different types of objects. Some objects will also implement an interface that provides specific functionality unique to that type of Active Directory object.

So how do we know what we can and cannot do? We study the object model that we want to work with. We read the documentation (ADSI is well documented on the Web), and we resort to a little good old-fashioned trial and error. As we work through examples in this book, you will see what works and what does not, and we will talk about why some things do not work.

ADSI Providers

One of ADSI's most endearing qualities is its ability to play well with others. This refers not only to its language independence, but also to how many directory services with which it can interact. Active Directory was not the first directory service on the block, and the Active Directory we know today definitely will not be its last version. In the ever-expanding corporate world, where companies routinely take over other companies and have to integrate information systems, there's a good chance you might run into another directory service with which you will have to work and play. Not to worry, though—ADSI has you covered.

Active Directory is just one of several directory services with which ADSI can communicate. To provide this kind of support, ADSI implements a provider-based architecture. This means that you, the programmer, specify the directory service provider you want to use, and ADSI takes care of the details. When you tell ADSI to create a user object, it looks at the provider and does exactly what that directory service expects to create a new user object.

Think of it like turning on a television. You could likely walk into any store right now and fire up every make and model of television sitting on the shelf. But do you know how those televisions work internally? Probably not, and you probably don't care either. Power circuits start supplying juice to the tuners, which get the signal from the cable and feed it into a processor, and sooner or later you wind up with a picture on the tube. Your main concern is that when you press the power button, the picture shows up on the screen. Let the television take care of the details. This is how we work with ADSI; our concern is working with the objects in Active Directory, and we will let ADSI handle the details.

Let's take a quick look at some of the providers ADSI supports. Obviously ADSI supports Active Directory. Because Active Directory is based on the Lightweight Directory Access Protocol (LDAP), we use the LDAP provider to connect to Active Directory. The LDAP provider is used for working with domain controllers, which most of our scripting activity will be focused on, but there is also a provider supplied for communicating with global catalog servers. For working with Microsoft Security Accounts Manager (SAM)–based domains (NT 4 and earlier), ADSI supplies a Windows NT provider. Novell's NetWare Directory Service (NDS) and Bindery Services (NetWare 3.12 and earlier) are supported as well. These, and a few others we will soon get to, are the major players.

Now we need to talk about locating and connecting with our provider of choice. To do this we will create a statement, which is something like a street address. We'll specify which object in the directory service we want to work with, and how we want to communicate with that object. See if this statement looks familiar: `http://www.sybex.com/sybexbooks.nsf/booklist/4305`.

It looks like a URL you would type into Internet Explorer, right? It's basically an address that says, "Using the HTTP protocol, find a web server called www.sybex.com, and on that server look in the `sybexbooks.nsf/booklist` folder and show me the 4305 file" (that is not exactly what it is doing, but work with me here!). Now look at this statement:

```
LDAP://CN=Scott,CN=Users,DC=zygort,DC=com
```

Following the same basic address idea (but reading the address portion from right to left), this says, "Using the LDAP protocol, find the domain named zygort.com, look in the Users container and show me any object with the common name of 'Scott.'" By specifying LDAP as the protocol to use, I am telling ADSI to communicate with a directory service that supports LDAP (which is probably Active Directory in our case). LDAP is the moniker of the statement, and the moniker is used to specify the protocol.

Table 18.1 lists the ADSI provider names (or monikers). We'll use these names to specify which directory service provider we want to work with.

TABLE 18.1:   ADSI Providers

PROVIDER NAME	DESCRIPTION
LDAP	Used with Windows 2000/2003/2008 Active Directory as well as other LDAP-compliant sources
WinNT	Used with Windows NT to access information in the SAM database
GC	Used with Windows 2000/2003/2008 Active Directory to access information stored on a global catalog server
NW	Used for Novell Directory Services (NetWare 4.x and later)
NWCOMPAT	Used for Novell Bindery Services (NetWare 3.x and earlier)
IIS	Used for accessing IIS data

As if the list in Table 18.1 were not enough, one more provider is available for accessing a directory service through an object linking and embedding database (OLE DB) connection. The name for this provider is `ADsDSOObject`. However, this is not a moniker; it is not used to reference an individual object in Active Directory. Instead, it is used for writing queries to pull information out of your directory service. When you think of OLE DB, think of databases. This provider will let you treat the directory service like a database. A programmer familiar with ActiveX Data Objects (ADO) can query the directory service for information and cycle through the results. This stream of data is read-only, which means you cannot do updates directly through it. If you are not familiar with ADO, rest assured; we will discuss it later in this chapter.

Now let's spend some time getting to know the objects we will work with in Active Directory. You are probably familiar with most of these objects on a high level, but now it is time to open the hood and get our hands a little dirty exploring what exactly is inside the data store known as Active Directory.

Active Directory Objects

By now you have created several users and other objects in Active Directory. You are probably so familiar with Active Directory Users and Computers (ADUC) that you could create a new user in your sleep, right? That's good—but that is also not so good, because what you know about users in ADUC is not what you're going to see through ADSI. It will take a little getting used to, and some good documentation, but it will be second nature to you soon enough.

Everything in Active Directory is stored as an object. Users are stored as user objects, computers are stored as computer objects, and so on. A user and a computer are obviously different types of entities, so it only makes sense that they are stored as different types of objects. Another commonly used term for objects is *entity*, but I will use the term *object*. So, what exactly is an object?

An object is basically a programming structure. In a nutshell, an object holds values that describe the object and the code that is designed to operate that object. Right now that explanation probably does you very little good, so try this analogy: Think of an object as a house. What do you know about a house? It usually has windows, it's usually painted one main color (unless it's the Partridge family house!), and it probably has switches that turn the lights on and off.

Properties

Think about the color of our house for a moment. What color is it? In our object, the color is stored as a *property*, sometimes called an *attribute*. Your house has other properties as well. How many windows does it have? Does it have a fireplace? Now consider a user object and think about the properties it might have. The first name, last name, and account name are some (but not all) of the properties of the user object.

These properties have names, and this is where things start to turn tricky during your first foray into ADSI. In ADUC, you know which field to type in to change a user's first name (I don't have to tell you that field name, do I?). But in ADSI you won't find the `first name` property anywhere. You won't find the `last name` property anywhere either, because that is simply not what these properties are named in the object itself.

Nope, you get to learn a whole new set of names that correspond to the fields you see in ADUC. For example, the First Name field corresponds to the `givenName` property in ADSI. The Last Name field corresponds to the `sn` property (short for *surname*). We will discuss the property names in more depth when we talk about the specific objects in Active Directory.

And no, I didn't mistype the `givenName` property. That is actually how the property name appears in the schema. When you look at the schema later on, the property name will be referred to as the `ldapDisplayName`. The formatting of the name is created using a method of composing programming names known as camel-casing. A variable or property name might be composed of several words. Those names can't have spaces in them (trust me; you do not want spaces in them!), so to visually set each word apart, the first letter of each word is capitalized, with the exception of the very first word. Of course, with every rule there are the occasional exceptions.

Methods

Going back to our house analogy, we have switches that turn on the lights, which is similar to invoking an object's method. You might hear the term *function* as well, but the proper term when working with objects is *method*. A method simply tells the object to do something; in the case of our house, we're turning on the lights. Other methods might be to open the garage door or lower the shades. Think about the things that a user object can do, such as setting a password. There is no password field in the user object, so the only way to set it is through a method call. Objects in Active Directory have a typical set of methods you can use, and some also have more specialized methods. For example, the Organization Unit object, because it is a type of container object, has a method to create new objects.

INTERFACES VS. LDAPDISPLAYNAME

Object properties can be accessed in one of two ways: through an interface or through Get/Put methods with the ldapDisplayName. After binding to an object, an interface can be applied to the object (depending on its type) that will associate a "friendly" name for the property to its ldapDisplayName. For example, accessing User.givenName is the same property as User.Get("givenName"). Not every property is mapped by the interface, and some binding methods will not use the full interface for the object at all.

Which method you use is entirely up to you, but we advise you to choose one and stick with it. The Get/Put methods are handy for two reasons: consistency and flexibility. You can always use a Get method to retrieve an object property, regardless of the applied interface. It is also much easier to use a string variable for the ldapDisplayName and change it on the fly in your script than it is to work around a group of hard-coded property names used by the interface.

Schema

As you probably remember, the Active Directory schema is where we define what makes up an object. The names that correspond to the fields in our standard administration tools are defined in the schema. To develop scripts that work successfully with Active Directory, we need to look at the schema and get a feel for how it works. Most administrators do not work with Active Directory at this level except when making schema modifications. In fact, to ensure consistent results, most schema modifications have been automated with scripts to some degree, so there is even less reason for administrators to open the schema tools.

Every object in Active Directory, whether it is a user, a computer, or anything else, was created from information stored in the schema. The schema contains the blueprints for every type of object that can be created in a particular implementation of Active Directory. It describes the properties for each object created from those blueprints. The blueprint for an object is known as the *class* for that object.

The terms *class* and *object* are used interchangeably all too often. A class is an abstract entity; it cannot actually do anything because it really does not exist as a "physical" object. The class exists only in the schema, and it exists only to create objects. The object is the physical implementation of the class we can work with in Active Directory. The process of creating the object is referred to as creating an *instance* of an object, or *instantiation*.

The terms *property* and *attribute* can also be used interchangeably, but in this case the practice is a little more acceptable. When we refer to an attribute, we are usually referring to the name of a property in the class definition, which has not yet been instantiated into an object. A property is used to refer to the actual value in the instantiated object.

Let's go back to our house analogy. Have you ever seen two houses that look almost identical, except that one is painted white and the other is painted beige? It is a good bet those houses were built from the same set of blueprints—a common practice in the building industry as well as in Active Directory. Every object in Active Directory comes from the same set of blueprints, whether it is a user, a computer, or whatever. This means that they are all created with the same attributes and methods. By changing a property associated with an object, such as the account name, we make it unique in our domain and set the appropriate values.

The schema supplied with a standard installation of Active Directory is well-documented and available on the Web. You can print the documentation and study it until you are blue in the face, but to really get a feel for how the schema is implemented in Active Directory, you need to see it in action. You can do this using the tools available with your Windows Server installation or by downloading the Windows Server Resource Kit.

Tools

Some of the tools we talk about in this section are designed for modifying the schema itself. Rest assured; we won't perform any updates in this book. You should not need special permissions to view the schema, and you definitely do not need membership in the Schema Admins group!

Let's start with the most basic tool, the `dsquery` utility, which is available after you install the `adminpack.msi` from the Windows Server 2008 CD. This utility lets us view the schema and properties of objects in Active Directory. To view a class's attributes, open a command prompt and run the following command; you will need to replace *<domain>* with the domain controller (DC) elements of your domain (such as `DC=zygort,DC=com`).

```
dsquery * cn=computer,cn=schema,cn=configuration,<domain>
-scope base-attr *
```

It's complete, but definitely not fun to read, as you can see in Figure 18.1.

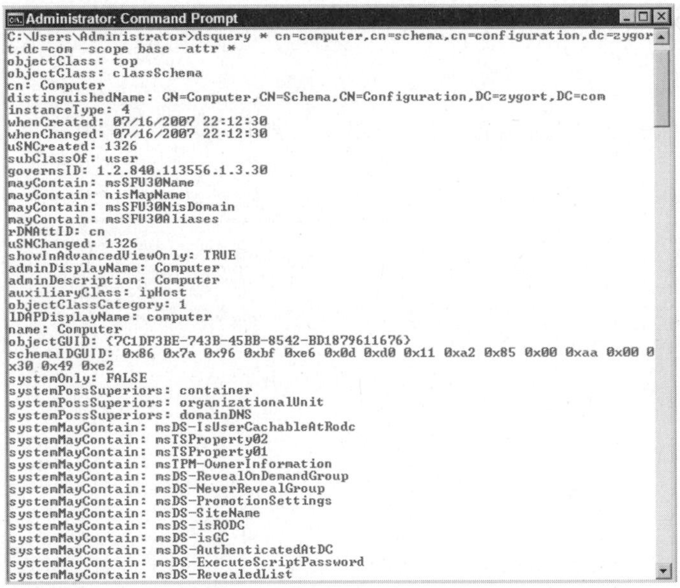

```
Administrator: Command Prompt
C:\Users\Administrator>dsquery * cn=computer,cn=schema,cn=configuration,dc=zygor
t,dc=com -scope base -attr *
objectClass: top
objectClass: classSchema
cn: Computer
distinguishedName: CN=Computer,CN=Schema,CN=Configuration,DC=zygort,DC=com
instanceType: 4
whenCreated: 07/16/2007 22:12:30
whenChanged: 07/16/2007 22:12:30
uSNCreated: 1326
subClassOf: user
governsID: 1.2.840.113556.1.3.30
mayContain: msSFU30Name
mayContain: nisMapName
mayContain: msSFU30NisDomain
mayContain: msSFU30Aliases
rDNAttID: cn
uSNChanged: 1326
showInAdvancedViewOnly: TRUE
adminDisplayName: Computer
adminDescription: Computer
auxiliaryClass: ipHost
objectClassCategory: 1
lDAPDisplayName: computer
name: Computer
objectGUID: {7C1DF3BE-743B-45BB-8542-BD1879611676}
schemaIDGUID: 0x86 0x7a 0x96 0xbf 0xe6 0x0d 0xd0 0x11 0xa2 0x85 0x00 0xaa 0x00 0
x30 0x49 0xe2
systemOnly: FALSE
systemPossSuperiors: container
systemPossSuperiors: organizationalUnit
systemPossSuperiors: domainDNS
systemMayContain: msDS-IsUserCachableAtRodc
systemMayContain: msTSProperty02
systemMayContain: msTSProperty01
systemMayContain: msTPM-OwnerInformation
systemMayContain: msDS-RevealOnDemandGroup
systemMayContain: msDS-NeverRevealGroup
systemMayContain: msDS-PromotionSettings
systemMayContain: msDS-SiteName
systemMayContain: msDS-isRODC
systemMayContain: msDS-isGC
systemMayContain: msDS-AuthenticatedAtDC
systemMayContain: msDS-ExecuteScriptPassword
systemMayContain: msDS-RevealedList
```

FIGURE 18.1
dsquery of computer class attributes

A friendlier option is the ADSI Schema Microsoft Management Console (MMC) snap-in. Prior to Windows Server 2008, this snap-in was available after installing the Windows Support Tools. With Windows Server 2008, it is included right out of the box, but the dynamic link library (DLL) must be registered before you can add it to the MMC console. The following command makes it available:

```
Regsvr32 schmmgmt.dll
```

You can now open an MMC console and add the Active Directory Schema snap-in (I like to save the console to easily open the ADSI Schema utility later), and dig into the object classes available in your Active Directory structure. By selecting an individual object (such as the computer object), you can view all the attributes that are available when an object is created in Active Directory based on that class.

Pay particular attention to the Type column; it tells you if an attribute is mandatory or optional (Figure 18.2). Mandatory attributes will be very important when we begin creating Active Directory objects in our scripts. Basically, you cannot create an object successfully unless you supply values for all mandatory attributes of an object class.

FIGURE 18.2

The ADSI Schema application

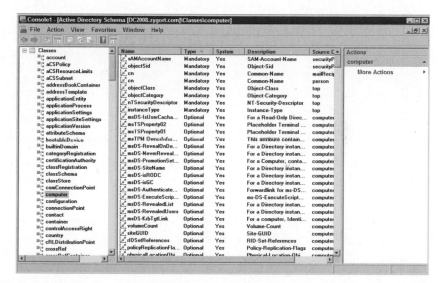

Still, the AD Schema tool isn't ideal for script writers working with Active Directory. My favorite tool for developing an Active Directory script used to be the Active Directory Viewer, which was available as part of the ADSI software-development kit. Alas, all good things must come to an end, and it is no longer available (unless you know someone with deep archives).

Microsoft provides Active Directory Explorer (AD Explorer for short) as a replacement for the Active Directory Viewer. This tool is part of the SysInternals tool suite written by Bryce Cogswell and Mark Russinovich. You can download it from `http://technet.microsoft.com/en-us/sysinternals/bb963907.aspx`.

AD Explorer is a great tool. For starters, it lets you view Active Directory objects and their properties. You can work not only with the domain objects, but (assuming you have the correct privileges) also with objects in the Schema and Configuration containers. One of my favorite features, hands down, is the ability to take a "snapshot" of the current Active Directory database. You can use this to take "before" and "after" snapshots of any Active Directory operation to see what has changed.

After you start AD Explorer you'll see options for connecting to a domain. If you leave all fields blank and click the OK button, AD Explorer will automatically connect to the default domain using your current credentials.

After connecting, you'll see a tree with branches that lead to the Schema and Configuration containers and with a branch that points to your domain. Start by expanding the domain branch and exploring the objects in your domain.

After downloading and installing the Windows Server Resource Kit (SRK), execute the viewer application (`adsvw.exe`). In the New window, select ObjectViewer and click OK. In the New Object window, deselect the User OpenObject check box and enter **LDAP://** along with your domain naming context into the Path field, as shown in Figure 18.3.

FIGURE 18.3
Active Directory
Explorer

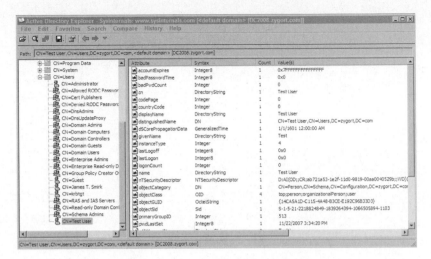

Spend some time using AD Explorer to select various objects, especially object types, and cycle through the properties. Make correlations between the actual property names and their friendly names in Active Directory. Print the documentation listing the properties of the objects you will deal with most frequently (users, computers, OUs, etc.) and note the properties of most interest to you. Even after a brief hiatus from writing Active Directory scripts, it is easy to forget the simplest of property names (such as sn).

Inheritance

When you are comfortable navigating the schema, let's get back to the business of mandatory and optional attributes. Mandatory attributes require a value before you can successfully create the object in Active Directory. If an optional attribute is empty, you can still create the object. Use the following dsquery statement to look at the computer class (cn=computer). Again, you will need to replace <domain> with the DC elements of your domain.

```
dsquery * cn=computer,cn=schema,cn=configuration,<domain>
-scope base Â -attr * | find "systemMustContain" /I
```

How many mandatory attributes for this class did you find? I'm guessing none. So does that mean you can just create a computer object without giving it so much as a name? Of course not. Just imagine how hard it would be to map a drive to a computer with no name. Every object has some mandatory properties; we just have to find them.

Confession time: I asked you to use dsquery for a reason; it shows you the definition of the one class (and only the one class) that was specified. Now try looking at the computer class with the MMC and Active Directory Schema snap-ins. You will get slightly different results, namely some additional attributes that happen to be mandatory. But if those mandatory properties are not defined in the computer class, where did they come from?

The answer lies in understanding the concept of *inheritance*. Just as your kids might inherit your hair color, classes can inherit attributes from parent classes. Using parent classes makes Active Directory more efficient. By defining attributes in a parent class and then inheriting those attributes into child classes, the class designer does not have to redefine the same attributes over and over for multiple classes. Think about it: why would you want to put an attribute called *name* into every single class you might ever create when you can create it once and let inheritance do the work for you?

The use of inheritance creates a hierarchical set of classes in the Active Directory schema. One class is inherited into another class until the final child classes are created and ready to use. The top-most class in the schema is top. The attributes (mandatory and optional) of top are then inherited by classes such as person and organizational-person.

So the mandatory attributes we are looking for actually lie in one or more of the parent classes. But who is the parent? Looking at the computer object's schema again, find the value of the subClassOf attribute. This attribute points to the parent class, which in the case of the computer class happens to be user. I bet you weren't expecting that, were you? Here is the ancestry of the computer class:

```
computer -> user -> organizational-person -> person -> top
```

As you work your way through each of these classes you will notice that mandatory attributes start appearing with the top class. The person class adds another, but the organizational-person and user classes don't add any. In addition, optional attributes are inherited from the parent classes. Eventually, we wind up with a fully formed computer class, completely defined and ready to use.

Now that you are getting the hang of inheritance, let's find out where something important—such as the account name—is defined. But this time, let's do it the easy way by using the MMC and Active Directory Schema snap-ins. The account-name property is stored as sAMAccountName. Looking at the computer object, you can see a Source Class column that points to the class that defines the account-name attribute. The source class for sAMAccountName is securityPrincipal; however, the securityPrincipal class is not in the inheritance diagram we saw earlier. If we did not inherit from securityPrincipal, how did that attribute get there?

Auxiliary Classes

To answer the question in the previous section, we must look at what kind of class we are talking about. Active Directory has four different types of classes (shown in Table 18.2). Some classes can be used to create objects and some classes cannot. Of the four types of classes, only structural classes can be instantiated.

TABLE 18.2:   Class Types

TYPE	CATEGORY	DESCRIPTION
88	0	These classes were defined before there was a specification to classify categories of classes. They behave like structural classes but should be treated as abstract.
Structural	1	Active Directory objects are most often created from these classes. This includes users, computers, and OUs.
Abstract	2	These classes provide attributes that child classes inherit. Active Directory objects cannot be created from these classes.
Auxiliary	3	These classes provide additional attributes to a structural class. Active Directory objects cannot be created from these classes.

When looking at a class's schema, you can determine the type of class by examining the `objectClassCategory` attribute. This attribute contains a number that corresponds to the class type.

`securityPrincipal` is an auxiliary class; it provides additional attributes to the structural class. This class is very important in that it allows positive identification of a created object, which is the first step in providing security. Because it is an auxiliary class, it cannot be instantiated.

Understanding inheritance and the role of classes in the Active Directory schema helps you write scripts that return the properties of the objects you are looking for. Even more importantly, if you develop your own scripts, inheritance makes your job a lot easier. If you know how one class implements an attribute, and that attribute is used in other classes because of inheritance, you already know how to use that attribute in all the other classes.

Common Active Directory Objects

We have talked about the schema and how it defines the attributes that make up an object in Active Directory. Now it is time to look more closely at the objects with which we will be dealing. We do not cover all the object classes or every single property and method here, but we do talk about the most common ones you will be working with as you develop your ADSI scripts.

As we look at the properties and methods, we mention some COM interfaces that implement those operations. ADSI implements core interfaces for all Active Directory objects and specific interfaces for specific object types. We do not go into the interfaces themselves, but we do mention the functionality they provide. The property names provided in the tables in the following sections are the `ldapDisplayNames` we use in our scripts.

Common Properties and Methods

The `IADs` interface, implemented by all ADSI objects, describes the basic features of every object. It provides identification, a reference to the Parent-container, and schema definition, and enables the object to load its properties into the local property cache and commit any changes made to the directory service. Tables 18.3 and 18.4 describe the properties and methods, respectively, common to all Active Directory objects.

TABLE 18.3: Common ADSI Properties

PROPERTY	DESCRIPTION
ADsPath	Active Directory path to the object.
distinguishedName	Fully qualified name; specifies the complete path to the object.
objectGUID	Globally unique ID of the object.
Name	Relative name (RN) of the object.
objectClass	Schema class of the object.
objectCategory	Category of the object. This is usually the same as the `objectClass` value, but not always.

TABLE 18.4: Common ADSI Methods

METHOD	DESCRIPTION
GetInfo	Loads all property values of the object into the local property cache
SetInfo	Writes property values from the local property cache to the directory service
Get	Gets a value by the property name
Put	Sets a value by the property name
GetEx	Gets property values from the local property cache
PutEx	Sets property values into the local property cache
GetInfoEx	Loads specific property values from the directory service

Container Properties and Methods

Container objects in Active Directory are designed to manage child objects, including their creation and removal. The IADsContainer interface implements most of this functionality and is used by containers and organizational units. Tables 18.5 and 18.6 describe the properties and methods, respectively, of the container object.

TABLE 18.5: Container Properties

PROPERTY	DESCRIPTION
Cn	Container's common name
Description	Container's description
distinguishedName	Container's distinguished name
Name	Container's name

TABLE 18.6: Container Methods

METHOD	DESCRIPTION
GetObject	Retrieves an interface to the child object in the container
Create	Creates an instance of a child object in the container
Delete	Removes a child object from the container
CopyHere	Copies a child object into the container
MoveHere	Moves a child object into the container

Organizational Units

Organizational units (OUs) manage other objects in the Active Directory hierarchy; they use the same properties and methods as the container. Note that OUs cannot be created inside a container object. This is a restriction of the Active Directory schema. The only way to change this behavior is by modifying the organizationalUnit class to allow the container object to be a possible superior to an organizational unit. Tables 18.7 and 18.8 show the properties and methods, respectively, of the Organizational Unit object.

Organizational units also have properties similar to those of user objects, such as telephone and fax numbers, but they are rarely used and difficult to access without a custom application.

TABLE 18.7:   Organizational-Unit Properties

PROPERTY	DESCRIPTION
Cn	Organizational unit's common name
Description	Organizational unit's description
distinguishedName	Organizational unit's distinguished name
Ou	Organizational unit's name
managedBy	Distinguished name of the organizational unit's manager
Name	Organizational unit's name

TABLE 18.8:   Organizational-Unit Methods

METHOD	DESCRIPTION
GetObject	Retrieves an interface to the child object in the container
Create	Creates an instance of a child object in the container
Delete	Removes a child object from the container
CopyHere	Copies a child object into the container
MoveHere	Moves a child object into the container

User Properties and Methods

The IADsInterface manages user accounts in the directory. This interface inherits from the IADs interface described earlier, so it also contains the properties and methods described with that interface. Because we will work extensively with the user object in our scripts, you should familiarize yourself with this object's properties and methods.

Two more important reminders: not all properties listed here will be available through the Active Directory Users and Computers console (the only way to access these properties is via ADSI or another utility application) and some properties will be set according to the value set for other properties. For example, setting the country property (co) automatically sets the country-abbreviation property (c). Table 18.9 shows the user object's properties.

TABLE 18.9: User Properties

PROPERTY	DESCRIPTION
sAMAccountName	Account name for the user
givenName	User's first name
middleName	User's middle name
Sn	User's last name (or surname)
Initials	User's initials
physicalDeliveryOfficeName	Office location
streetAddress	Address
countryCode	Country
postOfficeBox	Post office box
L	City
St	State
C	Country abbreviation
Co	Country
postalCode	ZIP (or postal) code
telephoneNumber	Telephone number
facsimileTelephoneNumber	Fax number
mobile	Mobile telephone number
ipPhone	VOIP telephone number
info	Notes section on the telephone tab
homePhone	Home telephone number
pager	Pager number
profilePath	Path to the user's profile
scriptPath	Path to the user's logon script

TABLE 18.9:   User Properties *(CONTINUED)*

PROPERTY	DESCRIPTION
homeDrive	Drive letter mapped to the user's home directory
homeDirectory	Path to the user's home directory
mail	Primary e-mail address
manager	Distinguished name of the user object that is this user's manager
accountDisabled	A set of flags that indicate if an account is disabled, locked out, password expiration is disabled, etc.
accountExpirationDate	Date the account expires, if set
company	Company
department	Department
departmentNumber	Department number
division	Division
employeeID	Employee ID
employeeNumber	Employee number
employeeType	Employee type
Drink	Yes, there is a drink property. (I kid you not!)

Another property to be aware of is memberOf, which returns a collection of group objects the user directly belongs to. However, this does not take into account any groups the user may belong to via group inheritance (groups that belong to other groups). Chapter 19, "Active Directory Scripts," describes a way around this issue. Table 18.10 shows the methods of the user object.

TABLE 18.10:   User Methods

METHOD	DESCRIPTION
SetPassword	Sets the user's password.
ChangePassword	Changes the password. The old password must be specified in addition to the new password.

Group Properties and Methods

The IADSGroup interface is used to manage group membership in Active Directory. This includes adding and removing users as well as checking for group membership. Tables 18.11 and 18.12 show the properties and methods of the group object.

TABLE 18.11: Group Properties

PROPERTY	DESCRIPTION
Cn	Organizational unit's common name
Description	Organizational unit's description
distinguishedName	Organizational unit's distinguished name
groupType	Bitmap representing the type of group
Ou	Organizational unit's name
managedBy	Distinguished name of the organizational unit's manager
Mail	E-mail address for the group
Name	Organizational unit's name
sAMAccountName	Account name of the group

TABLE 18.12: Group Methods

METHOD	DESCRIPTION
Add	Adds a new member to the group
Remove	Removes a member from the group
IsMember	Verifies an object is a member of the group

Computer Properties and Methods

The IADsComputer interface manages computer objects in Active Directory, including servers and workstations on the network. Because this interface inherits from the IADs interface, it already has the properties and methods described in that interface. If you browse through the properties in more detail, you will notice it also shares many properties with the user object. Table 18.13 shows the properties of the computer object.

TABLE 18.13: Computer Properties

NAME	DESCRIPTION
Cn	Computer's common name for the computer
Comment	Comment field
Department	Computer's department
Description	Computer's description
distinguishedName	Computer's distinguished name
Division	Computer's division
dNSHostName	Computer's DNS host name
Location	Computer's location
Name	Computer's name
managedBy	Distinguished name of the computer's manager
memberOf	Computer's group memberships
operatingSystem	Operating system detected on the machine
operatingSystemServicePack	Service-pack level of the operating system
operatingSystemVersion	Version number of the operating system
sAMAccountName	Computer's account name
serialNumber	Computer's serial number

The Basic ADSI Pattern

From a programming standpoint, when you develop your script for Active Directory, you will notice that it follows a basic pattern. Patterns are a good thing for programmers. Using a pattern means you do not have to reinvent the wheel or, in the case of script writing, figure out how to write a script that manipulates your directory service. The pattern we'll use in our ADSI scripts has three simple, basic steps and looks something like this:

1. Bind to an object in Active Directory. The object can be the top level of the domain, an OU in the domain, or an object (such as a user) in an OU.

2. Read the data and work with the object. This includes querying the object, finding the child objects, changing the object's properties, creating a new object, or deleting the object.

3. Save any changes you made to the object. Just like a word processor, if you don't save your work, no one can appreciate it (or blame you for it) later.

Rinse and repeat as needed.

Obviously this is not the complete list of steps. In fact, things can get complicated in a hurry. You might have to query a database or write to a file along the way, but those steps can be inserted into the basic pattern. For now we'll stick with the basics. Let's look at a simple example—adding a new user account:

```
Bind to the OU you want to create the user account in.
Create a user object. Set the mandatory properties of the object.
Save the new user object.
```

Creating one object requires only one pass through the pattern. To see an example that repeats the pattern, I will resort to a little pseudocode to give you the general idea. In this example, we want to modify the office location of 10 users that we already have in a list:

```
While not at the end of the user list
        Bind to the user object.
        Modify the office attribute
        Save the user object
Return to the top of the loop and move to the next user
```

I want to give you one more example, but this one is a bit more complex (albeit more real-world). We want to change the office location of a set of users again, but this time the users will belong to an OU in Active Directory.

```
Bind to the OU containing the users
Query the OU for user objects
While not at the end of the user list
Bind to the user object
Modify the office attribute
Save the user object
Return to the top of the loop and move to the next user
```

In this example, I actually used the pattern inside another pattern. Notice also that I didn't save the OU object because no changes were made to it. You could expand this pattern further to include a range of OUs.

You should be getting a feel for how most ADSI scripts that follow this pattern are going to work. On your own, take a few minutes and think of how to use this pattern to accomplish some of these tasks:

- ◆ Adding an OU to the domain

- ◆ Adding an OU underneath an existing OU

- ◆ Deleting a user from the domain

- ◆ Resetting a user's password

Local Property Cache

Before we get into the details of creating our ADSI scripts, it's important that you understand a little more about what ADSI does on your client machines as you go through the pattern just explained.

When you bind to an object in ADSI, a region of memory on your client machine—known as a *local property cache*—is set aside as a cache location for that object. As you read the object's property values in Active Directory, the values are stored locally in the cache. Placing a copy of the object in a local repository can speed up operations and provide a layer of safety for the scripts. Figure 18.4 shows the local property cache and how it interacts with Active Directory.

Because the script changes the object in the local cache, those changes could be discarded or just plain lost. If you want to undo all your changes, simply do not save the object. Likewise, if Fido comes along and decides your power cord would make an excellent chew toy, your work can be lost if you have not saved the object to Active Directory recently.

FIGURE 18.4
The local property cache

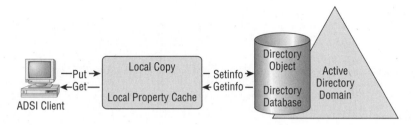

The key to the local property cache is to find the best time to save your work. Each time the `SetInfo` method is called to write your object out to Active Directory, you will incur some network overhead. Some scriptwriters set the object's mandatory properties, save it to Active Directory, set the object's optional properties, and save again. Some set all properties and save the object at one time. As you write your scripts, you will develop a style with which you are comfortable and that works in your network environment.

 Real World Scenario

TALKING NICE TO YOUR ELDERLY MAINFRAME

As the new guy on the college Network Administration team, Tom expected to be given his share of the grunt work. His first assignment was to synchronize student accounts between the aging mainframe and the new Active Directory installation. At first glance this seemed like a simple enough task. But there was one problem: the mainframe had no way to communicate directly with Active Directory.

Instead, a program was used to read a comma-separated file and import the contents into the mainframe's user catalog. Every week someone had to manually create and import a file with information about the new Active Directory accounts. With hundreds of accounts per week, this would take several hours of Tom's time.

There had to be an easier way. After all, Active Directory is a database and it should be possible to query it as such. With a little research, Tom wrote a script to execute a simple LDAP query that retrieved information from Active Directory. Soon his script was retrieving all the information the mainframe needed and writing it out to a text file to be consumed by the mainframe program.

After a few trial runs to work out the bugs, Tom's program was running by itself every week. Soon afterwards, the program to read and import the text file was also running automatically.

Now, rather than spending days on the task, Tom only spends a few moments to check the results of his Active Directory script.

Binding

You should have a pretty good grasp of the steps to take when writing an ADSI script. It is time to look at those steps in more detail, starting with binding. At this point we will start talking more in terms of actual VBScript code.

Binding is basically assigning a variable name to an object in Active Directory. That explanation is oversimplified, but it works for now. When we execute our script and want to read or change any attributes of an Active Directory object, we refer to the object by the variable name. The actual name of the variable does not matter, but it should be something that is easy to associate with the object being manipulated.

BINDING SYNTAX

The first step in binding to an object in Active Directory is to find where that object is in Active Directory. Every object has to reside somewhere, either under the root of the domain itself or maybe buried in the depths of an OU structure seven levels deep. Finding some objects is like looking for that mysteriously missing watch in your house. If your house is like mine, that usually means a search is required. For now let's assume that we know right where that object exists in Active Directory, and we can send the search party out to look for other objects later.

In VBScript we can use one statement to bind to an object in Active Directory. The statement itself has two important parts: the `Set` keyword and the `GetObject` function. The `Set` keyword binds a variable to an instance of an object; in our case the object resides in Active Directory. The `GetObject` function returns an instance of the requested object. The complete statement looks like this:

```
Set ADObject = GetObject("LDAP://CN=Scott,CN=Users,DC=zygort,DC=com")
```

There is one hitch to this method, and it is one of the most common problems when dealing with any directory-services script. What if the object you are trying to bind to does not exist or the object does not exist where you think it does?

First, before attempting to bind to any object in Active Directory, enable error trapping in your script. In VBScript you do this with the `On Error Resume Next` statement. The error trap lets errors occur in the script without causing the script to end prematurely. An intrinsic object in VBScript called the `Err` object holds the success or failure result of the last executing operation. You should check the `Number` property value of the `Err` object (`Err.Number`) immediately after you attempt to bind to the object. If the value is not zero, something has gone wrong and you might want to consider terminating the script.

If you choose not to check `Err.Number`, at least check the object after you attempt to bind to see if it is `Empty`. If the object does not exist in Active Directory, it will not populate the variable with any information, hence leaving it `Empty`. If the variable is `Empty`, warn the user and end the script gracefully if possible. The following example gives you a better idea of how to handle binding and its potential for disaster:

```
On Error Resume Next
Set ADObject = GetObject("LDAP://CN=Scott,CN=Users,DC=zygort,DC=com")
If IsEmpty(ADObject) Then
      WScript.Echo "The object does not exist"
      WScript.Quit
End If
' Do your magic to the object
```

The path to the object you want to bind to is one of the most common places errors can occur in your scripts. If you allow the user to enter the path to the object, you increase the chances of a bad path. With a few additional lines of code you can handle the situation more gracefully.

ADsPath

To bind to the Active Directory object we must know where it exists. For each object in Active Directory a path known as the ADsPath points to the object's current location; we use this path to bind to that object. The ADsPath is basically the distinguished name of the object preceded by the provider moniker (in the case of Active Directory that moniker is LDAP://). You can use the Active Directory Explorer to find the distinguishedName attribute of any object, as shown in Figure 18.5.

FIGURE 18.5
Finding the distinguishedName property in the Active Directory Explorer

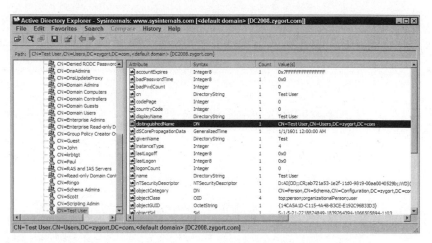

To bind to the user object in VBScript, we use the Set keyword to associate the variable name to the object in Active Directory. For this work we need to use the GetObject function to point to the object in Active Directory. GetObject connects to the directory service specified by the moniker, locates the object (if it exists where we say it does), and returns the object's properties to a location known as the local property cache. The following code shows how to bind a variable to a user object, and use that variable to read the user's last name:

```
Set User = GetObject("LDAP://CN=Scott,CN=Users,DC=zygort,DC=com")
Wscript.Echo User("sn")
```

An ADsPath is built with two parts: the protocol moniker for the directory service and the object's distinguished name. You should already be familiar with distinguished names, and we discussed directory service provider monikers earlier in this chapter. For Active Directory, we use the LDAP:// provider.

```
<moniker>://<distinguished name>
```

Variations on the distinguished name offer a few more options when it comes to binding to an object. In the following pages we will cover each of these variations in more detail and discuss when you would want to use them.

HARD-CODED BINDING

Binding an object in a domain is fairly straightforward. Part of the ADsPath points to the domain to be contacted. These are the DC components of the distinguished name. For example, the domain name in the following ADsPath is zygort.com:

```
LDAP://CN=Scott,CN=Users,DC=zygort,DC=com
```

Instead of binding to a user object, let's bind to the Default container that holds the user objects—the Users container.

```
LDAP://CN=Users,DC=zygort,DC=com
```

Let's take it a step further and imagine this script will list every user object in the Users container. That might be a very useful report! Now let's take that script to another domain, such as sybex.com. The script no longer works. Why?

Because the container it is trying to bind to—Users—is in the zygort.com domain. We've hard-coded the domain value in our script, and if the script cannot contact that domain the script will not work. If the script is able to contact the original domain it will not give us the results from our new domain.

The solution is simple enough: just rename the ADsPath of the Users container from zygort.com to sybex.com. Oh, and make sure you also change any other references throughout the *entire* script. Do not expect to take any script changes back to zygort.com, because it will not work again until you again rename the domain throughout the script. Sound like fun?

SERVERLESS BINDING

I like my scripts to be as portable as possible. I want to be able to take a script from one domain to another and do as little rewriting as possible, preferably none!

To bind to an object, the ADsPath must have a domain component. There is just no way around it. Thus, to make our scripts portable, we basically have to "teach" the script to fill in the domain components for itself. In Active Directory (and other LDAP services), the means to do just that is at our fingertips.

We can use a special object called RootDSE in our scripts. RootDSE is a unique object created on each domain controller. It provides information about the capabilities and directory services available on that domain controller. By reading the attributes of the RootDSE object, our script can find out in which domain our script is running, the path to the Schema container for the domain, the current time, and a host of other useful information.

We start by binding to the RootDSE object itself with the LDAP moniker. Because the RootDSE object provides us with the domain information, ADsPath contains no DC components.

```
Set RootDSE = GetObject("LDAP://RootDSE")
```

After binding to the RootDSE object, we can reference its attributes to find the information we need. Table 18.14 lists some of the most useful attributes of the RootDSE object. For a complete listing of the RootDSE attributes, visit http://msdn2.microsoft.com/en-us/library/ms684291.aspx.

TABLE 18.14: RootDSE Attributes

ATTRIBUTE	DESCRIPTION
configurationNamingContext	Returns the distinguished name of the Configuration container in the domain
currentTime	Returns the current time on the domain controller
defaultNamingContext	Returns the distinguished name of the domain of which the domain controller is a member
dnsHostName	Returns the DNS name of the domain controller
schemaNamingContext	Returns the distinguished name of the Schema container

As you can see, you can retrieve the distinguished names of several important containers through the RootDSE object. In our case, we want the distinguished name of the current domain. To find that we can read the defaultNamingContext attribute of the RootDSE object. The following code shows the entire process in action:

```
Set RootDSE = GetObject("LDAP://RootDSE")
Wscript.Echo RootDSE("defaultNamingContext")
' On my domain, this returns DC=zygort,DC=com
Set UserCN = GetObject("LDAP://CN=Users, " & _ RootDSE("defaultNamingContext"))
```

The process is simple: Start by binding a variable to the RootDSE object. With that variable, read the contents of the defaultNamingContext property, which returns the domain components of the current domain. Because our imaginary script was binding to the Users container of the domain, we prepended the LDAP moniker and container name to the value returned from the RootDSE object and submitted it to the GetObject function. The end result will be the UserCN object bound to the Users container (which still has a chance of failing, so always use the error trap discussed earlier!).

Binding to the RootDSE object is standard practice in most ADSI scripts. In addition to giving you lots of useful information about the domain itself, binding an object to the RootDSE object can also give you a performance boost. Later in this chapter we talk about how that works.

USING AN ALTERNATE DOMAIN CONTROLLER

So far all the binding statements we've seen have one thing in common: we have never specified a domain controller to use. Each ADsPath simply lists the domain components, but never a server name. To bind to an object and retrieve its information, we have to contact a domain controller for that domain. So which domain controller are we talking to?

Remember that domain controllers are peers in Active Directory, so each contains roughly the same information (keep in mind there is always some latency involved in replicated data between domain controllers). If your binding statement does not specify a domain controller, you should be talking to the same domain controller that authenticated your account when you logged on. To see which domain controller authenticated you, look at the %logonserver% environment variable.

Now, what happens if that domain controller is unavailable? DNS will be queried for other available domain-controller services on the local site. You should have one available, or you might (unintentionally) find your work being done at another site and discover that WAN lines do little to improve performance. If no domain controllers are available at your site, you should probably put this book down and find out why.

The recommended practice for writing ADSI scripts is to not specify a domain controller when binding to Active Directory objects. This lets Active Directory and DNS do their respective jobs, providing a list of available services and preferred service providers for your network location. A good domain administrator will have set up sites and services to be readily available to his or her users (and to their scripts).

However, if you are really picky about where your Active Directory work gets done, ADSI lets you specify the domain controller you want to communicate with. By changing the ADsPath to a different format, we can specify a domain controller and, optionally, the port to use if the directory service is running on a port other than the default (port 398). To support this the ADsPath can take on one of the following alternate formats:

```
LDAP://<domain controller>,<distinguished name>
LDAP://<domain controller>:<port>,<distinguished name>
```

Consider a few examples. The first two are typical examples of an ADsPath, and the rest are variations that specify to use the BranchOffice domain controller:

```
LDAP://DC=zygort,DC=com
LDAP://CN=Scott,CN=Users,DC=zygort,DC=com
LDAP://BranchOfficeDC
LDAP://BranchOfficeDC:5151
LDAP://BranchOfficeDC,CN=Scott,CN=Users,DC=zygort,DC=com
LDAP://BranchOfficeDC:5151,OU=Offices,DC=zygort,DC=com
```

This is not the recommended practice. Specifying a domain controller essentially ties the successful execution of your script to the status of the specified controller. You have also severely limited the portability of your script to other domains. Using the RootDSE object to obtain the current domain components still works, but unless that domain has a domain controller with the same name specified in the ADsPath, you will still be out of luck.

Having said all that, some situations do weigh in this technique's favor. Let's say you have a domain controller that is busy (perhaps performing double duty as a print server) and one that is idly waiting for authentication requests; which would you rather use? Trust us when we say that a heavy Active Directory script can bring a print server running on the domain controller to its virtual knees (this was how I learned to check which domain controller I was authenticating against).

Let's say you need to make a change for a specific site. You could make the change to your local domain controller and let replication propagate to the rest of the domain controllers. Or you could target a domain controller at that site, which makes the change available immediately to the local users. Eventually the change will replicate through the rest of the domain according to the replication schedule.

BINDING TO GLOBAL CATALOG SERVERS

While binding to a single-domain directory tree is good for most scripts, some situations may require information from a broader authority. For example, if your current domain is just one of a larger domain forest, you may need to bind to a global catalog server to find the data you need, which may be spread across the forest.

To summarize the global catalog server's functions, think of it as a domain controller that replicates a subset of domain information from each domain in a forest. Directory attributes that are defined as part of the *partial attribute set* are replicated to all domain controllers that have been configured as global catalog servers. Binding to the global catalog server and using it as the source of your queries can yield information for each domain in the forest.

Global catalog servers use separate TCP/IP ports (the global catalog server uses port 3268 by default) to separate directory queries from global catalog queries. ADSI already knows the default port for binding to the global catalog server; you do not need to specify the port unless an administrator has changed it. Instead, we only have to change the provider we want to use. To use the global catalog server, use GC:// instead of LDAP://, like so:

```
Set GC = GetObject("GC://RootDSE")
```

Notice that we can still use the RootDSE object when querying a global catalog server. In the next chapter, we will give you some scripts to work with the global catalog server and go over them in more detail.

GUID BINDING

To refresh your memory, a globally unique identifier (GUID) is a 128-bit value guaranteed to be unique in the span of the networked world (but I've never heard it called a money-back guarantee; I wonder why?). Active Directory not only identifies objects using distinguished names, but it also generates a GUID for each new object that is created. Although a distinguished name may change over time (as might its location in Active Directory), the same GUID remains with the object throughout its lifetime.

Knowing this, you can bind to an object using its GUID instead of its distinguished name, assuming you know the object's GUID beforehand of course. The beauty of this method is that you can always bind to *that* object, no matter where in the Active Directory tree it happens to be. When you see the code for this you'll also see the ugly side of binding to a GUID instead of a distinguished name:

```
Set MyObject = GetObject("LDAP://<GUID=AC54…91BF74,DC=zygort,DC=com>")
```

First, notice that I have enclosed the GUID piece of the ADsPath between a set of less-than (<) and greater-than (>) symbols. Because GUIDs are represented in hexadecimal notation, typing out the entire GUID would run well beyond the edge of the page or take up several lines of text, not to mention that it would not correspond to any object in any Active Directory tree but my own (I would hope!). To view the object's GUID you can use Active Directory Viewer or reference the object's GUID property that you bound to, as shown here:

```
Set MyObject = GetObject("LDAP://CN=Scott,CN=Users,DC=zygort,DC=COM")
WScript.Echo MyObject.Get("objectGUID")
' or
WScript.Echo MyObject.GUID
```

WELL-KNOWN GUIDS

Getting past the ugliness of GUIDs for everyday objects such as user and computers objects, knowing the GUID is critical to finding some containers. You can rename several of the commonly used standard containers in Active Directory, thus changing their distinguished names and potentially breaking our scripts. Microsoft knew this was possible and assigned each of these containers a consistent GUID (which defeats the purpose of a GUID, don't you think?) so they could always be bound to regardless of what their current name happens to be. Table 18.15 shows a list of these containers, referred to as *well-known GUIDs*.

TABLE 18.15:   Well-Known GUID Values

CONTAINER	WELL-KNOWN GUID
Users	A9D1CA15768811D1ADED00C04FD8D5CD
Computers	AA312825768811D1ADED00C04FD8D5CD
System	AB1D30F3768811D1ADED00C04FD8D5CD
DomainControllers	A361B2FFFFD211D1AA4B00C04FD7D83A
Infrastructure	2FBAC1870ADE11D297C400C04FD8D5CD
DeletedObjects	18F2FA80684F11D2B9AA00C04F79F805
LostAndFound	AB8153B7768811D1ADED00C04FD8D5CD

To use a well-known GUID we need to vary our binding syntax a bit (I know, you were just getting used to the last set of variations). In the next example we'll bind to the Users container of the zygort.com domain. For the sake of brevity we'll use the constant from the earlier file.

```
Set UsersCN = GetObject("LDAP://<WKGUID=" & WKGUID_USERS & ",DC=zygort,DC=com>"
```

Again, notice that I enclosed the GUID between a set of less-than (<) and greater-than (>) symbols. Using the keyword WKGUID= tells the query engine we are referencing a well-known GUID. You should notice that domain components are also included *inside* the symbols. These GUID values are consistent across all Active Directory domains, but we still need to specify the domain we are targeting. We can, however, retrieve domain components from the RootDSE object rather than hard-coding them.

INTERFACES

Now that you have a handle on binding with GUIDs, you should not use them in place of binding with distinguished names. (Don't you just hate it when people show you something cool and then tell you that you can't have it? Well, not to worry, I would never do that to you.)

Instead you should use them *in conjunction* with distinguished names. Why? Because, when binding with the GUID syntax, certain attributes and methods that worked when binding with distinguished names suddenly stop working. What's happening behind the scenes is that a different interface is used when you bind to the object using a GUID.

An interface is simply a contract between the client and object. The interface states, "I support attributes A, B, and C." If the client tries to use attribute D, E, or F, an error occurs. You know by now that different Active Directory classes (user, computer, etc.) sometimes have different attributes and methods, which are enabled by implementing class-specific interfaces on those objects. Depending on the object you bind to, you will wind up using an interface specific to that class—at least, until you try to bind using a GUID.

When binding using a GUID, ADSI does not use the interface for the class of the object you are binding to. GUID binding was not designed to support all functionality of an object class; rather it was designed to connect quickly to an object. Because it does not use the class-specific interface, overhead is low. In fact, as well as being replicated to every global catalog server (as part of the replica set), the GUID itself is an indexed attribute in Active Directory, which improves query performance.

So how do we regain our lost functionality? The answer is simple: bind with the GUID first, retrieve the distinguished name, then bind to the object using the distinguished name. This allows you to bind to the correct object no matter what its current name is, and gives you access to all the object's attributes and methods. The following is an example, from start to finish, of binding to the Users container from a domain:

```
Set RootDSE = GetObject("LDAP://RootDSE")
UsersGUID = "<WKGUID=" & WKGUID_USERS & "," & _
      RootDSE.Get("defaultNamingContext") & ">"
Set UsersGUIDCN = GetObject("LDAP:// " & UsersGUID)
Set UsersCN = GetObject("LDAP:// " & _ UsersGUIDCN.Get("distinguishedName"))
```

This code first binds to the RootDSE object and then creates a string that combines the well-known GUID from the constant value with the default naming context from the RootDSE object. This string is then used to bind to the Users container. When the distinguishedName property of the Users container is retrieved, we bind to the container again using the distinguished name of the container. We now have all the attributes and methods of the object that we are used to working with.

OpenDSObject

Permissions in Active Directory can be very selective, right down to the attribute level. Users typically do not have the permissions to create or delete objects. A network administrator might grant everyone access to view user location attributes, while granting only a managers group access to view homeTelephone attributes.

Until now we've authorized access to Active Directory using the credentials of the logged-on user. Active Directory naturally has a set of default security permissions in place to keep unauthorized users from creating, modifying, or (even worse) deleting objects. Depending on the task, we need to run our scripts in the security context of the account that has the rights to perform the tasks we have written the script to do.

A script runs in the security context of the currently logged-on user. By using the RunAs command, you can change the security context of script's running instance if you supply a valid username and password. Because the GetObject function does not accept a username and password as arguments, it must bind to an object using whatever security context the script is running.

To bind to an object using a different set of security credentials without using the RunAs command, we can use a function called OpenDSObject. This function takes four arguments in the following order: the object to bind, a username, a password, and the type of authentication mechanism to use. Using OpenDSObject in our script looks similar to this (but with a stronger password, one would hope!):

```
Set MyObject = _ OpenDSObject("LDAP://CN=Scott,CN=Users,DC=zygort,DC=com", _
   "ZYGORT\ScriptingAdmin", "P@sswOrd", ADS_SECURE_AUTHENTICATION)
```

Before continuing we must point out the danger at hand. Using this function puts a password in clear text to be seen by anyone with access to the script. *Do not use any account with domain administrator rights in this function!* Create a special, very restricted account with just enough rights to perform the task at hand—and give it a strong password.

Keep these next things in mind whenever you create a special account for automated scripts. First, give the account an inconspicuous name if possible (and make note of it somewhere!). Second, make sure the password on the account is very strong (again, make note of it somewhere!). Finally, and perhaps most importantly, make sure the password on the account does not expire—or one day your script will suddenly stop running.

You should also download the Script Encoder from Microsoft and apply it to any scripts that put a password in clear text. The Script Encoder essentially hides the code from prying eyes conducting a surface-level search by applying a known cipher to the code, rendering the code unreadable. When the code executes, the scripting engine reads and decodes the encoded script. However, the code is not encrypted and the cipher is well-known by this point. Cracking tools are freely available on the Web to reverse your encoded script into a readable form.

Another catch to using `OpenDSObject` is that you must already have a reference to an ADSI object before you can use it. Any object will do, and it need not be the object you want to work with at the moment. The trick is to bind to an object that does not require authentication, such as the LDAP object itself. So prior to calling `OpenDSObject`, we would execute the following line of code:

```
Set NonSecureObject = GetObject("LDAP:")
```

With those important warnings out of the way, let's look at the method in more detail. The `ADsPath` is nothing new to us by now. The password is simply a string value. The username is a string value as well, but it can take a number of formats:

Username: `ScriptingAdmin`

User principle name: `ScriptingAdmin@zygort.com`

Domain\username: `ZYGORT\ScriptingAdmin`

Distinguished name: `cn=ScriptingAdmin,cn=Users,dc=zygort,dc=com`

I should point out that while `OpenDSObject` has arguments for username and password, nothing says you *have* to use them! To use the current security context of the script, simply put the VBScript keyword `Nothing` in the `username` and `password` arguments. As you look at some of the authentication types that follow the next paragraph, you will notice some have less to do with security and more to do with performance—we can take advantage of that.

The specified authentication type is one of several constants defined elsewhere (see `\includes\ADSI_CONSTANTS.vbs`). These constants are hexadecimal values that set security flags on or off, depending on the security behavior desired. These flags form a bit mask so you can use the `OR` keyword to combine them and form the final bit mask. Note that the NDS and NWCompat providers support none of these options. The constants include the following authentication flags. (The hexadecimal value of each flag is shown in parentheses.)

ADS_SECURE_AUTHENTICATION (0x1): Uses secure authentication. When connecting to Active Directory, Kerberos is used if it is available; otherwise it uses NT LAN Manager (NTLM). If the username and password are NULL, the binding uses the security context of the running script.

ADS_USE_ENCRYPTION (0x2): Requests that ADSI use encryption for data exchanges over the network. This option is not supported by the WinNT provider.

ADS_USE_SSL (0x2): Attempts to encrypt the communications channel using SSL. This requires a certificate server to be installed on the domain to support SSL. This option is not supported by the WinNT provider.

ADS_READONLY_SERVER (0x4): Indicates that a writable server is not required for serverless binding. On a Windows NT network this allows ADSI to connect to either a Primary Domain Controller (PDC) or a Backup Domain Controller (BDC), because BDCs are read-only. On a Windows 2000 or 2003 network this flag has no effect because all domain controllers are writable.

ADS_NO_AUTHENTICATION (0x10): Explicitly requires no authentication. Active Directory attempts to establish a connection between the client script and the object but does not perform authentication. This flag requests an anonymous binding, which is equivalent to binding using the Everyone group credentials. This option is not supported by the WinNT provider.

ADS_FAST_BIND (0x20): Causes ADSI to expose only the base interfaces supported by all ADSI objects. This flag is not so much a security directive as a performance directive. Setting this flag allows the LDAP provider to skip several steps, thus improving performance.

ADS_USE_SIGNING (0x40): Verifies sent and received data. This should be set in conjunction with the ADS_SECURE_AUTHENTICATION flag. This option is not supported by the WinNT provider.

ADS_USE_SEALING (0x80): Uses Kerberos to encrypt data. This should be set in conjunction with the ADS_SECURE_AUTHENTICATION flag. This option is not supported by the WinNT provider.

ADS_USE_DELEGATION (0x100): Allows ADSI to delegate the user security context. This must be used to move objects between domains.

ADS_SERVER_BIND (0x200): Indicates the ADsPath includes a server name. Do not use this flag with serverless binding or if the binding syntax includes domain components. Using a server name without setting this flag can increase network traffic.

To define these flags as constants in your VBScript, change the 0x notation to the VBScript &H notation. For example, the ADS_USE_ENCRYPTION value of 0x2 would become &H2 in your VBScript.

PERFORMANCE CONSIDERATIONS

As we mentioned before, ADSI handles the mechanics of connecting to objects in the directory service for you, basically shielding you from the dirty work. This can be a good thing, but it can also be a bad thing because it makes it difficult to troubleshoot a poorly performing ADSI script.

Each time you bind to an object in Active Directory you create some overhead. DNS records may have to be accessed to find a domain controller. The schema may have to be referenced. Certainly the object itself will have to be located and its attributes read into the local property cache. You can modify your script to reduce the total amount of overhead generated when binding, especially when your script binds to many Active Directory objects in succession.

One of the simplest ways to improve performance is by taking advantage of connection caching. When you bind to an object in Active Directory, your script must first authenticate itself to the domain controller servicing the request. This authentication takes time, and repeating the authentication takes additional time. Connection caching simply keeps open one connection that has successfully authenticated to a domain controller and uses the same server for all subsequent object requests. When the script is ready to end, the connection is finally dropped by setting the object to Nothing (which also happens automatically when the script terminates). This is why opening a connection to the RootDSE object at the beginning of a script and leaving it open can be a simple and easy performance enhancement.

To achieve other performance gains, take advantage of some of the flags available through the OpenDSObject function. These flags basically tell ADSI to skip some steps that normally occur when you bind to an object. While eliminating steps obviously improves performance (less work takes less time to perform, right?), there are always trade-offs in terms of exactly which steps were skipped.

The first flag to consider is ADS_FAST_BIND, which allows the LDAP provider to skip the steps of verifying that the object exists and getting the object's class. If the object does not exist and you attempt to access one of its attributes or methods, an error occurs. Because the object's class is unknown, ADSI cannot use the class-specific interface for the object, meaning you will also lose the specific functionality of the object's class.

To use this flag successfully you should always be certain that the object(s) you need to work with exist, and run your code in an error trap. You should know what attributes and methods are available on the object. Only the base interface of the object is used, which exposes the `ADsPath`, `Class`, `GUID`, `Name`, and `Parent` attributes and the `Get`, `GetEx`, `GetInfo`, `GetInfoEx`, `Put`, `PutEx`, and `SetInfo` methods.

The other flag to consider is `ADS_SERVER_BIND`, which eliminates the steps of locating a domain controller on your behalf. This means you must take the initiative to provide a suitable server name in your `ADsPath`.

Reading Data

At some point after binding to an object, most scripts read the attributes of that object. Remember that ADSI always sets up a cached copy of our Active Directory objects in a region of memory called the local property cache. Even though we have a cache location, we have no data in that cache yet. Binding to the object doesn't download any of its attributes into the local property cache; that task is left to us. ADSI provides three methods for populating the local property cache: `GetInfo`, `Get`, and `GetInfoEx`.

Before I tell you the differences between them, I have to point out the issue of latency involved in ADSI scripting. Simply put, someone can change the value of an attribute in Active Directory after we've read it into the cache. By the same token, our script could change the value of an attribute immediately after someone else submitted a change for the same attribute. In either case, someone's going to be confused about why his or her change didn't take place. There are no provisions for "locking" the values of an object while we manipulate them. Essentially, the last change submitted to Active Directory wins.

GetInfo Method

The `GetInfo` method initializes the local property cache or refreshes the values stored in it. All of the object's supported attributes are loaded into the cache. This method also overwrites all existing values in the cache with the current values from Active Directory. This means if you haven't saved your work before you call `GetInfo`, all your changes will be lost. The method takes no arguments, so the code looks like this:

```
User.GetInfo
```

Get and GetEx Methods

The `Get` method retrieves object attribute values from the local property cache and is called with one attribute at a time. If the cache is already loaded with the object's attributes (via `GetInfo`, perhaps), you are ready to go. However, if the cache hasn't retrieved the attributes from Active Directory yet, the first call to the `Get` method implicitly invokes the `GetInfo` method to populate the local property cache.

The method takes one argument: the LDAP display name of the attribute to retrieve. It retrieves the value (assuming there is one) and returns it to a variable. The code to use the `Get` method looks like this:

```
UserFirstname = User.Get("givenName")
```

The `Get` method is also "implied" when you refer to the property name directly from the object. For example, here are two equivalent lines of code:

```
WScript.Echo User.Get("givenName")
WScript.Echo User.givenName
```

That seems simple enough, which usually means it's not. Some attributes return other objects. If this is the case you have to use the `Set` keyword in front of the variable, like this:

```
Set Security = User.Get("ntSecurityDescriptor")
```

We're not out of the woods yet! Some attributes in Active Directory contain more than one value as well (appropriately called *multivalued attributes*). These values return an array of values to the variable. Because an array is not considered an object, we can skip the `Set` keyword. The trick comes when reading the values of that attribute. Luckily, reading values from an array is simple:

```
PhoneNumbers = User.Get("otherHomePhone")
For each PhoneNumber in PhoneNumbers
    Wscript.Echo PhoneNumber
Next
```

As if that's not enough fun, ADSI returns a different type of structure if the multivalued attribute has only one value. When you use a home `PhoneNumber` attribute that contains only one value, ADSI returns it as a string type. If it has several values, it returns them in an array.

This is where the `GetEx` method comes into play, as does your newly acquired knowledge of the Active Directory schema. If you know an attribute is multivalued but you don't know how many values it contains, using the `GetEx` method always returns the attribute value(s) in an array. This saves you from having to look at the value returned, figure out if it is a string or an array, and then display the value(s) appropriately. Because the `GetEx` method always gives you an array, we can modify the previous code ever so slightly to accommodate the `GetEx` method:

```
PhoneNumbers = User.GetEx("otherHomePhone")
For each PhoneNumber in PhoneNumbers
    Wscript.Echo PhoneNumber
Next
```

There is one more catch to all of this reading and displaying data. This one has to do with the type of data returned by the attribute. Some attributes contain numbers and others contain characters or strings. Some contain more complex data, such as 64-bit unsigned integers. We'll talk about the details in the section "Active Directory Data Types."

GETINFOEX METHOD

This method is the middle ground between `GetInfo` and `Get`. First it reads the value of an attribute from Active Directory, not the local property cache; then it stores that value in the cache, overwriting the current value if one exists. Instead of refreshing the entire set of an object's attributes, you can use this method to refresh the value of selected attributes. Even better, this method can retrieve several specific attributes with one line of code, as you will see in a moment.

This method looks like it takes two arguments, but in its current version it really takes only one. The first argument is an array of attributes to retrieve. The second argument is reserved for later use, so for now we always set it to 0.

```
AttributeArray(0) = "AdsPath"
AttributeArray(1) = "givenName"
AttributeArray(2) = "sn"
User.GetInfoEx AttributeArray, 0
Wscript.Echo User.Get("AdsPath")    ' from the Local Property Cache
```

The following piece of code puts three values in `AttributeArray` and passes that array into the `GetInfoEx` method, which populates the local property cache with those three attributes. If you do not like populating an array one element at a time, the alternative is to use the `Array` function, like this:

```
User.GetInfoEx Array("AdsPath","givenName","sn"), 0
Wscript.Echo User.Get("Adspath")
```

The `Array` function takes a list of comma-separated values and returns them in an array. You can return that list directly into the first argument of the `GetInfoEx` method.

Saving Data

I know: in our ADSI pattern, saving your work is the last step. So why am I mentioning it now? First, it's a very important step. If you do not save your work, why run the script? Second, it is a short step and it is easy to forget. And it's a step that neither your script nor the scripting engine will complain about when you forget it. Your only clue (assuming the rest of your script functions properly) will be the lack of changes when you check Active Directory. Finally, we refer to it in upcoming sections, so it's good that you know what it does ahead of time.

As we said, saving your work is a short step. All you do is call the `SetInfo` method of the object you have been modifying. This writes out the current values of that object in the local property cache to the directory service itself. The method has no arguments, so the code to use it looks like this:

```
User.SetInfo
```

You can call `SetInfo` any time you want, but think about the lack of arguments in the method. That means you cannot save only certain attributes from the local property cache; it is an all-or-nothing deal. You can minimize the amount of network traffic by batching your changes to an object together and saving them at one time. A common practice when creating objects is to populate the mandatory attributes for the new object, save the object, populate whatever optional attributes you choose, and save again. Definitely do not call `SetInfo` after every attribute change you make!

After writing the object to the Active Directory, the `SetInfo` method queries the object for its values. As you will see in the next section, even if we do not explicitly set an attribute, Active Directory fills in certain attributes for us. At a minimum, when an object is first created, Active Directory ensures that the mandatory attributes for that class have values.

Modifying Data

You have seen how to bind to objects, how to read the object's attribute values, and how to save changes to those attributes. Now we can dive into the depths of actually modifying data in Active Directory. One last-minute reminder: always check that the object you've bound a variable to actually exists—that is to say, it does not have a value of `Nothing`. If you missed the target it is a lot easier to stop and adjust your aim than to keep firing errant shots into the hillside.

In this section, we talk about creating, modifying, and deleting objects. We will also talk more in-depth about the different data types that Active Directory uses and how to work with them.

By this point, you should know the first step is always to bind to an object. We will talk about which object you should bind to, but we won't go into depth about the binding process or creating specific classes of objects—we cover those topics in the next chapter, "Active Directory Scripts."

A word of warning: we are officially about to start playing with your Active Directory hierarchy for real. We highly recommend working with this book's scripting examples and downloadable material on a test domain. A virtual environment is ideal for these types of learning exercises.

CREATING OBJECTS

Creating an object in Active Directory requires you to make two decisions: what object do you want to create, and where in the hierarchy do you want to create that object? Thinking back to our Active Directory schema, remember there are a number of structural classes from which Active Directory is capable of creating an object. For the majority of directory structures you will use a standard set of classes: the user, the group, the organizational unit, and the container.

Once you have decided on the what and where, you can get to work. When we perform the binding step of our pattern, we want to bind to the container object that is going to hold our new object (either an OU or an actual container). For example, if I want to create a new user in an organization unit called Sybex, I would bind to the Sybex OU.

One mistake I have seen a few times by new ADSI scriptwriters is forgetting to bind to the container itself. Instead they bind to the root of the domain, create their new object, and then cannot find the object. At first they think their new user was created in the default container for that object (e.g., the Users container for new users), but that is not the case. ADSI does exactly what you tell it to do and creates that new object in the root of your Active Directory hierarchy. So be specific!

```
Set Parent = GetObject("LDAP://CN=Users,DC=zygort,DC=com")
```

To create the new object, we use the `Create` method of the Parent container. Because this method returns an object, we have to use the `Set` keyword. The `Create` method is available on any object capable of holding Active Directory objects and requires two arguments: the type of class to create and the Common Name (CN) value of the object:

```
Set NewUser = Parent.Create("user","CN=MyFirstUser")
```

The first argument (`"user"`) tells ADSI to refer to the `user` class to create the object. This is the LDAP display name for the class. The second argument (`"CN=MyFirstUser"`) gives ADSI a value to assign the Common Name of the object. This value must be unique in the container. Creating new objects within an error trap is a good practice in case an error occurs.

At this point you have a variable pointing to your new object. Now is the perfect time to start assigning values to the mandatory attributes of the object. One of the `user` object's mandatory attributes is `sAMAccountName` (we'll go more into the `Put` method in a moment).

```
NewUser.Put "sAMAccountName", "MyFirstUser"
```

Believe it or not, mandatory attributes are not mandatory in the sense that you have to fill them in yourself. Mandatory attributes such as `objectSid` (which is a GUID that you would not want to create yourself anyway!) are generated by the system in the event that you leave them empty when you save your object. Just for fun, I left the `sAMAccountName` attribute blank on my `NewUser` object, and the value I found in Active Directory was $L21000-QV9063NT6GK3. Definitely a secure name, but not one I would like to type in on a daily basis! So I changed it to `Scott`.

When you have finished assigning values to the attributes of your newly created object, do not forget to call the `SetInfo` method of the object:

```
NewUser.SetInfo
```

DELETING OBJECTS

You can delete objects in Active Directory several ways. The first is the most straightforward: simply bind to the object and call the `DeleteObject` method. The `DeleteObject` method takes one argument, which is reserved, so for now we simply use 0 as the argument value. This code shows how to delete a user:

```
Set UserToDelete = GetObject("CN=Scott,DC=zygort,DC=com")
UserToDelete.DeleteObject(0)
```

The second way to delete an object in Active Directory is similar to creating a user. We bind to the Parent container, call the `Delete` method, and specify the object class and name of the object to be removed. The code to remove a user looks like this:

```
Parent.Delete "user", "CN=Scott"
```

If a variable was bound to the object you removed, you need to set the variable to `Nothing`. In the local property cache, the object still exists. If you were to call the `SetInfo` method, your script would return an error. Basically, the local property cache would try to save changes to an object that no longer existed! Even worse, it would not be readily obvious why your script was failing; the error would occur on the `SetInfo` line of code. This code shows the entire process in action:

```
Set User = GetObject("LDAP://CN=Scott,CN=Users,DC=zygort,DC=com")
' Make and save changes to the user object here
Set Parent = GetObject("LDAP://CN=Users,DC=zygort,DC=com")
Parent.Delete "user", User.Name
Parent.SetInfo
Set User = Nothing
```

How do you know which deletion method to use? Think about the job your script is going to do. If you want to delete one object, use the `Delete` method. One binding followed by one deletion, and you are done. If you are examining many objects in a container, use the `DeleteObject` method. You bind only to the parent object as opposed to each individual leaf object to delete. Binding operations create overhead, so reducing that overhead helps your scripts perform better.

You also want to consider what type of objects you are deleting. Technically you can use either deletion method for container objects. The difference is that the `Delete` method generates an error if the container contains child objects below it, while the `DeleteObject` method deletes the container and everything below it in one fell swoop. While efficient, using the `DeleteObject` method on containers is also dangerous. How do you know if the container has any child objects? One sure way is to try deleting the container! If it has child objects it will return an error stating, "The directory service can perform the requested operation only on a leaf object."

Before deleting objects en masse, consider the repercussions of your action. As with databases, there is no Undo button if you wipe out the wrong object. If your script is the interactive sort, displaying an "OK to delete?" prompt might prevent the user from making a big mistake. In an automated script you will have to use your best judgment about when it is truly safe to delete an object.

Modifying Properties via Put and PutEx

The `Put` and `PutEx` methods modify an existing Active Directory object property. The property may or may not have a current value, but if a value does exist it will be overwritten. Remember that this changes only the values in the local property cache, not the directory service. To set your changes in the Active Directory, execute the `SetInfo` method.

When modifying the properties of an Active Directory object, you must first bind to it (of course!). Executing the `GetInfo` method populates the local data cache with the object's properties. You can then examine the current property values to determine which (if any) need to be modified, or you can begin making your changes immediately.

To change a property you must first know what kind of data type it holds and if it holds a single value or multiple values. We discuss Active Directory data types in the next section, but most of the values modified in scripts are simple string, date, or numeric values.

To assign a new value to properties that hold a single value you use the Put method. You specify the ldapDisplayName when you assign the new value.

```
User.Put("givenName") = "Scott"
```

Assigning values to a property that holds multiple values is a bit trickier. The first step is to decide if you want to overwrite all the values currently stored in the property or to simply append a new value to the existing values.

The PutEx method accepts three arguments: a numeric value that represents the operation to perform, the ldapDisplayName of the property to modify, and the values to use in the operation.

The numeric value representing the operation specifies what type of operation will take place on the property values. You may clear the current property values, update the current values, append a new value, or delete a property value. Values are usually assigned to a set of constants in the script.

```
Const ADS_PROPERTY_CLEAR = 1
Const ADS_PROPERTY_UPDATE = 2
Const ADS_PROPERTY_APPEND = 3
Const ADS_PROPERTY_DELETE = 4
```

Value arguments are almost always an array of values. The only exception is when you are clearing the current property values. The easiest way to create an array of new values to pass into the PutEx method is with the built-in function Array(). The Array() function is passed a comma-separated list of values that are then returned in an array structure. We will see this in action in the following sets of example code.

To clear the existing property values we would use the following code:

```
User.PutEx ADS_PROPERTY_CLEAR, "middleName", 0
```

Again, the only time you would not pass an array to the PutEx method is when clearing the property values. However, the method expects an argument, so we simply pass it the number 0.

When updating a property, the array in the third argument has two elements: the current value to be replaced and the new value.

```
User.PutEx ADS_PROPERTY_UPDATE, "otherTelephoneNumber", _
    Array(" (971) 555-1234", " (971) 555-1122")
```

To append additional values to a property, create an array of the new values and pass it to the PutEx method. If you pass a duplicate value to the property, it will be ignored.

```
User.PutEx ADS_PROPERTY_APPEND, "otherTelephoneNumber", _
    Array(" (971) 555-1111"," (971) 555-2222")
```

When removing a value from a property, the third argument contains an array of the current property values to remove. If one of the current values is not found it is ignored.

```
User.PutEx ADS_PROPERTY_DELETE, "otherTelephoneNumber", _
    Array("(971) 555-1122")
```

Active Directory Data Types

Active Directory holds several types of data in its attributes. To write a script that successfully displays and manipulates an Active Directory object's properties, you have to understand how the information in those properties is stored. Some properties store their data in simple strings or numeric values. Other properties return whole objects that you have to work with. In this section we look briefly at the some of the different Active Directory data types and show you how to work with them in your scripts.

DN (DISTINGUISHED NAME)

Not to be confused with the distinguishedName attribute, the DN data type links one Active Directory object to another. For example, the manager attribute links one user object to another. Most servers return an error if the DN value does not point to a valid Active Directory object. The DN property is treated as a string for reading and writing.

OCTETSTRING

An attribute of this data type is returned as an array of bytes, which represents a string of binary data. Normally these store security IDs and are returned as byte arrays. Byte arrays are typically set by the system; typically you will not work with them in VBScript. To see the value stored in an octet string you can use the following code (thanks to MVP Richard Mueller for reminding me how this works):

```
Set User = GetObject("LDAP://CN=Scott,CN=Users,DC=zygort,DC=com")
UserSID = User.Get("objectSID")
SIDString = ""
For X = 1 To LenB(UserSID)
SIDString = SIDString & " 0x" & _
Right("0" & Hex(AscB(MidB(UserSID, X, 1))), 2)
Next
WScript.Echo SIDString
```

DNWITHBINARY

This is also known as a distinguished name with an octet string.

CASEEXACTSTRING AND CASEIGNORESTRING

Attributes of these data types represent case-sensitive and case-insensitive strings, respectively. These strings may or may not contain Unicode strings. ADSI accepts and returns either kind of data type. Many of the Active Directory attributes use these two data types.

DIRECTORYSTRING

A DirectoryString attribute is a Unicode string that is treated as a CaseIgnoreString.

IA5STRING

An IA5String is treated as a CaseIgnoreString.

NUMERICSTRING

Attributes of this data type contain string values. All space characters are ignored during comparisons. ADSI does not verify that the value is actually numeric or contains spaces.

PRINTABLESTRING

Attributes of this data type contain string values. These strings are considered case-sensitive during comparisons. ADSI accepts any value without verifying that it is actually printable.

BOOLEAN

This attribute is stored as a 32-bit value. Zero is considered false and all other values are considered true.

UTCTIME

This attribute stores date and time information. Attributes of this data type are stored as an ASCII string. The date and time are represented in either the YYMMDDHHMM or YYMMDDHHMMSS format. Appended to this is either the character Z to indicate Greenwich Mean Time or the +/-HHMM format to indicate the offset from Greenwich Mean Time. In other words, adding the local time to the time offset should equal Greenwich Mean Time (`local + offset = GMT`).

ADSI accepts any string value without verifying that it is a valid time string. For ordering, the value is treated as an ASCII string, not as a date/time value.

GENERALIZEDTIME

This data type stores date and time information. Attributes of this data type are stored as an ASCII string. The date and time are represented in the same way as for the `UTCTime` data type except that the year value is represented with four characters instead of two. You should use this data type when extending the schema with a new date or time attribute.

INTEGER

This attribute is a 32-bit signed numeric value.

INTEGER8

This attribute is a 64-bit unsigned numeric value. Attributes of the `Integer8` data type can represent one of three different types of values: a date/time field, an interval field, or a counter field.

`Integer8` is also known as a *large integer*. Because VBScript does not know how to work with 64-bit values it is limited to 32-bit values. Therefore, these attributes are returned as COM objects implementing the `IADSLargeInteger` interface, which makes them a bit easier to deal with. This interface defines two properties—`HighPart` and `LowPart`—thus dividing the 64-bit integer into two 32-bit integers.

When storing a time value, `Integer8` represents time in intervals of 100 nanoseconds. Because one nanosecond is 1 billionth (.000000001) of a second, we are dealing with intervals of .0000001 second. One second is made of up 10 million of these intervals.

When storing a date/time value, this data type represents the number of intervals since midnight on January 1, 1601. Even with the `IADSLargeInteger` interface, we have to perform some math. For `Interval` values—such as the maximum password age—the following code should give us the value in minutes, hours, and days:

```
Const Int8Minutes = 600000000      '60 seconds * 10000000
Set Domain = GetObject("LDAP://DC=zygort,DC=com")
Set MaxPwdAgeLI = Domain.Get("maxPwdAge")
```

```
HighPart = MaxPwdAgeLI.HighPart
LowPart = MaxPwdAgeLI.LowPart
If LowPart < 0 Then HighPart = HighPart + 1
MaxPwdAge = Abs(HighPart * (2^32) + LowPart) / Int8Minutes
WScript.Echo "Maximum Password Age is " & MaxPwdAge & " minutes. "
WScript.Echo "Maximum Password Age is " & MaxPwdAge/60 & " hours. "
WScript.Echo "Maximum Password Age is " & MaxPwdAge/60/24 & " days. "
```

The math is not fun, but we will try to explain it. First we get the two 32-bit values from `HighPart` and `LowPart`. If `LowPart` is negative we add 1 to `HighPart`; otherwise the calculation will be off by a little over 7 minutes. This is just a "gotcha" of unsigned arithmetic (which VBScript doesn't like working with either), so we work around it with one line of code.

Next we shift the `HighPart` by 32 bits and add the value of `LowPart`. We want the absolute value of this calculation so it is enclosed in the `Abs` function. At this point we have the number of 100-nanosecond intervals that make up the value. Because we want the value in minutes, we divide the number of intervals by the number of intervals in a minute—60 seconds × (10,000,000 intervals in 1 second) = 60,000,000 intervals. Is this giving you a headache yet?

We took the more illustrative route to display the value in hours and days by doing the division in the `Echo` statement. You could easily have computed it right off the bat by changing the value of the constant to the proper number of intervals for an hour and a day.

For date/time values—such as the date the password was last set for a user object—the following code gives us the correct date and time value:

```
Set User = GetObject("LDAP://CN=Scott,CN=Users,DC=zygort,DC=com")
Set PwdLastSetLI = User.Get("PwdLastSet")
HighPart = PwdLastSetLI.HighPart
LowPart = PwdLastSetLI.LowPart
If LowPart < 0 Then HighPart = HighPart + 1
PwdLastSet = #1/1/1601# + _
(Abs((HighPart * (2^32)) + LowPart) /Int8Minutes) /  MinutesInDay
WScript.echo CDate(PwdLastSet)
```

The date from this code will be in Coordinated Universal Time (abbreviated UTC). It should be adjusted by the appropriate time-zone bias, which we can get from Windows Management Instrumentation (WMI) and add to our code. The bias is reported in number of minutes; for example the Central time zone is currently 6 hours, or 360 minutes, behind Greenwich Mean Time (GMT).

```
Set WMIService = GetObject("winmgmts:\\.\root\cimv2")
Set Items = WMIService.ExecQuery("Select * from Win32_TimeZone",,48)
For Each Item in Items
    Bias = Item.Bias
    DaylightSavings = Item.DaylightBias
Next
TimeBias = Bias - DayLightSavings
```

Be sure to also check for any daylight-savings adjustments that need to be made and add them to the time-zone value, as in the example. Finally, add the time-zone adjustment to the `Int8Minutes` value in the statement that computes the date.

```
PwdLastSet = #1/1/1601# + _
    (Abs((HighPart * (2^32)) + LowPart) / Int8Minutes + TimeBias) / MinutesInDay
```

Notice the use of parentheses in this statement. This is important, because if you remember the order of precedence from math class, you'll know that multiplication and division operations take place before addition and subtraction. This screws up the calculation and raises an error unless we use parentheses to add the Int8Minutes value to the time bias before dividing by the number of minutes in a day.

For Counter values we do not have to do any conversions at all.

Unfortunately you cannot reference any specific naming convention to determine what type the field represents (which of the three value types the attribute represents affects how you compute its value).

SECURITY DESCRIPTORS

Security descriptors contain the access control lists (ACLs) for Active Directory objects. When accessing one of these properties, ADSI returns an object with the IADSSecurityDescriptor interface. ACLs contain a list of access control entries (ACEs), each of which represents the rights to an object as assigned to either a user or a group. This list is exposed through the DiscretionaryACL property, which returns an object containing the individual entries. Creating a new ACE is beyond the scope of this book, but we can look at the entries with the following code (we discuss this in more detail in Chapter 19).

```
Set User = GetObject("LDAP://CN=Scott,CN=Users,DC=zygort,DC=com")
Set UserSec = User.Get("ntSecurityDescriptor")
WScript.Echo "Owner -> " & UserSec.Owner
WScript.Echo "Group -> " & UserSec.Group
Set DACL = UserSec.DiscretionaryACL
WScript.Echo "List Count -> " & DACL.AceCount
For Each Entry In DACL
    WScript.Echo "Trustee -->" & Entry.Trustee
    WScript.Echo "AccessMask -> " & Entry.AccessMask
    WScript.Echo "Ace Type --> " & Entry.AceType
Next
```

Searching for Data

Because Active Directory is a directory service, we are going to search it from time to time. One way to do this is by binding to each container and recursively searching through every Child container, one object at a time. This surely gets the job done, but the performance penalty is enough to make you never want to do it again.

Using the built-in search provider from ADSI, the ADSDSoObject provider, is a more efficient option. When used with the ActiveX Data Objects (ADO) library, ADSDSoObject provides a simple and powerful method to query Active Directory and process the results.

THE QUERY PATTERN

Let's start by defining a pattern to query Active Directory. This pattern is similar to the one we described earlier for working with Active Directory objects, and consists of the following six steps:

Select the search root. With Active Directory we select the container object we want to query. This can be the root of the domain or any Child container below it. To this container we bind a variable and use it as the base for our search.

Define a filter.   The filter defines the criteria the object must meet to be returned. This is usually based on object properties such as `objectClass` or `objectCategory`. The filter syntax can get very complicated and we will cover it in more detail soon.

Define the properties to retrieve.   These are the attributes you want to read from the objects in the result set. Leaving this portion empty returns all the object properties, but for most queries this is overkill.

Specify the scope.   The scope is the depth to which the search should go below the search root. The search can be limited to the search root itself, the search root and the immediate Child containers, or every container below the search root.

Execute the search.   This step passes the query to Active Directory for processing and then passes the results into an object we can process later.

Process the results.   In this step we go through the results one record at a time and display the returned property values or use them for further processing.

To execute our queries against Active Directory, let's use a set of objects designed for querying all kinds of data sources. The ADO type library has three objects we can use: `Connection`, `Command`, and `Recordset`.

The `Connection` object points to the data source, Active Directory in our case. The `Command` object executes the query and returns the result set in a `Recordset` object.

When we create instances of ADO objects, remember that these are not Active Directory objects, so we need to use the `CreateObject` function instead of `GetObject`. The object classes reside in the ADODB type library, so we have to reference the type library with the `ProgID` when we create the objects, as you will see in the code samples that follow.

SPECIFY THE SEARCH ROOT

The search root defines where in the Active Directory tree we want our search to begin. While the search root should almost always be a container or organizational unit object, technically you can use any object you want.

Rather than using the distinguished name of the container object, the search root is specified as an `ADsPath`. The search root can be a domain object, a global catalog server, or a member of one of the well-known container objects such as the `Configuration` container for querying the Active Directory schema.

The final step in constructing a search root is to enclose the `ADsPath` of the container object in angle brackets. Here are three examples of search roots:

```
<LDAP://DC=zygort,DC=com>
<LDAP://CN=Users,DC=zygort,DC=com>
<GC://DC=zygort,DC=com>
```

The search root value eventually finds a home in the `CommandText` property of the `Command` object. You can use the properties of the `RootDSE` object to find the values of the `defaultNamingContext` or `rootDomainNamingContext` to build the search root value on the fly rather than hard-coding it in your script.

DEFINE THE SEARCH FILTER

Undoubtedly the most difficult portion of the query process is constructing the search filter. Even for experienced query writers, writing a query typically starts simple and becomes more complex as the result set gets smaller and more focused, until finally only the desired data is returned. The search filter is the Active Directory equivalent of a SQL WHERE clause, but many would say it is less readable. We will take the syntax one step at a time and you'll have it under control in no time.

The basic filter syntax looks something like this:

```
( attribute = value )
```

With the code enclosed in parentheses, we compare a property to a value. We can check for equality (=), less than or equal to (<=), or greater than or equal to (>=). An approximately equal-to operator (~=) also exists but is ignored by Active Directory and treated as an equality comparison. Note that the less-than and greater-than operators are not supported, but you can achieve the same result with the operators we do have. If you want your filter to return all objects with a property value less than 50, you can create your filter to check that the property value is less than or equal to 49.

The search filters allow for exact matches or wildcard searches using the asterisk character (*). Most people are familiar with using the asterisk in wildcard searches, but its behavior in ADSI takes on two personalities. When used by itself it becomes a present operator and tests for the presence of a value in the attribute. When used with other characters, it tests for any number (including zero) of characters in the wildcard location. Wildcards can be used multiple times in the statement. Here are a few examples to give you an idea:

```
(attribute=*)       ' Present operator.
                    ' Matches objects that contain
                    ' a value in the attribute field
(attribute=*son)    ' Matches values ending in "son"
(attribute=A*)      ' Matches values beginning
                    ' with the letter A
(attribute=*ste*)   ' Matches values with "ste"
                    ' anywhere in the value
```

Using a wildcard does not guarantee that a value will contain anything in the wildcard location. The last example, `*ste*`, matches words like Stephen, Austen, or Paste. Wildcards nearly always return a large result set, so be prepared for a long query and a correspondingly long processing time on the result set.

Another useful operator we can employ in the value comparison is the Not operator, represented by an exclamation mark (!). The Not operator reverses the result of a comparison; in other words, if a statement was true it becomes false. Use this operation in front of the attribute value rather than with the equals sign.

```
(!givenName=Scott)   ' Returns all objects except those with a
                     ' givenName attribute of Scott
```

Now, remember those missing less-than or greater-than operators? By using the Not operator we can achieve the same result of those missing operators. Consider the following example:

```
(!attribute>=50)
```

This filter states that if an attribute value is greater than or equal to 50, it should *not* be returned (by way of the Not operator). This is the same as saying any value less than 50 *should* be returned. While the code does its job, it's a bad practice to get into and it can hurt your query performance.

Consider this: you are examining 1,000 records. The server takes x number of steps to perform a comparison. This gives us $x \times 1,000$ operations to get the final result set. An additional step per record is required to reverse the result of the comparison. Now we are looking at $(x + 1) \times 1,000$

operations to get the final result set. Each additional operation step takes more time to return the final result set. To optimize your queries, avoid the use of the Not operator whenever possible.

Finally, let's talk about handling those Active Directory attributes that implement bitmaps. We can still use bitmap attributes in our comparisons, but we have to use a set of comparisons defined by LDAP known as the *matching-rule object identifiers*, or matching-rule OIDs. Table 18.16 shows those rules.

TABLE 18.16:   Matching-Rule OIDs

MATCHING-RULE OID	DESCRIPTION
1.2.840.113556.1.4.803	Matches only if all bits from the attribute match the value. Equivalent to a bitwise AND operator.
1.2.840.113556.1.4.804	Matches if any bits from the attribute match the value. Equivalent to a bitwise OR operator.

To use the bitwise comparison rules, we have to specify the OID of the rule with the attribute, separated by colons on either side of the OID value. This makes the filter a little convoluted to read, so the following example explains it:

```
(groupType:1.2.840.113556.1.4.803:=2147483648)
```

Here we are looking at the groupType attribute. The bitwise AND rule performs the comparison. When we look at the groupType documentation we see that the bitmask that defines a group as a security group is the hexadecimal value 0x80000000, which translates to the numeric value 2147483648.

Let's finish by looking at these actual examples of a single-comparison filter:

```
(objectClass=user)        ' Returns objects of the user class
(objectCategory=person)   ' Returns objects of the person category
(sn=Fenster*)             ' Returns objects with the surname property
                          ' beginning with the letters "Fenster"
```

We've seen almost every variation of a single comparison we can use in a query. By itself, however, a single comparison isn't very powerful. By combining comparisons we can either narrow down our result set or make it larger. At this point things start to get more complicated; thus, as you make changes to your filter statement, you might want to consider keeping a copy of your last few filter statements to revert to in case you make a change in the wrong direction.

To combine single filters we group them inside a set of parentheses. In addition we need to specify exactly how we want to combine the results. Do we want to combine the results into one huge result set or do we want to specify that the result set has to satisfy each individual filter? The AND operator (&) and the OR operator (|) combine the individual results sets into the final result set. Here are a couple of examples to get you started:

```
(&(objectClass=user)(givenName=Scott))
(|(givenName=Scott)(givenName=Brad))
```

The first example uses the AND operator; this says that if objectClass is a user and the givenName attribute is Scott, then the row should be returned in the final result set. The second example uses the OR operator; this says if the givenName attribute is either Scott or Brad, then the row should be returned in the final result set.

In the next chapter we'll examine in detail queries specific to each type of Active Directory object.

DEFINE THE PROPERTIES TO RETRIEVE

We can specify which attributes we would like to view of the objects matching the filter criteria. The attribute search list is simply a comma-separated list of the attribute's LDAP display names. To see all the attributes you can use the wildcard character (*) in place of the list.

Returning all attributes is very wasteful of server and network resources. When you develop a script, if you are unsure which attributes you will need during the processing, you can rewrite the search-attribute list each time to add or remove an attribute from the processing section. When you are ready to put your script into production you should limit the attribute list to only those attributes used during processing.

One attribute you should keep in mind is ADsPath. If you need to modify any object attributes during processing, having the ADsPath allows you to bind to the object to make your changes.

SPECIFY THE SEARCH SCOPE

The search scope controls the depth of the query. This is the only optional portion of the Active Directory query because a default value (SubTree) is defined. Even though this is optional it is still good practice to keep your intentions clear by specifying the search scope. You can choose from three search scopes, as shown in Table 18.17.

TABLE 18.17: Search-Scope Options

SCOPE	DESCRIPTION
Base	Searches only the Search Root container.
OneLevel	Searches only the child objects of the Search Root container.
SubTree	The default search scope; this searches the Search Root container and all the child objects below, regardless of the depth of the child object.

EXECUTE THE SEARCH

At this point we have defined the search root, the filter, the attribute list, and the search scope. Now it is time to put them together and use them with the ADO objects and execute the query. We start with the Connection object, move on to the Command object, and use it to create a Recordset object. With the Recordset object full of data we move on to process the results.

ADO Connection Object

The Connection object points to the data source and is responsible for loading the appropriate data-source provider and validating the user credentials. To query Active Directory we use the ADsDSOObject as the provider.

```
Set Conn = CreateObject("ADODB.Connection")
Conn.Provider = "ADsDSOObject"
```

By default, the credentials of the user running the script are used for validation. We can specify an alternative set of credentials by setting the User ID and Password properties of the Connection object. We also have the option to encrypt the password for transmission across the network.

The last property, ADSI Flag, sets the authentication options for the connection. The authentication options are the same options we discussed in the "Binding" section. The default value is 0, which sets no authentication flags.

```
Conn.Properties("User ID") = "Scott"
Conn.Properties("Password") = "P@ssw0rd"
Conn.Properties("Encrypt Password") = True
Conn.Properties("ADSI Flag") = 0x1    ' Secure authentication
```

ADO Command Object

The Command object executes queries and other commands against a data source using the Connection object as the pathway. The ActiveConnection property is set to the Connection object.

```
Set Cmd = CreateObject("ADODB.Command")
Set Cmd.ActiveConnection = Conn
Cmd.CommandText = ADQuery    ' To be revealed soon
```

The CommandText property holds the Active Directory query we just built with the search root, filter, attribute list, and search scope. We will combine all four pieces into one statement for execution. When put together the statement will look something like this:

```
<LDAP://DC=zygort,DC=com>;(&(objectClass=User)(objectCategory=person));
    ADsPath,givenName,sn;subtree
```

Notice how we used semicolons to separate the individual parts of the query. We are going to use this statement as a string in the CommandText property of the Command object. The following example gives you an easy way to put the pieces together for the CommandText property:

```
SearchRoot = "<LDAP://DC=zygort,DC=com>"
Filter = " (&(objectClass=user)(objectCategory=person))
AttributeList = "ADsPath,givenName,sn"
Scope = "subTree"
Cmd.CommandText = SearchRoot & ";" & _
            Filter & ";" & _
            AttributeList & ";" & _
            Scope
```

By separating the Active Directory query into individual variable names and concatenating the strings together, the code becomes a bit easier to read and change later. Again, notice the semicolons separating each piece of the query.

Some additional properties of the Command object can also be useful. The Size Limit property limits the final result set's size. By default there is no limit. The TimeOut property sets the maximum time, in seconds, for the client to wait for results from the server. The default is no timeout. Setting this property even for smaller searches can act as a safety net in case network or other problems prevent a script from blocking indefinitely.

The Page Size property specifies the maximum number of results to be stored in a page of memory. When the Command object itself sets no default page size, Active Directory limits result returns to the first 1,000 items, regardless of the actual number of rows returned by the query. Therefore when the result set to be returned could contain more than 1,000 items, specifying a page-size value returns all the results, one page at a time until the end of the results. Setting the page size also improves performance by allowing the server to send the results one page at a time rather than waiting for the entire result set to be compiled. Paged searches also allow the client to stop the operation before the entire result set is returned. In a search operation that does not use pages, the client is blocked from doing anything else until the result set is compiled.

The Cache Results property specifies if the results should be cached on the client. This property is set to true by default. For large search operations, you may improve performance by setting this property to false.

The Sort By property sorts the result set on the server prior to returning it to the client. This property supports a comma-separated list of attributes to sort by, but Active Directory supports sorting only on a single key. Because the sorting is done on the server prior to the result set being returned to the client, this can severely slow down the performance of your queries.

```
Cmd.Properties("TimeOut") = 30
Cmd.Properties("Page Size") = 500
Cmd.Properties("Cache Results") = True
```

After setting the Command object properties we are ready to execute the command. To run the query, call the Execute method of the Command object. This method returns a Recordset object, so the code looks like this:

```
Set RS = Cmd.Execute
```

ADO Recordset Object

The Recordset object holds the results of the Active Directory query. More accurately, it holds the results of the query whether or not there are any results. Several properties of the ADO Recordset object allow you iterate through the query results and access the fields. Unlike binding to an object to access its properties, the Recordset is a read-only copy of data.

With a populated Recordset the only task remaining is to process the results. Keep in mind that we are processing Active Directory data, and some data types will return objects or multivalued properties that will have to be handled differently than straightforward values like integers and strings.

PROCESS THE SEARCH RESULTS

When the Recordset is first returned the current row marker is at the beginning of the file, making the BOF property true. If the query did not return any results the current row marker will also be at the end of the file, making the EOF property true. By checking the values of the BOF and EOF properties before processing the result set, you will know if the result is empty or not.

```
If RS.BOF and RS.EOF Then
    WScript.Echo "No results were found!"
End If
```

If the Recordset does contain results it is a simple matter to iterate through the result set. The only trick—and for some reason one of the easiest lines of code to forget—is to move the current row marker to the next row in the result set using a method called MoveNext. Each time we move to the next row in the Recordset we need to check if that row is at the end of the file with the EOF property. When we reach the end of the file it's time to stop processing the result set. Trying to move beyond the end of the result set will cause an error.

To iterate through the result set while checking for the end of the file, we can use a `Do-Until` loop. To retrieve the attribute values from the result set we can access the `Fields` property of the `Recordset` and supply the name of the attribute we want to retrieve. To refer to the `Fields` property of the `Recordset` object, we use the current row marker to retrieve the value of each attribute in the current row in the result set. The following code puts the pieces together:

```
Do Until RS.EOF
    WScript.Echo RS.Fields("ADsPath")
    RS.MoveNext
Loop
```

As you can see in this example we have printed out the value of the `ADsPath` property for each result. The `Fields` property allows you to enter either the field name (which should be the `ldapDisplayName` specified in the query) or the position of the field in the result set. This is also known as the ordinal value. Fields start at 0. In the query we've been building so far the selected attributes were `ADsPath`, `givenName`, and `sn`, respectively. `ADsPath` would be field 0, `givenName` would be field 1, and `sn` would be field 2. Accessing a field by ordinal value looks like this:

```
WScript.Echo RS.Fields(0)
```

When accessing a field by name the `Recordset` object looks up the field name and finds its ordinal position. Fields are stored in the `Recordset` in the same order they were defined in the query; therefore, you should already know the position of the field you want to access. You can increase your scripts' performance a bit by using ordinal values rather than field names.

Handling Errors

Rarely does a script get written perfectly the first time. When a script uses an outside resource, such as a database or a directory service, the chances that something could go wrong only increase. Now not only do you have to account for the usual scripting errors, but you also have to be prepared for errors that might occur on that resource.

You might encounter the following error types when developing a script:

- Syntax
- Runtime
- Logical

Syntax errors result when your script breaks the rules of the language. This is typically the result of misspelling something or using parentheses incorrectly when calling a subroutine. The interpreter will catch these for you, one line at a time, when you execute your script. It will even tell you what line number the error is on and what the error is. Using a good script editor (such as Sapien's PrimalScript) can help you avoid syntax mistakes by offering color-coding for recognized keywords, and IntelliSense to fill in the syntax for you. A good script editor also lets you see the line numbers of your script, which makes it easier to go directly to the offending line of code. Syntax errors are very common and easily fixed.

Runtime errors occur when your script attempts to do something and fails. Maybe it is trying to read a file that doesn't exist. It could be trying to divide a number by zero (always a classic!). The interpreter tells you what line the error occurred on and what error was reported when you execute your script. The chance for runtime errors increases when your script uses an external resource.

Logical errors occur when your script executes without crashing but does not produce the correct results. For example, if you design a script to create a user in Active Directory but the new user never gets created, your script has a logical error in it. Logical errors require more detective work because as far as the interpreter is concerned, your script does not have a problem.

This is where debuggers come in. A debugger lets you step through your code, execute one line at a time, and watch the results. A good debugger lets you view values in your script as they change and allows you to change them yourself. It also gives you the ability to jump over pieces of code that you know work and you do not want to waste your time with.

To execute a script in a debugger, add the //X option to the command line when you execute the script, as shown in the following example:

```
CScript //X MyBuggyScript.vbs
```

Figure 18.6 shows how you will be prompted to select a debugger if you have more than one debugger installed (unless you have already specified a debugger as the default). You might have a debugger installed already and not know it. Now we need to answer the question of which debugger you should use. There are two options from Microsoft, one of which is free and one of which you might already have.

FIGURE 18.6
Choosing a debugger

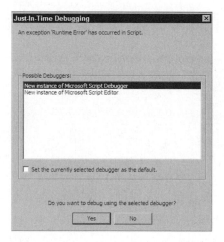

MICROSOFT SCRIPT DEBUGGER

Microsoft provides its Script Debugger as a free download. While it is far from the most powerful script editor available, it is definitely handy to have around. Be sure to download the correct version for your operating system (for Windows XP and above the file is scden10.exe). Table 18.18 presents the features of Microsoft's Script Debugger (see Figure 18.7).

When a debugging session begins, the first executable line of code is highlighted. At this point the highlighted line of code has not been executed. You can execute the line by pressing F8 or by selecting Debug ➤ Step. On the Debug menu you will see two other stepping options: Step Over (Shift+F8) and Step Out (Shift+Ctrl+F8).

The Step Over option allows you to execute a procedure (either a subroutine or a function) without actually stepping through the procedure itself. The procedure executes as it normally does, and debugging resumes at the line of code following the procedure call. This saves you debugging time by not having to continually step through a procedure that you already know works.

FIGURE 18.7

Microsoft Script
Debugger

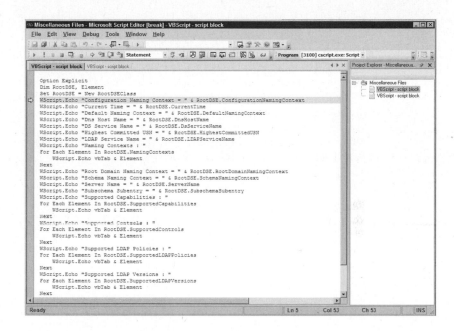

TABLE 18.18: Microsoft Script Debugger Features

FEATURE	DESCRIPTION
Breakpoints	Allows the user to specify a line of code to stop script execution and begin debugging
Bookmarks	Allows the user to jump to a bookmarked line of code
Command window	Displays or sets the value of a variable; executes subroutines or functions
Call stack	Displays the script call stack
Running documents	Displays the currently running scripts

You can also use the Step Over option on lines of code that do not call a procedure, and it will function like the Step Into option. This trick helps you avoid falling into a procedure by accident. Debugging is monotonous; you will find yourself pressing the F8 key absentmindedly. Without realizing it, you will step through lines of code in a procedure that you already know works. At that point you have to step the rest of the way through the procedure or use the Step Out option. By using the Step Over keys you can avoid the situation altogether.

The Step Out option allows you to execute a procedure and resume debugging on the line of code following the procedure call. This is more useful than it sounds, especially when you find yourself stepping through a long procedure call that you know works.

While you are stepping through your script code you will want to examine the values stored in your variables. You can do this from the Command window (select View ➤ Command Window from the menu). You cannot have the Command window open and step through the code at the same time. To view a variable's value enter a question mark followed by a space and the name of the variable, like this:

```
? MyVariable
```

The Command window retains the commands you entered, which allows you to view the variable's value later; simply scroll up to the command that displayed the value and press the Enter key. The new value appears immediately below the command, moving the old value (and all other statements in the window) down one line.

The Command window also lets you set or change the current value of a variable with a command such as this:

```
MyVariable = 100
```

Finally, the Command window allows you to execute a subroutine, procedure, or other line of valid VBScript code simply by entering it into the window and pressing Enter. Depending on the procedure you are executing, this can be useful in testing and resetting values in your script.

While Microsoft Script Debugger works, it is not my tool of choice. The Microsoft Script Editor offers a better script debugger, and you might already have it. If you have Microsoft Visual Studio installed, you will be doing yourself a favor by not installing Script Debugger, because it will change some of your system debugging settings in its favor.

Microsoft Script Editor

The second option is Microsoft's Script Editor, which comes as part of the Microsoft Office installation. This editor is installed with Word if you chose the HTML editing option with FrontPage; it offers a similar debugging experience that is much more powerful than Script Debugger. Many times I choose Script Editor simply because I don't need the extra overhead of Visual Studio to debug a Visual Basic script. (In updating this book Microsoft has elected to remove Script Editor from Word 2007. Luckily for us it is still available, just buried in a different location—which will be pointed out in a moment.)

Script Editor offers the same features as Script Debugger: breakpoints, bookmarks, an Immediate window in place of the Command window, call stack, and running documents. Script Editor also offers some additional features you might find useful; these are described in Table 18.19.

In fact, if you are looking for a decent, affordable editor with which to build your scripts, the Microsoft Script Editor (Figure 18.8) may be just the tool you need.

TABLE 18.19:   Additional Features

FEATURE	DESCRIPTION
DataTips	Pop-up windows that display the value of the variable currently under the mouse pointer
QuickWatch	A modal dialog window that quickly displays a variable value or an expression
Watch window	Displays selected variable values and expressions
Autos window	Displays variable values used in the current and previous statement
Locals window	Displays variable values local to the current procedure
Object browser	Displays object properties and methods and their arguments

FIGURE 18.8
Microsoft Script
Editor

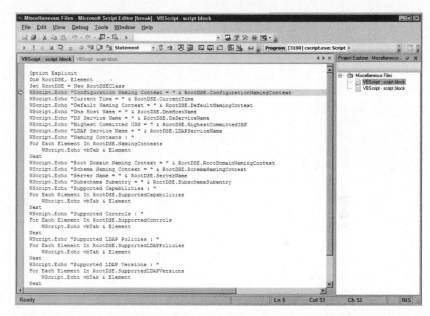

To execute Script Editor by itself, locate the MSE7.exe file. For Office 2003 installations, the file is in the \Program Files\Microsoft Office\Office11 folder. For Office 2007 installations, the file is in \Program Files\Common Files\Microsoft Shared\Office12.

When you select Script Editor as your debugger you may be prompted to select the program types you want to debug; Script will be the only option. Click the OK button to open the debugger; an arrow points to the first line of executable code. Again this line of code has not yet been executed. If you already have Script Editor open you can debug the script in the existing instance of Script Debugger or open a new instance.

When you're debugging a script, monitor the values of your variables and how they change throughout the execution of your script. Script Editor's tools are perfect for this. The DataTips pop-up windows allow you to place your mouse over a variable name and view its current value. By right-clicking the variable you can choose to add a watch or view a QuickWatch on the variable.

QuickWatch is a modal dialog window (see Figure 18.9); you cannot continue stepping through your code while it is open. This window can display the value of the variable you selected, or you can type another variable in the Expression field to view its value. You can type an expression, such as **25*25**, into the Expression field to have it evaluated, and you can create a Watch expression from the value by clicking the Add Watch button on the right side.

A Watch expression displays a variable's value or the result of an expression in a nonmodal window. This window can be docked in the editor or allowed to float, and it remains open while you step through your code, allowing you to see variable changes as they occur. Values that have changed display in red to alert you of the change.

To open the Watch window select Debug ➤ Windows ➤ Watch Window. You can use this window to add new Watch expressions simply by typing the expression into the next available line; you can also select lines and delete watches. All watches remain in the window until you remove them, even if the expression being watched is no longer valid.

When you watch a variable type with multiple values, such as an object or an array, the value's variables display in a tree view. You know a tree view is available if a plus sign displays to the left of the variable name. Click on the plus sign to expand the view, as shown in Figure 18.10.

FIGURE 18.9

Microsoft Script
Editor's QuickWatch
window

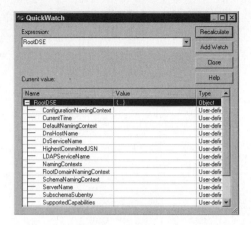

FIGURE 18.10

Microsoft Script
Editor's Watch
window

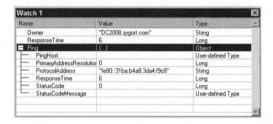

The Autos window displays a set of Watch expressions that the debugger controls, automatically displaying the values of the variables in the current and previous lines of code. In practice the Locals window is by far more useful than the Autos window when debugging.

The Locals window also displays a set of Watch expressions automatically, but these expressions correspond to all variables that are visible at the current location in your script. Think of it like a Watch window that automatically makes the changes for you. As you step into a procedure, any variables declared in that procedure are automatically added to the watch list. When you leave that procedure they are removed. To open the Locals window (shown in Figure 18.11), select Debug ➢ Windows ➢ Locals Window.

All windows that let you watch a variable also let you change the variable's value. Simply edit the value directly in the Value column, and the new value becomes available immediately. Keep in mind that this is truly effective only on variables that do not point to objects. You can modify the properties of an object but not the object reference itself.

FIGURE 18.11

Microsoft Script
Editor's Locals
window

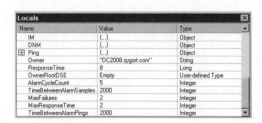

The object browser is not a debugging tool as much as it is an informational tool. You will use it mainly to probe the properties and methods of objects, giving you information about their functions, and arguments required by the methods.

Use the F11 key to step through code in Script Editor. To use the Step Over option press the F10 key. To step out of a procedure press Shift+F11.

You can also change the next line of code to be executed. By clicking and dragging the yellow arrow that points to the next line of code, you effectively change your script's execution path. You can either skip one or more lines of code entirely or re-execute a line of code.

As nice as the Microsoft Script Editor is (especially for the price), for heavy-duty scripting work you will want to invest in a heavy-duty editor. In my opinion the best in class is Sapien's PrimalScript editor. It works with the gamut of languages from VBScript to HTML to PowerShell and offers features such as built-in debugging and wizards. It's also a bit pricey, so do your own research into other scripting editors before choosing the editor that best suits your needs.

BREAKING YOUR CODE ON PURPOSE

Believe it or not the debugger is good for more than debugging. We already mentioned that Script Editor does indeed make a good script editor, but we are referring to using the debugger to actually break your script code. We would all like to think our scripts are bulletproof, but you can verify that only by actually firing bullets at them. It is time to start thinking about testing your scripts.

Watch windows let you change values. When you change values try using a value that is out of the ordinary and see how your script responds. Test a variety of data and note the outcome, especially every error code that is raised. By knowing the error codes ahead of time you can build effective error traps into your code to handle them when they arise.

You can also try a less code-invasive approach to testing your code. Unplug your computer from the network to simulate losing connectivity. Log in as different user, preferably one with reduced privileges, and execute your scripts. Test your script across slow links, dial-up, VPN—any remote-access system that might be in place. In a test domain you might even be able to load-test a domain controller while running your script.

The idea behind all this mayhem is to create a more robust script. Few things are as frustrating as a script that crashes halfway through its execution. Not only will you have to clean up whatever it left behind, you will also have to find out why it crashed, and fix the cause. Testing allows you to identify as many causes as possible ahead of time.

OPTION EXPLICIT

Even if you haven't used VBScript very long you've probably seen the statement `Option Explicit` at the beginning of a script. This setting causes the interpreter to stop script execution when it encounters a variable that you have not yet defined. This is possibly the easiest method for avoiding the dreaded logic error. Consider this code:

```
OneLongTextString = "Why in the world would I use Option Explicit?"
MsgBox OneLongTextStrng
```

This code displays an empty message box because it is trying to display a variable that didn't exist until that point. Without `Option Explicit` in effect the interpreter would recognize that the variable didn't exist and happily create it for you with no value assigned to it. This is obviously just a typographical error, but if you type like I do this scenario could be all too common.

Take the same code but add `Option Explicit` to the beginning. This time the code raises an error on the `MsgBox` line stating that the variable was not declared. We instantly know where the mistake is and zero in on the needed correction.

Always use `Option Explicit` and include it in any templates you create for scripts. It is very cheap insurance for avoiding logic errors.

ERROR TRAPS

In VBScript we can enable and disable an error trap with the `On Error` statement as shown here:

```
On Error Resume Next    ' enables the error trap
```

This statement tells the interpreter to continue executing the script if an error occurs, rather than abruptly ending the script. This is good in that your script does not crash halfway through a task. But it is bad in that if the error affects the rest of the script the results could be chaotic.

You can place the error-trap statement anywhere in your script. Placing the error-trap statement at the beginning of a script ensures that it remains in effect throughout the entire script. If you place it inside a procedure it will be in effect only until that procedure is finished. You can place error traps in multiple locations within the script.

The key to using an error trap is the `Err` object. The `Number` property of the `Err` object reports the error number of the last statement that was executing. If no error occurred, then `Err.Number` will equal 0. If `Err.Number` does not equal 0, a problem occurred that you will potentially have to deal with.

You do not have to check the value of `Err.Number` after every statement. However, you should always check it after "risky" statements. Risky statements are pieces of code that have a higher chance than most of raising an error. Message boxes, for example, seldom fail. Binding to an object in Active Directory, on the other hand, could fail for any number of reasons. You should always consider code that connects with a resource, such as Active Directory, to be risky.

When developing a script, many times I "hide" the error-trap statement in a comment to disable it. This allows the interpreter to tell me where my errors are during the initial phases of testing so I can zero in on syntax and runtime errors and fix them quickly. Using a comment reminds me to enable the error trap before I put the script into production.

ADSI and COM Errors

The errors returned by ADSI code are well-documented. There is also a strong possibility of errors coming from the COM system. In this section we look at the most common errors your Active Directory script could run into. The error codes are in hexadecimal format and the descriptions begin with the ADSI or COM constant name for the error code. ADSI errors are prefixed with LDAP_ and COM errors are prefixed with E_ADS_.

These constant names are not available directly in VBScript, which means that you will have to define your own constants to use them. In the next chapter you'll see how to make this a painless process.

This is not a complete list of possible script errors. You may encounter some VBScript errors along with ADSI and COM errors. In addition to your normal regimen of script testing you should perform a more invasive set of tests in the debugger. You should do this only in a safe test environment such as a virtual machine or a test domain. Try to see what kinds of errors result when you break your own script, then build your error traps to handle those errors.

CONNECTION ERRORS

Connection errors typically occur for simple reasons that are easy to correct. The LDAP server might be unavailable, especially if you specified a particular server. If you use `GetDSObject` and supply an alternate set of credentials, those credentials may not be valid (hint: did the password on the account expire?).

A referral usually occurs when you attempt to bind to a domain that is unavailable on your current network. This typically happens when you hard-code the domain into the script rather than retrieving the domain information from the RootDSE object. Finally, the LDAP server might require a stronger form of connection. Table 18.20 shows a brief list of error codes that ADSI might return when a connection fails.

TABLE 18.20:   ADSI Connection Error Codes

ADSI ERROR	ERROR TEXT	DESCRIPTION
0x800704C9	LDAP_CONNECT_ERROR	A connection could not be established.
0x8007052E	LDAP_INVALID_CREDENTIALS	The credentials supplied are invalid.
0x8007200E	LDAP_SERVER_BUSY	The LDAP server is too busy to service your request.
0x8007200F	LDAP_SERVER_UNAVAILABLE	An LDAP server is not available.
0x80072027	LDAP_AUTH_METHOD_NOT_SUPPORTED	The authentication method is not supported.
0x80072028	LDAP_STRONG_AUTH_REQUIRED	The LDAP server requires strong authentication.
0x8007202A	LDAP_AUTH_UNKNOWN	An unknown authentication error occurred.
0x8007202B	LDAP_REFERRAL	A referral occurred; check your LDAP syntax.
0x8007203A	LDAP_SERVER_DOWN	The LDAP server cannot be contacted.

SECURITY ERRORS

Security issues are also common in Active Directory scripts, particularly when those scripts are automated. Remember to configure your scripts to run in a security context with enough rights to perform the required actions. Always test your scripts using whatever security context will be used in production. Table 18.21 shows common security error codes ADSI might return.

TABLE 18.21:   ADSI Security Error Codes

ADSI ERROR	ERROR TEXT	DESCRIPTION
0x80070005	LDAP_INSUFFICIENT_RIGHTS	The security context of the script has insufficient rights to perform its actions.
0x8007052E	LDAP_INVALID_CREDENTIALS	The supplied credentials are invalid.
0x80072024	LDAP_ADMIN_LIMIT_EXCEEDED	Administration limit is exceeded on the server.
0x80072029	LDAP_INAPPROPRIATE_AUTH	The authentication is inappropriate.
0x8007202A	LDAP_AUTH_UNKNOWN	An unknown authentication error has occurred.

OPERATION ERRORS

Operation errors compose the majority of problems you will experience with ADSI scripts. Some errors have nothing to do with your script but indicate the server might be experiencing a problem. This frequently results in a timeout or server-unavailable error.

If an error points to an unknown or invalid object, verify that the AdsPath to the object is valid. Table 18.22 shows a list of common operational error codes ADSI might return.

TABLE 18.22: ADSI Operational Error Codes

ADSI ERROR	ERROR TEXT	DESCRIPTION
0x0	LDAP_SUCCESS	The operation succeeded.
0x80005000	E_ADS_BAD_PATHNAME	An invalid ADSI pathname does not point to an existing object in Active Directory. Verify the domain path.
0x80005004	E_ADS_UNKNOWN_OBJECT	An unknown object was requested. Verify the path to the object.
0x80005006	E_ADS_PROPERTY_NOT_SUPPORTED	The requested property is not supported. Verify the property name for the object.
0x80005009	E_ADS_OBJECT_UNBOUND	The ADSI object is not bound to a directory services object (call GetInfo).
0x8000500D	E_ADS_PROPERTY_NOT_FOUND	The property is not in the local property cache. Call GetInfo and verify the property is set on the server.
0x8000500E	E_ADS_OBJECT_EXISTS	The object already exists in Active Directory.
0x8000500F	E_ADS_SCHEMA_VIOLATION	The operation attempted to perform an action that the schema does not allow.
0x80005014	E_ADS_INVALID_FILTER	The filter syntax for the LDAP query is invalid.
0x8007001F	LDAP_OTHER	An unknown error has occurred.
0x800705B4	LDAP_TIMEOUT	The LDAP search timed out.
0x80071392	LDAP_ALREADY_EXISTS	The object already exists in Active Directory.
0x8007200A	LDAP_NO_SUCH_ATTRIBUTE	The attribute requested from an object does not exist.
0x8007200B	LDAP_INVALID_SYNTAX	The syntax of your LDAP query is invalid.
0x80072015	LDAP_NOT_ALLOWED_ON_NONLEAF	The attempted operation is not allowed on a nonleaf object such as a container.

TABLE 18.22:   ADSI Operational Error Codes *(CONTINUED)*

ADSI ERROR	ERROR TEXT	DESCRIPTION
0x80072023	LDAP_SIZELIMIT_EXCEEDED	The size limit on the query has been exceeded. Consider using the Page Size property.
0x80072030	LDAP_NO_SUCH_OBJECT	The requested object does not exist. Verify the path.
0x80072032	LDAP_INVALID_DN_SYNTAX	The distinguished name is invalid.
0x80072037	LDAP_NAMING_VIOLATION	A naming violation has occurred.
0x8007203C	LDAP_FILTER_ERROR	The search filter is invalid.
0x80072040	LDAP_NOT_SUPPORTED	An attempt has been made to access a feature of LDAP that is not supported by the server.

The Bottom Line

Connect to Active Directory using VBScript   Writing Active Directory scripts for your users will increase your productivity and lighten your workload. The first step is to connect to the current domain. A portable script does not reference a particular domain, but rather uses Active Directory itself to connect to the current domain.

Master It   Develop a script that connects to the current domain using the RootDSE object. Display the default naming context and current time of the domain.

Read and write the properties available in Active Directory objects   Being able to read and write the property values of objects in Active Directory is an important skill for a scripting administrator. After connecting to a given object in Active Directory, the script writer must know the name of the property as defined in the schema. The script writer must also remember to save any property changes to Active Directory.

Master It   Develop a script that connects to an object with the distinguished path CN=User1, DC=zygort,DC=com. First display the first and last name of the user. Next change the last name property to *Smith* and save the change to Active Directory.

Develop an LDAP query to retrieve objects from Active Directory   An LDAP query's format is different from the SQL queries you've probably seen before. The ability to write an effective LDAP query takes practice and requires a familiarity with the schema of your Active Directory domain.

Master It   Write an LDAP query to retrieve all objects of the OU class. Next narrow down the search to OUs beginning with *Sales*.

Write another LDAP query to find all objects of the user class that have a surname beginning with the letter *S*.

Chapter 19

Active Directory Scripts

In Chapter 18, "ADSI Primer," we looked at the various pieces of VBScript code used to build an Active Directory script. This chapter focuses on putting those pieces together into usable scripts. We also devote some time to examining different techniques you can incorporate into your scripts to customize them to suit your particular needs.

In this chapter you will learn to:

- ◆ Use the Windows Script File format (WSF)

- ◆ Use WSF to incorporate the functionality of an existing VBScript class into a new script

- ◆ Use VBScript classes to encapsulate Active Directory and other application functionality

- ◆ Write Visual Basic scripts to read and manage Microsoft Active Directory

We begin with some of the most commonly run scripts—those that deal with users and groups. Later we will work with scripts that submit queries to Active Directory. Finally we will look at scripts that deal with organizational units (OUs) and containers.

All script examples are available for download. Instead of reproducing the downloadable scripts line by line in this book, we will work on building a set of tools that allow you to create your own scripts in the future.

We will use a format of scripting files known as a Windows Script File (WSF). With this file format you can reference existing scripts and incorporate their functionality into your new script without copying and pasting lines of code. Using the WSF format you can reference existing type libraries, which allow you to take advantage of the constant declarations present in that type library.

Our scripts also make use of classes and objects coded in VBScript. That's right—we define our own objects in VBScript. This lets us define a set of functionality in a class—such as a user or group—and reuse that functionality in every script we create.

Fully documenting the use of Windows script files and VBScript classes is beyond the scope of this book, but to prepare you for the road ahead we will cover the basics. The primary functionality of the Windows script files we introduce is the ability to integrate external source files into our scripts. This has an effect similar to performing a copy-and-paste operation, but with only one line of code. Furthermore, if the external source file should ever be revised, every script that references that file will immediately use the updated code.

While we always encourage people to modify our sample code as they see fit, you should also always maintain a backup of the original code to fall back on if your modifications don't work out as planned. Always test your scripts in a lab environment before unleashing them in your production environment. And above all, don't be afraid to ask for assistance in any of the online forums or newsgroups.

Windows Script File Basics

Windows Script Files are written in an XML format. For our purposes these two elements must exist: `<job>` and `<script>`. A basic WSF file might look something like this:

```
<job>
<script language="VBScript">
WScript.Echo "This is a sample Windows script file."
</script>
</job>
```

XML files represent data. The use of bracketed tags (`<tag>`) is similar to the tags used in HTML, but the rules governing the use of tags are much stricter. All XML tags are case-sensitive. All tags must be closed in the same order in which they were opened. HTML parsers will simply ignore any tags that are out of order but the XML parser will throw a fit if proper nesting is not observed.

Element tags in XML can also employ attributes to further define the usage of the data stored in the element. In the `<script>` tag, the language of the script is specified as VBScript. The `<script>` tag can also use the `src` attribute to reference an external script.

```
<job>
<script language="VBScript" src="Output.vbs" />
<script language="VBScript">
Display "This is a sample Windows script file."
</script>
</job>
```

The first `<script>` tag references a script named `output.vbs`. The lack of a path statement usually means the file exists in the same folder as the referencing script. The tag also specifies the language of the external script as VBScript. External scripts are not confined to a single language; you can reference scripts written in any supported scripting language. Be sure to specify the appropriate language in the attribute.

While the previous example references only a single external file, you can reference as many files as you need. This enables you to create a new script using existing script functionality in a very short amount of time. It also allows you to update (or fix) the functionality in an external file and immediately use that new functionality in every script that references it. This can save potentially hundreds of hours of script updates.

VBScript Class Basics

Creating our own classes in VBScript is one of the most daunting tasks we will undertake as we create the scripting toolbox. It's also one of the most useful, because you can build your own new objects from scratch or extend existing objects without a programming suite such as Visual Studio, and without encountering the difficulties associated with distributing compiled objects and object libraries.

Recall from the previous chapter that classes are the blueprints for objects. We cannot use the code written in a class until we create an instance of the class. Because our VBScript classes essentially become part of the main script when they are referenced in the Windows script file, we can use the following syntax in our main script:

```
Set MyObject = New ObjectClass
```

Designing a class requires a slightly different train of thought than you might be used to when it comes to writing scripts; we tend to think in terms of getting input from the user and producing output for the user to read. As a general guideline, an object typically provides data, not output, for the main script. This separation of duties keeps our object relatively clean of extraneous code and focused on performing only the tasks it is designed to do. For example, we focus the user class on providing functionality specific to a user object in Active Directory—such as creating the user, getting and setting the user properties, and so forth. We leave the user input and output functions up to the main script.

We write a VBScript class as a structure. Inside the structure we define properties and methods that give the class object its functionality. Do not let the terms *property* and *method* intimidate you. Creating a property is just like creating a variable, and creating a method is just like creating a subroutine or function. Let's create a simple class to use as an example.

```
Class MySampleClass
Public FirstName
Public LastName
Public BirthDate

Public Function GetAge
    GetAge = DateDiff("yyyy",BirthDate,Now)
End Function

Public Sub DisplayFullName
    WScript.Echo FirstName & " " & LastName
End Sub
End Class
```

Eagle-eyed readers will notice I just broke my guideline about classes displaying output. Because this is only an example script, I'll let myself off with a warning.

The class begins with the keyword Class followed by the class name, and ends with the keywords End Class. These statements enclose our class structure. Within the structure we define the properties FirstName, LastName, and BirthDate, and the methods GetAge and DisplayFullName. To use this class in a script we might use the following code:

```
<job>
<script language="VBScript" src="MySampleClass.vbs" />
<script language="VBScript">
Set MyObject = New MySampleClass
MyObject.FirstName = "Tom"
MyObject.LastName = "Sawyer"
MyObject.BirthDate = #10/31/1970#
MyObject.DisplayFullName
WScript.Echo "is " & MyObject.GetAge & " years old."
Set MyObject = Nothing
</script>
</job>
```

Notice the main script itself is in the WSF format with a <script> tag referencing the external script MySampleClass.vbs, which holds the class definition. The object syntax should look familiar after dealing with objects in Chapter 18. A new `MyObject` object is created using the `Set` and `New` keywords. The object then references the properties and methods of the class. Finally the object is cleaned up by setting it equal to the keyword `Nothing`.

WHY DID YOU USE POUND SIGNS AROUND THAT DATE?

Assigning a value to an object's property can be tricky. Dates can be extra tricky because there are just so many different ways to interpret a date format, especially in different cultures! If I were to enclose the date in quotation marks, the date would be a string value that VBScript would have to convert to a date value. And VBScript converts that string to a date value only if it first successfully determined that the string value is, in fact, a valid date! One of the pitfalls of a forgiving language such as VBScript is that some ugly inefficiencies crop up in certain situations, such as date handling.

To avoid that ugliness we can enclose the date in pound signs. This format basically tells VBScript "This really is a date value; just assign it to the property!" and we can move on with the rest of our script.

Scope

In the class definition all statements are declared with the keyword `Public`. This operator defines the scope or visibility of a property or method. Think of the class; to expose anything inside the box to the outside (such as our main script) we have to create an opening in the box. We do this programmatically with the keyword `Public`. We can also create variables and procedures inside the box that only other procedures inside the box can see. These are declared with the keyword `Private`.

Why create a private variable or procedure? Although there are many reasons to create private variables and procedures, the most common reason is that they are simply not needed outside the object itself. Their functionality is confined inside the object, typically to manipulate the object itself or to refine some aspect of the object's behavior. Allowing access to them from outside the object could create unpredictable results.

Property Procedures

This leads to another facet of object-class design we must examine in the class variables themselves. In our example class all the variables were defined as `Public`, which allowed the main code to manipulate their values directly. Now think about what would happen if this excerpt of code were run in the main script:

```
MyObject.BirthDate = "Today"
WScript.Echo MyObject.GetAge
```

This would cause an error because the `DateDiff` function cannot convert `Today` into a date. This is a pitfall of declaring a variable itself as `Public`. We can control the value in the variable by using property procedures. Property procedures look exactly like regular procedure calls but they are treated as variables in the main code. Using property procedures allows you to programmatically control the values set in the main code. In the following example I will fix the `MySampleClass` definition for the `BirthDate` variable using property procedures:

```
Class MySampleClass
Private m_BirthDate
Public Property Get BirthDate
```

```
    BirthDate = m_BirthDate
End Property

Public Property Let BirthDate(Value)
If IsDate(Value) Then
    m_BirthDate = Value
Else
    Err.Raise 100,"MySampleClass","Invalid Date"
End If
End Property
End Class
```

First, the original `Public` variable was redefined as `Private`. It was also renamed by prefixing m_ to the beginning of the variable name. This notation commonly denotes a variable as private to the module (m_ for module). Next, two property procedures were added. The first property procedure has the keyword `Get` and the second has the keyword `Let`. `Get` procedures return a value to the calling code; in this case the value of the m_BirthDate variable. The `Let` procedure is used when the main code attempts to set a value for the variable. The new value is passed into the variable `Value`. In this example the new value is checked to see if it is a valid date. If it is, the new value is assigned to the private variable. If it is not valid, an error is raised. The main code requires no changes because the procedure name matches the original property name.

Class Initialization and Termination

An object's life always includes at least two events: the object is initialized and it is destroyed (or terminated). An object is initialized when an instance of the class is created. An object is destroyed when the object is set to `Nothing` (or the script ends and the object goes out of scope). Two optional pieces of code can be coupled to these events.

Two VBScript subroutines tie to these two events. These subroutine names are reserved and must be used to properly link the event to the subroutine. When the object is created the `Class_Initialize` subroutine is called. When the object is destroyed the `Class_Terminate` subroutine is called. Omitting either or both of these procedures is acceptable; the interpreter simply ignores their absence.

Using these two subroutines allows the object to set itself up for business when it is created and to close down shop when finished. In the `Class_Initialize` procedure, variables can be set up and given initial values. In the `Class_Terminate` procedure, any internal object can be set to `Nothing` and any other work necessary to clean up after the object can be performed.

Script Locations

Like most files on a system, script files tend to be saved wherever is most convenient. This is a very bad practice, especially when external script files are referenced. The path in the `src` attribute is very important and will cause a script to fail if it cannot find the external script. Organizing your script files will save you many hours of hair-loss treatment.

There are typically two types of scripts: *user-invoked* scripts for regular administrative duties such as creating new users, and *unattended* scripts, which are usually invoked by the Task Scheduler or in response to a defined server event. This can affect how and where you locate your scripts.

All scripts should be on a file-server share that is backed up regularly. Locating the script files on a share ensures they are accessible from any network computer, depending on share and NTFS security assigned to the folder.

Because all scripts execute within a security context, permissions on the subordinate share and folders are important to consider. For unattended script execution you should create a normal user account with very limited permissions and a very strong password (depending on your network security restrictions you might consider exempting the password from expiring). Unattended scripts can be located in a secured folder beneath the script share.

You must also factor into the layout the location of any scripts referenced by another script. Most of these resource scripts rarely change. I typically set up a separate folder named `includes` to store my resource files. This gives me a consistent path for my external script files no matter what location the main script is executing from. Figure 19.1 gives you an example of a folder hierarchy you might find useful.

FIGURE 19.1
Script folder hierarchy

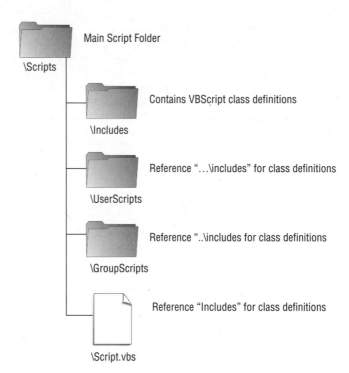

RootDSE Scripts

We will start by creating a fairly straightforward VBScript class to represent the RootDSE (Root DSA-Specific Entry) of an Active Directory domain, and then we'll use it in some scripts. Creating an instance of this class gives us an object whose properties we can reference when we need information from Active Directory's RootDSE object.

RootDSE Class

The RootDSE object initializes by creating a reference object to the RootDSE of the Active Directory domain. This object is assigned to a private variable. All of the RootDSE object properties are exposed through function calls.

```
Option Explicit
'=======================================================================
Class RootDSEClass
'=======================================================================
Private m_RootDSEObject
Private m_DomainObject
'=======================================================================
Private Sub Class_Initialize
   Set m_RootDSEObject = GetObject("LDAP://RootDSE")
End Sub
'=======================================================================
Private Sub Class_Terminate
   Set m_RootDSEObject = Nothing
End Sub
'=======================================================================
Public Function ConfigurationNamingContext
   ConfigurationNamingContext = _
      m_RootDSEObject.Get("configurationNamingContext")
End Function
'=======================================================================
Public Function CurrentTime
   CurrentTime = m_RootDSEObject.Get("currentTime")
End Function
'=======================================================================
Public Function DefaultNamingContext
   DefaultNamingContext = m_RootDSEObject.Get("defaultNamingContext")
End Function
'=======================================================================
Public Function DnsHostName
   DnsHostName = m_RootDSEObject.Get("dnsHostName")
End Function
'=======================================================================
Public Function DsServiceName
   DsServiceName = m_RootDSEObject.Get("dsServiceName")
End Function
'=======================================================================
Public Function HighestCommittedUSN
   HighestCommittedUSN = m_RootDSEObject.Get("highestCommittedUSN")
End Function
'=======================================================================
Public Function LDAPServiceName
   LDAPServiceName = m_RootDSEObject.Get("LDAPServiceName")
End Function
'=======================================================================
Public Function NamingContexts
' Returns an array!
   NamingContexts = m_RootDSEObject.Get("namingContexts")
End Function
'=======================================================================
```

```
Public Function RootDomainNamingContext
    RootDomainNamingContext = _
        m_RootDSEObject.Get("rootDomainNamingContext")
End Function
'====================================================================
Public Function SchemaNamingContext
    SchemaNamingContext = m_RootDSEObject.Get("schemaNamingContext")
End Function
'====================================================================
Public Function ServerName
    ServerName = m_RootDSEObject.Get("serverName")
End Function
'====================================================================
Public Function SubschemaSubentry
    SubschemaSubentry = m_RootDSEObject.Get("subschemaSubentry")
End Function
'====================================================================
Public Function SupportedCapabilities
' Returns an array!
    SupportedCapabilities = m_RootDSEObject.Get("supportedCapabilities")
End Function
'====================================================================
Public Function SupportedControls
' Returns an array!
    SupportedControls = m_RootDSEObject.Get("supportedControl")
End Function
'====================================================================
Public Function SupportedLDAPPolicies
' Returns an array!
    SupportedLDAPPolicies = m_RootDSEObject.Get("supportedLDAPPolicies")
End Function
'====================================================================
Public Function SupportedLDAPVersions
' Returns an array!
    SupportedLDAPVersions = m_RootDSEObject.Get("supportedLDAPVersion")
End Function
'====================================================================
Public Function SupportedSASLMechanisms
' Returns an array !
    SupportedSASLMechanisms = _m_RootDSEObject.Get("supportedSASLMechanisms")
End Function
'====================================================================
End Class
```

This object allows you to have a RootDSE object at your disposal in any script simply by adding a reference to the RootDSEObject.vbs script and creating an instance of the object. Now we can create some scripts to use this class and see it in action. All the following scripts use this same approach.

Viewing RootDSE Properties

This script uses the RootDSEClass class and simply calls each of the functions mapped to a RootDSE property. Keep in mind that some RootDSE properties contain an array of values, and that array is passed back to the main code. In the main code you must use a loop to cycle through each item in the array.

```
<job>
<script language="VBScript" src="includes\RootDSEClass.vbs" />
<script>
Option Explicit
Dim RootDSE, Element
Set RootDSE = New RootDSEClass
WScript.Echo "Configuration Naming Context = " & _
    RootDSE.ConfigurationNamingContext
WScript.Echo "Current Time = " & RootDSE.CurrentTime
WScript.Echo "Default Naming Context = " & RootDSE.DefaultNamingContext
WScript.Echo "DNS Host Name = " & RootDSE.DnsHostName
WScript.Echo "DS Service Name = " & RootDSE.DsServiceName
WScript.Echo "Highest Committed USN = " & RootDSE.HighestCommittedUSN
WScript.Echo "LDAP Service Name = " & RootDSE.LDAPServiceName
WScript.Echo "Naming Contexts : "
' this for-next structure is the loop
' each element in the naming contexts is cycled through
For Each Element In RootDSE.NamingContexts
    WScript.Echo vbTab & Element
Next
WScript.Echo "Root Domain Naming Context = " & _
    RootDSE.RootDomainNamingContext
WScript.Echo "Schema Naming Context = " & RootDSE.SchemaNamingContext
WScript.Echo "Server Name = " & RootDSE.ServerName
WScript.Echo "Subschema Subentry = " & RootDSE.SubschemaSubentry
WScript.Echo "Supported Capabilities : "
For Each Element In RootDSE.SupportedCapabilities
    WScript.Echo vbTab & Element
Next
WScript.Echo "Supported Controls : "
For Each Element In RootDSE.SupportedControls
    WScript.Echo vbTab & Element
Next
WScript.Echo "Supported LDAP Policies : "
For Each Element In RootDSE.SupportedLDAPPolicies
    WScript.Echo vbTab & Element
Next
WScript.Echo "Supported LDAP Versions : "
For Each Element In RootDSE.SupportedLDAPVersions
    WScript.Echo vbTab & Element
Next
WScript.Echo "Supported SASL Mechanisms : "
```

```
For Each Element In RootDSE.SupportedSASLMechanisms
    WScript.Echo vbTab & Element
Next
</script>
</job>
```

The RootDSE object is really simple—probably too simple for an actual class implementation such as this. But in this case it served a purpose: to familiarize you with the use of a VBScript class. Now we can proceed to some more complicated VBScript classes and their implementations.

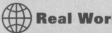 **Real World Scenario**

REINVENTING THE WHEEL

Jimmy was tasked with writing a complement of scripts to automate various Active Directory administrative tasks. One script had to examine how close each user's password was to expiring. Another had to verify that every manager belonged to a special set of groups. Still another script had to examine each object in a set of organizational units to verify that only computer accounts existed. Each script was to run at night, unattended, sending the results of each script either to an e-mail address or to a log file.

While designing the scripts Jimmy realized that each one had similar functions. Each script connected to Active Directory. Each script ran some type of query. Some scripts sent results to an e-mail address, some to a log file. A lot of functionality was duplicated. Rather than reinventing the wheel for each script, Jimmy realized he could reuse the same code in different scripts.

The easy solution was to simply copy and paste the relevant code from one script to another. But then it happened: Jimmy made a mistake. During testing he realized he made a similar error in connecting to Active Directory. The error was easily fixed, but now he had to fix the error on every script he had copied the original code to. The prospect of having to fix the same error in multiple scripts wasn't appealing, to say the least.

Jimmy knew that other programming languages support the ability to grab the code from one module and use it in another program. This would allow him to write (and fix) the supporting code in one place, yet still incorporate its functionality in multiple scripts. Dynamic link libraries (DLLs) do this all the time. Surely VBScript supported some way of doing the same.

The answer was again actually very simple: he changed the format. He found that by placing his VBScript code in the WSF format he could reference an outside code file in a completely new script. He began by placing the code that connected to Active Directory in a separate .vbs file, then referenced that file in a new script in the WSF format. It worked! He immediately rewrote the other scripts to use the new format and include the external .vbs file. When he changed to the .vbs file, every script used the new change upon the next execution. Perfect!

Jimmy continued to expand his script library using this technique. He wrote new scripts from the beginning to take advantage of the library of functions that had already been written and proved effective. Development time for new scripts was cut dramatically. More design time was spent on the primary function of each script rather than on reinventing the same functionality over and over again.

Domain Scripts

A number of other objects stored in Active Directory use domain information. The best and most familiar example is information about the password expiration on the domain. By implementing the domain object as a class in our VBScript we can save ourselves some work by making some less-intuitive information—such as the values of the well-known GUIDs—available through the use of the class.

DomainClass

The domain object can be used to access the default domain and its properties. When the object initializes it creates a temporary object referencing the RootDSE of the domain. After using the object to get the default naming context of the domain it de-references the object.

One of the most frustrating things about VBScript classes is their lack of support for constants as class members. In other words, a constant can't be declared and used throughout the class definition. To work around this, several private variables are declared and then given their values in the Class_Initialize procedure.

Different functions are used in the class to get information from the domain. The GetProperty function is passed the property name to retrieve. From the previous chapter you learned that the values stored in properties can be either a normal string or number value, or they can return an object.

In most cases a LargeInteger value will be returned, which we can assume represents either a time or counter value. Regardless of the value represented, it is still a 64-bit integer that must be converted to view. To handle this possibility, the code in the GetProperty procedure looks to see if an object was returned. If so the object is converted into a 32-bit integer before returning to the calling code.

Password properties are stored as a bitmap in the pwdProperties property of the domain. To determine what properties are set, the constant name for the property is passed into the GetPasswordProperty function as a string. A logical AND operation is performed on the property bitmap and the appropriate value to determine if the bit is set.

```
Option Explicit
'=====================================================================
Class DomainClass
'=====================================================================
' Private and public variables
Private m_DomainObject
Private m_DefaultNamingContext
'=====================================================================
Private Sub Class_Initialize
Dim RootDSE
Set RootDSE = GetObject("LDAP://RootDSE")
m_DefaultNamingContext = RootDSE.Get("defaultNamingContext")
Set m_DomainObject = GetObject("LDAP://" & m_DefaultNamingContext)
Set RootDSE = Nothing
End Sub
'=====================================================================
Private Sub Class_Terminate
Set m_DomainObject = Nothing
End Sub
```

```
'===========================================================================
Public Function GetProperty(PropertyName)
On Error Resume Next
If IsObject(m_DomainObject.Get(PropertyName)) Then
    Dim PropertyObject, PropertyValue
    Set PropertyObject = m_DomainObject.Get(PropertyName)
    If PropertyObject.LowPart = 0 Then
        PropertyValue = 0
    Else
        PropertyValue = Int(Abs((PropertyObject.HighPart * 2^32) _
                            + PropertyObject.LowPart)/600000000)
End If
    GetProperty = PropertyValue
Else
    GetProperty = m_DomainObject.Get(PropertyName)
End If
End Function
'===========================================================================
Public Function GetPasswordProperty(PropertyName)
Dim PasswordProperties
PasswordProperties = m_DomainObject.Get("pwdProperties")
Select Case LCase(PropertyName)
    Case "domain_password_complex"
        GetPasswordProperty = CBool(PasswordProperties And _
                DOMAIN_PASSWORD_COMPLEX)
    Case "domain_password_no_anon_change"
        GetPasswordProperty = CBool(PasswordProperties And _
                DOMAIN_PASSWORD_NO_ANON_CHANGE)
    Case "domain_password_no_clear_change"
        GetPasswordProperty = CBool(PasswordProperties And _
            DOMAIN_PASSWORD_NO_CLEAR_CHANGE)
    Case "domain_lockout_admins"
        GetPasswordProperty = CBool(PasswordProperties And _
            DOMAIN_LOCKOUT_ADMINS)
    Case "domain_password_store_cleartext"
        GetPasswordProperty = CBool(PasswordProperties And _
            DOMAIN_PASSWORD_STORE_CLEARTEXT)
    Case "domain_refuse_password_change"
        GetPasswordProperty = CBool(PasswordProperties And _
            DOMAIN_REFUSE_PASSWORD_CHANGE)
    Case Else
        GetPasswordProperty = "Unknown Property"
End Select
End Function
'===========================================================================
Public Function GetPathFromWKGuid(WKGuidName)
Dim WKGuid, GuidObject
Select Case LCase(WKGUIDName)
    Case "users" : WKGuid = _
            "a9d1ca15768811d1aded00c04fd8d5cd"
```

```
    Case "computers" : WKGuid = _
            "aa312825768811d1aded00c04fd8d5cd"
    Case "systems" : WKGuid = _
            "ab1d30f3768811d1aded00c04fd8d5cd"
    Case "domaincontrollers" : WKGuid = _
            "a361b2ffffd211d1aa4b00c04fd7d83a"
    Case "infrastructure" : WKGuid = _
            "2fbac1870ade11d297c400c04fd8d5cd"
    Case "deletedobjects" : WKGuid = _
            "18e2ea80684f11d2b9aa00c04f79f805"
    Case "lostandfound" : WKGuid = _
            "ab8153b7768811d1aded00c04fd8d5cd"
    Case Else
        Err.Raise 120,m_ErrSource, _
                "Unknown well-known GUID specified."
        GetPathFromWKGuid = ""
        Exit Function
End Select
On Error Resume Next
Set GuidObject = GetObject("LDAP://<WKGuid=" & _
                    WKGuid & "," & m_DefaultNamingContext & ">")
If Err.Number = 0 Then
    GetPathFromWKGuid = GuidObject.Get("distinguishedName")
Else
    GetPathFromWKGuid = "Error binding to Well-Known GUID"
End If
Set GuidObject = Nothing
End Function
'=======================================================================
Public Function GetDomainControllers
' This returns a Dictionary Object!
Dim DCList, NTDSObject, Server
DCList = m_DomainObject.GetEx("masteredBy")
Set GetDomainControllers = WScript.CreateObject("Scripting.Dictionary")
For Each NTDSObject in DCList
    Set Server = _
        GetObject(GetObject("LDAP://" & NTDSObject).Parent) _
    GetDomainControllers.Add Server.Get("dNSHostName"), Nothing
Next
End Function
'=======================================================================
Public Property Get m_ErrSource
    m_ErrSource = "DomainObject"
End Property
Public Property Get DOMAIN_PASSWORD_COMPLEX
    DOMAIN_PASSWORD_COMPLEX = &H1
End Property
Public Property Get DOMAIN_PASSWORD_NO_ANON_CHANGE
    DOMAIN_PASSWORD_NO_ANON_CHANGE = &H2
End Property
```

```
Public Property Get DOMAIN_PASSWORD_NO_CLEAR_CHANGE
    DOMAIN_PASSWORD_NO_CLEAR_CHANGE = &H4
End Property
Public Property Get DOMAIN_LOCKOUT_ADMINS
    DOMAIN_LOCKOUT_ADMINS = &H8
End Property
Public Property Get DOMAIN_PASSWORD_STORE_CLEARTEXT
    DOMAIN_PASSWORD_STORE_CLEARTEXT = &H16
End Property
Public Property Get DOMAIN_REFUSE_PASSWORD_CHANGE
    DOMAIN_REFUSE_PASSWORD_CHANGE = &H32
End Property
'=====================================================================
End Class
```

WHY ARE THE DOMAIN OBJECT CONSTANTS DEFINED IN PROPERTY PROCEDURES?

The simple answer is that we need those constants defined somewhere. The alternative is to hard-code the constant value into every line of code that requires it, and trust us when we say that is *not* a road you want to go down. The problem is that VBScript classes don't support class-level constants—for example, in our sample class the variable m_DomainObject is at the top of the class definition. Notice that the variable is also not defined within the body of any procedure. This gives the variable a class-level scope, which basically means the variable is "visible" from any location in the class (because it is defined as Private it is not visible outside of the class).

Normally we use the keyword Const to define a constant. This reserves memory for the variable, assigns it a value, and prevents the code from changing it when the script executes. Unfortunately, VBScript classes do not support the Const keyword at the class level. So we have to work around it somehow.

One option is to simply define the constants as variables. This would work perfectly well except that you could inadvertently change the value and never be the wiser (that is, until you have to debug your script for the unexpected results). I don't want to deal with that possibility.

Our solution is to define the constants as properties of the class, but only define the Get procedure, which returns the value of the constant. By not defining a Let procedure for the property we effectively make the property read-only, which fits the definition of a constant.

You might notice that the properties are also defined with the Public scope. That allows us to access those constant values from our new scripts as well! You'll see this design at work in most of the remaining class definitions.

View Domain Account Policies

This script uses the DomainClass class to find the default domain password policies. The password-age properties return a value in minutes, and it is then converted into a value representing days.

```
<job>
<script language="VBScript" src="includes/DomainClass.vbs" />
<script>
Option Explicit
Dim Domain
```

```
Set Domain = New DomainClass
WScript.Echo "Lockout Duration  = " & _
    Domain.GetProperty("lockoutDuration") & " minutes."
WScript.Echo "Lockout Threshold = " & _
    Domain.GetProperty("lockoutThreshold") & " attempts."
WScript.Echo "Lockout Observation Window = " & _
    Domain.GetProperty("lockoutObservationWindow") & " minutes."
WScript.Echo "Maximum Password Age = " & _
    Domain.GetProperty("maxPwdAge") / 60 / 24 & " days."
WScript.Echo "Minimum Password Age = " & _
    Domain.GetProperty("minPwdAge") / 60 / 24 & " days."
WScript.Echo "Minimum Password Length = " & _
    Domain.GetProperty("minPwdLength") & " characters."
WScript.Echo "Password History Length = " & _
    Domain.GetProperty("pwdHistoryLength") & " passwords remembered."
</script>
</job>
```

View Domain Password Policies

This script uses the DomainClass class to view the current settings for the domain's password policy. The string value passed into GetPasswordProperty is the same as the constant defined for the property bitmask.

```
<job>
<script language="VBScript" src="includes\DominObject.vbs" />
<script>
Option Explicit
Dim Domain
Set Domain = New DomainObject
WScript.Echo "Complex Passwords Enabled  = " & _
Domain.GetPasswordProperty("domain_password_complex")
WScript.Echo "No Anonymous Changes  = " & _
    Domain.GetPasswordProperty("domain_password_no_anon_change")
WScript.Echo "No Clear Change  = " & _
    Domain.GetPasswordProperty("domain_password_no_clear_change")
WScript.Echo "Lockout Admins  = " & _
    Domain.GetPasswordProperty("domain_lockout_admins")
WScript.Echo "Store Password in Clear Text  = " & _
    Domain.GetPasswordProperty("domain_password_store_cleartext")
WScript.Echo "Refuse Password Change  = " & _
    Domain.GetPasswordProperty("domain_refuse_password_change")
</script>
</job>
```

Active Directory Query Scripts

Before we get into creating and using classes to represent various objects in Active Directory (such as users and computers), let's take a look at how to query Active Directory (AD). Building and executing queries in AD is often the basis for additional operations on other objects. For example, to change the value of a property for users on the domain you first have to collect a list of users on the domain! That is best done with a query, so creating a class to help us quickly build AD queries makes a lot of sense.

QueryClass

The QueryClass class simplifies creating and executing queries against AD. Several steps must be performed to create an AD query: selecting the search root, creating the filter, selecting the attributes, and defining the search scope.

The script typically uses several ActiveX Data Objects (ADOs) to define and execute the query. A Connection object defines a connection to an AD source. A Command object defines, controls, and executes the query itself. The results are returned in a Recordset object. With the QueryClass class the ADO objects are created and controlled within the object itself.

The main script first creates an instance of the QueryClass class. Then the search root, filter, attributes, and search scope are defined by setting their respective properties in the QueryClass. Finally the query is executed by calling the ExecuteQuery function of the object. The results are returned in a Recordset; the main script iterates through the recordset and processes the results.

In the previous chapter we discussed the effect the Command object properties have on the query result set and performance. Those properties are defined in a Dictionary object, which stores the property name as the key. The properties are loaded into the Dictionary object in the Class_Initialize procedure. You can change these defaults to suit your environment as necessary. To change the properties prior to executing the query, call the SetProperty procedure and pass in the property name and new value.

Two private utility functions appear at the bottom of the script. These functions examine the value entered for the SearchRoot property. The function FormatAdsPath attempts to correctly format the LDAP path entered. The function ADObjectExists checks AD for the existence of the specified search root. These utility functions also appear in other object classes.

```
Option Explicit
'=========================================================================
Class QueryClass
'=========================================================================
Private m_cn, m_cmd
Private m_SearchRoot
Private m_FilterText
Private m_Attributes
Private m_SearchScope
Private m_CmdProperties
'=========================================================================
Private Sub Class_Initialize
Set m_cn = WScript.CreateObject("ADODB.Connection")
m_cn.Provider = "ADsDSOObject"
Set m_cmd = WScript.CreateObject("ADODB.Command")
Set m_CmdProperties = WScript.CreateObject("Scripting.Dictionary")
m_CmdProperties.Add "Asynchronous", False
m_CmdProperties.Add "Cache results", True
m_CmdProperties.Add "Chase referrals",ADS_CHASE_REFERRALS_EXTERNAL
m_CmdProperties.Add "Column Names Only", False
m_CmdProperties.Add "Deref Aliases", False
m_CmdProperties.Add "Page size", 1000
```

```vb
m_CmdProperties.Add "SearchScope", ADS_SCOPE_SUBTREE
m_CmdProperties.Add "Size Limit", 0' No limit
m_CmdProperties.Add "Sort On", ""' No sort
m_CmdProperties.Add "Time Limit", 600      ' 600 seconds = 10 Minutes
m_CmdProperties.Add "Timeout", 600
m_SearchScope = "subtree"                   ' Set a default scope
End Sub
'========================================================================
Private Sub Class_Terminate
m_cn.Close
Set m_cn = Nothing
Set m_cmd = Nothing
Set m_CmdProperties = Nothing
End Sub
'========================================================================
Public Property Get FilterText
   FilterText = m_FilterText
End Property

Public Property Let FilterText(FilterValue)
   m_FilterText = FilterValue
End Property
'========================================================================
Public Property Get Attributes
   Attributes = m_Attributes
End Property

Public Property Let Attributes(AttributeList)
   m_Attributes = AttributeList
End Property
'========================================================================
Public Property Get Scope
   Scope = m_SearchScope
End Property

Public Property Let Scope(ScopeText)
   Select Case UCase(ScopeText)
      Case "BASE" : m_SearchScope = "base"
      Case "ONELEVEL" : m_SearchScope = "onelevel"
      Case "SUBTREE" : m_SearchScope = "subtree"
      Case Else
         Err.Raise 100, m_ErrSource, "Invalid Scope"
         m_SearchScope = "subtree"' Set a default scope
   End Select
End Property
'========================================================================
Public Property Get SearchRoot
   SearchRoot = m_SearchRoot
End Property
```

```
Public Property Let SearchRoot(AdsPath)
   If ADObjectExists(AdsPath) Then
      m_SearchRoot = "<" & FormatAdsPath(AdsPath) & ">"
   Else
      Err.Raise 101, m_ErrSource, "Invalid AdsPath"
   End If
End Property
'=======================================================================
Public Sub SetProperty(PropertyName,PropertyValue)
If m_CmdProperties.Exists(PropertyName) Then
   m_CmdProperties(PropertyName) = PropertyValue
Else
   Err.raise 105, m_ErrSource, "Unknown command property"
End If
End Sub
'=======================================================================
Public Function ExecuteQuery
Dim CmdProperty
If IsEmpty(m_SearchRoot) Then
   Err.Raise 102, m_ErrSource, "No search root defined"
   Exit Function
End If
If IsEmpty(m_Attributes) Then
   Err.Raise 103, m_ErrSource, "No attributes defined"
End If
m_cn.Open
m_cmd.ActiveConnection = m_cn
For Each CmdProperty In m_CmdProperties.Keys
    m_cmd.Properties(CmdProperty) = m_CmdProperties(CmdProperty)
Next
m_cmd.CommandText = m_SearchRoot & ";" & _
                    m_FilterText & ";" & _
                    m_Attributes & ";" & _
                    m_SearchScope
Set ExecuteQuery = m_cmd.Execute
End Function
'=======================================================================
Private Function ADObjectExists(ADsPath)
Dim ADObject, LDAPObject
ADSPath = FormatAdsPath(AdsPath)
On Error Resume Next
Set LDAPObject = GetObject("LDAP:")
Set ADObject = _
    LDAPObject.OpenDSObject(ADSPath,vbNullString,vbNullString, _
                            ADS_FAST_BIND)
If Err.Number = 0 Then
   ADObjectExists = True
Else
   ADObjectExists = False
End If
```

```
    Set ADObject = Nothing
    Set LDAPObject = Nothing
    End Function
    '=====================================================================
    Private Function FormatAdsPath(ADsPath)
    If Not CBool(Instr(ADsPath,"LDAP://")) Then
        FormatAdsPath = "LDAP://" & ADsPath
    Else
        FormatAdsPath = AdsPath
    End If
    End Function
    '=====================================================================
    Public Property Get m_ErrSource
    m_ErrSource = "QueryClass"
    End Property
    Public Property Get ADS_CHASE_REFERRALS_NEVER
        ADS_CHASE_REFERRALS_NEVER = &H00
    End Property
      Public Property Get ADS_CHASE_REFERRALS_SUBORDINATE
        ADS_CHASE_REFERRALS_SUBORDINATE = &H20
    End Property
    Public Property Get ADS_CHASE_REFERRALS_EXTERNAL
        ADS_CHASE_REFERRALS_EXTERNAL = &H40'  Default
    End Property
    Public Property Get ADS_CHASE_REFERRALS_ALWAYS
        ADS_CHASE_REFERRALS_ALWAYS = &H60
    End Property
    Public Property Get ADS_SCOPE_BASE
        ADS_SCOPE_BASE = 0
    End Property
    Public Property Get ADS_SCOPE_ONELEVEL
        ADS_SCOPE_ONELEVEL = 1
    End Property
    Public Property Get ADS_SCOPE_SUBTREE
        ADS_SCOPE_SUBTREE = 2
    End Property
    Public Property Get ADS_FAST_BIND
        ADS_FAST_BIND = &H20
    End Property
    '=====================================================================
    End Class
```

Using the QueryClass

This class requires you to set only four properties: the SearchRoot, the Attributes to be returned, the Scope of the search, and the FilterText. After setting those four properties, you can call the ExecuteQuery method and assign the result to an object. The resulting object is an ADO Recordset.

You must loop through Recordsets until the Recordset's EOF property is True. Don't forget to execute the MoveNext method of the Recordset in the loop!

The `QueryClass` object is the third VBScript class we have examined. As you look at the code for the class itself and then at the code for the script that uses the class, notice the difference in their sizes. While the class code is large (and they are going to get larger yet!), the script that uses the class is relatively small. When you consider the time savings in both writing and then debugging code, using classes in your scripts should prove to be more cost- and time-effective than writing several stand-alone scripts.

Search for User Accounts

This script uses the `QueryClass` class to return a list of the user objects in the specified Active Directory domain. The domain is specified by using the `RootDSEClass`, which we examined earlier, and retrieving the default naming convention property.

```
<job>
<script language="VBScript" src="includes\RootDSEClass.vbs" />
<script language="VBScript" src="includes\QueryClass.vbs" />
<script>
Dim RootDSE
Set RootDSE = New RootDSEClass
Dim Query
Set Query = New QueryClass
Query.SearchRoot = RootDSE.DefaultNamingContext
Query.Attributes = "cn,AdsPath"
Query.Scope = "subtree"
Query.FilterText = "(&(objectClass=user)(objectCategory=person))"
Dim Results
Set Results = Query.ExecuteQuery
Do Until Results.eof
   WScript.Echo Results.Fields(0) & "," & Results.Fields(1)
   Results.MoveNext
Loop
Set QueryObject = Nothing
Set RootDSE = Nothing
</script>
</job>
```

Search for Computer Accounts

This script uses the `QueryClass` class to return a list of the computer objects in the specified Active Directory domain.

```
<job>
<script language="VBScript" src="includes\RootDSEClass.vbs" />
<script language="VBScript" src="includes\QueryClass.vbs" />
<script>
Dim RootDSE
Set RootDSE = New RootDSEClass
Dim Query
Set Query = New QueryClass
Query.SearchRoot = RootDSE.DefaultNamingContext
```

```
Query.Attributes = "cn,AdsPath"
Query.Scope = "subtree"
Query.FilterText = "(&(objectClass=computer)(objectCategory=computer))"
Dim Results
Set Results = Query.ExecuteQuery
Do Until Results.eof
    WScript.Echo Results.Fields(0) & "," & Results.Fields(1)
    Results.MoveNext
Loop
Set QueryObject = Nothing
Set RootDSE = Nothing
</script>
</job>
```

Search for Groups

This script uses the QueryClass class to return a list of the group objects in the specified Active Directory domain.

```
<job>
<script language="VBScript" src="includes\RootDSEClass.vbs" />
<script language="VBScript" src="includes\QueryClass.vbs" />
<script>
Dim RootDSE
Set RootDSE = New RootDSEClass
Dim Query
Set Query = New QueryClass
Query.SearchRoot = RootDSE.DefaultNamingContext
Query.Attributes = "cn,AdsPath"
Query.Scope = "subtree"
Query.FilterText = "(&(objectClass=group)(objectCategory=group))"
Dim Results
Set Results = Query.ExecuteQuery
Do Until Results.eof
    WScript.Echo Results.Fields(0) & "," & Results.Fields(1)
    Results.MoveNext
Loop
Set QueryObject = Nothing
Set RootDSE = Nothing
</script>
</job>
```

Search for Organizational Units

This script uses the QueryClass class to return a list of OUs in the specified AD domain. If you don't see all the objects you expect, remember that an OU is different from a container, and this script is looking only for OUs. We'll give you a script to find the containers next.

```
<job>
<script language="VBScript" src="includes\RootDSEClass.vbs" />
```

```
<script language="VBScript" src="includes\QueryClass.vbs" />
<script>
Dim RootDSE
Set RootDSE = New RootDSEClass
Dim Query
Set Query = New QueryClass
Query.SearchRoot = RootDSE.DefaultNamingContext
Query.Attributes = "name,AdsPath"
Query.Scope = "subtree"
Query.FilterText = "(objectClass=organizationalUnit)"
Dim Results
Set Results = Query.ExecuteQuery
Do Until Results.eof
    WScript.Echo Results.Fields(0) & "," & Results.Fields(1)
    Results.MoveNext
Loop
Set QueryObject = Nothing
Set RootDSE = Nothing
</script>
</job>
```

Search for Containers

This script uses the QueryClass class to return a list of containers in the specified Active Directory domain. Remember that OUs and containers may look the same in Active Directory Users and Computers (ADUC), but they are different objects as far as Active Directory is concerned. In fact, you might see some containers that you've never noticed in ADUC.

```
<job>
<script language="VBScript" src="includes\RootDSEClass.vbs" />
<script language="VBScript" src="includes\QueryClass.vbs" />
<script>
Dim RootDSE
Set RootDSE = New RootDSEClass
Dim Query
Set Query = New QueryClass
Query.SearchRoot = RootDSE.DefaultNamingContext
Query.Attributes = "name,AdsPath"
Query.Scope = "subtree"
Query.FilterText = "(objectClass=container)"
Dim Results
Set Results = Query.ExecuteQuery
Do Until Results.eof
    WScript.Echo Results.Fields(0) & "," & Results.Fields(1)
    Results.MoveNext
Loop
Set QueryObject = Nothing
Set RootDSE = Nothing
</script>
</job>
```

Search for Containers and OUs

Now that we've covered querying for OUs and containers separately, let's put them together with this script. Be careful when typing the `FilterText` property of the `Query` object; the opening and closing parentheses must be properly paired together (I've made this mistake myself more times than I can count)! We've split the line up for easier reading.

```
<job>
<script language="VBScript" src="includes\RootDSEClass.vbs" />
<script language="VBScript" src="includes\QueryClass.vbs" />
<script>
Dim RootDSE
Set RootDSE = New RootDSEClass
Dim Query
Set Query - New QueryClass
Query.SearchRoot = RootDSE.DefaultNamingContext
Query.Attributes = "name,AdsPath"
Query.Scope = "subtree"
Query.FilterText = _
   "((objectClass=container)" & _
     "(objectClass=organizationalUnit))"
Dim Results
Set Results = Query.ExecuteQuery
Do Until Results.eof
   WScript.Echo Results.Fields(0) & "," & Results.Fields(1)
   Results.MoveNext
Loop
Set QueryObject = Nothing
Set RootDSE = Nothing
</script>
</job>
```

User Scripts

Finally we get to start building classes that represent real Active Directory objects, starting with the User object. The User object is possibly the most-used object in AD; it is constantly being created, deleted, and modified in one way or another. Again, our goal here is to use a class to reduce some of the complexity of the ADSI object model.

UserClass

The UserClass class obviously represents a User object in Active Directory. To use this object it must be instantiated like the other classes and then either bound to an existing User object in AD or used to create a new user. User properties can then be modified, the password reset, or the account unlocked. The group membership of the user can be returned, a group can be joined, or the group membership can be copied from another user. Finally, the object can be saved to AD.

The Create method is used to create a new user. This method takes three arguments: the ADsPath to the container that will hold the User object, the Common Name (CN) of the new object, and the Security Account Manager (SAM) account name of the new object. The object is created and saved to Active Directory and a reference to the new User object is returned.

To bind to an existing user we employ the `BindToUser` method, which only takes the `ADsPath` to the object as an argument. A reference is returned to the object. When the reference is returned it may be ignored if you don't need it, as you will see in the example scripts that follow the class definition.

```
Option Explicit
'===================================================================
Class UserClass
'===================================================================
Private Sub Class_Initialize
End Sub
'===================================================================
Private Sub Class_Terminate
End Sub
'===================================================================
' Private and public variables
Private m_UserObject
'===================================================================
Public Function BindToUser(UserPath)
If ADObjectExists(UserPath) Then
   Set m_UserObject = GetObject(FormatAdsPath(UserPath))
   m_UserObject.GetInfo
   Set BindToUser = m_UserObject
Else
   Err.Raise 102,m_ErrSource,"Object does not exist"
End If
End Function
'===================================================================
Public Function Create(ContainerPath,CN,AccountName)
If CN = "" Or ContainerPath = "" Or AccountName = "" Then
   Err.Raise 101,m_ErrSource,"Missing arguments"
   Exit Function
End If
Dim Container
If ADObjectExists(ContainerPath) Then
   Set Container = GetObject(FormatAdsPath(ContainerPath))
   Set m_UserObject = Container.Create("user",FormatCN(CN))
   m_UserObject.Put "sAMAccountName", AccountName
   m_UserObject.SetInfo
   m_UserObject.GetInfo
   Set Create = m_UserObject
Else
   WScript.Echo "Error connecting to container!"
   WScript.Quit(1)
End If
End Function
'===================================================================
Public Function Copy(Destination,CN,AccountName)
If CN = "" Or AccountName = "" Then
   Err.Raise 101,m_ErrSource,"Missing arguments"
   Exit Function
```

```
      End If
   If ADObjectExists(Destination) Then
      Dim PropertiesToCopy
      PropertiesToCopy = _
         Array("company","co","c","l","st","zipcode","scriptPath")
      Dim Container, ObjectCopy
      Set Container = GetObject(FormatAdsPath(Destination))
      Set ObjectCopy = Container.Create("user","CN=" & FormatCN(CN))
      ObjectCopy.Put "sAMAccountName", AccountName
      ObjectCopy.SetInfo
      ObjectCopy.GetInfo
      Dim PropertyName
      On Error Resume Next
      For Each PropertyName In PropertiesToCopy
         ObjectCopy.Put PropertyName,m_UserObject.Get(PropertyName)
      Next
      ObjectCopy.SetInfo
      Set Copy = ObjectCopy
   Else
      Err.Raise 109,m_ErrSource,"Destination does not exist"
   End If
   End Function
'=======================================================================
Public Property Get AccountEnabled
   AccountEnabled = Not(m_UserObject.AccountDisabled)
End Property
'=======================================================================
Public Property Let AccountEnabled(EnableValue)
If CBool(EnableValue) Then
   m_UserObject.AccountDisabled = False
Else
   m_UserObject.AccountDisabled = True
End If
End Property
'=======================================================================
Public Property Let Password(NewPassword)
   m_UserObject.SetPassword(CStr(NewPassword))
End Property
'=======================================================================
Public Property Get PasswordDoesntExpire
PasswordDoesntExpire = _
CBool(m_UserObject.Get("userAccountControl") And _
   ADS_UF_DONT_EXPIRE_PASSWD)
End Property
'=======================================================================
Public Property Let PasswordDoesntExpire(ExpireValue)
Dim NewValue
If CBool(ExpireValue) Then
   NewValue = CalculateBitMask _
```

```
            (m_UserObject.Get("userAccountControl"), _
          ADS_UF_DONT_EXPIRE_PASSWD,True)
    Else
       NewValue = CalculateBitMask _
            (m_UserObject.Get("userAccountControl"), _
          ADS_UF_DONT_EXPIRE_PASSWD,False)
    End If
    m_UserObject.Put "userAccountControl", NewValue
    End Property
    '=================================================================
    Public Property Get LockedOut
       LockedOut = m_UserObject.IsAccountLocked
    End Property
    '=================================================================
    Public Sub UnlockAccount
    If CBool(m_UserObject.IsAccountLocked) Then
       m_UserObject.IsAccountLocked = False
    End If
    End Sub
    '=================================================================
    Public Property Get PasswordExpired
    PasswordExpired = CBool(m_UserObject.Get("userAccountControl") _
                    And ADS_UF_PASSWORD_EXPIRED)
    End Property
    '=================================================================
    Public Function Move(Destination)
    If ADObjectExists(Destination) Then
       m_UserObject.MoveHere FormatAdsPath(Destination), _
           m_UserObject.Get("distinguishedName")
    Else
       Err.Raise 109,m_ErrSource,"Invalid object or destination"
    End If
    End Function
    '=================================================================
    Public Property Get Groups
    ' Returns a Dictionary object!
    Dim GroupList, Group
    Set GroupList = WScript.CreateObject("Scripting.Dictionary")
    For Each Group In m_UserObject.GetEx("memberOf")
       GroupList.Add Group,0
    Next
    Set Groups = GroupList
    End Property
    '=================================================================
    Public Property Get AllGroups
    ' Returns a Dictionary object!
    Dim GroupList
    Set GroupList = WScript.CreateObject("Scripting.Dictionary")
    GetMembership m_UserObject.Get("distinguishedName"),GroupList
    Set AllGroups = GroupList
```

```
End Property
'========================================================================
Private Function GetMembership(ObjectAdsPath,List)
Dim tmpObject, Group
Set tmpObject = GetObject(FormatAdsPath(ObjectAdsPath))
On Error Resume Next
For Each Group In tmpObject.GetEx("memberOf")
   If Err.Number = 0 Then
      If Not(List.Exists(Group)) Then
         List.Add Group,0
         GetMembership Group,List
      End If
   End If
   Err.Clear
Next
End Function
'========================================================================
Public Sub CopyGroupsFromUser(UserPath)
If ADObjectExists(UserPath) Then
   Dim GroupsToCopy
   Dim CopyObject
   Set CopyObject = GetObject(FormatAdsPath(UserPath))
   On Error Resume Next
   GroupsToCopy = CopyObject.GetEx("memberOf")
   If Err.Number <> 0 Then
      Dim Group, GroupObject
      For Each Group In GroupsToCopy
         Set GroupObject = GetObject(FormatAdsPath(Group))
         GroupObject.PutEx ADS_PROPERTY_APPEND, _
            "member", Array(UserPath)
         GroupObject.SetInfo
      Next
   End If
Else
   WScript.Echo "User " & UserPath & " does not exist."
   WScript.Quit(1)
End If
End Sub
'========================================================================
Public Sub JoinGroup(GroupPath)
If ADObjectExists(GroupPath) Then
   Dim GroupObject
   Set GroupObject = GetObject(FormatAdsPath(GroupPath))
   GroupObject.PutEx ADS_PROPERTY_APPEND, _
      "member", Array(m_UserObject.Get("distinguishedName"))
   GroupObject.SetInfo
Else
   WScript.Echo "Group " & GroupPath & " does not exist."
   WScript.Quit(1)
End If
```

```
End Sub
'=========================================================================
Public Sub Save
m_UserObject.SetInfo
m_UserObject.GetInfo
End Sub
'=========================================================================
Public Property Get PropertyList
' Returns a Dictionary object!
Dim Properties
Set Properties = WScript.CreateObject("Scripting.Dictionary")
Dim PropertyIndex, PropertyValue
For PropertyIndex = 0 To (m_UserObject.PropertyCount - 1)
    For Each PropertyValue In m_UserObject.Item(PropertyIndex).Values
        If Not (Properties.Exists( _
            m_UserObject.Item(PropertyIndex).Name)) Then
                Properties.Add _
                    m_UserObject.Item(PropertyIndex).Name, _
                    GetADsTypeValue(CInt( _
                        PropertyValue.AdsType),PropertyValue)
        End If
    Next
Next
Set PropertyList = Properties
End Property
'=========================================================================
Public Sub SetProperty(PropName,PropValue)
On Error Resume Next
m_UserObject.Put PropName,PropValue
If Err.Number <> 0 Then
    WScript.Echo "Error setting property " & PropName
End If
End Sub
'=========================================================================
Public Sub MultiPropertyClear(PropertyName)
    m_UserObject.PutEx ADS_PROPERTY_CLEAR,PropertyName,0
End Sub
'=========================================================================
Public Sub MultiPropertyUpdate(PropertyName, PropertyArray)
    m_UserObject.PutEx ADS_PROPERTY_UPDATE,PropertyName,PropertyArray
End Sub
'=========================================================================
Public Sub MultiPropertyAppend(PropertyName, PropertyArray)
    m_UserObject.PutEx ADS_PROPERTY_APPEND,PropertyName,PropertyArray
End Sub
'=========================================================================
Public Sub MultiPropertyDelete(PropertyName, PropertyArray)
    m_UserObject.PutEx ADS_PROPERTY_DELETE,PropertyName,PropertyArray
End Sub
```

```
'=======================================================================
Private Function ADObjectExists(ADsPath)
Dim ADObject, LDAPObject
ADSPath = FormatAdsPath(AdsPath)
On Error Resume Next
Set LDAPObject = GetObject("LDAP:")
Set ADObject = LDAPObject.OpenDSObject( _
   ADsPath,vbNullString,vbNullString,ADS_FAST_BIND)
If Err.Number = 0 Then
   ADObjectExists = True
Else
   ADObjectExists = False
End If
Set ADObject = Nothing
Set LDAPObject = Nothing
End Function
'=======================================================================
Private Function GetADsTypeValue(AdsType,AdsValue)
Select Case CInt(adsType)
   Case 1 : GetADsTypeValue = AdsValue.DNString
   Case 2 : GetADsTypeValue =  AdsValue.CaseExactString
   Case 3 : GetADsTypeValue =  AdsValue.CaseIgnoreString
   Case 4 : GetADsTypeValue =  AdsValue.PrintableString
   Case 5 : GetADsTypeValue =  AdsValue.NumericString
   Case 6 : GetADsTypeValue =  CStr(AdsValue.Boolean)
   Case 7 : GetADsTypeValue =  AdsValue.Integer
   Case 8 : GetADsTypeValue =  "Octet String"
   Case 9 : GetADsTypeValue =  AdsValue.UTCTime
   Case 10 :
         Dim PropertyLargeInteger, LargeIntegerValue
         Dim LargeIntegerDate, DateHigh, DateLow
         Set PropertyLargeInteger = AdsValue.LargeInteger
         DateHigh = PropertyLargeInteger.HighPart
         DateLow = PropertyLargeInteger.LowPart
         If DateLow < 0 Then
            DateHigh = DateHigh + 1
         End If
         If (DateHigh = 0) And (DateLow = 0 ) Then
            LargeIntegerDate = #1/1/1601#
         Else
            LargeIntegerDate = #1/1/1601# + (((DateHigh * _
                     (2 ^ 32)) + DateLow)/600000000)/1440
         End If
         If IsDate(LargeIntegerDate) And _
               LargeIntegerDate > #1/1/1970# Then
            GetADsTypeValue = LargeIntegerDate
         Else
            GetADsTypeValue = _
               PropertyLargeInteger.HighPart * 2^32 + _
```

```
                        PropertyLargeInteger.LowPart
            End If
      Case 11 : GetADsTypeValue = "Provider Specific"
      Case 12 : GetADsTypeValue = "Object Class"
      Case 13 : GetADsTypeValue = "Case Ignore List"
      Case 14 : GetADsTypeValue = "Octet List"
      Case 15 : GetADsTypeValue = "Path"
      Case 16 : GetADsTypeValue = "Postal Address"
      Case 17 : GetADsTypeValue = "TimeStamp"
      Case 18 : GetADsTypeValue = "BackLink"
      Case 19 : GetADsTypeValue = "Typed Name"
      Case 20 : GetADsTypeValue = "Hold"
      Case 21 : GetADsTypeValue = "Net Address"
      Case 22 : GetADsTypeValue = "Replica Pointer"
      Case 23 : GetADsTypeValue = "Fax Number"
      Case 24 : GetADsTypeValue = "Email"
      Case 25 : GetADsTypeValue = "NT Security Descriptor"
      Case 26 : GetADsTypeValue = "Unknown"
      Case Else : GetADsTypeValue = "Unknown - " & _
                     AdsValue.adsType
   End Select
End Function
'=====================================================================
Private Function FormatCN(CNValue)
FormatCN = Replace(CNValue,"LDAP://","")
If Left(FormatCN,3) <> "CN=" Then
   FormatCN = "CN=" & FormatCN
End If
End Function
'=====================================================================
Private Function FormatAdsPath(ADsPath)
If CBool(Instr(ADsPath,"LDAP://")) Then
   FormatAdsPath = AdsPath
Else
   FormatAdsPath = "LDAP://" & ADsPath
End If
End Function
'=====================================================================
Private Function CalculateBitMask(CurrentMask,NewMask,EnableFlag)
If CBool(EnableFlag) Then
   CalculateBitMask = CurrentMask Or NewMask
Else
   If CurrentMask And NewMask Then
      CalculateBitMask = CurrentMask Xor NewMask
Else
      CalculateBitMask = CurrentMask
   End If
End If
End Function
'=====================================================================
```

```
Public Property Get m_ErrSource
   m_ErrSource = "UserClass"
End Property
' ADS Constants defined as readonly properties of the class
Public Property Get ADS_UF_ACCOUNTDISABLE
' The user account Is disabled
   ADS_UF_ACCOUNTDISABLE =  &H2
End Property
Public Property Get ADS_UF_HOMEDIR_REQUIRED
' The home directory Is required
   ADS_UF_HOMEDIR_REQUIRED = &H8
End Property
Public Property Get ADS_UF_LOCKOUT
'The account Is currently locked out
   ADS_UF_LOCKOUT = &H10
End Property
Public Property Get ADS_UF_PASSWD_NOTREQD
' No password is required
   ADS_UF_PASSWD_NOTREQD = &H20
End Property
Public Property Get ADS_UF_PASSWD_CANT_CHANGE
' The user cannot change the password. This flag can be read,
' but not set directly.
   ADS_UF_PASSWD_CANT_CHANGE = &H40
End Property
Public Property Get ADS_UF_ENCRYPTED_TEXT_PASSWORD_ALLOWED
' The user can send an encrypted password
   ADS_UF_ENCRYPTED_TEXT_PASSWORD_ALLOWED = &H80
End Property
Public Property Get ADS_UF_TEMP_DUPLICATE_ACCOUNT
' This is an account for users whose primary account is in
' another domain.
' This account provides user access to this domain,
' but not to any domain that trusts this domain.
   ADS_UF_TEMP_DUPLICATE_ACCOUNT = &H100
End Property
Public Property Get ADS_UF_NORMAL_ACCOUNT
' This is a default account type that represents a typical user
   ADS_UF_NORMAL_ACCOUNT = &H200
End Property
Public Property Get ADS_UF_INTERDOMAIN_TRUST_ACCOUNT
' This is a permit to trust account for a system domain that
' trusts other domains
   ADS_UF_INTERDOMAIN_TRUST_ACCOUNT = &H800
End Property
Public Property Get ADS_UF_DONT_EXPIRE_PASSWD
' When Set, the password will Not expire on this account
   ADS_UF_DONT_EXPIRE_PASSWD = &H10000
End Property
Public Property Get ADS_UF_SMARTCARD_REQUIRED
```

```
' When set, this flag will force the user to log on using a smart card
  ADS_UF_SMARTCARD_REQUIRED = &H40000
End Property
Public Property Get ADS_UF_TRUSTED_FOR_DELEGATION
' When Set, the service account is trusted for Kerberos delegation.
  ADS_UF_TRUSTED_FOR_DELEGATION = &H80000
End Property
Public Property Get ADS_UF_NOT_DELEGATED
' When set, the security context of the user will not be delegated
' to a service even if the service account is set as trusted for
' Kerberos delegation.
  ADS_UF_NOT_DELEGATED = &H100000
End Property
Public Property Get ADS_UF_PASSWORD_EXPIRED
' The user password has expired. It is read-only and cannot be set.
  ADS_UF_PASSWORD_EXPIRED = &H800000
End Property
'=====================================================================
' OpenDSObject Constants
Public Property Get ADS_SECURE_AUTHENTICATION
  ADS_SECURE_AUTHENTICATION = &H1
End Property
Public Property Get ADS_USE_ENCRYPTION
  ADS_USE_ENCRYPTION = &H2
End Property
Public Property Get ADS_USE_SSL
  ADS_USE_SSL = &H2
End Property
Public Property Get ADS_READONLY_SERVER
  ADS_READONLY_SERVER = &H4
End Property
Public Property Get ADS_PROMPT_CREDENTIALS
  ADS_PROMPT_CREDENTIALS = &H8
End Property
Public Property Get ADS_NO_AUTHENTICATION
  ADS_NO_AUTHENTICATION = &H10
End Property
Public Property Get ADS_FAST_BIND
  ADS_FAST_BIND = &H20
End Property
Public Property Get ADS_USE_SIGNING
  ADS_USE_SIGNING = &H40
End Property
Public Property Get ADS_USE_SEALING
  ADS_USE_SEALING = &H80
End Property
Public Property Get ADS_USE_DELEGATION
  ADS_USE_DELEGATION = &H100
End Property
```

```
Public Property Get ADS_SERVER_BIND
    ADS_SERVER_BIND = &H200
End Property
'=======================================================================
Public Property Get ADS_PROPERTY_CLEAR
    ADS_PROPERTY_CLEAR = 1
End Property
Public Property Get ADS_PROPERTY_UPDATE
    ADS_PROPERTY_UPDATE = 2
End Property
Public Property Get ADS_PROPERTY_APPEND
    ADS_PROPERTY_APPEND = 3
End Property
Public Property Get ADS_PROPERTY_DELETE
    ADS_PROPERTY_DELETE = 4
End Property
'=======================================================================
End Class
```

BUT CLASS_INITIALIZE AND CLASS_TERMINATE ARE EMPTY!

Think of these empty procedures as placeholders. The idea is simple: if later in the cycle of script management we realize it would be to our advantage to put some code in those procedures, they are already there and ready to be filled in. It also comes in handy if you decide you would like to use these classes as templates for your own classes, and your new classes will make use of the Initialize and Terminate procedures.

Create a New User

This script uses the UserClass to create a new user. The ADsPath to the container, the CN, and the SAM account name for the new object are passed to the Create method of the class. After successfully executing the Create method, the new User object is created but is essentially blank.

A few additional properties are then set for the new user account—first name (givenName property), last name (sn property), and a new password. This script can easily be modified to accept these values from the command line.

When using this class to set properties for the new User object, note that the properties are not saved to the User object automatically. Rather the object is saved only after setting all the new properties. This design decision prevents multiple trips to the domain controller as each property is set. The class design can easily be modified to enable this behavior if desired.

```
<job>
<script language="VBScript" src="includes\UserClass.vbs" />
<script>
Option Explicit
Dim UserObject
Set UserObject = New UserClass
UserObject.Create _
```

```
     "LDAP://CN=Users,DC=zygort,DC=com","ScriptUser","ScriptTest"
UserObject.AccountEnabled = True
UserObject.SetProperty "givenName", "Script"
UserObject.SetProperty "sn", "User"
UserObject.Password = "P@ssw0rd"
UserObject.Save
</script>
</job>
```

List User Properties

When not creating a new User object, all operations on User objects begin by binding to the User object in Active Directory with the BindToUser method. This method takes only the ADsPath to the User object as an argument.

A Dictionary object is returned by the PropertyList method of the class. The key value holds the property name, and the value (obviously) holds that property's value. A simple For-Next loop iterates through the property list. Note that the list contains only properties for values that have been set on the User object.

```
<job>
<script language="VBScript" src="includes\UserClass.vbs" />
<script>
Option Explicit
Dim UserObject
Set UserObject = New UserClass
UserObject.BindToUser "CN=ScriptUser,CN=Users,DC=zygort,DC=com"
Dim PropertyList, Prop
Set PropertyList = UserObject.PropertyList
For Each Prop In PropertyList.Keys
    WScript.Echo Prop & "=" & PropertyList(Prop)
Next
</script>
</job>
```

Set User Properties

Setting user properties is one of the most common operations on User objects. Begin by binding to the User object, then set the property using the SetProperty method. This method takes the property name (the LDAP display name) and the new value as arguments.

After setting new property values on the User object, be sure to call the Save method. This method essentially executes a SetInfo method on the User object itself and writes the information back to Active Directory. This saves network traffic to the domain controller and allows your script to backtrack out of an operation if necessary.

The last property set does not use the SetProperty method, but rather sets a property of the UserClass called PasswordDoesntExpire. This one requires a little more explanation. The actual property that controls the password expiration on the user object is stored as a bitmap in the userAccountControl property. Rather than force the script writer to memorize or build the new bitmap for the intended result, certain "bits" of the bitmap have been exposed through properties in the class, which will manipulate the bitmap for you. As homework, look at the code for the property Let PasswordDoesntExpire procedure and figure out how it works.

```
<job>
<script language="VBScript" src="includes\UserClass.vbs" />
<script>
Option Explicit
Dim UserObject
Set UserObject = New UserClass
UserObject.BindToUser "CN=ScriptUser,CN=Users,DC=zygort,DC=com"
UserObject.SetProperty "givenName", "FirstName"
UserObject.SetProperty "sn", "LastName"
UserObject.SetProperty "", ""
UserObject.PasswordDoesntExpire = True
UserObject.Save
</script>
</job>
```

Set User Password

This script lets you bind to a User object and reset the user's password. Don't forget to save the object when you have finished. This example uses a simple string value. This script can (and probably should) be updated with your own code to generate a pseudo-random and stronger password.

```
<job>
<script language="VBScript" src="includes\UserClass.vbs" />
<script>
Option Explicit
Dim UserObject
Set UserObject = New UserClass
UserObject.BindToUser "CN=ScriptUser,CN=Users,DC=zygort,DC=com"
UserObject.Password = "P@ssw0rd"
UserObject.Save
</script>
</job>
```

Set Password Not to Expire

This script allows you to bind to a User object and change settings so the password does not expire. Changing the assignment value to False re-enables password expiration.

```
<job>
<script language="VBScript" src="includes\UserClass.vbs" />
<script>
Option Explicit
Dim UserObject
Set UserObject = New UserClass
UserObject.BindToUser "CN=ScriptUser,CN=Users,DC=zygort,DC=com"
```

```
UserObject.PasswordDoesntExpire = True
UserObject.Save
</script>
</job>
```

Unlock a User Account

This script binds to a user account, and if the account is locked out it will be unlocked. This script can be modified to run on the result set of a query that scanned Active Directory for locked User objects.

```
<job>
<script language="VBScript" src="includes\UserClass.vbs" />
<script>
Option Explicit
Dim UserObject
Set UserObject = New UserClass
UserObject.BindToUser "CN=ScriptUser,CN=Users,DC=zygort,DC=com"
If UserObject.LockedOut Then
    UserObject.UnlockAccount
End If
UserObject.Save
</script>
</job>
```

Enable and Disable a User Account

By default a new user account is disabled. This script demonstrates how to enable and disable a user account with the UserClass object. Setting the AccountEnabled property for the object to True enables the account, while False disables it.

```
<job>
<script language="VBScript" src="includes\UserClass.vbs" />
<script>
Option Explicit
Dim UserObject
Set UserObject = New UserClass
UserObject.BindToUser "CN=ScriptUser,CN=Users,DC=zygort,DC=com"
If UserObject.AccountEnabled Then
    UserObject.AccountEnabled = False
Else
    UserObject.AccountEnabled = True
End If
UserObject.Save
</script>
</job>
```

List Group Membership of a User

This script lists a user's immediate group membership. By *immediate group membership*, I am refer-ring to the group membership that you can see in the Members Of tab of the User object. Remember that while a user can belong to a group, that group can be a member of another group. This script does not list those groups.

```
<job>
<script language="VBScript" src="includes\UserClass.vbs" />
<script>
Option Explicit
Dim UserObject
Set UserObject = New UserClass
UserObject.BindToUser "CN=ScriptUser,CN=Users,DC=zygort,DC=com"
Dim GroupList, Group
Set GroupList = UserObject.Groups
For Each Group In GroupList.Keys
    WScript.Echo Group
Next
</script>
</job>
```

List All Group Memberships of a User

This script lists a user's immediate group membership plus group memberships of the user groups. Nested group membership can cause different security problems, simply because the group-membership hierarchy is difficult to see in ADUC. This script reads the value of the UserClass object's AllGroups property, whereas the earlier script (which only reads the immediate group membership) reads the value of the Groups property.

```
<job>
<script language="VBScript" src="includes\UserClass.vbs" />
<script>
Option Explicit
Dim UserObject
Set UserObject = New UserClass
UserObject.BindToUser "CN=ScriptUser,CN=Users,DC=zygort,DC=com"
Dim GroupList, Group
Set GroupList = UserObject.AllGroups
For Each Group In GroupList.Keys
    WScript.Echo Group
Next
</script>
</job>
```

Join the User to a Group

There are two ways for a user to join a group via scripting. One is to bind to the group and add a new member (this will be demonstrated when we examine the GroupClass class). The other, demonstrated in the script that follows, binds to the user and joins that user to the group by calling the JoinGroup method of the UserClass object and passing the ADsPath of the group to join.

```
<job>
<script language="VBScript" src="includes\UserClass.vbs" />
```

```
<script>
Option Explicit
Dim UserObject
Set UserObject = New UserClass
UserObject.BindToUser "CN=ScriptUser,CN=Users,DC=zygort,DC=com"
UserObject.JoinGroup "LDAP:\\CN=ScriptGroup,CN=Users,dc=zygort,dc=com"
UserObject.Save
</script>
</job>
```

Copy a User Object

The process of creating new user accounts can be made simpler (and less susceptible to errors) by using a template user account as the basis for creating a new user account. Calling the Copy method of the UserClass object and passing the container, the Common Name (CN), and the SAM account name of the new user account can do this task for you. You will also want to set an initial password on the new account.

```
<job>
<script language="VBScript" src="includes\UserClass.vbs" />
<script>
Option Explicit
Dim UserObject, NewUserObject
Set UserObject = New UserClass
UserObject.BindToUser "CN=TemplateUser,CN=Users,DC=zygort,DC=com"
Set NewUserObject = UserObject.Copy _
    "LDAP://CN=Users,DC=zygort,DC=com","CopiedUser","CopiedUser"
NewUserObject.Password = "P@ssw0rd"
NewUserObject.Save
</script>
</job>
```

Copy Group Membership to Another User

Group membership is a constant source of aggravation for user administrators. A common practice is to create a template user account, which you then copy as new users are added. This script demonstrates how to take advantage of a template user account's existing group membership (specifically immediate group membership) by reading the template object's group membership and joining the bound User object to those groups.

```
<job>
<script language="VBScript" src="includes\UserClass.vbs" />
<script>
Option Explicit
Dim UserObject
Set UserObject = New UserClass
UserObject.BindToUser "CN=ScriptUser,CN=Users,DC=zygort,DC=com"
UserObject.CopyGroupsFromUser _
```

```
        "LDAP:\\CN=TemplateUser,CN=Users,dc=zygort,dc=com"
    UserObject.Save
    </script>
    </job>
```

Move a User Object

Because a good Active Directory hierarchy uses containers (and/or organizational units) to organize objects, eventually you will have to deal with user accounts moving from one container object to another. Calling the Move method and passing the ADsPath of the destination container will move the bound User object to its new home.

```
    <job>
    <script language="VBScript" src="includes\UserClass.vbs" />
    <script>
    Option Explicit
    Dim UserObject, NewUserObject
    Set UserObject = New UserClass
    UserObject.BindToUser "CN=ScriptUser,CN=Users,DC=zygort,DC=com"
    UserObject.Move "LDAP://OU=Test,DC=zygort,DC=com"
    UserObject.Save
    </script>
    </job>
```

Group Scripts

We've looked at groups in the User class, and now it is time to start working with Group objects all on their own. To do this we are going to build a GroupClass class, which we can use in later scripts to easily build and manipulate real Active Directory Group objects.

GroupClass

Many of the functions of the GroupClass class mirror those found in UserClass. When developing scripts with this class, using a common design helps by not making you learn an entirely new set of properties and functions for every class your scripts utilize.

A few additional aspects must be noted when dealing with groups. Groups can be one of two types: security or distribution. They can also have one of three scopes: universal, global, or domain local. You must specify each of these when creating a new group. VBScript uses constant values to internally denote the type and scope of a group. At the bottom of the GroupClass code we have made these available through public properties to make life easier. (We have also given them friendlier names than you would find in the Microsoft documentation.)

```
    Option Explicit
    '================================================================
    Class GroupClass
    '================================================================
    Private Sub Class_Initialize
    End Sub
    '================================================================
```

```
Private Sub Class_Terminate
End Sub
'==========================================================================
' Private and public variables
Private m_GroupObject
'==========================================================================
Public Function BindToGroup(GroupPath)
If ADObjectExists(GroupPath) Then
    Set m_GroupObject = GetObject(FormatAdsPath(GroupPath))
    m_GroupObject.GetInfo
    Set BindToGroup = m_GroupObject
Else
    Err.Raise 102,m_ErrSource,"Object does not exist"
End If
End Function
'==========================================================================
Public Function Create _
    (ContainerPath,CN,AccountName,GroupType,GroupScope)
If CN = "" Or ContainerPath = "" Or GroupType = "" Then
    Err.Raise 101,m_ErrSource,"Missing arguments"
    Exit Function
End If
Dim Container
If ADObjectExists(ContainerPath) Then
    Set Container = GetObject(FormatAdsPath(ContainerPath))
    Set m_GroupObject = Container.Create("group",FormatCN(CN))
    m_GroupObject.Put "groupType", GroupType Or GroupScope
    m_GroupObject.Put "sAMAccountName", AccountName
    m_GroupObject.SetInfo
    m_GroupObject.GetInfo
    Set Create = m_GroupObject
Else
    WScript.Echo "Container does not exist!"
    WScript.Quit(1)
End If
End Function
'==========================================================================
Public Property Get GroupType
If CBool(m_GroupObject.Get("groupType") And SECURITY_GROUP) Then
    GroupScope = "Security"
Else
    GroupScope = "Distribution"
End If
End Property
'==========================================================================
Public Property Let GroupType(TypeValue)
Select Case LCase(TypeValue)
    Case "distribution" : m_GroupType = DISTRIBUTION_GROUP
```

```
   Case "security" : m_GroupType = SECURITY_GROUP
End Select
End Property
'==================================================================
Public Property Get GroupScope
CheckForBoundObject
If CBool(m_GroupObject.Get("groupType") And GLOBAL_GROUP) Then
   GroupScope = "Global"
Else
   If CBool(m_GroupObject.Get("groupType") And _
   DOMAIN_LOCAL_GROUP) Then
      GroupScope = "Domain Local"
   Else
      GroupScope = "Universal"
   End If
End If
End Property
'==================================================================
Public Property Let GroupScope(TypeValue)
Select Case lcase(TypeValue)
   Case "global" : m_GroupScope = GLOBAL_GROUP
   Case "domain local" : m_GroupScope = DOMAIN_LOCAL_GROUP
   Case "universal" : m_GroupType = UNIVERSAL_GROUP
End Select
End Property
'==================================================================
Public Sub AddMember(Member)
If ADObjectExists(Member) Then
   On Error Resume Next
   m_GroupObject.Add FormatAdsPath(Member)
Else
   WScript.Echo "Member " & Member & " does not exist."
End If
End Sub
'==================================================================
Public Sub RemoveMember(Member)
   m_GroupObject.Remove FormatAdsPath(Member)
End Sub
'==================================================================
Public Property Get Members
' returns a Dictionary object!
Dim MemberList
Set MemberList = WScript.CreateObject("Scripting.Dictionary")
For each Member in m_GroupObject.Members
   MemberList.Add Member.Name,0
Next
Set Members = MemberList
End Property
'==================================================================
```

```
Public Property Get AllMembers
' Returns a Dictionary object!
Dim MemberList
Set MemberList = WScript.CreateObject("Scripting.Dictionary")
GetMembership m_GroupObject.AdsPath,MemberList
Set AllMembers = MemberList
End Property
'=====================================================================
Private Function GetMembership(ObjectAdsPath,List)
Dim tmpObject, Member
Set tmpObject = GetObject(FormatAdsPath(ObjectAdsPath))
On Error Resume Next
For Each Member In tmpObject.Members
   If Err.Number = 0 Then
      If Not(List.Exists(Member.Name)) Then
         List.Add Member.Name,0
         If Member.Class = "group" Then
            GetMembership Member.AdsPath,List
         End If
      End If
   End If
   Err.Clear
Next
End Function
'=====================================================================
Public Property Get MemberOf
' Returns a Dictionary object!
Dim MemberList, Member
Set MemberList = WScript.CreateObject("Scripting.Dictionary")
On Error Resume Next
For Each Member In m_GroupObject.GetEx("memberOf")
   MemberList.Add Member,0
Next
Set MemberOf = MemberList
End Property
'=====================================================================
Public Property Get Manager
   Manager = m_GroupObject.Get("managedBy")
End Property
'=====================================================================
Public Property Let Manager(ManagerPath)
If ADObjectExists(ManagerPath) Then
   m_GroupObject.Put "managedBy", FormatCN(ManagerPath)
End If
End Property
'=====================================================================
Public Sub SetProperty(PropName,PropValue)
On Error Resume Next
m_GroupObjectObject.Put PropName,PropValue
```

```
If Err.Number <> 0 Then
   WScript.Echo "Error setting property " & PropName
End If
End Sub
'=======================================================================
Public Sub DisplayProperties
Dim Element
For Each Element In m_PropertyList.Keys
   WScript.Echo Element & " = " & m_PropertyList(Element)
Next
End Sub
'=======================================================================
Public Sub Save
m_GroupObject.SetInfo
m_GroupObject.GetInfo
End Sub
'=======================================================================
Private Function GetADsTypeValue(AdsType,AdsValue)
Select Case CInt(adsType)
   Case 1 : GetADsTypeValue = AdsValue.DNString
   Case 2 : GetADsTypeValue =  AdsValue.CaseExactString
   Case 3 : GetADsTypeValue =  AdsValue.CaseIgnoreString
   Case 4 : GetADsTypeValue =  AdsValue.PrintableString
   Case 5 : GetADsTypeValue =  AdsValue.NumericString
   Case 6 : GetADsTypeValue =  CStr(AdsValue.Boolean)
   Case 7 : GetADsTypeValue =  AdsValue.Integer
   Case 8 : GetADsTypeValue =  "Octet String"
   Case 9 : GetADsTypeValue =  AdsValue.UTCTime
   Case 10 :
      Dim PropertyLargeInteger, LargeIntegerValue
      Dim LargeIntegerDate, DateHigh, DateLow
      Set PropertyLargeInteger = AdsValue.LargeInteger
      DateHigh = PropertyLargeInteger.HighPart
      DateLow = PropertyLargeInteger.LowPart
      If DateLow < 0 Then
         DateHigh = DateHigh + 1
      End If
      If (DateHigh = 0) And (DateLow = 0 ) Then
         LargeIntegerDate = #1/1/1601#
      Else
         LargeIntegerDate = #1/1/1601# + (((DateHigh * _
                  (2 ^ 32)) + DateLow)/600000000)/1440
      End If
      If IsDate(LargeIntegerDate) And _
      LargeIntegerDate > #1/1/1970# Then
         GetADsTypeValue = LargeIntegerDate
      Else
         GetADsTypeValue = _
            PropertyLargeInteger.HighPart * 2^32 + _
```

```
                    PropertyLargeInteger.LowPart
            End If
        Case 11 : GetADsTypeValue = "Provider Specific"
        Case 12 : GetADsTypeValue = "Object Class"
        Case 13 : GetADsTypeValue = "Case Ignore List"
        Case 14 : GetADsTypeValue = "Octet List"
        Case 15 : GetADsTypeValue = "Path"
        Case 16 : GetADsTypeValue = "Postal Address"
        Case 17 : GetADsTypeValue = "TimeStamp"
        Case 18 : GetADsTypeValue = "BackLink"
        Case 19 : GetADsTypeValue = "Typed Name"
        Case 20 : GetADsTypeValue = "Hold"
        Case 21 : GetADsTypeValue = "Net Address"
        Case 22 : GetADsTypeValue = "Replica Pointer"
        Case 23 : GetADsTypeValue = "Fax Number"
        Case 24 : GetADsTypeValue = "Email"
        Case 25 : GetADsTypeValue = "NT Security Descriptor"
        Case 26 : GetADsTypeValue = "Unknown"
        Case Else : GetADsTypeValue = "Unknown - " & AdsValue.adsType
    End Select
End Function
'========================================================================
Private Function ADObjectExists(ADsPath)
Dim ADObject, LDAPObject
ADSPath = FormatAdsPath(AdsPath)
On Error Resume Next
Set LDAPObject = GetObject("LDAP:")
Set ADObject = _
    LDAPObject.OpenDSObject(ADsPath,vbNullString,vbNullString, _
ADS_FAST_BIND)
If Err.Number = 0 Then
    ADObjectExists = True
Else
    ADObjectExists = False
End If
Set ADObject = Nothing
Set LDAPObject = Nothing
End Function
'========================================================================
Private Function FormatAdsPath(ADsPath)
If CBool(Instr(ADsPath,"LDAP://")) Then
    FormatAdsPath = AdsPath
Else
    FormatAdsPath = "LDAP://" & ADsPath
End If
End Function
'========================================================================
Private Function FormatCN(CNValue)
FormatCN = Replace(CNValue,"LDAP://","")
```

```
    If Left(FormatCN,3) <> "CN=" Then
        FormatCN = "CN=" & FormatCN
    End If
    End Function
    '========================================================================
    Public Property Get m_ErrSource
        m_ErrSource = "GroupClass"
    End Property
    Public Property Get ADS_PROPERTY_CLEAR
        ADS_PROPERTY_CLEAR = 1
    End Property
    Public Property Get ADS_PROPERTY_UPDATE
        ADS_PROPERTY_UPDATE = 2
    End Property
    Public Property Get ADS_PROPERTY_APPEND
        ADS_PROPERTY_APPEND = 3
    End Property
    Public Property Get ADS_PROPERTY_DELETE
        ADS_PROPERTY_DELETE = 4
    End Property
    Public Property Get ADS_FAST_BIND
        ADS_FAST_BIND = &H20
    End Property
    '========================================================================
    ' I'm taking a little liberty in renaming these constants to something
    ' more friendly than ADS_GROUP_TYPE_DOMAIN_LOCAL_GROUP
    Public Property Get DISTRIBUTION_GROUP
        DISTRIBUTION_GROUP = &h0
    End Property
    Public Property Get GLOBAL_GROUP
        GLOBAL_GROUP = &h2
    End Property
    Public Property Get DOMAIN_LOCAL_GROUP
        DOMAIN_LOCAL_GROUP = &h4
    End Property
    Public Property Get UNIVERSAL_GROUP
        UNIVERSAL_GROUP = &h8
    End Property
    Public Property Get SECURITY_GROUP
        SECURITY_GROUP = &h80000000
    End Property
    '========================================================================
    End Class
```

Creating a New Group

To create a new group, start by creating an instance of the GroupClass class. Next call the Create method and pass it the ADsPath of the parent container, the CN of the group, the SAM account name of the group, and finally the group type (security or distribution) and group scope (domain local, global, or universal).

In the `GroupClass` class the constants that define the group are exposed as read-only properties. After you have created an instance of the class you can read these property values from the instantiated object. In this example, the last argument uses the `Security_Group` and `Domain_Local_Group` properties to define the group type and scope.

```
<job>
<script language="VBScript" src="includes\GroupClass.vbs" />
<script>
Option Explicit
Dim GroupObject
Set GroupObject = New GroupClass
GroupObject.Create _
    "CN=Users,DC=zygort,DC=com","ScriptGroup","ScriptGroup", _
    GroupObject.Security_Group,GroupObject.Domain_Local_Group
</script>
</job>
```

To define the group type, use the `Security_Group` and `Distribution_Group` properties. Use `Domain_Local_Group`, `Global_Group`, and `Universal_Group` to define the group scope. Purists will probably notice that these are not the actual ADSI constant names. In the interest of readability, we have taken the liberty of exposing the properties by using names that are much friendlier to read than ADS_GROUP_TYPE_DOMAIN_LOCAL_GROUP.

List Group Members

This script lists the immediate members of a group. Start by binding to the group, then set a variable equal to the `Members` property. This property returns a `Dictionary` object containing a list of group members in the `Key` field. The value field will contain 0.

```
<job>
<script language="VBScript" src="includes\GroupClass.vbs" />
<script>
Option Explicit
Dim GroupObject, GroupMembers, Member
Set GroupObject = New GroupClass
GroupObject.BindToGroup "CN=ScriptGroup,CN=Users,DC=zygort,DC=com"
Set GroupMembers = GroupObject.Members
For Each Member In GroupMembers.Keys
    WScript.Echo Member
Next
</script>
</job>
```

List All Group Members

This script lists the immediate members of a group, as well as the group membership of any subordinate groups. After binding to the group with the `GroupClass` class, set a variable equal to the `AllMembers` property of the object. This property returns a `Dictionary` object with a list of group members in the `Key` field. The value field will contain 0.

Please note that the Members and AllMembers properties will (usually) return different result sets. Be sure to use the property that will return the specific set of members you are looking for.

```
<job>
<script language="VBScript" src="includes\GroupClass.vbs" />
<script>
Option Explicit
Dim GroupObject, GroupMembers, Member
Set GroupObject = New GroupClass
GroupObject.BindToGroup "CN=ScriptGroup,CN=Users,DC=zygort,DC=com"
Set GroupMembers = GroupObject.AllMembers
For Each Member In GroupMembers.Keys
    WScript.Echo Member
Next
</script>
</job>
```

List a Group's Group Membership

This script lists the groups that the bound group is a member of (for example, the ScriptTest group might belong to the DomainScripters group). Begin by binding to the group, then set a variable equal to the MemberOf property of the group. This property returns a Dictionary object. We can then iterate through the items in the Dictionary object with a For-Next loop.

```
<job>
<script language="VBScript" src="includes\GroupClass.vbs" />
<script>
Option Explicit
Dim GroupObject, GroupMember, Member
Set GroupObject = New GroupClass
GroupObject.BindToGroup "CN=ScriptGroup,CN=Users,DC=zygort,DC=com"
Set GroupMember = GroupObject.MemberOf
For Each Member In GroupMember
    WScript.Echo Member
Next
</script>
</job>
```

Add a New Group Member

One of the primary scripting tasks of a group is adding (and later removing) members to the group. Start by binding the GroupClass to the group, then call the AddMember method and pass it the ADsPath of an existing User object in Active Directory.

```
<job>
<script language="VBScript" src="includes\GroupClass.vbs" />
<script>
Option Explicit
Dim GroupObject
Set GroupObject = New GroupClass
```

```
GroupObject.BindToGroup "CN=ScriptGroup,CN=Users,DC=zygort,DC=com"
GroupObject.AddMember "LDAP://CN=Scott,CN=Users,DC=zygort,DC=com"
</script>
</job>
```

Remove a Group Member

We can't have a script to add members to a group without a script to remove members. Bind to the group, call the RemoveMember method, and specify the ADsPath of the group member to remove.

```
<job>
<script language="VBScript" src="includes\GroupClass.vbs" />
<script>
Option Explicit
Dim GroupObject
Set GroupObject = New GroupClass
GroupObject.BindToGroup "CN=ScriptGroup,CN=Users,DC=zygort,DC=com"
GroupObject.RemoveMember "LDAP://CN=Scott,CN=Users,DC=zygort,DC=com"
</script>
</job>
```

Change the Group Manager

This script allows you to change a group's manager. The manager is exposed through the Manager property and should be passed the ADsPath to an existing User object in Active Directory.

```
<job>
<script language="VBScript" src="includes\GroupClass.vbs" />
<script>
Option Explicit
Dim GroupObject
Set GroupObject = New GroupClass
GroupObject.BindToGroup "CN=ScriptGroup,CN=Users,DC=zygort,DC=com"
GroupObject.Manager = "CN=Scott,CN=Users,DC=zygort,DC=com"
GroupObject.Save
</script>
</job>
```

Computer Scripts

Several management tasks involve Computer objects in Active Directory. To deal with these tasks through VBScript, we create a class to do the grunt work for us just as we did with the UserClass and GroupClass classes.

ComputerClass

Many ComputerClass class functions mirror those found in UserClass and GroupClass. This means you can use the same method calls and property names you used with the other VBScript classes presented in this chapter, rather than learn a new set for every class.

```
Option Explicit
'=============================================================================
Class ComputerClass
'=============================================================================
' Private and public variables
Private m_ComputerObject
'=============================================================================
Private Sub Class_Initialize
End Sub
'=============================================================================
Private Sub Class_Terminate
End Sub
'=============================================================================
Public Sub BindToComputer(ComputerPath)
If ADObjectExists(ComputerPath) Then
   Set m_ComputerObject = GetObject(FormatAdsPath(ComputerPath))
   m_ComputerObject.GetInfo
   Set BindToUser = m_ComputerObject
Else
   Err.Raise 102,m_ErrSource,"Object does not exist"
End If
End Sub
'=============================================================================
Public Function Create(ContainerPath,CN,AccountName)
If CN = "" Or ContainerPath = "" Or AccountName = "" Then
   Err.Raise 101,m_ErrSource,"Missing arguments"
   Exit Function
End If
Dim Container
If ADObjectExists(ContainerPath) Then
   Set Container = GetObject(FormatAdsPath(ContainerPath))
   Set m_ComputerObject = Container.Create("computer",FormatCN(CN))
   m_ComputerObject.Put "sAMAccountName", AccountName & "$"
   m_ComputerObject.Put "userAccountControl", _
                        ADS_UF_WORKSTATION_TRUST_ACCOUNT
   m_ComputerObject.SetInfo
   m_ComputerObject.GetInfo
   Set Create = m_ComputerObject
Else
   WScript.Echo "Error connecting to container!"
   WScript.Quit(1)
End If
End Function
'=============================================================================
Public Sub Move(Destination)
If ADObjectExists(Destination) Then
   Dim NewContainer
   Set NewContainer = GetObject(FormatAdsPath(Destination))
   NewContainer.MoveHere m_ComputerObject.AdsPath, _
                         m_ComputerObject.Name
```

```
End If
End Sub
'=====================================================================
Public Sub SetProperty(PropName,PropValue)
On Error Resume Next
m_ComputerObject.Put PropName,PropValue
If Err.Number <> 0 Then
   WScript.Echo "Error setting property " & PropName
End If
End Sub
'=====================================================================
Public Sub MultiPropertyClear(PropertyName)
   m_ComputerObject.PutEx ADS_PROPERTY_CLEAR,PropertyName,0
End Sub
'=====================================================================
Public Sub MultiPropertyUpdate(PropertyName, PropertyArray)
m_ComputerObject.PutEx _
   ADS_PROPERTY_UPDATE,PropertyName,PropertyArray
End Sub
'=====================================================================
Public Sub MultiPropertyAppend(PropertyName, PropertyArray)
m_ComputerObject.PutEx _
   ADS_PROPERTY_APPEND,PropertyName,PropertyArray
End Sub
'=====================================================================
Public Sub MultiPropertyDelete(PropertyName, PropertyArray)
m_ComputerObject.PutEx _
   ADS_PROPERTY_DELETE,PropertyName,PropertyArray
End Sub
'=====================================================================
Public Sub Reset
On Error Resume Next
m_ComputerObject.SetPassword m_ComputerObject.Name
If Err.Number = 0 Then
   WScript.Echo "Computer " & m_ComputerObject.Name & " was reset."
   WScript.Echo "       It must now rejoin the domain!"
Else
   WScript.Echo "Error resetting computer account " & _
                m_ComputerObject.Name
End If
End Sub
'=====================================================================
Public Sub Save
m_ComputerObject.SetInfo
m_ComputerObject.GetInfo
End Sub
'=====================================================================
Private Function ADObjectExists(ADsPath)
Dim ADObject, LDAPObject
```

```
ADSPath = FormatAdsPath(AdsPath)
On Error Resume Next
Set LDAPObject = GetObject("LDAP:")
Set ADObject = _
    LDAPObject.OpenDSObject(ADsPath,vbNullString,vbNullString, _
                            ADS_FAST_BIND)
If Err.Number = 0 Then
    ADObjectExists = True
Else
    ADObjectExists = False
End If
Set ADObject = Nothing
Set LDAPObject = Nothing
End Function
'=====================================================================
Private Function FormatAdsPath(ADsPath)
If CBool(Instr(ADsPath,"LDAP://")) Then
    FormatAdsPath = AdsPath
Else
    FormatAdsPath = "LDAP://" & ADsPath
End If
End Function
'=====================================================================
Private Function FormatCN(CNValue)
FormatCN = Replace(CNValue,"LDAP://","")
If Left(FormatCN,3) <> "CN=" Then
    FormatCN = "CN=" & FormatCN
End If
End Function
'=====================================================================
Public Property Get ADS_FAST_BIND
    ADS_FAST_BIND = &H20
End Property
Public Property Get m_ErrSource
    m_ErrSource = "ComputerClass"
End Property
Public Property Get ADS_UF_WORKSTATION_TRUST_ACCOUNT
    ADS_UF_WORKSTATION_TRUST_ACCOUNT = &H1000
End Property
'=====================================================================
End Class
```

Create a Computer Account

Creating a computer account is a common administrative function. After creating a new instance of the ComputerClass class, call the Create method. The Create method takes three arguments: the ADsPath of the computer account's container, the CN, and the SAM account name of the new computer account.

After you create the new computer account you can continue to set any additional properties with the SetProperty method. This method takes two arguments: the property name and the new value. After you set the property values be sure to call the Save method to write the new property values back to Active Directory.

```
<job>
<script language="VBScript" src="includes\ComputerClass.vbs" />
<script>
Option Explicit
Dim ComputerObject
Set ComputerObject = New ComputerClass
ComputerObject.Create _
    "LDAP://OU=Test,DC=zygort,DC=com","ScriptComputer","ScriptComputer"
ComputerObject.SetProperty "description", "Scripting Test Computer"
ComputerObject.Save
</script>
</job>
```

Move a Computer Account

Computer accounts sometimes need to be moved between containers so the proper set of Group Policy Objects (GPOs) can be applied. After you bind to the Computer object in Active Directory, call the Move method and pass the ADsPath of the new container as the argument.

```
<job>
<script language="VBScript" src="includes\ComputerClass.vbs" />
<script>
Option Explicit
Dim ComputerObject
Set ComputerObject = New ComputerClass
ComputerObject.BindToComputer _
    "LDAP://CN=ScriptComputer,CN=Computers,DC=zygort,DC=com", _
        "ScriptComputer","ScriptComputer"
ComputerObject.Move "LDAP://OU=Test,DC=zygort,DC=com"
</script>
</job>
```

Reset a Computer Account

Like user accounts, computer accounts have passwords, and these passwords sometimes need to be reset. Use the ComputerClass object's Reset method to perform this task. This is actually a function call in the class that will return True if the reset operation was successful. In the following script, the result of the Reset method is used to display a message to the user about the outcome of the operation.

```
<job>
<script language="VBScript" src="includes\ComputerClass.vbs" />
<script>
Option Explicit
Dim ComputerObject
Set ComputerObject = New ComputerClass
```

```
ComputerObject.BindToComputer _
   "LDAP://CN=ScriptComputer,OU=Test,DC=zygort,DC=com"
If ComputerObject.Reset Then
   WScript.Echo "Computer account was successfully reset."
   WScript.Echo "Please rejoin the computer to the domain!"
Else
   WScript.Echo "An error occurred resetting the computer account."
End If
</script>
</job>
```

Organizational-Unit Scripts

Organizational units tend to be fairly static structures in an Active Directory hierarchy. In fact the structure of a well-thought-out hierarchy almost never changes except in response to changes within the organization itself, such as reorganizations or new business acquisitions.

OUClass

Now it's time to build a class to represent the OU object and its capabilities. Be aware that not all the functionality you have for an OU in the graphical administration tools is available to you as a programmer. One of the most requested features in the newsgroups—the ability to create GPOs—is not yet available to programmers. However, the ability to link GPOs to organizational units is within our grasp.

```
Option Explicit
Class OUClass
'====================================================================
' Private and public variables
Private m_OUObject
'====================================================================
Private Sub Class_Initialize
End Sub
'====================================================================
Private Sub Class_Terminate
End Sub
'====================================================================
Public Function BindToOU(OUPath)
If ADObjectExists(OUPath) Then
   Set m_OUObject = GetObject(FormatAdsPath(OUPath))
   m_OUObject.GetInfo
   Set BindToOU = m_OUObject
Else
   Err.Raise 102,m_ErrSource,"Object does not exist"
End If
End Function
'====================================================================
Public Sub Create(ContainerPath,CN)
If CN = "" Or ContainerPath = "" Then
```

```
        Err.Raise 101,m_ErrSource,"Missing arguments"
        Exit Sub
    End If
    Dim Container
    If ADObjectExists(ContainerPath) Then
        Set Container = GetObject(FormatAdsPath(ContainerPath))
        Set m_OUObject = Container.Create("organizationalUnit",FormatCN(CN))
        m_OUObject.SetInfo
        m_OUObject.GetInfo
        Set Create = m_OUObject
    Else
        WScript.Echo "Error connecting to container!"
        WScript.Quit(1)
    End If
    End Sub
    '=======================================================================
    Public Sub Delete
        m_OUObject.DeleteObject(0)
    End Sub
    '=======================================================================
    Public Sub Move(Destination)
    Dim NewContainer
    Set NewContainer = GetObject(FormatAdsPath(Destination))
    NewContainer.MoveHere m_OUObject.AdsPath, m_OUObject.Name
    m_OUObject.MoveHere FormatAdsPath(Destination),FormatCN(Destination)
    End Sub
    '=======================================================================
    Public Property Get ChildCount
    m_OUObject.GetInfoEx Array("msDS-Approx-Immed-Subordinates"),0
    ChildCount = m_OUObject.Get("msDS-Approx-Immed-Subordinates")
    End Property
    '=======================================================================
    Public Property Get ChildObjects
    ' This returns a Dictionary object!
    Dim Child
    Set ChildObjects = WScript.CreateObject("Scripting.Dictionary")
    For Each Child in m_OUObject
        ChildObjects.Add Child.Name, Child.Class
    Next
    End Property
    '=======================================================================
    Public Sub LinkGPO(GPOName)
    Dim SearchRoot,FilterText,Attributes,SearchScope,GPOPath
    Dim RootDSE
    Set RootDSE = "LDAP://RootDSE"
    SearchRoot = "<LDAP://cn=policies,cn=system," & _
        RootDSE.Get("defaultNamingContext") & ">;"
    Set RootDSE = Nothing
```

```vbscript
    FilterText = _
        "(&(objectcategory=grouppolicycontainer)" & _
        "(objectclass=grouppolicycontainer)" & _
        "(displayname=" & GPOName & "));"
    Attributes = "AdsPath"
    SearchScope = "OneLevel"
    Dim Cn, Cmd, Results
    Set Cn = CreateObject("ADODB.Connection")
    Set Cmd = CreateObject("ADODB.Command")
    Cmd.ActiveConnection = Cn
    Cmd.CommandText = SearchRoot & ";" & FilterText & ";" & _
    Attributes & ";" & SearchScope
    Set Results = Cmd.Execute
    Select Case Results.RecordCount
        Case 0
            WScript.Echo "No GPO found named " & GPOName
            WScript.Quit(1)
        Case 1
            GPOPath = Results.Fields(0)
        Case Else
            WScript.Echo "More than 1 matching GPO found!"
            WScript.Quit(1)
    End Select
    Set Results = Nothing
    Set Cmd = Nothing
    Set Cn = Nothing
    On Error Resume Next
    Dim CurrentGPOLinks
    CurrentGPOLinks = m_OUObject.Get("gpLink")
    If Err.Number > 0 Then
        WScript.Echo "Error retrieving current GPO Links"
    End If
    On Error GoTo 0
    m_OUObject.Put "gpLink",CurrentGPOLinks & "[" & GPOPath & ";0]"
End Sub
'=====================================================================
Private Function ADObjectExists(ADsPath)
Dim ADObject, LDAPObject
ADSPath = FormatAdsPath(AdsPath)
On Error Resume Next
Set LDAPObject = GetObject("LDAP:")
Set ADObject = _
    LDAPObject.OpenDSObject(ADsPath,vbNullString,vbNullString, _
                        ADS_FAST_BIND)
If Err.Number = 0 Then
    ADObjectExists = True
Else
ADObjectExists = False
End If
```

```
Set ADObject = Nothing
Set LDAPObject = Nothing
End Function
'=====================================================================
Private Function FormatAdsPath(ADsPath)
If CBool(Instr(ADsPath,"LDAP://")) Then
    FormatAdsPath = AdsPath
Else
    FormatAdsPath = "LDAP://" & ADsPath
End If
End Function
'=====================================================================
Public Property Get m_ErrSource
    m_ErrSource = "OUClass"
End Property
Public Property Get ADS_FAST_BIND
    ADS_FAST_BIND = &H20
End Property
'=====================================================================
End Class
```

Create a New Organizational Unit

Creating a OU unit is similar to creating all the other objects we have looked at so far. Start by creating an instance of the OUclass class, then call the Create method and supply the ADsPath of the parent container and name of the new OU.

```
<job>
<script language="VBScript" src="includes\OUClass.vbs" />
<script>
Option Explicit
Dim OUObject
Set OUObject = New OUClass
OUObject.Create "LDAP://OU=Test,DC=zygort,DC=com","ScriptOU"
OUObject.SetProperty "description", "Scripting OU"
OUObject.Save
</script>
</job>
```

Delete an Organizational Unit

To delete an organizational unit, first bind to the OU and call the Delete method of the OUClass object. A check is performed first against the object's ChildCount property to guard against deleting an OU that contains child objects.

```
<job>
<script language="VBScript" src="includes\OUClass.vbs" />
<script>
Option Explicit
Dim OUObject
```

```
Set OUObject = New OUClass
OUObject.BindToOU "LDAP://OU=Test,DC=zygort,DC=com"
If OUObject.ChildCount = 0 Then
    OUObject.Delete
Else
    WScript.Echo "This OU contains child objects, aborting delete."
End If
</script>
</job>
```

List Child Objects in an Organizational Unit

When reorganizing the hierarchy of OUs in Active Directory, you may find it useful to get a list of child objects in an existing OU. If you bind to the OU, the `ChildObjects` property returns a `Dictionary` object with a list of the organizational unit's child objects, which you can then iterate through and perform additional operations on.

```
<job>
<script language="VBScript" src="includes\OUClass.vbs" />
<script>
Option Explicit
Dim OUObject, ChildObjects, ChildObj
Set OUObject = New OUClass
OUObject.BindToOU "LDAP://OU=Test,DC=zygort,DC=com"
If OUObject.ChildCount > 0 Then
    Set ChildObjects = OUObject.ChildObjects
    For Each ChildObj In ChildObjects.Keys
        WScript.Echo ChildObj & ", " & ChildObjects(ChildObj)
    Next
Else
    WScript.Echo "OU contains no child objects"
End If
</script>
</job>
```

Excel Scripts

Beyond administrative use, scripting is used to gather data from Active Directory. Query results (see the discussion of `QueryClass` earlier in this chapter) can be displayed as command-line output that can be redirected to a text file. The text file can then be loaded into Excel. If the data was formatted correctly in the output file (for example, with commas separating the fields), the data can be imported into separate columns—which might then need to be reformatted, with column headers added and all those other fun tasks that turn data into information.

The other option is to access Excel directly from VBScript. If Excel is loaded on the computer that is running the script, an instance of the `Excel.Application` object can be created. You must then learn to use the object model that encompasses Excel to properly send your data to an Excel spreadsheet. The Excel object is not a trivial set of properties and methods.

To see what object model makes up Excel, fire up Excel, open the Visual Basic editor (Tools ➢ Macros ➢ Visual Basic Editor), and press the F2 key. This opens the Object Browser window, which you might want to maximize. First you will see the objects in all the loaded modules, so click the drop-down box in the upper-left corner (which should contain <All Libraries>) and select Excel. Now you will see only the objects, properties, methods, and enumerations that deal with Microsoft Excel.

Although we can't possibly cover everything you see, let's go through a simple example. Find the Application object in the left window and select it. The right window now shows the properties and methods of the Application object. Select the ActiveCell property (see Figure 19.2). The property definition will display in the bottom window. Notice that the property will return a Range object. Click on the underlined word *Range* in the bottom window to select the Range object. Unfortunately you don't see much information about the object? Figure 19.2 shows the Object Browser in action.

Scripting Excel can be a complex task, but we hope that the following ExcelClass definition will make things easier. Rather than navigating through the Excel object model, the class provides the functionality that allows movement from cell to cell and formats the data. This is not a full-featured class for handling Excel scripting, but it is plenty to get you started—and of course you can expand it as you see fit.

FIGURE 19.2

The Object Browser

ExcelClass

The ExcelClass class is more complicated than other class definitions we have seen so far. Because we have not yet discussed anything about Excel, we need to take a few minutes to discuss the methodology used by the ExcelClass class before we start using it. It is important to remember that this class acts as a middleman between your script and the Excel application.

Most result sets are processed from left to right, top to bottom. Excel uses columns and rows. While columns are labeled with alphabetic letters, they are really represented by numbers.

Every instantiated ExcelClass object has only one active cell. This cell has a value assigned to or read from it. To get or set the value of the active cell, use the object's CellValue property. Two methods are also available to read or set the values of any cells in the worksheet. The GetAbsoluteCellValue method takes two arguments: the row and column of the cell to read. The SetAbsoluteCellValue method takes three arguments: the row and column of the cell and the value to set in that cell. These methods are very useful in making comparisons between cells in a workbook.

The active cell can have certain properties set through the class. The foreground, or text, color is set through the CellForeColor property. The background color can be set with the CellBackColor property. These are not the actual property names exposed by the Excel object model, but these names are more intuitive than referencing the `Cell.Interior.Color` property.

You can also manipulate the cell's font characteristics. The `CellFont` property can set or read the font name. The `CellFontSize` can set or read the size of the font. The `CellBold` property can be set to `True` or `False` to make the font style bold or normal, respectively.

Setting the same font characteristics for every cell can be wasteful, so you can use a handful of methods in the `ExcelClass` class to manipulate them on a larger scale. To set the background or foreground colors on an entire column, you can use the `SetColumnBackColor` and `SetColumnForeColor` methods, respectively. The `SetRowBackColor` and `SetRowForeColor` methods do the same on a row basis. All of these methods (notice they are not properties!) take two arguments: the column or row number and the color value to set. At the present time these methods cannot handle ranges of columns or rows.

Your script can also change the row height and column width. The `CurrentRowHeight` and `CurrentColumnWidth` properties access the current column and row properties of the active cell. To change a specific row or column, you may use the `SetRowHeight` and `SetRowWidth` methods and pass the row or column number and height or width as arguments.

Navigating, or moving, the active cell is a common task and there are several methods available for doing so. Because reading or populating a spreadsheet is done one cell at a time, from right to left and top to bottom, it makes sense to use navigation methods that reflect this. Those methods are `NextColumn` and `NextRow`. The `NextColumn` method moves the active cell one column to the right, and the `NextRow` method moves it one row down. (Note that the `NextRow` method does not move the active cell to the first column! To move the active cell to the first column on the next row, call the `StartNewRow` method. Do not confuse these two methods.)

To locate the current active cell, you can reference the object's `Row` and `Column` properties. These return the numeric value of the row and column. To translate the numeric value of the column into the standard alphabetic representation, you can pass the column number to the object's `GetColumnLetters` method. You can also set the value for the current row and column if you want. Because several other methods are available for moving the active cell, I would avoid setting the row and column values directly.

Other navigational methods are also provided. The `MoveAbsoluteCell` method takes two arguments—the row number and column number—and moves the active cell to that specific cell. When looking at a spreadsheet in Excel, remember that the columns are represented by letters, and while you could mentally translate those alphabetic values into their numeric equivalents, we have provided a method to do it for you. Call the `GetColumnNumber` method and pass the string value of the column (case is ignored) to the method, and it will return the column number.

You can also move a number of cells relative to the active cell. The `MoveRelativeCell` method takes two arguments: the number of rows (positive or negative) to move and the number of columns (positive or negative) to move from the active cell.

You might need to populate two or more worksheets with information. The `NewWorksheet` method creates a new worksheet in the current workbook and makes it the active worksheet. The active cell is set to A1 and you can immediately begin entering data.

To save a workbook, use the `SaveWorkbook` method, passing it the filename you want to use. If you attempt to exit the script without saving the workbook, Excel will prompt you to save your work (you've run into this behavior before with at least one other application, right?). If you truly want to exit without saving your work, set the `QuitWithoutSaving` property of the object to `True` before the script ends.

To open an existing workbook, create an instance of the ExcelClass class and call the OpenWorkbook method, passing it the filename of the spreadsheet to open. The active cell will be on the first worksheet, cell A1.

By default the spreadsheet is not visible while you are working with it (though you can tell Excel is running if you examine the running processes under Task Manager). To see what is going on you can execute the Show method. To hide the spreadsheet execute the Hide method.

```
Option Explicit
'=====================================================================
Class ExcelClass
'=====================================================================
' Private and public variables
Private m_ExcelObject
Private m_ActiveWorkbook, m_ActiveSheet
Private m_CurrentRow, m_CurrentColumn
Private m_QuitWithoutExiting
Private m_ErrSource
'=====================================================================
Private Sub Class_Initialize
Set m_ExcelObject = WScript.CreateObject("Excel.Application")
m_ErrSource = "ExcelObject"
m_QuitWithoutExiting = False
End Sub
'=====================================================================
Private Sub Class_Terminate
If m_QuitWithoutExiting Then
   m_ExcelObject.Visible = True
Else
   m_ActiveWorkbook.Close
   m_ExcelObject.Application.Quit
End If
Set m_ActiveSheet = Nothing
Set m_ActiveWorkbook = Nothing
Set m_ExcelObject = Nothing
End Sub
'=====================================================================
Public Property Get Row
   Row = m_CurrentRow
End Property

Public Property Let Row(RowValue)
If IsNumeric(RowValue) Then
   m_CurrentRow = RowValue
Else
   Err.Raise 101,m_ErrSource,"Row must be a number"
End If
End Property
'=====================================================================
Public Property Get Column
   Column = m_CurrentColumn
```

```
End Property

Public Property Let Column(ColumnValue)
If IsNumeric(ColumnValue) Then
   m_CurrentColumn = ColumnValue
   Else
   Err.Raise 102,m_ErrSource,"Column must be a number"
End If
End Property
'===================================================================
Public Property Get QuitWithoutExiting
   QuitWithoutExiting = m_QuitWithoutExiting
End Property

Public Property Let QuitWithoutExiting(ExitValue)
   m_QuitWithoutExiting = ExitValue
End Property
'===================================================================
Public Sub SetColumnForeColor(Column,ColorValue)
   m_ActiveSheet.Columns(Column).Font.Color = ColorValue
End Sub
'===================================================================
Public Sub SetColumnBackColor(Column,ColorValue)
   m_ActiveSheet.Columns(Column).Interior.Color = ColorValue
End Sub
'===================================================================
Public Sub SetRowForeColor(Row,ColorValue)
   m_ActiveSheet.Rows(Row).Font.Color = ColorValue
End Sub
'===================================================================
Public Sub SetRowBackColor(Row,ColorValue)
   m_ActiveSheet.Rows(Row).Interior.Color = ColorValue
End Sub
'===================================================================
Public Property Get CellValue
   CellValue = m_ActiveSheet.Cells(m_CurrentRow,m_CurrentColumn).Value
End Property

Public Property Let CellValue(NewValue)
   m_ActiveSheet.Cells(m_CurrentRow,m_CurrentColumn).Value = NewValue
End Property
'===================================================================
Public Property Get CurrentColumnWidth
CurrentColumnHeight = _
   m_ActiveSheet.Columns(m_CurrentColumn).ColumnWidth
End Property

Public Property Let CurrentColumnWidth(WidthValue)
If IsNumeric(WidthValue) Then
   m_ActiveSheet.Columns(m_CurrentColumn).ColumnWidth = WidthValue
```

```
   End If
   End Property
   '========================================================================
   Public Sub SetColumnWidth(Column,WidthValue)
   If IsNumeric(Column) Then
      If IsNumeric(WidthValue) Then
         m_ActiveSheet.Columns(Column).ColumnWidth = WidthValue
      Else
         Err.Raise 104,m_ErrSource,"Width must be a number"
      End If
   Else
      Err.Raise 103,m_ErrSource,"Column must be a number"
   End If
   End Sub
   '========================================================================
   Public Property Get CurrentRowHeight
      CurrentRowHeight = m_ActiveSheet.Rows(m_CurrentRow).RowHeight
   End Property

   Public Property Let CurrentRowHeight(WidthValue)
   If IsNumeric(WidthValue) Then
      m_ActiveSheet.Rows(m_CurrentRow).RowHeight = WidthValue
   End If
   End Property
   '========================================================================
   Public Sub SetRowHeight(Row,WidthValue)
   If IsNumeric(Row) Then
      If IsNumeric(WidthValue) Then
         m_ActiveSheet.Rows(Row).RowHeight = WidthValue
      Else
         Err.Raise 104,m_ErrSource,"Width must be a number"
      End If
   Else
      Err.Raise 103,m_ErrSource,"Row must be a number"
   End If
   End Sub
   '========================================================================
   Public Property Get CellForeColor
   CellForeColor = _
      m_ActiveSheet.Cells(m_CurrentRow,m_CurrentColumn).Font.Color
   End Property

   Public Property Let CellForeColor(ColorValue)
   m_ActiveSheet.Cells(m_CurrentRow,m_CurrentColumn).Font.Color = _
                                                     ColorValue
   End Property
   '========================================================================
```

```
Public Property Get CellBackColor
CellBackColor = _
   m_ActiveSheet.Cells(m_CurrentRow,m_CurrentColumn).Interior.Color
End Property

Public Property Let CellBackColor(ColorValue)
m_ActiveSheet.Cells(m_CurrentRow,m_CurrentColumn).Interior.Color = _
                                                        ColorValue
End Property
'====================================================================
Public Property Get CellFont
CellFont = _
   m_ActiveSheet.Cells(m_CurrentRow,m_CurrentColumn).Font.Name
End Property

Public Property Let CellFont(FontValue)
m_ActiveSheet.Cells(m_CurrentRow,m_CurrentColumn).Font.Name = _
                                                  FontValue
End Property
'====================================================================
Public Property Get CellBold
CellBold = _
   m_ActiveSheet.Cells(m_CurrentRow,m_CurrentColumn).Font.Bold
End Property

Public Property Let CellBold(BoldValue)
If BoldValue Then
   m_ActiveSheet.Cells(m_CurrentRow,m_CurrentColumn).Font.Bold = _
                                                        True
Else
   m_ActiveSheet.Cells(m_CurrentRow,m_CurrentColumn).Font.Bold = _
                                                        False
End If
End Property
'====================================================================
Public Property Get CellFontSize
CellFontSize = _
   m_ActiveSheet.Cells(m_CurrentRow,m_CurrentColumn).Font.Size
End Property

Public Property Let CellFontSize(SizeValue)
If IsNumeric(SizeValue) And SizeValue >= 8 Then
   m_ActiveSheet.Cells(m_CurrentRow,m_CurrentColumn).Font.Size = _
                                                  SizeValue
Else
   Err.Raise 106,m_ErrSource,"Invalid font size"
End If
End Property
'====================================================================
```

```
Public Sub NewWorkBook
Set m_ActiveWorkbook = m_ExcelObject.Workbooks.Add
' Set m_ActiveSheet to the first worksheet in the workbook
Set m_ActiveSheet = m_ActiveWorkbook.Worksheets(1)
m_CurrentRow = 1
m_CurrentColumn = 1
End Sub
'=====================================================================
Public Sub NewWorksheet
Set m_ActiveSheet = m_Worksheets.Add
m_CurrentRow = 1
m_CurrentColumn = 1
End Sub
'=====================================================================
Public Property Get Worksheet
Worksheet = m_ActiveSheet.Name
End Property

Public Property Let Worksheet(WorksheetValue)
If IsNumeric(WorkSheetValue) Then
    If WorksheetValue <= m_ExcelObject.Worksheets.Count Then
        Set m_ActiveSheet = m_ExcelObject.Worksheets(WorksheetValue)
        m_CurrentRow = 1
        m_CurrentColumn = 1
    Else
        Err.Raise 111,m_ErrSource,"Invalid worksheet"
    End If
Else
    Dim WSCount
    For WS = 1 To m_ExcelObject.Worksheets.Count
        If m_ExcelObject.Worksheets(WS).Name = WorkSheetValue Then
            Set m_ActiveSheet = m_ExcelObject.Worksheets(WS)
            Exit For
        End If
    Next
End If
End Property
'=====================================================================
Public Sub MoveAbsoluteCell(Row,Column)
If IsNumeric(Row) Then
    m_CurrentRow = Row
Else
    Err.Raise 101,m_ErrSource,"Row must be a number"
End If
If IsNumeric(Column) Then
    m_CurrentColumn = Column
Else
    Err.Raise 102,m_ErrSource,"Column must be a number"
End If
```

```
End Sub
'==================================================================
Public Sub MoveRelativeCell(Row,Column)
If IsNumeric(Row) Then
    m_CurrentRow = m_CurrentRow + Row
Else
    Err.Raise 101,m_ErrSource,"Row must be a number"
End If
If IsNumeric(Column) Then
    m_CurrentColumn = m_CurrentColumn + Column
Else
    Err.Raise 102,m_ErrSource,"Column must be a number"
End If
End Sub
'==================================================================
Public Function GetColumnNumber(Column)
Select Case Len(Column)
Case 1
    GetColumnNumber = Asc(UCase(Column)) - 64
Case 2
    GetColumnNumber = (Asc(UCase(Left(Column,1))) -64) * 26 + _
                      Asc(UCase(Right(Column,1))) - 64
End Select
End Function
'==================================================================
Public Function GetColumnLetters(Column)
If Column \ 26 > 0 Then
    Dim FirstLetter, SecondLetter
    FirstLetter = Chr((Column \ 26) + 64)
    SecondLetter = Chr((Column Mod 26) + 64)
    GetColumnLetters = FirstLetter & SecondLetter
Else
    GetColumnLetters = Chr(Column + 64)
End If
End Function
'==================================================================
Public Sub NextRow
    m_CurrentRow = m_CurrentRow + 1
End Sub
'==================================================================
Public Sub PreviousRow
If (m_CurrentRow - 1) > 0 Then
    m_CurrentRow = m_CurrentRow - 1
End If
End Sub
'==================================================================
Public Sub NextColumn
    m_CurrentColumn = m_CurrentColumn + 1
End Sub
'==================================================================
```

```
Public Sub PreviousColumn
If (m_CurrentColumn - 1) > 0 Then
    m_CurrentColumn = m_CurrentColumn - 1
End If
End Sub
'====================================================================
Public Sub StartNewRow
m_CurrentRow = m_CurrentRow + 1
m_CurrentColumn = 1
End Sub
'====================================================================
Public Sub OpenWorkBook(Filename)
On Error Resume Next
m_ExcelObject.Workbooks.Open FileName
If Err.Number <> 0 Then
    Err.Raise Err.Number,m_ErrSource,Err.Description
End If
Set m_ActiveWorkbook = m_ExcelObject.Workbooks(1)
Set m_ActiveSheet = m_ActiveWorkbook.Worksheets(1)
m_CurrentRow = 1
m_CurrentColumn = 1
End Sub
'====================================================================
Public Sub SaveWorkBook(FileName)
    m_ActiveWorkbook.SaveAs FileName
End Sub
'====================================================================
Public Property Get ActiveSheetName
    ActiveSheetName = m_ActiveSheet.Name
End Property

Public Property Let ActiveSheetName(NameValue)
    m_ActiveSheet.Name = NameValue
End Property
'====================================================================
Public Function GetAbsoluteCellValue(Row,Column)
If IsNumeric(Row) Then
    If IsNumeric(Column) Then
        GetAbsoluteCellValue = _
            m_ActiveSheet.Cells(Row,Column).Value
    Else
        Err.Raise 102,m_ErrSource,"Column must be a number"
    End If
Else
    Err.Raise 101,m_ErrSource,"Row must be a number"
End If
End Function
'====================================================================
```

```
Public Sub SetAbsoluteCellValue(Row,Column,CellValue)
If IsNumeric(Row) Then
    If IsNumeric(Column) Then
        m_ActiveSheet.Cells(Row,Column).Value = CellValue
    Else
        Err.Raise 102,m_ErrSource,"Column must be a number"
    End If
Else
    Err.Raise 101,m_ErrSource,"Row must be a number"
End If
End Sub
'=====================================================================
Public Sub Hide
    m_ExcelObject.Visible = True
End Sub
'=====================================================================
Public Sub Show
    m_ExcelObject.Visible = True
End Sub
'=====================================================================
End Class
```

Export Users to Excel

This script demonstrates how to create an Excel spreadsheet with a list of User objects and their ADsPaths. It uses the QueryClass class to find the User object and the ExcelClass class to write the results to an Excel spreadsheet.

The QueryClass object is instantiated as you have seen before, and the values for the searchroot, attributes, scope, and filtertext are supplied. The resulting record set, Results, is then iterated through.

Before we start processing the results the ExcelClass object is instantiated. This creates an instance of the Excel application in memory, but since we have not set the Visible property of the object to True, it will not be displayed. A new workbook is created with the NewWorkbook method. The active cell is the first cell in the workbook, A1 by default, which is given the value from the first field of the Recordset. For demonstration purposes the foreground color is changed to red and the background color is changed to blue. The NextColumn method moves the active cell to the next column in the workbook, B1, and the value is assigned. The cell's font is changed to Arial Narrow for demonstration. The StartNewRow method moves the active cell to the first column in the next row, much like sending a CRLF (carriage return–line feed) to a text file. The Recordset point is then moved to the next record and the process repeats.

The last section of the code demonstrates how to set the foreground color for an entire column and how to set the height for a row. This is a simple example to get you started. The main purpose is to get you used to the idea of navigating the Excel spreadsheet using the ExcelClass object.

```
<job>
<script language="VBScript" src="includes\RootDSEClass.vbs" />
<script language="VBScript" src="includes\QueryClass.vbs" />
<script language="VBScript" src="includes\ExcelClass.vbs" />
<script>
```

```
Dim RootDSE
Set RootDSE = New RootDSEClass
Dim Query
Set Query = New QueryClass
Query.SearchRoot = "CN=Users,DC=zygort,DC=org"
Query.Attributes = "cn,AdsPath"
Query.Scope = "subtree"
Query.FilterText = "(&(objectClass=user)(objectCategory=person))"
Dim Results
Set Results = Query.ExecuteQuery
Set Excel = New ExcelClass
Excel.NewWorkbook
Do Until Results.eof
    Excel.CellValue = Results.Fields(0)
    Excel.NextColumn
    Excel.CellValue = Results.Fields(1)
    Excel.StartNewRow
    Results.MoveNext
Loop
Excel.QuitWithoutExiting = True
Set Query = Nothing
Set RootDSE = Nothing
</script>
</job>
```

Import Users from Excel

This script uses the `ExcelClass` and `UserClass` classes to read a list of settings from an Excel spreadsheet and populate Active Directory with the users and their information. This can be a bit tricky, especially if you want to maintain flexibility in your script, so let me explain what we were trying to do here.

First, we do not like locking anyone into a given format. That means we want users to be able to modify the spreadsheet as they see fit, and the script should adapt to it. However, to meet the requirements for adding users (specifically through the `Create` method of the `UserClass` object), three elements are required: the parent container, the Common Name, and the sAMAccountName. Other that that, anything should go.

To accomplish this, the first row is reserved for the `lDAPDisplayName` of the property you want to set. The only three required columns are Container, CN, and sAMAccountName, which we have placed as the first three spreadsheet columns. After those columns enter the `lDAPDisplayName` for any other properties you want to set on the first row. Then fill in the properties for the individual users that correspond to those properties on the subsequent lines.

The script begins by opening the spreadsheet and skipping the first row of property names. Each subsequent row of properties is read and stored in either a variable (for the required properties) or in a `Dictionary` object (for the optional properties). If all required properties are included the `UserClass` object is instantiated, the new `User` object is created, and the optional properties are set. This procedure repeats for each row in the spreadsheet.

```
<job>
<script language="VBScript" src="includes\ExcelClass.vbs" />
<script language="VBScript" src="includes\UserClass.vbs" />
<script>
```

```
Dim EndOfRow, EndOfFile
EndOfRow = False
EndOfFile = False
Set Excel = New ExcelClass
Excel.OpenWorkbook "NewUsers.xls"
' First row is the lDAPDisplayName, skip it
Excel.NextRow
Dim User
Do Until EndOfFile
    If Excel.CellValue = "" Then
        EndOfFile = True
    Else
        Dim Container, CN, sAMAccountName, OtherProperties
        Set OtherProperties = _
            WScript.CreateObject("Scripting.Dictionary")
            Do Until EndOfRow
                If Excel.GetAbsoluteCellValue(1,Excel.Column) = "" Then
                    EndOfRow = True
                Else
                    Select Case _
                        LCase(Excel.GetAbsoluteCellValue(1,Excel.Column))
                        Case "container"
                            Container = Excel.CellValue
                        Case "cn"
                            CN = Excel.CellValue
                        Case "samaccountname"
                            sAMAccountName = Excel.CellValue
                        Case Else
                            If Not(Excel.CellValue = "") Then
                                OtherProperties.Add _
                                    Excel.GetAbsoluteCellValue(1,Excel.Column), _
                                    Excel.CellValue
                            End If
                    End Select
                    WScript.Echo _
                        Excel.GetAbsoluteCellValue(1,Excel.Column) & _
                            "=" & Excel.CellValue
                    Excel.NextColumn
                End If
        Loop
        If Not(Container = "" And CN = "" And sAMAccountName = "") Then
            Dim UserObject
            UserObject = New UserClass
            UserObject.Create Container,CN,sAMAccountName
            Dim PropName
            For Each PropName In OtherProperties.Keys
                UserObject.SetProperty PropName, _
                                        OtherProperties(PropName)
            Next
            UserObject.Save
```

```
        Else
            WScript.Echo "Missing required values in row " & Excel.Row
        End If
        Excel.StartNewRow
        EndOfRow = False
    End If
Loop
</script>
</job>
```

Arguments Class

Now that we've gotten through the scripts in this chapter, it's time to point out one flaw they all have. Many of the Active Directory elements such as ADS Path, Common Name, etc., have been hard-coded into the script. This was done for one simple reason: space.

A good script allows the user to pass arguments on the command line. This gives the script the flexibility to match the situation. It also adds a layer of complexity to the script that can take up a significant amount of space with every script in this (and the next) chapter. But we do want to give you a tool to help you add command-line argument handling to your scripts.

Let's get something out in the open: dealing with command-line arguments is not fun. It tends to be messy because you can't always trust the person running the script to know exactly how to run the script (even if that person is you). Therefore you must put safeguards in your script to weed out the good arguments from the bad.

To make life a little easier, we've given you a class to help you script command-line arguments. It is not the complete solution; you will still have to rewrite your scripts to evaluate the arguments (it's not much work and we'll give you a few examples). But it does give you a simple framework from which to start.

To start you need to know that arguments can take one of two forms on the command line: they can appear by themselves or they can be qualified with a name, as in this example:

```
CScript CreateUser.wsf /FirstName:Test User
```

Can you spot the two arguments? The first one is pretty obvious: `FirstName:Test`. In actuality, `FirstName` is the name assigned to the value `Test`. This is called a named Argument in VBScript, and it's really the correct way to pass arguments to a script. Every value is assigned a proper name, so you know what to do with it in your script.

But the second argument is a little harder to spot; it's the value `User`. Unfortunately nothing else on the command line specifies exactly what the `User` value is for. The idea is that the person running the script will type the arguments in the correct order for the script to execute properly. This is a bad practice, and one this class is designed to help you take control of.

Simply creating an instance of this class causes it to gather all the command-line arguments passed to the script. It doesn't matter if the user typed in arguments using the slash (/) prefix, as shown in the most recent example, or simply qualified the arguments using a colon or equals-sign delimiter; they will all be gathered and placed into a `Dictionary` object for easy retrieval. For example, all of the following are valid argument types:

```
CScript MyScript.wsf /A:1 B:2 C=3 /D=4
```

In this example the `Arguments` class gathers the arguments A, B, C, and D, and assigns their respective values. This kind of flexibility makes your scripts very easy to use (as well as tolerant of mistakes like "whoops, I meant to use a colon, not the equals sign!").

Along with retrieving the command-line arguments, the class allows you to check for a set of required arguments. This is done by passing a comma-separated list of argument names to a function, which returns a true value if all the argument names exist.

To retrieve an argument's value, simply call the function GetArgument and pass the name of the argument to retrieve. Before retrieving an argument it's a good idea to make sure it exists first, which you can do with the function ArgumentExists.

```
Class ArgumentsClass
Private m_Arguments

Private Sub Class_Initialize
Set m_Arguments = CreateObject("Scripting.Dictionary")
If WScript.Arguments.Count > 0 Then
    For Each Argument In WScript.Arguments
        ArgArray = Split(Replace(Argument,"=",":"),":")
        If UBound(ArgArray) = 0 Then
            m_Arguments.Add m_Arguments.Count, Argument
        Else
            Key = Replace(ArgArray(0),"/","")
            If Not(m_Arguments.Exists(Key)) Then
                m_Arguments.Add _
                    Replace(ArgArray(0),"/",""), _
                    ArgArray(1)
            End If
        End If
    Next
End If
End Sub

Private Sub Class_Terminate
Set m_Arguments = Nothing
End Sub

Public Function RequiredArgumentsExist(ByVal KeysCSV)
Dim KeyArray, Key
KeyArray = Split(KeysCSV,",")
RequiredArgumentsExist = True
For Each Key In KeyArray
    If Not (m_Arguments.Exists(Key)) Then
        RequiredArgumentsExist = False
        Exit Function
    End If
Next
End Function

Public Function ArgumentExists(ByVal Key)
If m_Arguments.Exists(Key) Then
    ArgumentExists = True
Else
```

```
        ArgumentExists = False
    End If
    End Function

    Public Function GetArgument(ByVal Key)
    If m_Arguments.Exists(Key) Then
        GetArgument = m_Arguments(Key)
    Else
        GetArgument = ""
    End If
    End Function

    Public Property Get Count
        Count = m_Arguments.Count
    End Property

    End Class
```

Now that you've seen the contents of the `Arguments` class, we'll show you a few examples of how to integrate it into your scripts. Before you start adding code you must think about the arguments your script requires and make a list. Let's look at a classic script—resetting a user's password—and see the process in action:

```
<job>
<script language="VBScript" src="includes\UserClass.vbs" />
<script>
' This is the original script
Option Explicit
Dim UserObject
Set UserObject = New UserClass
UserObject.BindToUser "CN=ScriptUser,CN=Users,DC=zygort,DC=com"
UserObject.Password = "P@ssw0rd"
UserObject.Save
</script>
</job>
```

Looking at the script, you should see two hard-coded values that we can turn into command-line arguments: the LDAP path of the user and the new password. The user's LDAP path is a required argument; we can't proceed without knowing it. But we can treat the password as an optional argument. The script can use a standard password if a new password isn't supplied on the command line.

Now that you know what arguments to look for on the command line, we can modify the script to handle them using the `Arguments` class.

First add a reference to the `ArgumentsClass.vbs` script. Next create an instance of the `ArgumentsClass` object in your script. You'll want to check for the presence of the required arguments right away, because missing any bit of required information is a show-stopper.

```
<job>
<script language="VBScript" src="includes\UserClass.vbs" />
<script>
' This is the original script
Option Explicit
```

```
Set Arguments = New ArgumentsClass
If Not(Arguments.RequiredArgumentsExist("User")) Then
    WScript.Echo "Missing a required argument!"
    ' Display the proper syntax message here
    WScript.Quit(1)
End If
```

Satisfied that we have the required argument, we can move on. The `UserObject` is created and bound to the specified argument.

```
UserObject.BindToUser Arguments.GetArgument("User")
```

Finally we reset the password. Because the `Password` argument is optional we need to check for its existence. If it wasn't passed on the command line we'll use the default password value.

```
If Arguments.ArgumentExists("Password") Then
    UserObject.Password = _
        Arguments.GetArgument("Password")
Else
    UserObject.Password = "P@ssw0rd"
End If
UserObject.Save
```

We're done; this script can now accept command-line arguments. To execute the new script, the command line might look something like the following:

```
CScript.exe ResetPassword.wsf
    /User:CN=Scott,CN=Users,DC=zygort,DC=com
    /Password:NewP@ssword
```

Before you jump into rewriting the rest of your scripts, think about doing a bit more work. For example, the script does nothing to validate the LDAP path of the user that was passed in. As we said, handling command-line arguments adds a layer of complexity to your scripts and that layer can get very deep if you let it.

The Bottom Line

Use the Windows Script File to incorporate the functionality of an existing VBScript class into a new script When developing scripts, especially a lot of scripts, it makes sense to avoid reinventing code you've already written. Code reuse in VBScript used to be a copy-and-paste operation. With the Windows Script File (WSF) this is not the case. The script code that exists in another file can be referenced by the WSF script, which saves time and unneeded duplication.

Master It You are writing a new script to perform some user maintenance. Your script needs to create a password based on a key value. A function named `CreatePassword` has already been written to create the password and exists in the file `Password.vbs`. Create a new WSF file that can use the existing function. Display the password that would be generated by the key value `John Smith`.

Use VBScript classes to encapsulate Active Directory and other application functionality A class is simply a blueprint for creating an object. In VBScript we create our own classes using VBScript code. A number of functions deal specifically with Active Directory objects, such as users and groups. By grouping those functions into a class based on the particular object, we can accomplish two things: we can keep our main script clean and focused on the task at hand, and we can reuse the same class code in several different scripts (with the help of WSF files).

Master It   In this chapter we created a class to represent an Active Directory user. The class is named UserClass and is contained in a file named UserClass.vbs. Create a new script that creates a new instance of an Active Directory user (you can pick the user) and display the user's first name, last name, and telephone properties.

Develop Visual Basic scripts to read and manage Microsoft Active Directory   Writing scripts to manage Active Directory has some clear benefits. First, a script can perform several operations on Active Directory in one fell swoop, saving the administrator time. Second, a script performs the operations the same way every time the script is running, keeping Active Directory objects consistent and uniform. Finally, a script runs at any time of day or night, weekday or weekend. This allows the administrator to offload routine maintenance tasks—many of which are best performed during off-hours—to the script.

Master It   Using the classes presented in this chapter, develop a script that queries Active Directory for all groups. Export a list of all groups to Excel. Save the workbook with the name GroupList.xls.

Chapter 20

Monitoring Active Directory

In this chapter we will create scripts for monitoring your Active Directory installation. Microsoft already has an excellent server product, Microsoft System Center Operations Manager (SCOM), that supports a feature pack designed to manage Active Directory. This server product is, unfortunately, priced beyond the budget of many IT departments.

In this chapter, you will learn to:

- ◆ Use WMI to monitor the health of Active Directory servers
- ◆ Write scripts to monitor the health of Active Directory

Active Directory Management Pack (ADMP) functionality is documented on the Microsoft System Center Operations Manager website. From that documentation you learn what each individual monitoring task is designed to do and how often each task executes. We can use this information to build a VBScript to replicate the original task, and we can use the Task Scheduler to execute the script on a regular schedule.

Following the same modular approach to script writing as you saw in the previous chapter, we will use the Windows script file (WSF) format for our scripts. Along the way, we'll build a few additional VBScript classes to use (and reuse) in our scripts. Of course all these scripts are available for download.

In this module you will also be introduced to Windows Management Instrumentation (WMI). WMI provides a standard interface we can take advantage of to monitor not only Active Directory functions, but also most functions and settings on a local or remote computer.

OutputClass

In terms of output, monitoring scripts are quite different when compared with other scripts. What kind of information do we expect a monitoring script to provide? Most of the time we don't want information from the script unless it finds something wrong, in which case we want to know about the problem right away.

The OutputClass class object acts as a smart equivalent to the Wscript.Echo method. Rather than calling the Wscript.Echo method directly, you would instead instantiate an instance of the OutputClass and call the object's Display method. The object then decides, based on its own information, whether to actually display the output.

Why would we want to avoid displaying output from a script? Consider that when a script is executed with the WScript engine, the user sees output in the form of a dialog box. The script execution is blocked until the user responds to the dialog box. Considering how often these monitoring scripts are designed to execute, this could quickly irritate the user. Therefore, by using this class as a "middle-man" in displaying output, we give the script a built-in method to avoid the blocking behavior of dialog boxes.

Of course this blocking is not an issue when executing a script with the CScript engine because output is sent to a command prompt window. Normally when scripts are scheduled by means of the Task Scheduler, CScript.exe is specified as the script engine. This leads to a command-prompt box popping up each time a script executes, and then disappearing when the script has completed. This can be equally irritating to the user.

The question then becomes, which behavior are we looking for? As we go over the code for the monitoring scripts, you will notice that we have designed them to serve a dual purpose: in addition to raising an alert to potential problems, they can also be used to present the monitored data to the user. This allows us to use one script for both alerts and potential problem diagnoses with Active Directory, depending on which engine we use to run the script.

Therefore, when scheduling our scripts with the Task Scheduler we want to specify the WScript.exe scripting engine. To view the output from the script, use the CScript.exe engine.

The class itself is very simple. It starts by determining which scripting engine is executing the script. If the scripting engine is WScript.exe, the default behavior is to suppress the output; otherwise, the script output is displayed as normal. You can also use the SuppressOutput property to manually control the script output. Setting the property to True suppresses the script output, while setting it to False allows the output to be displayed.

The last method of the class is ModalAlert. This method displays a system modal dialog box with the message passed to the method. This is a quick and easy way of interrupting the user with an important message, such as an alert to an impending problem with Active Directory.

This only scratches the surface of what you can accomplish with a class like OutputClass. If your scripts use the same dialog-box settings continuously you could add a method similar to ModalAlert to reliably re-create the same dialog box time and time again.

```
'=====================================================================
Class OutputClass
'=====================================================================
' Private and public variables
Private m_SuppressOutput
'=====================================================================
Private Sub Class_Initialize
    If Instr(LCase(WScript.FullName),"wscript.exe") > 0 Then
        SuppressOutput = True
    Else
        SuppressOutput = False
    End If
End Sub
'=====================================================================
Private Sub Class_Terminate
End Sub
'=====================================================================
Public Property Get SuppressOutput
    SuppressOutput = m_SuppressOutput
End Property

Public Property Let SuppressOutput(SuppressValue)
    m_SuppressOutput = CBool(SuppressValue)
End Property
'=====================================================================
```

```
Public Function Display(Message)
If Not(m_SuppressOutput) Then
    WScript.Echo Message
End If
End Function
'================================================================
Public Sub ModalAlert(Message)
    MsgBox Message,vbExclamation+vbOKOnly+vbSystemModal,"ALERT!"
End Sub
'================================================================
End Class
```

Windows Management Instrumentation

Windows Management Instrumentation (WMI) is a cornerstone technology when it comes to monitoring systems, whether client or server. You might also hear it referred to as Web-Based Enterprise Management (WBEM). WMI is Microsoft's implementation of an industry initiative to standardize management of systems in an enterprise environment.

WMI is ready to use in Windows 2003, XP, and Windows 2000 operating systems. In Windows NT 4.0 SP4 and Windows 98 or (gasp!) 95, WMI is available as a downloadable component.

WMI uses a Common Information Model (CIM) to represent systems, the applications on those systems, networks, devices on those networks, and a variety of other managed components. The goal of CIM is to present a view of the logical and physical elements of a system. It is also object-oriented and extensible.

One of WMI's biggest strengths is its ability to pull or set configuration data on remote computers as well as the local system. The name of the system to connect to is passed in a connection string; if the system name can be resolved an attempt is made to access the WMI repository on that system. On the surface it seems simple enough. Remember, however, that we are remotely accessing and potentially modifying a system. Network administrators tend to keep a close eye on this practice and to restrict it where appropriate.

One of those restrictions is in the Windows Firewall. When enabled (which it is by default in Server 2008), WMI requests are denied. This usually results in an error message such as "RPC Server Unavailable." WMI must be allowed to establish a Distributed Component Object Model (DCOM) connection to the remote computer. Figure 20.1 shows how DCOM communication must get through the firewall on both the local and the remote client.

FIGURE 20.1
WMI and DCOM
communication

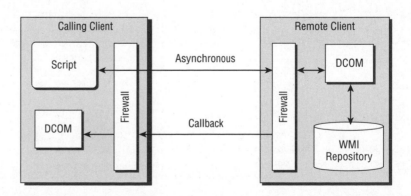

A full discussion of WMI programming is well beyond the scope of this chapter, but we will cover the basics to help you understand how the WMIClass (discussed in the next section) works.

The process begins by establishing a connection to the WMI repository on the remote computer. Several different methods are available for connecting to the remote computer, but for the purposes of our reusable VBScript object, we opted to use a flexible approach. Specifically, the WMIClass uses an object called SWBemLocator.

SWBemLocator obtains an object that represents the connection to the WMI repository. The connection is created by calling the object's ConnectServer method. The method takes four arguments: the name of the system to connect to, the WMI namespace to connect to, the username, and the password to establish the connection. You should be familiar with three of those arguments, but the WMI namespace might require a little more explanation.

A WMI namespace is a method of grouping similar WMI classes together. During installation a WMI provider first registers its namespace with the system and then registers all the classes that will reside within that namespace. For example, all Win32 WMI classes can be found in the root\cimv2 namespace.

To give you an idea of the query possibilities available with WMI, Table 20.1 lists some of the most useful Win32 WMI classes and their properties. This is far from a comprehensive list; for more information visit Microsoft's website and search for WMI.

TABLE 20.1: Commonly Used Win32 WMI Classes and Their Properties

CLASS	DESCRIPTION AND PROPERTIES
Win32_ComputerSystem	Represents the computer operating system. Useful properties include Name, Domain, DomainRole, PartOfDomain, Roles, and UserName.
Win32_DiskDrive	Represents the physical disk drives in the system. Useful properties include Name, Model, Size, and Status.
Win32_LogicalDisk	Represents both physical and mapped drives. Useful properties include Name, DriveType, FileSystem, and Size.
Win32_NetworkAdapterConfiguration	Represents the network adapters in a system. Useful properties include Caption, DHCPEnabled, DNSDomain, IPAddress, IPSubnet, DefaultIPGateway, and MACAddress.
Win32_OperatingSystem	Represents the operating system. Useful properties include Caption, BootDevice, CurrentTimeZone, CSName, FreePhysicalMemory, FreeVirtualMemory, SystemDrive, ServicePackMajorVersion, and Version.
Win32_Process	Represents the processes running on a system. Useful properties include CommandLine, ExecutablePath, ProcessID, and ParentProcessID.
Win32_Processor	Represents the system processor(s). Useful properties include Name, Availability, CPUStatus, MaxClockSpeed, CurrentClockSpeed, and Status.

TABLE 20.1:   Commonly Used Win32 WMI Classes and Their Properties *(CONTINUED)*

CLASS	DESCRIPTION AND PROPERTIES
Win32_Service	Represents the running services on a system. Useful properties include Caption, Name, PathName, Started, StartMode, StartName, and State.
Win32_Share	Represents the shared resources on a system. Useful properties include Name, Path, Type, and Status.

To get a better idea of what is available in WMI, let's look at a few tools. The first is a built-in utility named WbemTest.exe. This tool allows you to browse the wealth of WMI information on a system. It is installed with Windows 2000, Windows 2003, and Windows XP, and is available as a download for other systems. To start WbemTest, click Start ➢ Run and enter **WbemTest**.

The first step in working with WMI is to connect to the system you want to examine. The first dialog box is presented with about 13 disabled buttons, which might give you the impression that you already have a problem. You don't—you just haven't connected yet. Figure 20.2 shows the WbemTest dialog box in an unconnected state.

In the upper-right corner is a button labeled Connect. Click it to display the Connect dialog box, as shown in Figure 20.3. This dialog box allows you to specify any necessary connection information. The Namespace field allows you to specify a system and a namespace to connect to. If your current security credentials are not enough to connect to the WMI repository, you can supply an alternate set of security information in the User, Password, and Authority fields.

By default, the Namespace field says "root\default" (on Windows XP the field is sometimes not labeled). Let's change that to "root\cimv2" and click the Connect button. This returns us to the WbemTest dialog box, where all the buttons should now be enabled. You'll also see the namespace we entered in the Connect dialog box listed under the Namespace label. We can now start to explore WMI.

Start by clicking the Enum Classes button. You'll see the Superclass Info dialog box, shown in Figure 20.4. Because we are not going to narrow down our search we can leave it blank and click the OK button.

FIGURE 20.2
WbemTest dialog box
(not connected)

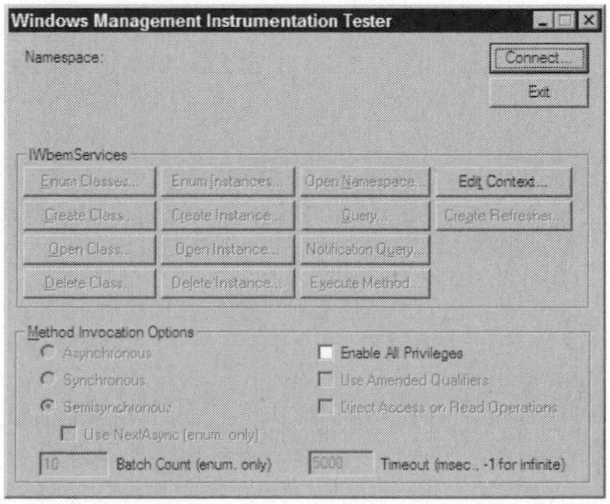

FIGURE 20.3
Connect dialog box

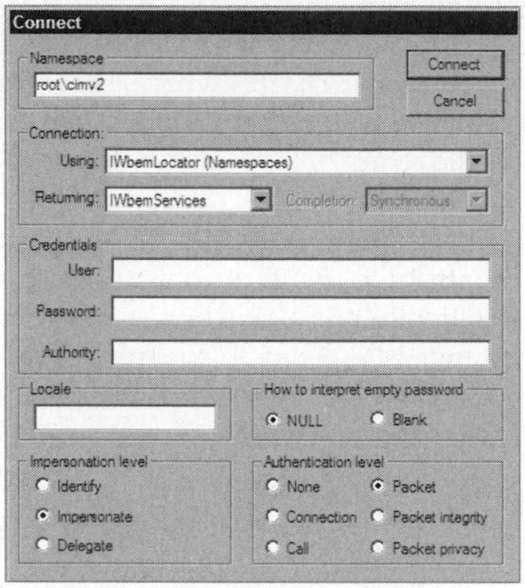

FIGURE 20.4
Superclass Info
dialog box

This returns the Query Result dialog box shown in Figure 20.5. This box lists the results of our query for all the base-level classes. As you scroll through the list you'll notice a few common prefixes to the classes (e.g., `CIM_`, `Win32_`, and `Msft_`). You'll also see two buttons for adding or deleting top-level classes to the WMI repository. We'll avoid that for now and go on to actually writing a few WMI queries, so click the Close button to return to the `WbemTest` dialog box.

The WMI Query Language (WQL) is used for writing queries in WMI. If you are familiar with Structured Query Language (SQL)—used by most database packages—this will seem very familiar to you. For the rest we'll cover the elements of a query along the way.

A query has two essential clauses: the `Select` clause, which is a list of attributes to return, and the `From` clause, which lists the data source that contains the information. In the `Select` clause we can submit a comma-separated list of individual attributes to return or we can use the asterisk (*) as a wildcard, which means "give me all the attributes." When developing queries, start by using the wildcard. You will get more information than you need at first, but you can whittle it down as you refine the query.

FIGURE 20.5
Query Result
dialog box

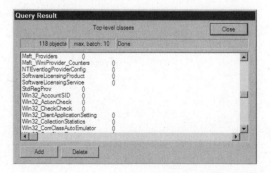

To write and submit a query, click the Query button. This brings up the Query dialog box, shown in Figure 20.6, which has a large text field where we will enter our query. We'll start with a very simple query to list the local computer system attributes. The query text is **Select * From Win32_ComputerSystem**. Enter the query in the Enter Query field and click the Apply button.

This should return only one result, shown in Figure 20.7—namely, your local computer. It doesn't seem like much information at first, but double-click on the single result.

You now see the Object Editor dialog box, shown in Figure 20.8. This dialog box allows you to browse the attributes for the instance of the Win32_ComputerSystem class that our query returned. The information in this dialog box, particularly the attribute names, is useful to note when developing your own WMI queries. When you have finished reviewing the results, click the Close button in the Object Editor dialog box, then click the Close button in the Query Results dialog box to return to the WbemTest dialog box.

FIGURE 20.6
Query dialog box

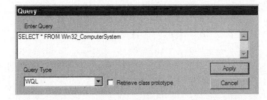

FIGURE 20.7
Query Result dialog box

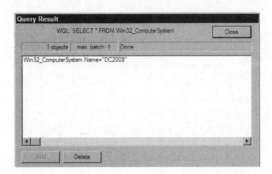

FIGURE 20.8
Object Editor dialog box

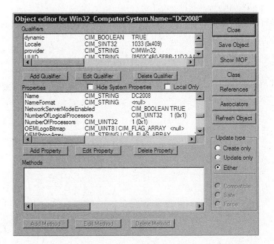

We've seen a simple two-part WMI query using only the Select and From clauses, which returned only a single result. Let's submit another query that gives us more to work with. Click the Query button and enter the following WMI query: **Select * from Win32_LogicalDisk**. Your results will look different from ours (which are displayed in Figure 20.9) but will list the physical and mapped disks.

By looking at the results you can probably guess which drives are local and which are mapped. If we want to write a WMI query that returns only the local or only the mapped drives, we have to find something that differentiates the two. In your own result set, examine the value of the DriveType attribute for a local and a mapped drive. According to Microsoft's documentation, the DriveType of a local disk is 3, a network drive is 4, and a CD-ROM is 5. Therefore, to write a WMI query that targets only mapped drives, we need to add a clause to limit the result set to instances where the DriveType attribute is 4.

A Where clause limits the result set of a query. You add the Where clause after the From clause in a query. Close the current Query Results dialog box and execute the following new query: **Select * from Win32_LogicalDisk Where DriveType='4'** (in this case the single quotes around the 4 are optional, but we've found that it is a good habit to get into when specifying Where-clause values). Figure 20.10 shows our results.

Finally, to query for the local drives we can modify the Where clause to look for both local disks and CD-ROM drives. The Where clause supports logical operators just like the VBScript If-Then statement. Close the current Query Results dialog box and execute the following query: **Select * from Win32_LogicalDisk Where DriveType='3' or DriveType='5'**.

WbemTest is an excellent tool that lets you practice and hone your WMI queries before committing them to a script. You can continue to write and experiment with WMI queries without fear of causing irreparable harm to your system. The worst outcome is that WbemTest might lock up and you'll have to restart it, so feel free to explore.

FIGURE 20.9
Win32_LogicalDisk
query results

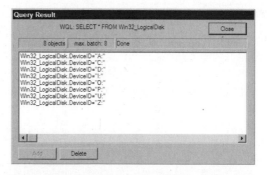

FIGURE 20.10
Network-drive
query results

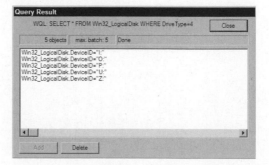

If you would like some additional help in the form of prewritten WMI queries, we have another tool for your consideration: a free download from Microsoft called Scriptomatic 2.0. (The URL is long and complicated so do a Google search on the keywords "Scriptomatic 2 download" to find a link to it.) Download the compressed executable file from Microsoft, extract the files, and double-click the `ScriptomaticV2.hta` file to execute. Figure 20.11 shows the Scriptomatic tool after initializing. After using it a few times you will find it to be one of the most invaluable tools at your disposal.

The Scriptomatic tool is a hypertext application (HTA), which means it is essentially a local web application. You can open the `ScriptomaticV2.hta` file in a text editor to see how it does its magic. Scriptomatic begins by loading all the namespaces available on the local computer. The default namespace is `root\CIMv2` but you can choose any other namespace with the WMI Namespace drop-down. After selecting the appropriate namespace, use the WMI Class drop-down to select the class you want to query.

As you can see in Figure 20.11, we have selected the `Win32_LogicalDisk` class. The Scriptomatic tool created a VBScript that queries the class and displays all the class's attributes. To see the script in another programming language select that language from the Language frame on the right side.

To run the script, click the Run button near the top of the window. A list of output choices displays on the right side; by default the output is sent to a command prompt window. When you select the Plain Text output option a file named `Output.txt` is created, filled, and opened in Notepad. The HTML output option creates an `Output.htm` file and opens it in Internet Explorer, as shown in Figure 20.12. We'll leave it as an exercise for you to discover the results of the remaining output options.

You can save the script Scriptomatic created by clicking the Save button and supplying a path. You can also copy and paste the script into your script editor and modify it to suit your needs. Again, the best way to discover the Scriptomatic tool's true potential is to experiment with it. `ScriptomaticV2.hta` includes a `read_me.doc` file that describes more of the tool's functionality, along with a dose of humor from its creators, The Microsoft Scripting Guys.

FIGURE 20.11
Scriptomatic 2.0 tool

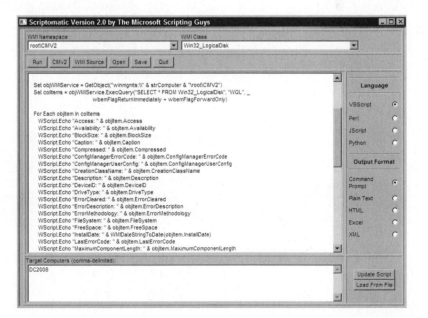

FIGURE 20.12
Scriptomatic HTML
output

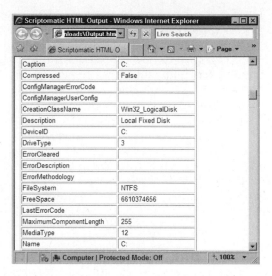

The Scriptomatic tool produces code with a few common traits. The code uses an array of computer names, allowing you to run the same WMI query on multiple computers. It uses the same method of executing the WMI query. It also uses a For Each loop to cycle through each instance of the class in the query result set. You might question if this is necessary for all WMI classes—it really is.

The CIM itself defines many base classes that are inherited by other classes in the repository. These classes represent the hardware and software in a system. All WMI classes support multiple instances of any given class, which makes WMI flexible enough to represent any computer configuration imaginable.

Multiple class instances can also complicate the task of processing WMI data. Let's look at a simple computer system. We typically have a motherboard, at least one processor, and at least one hard drive (we didn't say it was a *complete* system). These would be represented by one instance of the Win32_MotherboardDevice class, one instance of the Win32_Processor class for each processor, and one instance of the Win32_DiskDrive class for each hard drive.

To get information about the processor we would execute a WMI query such as **Select * from Win32_Processor**. The query simply says "Get all properties of all the instances of the Win32_ Processor class." If you want the query to be more efficient you can specify only the properties you are interested in.

After executing the query you will process each instance of the Win32_Processor class that was returned. Depending on the computer system, this makes perfect sense. Servers tend to have multiple processors, while desktop clients tend to have a single processor. We cannot guarantee that every computer we contact has only one processor; therefore it makes sense to treat each query result set as if it contains more than one instance of the WMI class. The following example code shows how to execute a WMI query and process the result set:

```
WMIQuery = "Select * From Win32_Processor"
Set ResultSet = WMILocator.ExecQuery(WMIQuery)
For Each Result in ResultSet
    WScript.Echo "Current Speed=" & Result.CurrentClockSpeed
    WScript.Echo "Max Speed=" & Result.MaxClockSpeed
Next
```

However, most common computer systems have only one motherboard, correct? While it might not make sense to treat the query result set as if there is only one instance of the `Win32_MotherboardDevice` class, this is still how it should be treated. In fact, all query results should be treated as if they might have multiple instances of the WMI class. The WMI query is always going to return a collection of instances, even if there is only one instance in that collection.

That said, there is a shortcut you can take if you are absolutely sure there is only one instance of a class or if you want to process only the first instance in the collection. By executing an `Exit For` command after processing the properties of the first instance, you can bypass the rest of the loop. The following code example shows how to do this with the `Win32_MotherboardDevice` class:

```
WMIQuery = "Select * From Win32_MotherboardDevice"
Set ResultSet = WMILocator.ExecQuery(WMIQuery)
For Each Result in ResultSet
   WScript.Echo "Caption=v & Result.Caption
   WScript.Echo "Description=" & Result.Description
   Exit For   ' Displays only the first motherboard's data
Next
```

Now that you have seen some of the basic WMI concepts, it is time to start using it. As with other useful pieces of code, we have created a `WMIClass` VBScript class for you.

 Real World Scenario

MONITORING ON A BUDGET

A school district moved over to an Active Directory system for managing student and personnel account information, and the district IT manager was very concerned about the uptime of the servers running the Active Directory services. He looked at different solution providers, researching product after product, when he noticed that most projects depend, in one form or another, on the WMI services. Given that it was late in the school's budget year and his unused budget money had already been reappropriated for other projects in the school district, he decided to look at implementing a monitoring solution himself.

Sifting through Microsoft's documentation about their System Center Operations Manager product, he found the parameters that defined a healthy Active Directory server. After a few search-engine queries about implementing WMI, he implemented a set of queries to run against each server and to generate a report about the health of each server. Besides saving a considerable amount of money on a monitoring solution, he found he also better understood what was going on with his Active Directory servers.

WMIClass

The `WMIClass` class is designed for two purposes. First, it has a set of methods for monitoring Active Directory. The WMI queries are contained in the appropriate method and the output is typically packaged in a dictionary object to pass back to the calling script. The second purpose is that it gives you a template of sorts to follow for creating your own WMI queries. Looking closely, you will see the methods tend to follow a predictable and repeatable pattern.

Creating the WMI class was not an easy task, mentally. We had to choose from several different approaches—from a generic and open-ended framework to a specific case-by-case methodology. For the purposes of the book format we opted for a more specific approach. This allowed us to package the query results in a specific manner for consumption by the calling script. The generic approach would have required more "programming gymnastics" than we wanted to subject you to.

While the methods used to submit a WMI query to a target system are fairly straightforward, actually connecting to the target system is not. A few different methods are available. The main reason for this is security. Generally speaking, the code submitted in this book is intended for system administrators. As such, most of the code should run just fine with the user's security credentials. However, because this might not always be true, we decided to use a WMI connection object that would easily allow a different set of security credentials to be passed to the target system.

The SWBemLocator object creates and opens a connection to the WMI namespace on the target computer. The ConnectServer method connects to the system; this method allows us to pass in a username and password if the current user does not have adequate security rights. Other connection methods either don't have this provision or require a few more hoops through which to jump. By default, the username and password (set by the m_Username and m_Password variables, respectively) are set to a blank string. By leaving these fields blank we ensure the ConnectServer method uses the current security context when connecting to the target server.

As we mentioned earlier, the methods in this VBScript class follow a pattern. You can reuse this pattern to create your own WMI query functions. When the class is instantiated by a calling script, an instance of SWBemLocator is created for use in the class's method calls. In the course of each method, this object connects to and returns a reference object to the WMI namespace on the target system. This reference object submits the WMI query.

Each method starts by building the WMI query itself. The object that connects to the target server, and the WMI query is submitted. The results are processed and packaged in the appropriate manner and sent back to the calling script. Results are packaged differently in each method, but most methods shown here use a dictionary object to return the results to the client:

```
Option Explicit
'===================================================================
Class WMIClass
'===================================================================
Private m_UserName
Private m_Password
Private m_ADLogFile
Private WMILocator, WMIService, WMIQuery
Private Results, Result
'===================================================================
Private Sub Class_Initialize
m_UserName = ""
m_Password = ""
Set WMILocator = CreateObject("WbemScripting.SWBemlocator")
End Sub
'===================================================================
Private Sub Class_Terminate
End Sub
'===================================================================
Public Property Get UserName
UserName = m_UserName
End Property

Public Property Let UserName(NameValue)
```

```
m_UserName = Trim(NameValue)
End Property
'=======================================================================
Public Property Get Password
Password = m_Password
End Property


Public Property Let Password(PasswordValue)
m_Password = Trim(PasswordValue)
End Property
'=======================================================================
Public Function GetProcessorTimeForProcess(Server,Process)
' Returns a Dictionary Object
WMIQuery = "Select Name, PercentProcessorTime " & _
   "From Win32_PerfFormattedData_PerfProc_Process"
If IsArray(Process) Then
   Dim ServiceCount, X, WhereClause
   WhereClause = " Where "
   ServiceCount = UBound(Service)
   For X = 0 To UBound(Service)
      WhereClause = WhereClause & "name='" & Service(X) & "' or "
   Next
   WhereClause = Left(WhereClause,Len(WhereClause) - 4)
   WMIQuery = WMIQuery & WhereClause
Else
   WMIQuery = WMIQuery & " Where name='" & Process & "'"
End If
Set WMIService = WMILocator.ConnectServer _
   (Server,"\root\CIMV2",m_Username,m_Password)
Set Results = WMIService.ExecQuery(WMIQuery,,48)
Set GetProcessorTimeForProcess = _
   WScript.CreateObject("Scripting.Dictionary")
For Each Result in Results
   GetProcessorTimeForProcess.Add Result.Name, _
      CInt(Result.PercentProcessorTime)
Next
End Function
'=======================================================================
Private Function TweakDate(TimeWritten)
' TimeWritten comes back in this format: 20050330085208.000000-360
' It needs a bit of tweaking to display properly
Dim Year,Month,Day,Hour,Minute
Year = Left(TimeWritten,4)
Month = Mid(TimeWritten,5,2)
Day = Mid(TimeWritten,7,2)
Hour = Mid(TimeWritten,9,2)
Minute = Mid(TimeWritten,11,2)
TweakDate = Month & "/" & Day & "/" & Year & " " & Hour & ":" & Minute
End Function
'=======================================================================
```

```
Public Function GetServiceState(Server,Service)
' Returns a Dictionary Object
WMIQuery = "Select Name, State From Win32_Service"
If IsArray(Service) Then
   Dim ServiceCount, X, WhereClause
   WhereClause = " Where "
   ServiceCount = UBound(Service)
   For X = 0 To UBound(Service)
      WhereClause = WhereClause & "name='" & Service(X) & "' or "
   Next
   WhereClause = Left(WhereClause,Len(WhereClause) - 4)
   WMIQuery = WMIQuery & WhereClause
Else
   WMIQuery = WMIQuery & " Where name='" & Service & "'"
End If
Set WMIService = WMILocator.ConnectServer _
   (Server,"\root\CIMV2",m_Username,m_Password)
Set Results = WMIService.ExecQuery(WMIQuery,,48)
Set GetServiceState = WScript.CreateObject("Scripting.Dictionary")
For Each Result In Results
   GetServiceState.Add Result.Name, Result.State
Next
End Function
'======================================================================
Public Function GetAvailableSpace(Server,DriveLetter)
' This value is returned in BYTES, not Megabytes or Gigabytes
WMIQuery = "Select FreeSpace From Win32_LogicalDisk " & _
           "Where DeviceID='" & DriveLetter & "'"
Set WMIService = WMILocator.ConnectServer _
   (Server,"\root\CIMV2",UserName,Password)
Set Results = WMIService.ExecQuery(WMIQuery,,48)
For Each Result In Results
   GetAvailableSpace = Result.FreeSpace
Next
End Function
'======================================================================
Public Function GetTrustInfo(Server)
' This function returns a Dictionary Object!
WMIQuery = "Select * from Microsoft_DomainTrustStatus"
Set WMIService = WMILocator.ConnectServer _
   (Server,"\root\MicrosoftActiveDirectory",UserName,Password)
Set Results = WMIService.ExecQuery(WMIQuery,,48)
Set GetTrustInfo = WScript.CreateObject("Scripting.Dictionary")
Dim ResultString
For Each Result In Results
' The value contains a comma-delimited list.
' 0 = Trusted Domain, 1 = Trust Direction, 2 = Trust Type
' 3 = Trust attributes
' 4 = Trust Status
```

```
            ResultString = Result.TrustedDomain
            Select Case Result.TrustDirection
               Case 1 : ResultString = ResultString & ",Inbound"
               Case 2 : ResultString = ResultString & ",Outbound"
               Case 3 : ResultString = ResultString & ",Bidirectional"
            End Select
            Select Case Result.TrustType
               Case 1 : ResultString = ResultString & ",Downlevel"
               Case 2 : ResultString = ResultString & ",Uplevel"
               Case 3 : ResultString = ResultString & ",Kerberos Realm"
               Case 4 : ResultString = ResultString & ",DCE"
            End Select
            Select Case Result.TrustAttributes
               Case &h1 : ResultString = ResultString & ",Non-transitive"
               Case &h2 : ResultString = ResultString & ",Uplevel Clients Only"
               Case &h40000 : ResultString = ResultString & ",Tree Parent"
               Case &h80000 : ResultString = ResultString & ",Tree Root"
               Case Else
                   ResultString = ResultString & "," & Result.TrustAttributes
            End Select
            ResultString = ResultString & "," & Result.TrustIsOk
            GetTrustInfo.Add Result.FlatName, ResultString
      Next
      End Function
      '=======================================================================
      End Class
```

CPU Overload

This script monitors the Local Security Authority Subsystem Service (LSASS) CPU utilization on each domain controller and alerts the user when the process's percentage of CPU use exceeds a designated threshold.

The script starts by getting a list of all domain controllers from the DomainClass object. It then cycles through each domain controller and uses the WMIClass object to retrieve the percentage of processor time used by the LSASS process. The percentage at which an alarm is raised is set by the ThresholdAlarm constant, so feel free to modify this to suit your needs and schedule.

At first, raising an alarm when CPU utilization surpassed the threshold value seemed simple enough. However, we all know that every process has spikes. For example, when you start Task Manager and click the Performance tab, you usually see a small spike right away. That spike occurs when you start the Task Manager itself, and does not indicate a system problem. The same is true of the LSASS process. It may experience a series of spikes lasting a few seconds or a few minutes. These spikes tend to occur as groups of users log onto the system, and probably are not a cause for alarm.

Therefore, the process of raising an alarm takes some additional steps. If the process is above the designated threshold we start another loop to watch that particular domain controller for a bit longer. The script checks the domain controller every 2 seconds for 5 cycles (which means the domain controller is monitored for an additional 10 seconds). The average CPU usage of the LSASS process is computed, and if that average is still above the threshold value, an alarm is raised. You can adjust these settings by changing the values of the AlarmCycleCount and TimeBetweenAlarmSamples constants.

```vbscript
<job>
<script language="VBScript" src="..\includes\OutputClass.vbs" />
<script language="VBScript" src="..\includes\WMIClass.vbs" />
<script language="VBScript" src="..\includes\DomainClass.vbs" />
<script>
Option Explicit
Dim Output
Set Output = New OutputClass
Dim WMI
Set WMI = New WMIClass
Dim Domain
Set Domain = New DomainClass
Dim Servers, Server
Set Servers = Domain.GetDomainControllers
' Threshold percentage to trigger some concern
Const ThresholdAlarm = 80
' Number of cycles above threshhold to raise alarm
Const AlarmCycleCount = 5
' Time between 'alarm mode' samples
' The time value is in milliseconds
Const TimeBetweenAlarmSamples = 2000
Output.Display "Getting LSASS process CPU Usage"
For Each Server In Servers.Keys
   Dim ProcessorTime
   Set ProcessorTime = WMI.GetProcessorTimeForProcess(Server,"lsass")
   Dim PTime
   PTime = CInt(ProcessorTime("lsass"))
   Output.Display Server & " - " & PTime & "%"
   If PTime >= ThresholdAlarm Then
      Output.Display "Watching " & Server & " for alarm."
      Dim AlarmCycles
      ' Start at 2 because we already have the first sample.
      For AlarmCycles = 2 To AlarmCycleCount
         Set ProcessorTime = _
            WMI.GetProcessorTimeForProcess(Server,"lsass")
         PTime = PTime + ProcessorTime("lsass")
         WScript.Sleep(TimeBetweenAlarmSamples)
      Next
      If (PTime / AlarmCycleCount) >= ThresholdAlarm Then
         Output.ModalAlert Server & _
            " is above the lsass threshold."
      End If
   End If
Next
</script>
</job>
```

RegistryClass

Every so often you'll need to access the registry from a script. As with other scripting tasks, there are usually a few ways to accomplish it. For example, one of the easiest methods is to use the `shell` object with the `RegRead`, `RegWrite`, and `RegDelete` methods. Unfortunately, these don't address the needs of remote registry management.

However, WMI comes to the rescue by supplying a provider to handle registry queries and updates. This provider gives us the ability to enumerate both keys and values residing under a key, retrieve values, create keys and values, delete keys and values, and check the access privileges of the current user on a key. It can perform all of these functions on either a local or a remote computer. The implementation is a little cumbersome, so we have enclosed it in a VBScript class and added a few functions to make it a bit easier to use. The result is the `RegistryClass` class.

The class begins by assuming the local computer is the target of our registry functions. In the `Class_Initialize` method you'll see the variable `m_Server` is set to a period, which represents the local machine. To target a remote server, set the `Server` property to the name of the remote server.

Before any operations can be performed on the registry, the client must connect to the target server by invoking the `Connect` method of the `RegistryClass` object. After successfully connecting to the registry provider, you can work with any registry keys to which you have rights.

One of the more cumbersome aspects of using the WMI registry provider is the requirement to supply the tree and key path as separate arguments. You must also supply the tree value as a specific unsigned integer that corresponds to the desired tree. For example, the HKEY_LOCAL_ MACHINE tree is defined by the hexadecimal number 80000002. The enumerations are supplied as public read-only properties in the class. Because almost every registry path is viewed as a single line of text with the tree at the beginning of the path, we have designed this class's methods to accept the registry path in the same manner. The method parses the tree from the key path and uses the appropriate tree value for calling the WMI methods. For example, to view the keys underneath a particular key, you can use the `GetKeys` method and pass the key path as a single string, like this:

```
Set Registry = New RegistryClass
Set KeyList = Registry.GetKeys("HKLM\Software\Microsoft")
```

The `GetKeys` method returns a dictionary object populated with a list of keys underneath the submitted key path. The `GetKeyValues` method returns a dictionary object populated with the value names and their current values underneath the submitted key path.

The `GetValue` function returns a single value. It requires the key path, the name of the value, and the type of the value passed as arguments. The type of value should be one of the publicly exposed value-type properties in the class, such as REG_SZ, REG DWORD, etc. The following code demonstrates its use:

```
Set Registry = New RegistryClass
MyValue = Registry.GetValue _
   ("HKLM\Software\Microsoft","MyValue",Registry.REG_SZ)
```

The `DeleteKey` and `DeleteValue` methods delete keys and values, respectively. Both require the key path as the first argument, and the `DeleteValue` method also requires the value name.

The `CreateKey` and `CreateValue` methods create keys and values, respectively. Both require the key path as the first argument. The `CreateValue` method also requires a value name, the new value, and the value type as arguments. The value type is also passed as one of the public value-type properties, as this code demonstrates:

```
Set Registry = New RegistryClass
Registry.CreateValue_
   ("HKLM\Software\Microsoft","MyValue",0,Registry.REG_SZ)
```

Before turning you loose with this registry class we must reiterate the standard registry warning that you have heard many times before. Changes to the registry take effect immediately and can have a disastrous effect on your system. Make changes to the registry at your own risk. Always be sure to test your registry changes on a system you can afford to wipe out in case of an accident. Testing in an environment such as Virtual PC or VMWare is ideal because you can easily undo your changes in the event of a mishap.

```
Option Explicit
'===================================================================
Class RegistryClass
'===================================================================
' Private and public variables
Private m_Registry
Private m_Server
'===================================================================
Private Sub Class_Initialize
    m_Server = "."
End Sub
'===================================================================
Private Sub Class_Terminate
    Set m_Registry = Nothing
End Sub
'===================================================================
Public Property Get Server
    Server = m_Server
End Property

Public Property Let Server(ServerName)
    m_Server = Trim(ServerName)
End Property
'===================================================================
Public Sub Connect
Set m_Registry = _
    GetObject("winmgmts:{impersonationLevel=impersonate}!\\" & _
        m_Server & "\root\default:StdRegProv")
End Sub
'===================================================================
Public Function GetKeys(Key)
' Returns a Dictionary Object!
Set GetKeys = WScript.CreateObject("Scripting.Dictionary")
Dim Keys(), KeyCount
m_Registry.EnumKey GetTree(Key),GetSubKey(Key), Keys
For KeyCount = 0 to UBound(Keys)
   GetKeys.Add Keys(KeyCount), Nothing
```

```
Next
End Function
'======================================================================
Public Function GetKeyValues(Key)
' Returns a Dictionary object!
Dim Values(), ValueType()
m_Registry.EnumValues GetTree(Key), GetSubKey(Key), Values, ValueType
Set GetKeyValues = WScript.CreateObject("Scripting.Dictionary")
If Not IsNull(Values) Then
Dim ValueCount, Value
    For ValueCount = 0 To UBound(Values)
        Select Case ValueType(ValueCount)
            Case REG_SZ
                m_Registry.GetStringValue _
                    GetTree(Key), GetSubKey(Key), Values(ValueCount), Value
                GetKeyValues.Add _
                    CheckValueName(Values(ValueCount)), CheckValue(Value)
            Case REG_EXPAND SZ
                m_Registry.GetExpandedStringValue _
                    GetTree(Key), GetSubKey(Key), Values(ValueCount), Value
                GetKeyValues.Add _
                    CheckValueName(Values(ValueCount)), CheckValue(Value)
            Case REG_BINARY
                m_Registry.GetBinaryValue _
                    GetTree(Key), GetSubKey(Key), Values(ValueCount), Value
                GetKeyValues.Add _
                    CheckValueName(Values(ValueCount)), Join(Value,"")
            Case REG_DWORD
                m_Registry.GetDWORDValue _
                    GetTree(Key), GetSubKey(Key), Values(ValueCount), Value
                GetKeyValues.Add _
                    CheckValueName(Values(ValueCount)), CheckValue(Value)
            Case REG_MULTI_SZ
                m_Registry.GetMultiStringValue _
                    GetTree(Key), GetSubKey(Key), Values(ValueCount), Value
                GetKeyValues.Add _
                    CheckValueName(Values(ValueCount)), Join(Value,",")
        End Select
    Next
End If
End Function
'======================================================================
Public Function GetValue(Key,ValueName,KeyType)
Dim KeyValue
Select Case KeyType
    Case REG_SZ
        m_Registry.GetStringValue _
            GetTree(Key), GetSubKey(Key), ValueName, GetValue
    Case REG_EXPAND_SZ
        m_Registry.GetExpandedStringValue _
```

```
                     GetTree(Key), GetSubKey(Key), ValueName, GetValue
        Case REG_BINARY
          m_Registry.GetBinaryValue _
             GetTree(Key), GetSubKey(Key), ValueName, KeyValue
          GetValue = Join(KeyValue,"")
        Case REG_DWORD
          m_Registry.GetDWORDValue _
             GetTree(Key), GetSubKey(Key), ValueName, GetValue
        Case REG_MULTI_SZ
          m_Registry.GetMultiStringValue _
             GetTree(Key), GetSubKey(Key), ValueName, KeyValue
          GetValue = Join(KeyValue,",")
    End Select
    End Function
    '==================================================================
    Private Function CheckValueName(ValueName)
    If ValueName = "" Then
       CheckValueName = "(Default)"
    Else
       CheckValueName = ValueName
    End If
    End Function
    '==================================================================
    Private Function CheckValue(Value)
    If Value = "" Then
       CheckValue = "(value not set)"
    Else
       CheckValue = Value
    End If
    End Function
    '==================================================================
    Public Function CreateKey(Key)
       CreateKey = m_Registry.CreateKey(GetTree(Key),GetSubKey(Key))
    End Function
    '==================================================================
    Public Function CheckAccess(Key,AccessLevel)
    m_Registry.CheckAccess _
       GetTree(Key),GetSubKey(Key),AccessLevel,CheckAccess
    End Function
    '==================================================================
    Public Function DeleteKey(Key)
       DeleteKey = m_Registry.DeleteKey(GetTree(Key),GetSubKey(Key))
    End Function
    '==================================================================
    Public Function DeleteValue(Key, ValueName)
    DeleteValue = _
       m_Registry.DeleteValue(GetTree(Key),GetSubKey(Key),ValueName)
    End Function
    '==================================================================
```

```
Public Function CreateValue(Key,ValueName,KeyValue,KeyType)
Select Case KeyType
   Case REG_SZ
      CreateValue = m_Registry.SetStringValue _
         (GetTree(Key),GetSubKey(Key),ValueName,KeyValue)
   Case REG_EXPAND_SZ
      CreateValue = m_Registry.SetExpandedStringValue _
         (GetTree(Key),GetSubKey(Key),ValueName,KeyValue)
   Case REG_BINARY
      CreateValue = m_Registry.SetBinaryValue _
         (GetTree(Key),GetSubKey(Key),ValueName,KeyValue)
   Case REG_DWORD
      CreateValue = m_Registry.SetDWORDValue _
         (GetTree(Key),GetSubKey(Key),ValueName,KeyValue)
   Case REG_MULTI_SZ
      CreateValue = m_Registry.SetMultiStringValue _
         (GetTree(Key),GetSubKey(Key),ValueName,KeyValue)
End Select
End Function
'=====================================================================
Private Function GetTree(KeyValue)
Dim TreeName
Select Case Left(KeyValue,InStr(KeyValue,"\")-1)
   Case "HKCR" : GetTree = HKCR
   Case "HKCU" : GetTree = HKCU
   Case "HKLM" : GetTree = HKLM
   Case "HKU"  : GetTree = HKU
   Case "HKCC" : GetTree = HKCC
   Case Else
      GetTree = Nothing
End Select
End Function
'=====================================================================
Private Function GetSubKey(KeyValue)
   GetSubKey = Right(KeyValue,Len(KeyValue)-InStr(KeyValue,"\"))
End Function
'=====================================================================
' Tree enumerations
Public Property Get HKCR
   HKCR = &H80000000
End Property
Public Property Get HKCU
   HKCU = &H80000001
End Property
Public Property Get HKLM
   HKLM = &H80000002
End Property
Public Property Get HKU
   HKU = &H80000003
```

```vb
        End Property
        Public Property Get HKCC
            HKCC = &H80000005
        End Property
        '=========================================================================
        ' Key Value Type enumerations
        Public Property Get REG_SZ
            REG_SZ = 1
        End Property
        Public Property Get REG_EXPAND_SZ
            REG_EXPAND_SZ = 2
        End Property
        Public Property Get REG_BINARY
            REG_BINARY = 3
        End Property
        Public Property Get REG_DWORD
            REG_DWORD = 4
        End Property
        Public Property Get REG_MULTI_SZ
            REG_MULTI_SZ = 7
        End Property
        '=========================================================================
        ' Key Access Rights enumerations
        Public Property Get KEY_QUERY_VALUE
            KEY_QUERY_VALUE = &H1
        End Property
        Public Property Get KEY_SET_VALUE
            KEY_SET_VALUE = &H2
        End Property
        Public Property Get KEY_CREATE_SUB_KEY
            KEY_CREATE_SUB_KEY = &H4
        End Property
        Public Property Get KEY_ENUMERATE_SUB_KEYS
            KEY_ENUMERATE_SUB_KEYS = &H8
        End Property
        Public Property Get KEY_NOTIFY
            KEY_NOTIFY = &H10
        End Property
        Public Property Get KEY_CREATE_LINK
            KEY_CREATE_LINK = &H20
        End Property
        Public Property Get DELETE
            DELETE = &H10000
        End Property
        Public Property Get READ_CONTROL
            READ_CONTROL = &H20000
        End Property
        Public Property Get WRITE_DAC
            WRITE_DAC = &H40000
```

```
    End Property
    Public Property Get WRITE_OWNER
        WRITE_OWNER = &H80000
    End Property
    '=========================================================================
    End Class
```

AD-Database and Log-File Free Space

Every Active Directory database needs free disk space to grow. The AD transaction log files also need free space. This script monitors the amount of available disk space on the drives holding the AD database and log files and raises an alert if the available disk space drops below a given amount.

The script begins by retrieving a list of domain controllers from a `DomainClass` object. The location of the AD database and log files may be different on each domain controller. An advantage of the Microsoft Operations Manager is that it installs a COM helper object known as the `OOMADs`, which can be used to make several system calls not available through regular VBScript objects.

For our script to locate these files, we must read some values from the registry of the domain controller. We can do this by using an instance of the `RegistryClass` class described in the previous section. We can find the location of the AD database and log files in the following registry key:

HKLM\System\CurrentControlSet\Services\NTDS\Parameters

The database location is stored in the value `DSA Database file` and the log file location is stored in the value `Database log files path`. The script is interested in only the drive letter rather than the full path. The `WMIClass` object's `GetAvailableSpace` method is called and the server and drive letter are passed as arguments. This method executes a WMI query on the server and returns the amount of available space in bytes. Because most people are accustomed to reading drive-space values in gigabytes rather than bytes, the number is converted into a gigabyte format.

The minimum amount of free drive space is set by the `DBThreshold` constant for the AD database and by the `LogThreshold` constant for the log files. It is important to note here that the value used for each of these constants depends on how we chose to display the value of available space. The script currently displays the value in gigabytes, so the `DBThreshold` value of 1 means 1 GB. If we decide to lower the threshold to 500 MB we must change two items in the code. The first is the value in the `DBThreshold` constant itself. The second is the following code:

```
    DBFreeSpace = FormatNumber _
        (WMI.GetAvailableSpace(Server,DBDrive) / GB)
```

The constant `GB` refers to the number of bytes in a single gigabyte. Constants are also defined in the script for megabytes (`MB`) and kilobytes (`KB`). We simply need to substitute `MB` for `GB` in the script.

You can follow a similar procedure to change the log-files threshold. The value of the `LogThreshold` constant and the line of code setting the `LogFreeSpace` variable would be changed, as described earlier.

```
    <job>
    <comment>
    Microsoft SCOM runs a script similar to this
    every 15 minutes in response to an event rule.
    Schedule to your own liking.
    </comment>
    <script language="VBScript" src="..\includes\RegistryClass.vbs" />
```

```
<script language="VBScript" src="..\includes\DomainClass.vbs" />
<script language="VBScript" src="..\includes\WMIClass.vbs" />
<script language="VBScript" src="..\includes\OutputClass.vbs" />
<script>
Option Explicit
' Adjust thresholds to your minimum DB and Log free space.
' It currently uses Gigabytes as the unit of measure.
Const DBThreshold = 1
Const LogThreshold = 1
' Registry keys pointing to the AD Database and log file locations.
Const ADKey = "HKLM\System\CurrentControlSet\Services\NTDS\Parameters"
Const DBValue = "DSA Database file"
Const LogValue = "Database log files path"
' Number of bytes in a kilobyte, megabyte, and gigabyte.
Const KB = 1024
Const MB = 1048576
Const GB = 1073741824
Dim Registry
Set Registry = New RegistryClass
Dim Domain
Set Domain = New DomainClass
Dim Output
Set Output = New OutputClass
Dim WMI
Set WMI = New WMIClass
Dim Servers, Server
Set Servers = Domain.GetDomainControllers
For Each Server In Servers
   Dim DBDrive, LogDrive
   Dim DBFreeSpace, LogFreeSpace
   Registry.Server = Server
   Registry.Connect
   DBDrive = Left _
      (Registry.GetValue(ADKey,DBValue,Registry.REG_SZ),2)
   LogDrive = Left _
      (Registry.GetValue(ADKey,LogValue,Registry.REG_SZ),2)
   DBFreeSpace = FormatNumber _
      (WMI.GetAvailableSpace(Server,DBDrive) / GB)
   If DBDrive = LogDrive Then
      LogFreeSpace = DBFreeSpace
   Else
      LogFreeSpace = FormatNumber _
         (WMI.GetAvailableSpace(Server,LogDrive) / GB)
   End If
   Output.Display Server
   Output.Display "DBDrive = " & DBFreeSpace
   Output.Display "LogDrive = " & LogFreeSpace
   If DBFreeSpace < DBThreshold Then
      Output.ModalAlert _
```

```
           Server & " is low on DB space (" & DBFreeSpace & ")"
         End If
         If LogFreeSpace < LogThreshold Then
           Output.ModalAlert _
             Server & " is low on log space (" & LogFreeSpace & ")"
         End If
       Next
     </script>
     </job>
```

Active Directory Essential Services

For Active Directory to function correctly, several services must be operational. Those services include the File Replication Service (FRS), the Intersite Messaging Service (IsmServ), the Kerberos Key Distribution Center (KDC), the NetLogon service (NetLogon), and the Windows Time (W32Time) service. These services are almost always running on each domain controller. The script covered in this section alerts the user when one or more of these services is not running.

The script begins by retrieving a list of domain controllers from a `DomainClass` object. The `GetServiceState` method of a `WMIClass` object is called, which submits a query to each server to check the current state of each service. The method returns the state of each service in a dictionary object. If any service is not currently in the running state, a modal alert dialog box alerts the user.

```
<job>
<comment>
Microsoft SCOM runs a script similar to this
every 11 minutes. Schedule to your own liking.
</comment>
<script language="VBScript" src="..\includes\OutputClass.vbs" />
<script language="VBScript" src="..\includes\WMIClass.vbs" />
<script language="VBScript" src="..\includes\DomainClass.vbs" />
<script>
Option Explicit
Dim Output
Set Output = New OutputClass
Dim WMI
Set WMI = New WMIClass
Dim Domain
Set Domain = New DomainClass
Dim Servers, Server
Set Servers = Domain.GetDomainControllers
Dim StateList, State
For Each Server In Servers.Keys
   Output.Display "Checking Active Directory Services on " & Server
   Set StateList = _
     WMI.GetServiceState(Server, _
              Array("ntfrs","ismserv","kdc","Netlogon","w32time"))
   For Each State In StateList.Keys
     Output.Display State & " " & StateList(State)
       If Not(StateList(State) = "Running") Then
```

```
                    Output.ModalAlert Server & " - " & State & _
                                    " is not running!"
            End If
        Next
    Next
</script>
</job>
```

Active Directory Response Time

Because Active Directory is only as fast as the servers supporting it, checking the responsiveness of your domain controllers makes good sense. The following script does just that.

The script begins by retrieving a list of domain controllers by using a DomainClass object, and then attempts to bind to the RootDSE of each domain controller. The response time for the bind operation is measured, and if the response time exceeds our maximum (set by the MaxResponseTime constant) the script pays a little more attention to the server. The bind operation is attempted a few more times (set by the AlarmCycleCount constant) and the response time is measured. It's possible that the domain controller server is busy servicing other requests and we don't want to raise a false alarm. If the average of the response time still exceeds our maximum, a modal alert dialog box alerts the user.

```
<job>
<comment>
Microsoft SCOM runs a script similar to this
every 5 minutes in response to an event rule.
Schedule to your own liking.
</comment>
<script language="VBScript" src="..\includes\DomainClass.vbs" />
<script language="VBScript" src="..\includes\OutputClass.vbs" />
<script>
Option Explicit
Dim Domain
Set Domain = New DomainClass
Dim Output
Set Output = New OutputClass
Dim Servers, Server
Set Servers = Domain.GetDomainControllers
' Number of cycles to sample response
Const AlarmCycleCount = 5
' Time between 'alarm mode' samples
Const TimeBetweenAlarmSamples = 2000
' Maximum number of failures
Const MaxFailures = 2
' Maximum response time in seconds
Const MaxResponseTime = 2
Dim LDAPString
Dim TimeStart, TimeStop, ResponseTime
On Error Resume Next
For Each Server In Servers.Keys
    Dim TestServer
```

```
LDAPString = "LDAP://" & Server & "/RootDSE"
TimeStart = Timer
Set TestServer = GetObject(LDAPString)
TimeStop = Timer
If Err.Number = 0 Then
    ResponseTime = TimeStop - TimeStart
    Output.Display Server & " responded in " & _
                    ResponseTime & " seconds."
    If ResponseTime > MaxResponseTime Then
        For AlarmCycles = 2 To AlarmCycleCount
            TimeStart = Timer
            Set TestServer = GetObject(LDAPString)
            TimeStop = Timer
            WScript.Sleep(TimeBetweenAlarmCycles)
            ResponseTime = ResponseTime + (TimeStop - TimeStart)
        Next
        ResponseTime = ResponseTime / AlarmCycleCount
        If ResponseTime >= MaxResponseTime Then
            Output.ModalAlert Server & " is averaging " & _
                            ResponseTime & " to respond."
        End If
    End If
Else
    ' Server failed to respond.
    Err.Clear
    Dim AlarmCycles, FailureCounter
    FailureCounter = 1 ' It's failed once already
    For AlarmCycles = 2 To AlarmCycleCount
        Set TestServer = GetObject(LDAPString)
        If Err.Number <> 0 Then
            FailureCounter = FailureCounter + 1
        End If
        WScript.Sleep(TimeBetweenAlarmCycles)
    Next
    If FailureCounter >= MaxFailures Then
        Output.ModalAlert Server & " has failed to respond " & _
                        FailureCounter & " times!"
    End If
End If
Next
</script>
</job>
```

Global Catalog Server Response

Global catalog server response time is important to many domain and forest operations. A Microsoft Operations Manager script runs in response to an event that measures the response time of the global catalog server. Because we are not dealing with events in our scripts, we have simulated that script functionality; you may schedule it or run it manually.

The script begins by gathering a list of global catalog servers serving the domain. This is done in the function GetGlobalCatalogServers, which returns a dictionary object. Global catalog information is stored in the configuration naming context of the domain and can be found by using the ADSI query:

```
(&(objectcategory=ntdsdsa)(options=1))
```

Equipped with the list of global catalog servers, the script proceeds to test the servers for responsiveness. A query is submitted to each global catalog server and the response is timed. The query submitted to the server must be successful on a consistent basis and not cause a significant performance hit to the server. The documentation on the Active Directory Management Pack for Microsoft Operations Manager lists the following query as one that meets those criteria:

```
(objectCategory=DMD)
```

If the response time exceeds our maximum (set by the MaxResponseTime constant), pay more attention to the server. The query is submitted a few more times (set by the AlarmCycleCount constant) and response time is measured. The global catalog server may simply be experiencing a period of heavy activity, and we do not want to raise a false alarm. If the average of the response time still exceeds our maximum, a modal alert dialog box alerts the user.

```
<job>
<comment>
Microsoft SCOM runs a script similar to this
every 5 minutes in response to an event rule.
Schedule to your own liking.
</comment>
<script language="VBScript" src="..\includes\RootDSEClass.vbs" />
<script language="VBScript" src="..\includes\QueryClass.vbs" />
<script language="VBScript" src="..\includes\OutputClass.vbs" />
<script>
Option Explicit
Dim RootDSE
Set RootDSE = New RootDSEClass
Dim Output
Set Output = New OutputClass
Dim GCServers, GCServer
Set GCServers = GetGlobalCatalogServers
' Number of cycles to sample response
Const AlarmCycleCount = 3
' Time between 'alarm mode' samples
Const TimeBetweenAlarmSamples = 2000
' Maximum response time in seconds
Const MaxResponseTime = 2
Dim GCQuery
Set GCQuery = New QueryClass
GCQuery.FilterText = "(objectCategory=DMD)"
GCQuery.Attributes = "distinguishedName"
GCQuery.Scope = "SubTree"
Dim TimeStart, TimeStop, ResponseTime
For Each GCServer In GCServers.Keys
```

```
    Output.Display "Querying " & GCServer
    GCQuery.RawSearchRoot = "GC://" & GCServer
    Dim Results
    TimeStart = Timer
    Set Results = GCQuery.ExecuteQuery
    TimeStop = Timer
    If Results Is Nothing Then
        Output.ModalAlert GCServer & " returned nothing!"
    Else
        Output.Display GCServer & " returned " & _
                    Results.RecordCount & " records."
        If Results.RecordCount = 0 Then
            Output.ModalAlert GCServer & _
                        " returned no results from query attempt!"
        End If
        ResponseTime = TimeStop - TimeStart
        Output.Display GCServer & " responded in " & _
                    ResponseTime & " seconds."
        If ResponseTime > MaxResponseTime Then
            For AlarmCycles = 2 To AlarmCycleCount
                TimeStart = Timer
                Set Results = GCQuery.ExecuteQuery
                TimeStop = Timer
                WScript.Sleep(TimeBetweenAlarmCycles)
                ResponseTime = ResponseTime + (TimeStop - TimeStart)
            Next
            ResponseTime = ResponseTime / AlarmCycleCount
            If ResponseTime >= MaxResponseTime Then
                Output.ModalAlert GCServer & " is averaging " & _
                            ResponseTime & " to respond."
            End If
        End If
    End If
    GCQuery.Close
Next
'======================================================================
Function GetGlobalCatalogServers
' Find the Global Catalog Servers in this forest
' Returns a Dictionary Object!
Dim Query
Set Query = New QueryClass
Query.Searchroot = RootDSE.ConfigurationNamingContext
Query.FilterText = "(&(objectcategory=ntdsdsa)(options=1))"
Query.Attributes = "distinguishedName"
Query.Scope = "SubTree"
Dim Results
Set GetGlobalCatalogServers
WScript.CreateObject("Scripting.Dictionary")
Set Results = Query.ExecuteQuery
```

```
      Do Until Results.EOF
         Dim Server
         Set Server = GetObject(GetObject("LDAP://" & _
             Results.Fields(0)).Parent)
         GetGlobalCatalogServers.Add Server.Get("dNSHostName"), Nothing
         Results.MoveNext
   Loop
   Set Query = Nothing
   End Function
   </script>
   </job>
```

Lost and Found Object Count

Active Directory contains a lost-and-found container for orphaned objects. When objects start showing up in this container the administrator should examine them and determine whether to delete them or move them into another container. Of course, this requires actually remembering to check the lost-and-found container on a regular basis. This script checks the container for you and raises an alert when objects appear in it.

```
   <job>
   <comment>
   Microsoft SCOM runs a script similar to this
   every 120 minutes. Schedule to your own liking.
   </comment>
   <script language="VBScript" src="..\includes\DomainClass.vbs" />
   <script language="VBScript" src="..\includes\OutputClass.vbs" />
   <script>
   Option Explicit
   ' Microsoft Operations Manager runs a script similar to this
   ' every 120 minutes. Schedule to your own liking.
   ' Change the Threshold value to your desired threshold
   Const Threshold = 10
   Dim Domain
   Set Domain = New DomainClass
   Dim Output
   Set Output = New OutputClass
   Dim LostAndFound, ObjectCount
   LostAndFound = Domain.GetPathFromWKGuid("LostAndFound")
   WScript.Echo "Lost and Found container path is " & LostAndFound
   Set LostAndFound = GetObject("LDAP://" & _
      Domain.GetPathFromWKGuid("LostAndFound"))
   LostAndFound.GetInfoEx Array("msDS-Approx-Immed-Subordinates"),0
   ObjectCount = LostAndFound.Get("msDS-Approx-Immed-Subordinates")
   Output.Display "Lost and Found container holds " & ObjectCount & _
                   " objects."
   If ObjectCount > Threshold Then
      Output.ModalAlert "Lost and Found object count (" & _
                      ObjectCount & ")" & _
```

```
                           " is greater than the threshold value (" & _
                         Threshold & ")"
    End If
    </script>
    </job>
```

PingClass

If you ask any administrator what her or his first course of action would be to diagnose an unresponsive system, we're betting 9 out of 10 would say, "ping it." However, in VBScript a native method is not available to perform the simple act of pinging a network system. This is not to say it can't be done, however.

One alternative is to purchase a custom library of objects, such as those from ActiveXperts (www.activexperts.com). Another option is to create a Shell object, execute the ping.exe command, capture the output stream, and parse the results from that stream of text. Trust us—it's not fun.

Our alternative is to use WMI. The Win32_PingStatus class provides all the values returned by the ping command. By enclosing its functionality in a VBScript class, we can easily reuse it in any script we want. Most of the Win32_PingStatus class properties are read-only, so we have no need to expose them in our class as writeable properties.

The main PingClass class method is PingHost. The address of the server to ping is passed to the method as its only argument. The address can be passed as a DNS name, a NetBIOS name, or an IP address. When passing the address as a name, be sure you have the proper services available to resolve that name to its IP address (DNS, WINS, or a local HOSTS or LMHOSTS file).

The PingHost method executes a WMI query to ping the system. The method returns True to the calling script if the ping is successful, or False if it fails. The values from the ping command—such as response time, protocol address, and status code—are set as read-only properties of the PingClass object.

```
    Option Explicit
    '=================================================================
    Class PingClass
    '=================================================================
    ' Private and public variables
    Private m_PingWMIService
    Private m_PrimaryAddressResolutionStatus
    Private m_ProtocolAddress
    Private m_ResponseTime
    Private m_StatusCode
    Private m_StatusCodeMessage
    '=================================================================
    Private Sub Class_Initialize
    Set m_PingWMIService = _
        GetObject _
          ("winmgmts:{impersonationLevel=impersonate}//./root/cimv2")
    End Sub
    '=================================================================
    Private Sub Class_Terminate
    Set m_PingWMIService = Nothing
    End Sub
    '=================================================================
```

```
Public Function PingHost(Host)
Dim PingQuery
PingQuery = "SELECT * FROM Win32_PingStatus WHERE Address = '" & _
Host & "'"
Dim WMIPingResults, Result
Set WMIPingResults = m_PingWMIService.ExecQuery(PingQuery)
For Each Result In WMIPingResults
    m_PrimaryAddressResolutionStatus = Result.PrimaryAddressResolutionStatus
    m_ProtocolAddress = Result.ProtocolAddress
    m_ResponseTime = Result.ResponseTime
    m_StatusCode = Result.StatusCode
    If Result.StatusCode = 0 Then
        PingHost = True
    Else
        PingStatus = False
    End If
Next
End Function
'=================================================================
Public Property Get PrimaryAddressResolutionStatus
    PrimaryAddressResolutionStatus = m_PrimaryAddressResolutionStatus
End Property
'=================================================================
Public Property Get ProtocolAddress
    ProtocolAddress = m_ProtocolAddress
End Property
'=================================================================
Public Property Get ResponseTime
    ResponseTime= m_ResponseTime
End Property
'=================================================================
Public Property Get StatusCode
    StatusCode = m_StatusCode
End Property
'=================================================================
Public Property Get StatusCodeMessage
    StatusCodeMessage = GetStatusMessage(m_StatusCode)
End Property
'=================================================================
Private Function GetStatusMessage(Code)
Select Case Code
    Case 0 : StatusCodeMessage = "Success"
    Case 11001 : StatusCodeMessage = "Buffer Too Small"
    Case 11002 : StatusCodeMessage = "Destination Net Unreachable"
    Case 11003 : StatusCodeMessage = "Destination Host Unreachable"
    Case 11004 : StatusCodeMessage = "Destination Protocol Unreachable"
    Case 11005 : StatusCodeMessage = "Destination Port Unreachable"
    Case 11006 : StatusCodeMessage = "No Resources"
    Case 11007 : StatusCodeMessage = "Bad Option"
    Case 11008 : StatusCodeMessage = "Hardware Error"
```

```
        Case 11009 : StatusCodeMessage = "Packet Too Big"
        Case 11010 : StatusCodeMessage = "Request Timed Out"
        Case 11011 : StatusCodeMessage = "Bad Request"
        Case 11012 : StatusCodeMessage = "Bad Route"
        Case 11013 : StatusCodeMessage = "TimeToLive Expired Transit"
        Case 11014 : StatusCodeMessage = "TimeToLive Expired Reassembly"
        Case 11015 : StatusCodeMessage = "Parameter Problem"
        Case 11016 : StatusCodeMessage = "Source Quench"
        Case 11017 : StatusCodeMessage = "Option Too Big"
        Case 11018 : StatusCodeMessage = "Bad Destination"
        Case 11032 : StatusCodeMessage = "Negotiating IPSEC"
        Case 11050 : StatusCodeMessage = "General Failure"
        Case Else : StatusCodeMessage = "Unknown Status Code"
    End Select
    End Function
    '=================================================================
    End Class
```

Operations Master Response

This script checks the Active Directory operations masters for responsiveness. The Flexible Single Master Operations (FSMO) roles include the PDC Emulator, the RID Master, the Infrastructure Operations Master, the Domain Naming Operations Master, and the Schema Operations Master. The health and availability of the servers that hold these operations master roles is crucial.

The script starts by finding the server that owns each FSMO role. This entails finding the object in Active Directory linked to each role, followed by binding to that object to discover its DNS name. Each distinct server is added to a dictionary object with a comma-separated list of the roles that server holds.

The dictionary object allows the script to be more efficient. It is not uncommon in an AD installation to have one server hold multiple FSMO roles. In that case the dictionary object allows us to check the responsiveness of each server once, regardless of the number of roles it owns.

This script makes use of the `PingClass` described in the previous section. We start by sending a ping to check that the server is alive and responding to network traffic.

If the ping is successful an attempt is made to bind to the servers' `RootDSE`. If the ping is not successful or takes longer to respond than we consider to be acceptable (configured with the `MaxResponseTime` constant), the server is pinged a few additional times to verify that it really is being unresponsive. If the server is still unresponsive a modal alert is raised.

```
<job>
<comment>
Microsoft SCOM runs a script similar to this
every 5 minutes. Schedule to your own liking.
</comment>
<script language="VBScript" src="..\includes\RootDSEClass.vbs" />
<script language="VBScript" src="..\includes\OutputClass.vbs" />
<script language="VBScript" src="..\includes\PingClass.vbs" />
<script>
Option Explicit
' Number of cycles to sample response
```

```
Const AlarmCycleCount = 5
' Time between 'alarm mode' samples
Const TimeBetweenAlarmSamples = 2000
' Maximum number of failures
Const MaxFailures = 2
' Maximum response time in seconds
Const MaxResponseTime = 2
' Delay between ping attempts
Const TimeBetweenAlarmPings = 2000
Dim RootDSE
Set RootDSE = New RootDSEClass
Dim Output
Set Output = New OutputClass
Dim RoleOwners
Set RoleOwners = WScript.CreateObject("Scripting.Dictionary")
Dim FSMORoleOwner,RoleOwner,Host
Dim PDC,RID,SM,IM,DNM
' Find the PDC Emulator
Set PDC = GetObject("LDAP://" & RootDSE.DefaultNamingContext)
Set FSMORoleOwner = GetObject("LDAP://" & PDC.fsmoRoleOwner)
Set RoleOwner = GetObject(FSMORoleOwner.Parent)
Host = RoleOwner.Get("dNSHostName")
Output.Display "PDC Emulator = " & Host
RoleOwners.Add Host, "PDC Emulator"
' Find the RID Master
Set RID = GetObject("LDAP://cn=RID Manager$,cn=system," & _
    RootDSE.DefaultNamingContext)
Set FSMORoleOwner = GetObject("LDAP://" & RID.fsmoRoleOwner)
Set RoleOwner = GetObject(FSMORoleOwner.Parent)
Host = RoleOwner.Get("dnsHostName")
Output.Display "RID Master = " & Host
If RoleOwners.Exists(Host) Then
    RoleOwners(Host) = RoleOwners(Host) & ",RID Master"
Else
    RoleOwners.Add Host,"RID Master"
End If
' Find the Schema Master
Set SM = GetObject("LDAP://" & RootDSE.SchemaNamingContext)
Set FSMORoleOwner = GetObject("LDAP://" & SM.fsmoRoleOwner)
Set RoleOwner = GetObject(FSMORoleOwner.Parent)
Host = RoleOwner.Get("dnsHostName")
Output.Display "Schema Master = " & Host
If RoleOwners.Exists(Host) Then
    RoleOwners(Host) = RoleOwners(Host) & ",Schema Master"
Else
    RoleOwners.Add Host,"Schema Master"
End If
' Find the Infrastructure Master
Set IM = GetObject("LDAP://cn=Infrastructure," & _
```

```
         RootDSE.DefaultNamingContext)
Set FSMORoleOwner = GetObject("LDAP://" & IM.fsmoRoleOwner)
Set RoleOwner = GetObject(FSMORoleOwner.Parent)
Host = RoleOwner.Get("dnsHostName")
Output.Display "Infrastructure Master = " & Host
If RoleOwners.Exists(Host) Then
   RoleOwners(Host) = RoleOwners(Host) & ",Infrastructure Master"
Else
   RoleOwners.Add Host,"Infrastructure Master"
End If
' Domain Naming Master
Set DNM = GetObject("LDAP://cn=Partitions," & _
   RootDSE.ConfigurationNamingContext)
Set FSMORoleOwner = GetObject("LDAP://" & DNM.fsmoRoleOwner)
Set RoleOwner = GetObject(FSMORoleOwner.Parent)
Host = RoleOwner.Get("dnsHostName")
Output.Display "Domain Naming Master = " & Host
If RoleOwners.Exists(Host) Then
   RoleOwners(Host) = RoleOwners(Host) & ",Domain Naming Master"
Else
   RoleOwners.Add Host,"Domain Naming Master"
End If
Dim Ping
Set Ping = New PingClass
Dim Owner, ResponseTime, OwnerRootDSE
For Each Owner In RoleOwners.Keys
   Output.Display "Pinging " & Owner
   If Ping.PingHost(Owner) Then
      ResponseTime = Ping.ResponseTime
      Output.Display Owner & " is responding at " & _
                  ResponseTime & "ms."
      If ResponseTime > MaxResponseTime Then
         For AlarmCycles = 2 To AlarmCycleCount
            WScript.Sleep(TimeBetweenAlarmCycles)
            Ping.PingHost(Owner)
            ResponseTime = ResponseTime + Ping.ResponseTime
            WScript.Sleep(TimeBetweenAlarmPings)
         Next
         ResponseTime = ResponseTime / AlarmCycleCount
         If ResponseTime >= MaxResponseTime Then
            Output.ModalAlert Server & " is averaging " & _
                           ResponseTime & " to respond."
         End If
      End If
      On Error Resume Next
      Set OwnerRootDSE = GetObject("LDAP://" & Owner & "/RootDSE")
      If Err.Number = 0 Then
         Output.Display Owner & " connected via RootDSE."
      Else
```

```
            Err.Clear
            Output.ModalAlert Owner & " failed to bind to RootDSE!"
         End If
      Else
         Output.ModalAlert Owner & " is not responding."
      End If
   Next
   </script>
   </job>
```

Monitor Trust Relationships

Our last script is a simple one. It starts by obtaining a list of trusts and their current properties from the WMI provider \root\MicrosoftActiveDirectory, which is returned from the WMIClass object by calling the GetTrustInfo method and passing it the name of a domain controller to contact. In this case contacting every domain controller for this information is unnecessary, so we selected one local domain controller to query.

The GetTrustInfo method returns a dictionary object. The key is the trust name and the value is a comma-separated list of the trust properties. The property names are listed as comments in the following code. The main property we are interested in is TrustIsOK. If the trust is OK it returns True. If this value is False an alert is raised.

```
<job>
<comment>
Microsoft SCOM runs a script similar to this
every 17 minutes. Schedule to your own liking.
</comment>
<script language="VBScript" src="..\includes\WMIClass.vbs" />
<script language="VBScript" src="..\includes\OutputClass.vbs" />
<script language="VBScript">
Option Explicit
Dim WMI
Set WMI = New WMIClass
Dim DC, TrustList, Trust
' Set DC to the domain server to contact
DC = "DC1.zygort.com"
Set TrustList = WMI.GetTrustInfo(DC)
Dim Output
Set Output = New OutputClass
Dim TrustProperties
For Each Trust In TrustList.Keys
   TrustProperties = Split(TrustList(Trust),",")
   ' 0 = Trusted Domain, 1 = Trust Direction, 2 = Trust Type
   ' 3 = Trust attributes
   ' 4 = TrustIsOK (aka Trust Status)
   Output.Display "Trust : " & Trust
   Output.Display "Trusted Domain: " & TrustProperties(0)
   Output.Display "Trust Direction: " & TrustProperties(1)
   Output.Display "Trust Type: " & TrustProperties(2)
```

```
    Output.Display "Attributes: " & TrustProperties(3)
    Output.Display "Status: " & TrustProperties(4)
    Output.Display "----------"
    If Not(TrustProperties(4)) Then
        Output.ModalAlert "Trust " & Trust & _
            " has a failure code (" & TrustProperties(4) & ")"
    End If
Next
</script>
</job>
```

The Bottom Line

Use WMI to monitor the health of Active Directory servers   Windows Management Instrumentation (WMI) services provide a wide range of pertinent performance information for a given server. Active Directory relies on the performance and availability of several Windows services, such as File Replication Service (FRS), Intersite Messaging Service (IsmServ), Kerberos Key Distribution Center (KDC), NetLogon service (NetLogon), and Windows Time (W32Time) service. Monitoring these services is a key step in maintaining your Active Directory infrastructure.

> **Master It**   Develop a script that queries the current status of the FRS, Netlogon, and W32Time services. The script should query three different servers named AD_Server1, AD_Server2, and AD_Server3. Report the results for each server.

Write scripts to monitor the health of Active Directory   Microsoft's System Center Operations Manager (SCOM)—one of several methods for monitoring Active Directory—features an AD Management Pack specifically for monitoring the health of Active Directory. When actively monitoring several Microsoft products and services, SCOM is an ideal product. But for simply monitoring Active Directory we can replicate the functionality of SCOM's AD Management Pack with our own set of scripts.

> **Master It**   Develop a script that monitors a specific Active Directory server named AD_Server1. Query the status of the FRS and Netlogon services. Check the available disk space of the drives.

Chapter 21

Managing Active Directory with PowerShell

By this point you've seen how to use VBScript to manage Active Directory using the ADSI interface. If you've skipped ahead to this chapter, anticipating all the PowerShell goodness to learn, we strongly suggest you jump back to Chapter 19 to learn about the Active Directory Services Interface (ADSI). This is the first step we'll employ in our PowerShell journey.

Next you'll see how PowerShell uses .NET Framework functionality, specifically the Directory-Services objects, to manage Active Directory. Finally we'll look at the goodness provided by installing the PowerShell Community Extensions (PCX) and the Active Directory provider installed by PCX the package.

In this chapter, you will learn to:

- ◆ Use PowerShell cmdlets, piping them together to produce a result set

- ◆ Use Quest's Active Directory Management cmdlets

- ◆ Manage Active Directory using Quest's Active Directory Management and PowerShell cmdlets

Microsoft is putting a lot of its eggs in the PowerShell basket when it comes to management of its server products. Everything from Exchange Server 2007 to the new line of System Center products have built their management interfaces on PowerShell rather than on COM-based objects. This new approach has actually delayed the Windows-based management utilities (many of these were resolved in the first service pack for the product). For you, the administrator, this means that the PowerShell environment is your one-stop spot for management.

PowerShell Basics

Welcome to the brave new world of PowerShell, a re-introduction to Windows administrators of good old command-line administration. More than just the old command prompt, PowerShell is a new environment. It has the ability to execute all existing command-line utilities as well as a new set of utilities known as cmdlets (pronounced command-lets). Cmdlets are specific to the Power-Shell environment and are not available in the standard command-prompt window.

But what really gives PowerShell its—well—power is its ability to harness the immense functionality stored within the .NET Framework. Within the Framework are objects and functions capable of connecting to, querying, and managing Active Directory without using the COM-based ADSI interface.

PowerShell Installation

Installing PowerShell is very simple. The only mandatory prerequisite is the installation of .NET Framework 2.0 or higher. Soon all Microsoft operating systems will have the Framework included, so the only task will be to install the PowerShell environment itself.

INSTALLING THE .NET FRAMEWORK

PowerShell requires the Microsoft .NET Framework version 2.0 or higher. Windows Server 2008 already has this version installed and ready to use. For other Microsoft operating systems, this means you have a little work to do. Navigate to the following URL, download the package, and install it on the system you will be running PowerShell from:

```
www.microsoft.com/downloads/details.aspx?FamilyID=0856eacb-4362-4b0d-8edd-
aab15c5e04f5&displaylang=en
```

INSTALLING MICROSOFT POWERSHELL

Microsoft's new Server Manager console makes installing PowerShell easy because PowerShell is considered a feature application to Windows Server 2008.

Start by opening the Server Manager console (if it isn't already open). Scroll down to the Features Summary section and click the link Add Features. Select the item labeled Windows PowerShell, as shown in Figure 21.1. Click the Next button, then the Install button on the next dialog screen.

To install PowerShell on a different Microsoft operating system, you first need to download the PowerShell package from `http://support.microsoft.com/kb/926139`.

At the time of this writing PowerShell Version 2.0 was in its Community Technology Preview (CTP) release. By the time Windows Server 2008 is released it might very well be the standard version (it might even be installed by default on Windows Server 2008). Regardless, the commands and techniques discussed in this chapter should not change between versions.

FIGURE 21.1
Adding PowerShell to
Windows Server 2008

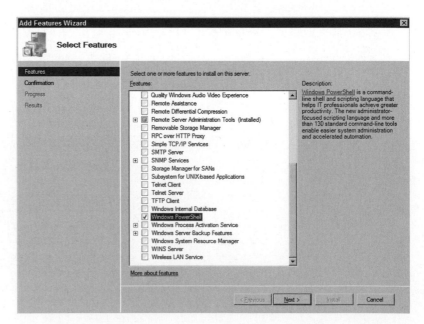

Getting Started in PowerShell

Starting the PowerShell environment is not unlike starting the Command Prompt window. Click on Start ➤ Programs ➤ Windows PowerShell (you might want to create a couple of convenient shortcuts to make this easier).

The PowerShell window looks like the familiar Command Prompt window. For the most part, everything you know how to do in the Command Prompt window will work in the PowerShell window. But you need to understand that the command interpreter is not the same, so your results are going to look a little different.

Let's start with our old friend the `dir` command to see this in action. In Figure 21.2 I've opened a Command Prompt window and the PowerShell window and have executed the `dir` command in both.

We still get the same information from both commands, but the format is a little different. The reason for this is simple: in PowerShell we are not actually executing the `dir` command. We are running a PowerShell command called `Get-ChildItem`.

Like most command interpreters, PowerShell prefers its way of executing commands over another interpreter's. So the first thing PowerShell does is look for its own matching command, which it won't find. Next it looks through its list of aliases (more on this list in a moment) for a match. In that list it finds that the `dir` command is simply an alias for the `Get-ChildItem` command, and executes it.

Microsoft was kind enough to preload a number of aliases for us, mapping our familiar command-prompt commands to its new PowerShell siblings. To view the current alias list, enter the following command:

    alias

FIGURE 21.2

The DIR command produces slightly different results in the Command Prompt and PowerShell windows.

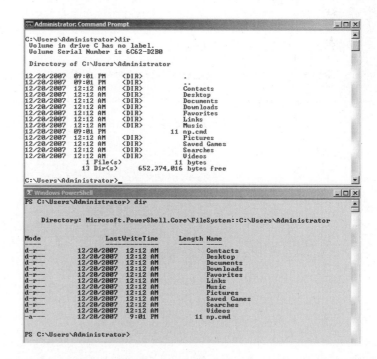

A simple command, right? But the output might leave something to be desired. For example, the first field, CommandType, is the same for every line. Well, duh; we were expecting a list of aliases, right? So we can probably lose that field without much worry. We can also put the list in some semblance of order without much effort. Try the following commands to see how easy it is:

```
alias | select name, definition | sort name
alias | select name, definition | sort definition
alias | select name, definition | sort name | fl
```

Each command produces roughly the same information but each formats the output a little differently. These are simple examples of piping commands together, but it gives you an idea of the path we are heading down with PowerShell. We are going to be piping together several small, specialized commands to achieve some very nice results in our scripts.

As a short exercise before moving on, look through the alias list we just produced. You already know the dir command is an alias; can you spot the other aliases we've just used in the commands?

SCRIPT-EXECUTION POLICY

Before we go on we have to make one adjustment to our PowerShell environment. By default, PowerShell runs under an execution policy called Restricted, which allows you to run only interactively within the environment. This policy does not allow you to run any scripts. Plus, it's easy to forget until the first time you try to run a script and the system balks at you, so let's just address it now.

To fix the restriction, we need to execute the Set-ExecutionPolicy cmdlet and specify a new policy. There are four policies, as shown in Table 21.1.

TABLE 21.1:   Script-Execution Policies

POLICY	DESCRIPTION
Restricted	Interactive mode, no script execution
Unrestricted	All scripts can be run.
AllSigned	Only signed scripts can be run.
RemoteSigned	Remote scripts must be signed before they can be run.

In a test environment it is permissible to set the execution policy to Unrestricted. In a production environment it is much safer to use either RemoteSigned (my personal choice) or AllSigned. The command to set the execution policy is as follows:

```
Set-ExecutionPolicy RemoteSigned
```

Creating and signing scripts is beyond the scope of this book, but Scott Hanselman provides an excellent walk-through on the topic at the following URL: www.hanselman.com/blog/ SigningPowerShellScripts.aspx.

POWERSHELL CMDLETS

It's time to introduce you to cmdlets. That isn't a typo—it's actually pronounced "command-lets," and this is the name by which PowerShell commands are called. Technically these represent the smallest unit of functionality on the PowerShell environment, so they were given their own special name.

In our alias list, you might have noticed that the PowerShell cmdlets follow a similar naming format. Specifically, each starts with a verb (such as Get, Write, or Start), followed by a dash, and finishes up with a noun (such as Output or Item). This verb-noun pairing format is used with all PowerShell cmdlets, even cmdlets created by third parties.

To view a complete list of available cmdlets, run the cmdlet Get-Command. The standard set of PowerShell cmdlets numbers almost 130, and that number may be larger if you've added the management snap-ins to other server products such as Exchange or System Center Operations Manager.

Learning a new set of commands takes time and practice; there is just no way around it. Of course, PowerShell provides a cmdlet called Get-Help to help us learn how to use cmdlets. Execute the following commands to get a feel for the Get-Help cmdlet in action:

```
Get-Help Select-Object
Get-Help Select-Object -detailed
Get-Help Select-Object -full
```

By adding the parameters -detailed and -full, the get-help cmdlet gives us greater details about the specified command. This is especially useful for understanding the important concept of proper parameter usage in cmdlets.

PowerShell accepts two types of parameter passing: *positional* and *named*. Positional parameter passing simply means to put one parameter after another on the command line. Using the Get-Help cmdlet, you can determine the order in which the parameters are expected to appear for any specified cmdlet. Named parameter passing uses the parameter name, prefixed with a dash, to specify which piece of information should be assigned to which parameter. Review the parameter list for the cmdlet Select-Object and then try the following examples to see both types of parameter passing in action:

```
alias | select name, definition
alias | select -property name, definition
alias | select name, definition -first 5
```

The first command uses positional parameters and the second uses named parameters, but what about the third command? It uses both positional *and* named parameters (we didn't say you had to use exclusively one or the other, did we?). Being able to use both types of parameters gives us a lot of freedom when it comes to running commands.

Before moving on, let us add one more bit of information about parameters: when in doubt, use named parameters. If you are getting unexpected results from a command, switch to named parameters. Named parameters take the guesswork out of determining which piece of information a cmdlet is evaluating, so take advantage of them (especially in scripts).

COMMON POWERSHELL CMDLETS

The PowerShell environment comes with a feature-rich set of cmdlets. We will use some of these cmdlets in our Active Directory scripting, but it's a good idea to get familiar with them and their purpose before using them.

Table 21.2 shows a quick list of the commonly–used PowerShell cmdlets. The table includes the cmdlet's alias (when the cmdlet has one) and a short description of its job. In the rest of this chapter, we usually refer to the cmdlet by its full name, but in the code we will use the alias value to save space (not to mention saving typing).

TABLE 21.2:   Commonly Used PowerShell cmdlets

CMDLET	ALIAS	DESCRIPTION
Get-Command	gcm	Gets basic information about the current set of cmdlets
Foreach-Object	foreach	Performs an operation on each object in an input stream
Format-Table	ft	Formats output as a table
Format-List	fl	Formats output as a list
Get-Content	gc, type	Gets the content of an item, such as a file
Get-Date		Gets the current date and time
Get-Member	gm	Gets information about the members of an object
Measure-Object		Measures characteristics of a set of objects, such as count
New-Alias	nal	Creates a new alias for a cmdlet
Out-File		Directs output to a specified file
Out-Printer	lp	Directs output to a printer
Out-Null		Deletes output rather than displaying it in the console
Read-Host		Reads input from the console
Select-Object	select	Specifies which properties of an object should be returned
Set-Content	sc	Appends or replaces the contents of an item, such as a file
Where-Object	where	Filters objects to be passed on to the next cmdlet in a pipe
Write-Host		Displays object values in the console.alias

Note that PowerShell cmdlets and parameter values are not case-sensitive.

Now it's time to take a few moments and play with the cmdlets shown in the table (if you haven't already). The following code examples show some of those cmdlets in use; it would be good to understand their role in the code examples.

USING OBJECTS IN POWERSHELL

Now that you've seen how to get output from a cmdlet, let's look at that output in more detail.

First, and possibly most importantly, PowerShell treats darn near everything as an object. Even simple bits of information such as text or dates are actually Integer and DateTime objects to Power-Shell (as they are defined in the .NET Framework). Treating text and dates as objects may seem like overkill, but it gives you advantages that aren't visible on the surface. Let's look at some examples in the following code:

```
$myValue = "This is a text string"
$myValue.GetType()          # String object
$myValue.Length             # length of the string
$myValue.SubString(10,4)    # extract 4 characters
                            # starting at position 10
$myValue.Replace(" ","-")   # replace spaces with dashes
$myValue.Split(" ")[3]      # 4th word in the string

$currentTime = [DateTime]::Now
                            # get the current time
$currentTime.GetType()      # DateTime object
$currentTime.AddHours(4)    # add 4 hours to the time
$currentTime.DayOfWeek      # display day of the week
$currentTime.Hour           # display the hour value
$currentTime.IsDaylightSavingsTime()
                            # is daylight savings in
                            # effect?
$currentTime.ToString       # format the date and time
(New-TimeSpan $(Get-Date) $currentTime).Minutes
                            # how many minutes have
                            # elapsed ?
```

The commands presented in this code are really just parlor tricks with a few of the simple object types available in the .NET Framework, but they should give you some ideas about how powerful objects (even really simple ones) can be!

PowerShell mastery is a long and arduous journey, and I think the only people to truly achieve enlightenment are those who were on the team that developed it. Luckily they've given us some guide books. To that end I suggest you read Bruce Payette's book *Windows PowerShell in Action* or Lee Holmes's *Windows PowerShell Cookbook*. Or both!

Adding Cmdlets through Snap-Ins

By this point you might have noticed we haven't seen any cmdlets that really have anything to do with Active Directory. There's a reason for that: there are none. At least not yet.

In the development cycle of recent Microsoft products (such as Windows Server 2008), Power-Shell was actually a latecomer to the build. With Microsoft's PowerShell push in the Exchange Server and Operations Manager Server products, it was a natural decision for Microsoft to include Power-Shell with Windows Server 2008, but the developers didn't have time to create any cmdlets specifi-cally for managing Active Directory.

But thanks to the folks at Quest Software, that doesn't mean we're up a creek. They were kind enough to write a set of Active Directory Management cmdlets and make them freely available on the Web. Open your web browser and navigate to the following URL to download and install the Management Shell for Active Directory: www.quest.com/activeroles-server/arms.aspx. While you are there be sure to download the Administrator's Guide too!

Installing the Management Shell for Active Directory makes a PowerShell *snap-in* available. A snap-in is basically a bundle of PowerShell functionality, usually specific to a task or server product, that we can incorporate into our PowerShell session as needed. However snap-ins are not loaded by default so we need to execute the following command to get access to the new set of cmdlets:

```
Add-PSSnapin Quest.ActiveRoles.ADManagement
```

To make the cmdlets available for all system users we can simply place this command in the system profile, which we'll talk about next.

Modifying the Profile

Old-timers among us will remember the name `autoexec.bat`—the batch file that ran whenever we started the system and it was used to (among other things) set up the environment to our own tastes. We can do something similar with *profiles* in PowerShell.

A profile is simply a text file named `profile.ps1` residing in one of the special locations known to PowerShell. These profiles are PowerShell scripts that execute each time the PowerShell environment starts. To keep things simple we'll talk about the two most obvious profiles: your personal profile and the system profile. Their locations are listed in Table 21.3.

TABLE 21.3:   PowerShell Profile Locations

PROFILE	LOCATION
Personal	`%UserProfile%\WindowsPowerShell`
System	`%SystemRoot%\System32\WindowsPowerShell\v1.0`

Your personal profile is unique to you, so you can tailor it any way you like. Items such as your own aliases and prompt functions go in this file. The system profile is executed for every system user when PowerShell starts. Items such as global functions and snap-ins go in this file. As we start creating our own Active Directory functions we will put them in the system profile to make them available to every system user.

CUSTOMIZING YOUR POWERSHELL PROMPT

One of the first things I change in my PowerShell profile is the prompt. By now I'm sure you've noticed how long PowerShell commands can be. As we start piping different cmdlets together the command gets longer and more difficult to read. For that reason I create a function named Prompt to modify the default appearance of my command-line prompt. It displays "PS" to remind me that I'm in the Power-Shell environment, followed by the current location. It then drops to the next line and presents a simple > symbol for my next command. You can type this command at any time but it's best to put it in either your personal profile or the system profile.

```
Function prompt
{
"PS " + (get-location).Path + [System.Environment]::NewLine + "> "
}
```

Creating PowerShell Scripts for Active Directory

In the previous three chapters our VBScripts used a COM object called the Active Directory Services Interface (ADSI). Because PowerShell supports the creation of COM objects, we could just rewrite the previous scripts using PowerShell's syntax. But that would create a lot of unnecessary work for us. Especially when the kind people at Quest Software have made a set of Active Directory management cmdlets (available to the public) that cover 90 percent of the management tasks we want to perform. Rather than reinvent the wheel (and potentially cause a flat tire), we will look at how to use the Quest Active Directory cmdlets.

In addition to the new Active Directory cmdlets, we will create a set of helper functions that will make our job easier when it comes to using the Quest Active Directory cmdlets. You will also see how to use the standard set of PowerShell cmdlets in conjunction with the Quest cmdlets.

Management Shell Scripts

Now for the part we've all been waiting for: creating PowerShell scripts to manage Active Directory. We'll start with the basics of the Quest Active Directory Management cmdlets, then we'll look at creating helper functions for these cmdlets to make them easier to work with. Finally we'll combine the Active Directory cmdlets with our helper functions, along with many of the standard PowerShell cmdlets, and start managing Active Directory.

POWERSHELL EDITORS

As we start writing PowerShell commands and scripts we should spend a moment examining some tools that might help us. You can choose whether to use the tools we suggest; fortunately most have a free evaluation period you should take advantage of.

PowerShell scripts are simply text files. You do not need a special editor to create a PowerShell script file. However a good editor makes using PowerShell more enjoyable and reduces errors. Features such as IntelliSense can make a world of difference when trying to solve problems with PowerShell.

Because PowerShell is relatively new, the choice of products is limited. Sapien added PowerShell support to its outstanding PrimalScript product, but as much as I adore PrimalScript I've found myself using a different tool for PowerShell, as you'll see in a moment.

Another tool to look at is also from the good people at Quest Software; it's called PowerGUI. This tool creates a graphical interface that allows you to select a function then creates the code for you. PowerGUI is free and can save time in your coding efforts, so download it and give it a try.

Our personal choice comes from Shell Tools, a new company that released a set of tools specifically for PowerShell called PowerShell Analyzer and PowerShell Plus. PowerShell Plus is a great product; it gives you the command-line environment with IntelliSense support for available functions and loaded cmdlets. As I develop a command or script, I find myself working in PowerShell Plus more often than any in other PowerShell tool.

USING QUEST'S ACTIVE DIRECTORY MANAGEMENT CMDLETS

In this section we are going to use the Active Directory cmdlets made available through the Quest Management Shell for the Active Directory snap-in. All the cmdlets are well documented in the Administrator's Guide, but take a quick look in Table 21.4 at the cmdlets we'll be using most.

This is not a comprehensive list, but as you can see, almost every function we'll likely perform through scripting is available as a cmdlet. However there are some things we can do to make working with cmdlets a little easier.

TABLE 21.4:   The Quest Management Shell for Active Directory Cmdlets

CMDLET	DESCRIPTION
New-QADUser	Creates a user object
Get-QADUser	Retrieves a user object
Set-QADUser	Sets the attributes of a user object
Enable-QADUser	Enables a user object
Disable-QADUser	Disables a user object
Unlock-QADUser	Unlocks a user object
New-QADGroup	Creates an Active Directory group object
Get-QADGroup	Retrieves an Active Directory group object
Set-QADGroup	Sets the attributes of a group object
Get-QADGroupMember	Retrieves the members of a group
Add-QADGroupMember	Adds user object(s) to a group
Remove-QADGroupMember	Removes user object(s) from a group
Get-QADComputer	Retrieves a computer object
Get-QADObject	Retrieves an Active Directory object (user, computer, OU, etc.)
Set-QADObject	Sets the properties of an Active Directory object
New-QADObject	Creates a new Active Directory object. The type of object must be specified
Move-QADObject	Moves an Active Directory object between containers
Rename-QADObject	Renames an existing Active Directory object
Remove-QADObject	Deletes an Active Directory object (user, computer, OU, etc.)

When working with the Quest Active Directory cmdlets, many times we must specify the Active Directory object we want to manipulate, either through the -Identity parameter (we will discuss the cmdlet parameters later in this chapter) or by piping a list into the input stream of the cmdlet.

You can specify the Active Directory object's identity by using the distinguished name (DN), the security ID (SID) of the object, the user principle name (UPN), or domain\name value of the object. The distinguished name is the most accurate for specifying the desired object, but the syntax can be a little much to type. For example, a typical DN might look like this:

```
CN=Business User 01,OU=Business,DC=zygort,DC=com
```

NEVER TOO LATE TO LEARN A NEW LANGUAGE

Managing Active Directory became very tedious. The Active Directory Users and Computers console didn't always have the functionality Tom needed to produce the results his manager wanted. As the network IT staff started rolling out Windows Server 2008, the situation only looked to get worse.

During his few free minutes Tom began looking at the documentation for a new environment being touted by Microsoft—PowerShell. He knew it was a key management piece for his company's new Exchange Server and Operations Manager Server products. Entirely command–line driven, its goal was to simplify management operations by allowing administrators to accomplish a given goal by stringing together sets of complementary functions. Tom saw how it worked with Exchange management and searched for a solution to do the same with Active Directory.

He found that Quest Software had released a set of command-line utilities (called cmdlets) specifically for Active Directory. After installing PowerShell and the new utilities, Tom learned how quickly he could accomplish a task at the command line. For many tasks he could finish the job in less time than it took to fire up the ADUC console. After a few weeks of using PowerShell, he began creating additional scripts and functions to automate several of his daily time-consuming chores. Suddenly Windows Server 2008 didn't look to be such a daunting management task after all.

The DN might be an accurate way to specify an object, but it's not fun to type over and over again. To that end, we've created a set of PowerShell helper functions to do the work. These functions not only provide an object's DN, but if more than one object is found matching our criteria, they allow the user to select the match from a list. We'll look at those helper functions in the next section.

Active Directory Helper Functions

In this section we'll start getting our hands dirty with some actual Active Directory PowerShell code. Earlier in this chapter we talked about the PowerShell profile. To recap, the profile can be a repository of commonly used functions and definitions. The helper functions that follow are relatively short, so you can place them in either your personal profile or the system profile. This makes them easily accessible from the command line and other cmdlets you might want to use them with.

In our helper functions we will use objects within the .NET Framework for retrieving information from Active Directory rather than recoding our earlier VBScript code that used the ADSI object. The `System.DirectoryServices` namespace in the Framework contains several Active Directory objects we can use. We will take advantage of the `DirectorySearcher` class to find the distinguished names of the objects we plan on managing.

DEVELOP YOUR OWN SCRIPTING STYLE

Before we dive into the code, you should be clear about one aspect of scripting, especially PowerShell scripting: there isn't necessarily a right way and a wrong way to do it. With time and practice I've developed my own way of writing code, which is sure to be different from someone else's way. If we both produce the same results we both did it right. As you start working more with PowerShell, you'll develop your own style as well, which may be much different than mine. And I'm OK with that, as long as you produce the correct result and you are comfortable writing the code your own way. So go for it!

THE GET-ADROOTDSEPROPERTY FUNCTION

This function is designed strictly to give you information contained in the RootDSE directory object. When invoking the function, specify the name of the RootDSE property you want to retrieve, as shown in these examples:

```
> Get-ADRootDSEProperty DefaultNamingContext
DC=zygort,DC=com
> Get-ADRootDSEProperty dnsHostName
CN=Schema,CN=Configuration,DC=zygort,DC=com
> Get-ADRootDSEProperty isSynchronized
TRUE
> Get-ADRootDSEProperty domainFunctionality
Windows Server 2008 Domain Mode
```

Here is the function:

```
function Get-ADRootDSEProperty(
    [string]$property)
{
$RootDSE = [ADSI]"LDAP://RootDSE"
switch($property)
{
    "defaultNamingContext"
        { $RootDSE.defaultNamingContext }
    "configurationNamingContext"
        { $RootDSE.configurationNamingContext }
    "rootDomainNamingContext"
        { $RootDSE.rootDomainNamingContext }
    "schemaNamingContext"
        { $RootDSE.schemaNamingContext }
    "subschemaSubentry"
        { $RootDSE.subschemaSubentry }
    "currentTime"
        { $RootDSE.currentTime }
    "dsnHostName"
        { $RootDSE.dnsHostName }
    "domainControllerFunctionality"
        {
        switch
        ($RootDSE.domainControllerFunctionality)
            {
                0 { "Windows 2000 Mode" }
                2 { "Windows 2003 Mode" }
                3 { "Windows 2008 Mode" }
            }
        }
    "domainFunctionality"
```

```
            {
        switch($RootDSE.domainFunctionality)
            {
                0 { "2000 Domain Mode" }
                1 { "2003 Interim Domain Mode" }
                2 { "2003 Domain Mode" }
                3 { "2008 Domain Mode" }
            }
        }
    "dsServiceName"
        { $RootDSE.dsServiceName }
    "highestCommittedUSN"
        { $RootDSE.highestCommittedUSN }
    "isGlobalCatalogReady"
        { $RootDSE.isGlobalCatalogReady }
    "isSynchronized"
        { $RootDSE.isSynchronized }
    "serverName"
        { $RootDSE.serverName }
    "supportedCapabilities"
        { $RootDSE.supportedCapabilities }
    "supportedControl"
        { $RootDSE.supportedControl }
    "supportedLDAPPolicies"
        { $RootDSE.SupportedLDAPPolicies }
    "supportedLDAPVersion"
        { $RootDSE.SupportedLDAPVersion }
    "supportedSASLMechanisms"
        { $RootDSE.supportedSASLMechanisms }
    default
        { "Unknown Property $property" }
    }
}
```

THE GET-ADROOTDN FUNCTION

This function returns the distinguished name of the current Active Directory root. It takes no arguments, as shown in the following example:

```
> Get-ADRootDN
DC=zygort,DC=com
```

Here is the function:

```
function Get-ADRootDN
{
return ( New-Object System.DirectoryServices.DirectoryEntry) .distinguishedName
}
```

THE FIND-ADUserDN FUNCTION

This function returns the distinguished name of a specified user object. When calling this function, specify the account name of the user object you want to find. Following are some examples of this function:

```
> Find-ADUserDN BusinessUser01
CN=BusinessUser01,OU=Business Users,DC=zygort,DC=com

> Find-ADUserDN Business
0: CN=BusinessUser01,OU=Business Users,DC=zygort,DC=com
1: CN=BusinessUser02,OU=Business Users,DC=zygort,DC=com
2: CN=BusinessUser03,OU=Business Users,DC=zygort,DC=com
More than one match found!
Select user: 1
1: CN=BusinessUser02,OU=Business Users,DC=zygort,DC=com

> $User = Find-ADUserDN("BusinessUser01")
> $User
CN=BusinessUser01,OU=Business Users,DC=zygort,DC=com
```

Here is the function:

```
Function Find-ADUserDN (
    [string]$AccountName)
{
if ($AccountName.length -eq 0)
    { Write-Host "Missing Account Name!"; exit }
$root = Get-ADRootDN
$searcher = new-Object
    System.DirectoryServices.DirectorySearcher($root)
$searcher.filter =
 "(&(objectClass=user)(sAMAccountName=*$AccountName*))"
$DNName = "distinguishedname"
$searcher.propertiesToLoad.Add($DNName) | out-null
$searchResults = $searcher.findall()
switch ($searchResults.Count)
{
    0 { Write-Host "No match found!" }
    1 {
       $dn = $searchResults[0].properties[$DNName]
       }
    default
    {
       $count = 0
       foreach($result in $searchResults)
       {
           Write-Host $count ": "
               $result.properties[$DNName]
           $count++
```

```
        }
        Write-Host "More than one match found!"
        $choice = Read-Host "Select user: "
        $dn = searchResults[$choice].properties[$DNName]
    }
}
$
return $dn
}
```

THE CHECK-ADUSEREXISTS FUNCTION

This function verifies that a user account exists in Active Directory. In a script or function it's easier to find out if an object exists in Active Directory before we try to manipulate it. This function itself returns true or false, as shown in the examples here:

```
> Check-ADUserExists BusinessUser01
True


> Check-ADUserExists BusinessUser99
False


> If (Check-ADUserExists("BusinessUser01")) { "OK!" }
OK!
```

Here is the function:

```
function Check-ADUserExists (
    [string]$AccountName)
{
if ($AccountName.length -eq 0)
    {Write-Host "Missing Account Name!"; exit }
$root = Get-ADRootDN
$searcher = new-Object
    System.DirectoryServices.DirectorySearcher($root)
$searcher.filter
  "(&(objectClass=user)(sAMAccountName=$AccountName*))"
$searchResults = $searcher.findall()
if ($searchResults.Count -gt 0) {$TRUE} else {$FALSE}
}
```

THE FIND-ADOUDN FUNCTION

This function returns the distinguished name of a specified organizational unit object. When calling this function, specify the name of the OU object you want to find. Following are some examples of this function:

```
> Find-ADOUDN "Business Users"
CN=Business Users,OU=Business Users,DC=zygort,DC=com
```

```
> Find-ADOUDN Business
0: CN=Business Users,DC=zygort,DC=com
1: CN=Business Computers,DC=zygort,DC=com
More than one match found!
Select user: 0
CN=Business Users,DC=zygort,DC=com

> $OU = Find-ADUserDN("Business Users")
> $OU
CN=Business Users,DC=zygort,DC=com
```

Here is the function:

```
Function Find-ADOUDN (
    [string]$OUName)
{
if ($OUName.length -eq 0)
    { Write-Host "Missing OU Name!"; exit }
$root = Get-ADRootDN
$searcher = new-Object
    System.DirectoryServices.DirectorySearcher($root)
$searcher.filter =
  "(&(objectClass=organizationalUnit)(name=*$OUName*))"
$DNName = "distinguishedname"
$searcher.propertiesToLoad.Add($DNName) | out-null
$searchResults = $searcher.findall()
switch ($searchResults.Count)
{
    0 { Write-Host "No match found!"; exit }
    1 { $dn = $searchResults[0].properties[$DNName] }
    default
    {
      $count = 0
      foreach($result in $searchResults)
      {
          Write-Host $count ": "
              $result.properties[$DNName]
          $count++
      }
      Write-Host "More than one match found!"
      $choice = Read-Host "Select OU: "
      $dn = $searchResults[$choice].properties[$DNName]
    }
}
return $dn
}
```

THE FIND-ADCOMPUTERDN FUNCTION

This function returns the distinguished name of a specified computer object. When calling this function, specify the name of the computer object you want to find. Following are some examples of this function:

```
> Find-ADComputerDN Vista01
CN=Vista01,OU=Business Computers,DC=zygort,DC=com

> Find-ADComputerDN Vista
0: CN=Vista01,OU=Business Computers,DC=zygort,DC=com
1: CN=Vista02,OU=Business Computers,DC=zygort,DC=com
2: CN=Vista03,OU=Business Computers,DC=zygort,DC=com
More than one match found!
Select user: 2
1: CN=Vista03,OU=Business Computers,DC=zygort,DC=com

> $OU = Find-ADComputerDN("Vista02")
> $OU
CN=Vista02,OU=Business Computers,DC=zygort,DC=com
```

Here is the function:

```
Function Find-ADComputerDN (
    [string]$Computer)
{
if ($Computer.length -eq 0)
    { Write-Host "Missing Computer Name!"; exit }
$root = Get-ADRootDN
$searcher = new-Object
    System.DirectoryServices.DirectorySearcher($root)
$searcher.filter =
  "(&(objectClass=computer)(name=*$Computer*))"
$DNName = "distinguishedname"
$searcher.propertiesToLoad.Add($DNName) | out-null
$searchResults = $searcher.findall()
switch ($searchResults.Count)
{
    0 { Write-Host "No match found!"; exit }
    1 { $dn = $searchResults[0].properties[$DNName] }
    default
    {
      $count = 0
      foreach($result in $searchResults)
      {
          Write-Host $count ": "
              $result.properties[$DNName]
          $count++
```

```
        }
        Write-Host "More than one match found!"
        $choice = Read-Host "Select Computer: "
        $dn = $searchResults[$choice].properties[$DNName]
    }
}
return $dn
}
```

THE FIND-ADGROUPDN FUNCTION

This function returns the distinguished name of a specified group object. When calling this function, specify the name of the group object you want to find. Examples of this function are shown here:

```
> Find-ADGroupDN Shipping
CN=Shipping,OU=Security Groups,DC=zygort,DC=com


> Find-ADGroupDN Admin
0: CN=Administrators,CN=Builtin,DC=zygort,DC=com
1: CN=Schema Admins,CN=Users,DC=zygort,DC=com
2: CN=Enterprise Admins,CN=Users,DC=zygort,DC=com
3: CN=Domain Admins,CN=Users,DC=zygort,DC=com
4: CN=DnsAdmins,CN=Users,DC=zygort,DC=com

More than one match found!
Select user: 3
3: CN=Domain Admins,CN=Users,DC=zygort,DC=com

> $OU = Find-ADGroupDN("Domain Admins")
> $OU
CN=Domain Admins,CN=Users,DC=zygort,DC=com
```

Here is the function:

```
Function Find-ADGroupDN (
    [string]$GroupName)
{
if ($GroupName.length -eq 0)
    { Write-Host "Missing Group Name!"; exit }
$root = Get-ADRootDN
$searcher = new-Object
    System.DirectoryServices.DirectorySearcher($root)
$searcher.filter =
    "(&(objectClass=group)(Name=*$GroupName*))"
$DNName = "distinguishedname"
$searcher.propertiesToLoad.Add($DNName) | out-null
$searchResults = $searcher.findall()
switch ($searchResults.Count)
{
    0 { Write-Host "No match found!"; exit }
```

```
  1 { $dn = $searchResults[0].properties[$DNName]}
  default
  {
    $count = 0
    foreach($result in $searchResults)
    {
        Write-Host $count ": "
            $result. properties[$DNName]
        $count++
    }
    Write-Host "More than one match found!"
    $choice = Read-Host "Select group: "
    $dn = $searchResults[$choice].properties[$DNName]
  }
}
return $dn
}
```

Using the Quest Active Directory Cmdlets

In this section we will get into the Quest Active Directory cmdlets. These cmdlets are designed for the most common management tasks in Active Directory, which saves us from writing a lot of Power-Shell code functions ourselves. Before we start talking about the cmdlets, now is a good time to review the documentation (you did download the Administrator's Guide with the installation package, didn't you?).

In the documentation you'll see several charts of parameters for the different cmdlets. You do not need to memorize these parameters, but we will definitely be using some of them. One of the most important is `-Identity`. This parameter is used in several of the Quest Active Directory cmdlets to specify the target object. The value we pass to this parameter can be a distinguished name (DN), a user principle name (UPN), the object's security ID (SID), or the domain\name of the object (such as zygort\accountant). Using the helper functions created earlier in this chapter makes working with the `-Identity` parameter much easier.

You may see helper functions used in a syntax that doesn't make much sense. That syntax will look something like this:

```
-Identity $(Find-ADUserDN("Business User01"))
```

This format looks a little cryptic; here's what it does: First it executes the `Find-ADUserDN` function, which returns the distinguished name of the target object. Then it passes this value to the `-Identity` parameter. We are simply wrapping up the function for the parameter to handle.

LISTING USERS

To list all users we can use the Quest Active Directory cmdlet `Get-QADUser` without any parameters. We can also use the `Select-Object` and `Sort-Object` cmdlets to make the output easier to read, as shown here:

```
Get-QADUser
(Get-QADUser | Measure-Object).Count
Get-QADUser | Select Name, DN | Sort DN
```

The `Get-QADUser` cmdlet gives us an easy way to produce a list of user objects that are either disabled or locked. This cmdlet has two parameters designed expressly for this purpose. To find currently disabled user objects we will use the `-Disabled` parameter, as shown here:

```
Get-QADUser -Disabled
(Get-QADUser -Disabled | Measure-Object).Count
```

To find currently locked user object we will use the `-Locked` parameter, as shown here:

```
Get-QADUser -Locked
(Get-QADUser -Locked | Measure-Object).Count
```

The output from either of these commands can be piped into another cmdlet to enable or unlock the user objects, as needed. We will cover that operation later in this chapter.

Many of the Quest Active Directory cmdlets utilize the parameter `-IncludeAllProperties`. This parameter takes no arguments and causes the cmdlet to return all the properties associated with the Active Directory object type. To see the properties returned by including this parameter, we can pipe the output into the `Get-Member` cmdlet, as shown here:

```
Get-QADUser -IncludeAllProperties | Get-Member
```

Here's a tip: you can use the `Get-Member` cmdlet with other cmdlets to view the properties and methods they expose. This is a great way to get more familiar with the various cmdlets.

You'll be presented with a scrolling list of items. Pay attention to the second column; any item labeled Property is data you can read. You might note that the names listed do not correspond with their Active Directory attributes, and that's alright! The cmdlet is just doing some interpreting for us. Let's take a look at some commands that show us more details about the users:

```
Get-QADUser -IncludeAllProperties |
    Select LastName, FirstName, Email |
    Sort LastName, FirstName
Get-QADUser -IncludeAllProperties |
    Where { $_.Email -match "@zygort.com" } |
    Select DisplayName, Email |
    Sort DisplayName
(Get-QADUser | Measure-Object).Count
```

The preceding commands demonstrate how easy it is to pipe cmdlets together to get the results you want. You can use this approach with several of the other cmdlets we will look at in this chapter, so feel free to experiment!

CREATING A USER

To create a new user we will use the `New-QADUser` cmdlet from Quest. This is one of the most difficult cmdlets in the set to use, simply because there is a lot that goes into properly creating a new user. To that end, we've created a function that helps you use this cmdlet. Before we get there though, let's look at some of the important parameters of the cmdlet.

The cmdlet requires only a couple of parameters. First we must specify the name of the new user object to create through the `-Name` parameter. We must also specify the new user object's parent container with the `-ParentContainer` parameter. You can specify the password for the new user object with the `-UserPassword` parameter. Following is a simple example of this cmdlet in action:

```
New-QADUser -Name "ShippingUser01"
    -ParentContainer "OU=Shipping,DC=Zygort,DC=com"
    -UserPassword "1b@dP@ssword"
```

Note that user accounts created with the `New-QADUser` cmdlet are automatically disabled. (You'll soon see how easy it is to enable them, and you can even incorporate the code into this function.)

We have a few options for setting additional user-object attributes through the `New-QADUser` cmdlet. This cmdlet makes a common set of user attributes available through the parameters listed in Table 21.5.

TABLE 21.5: New-QADUser Parameter Names for Active Directory User Attributes

ATTRIBUTE	ACTIVE DIRECTORY PROPERTY
`-City`	l
`-Company`	company
`-Description`	description
`-DisplayName`	displayName
`-Fax`	facsimileTelephoneNumber
`-FirstName`	givenName
`-HomePhone`	homePhone
`-Initials`	initials
`-LastName`	sn
`-Manager`	manager
`-MobilePhone`	mobile
`-Notes`	info
`-Office`	physicalDeliveryLocation
`-Pager`	pager
`-Telephone`	telephoneNumber
`-PostalCode`	postalCode

TABLE 21.5: New-QADUser Parameter Names for Active Directory User Attributes *(CONTINUED)*

ATTRIBUTE	ACTIVE DIRECTORY PROPERTY
-PostOfficeBox	postOfficeBox
-SamAccountName	samAccountName
-StateOrProvidence	st
-StreetAddress	streetAddress
-Title	title
-UserPrincipalName	userPrincipalName
-WebPage	wwwHomePage

To modify any other attributes, you must use a structure known as an *associative array*. This structure is basically a dictionary in memory; it holds keys and value pairs of information. Creating an associative array is fairly simple, as shown in the following example:

```
$attributes = @{""="";""=""}
```

Syntax is important in this case! First we specify the array name (in this case, $attributes) using an array structure that starts with the at (@) symbol. Notice the use of curly braces rather than parentheses or square brackets; this specifies we want to create an associative array. Use a semicolon to separate the key/value pairs. This array is then assigned using the -ObjectAttributes parameter of the cmdlet.

One catch to assigning attributes involves multivalued attributes in Active Directory (such as the otherTelephone attribute). The associative array above ($attributes) holds one value per attribute name. To solve this problem we have to create a one-dimensional array, populate it with the desired values, and then assign it to an attribute name in the first associative array.

Creating a one-dimensional array is similar to creating the associative array, except this time we will use parentheses rather than the curly braces, as shown in this example:

```
$otherPhones = @("555-971-1234","555-971-1235")
```

To assign the one-dimensional array to the associative array we would use the following code:

```
@attributes = @{"otherTelephone"=$otherPhones}
```

That should cover the major points of interest in using the New-QADUser cmdlet; now let's create a function that puts it to use. The code that follows prompts the user for information necessary to create the user. It uses both the cmdlet parameters to assign the required information and an associative array to assign other user attributes. The array $PropertiesToAdd can be modified to support any additional attributes you want to include; simply create a key/value pair with the prompt value followed by the Active Directory attribute name.

```
Function Create-ADUser
```

```
{
# add constant attributes to this array
$attributes = @{
    "company"="Zygort";
    "wwwHomePage"="http://www.zygort.com"}

$Pre2000Domain = "Zygort"
$Domain= "zygort.com"

$PropertiesToAdd = @{
    "DisplayName"="displayName";
    "LastName"="sn";
    "FirstName"="givenName"}

# Get the mandatory attributes
$ParentCN = Find-ADOUDN
    (read-Host "Enter Parent Container")
do {
    $AccountName = read-Host "Enter account Name"
} while (Check-ADUserExists($AccountName) -eq $true)
$UPN = "$AccountName@$Domain"
$Name = "$Pre2000Domain\$AccountName"

$PasswordLength = 6
do {
 $Password = read-Host "Enter password" -AsSecureString
} while ($Password.Length -lt $PasswordLength)

ForEach ($p in $PropertiesToAdd.Keys)
{
    $answer = read-Host "Enter value for $p"
    $attributes.Add($PropertiesToAdd[$p],$answer)
}
New-QADUser -Name $Name
    -UserPrincipalName $UPN
    -sAMAccountName $AccountName
    -ParentContainer $ParentCN
    -UserPassword $Password
    -ObjectAttributes $attributes}
```

In this example the Read-Host cmdlet uses a parameter named -AsSecureString. This parameter does not echo the characters as they are typed, but rather uses symbols as placeholders. This is good to use when entering any sensitive information.

SETTING USER PROPERTIES

To set user attributes on an existing user object we can use the Set-QADUser cmdlet. This cmdlet has parameters identical to the New-QADUser cmdlet for setting a specific set of user attributes (as shown in Table 21.5) and uses an associative array to set any other user attributes.

To provide the distinguished name to the -Identity parameter we can use the Find-ADUserDN function, as shown here:

```
Set-QADUser -Identity $(Find-ADUserDN(BusinessUser02))
    -Description "Business User 02"
    -Telephone "555-971-9725"
```

ENABLING A USER

To enable a user object we can use the Quest Active Directory cmdlet Enable-QADUser. The cmdlet itself is simple; all we have to do is pass the identity of the user object to enable. There are a few methods we can use to accomplish this:

```
Enable-QADUser -Identity $(Find-ADUserDN(TempUser01))
Find-ADUserDN TempUser01 | Enable-QADUser
Find-ADUserDN Temp | Enable-QADUser
```

ENABLE ALL DISABLED USERS FUNCTION

We can also use the Get-QADUser cmdlet to find and unlock all disabled accounts in one fell swoop. The one problem with this approach is the Guest account is disabled by default for security. Because that's one account we don't want to touch, we can add the Where-Object cmdlet in to exclude the Guest account from being enabled.

```
Function Enable-AllDisabledUsers
{
Get-QADUser -Disabled | Where {$_.Name -ne "Guest"| | Enable-QADUser
}
```

DISABLING A USER

To disable a user object we can use the Quest Active Directory cmdlet Disable-QADUser. Just like with the Enable-QADUser cmdlet, all we have to do is pass the identity of the user object to disable, as shown here:

```
Disable-QADUser -Identity $(Find-ADUserDN(TempUser01))
Find-ADUserDN tempUser01 | Disable-QADUser
Find-ADUserDN Temp | Disable-QADUser
```

UNLOCKING A USER

To unlock a user object we can use the Quest Active Directory cmdlet Unlock-QADUser. This cmdlet is also simple; all we have to do is pass the identity of the user object to disable, as shown here:

```
Find-ADUserDN tempUser01 | Unlock-QADUser
Find-ADUserDN Temp | Unlock-QADUser
```

To unlock all currently locked users, we can pipe the results of the Get-QADUser cmdlet, with the -Locked parameter, into the Unlock-QADUser cmdlet, as shown here:

```
Get-QADUser -Locked | Unlock-QADUser
```

Keep in mind that this is a blanket approach to unlocking accounts and will easily unlock accounts that could have been locked for the correct reasons. Therefore you might want to filter the results of the `Get-QADUser`. For example, if locked accounts are moved to an OU named Locked Accounts we can filter the results as shown here:

```
Get-QADUser -Locked |
    Where {$_.DN -ne "OU=Locked Accounts"} |
    Unlock-QADUser
```

CREATING AN ORGANIZATIONAL UNIT

To create a new organizational unit we can use the Quest Active Directory cmdlet `New-QADObject`. When using this cmdlet, we have to specify the type of Active Directory object we want to create. We must also specify the parent container and name of the new object, as shown here:

```
New-QADObject
    -Type "organizationalUnit"
    -ParentContainer $(Find-ADOUDN("Business"))
    -Name "Shipping"
```

LISTING GROUPS

Obtaining a list of groups is easy with the `Get-QADGroup` cmdlet. To make the results a little more readable we can pipe the output into the `Select-Object` and `Sort-Object` cmdlets. The examples shown here illustrate some different ways of listing the group information:

```
Get-QADGroup | Select Name, DN | Sort Name
Get-QADGroup -IncludeAllProperties |
    Select Name, ParentContainer, GroupType, GroupScope
(Get-QADGroup | Measure-Object).Count
```

The `Get-QADGroup` cmdlet also supports filtering based on the group type, group scope, and/or LDAP query. The cmdlet has two parameters, `-GroupType` and `-GroupScope`, for filtering based on the group type and scope, respectively. With these two parameters at our disposal, using an LDAP query is normally not necessary. Following are some examples:

```
Get-QADGroup -GroupType "Distribution"
Get-QADGroup -GroupScope "Global"
Get-QADGroup -GroupScope "Security"
    | Measure-Object | Select Count
Get-QADGroup -GroupType "Security" -GroupScope "Global"
```

CREATING A GROUP

We can create a new group in Active Directory with the `New-QADGroup` cmdlet. We need to supply a few required parameters, including `-Name` and `-ParentContainer`. We can also supply the `-Description` parameter to give some meaning to the group and its purpose.

```
New-QADGroup
    -Name "BusinessGroup"
    -ParentContainer $(Find-ADOUDN("Business"))
    -Description "Business Department Users"
```

LISTING GROUP MEMBERS

We can use the `Get-QADGroupMember` cmdlet to produce a membership list for almost any group in Active Directory, as shown in this example:

```
Get-QADGroupMember $(Find-ADGroupDN("Managers"))
(Get-QADGroupMember $(Find-ADGroupDN("Managers")) |
    Measure-Object).Count
```

Earlier in this chapter you saw how to list groups in Active Directory. With a little creative plumbing we can pipe the two commands together to get a membership listing of each group in the domain.

```
Get-QADGroup |
    Foreach {
        "`n$_.Name;"---------";
        Get-QADGroupMember $_.DN
    }
```

Because some groups are "special," you will see a few errors go by. But that's alright; it should still achieve the result we want. We've put some additional formatting in the command to improve its readability, which is helpful when producing any long stream of data.

ADDING A GROUP MEMBER

The `Add-QADGroupmember` cmdlet adds an Active Directory object to a group. This cmdlet uses two parameters: `-Identity` to specify the group and `-Member` to specify the object to add to the group's membership.

```
Add-QADGroupMember
    -Identity $(Find-ADGroupDN("Business Users"))
    -Member $(Find-ADUserDN("BusinessUser01"))
Add-QADGroupmember
    -Identity $(Find-ADGroupDN("SCCM Servers"))
    -Member $(Find-ADComputerDN("SCCM01"))
```

Remember: group members are not always users. In the second example we've added the computer SCCM01 to the group SCCM Servers.

The `-Member` parameter is not limited to one object at a time. It accepts a comma-separated list of objects to add to the group membership. The trick to this when using our distinguished name helper function is to use the helper function for each separate object, and to separate each returned value from each helper function by suing commas. The following example clarifies how this looks:

```
Add-QADGroupMember
    -Identity $(Find-ADGroupDN("Business Users"))
    -Member $(Find-ADUserDN("BusinessUser01")),
            $(Find-ADUserDN("BusinessUser02")),
            $(Find-ADUserDN("BusinessUser03"))
```

REMOVING A GROUP MEMBER

The `Remove-QADGroupMember` cmdlet removes objects from Active Directory groups. Its syntax is identical to that of the `Add-QADGroupMember` cmdlet. The `-Identity` parameter specifies the group, while the `-Member` parameter specifies which objects to remove from the group. The

-Member property accepts a comma-separated list of objects to be removed from the group as it does in the Add-QADGroupMember cmdlet. The examples here show the cmdlet in action:

```
Remove-QADGroupMember
    -Identity $(Find-ADGroupDN("Business Users"))
    -Member $(Find-ADUserDN("BusinessUser01"))
Add-QADGroupmember
    -Identity $(Find-ADGroupDN("SCCM Servers"))
    -Member $(Find-ADComputerDN("SCCM01"))
Add-QADGroupMember
    -Identity $(Find-ADGroupDN("Business Users"))
    -Member $(Find-ADUserDN("BusinessUser01")),
            $(Find-ADUserDN("BusinessUser02")),
            $(Find-ADUserDN("BusinessUser03"))
```

LISTING COMPUTERS

The Get-QADComputer cmdlet generates a list of computers in the domain. This cmdlet can produce a wealth of information if you specify the -IncludeAllParameters parameter. Of course, we can improve the readability by piping the result set through the Select-Object and Where-Object cmdlets, as shown in the examples here:

```
Get-QADComputer
Get-QADComputer -IncludeAllProperties |
    Select Name, ParentContainer, ComputerRole
Get-QADComputer -IncludeAllProperties |
    Where {$_.OSVersion -lt "6.0"} |
    Select Name, OSName, OSVersion, OSServicePack
(Get-QADComputer | Measure-Object).Count
Get-QADComputer -IncludeAllProperties |
    Where {$_.OSVersion -lt "6.0"} |
    Measure-Object | Select Count
```

SELECTING VALUES FOR COMPARISONS

In the preceding examples you'll notice the OSVersion property of the object used in the Where-Object cmdlet for comparison in the Where-Object cmdlet. The OSVersion value is convenient to use in a comparison when searching for computers with specific operating systems, but it is not guaranteed to be unique between client and server operating systems. For a more accurate result set you should include values for other attributes, such as OSName, ComputerRole, and OSServicePack.

The cmdlet also has parameters that narrow down the result set: the -ComputerRole parameter allows us to return either DomainController or Member systems, and the -SearchRoot parameter confines our search to a specific subtree of the domain. The following examples illustrate these parameters in use:

```
Get-QADComputer -ComputerRole "DomainController"
Get-QADComputer
    -SearchRoot $(Find-ADOUDN("Business Computers"))
```

MOVING USERS

To move Active Directory objects, use the Move-QADObject cmdlet. This cmdlet moves any object specified so we need to be very careful in passing the identity of the Active Directory object we want to move.

```
Move-QADObject
    -Identity $(Find-ADUserDN("Manager03"))
    -NewParentContainer $(Find-ADOUDN("Shipping"))
Move-QADObject
    -Identity $(Find-ADComputerDN("UPSSystem"))
    -NewParentContainer $(Find-ADOUDN("Shipping"))
Move-QADObject
    -Identity $(Find-ADGroupDN("Shippers"))
    -NewParentContainer $(Find-ADOUDN("Shipping"))
Move-QADObject
    -Identity $(Find-ADOUDN("ShippingEast"))
    -NewParentContainer $(Find-ADOUDN("Shipping"))
```

For added security we can specify the -Confirm parameter with the cmdlet. We will need to verify the operation before it actually takes place.

Note that moving objects can fail if the accidental deletion attribute is set on the object to be moved.

DELETING USERS, ORGANIZATIONAL UNITS, GROUPS, AND COMPUTERS

The Remove-QADObject cmdlet deletes Active Directory objects. This cmdlet removes any object specified, so we need to be very careful in passing the identity of the Active Directory object we want to remove.

A warning prompt displays before the object is removed; however, adding the -Force parameter overrides this behavior.

```
Remove-QADObject
    -Identity $(Find-ADUserObject("Temp"))
Remove-QADObject
    -Identity $(Find-ADOUDN("Shipping"))
Remove-QADObject
    -Identity $(Find-ADGroupDN("ShippingUsers"))
Remove-QADObject
    -Identity $(Find-ADComputerDN("Vista01"))
```

This cmdlet can also be on the receiving end of a pipe. For example, we could produce a list of computers in a particular organizational unit and then pass that list to the Remove-QADObject cmdlet.

```
Get-QADComputer
    -SearchRoot $(Find-ADOUDN("OldComputers")) |
    Remove-QADObject
```

Note that if you have protected an object from accidental deletion, PowerShell will not circumvent that designation. You must remove the accidental deletion protection attribute before you can successfully remove the object.

The Bottom Line

Use PowerShell cmdlets, piping them together to produce a result set   Piping the output from one cmdlet to the input stream of another is one of the most powerful features of PowerShell. Effectively piping cmdlets together is an essential skill of a PowerShell user.

Master It   Using the standard set of PowerShell cmdlets, create a command that counts the number of entries in the current directory. Show at least two commands to get the information.

Use the Quest Active Directory Management cmdlets   The Quest Active Directory Management cmdlets make easy work of managing Active Directory from the command line. You must understand what each cmdlet does to accomplish the management task at hand quickly and efficiently.

Master It   First create a command to find all locked accounts in the domain. Then expand the command to unlock those accounts.

Manage Active Directory using the Quest Active Directory Management and PowerShell cmdlets   Combining the Quest Active Directory Management cmdlets with the standard set of PowerShell cmdlets gives you a much wider range of solutions to management tasks. It is important to understand how these cmdlets can function together in a command.

Master It   First create a list of security groups on the server. Then find the number of users that belong to each group.

Appendix A

The Bottom Line

Each of The Bottom Line sections in the chapters suggest exercises to deepen skills and understanding. Sometimes there is only one possible solution, but often you are encouraged to use your skills and creativity to create something that builds on what you know and lets you explore one of many possible solutions.

Chapter 1: Active Directory Fundamentals

In this chapter we discussed the AD DS Flexible Single Master Operations (FSMO) roles and what tasks they perform. Special care must be taken when designing an AD DS environment, because these roles do not have redundancy built in.

Identify the five FSMO roles and explain each role's function Designing your AD DS environment can often prove to be challenging. There is a delicate balance between designing an efficient replication topology and keeping the design easy to administer.

Master It There are five FSMO roles in any AD DS environment. Learn what each role is, what its function is, and where it is located on the network.

Master It Solution

Schema Master—The Schema Master is the one domain controller within the forest that is allowed to access and modify the portion of the AD DS database that holds the schema. The schema partition, sometimes known as the schema naming context, resides on every domain controller within the forest, but can be modified only on this one domain controller.

Domain Naming Master—The Domain Naming Master is the system that is responsible for making sure that domain names are unique and available when you're adding or removing domains from your forest.

Infrastructure Master—The Infrastructure Master checks other domains in the forest for changes to objects. If it finds a change to an object in another domain, it will update the attributes for any instances of that object, and then the changes will be replicated to other domain controllers from its domain.

Relative Identifier (RID) Master—The RID Master is responsible for making sure that each security principal within the domain has a unique identifier.

Primary Domain Controller (PDC) Emulator—The PDC Emulator acts as the PDC for any Windows NT domain controllers that may reside on a mixed-mode network. The PDC Emulator is also responsible for time synchronization and password changes for pre–Windows 2000 clients.

Design FSMO placement according to AD DS best practices and business requirements Proper FSMO design and server placement are important to your AD DS design for service availability and performance.

Master It   You are designing the FSMO role placement in your AD DS environment. You have one forest and two domains. DomainA is a root domain that is used to protect certain resources from the main domain (DomainB). DomainA consists of two domain controllers: ServerA-1 and ServerA-2. DomainB consists of three domain controllers: ServerB-1, ServerB-2, and ServerB-3. ServerB-1 and ServerB-2 are also global catalog servers. All user accounts are located in DomainB except for administrative and service accounts.

Master It Solution   Place the Schema Master role on ServerA-1. It is also good practice to remove all users from the Schema Admins group until you need to make a change that requires a schema change or update.

Place the Domain Naming Master role on ServerA-2. This is a forestwide role and should be separated from the other domain if possible.

Place the Infrastructure Master role on ServerB-3. The Infrastructure Master role should not reside on the same server that hosts the global catalog.

Place the RID Master on ServerB-2. The RID Master should reside in the site where most user accounts are created.

Place the PDC Emulator on ServerB-1. This server should also be located in the same site where most accounts are created, but because of this role's added functionality, it should be on a server separate from the other servers and roles.

Chapter 2: Domain Name System Design

The importance of Microsoft Server 2008 DNS in Active Directory Domain Services   DNS is the backbone of Active Directory. While other DNS servers, such as BIND, may allow you to run Active Directory, certain Active Directory features are available only with Microsoft Windows Server–based DNS servers.

Master It   You are designing your Active Directory domain infrastructure that consists of multiple physical locations. Your domain will consist of Windows 2008 servers only. You want to implement a DNS infrastructure that provides you with a simple and easy way to manage DNS replication topology.

Master It Solution   Windows 2008-based DNS servers allow you to configure Active Directory–integrated zones, which automatically replicate DNS information for the zone to other domain controllers in the environment.

How to protect DNS data and keep it accurate   As the adage goes, garbage in, garbage out. Protecting DNS data and keeping the data accurate are key to the reliability and performance of your DNS infrastructure.

Master It   You've just completed your DNS design and implementation. You now need to make sure your DNS servers are protected from attack and from data corruption.

Master It Solution   Allow only secure dynamic updates, and configure IPSec so you can ensure that only "allowed" computers are updating records and that the data transmissions are secure when replication is taking place.

Disable recursion (on servers that are not configured as forwarders) to keep your servers safe from denial-of-service attacks.

Design a resilient zone-transfer topology. You may want to allow zone transfers to only DNS servers authorized to receive the transfers.

Chapter 3: Active Directory Domain Services Forest and Domain Design

In this chapter we reviewed AD DS forest and domain design criteria. There are many decisions to be made to help shape the layout of your forest and domain structures.

When to use a single forest or use multiple forests   Forest design is the first step in a very crucial design plan regarding your AD DS environment. Creating a forest design that meets your business and administrative goals is key to a successful design.

Master It   You are creating an AD DS design that consists of five physical locations. You have a centralized administration model, and all AD DS management is done by administrators at your location. You have one business unit that runs an application that requires schema changes upon each update.

Master It Solution   Deploy two forests for this implementation. Typically, you want to deploy as few forests as possible in a centralized management model. In this case, you should keep the application that requires frequent schema changes in a separate forest. Because the schema is forestwide, any changes to it affect the entire forest and all domains in that forest. If the applications caused adverse affects with the schema in this scenario, it would be limited to just that business unit and not the entire organization.

When to use a single domain or use multiple domains   The next step in your AD DS design is to determine your domain structure.

Master It   Business requirements state that you must keep a business unit's accounts and information separate from the rest of the company. You want to allow for this requirement while still using a simple administrative model.

Master It Solution   Because the requirements are that only user accounts and data are separate, there is no need for a separate forest. You can design a single forest and use a common schema and administrative model while separating the business unit into its own domain. This will allow that domain to operate in a separate, secure manner while still being maintained by a common schema and centralized administrators.

Which forest and domain functional levels to choose   If you are upgrading to Windows Server 2008, or you have requirements for Windows 2000 or 2003 domain controllers, you will have to determine which forest and domain functional levels you should use.

Master It   You have an environment that consists of one Active Directory 2003 forest with three Active Directory domains. Three domains were created because of password policy differences between the business units in each domain.

You are planning an upgrade to Windows Server 2008 on all of your domain controllers. Along with the upgrade to the servers, you would also like to simplify administration.

Master It Solution   When you move to a Windows Server 2008 domain functional level, you can take advantage of fine-grained password polices that were introduced in Windows Server 2008. This will allow you to consolidate your three domains into one domain and to configure password policies at the OU or group level instead of at the domain level.

Chapter 4: Organizing the Physical and Logical Aspects of AD DS

In this chapter we discussed proper planning and design related to the physical and logical aspects of AD DS. A proper design is crucial to the success of your implementation.

Design an efficient AD DS replication infrastructure   Designing your AD DS environment can often prove challenging. There is a delicate balance between designing an efficient replication topology and keeping the design easy to administer.

Master It   You have a centralized data center and five remote branch offices: New York, Chicago, Atlanta, Peoria, and Bloomington. New York, Chicago, and Atlanta are connected to the data center via T3 connections. Two of the branch offices (Peoria and Bloomington) are connected to the Chicago branch office through a fractional T1 line, connecting at 512 Kb. The Peoria and Bloomington offices need to authenticate to AD DS, but all applications run local to the workstations. You must create a site topology that meets the authentication requirements while keeping down hardware costs and administrative overhead.

Master It Solution   Create three Sites in AD DS, one each for New York, Chicago, and Atlanta. Place the domain controllers and other objects for Peoria and Bloomington into the Chicago site. This will eliminate the need for a domain controller at the remote branch, while still supplying authentication into AD DS.

Design an organizational unit (OU) structure that fits your environment   There are many different ways to design an OU structure. Through proper assessment and planning you can develop a plan that fits your business model and has a logical administrative model.

Master It   You are designing an OU structure for your company. Your company employs junior administrators that are responsible for different remote sites. Two administrators are assigned to each remote site. You send out software updates to different departments via Group Policy. You must determine the best plan for an OU structure based on these requirements and business practices.

Master It Solution   Create a mixed OU structure, based on location first, then on department. Delegate administration to each location's OU to the proper administrators assigned to that location. Inside each OU, create departmental OUs to assign or publish software via Group Policy. This will allow the branch administrators to control their own location, and will meet the software-deployment requirement by allowing administrators to assign or publish software based on departments.

Chapter 5: Flexible Single Master Operations Design

In this chapter we discussed the AD DS Flexible Single Master Operations (FSMO) roles and what tasks they perform. Special care must be taken when designing an AD DS environment, because these roles do not have redundancy built in.

Identify the five FSMO roles and explain each role's function   Designing your AD DS environment can often prove to be challenging. There is a delicate balance between designing an efficient replication topology and keeping the design easy to administer.

Master It   There are five FSMO roles in any AD DS environment. Learn what each role is, what its function is, and where it is located on the network.

Master It Solution

Schema Master—The Schema Master is the one domain controller within the forest that is allowed to access and modify the portion of the AD DS database that holds the schema. The schema partition, sometimes known as the schema naming context, resides on every domain controller within the forest, but can be modified only on this one domain controller.

Domain Naming Master—The Domain Naming Master is the system that is responsible for making sure that domain names are unique and available when you're adding or removing domains from your forest.

Infrastructure Master—The Infrastructure Master checks other domains in the forest for changes to objects. If it finds a change to an object in another domain, it will update the attributes for any instances of that object, and then the changes will be replicated to other domain controllers from its domain.

Relative Identifier (RID) Master—The RID Master is responsible for making sure that each security principal within the domain has a unique identifier.

Primary Domain Controller (PDC) Emulator—The PDC Emulator acts as the PDC for any Windows NT domain controllers that may reside on a mixed-mode network. The PDC Emulator is also responsible for time synchronization and password changes for pre–Windows 2000 clients.

Design FSMO placement according to AD DS best practices and business requirements
Proper FSMO design and server placement are important to your AD DS design for service availability and performance.

Master It You are designing the FSMO role placement in your AD DS environment. You have one forest and two domains. DomainA is a root domain that is used to protect certain resources from the main domain (DomainB). DomainA consists of two domain controllers: ServerA-1 and ServerA-2. DomainB consists of three domain controllers: ServerB-1, ServerB-2, and ServerB-3. ServerB-1 and ServerB-2 are also global catalog servers. All user accounts are located in DomainB except for administrative and service accounts.

Master It Solution Place the Schema Master role on ServerA-1. It is also good practice to remove all users from the Schema Admins group until you need to make a change that requires a schema change or update.

Place the Domain Naming Master role on ServerA-2. This is a forestwide role and should be separated from the other domain if possible.

Place the Infrastructure Master role on ServerB-3. The Infrastructure Master role should not reside on the same server that hosts the global catalog.

Place the RID Master on ServerB-2. The RID Master should reside in the site where most user accounts are created.

Place the PDC Emulator on ServerB-1. This server should also be located in the same site where most accounts are created, but because of this role's added functionality, it should be on a server separate from the other servers and roles.

Chapter 6: Managing Accounts: User, Group, and Computer

Create different account types and edit properties associated with them There are two different account types: security principal accounts and non–security principal accounts. Security principal accounts comprise user, security group, and computer accounts. Non–security principal accounts comprise contacts and distribution groups.

> **Master It** Your company is preparing a new marketing campaign. The Marketing group currently consists of five employees. Marketing has just hired three new internal employees and four external employees that will be working on a contract basis.
>
> You need to create the new accounts and create a mailing list so all of the users can communicate. The external users should not have access to any network resources.
>
> **Master It Solution** Create three new user accounts for the three new internal employees. Create contact accounts for the four external employees. Because contact accounts are non–security principal accounts, they will not have access to the internal network.
>
> Create a new Distribution Group and add the five existing user accounts, three internal user accounts, and four external user accounts inside the Distribution Group. The Distribution Group is a non–security principal account that can contain both security principal and non–security principal accounts.

Use built-in and downloadable utilities to manage user, group, and computer accounts AD DS includes many tools and utilities to manage and configure user, group, and computer accounts. There are also many Microsoft utilities and third-party tools you can download and use in your environment to help manage these accounts.

> **Master It** You have just received a request to add 100 new users to your domain. When you create these users, you must populate the account with information such as department, phone number, manager, and location.
>
> **Master It Solution** While you could use ADUC to create the new accounts, the information that is required must be entered manually after the user is created. Using a third-party tool such as DSADD, you can define the required information during the creation of the account. The user accounts can also be created en masse to save time with repetitive tasks of manually entering information. The built-in tools are often not sufficient for these types of bulk creation or modification tasks.

Chapter 7: Maintaining Organizational Units

In this chapter we discussed effective ways to access, control, and monitor objects in your organizational units. There are many different tools that you can use to define, control, and monitor activity.

Manage access to objects within your organizational units There are two ways to control access to Active Directory objects in an OU: rights and permissions.

Rights define a task that a person or group is allowed to perform; permissions define the access a user or group has to a particular object.

> **Master It** You have created a new folder named BlueprintArchive under a share named Blueprints. Administrators and members of the BPEngineering group are the only users that should have access to the BluePrints share. John Kaminski requires access to the BlueprintArchive folder but making him a member of the BPEngineering group will give him too much access.
>
> You explicitly grant John Kaminski the Read permission at the BlueprintArchive folder. You notice that John Kaminski is able to remove files from the folder, as well as create new folders. Using the tools you learned about in this chapter, you need to determine how John Kaminski

is able to perform these tasks and lock the folder down so John Kaminski only has read access to this particular folder.

Master It Solution

1. Navigate to the FinanceArchive folder.

2. Right-click and select Properties.

3. Click on the Security tab.

4. Click on the button labeled Advanced.

5. Click on the tab named Effective Permissions.

6. Click Select and enter the name of the user who should have access to the BluePrints share.

7. Verify the effective permissions At this point you see that John Kaminski has more than just read permissions. You must now determine where he is receiving the permissions.

8. Click Cancel and view the advanced security settings for the folder.

9. View the permission entries to see if John Kaminski is getting an inherited permission from another group he belongs to.

At this point you see that the Users group is listed as having an inherited permission from a parent folder. John Kaminski is getting his permissions from this group. You must now lock down the folder to remove all users except John Kaminski and assign John Kaminski the read permission.

1. Click Edit.

2. Uncheck the box labeled Include Inheritable Permissions from This Object's Parent.

3. When the Windows Security box appears, click Copy.

4. Highlight Users and click the box labeled Remove.

5. Click Apply and OK.

6. Click the Effective Permissions tab and check the permissions once again for John Kaminski. They should now be correct and list read permissions.

Manage administrative control of the objects within your organizational units Administrators can define the other administrators (such as branch administrators or junior administrators) who have access to manage the OUs or objects within the OUs. This can be accomplished by delegating control over certain OUs to these administrative users.

Master It Your company has just hired a new administrator who is assigned to the Berwick, Illinois branch. Previously, all resources from this office were part of the Galesburg OU. The new administrator will take over the management of users and computers for the Berwick branch.

Master It Solution Please see the following:

1. From ADUC, create a new OU named Berwick.

2. Create sub-OUs as you wish, such as computers, users, etc.

3. Right-click the Berwick OU and select Delegate Control.

4. At the Welcome to the Delegation of Control Wizard screen, click Next.

5. At the Users or Groups screen, click Add.

6. Select the name of the new administrator from AD DS and click OK.

7. Click Next.

8. At the Tasks to Delegate window, select the tasks you would like to assign to the Berwick administrator and then select Next.

9. At the Completing the Delegation of Control Wizard select Finish.

Monitor the activity of the objects within your organizational units   As you are creating your OU structure, creating AD DS objects, assigning rights and permissions, and delegating control over these OUs to other administrators, it is a good idea to keep tabs on what is going on by creating or modifying audit settings on the objects that reside in those OUs.

Master It   Expanding on our preceding example, now that you have delegated control to the Berwick OU to the Berwick admin, you want to audit activity to the OU.

Master It Solution   Please see the following:

1. Open the Group Policy Management MMC.

2. Navigate to the Berwick OU.

3. Right click on the Berwick OU and select Create a GPO in This Domain, and Link It Here.

4. Give the new GPO a name, such as Berwick Audit, and select OK.

5. Right-click your new GPO and select Edit.

6. Navigate to Computer Configuration ➢ Windows Settings ➢ Security Settings ➢ Local Policies ➢ Audit Policy.

7. Select the policies on the right side of the screen that you want to track, and change the policy accordingly. Your options are to track success, failure, or both.

8. Close the Group Policy Management MMC.

Chapter 8: Managing Group Policy

Identify the different group policy types   Microsoft has changed the format of group policy templates so that they are easier to manage. Instead of using a proprietary format, the new group policy templates that are used with Vista and Windows Server 2008 are based on XML.

Master It   Administrative templates are formatted using two different markup languages. What formats are they created in and which operating systems support the group policies that are configured with each?

Master It Solution   The original group policy administrative templates were created using a proprietary markup language, and used an extension of .adm. With Windows Vista and later operating systems, XML became the markup language for administrative templates. Administrative templates that use XML have an .admx extension.

It doesn't matter which markup language is used for the administrative template; the group policy can still be applied to any supported operating system.

Use the Group Policy Management Editor   The Group Policy Management Editor allows you to configure settings that will be used to manage systems when they initially start. The settings that are initially used are not enforced, so the user that logs onto the system can make configuration changes.

Master It   When working with the Group Policy Management Editor, you want to set initial settings for client systems, but you also want to allow the user to be able to make changes to the settings. What section of the GPO would you use to configure these settings?

Master It Solution   GPOs now have two sections that you can use to configure settings: Policies and Preferences. Preferences are used to set "baseline" settings that a user can change. Policies are enforced, and the user is not allowed to change them.

Use the Group Policy Management Console   The Group Policy Management Console makes managing group policies much easier than using just the Group Policy Object Editor and Active Directory Users and Computers. The tools that are included in the GPMC include a Group Policy Results wizard that allows you to determine how the GPOs applied to a user or computer, the Group Policy Modeling wizard, which allows you to determine how GPO will affect a user or computer, and the ability to create Starter GPOs.

Master It   You have identified settings within your group policies that you want to include in all GPOs. These settings are primarily comments you want to make sure are included when other administrators edit the GPOs, but they also contain configuration settings you want to make sure are included in each GPO. How would you go about creating an easy way to apply these settings?

Master It Solution   Starter GPOs are used to create a baseline of settings that will be common to all GPOs that are created from the starter GPOs.

Chapter 9: Managing Active Directory Security

In this chapter we discussed Active Directory security, from the basics of AD security to securing AD objects to new tools introduced in Windows Server 2008 that can aid in your security plans.

The Basics of Active Directory security   Understanding the key terms and security processes is key to planning security in your environment.

Master It   Define the five following terms and give examples of how they all work together:

◆   Security principals

◆   Access control lists

◆   Access tokens

◆   Authentication

◆   Authorization

Master It Solution

Security principals—Users, computers, and service accounts that can be authenticated to Active Directory.

Access control lists—The Access control lists control access to resources in the domain.

Access tokens—Access tokens consist of the user's SID, the SIDs for any groups to which the user belongs, and the user's rights and privileges.

Authentication—Authentication is the process that ensures the person who is trying to access the network is who he or she says.

Authorization—Authorization is the process of checking a security principal to validate rights and permissions.

Security principals are objects in AD DS that can be assigned a permission to access a resource. The first step to gain access to that resource is to authenticate to the network.

When you authenticate to the network, you validate that you are who you say you are and that you have the right to be there. Once you have authenticated to the network, you are given an access token.

The access token consists of the security principal's SID, the SIDs for any groups to which the security principal belongs, and the security principal's rights and privileges.

The access token is validated against the entries within the access control list to make sure the user has permissions to access the resource. This is known as authorization. If the user is authorized to use the resource, he or she is granted access.

How to Secure AD DS objects   There are many tools you can use to help secure your AD DS objects. Threats can come at you from internal or external users, and you must be prepared for any threat.

Master It   List steps you can take to protect your AD DS objects from accidental harm and malicious users, including steps you can take to track down what happened and who could have done the damage.

Master It Solution   One of the first steps you can take is to secure well-known accounts. Make sure the built-in accounts in your environment are disabled, because these accounts will often be the first accounts used in hacking attempts.

DNS should also be protected so a malicious user cannot bring down your DNS environment with a denial-of-service attack nor change entries so communication with an important server is spoofed.

Secure the AD DS database. If the AD DS database falls into the wrong hands, it could be disastrous to your domain.

Turn on auditing for all domain controllers to see who is making changes or attempting to make changes.

Physically secure your domain controllers. Lock servers in a data center and lock the racks where the servers reside. If physical security cannot be guaranteed, disable external ports that would allow data to be copied, lock down the server with the Syskey utility, or consider implementing a Windows Server 2008 RODC at that location.

Chapter 10: Managing Access with Active Directory Services

Install and manage Active Directory Federation Services   Active Directory Federation Services allows you to control access to resources within your organization. When using AD FS, you do not have to create the traditional trust relationships between your forest and an external organization's forest; you can use web-based access rights to manage who is allowed to access the resources. Both organizations have to create the federated access, but once it's in place, it is much easier to maintain than the traditional methods.

Master It Jamie is configuring the resource-partner side of the AD FS installation. The partner organization is going to be responsible for the account-partner side of the solution. Jamie is trying to decide which of the Certificate Services options she would like to use. Should she create her own certificate using her own root certification authority, use a certificate signed by a third-party root certification authority (CA), or use a self-signed certificate?

Master It Solution Two of the three options mentioned could be used. The best method would be to use a third-party trusted root certification authority to sign the certificate. Using her own CA, she would have to make sure that the partner organization imported her trusted root certificate into the trusted root certificate store on all of the systems that would be using the federated trust. Using a self-signed certificate is not recommended because of the amount of additional administrative overhead it would incur.

Install and manage Active Directory Lightweight Directory Services Applications and services can use Active Directory Domain Services as a storage location for configuration information and data. However, to do so usually entails extending the Active Directory schema. Instead, you can use Active Directory Lightweight Directory Services to create a new directory-service container to use for application and service storage. As a bonus, the AD LDS container can be replicated to only the systems that need to host it instead of being hosted on all of the domain controllers.

Master It Nick needs a configuration database for an application he is developing. He wants a local copy of the database on system where the application is installed. What criteria should he consider when determining whether he will use AD DS or AD LDS for his application?

Master It Solution When trying to decide whether to use AD DS or AD LDS for the configuration data, Nick needs to determine if he will be allowed to extend the AD DS schema. If not, he will have to use AD LDS to store the information. He should also consider where the data need to be replicated. If he wants to store the configuration data on all systems that will have a copy of the application, and some of those systems are not domain controllers, he will have to use AD LDS. AD LDS will also allow him to replicate the configuration data to only systems that have the application installed.

Use DSDBUtil to manage Active Directory Lightweight Directory Services AD DS has the NTDSUtil utility for managing the database. To manage the AD LDS database, you use the DSDBUtil utility.

Master It DeAnn needs to change the SSL port used when accessing an AD LDS instance so that it meets the company's new communication standards. How would she make the change so that SSL communications uses port 58445?

Master It Solution After entering the DSDBUtil utility, she needs to activate the proper AD LDS instance and then enter the command SSL `Port 58445`.

Chapter 11: Managing Active Directory Rights Management Services

Understanding rights-management servers The AD RMS Server is a server component that will issue RMS certificates and licenses, enroll servers and users, perform administrative functions, and manage licensing of rights-protected information.

Master It Shannon is the administrator of a large nationwide distribution company. She is implementing AD RMS servers for different departments in different geographical regions. She has installed the Root Certification server, but the consultant, Jami, said Shannon needs to install one more server in each geographical region before she can distribute license roles geographically. What server should Shannon install to distribute publish and use licenses geographically?

Master It Solution Shannon should install the license server. The license server issues only publish and use licenses. It delegates control of RMS publish and use licenses to individual departments so that the individual departments can have more control over their licenses. The License Cluster server should be installed and configured in a cluster to provide fault tolerance and load balancing.

Understanding certificates Understanding certificates and their uses is important in an AD RMS environment. The certificates that clients use are stored in the users' profile; however, you must understand the certificates' usage if you have to troubleshoot AD RMS licensing issues.

Master It Juan works as an AD RMS administrator for a medium-size bank in Toronto. While installing a new AD RMS server on the domain, Juan found there are multiple certificates installed on each client's machine. He is unable to identify RACs. How can he identify them?

Master It Solution Juan must understand the certificate extensions and their storage location. When the certificates are stored in a user's profile, you need to know what extension is used.

A rights account certificate (RAC) is issued by an RMS server to associate a user's account with specific computers. If a user logged on to multiple computers—for example office desktop, laptop, home desktop, and kiosk machine—the user would have received an RMS RAC on every computer that he or she logged into. The RAC identifies users either by a Windows Security ID (SID) or a Passport Unique ID (PUID). An RAC uses the GIC prefix and is stored in %USERPROFILE%\AppData\Local\Microsoft\DRM.

Troubleshoot decryption of contents Understanding licenses and their uses is important in an Active Directory Rights Management Services (AD RMS) environment. Licenses are required for encrypting and decrypting message contents.

Master It Spiros is the administrator of a large manufacturing company in Greece. His company is often the target of hackers that are interested in trade secrets and intellectual property. To address these issues, Spiros has implemented AD RMS in his organization. After he installed it, he began receiving a lot of help desk calls complaining that users are unable to get the use license. He has to explain the term *use license* to his manager, Demi. How should he explain it?

Master It Solution Spiros must understand the purpose and usage of the publish license and use license. AD RMS Server issues a publish license, also known as issuance license, to define usage policies for the content, which includes usage rights along with the list of authorized users who can request a use license. AD RMS Server also issues a use license, also known as end-user license (EUL), which is required for decrypting the content and for enforcing policies and content permissions so that only intended clients will be able to decrypt and view the protected document. Every document you protect requires its own use license.

Know the importance of RMA in an AD RMS infrastructure Understanding RMS-aware applications is important in an AD RMS environment. Although other AD RMS components (such the AD RMS cluster, Root Certification server, license cluster, server licensor certificate (SLC), client licensor certificate (CLC), and so on) are equally important to understand and implement, understanding AD RMS–aware applications is important to troubleshooting and open RMS-protected application.

Master It Elanda is planning to use AD RMS for remote users. She is responsible for identifying tools, utilities, and implementation strategies to enable RMS for remote users who do not have RMS-aware applications installed on their machines. Which applications can she use to view documents in Microsoft Internet Explorer when an intended application is not available?

Master It Solution Microsoft Office 2003 and 2007 (Enterprise Edition) are RMS-enabled. If Elanda's application is not RMS-aware, or if there is no native RMS functionality available for her application, she may have to use add-ons to RMS-enable those applications. One significant feature of the RMS system is that it allows users to view rights-managed documents in Internet Explorer when an intended application is not available; however, they must download and install the Rights Management Add-on for Internet Explorer (RMA), which allows users to view but not modify the rights-protected document. RMA is an RMS-based technology, and any application built to support AD RMS technology can take advantage of RMA. Microsoft also offers Windows RMS SDK, which can be used to RMS-enable applications.

Chapter 12: Managing Active Directory Certificate Services

In this chapter we looked at Active Directory Certificate Services, what's new in Windows Server 2008, and how to configure and manage AD CS.

Because AD CS services are integral to an organization's security configuration, it is important to understand the differences between enterprise and stand-alone CAs, how to implement a CA, and how to properly manage a CA.

Identify the differences between a stand-alone CA and an enterprise CA and know their uses
Before you can install AD CS you must have a thorough understanding of the types of CAs that are available in Windows Server 2008 so that you can select the right one.

Master It Two types of CAs are available in Windows Server 2008. Learn what they are, the prerequisites for installing them, and the differences between the services they provide.

Master It Solution

Enterprise CA—Requires Active Directory, and the host computer must be a member of that domain. IIS with Active Server Pages is required for the web interface. An enterprise CA supports the use of certificate templates. Because Active Directory is used to confirm requester identity, the certificate-application process is greatly simplified. Additionally, both user certificates and the CRL are published in AD DS.

Stand-alone CA—Active Directory is not required. These CAs are less automated, require more input from users when completing a certificate request, and do not support the use of certificate templates. Stand-alone CAs cannot be used to provide certificates for smart-card authentication to a domain. They are generally used when organizations need to utilize an extranet or the Internet.

Install your first CA Before implementing Certificate Services, most organizations will need to install a number of different CAs. It is important to know which is the starting CA.

Master It When tasked with setting up Certificate Services for her company, Mary needs to select the correct type of CA to start with.

Master It Solution   Install a root CA that will provide the foundation for the Certificate Services for the organization. This CA will also establish the basic rules for issue, use, and revocation of all certificates in the PKI.

For security purposes, once the root CA has been created and its initial certificate has been created and distributed, the root CA should be taken offline and placed in a highly secure location. Subordinate issuing CAs should be used for the actual distribution of certificates to users.

Understanding CA management procedures   Installing Certificate Services is only part of the story. Most administrators' duties involve the care and feeding of the CA servers. For a CA administrator, it is important to understand the types of tasks that need to be performed.

Master It   Understanding the types of maintenance tasks that must be performed on CA servers is critical to keeping those servers functioning properly.

Master It Solution   A CA administrator will perform two categories of management tasks: recurring and infrequent.

Recurring tasks are those performed on a daily or weekly basis. These include issuing certificates to users, revoking certificates that are no longer needed, and publishing the CRL.

Infrequent tasks are generally performed only when initially deploying a CA server, or when major changes need to be made to the CA. These include the deployment of certificate templates, performing key-archival and key-recovery services, and configuring security policies.

Chapter 13: Managing the Flexible Single Master Operations Roles

FSMO roles by their nature are special domain controllers that contain roles that can be a single point of failure for that particular role. Special planning and steps are necessary to ensure these roles can be moved or brought back up in a meaningful time frame.

Determine which servers hold the FSMO roles   The first step in FSMO planning and management is determining which domain controllers hold which FSMO roles. You can do this by checking the built-in AD DS tools or by using downloadable tools from Microsoft.

Master It   Determine which domain controllers in the environment hold FSMO roles.

Master It Solution   You can use the following built-in AD DS tools to determine the FSMO role holders:

Active Directory Users and Computers—Use this tool to determine the domain-specific FSMO roles of Infrastructure Master, RID Master, and PDC Emulator.

Active Directory Domains and Trusts—Use this tool to determine which domain controller contains the forest-specific role of Domain Naming Master.

Active Directory Schema—Use this tool to determine which domain controller contains the Schema Master FSMO role. To gain access to the Schema Admin tool, you must register the proper DLL file as described earlier in the chapter.

You can also use the following downloadable utilities to view the FSMO roles:

◆   `ReplMon`

◆   `dsquery`

- ◆ dcdiag

- ◆ dumpfsmos

- ◆ netdom

Transfer FSMO roles between servers   There will be times when you must transfer FSMO roles from one server to another—usually when you want to demote a server, to bring a server offline for a period of time, or to spread out the roles among servers if one server has multiple roles.

Master It   Use the built-in AD DS tools to transfer roles from one server to another.

Master It Solution

Schema Master:

Register the schema DLL.

Open MMC and add the snap-in Active Directory Schema.

Right-click on Active Directory Schema and select Change Domain Controller (make this the domain controller that you want to be the Schema Master).

Right-click on the domain controller and select Operations Masters.

Click the Change button, and transfer the role to the domain controller you want to use as the Schema Master.

Domain Naming Master:

Open Active Directory Domains and Trusts.

Right-click on Active Directory Domains and Trusts and select Change Domain Controller (make this the domain controller that you want to be the Domain Naming Master).

Right-click on the domain controller and select Operations Masters.

Click the Change button, and transfer the role to the domain controller you want to use as the Domain Naming Master.

Infrastructure Master:

Open Active Directory Users and Computers.

Right-click on Active Directory Users and Computers and select Change Domain Controller (make this the domain controller that you want to be the Infrastructure Master).

Right-click on the domain controller and select Operations Masters.

Click on the Infrastructure tab.

Click the Change button, and transfer the role to the domain controller you want to use as the Infrastructure Master.

RID Master:

Open Active Directory Users and Computers.

Right-click on Active Directory Users and Computers and select Change Domain Controller (make this the domain controller that you want to be the RID Master).

Right-click on the domain controller and select Operations Masters.

Click on the RID tab.

Click the Change button, and transfer the role to the domain controller you want to use as the RID Master.

PDC Emulator:

Open Active Directory Users and Computers.

Right-click on Active Directory Users and Computers and select Change Domain Controller (make this the domain controller that you want to be the PDC Emulator).

Right-click on the domain controller and select Operations Masters.

Click on the PDC tab.

Click the Change button, and transfer the role to the domain controller you want to use as the PDC Emulator.

Seize FSMO roles   If a domain controller that holds a FSMO role is down or unresponsive, you may need to seize a FSMO role.

Master It   You must be able to seize each FSMO role in case a role resides on a server that has crashed or is unresponsive.

Master It Solution   To seize a FSMO role, use the NTDSUtil program on Windows Server. This will allow you to seize any FSMO role on any server. A detailed explanation for each role is described in the chapter.

Chapter 14: Maintaining the Active Directory Database

Keeping the AD DS database in good health is essential to keeping your environment running its best. You may have to manage the AD DS database manually to perform certain tasks.

Defragment the AD DS database   The AD DS database performs certain maintenance tasks automatically on a regular basis. One thing it cannot do is rid itself of the "white space" that occurs as you delete items from the database.

Master It   Chris is the administrator of a large AD environment that contains user accounts for 1,000 temporary employees that work as seasonal help every year. When the seasonal work is done for these users, the user accounts are disabled and then eventually deleted. How can Chris determine how much white space is contained in his database and then reclaim that space?

Master It Solution   Chris starts by changing the Garbage Collection Logging value to reveal how much space in the AD DS database is considered white space. This will give him an idea of how much data can be recovered by running an offline defrag.

Chris then takes the domain controller offline.

The third step Chris performs is to actually run the offline defragmentation. This is accomplished by running the NTDSUtil program.

The final step is to bring the domain controller back online and check the event log for any errors.

Use NTDSUtil to manage the AD DS database   The main tool you will use to manage the AD DS database manually is the NTDSUtil command-line utility.

Master It   There are many functions of the NTDSUtil command-line utility. Name the functions that relate directly to managing the AD DS database.

Master It Solution   With NTDSUtil, you can perform the following tasks on the AD DS database:

Check database integrity

Recover the database

Compact the database

Move the database

Move the log files

Remove orphaned objects

Maintain security accounts

Implement best practices for optimizing the AD DS database   Taking a proactive approach with the AD DS database is key to maintaining the database in good health. Following best practices may help eliminate the need for the troubleshooting and recovery options that we discussed earlier.

Master It   When working with the AD DS database, what are the best practices you should follow to help alleviate downtime and poor performance?

Master It Solution   When troubleshooting the Directory Services, increase the logging level gradually to isolate the problem if the problem isn't apparent.

Always use the Recover option in the NTDSUtil command-line utility to commit all transactions to the database prior to running any other utilities.

Don't run an offline defragmentation on the database unless you have deleted a large number of objects or you are planning to move the database and want to reduce its size.

If any domain controller fails during demotion, make sure you remove the associated metadata from the database and remove all of the object information using ADSI Edit.

If the last domain controller for a domain fails during demotion, make sure you remove the associated metadata from the database.

Move the transaction log files to their own drive to increase the domain controller's efficiency.

If the RID Master role is inadvertently seized while the original is still functioning but offline, check for duplicate SIDs when the original is returned to the network.

Chapter 15: Microsoft's Troubleshooting Methodology for Active Directory

Having a good troubleshooting methodology will help you when problems related to Active Directory arise. Understanding the troubleshooting roadmap will save troubleshooting time.

The six essential steps of the troubleshooting methodology   Troubleshooting AD DS problems can be very time-consuming. Having a solid plan of action when problems arise can save you time and effort.

Master It   AD DS replication to all remote sites is failing. You must come up with a plan of action to determine where the problem lies.

Master It Solution   You can determine the problem by using the six-step Microsoft methodology for AD DS. The steps comprise the following:

◆ Discover and document the problem.

◆ Identify the components involved.

◆ Verify client health.

◆ Verify network path.

◆ Verify server health.

◆ Verify services health.

Proactive steps to take to help circumvent problems   Proactive planning is always better than reactive troubleshooting. There are many proactive steps that you can take to help cut down on problems that may arise.

Master It   After a severe network outage, Nick decides to design a proactive plan for checking AD DS health and stability. What should Nick include in his network plan to help discover potential problems?

Master It Solution   Nick's proactive plan should include the following steps to help circumvent any potential problems:

◆ Regularly back up the system state.

◆ Periodically test troubleshooting and recovery plans.

◆ Rapidly evaluate and deploy updates.

◆ Use and update antivirus software.

◆ Improve the physical computing environment.

◆ Monitor performance and event logs.

◆ Document hardware and software changes.

◆ Plan for hardware and software updates.

◆ Test changes in a lab environment before implementing them in production.

◆ Use compatible and tested hardware.

Chapter 16: Troubleshooting Problems Related to Network Infrastructure

There are many tools available for troubleshooting issues related to network infrastructure. Most of these tools help you troubleshoot issues related to name resolution and DHCP.

Use tools to troubleshoot name-resolution problems   Problems related to name resolution can be difficult to troubleshoot. Where the issue lies—with DNS or with WINS—will determine which tools you will use.

Master It   You are having a problem with AD DS database replication. You need to determine why replication is failing between servers.

Master It Solution   Start by isolating the problem. Check the event logs to determine which server is not communicating properly. After determining the name of the server, ping the server to determine if the server responds, or if the name resolves. If the name does not resolve, check the DNS configuration of the server by using the tools nslookup and DNSLint. After reviewing the results from these tools, you should have enough information to correct the problem.

Troubleshoot WINS issues   Often, communication problems or name-resolution problems occur with computers that use WINS.

> **Master It**   You are trying to communicate with a workstation that is named CAD01. The IP address of this workstation is 10.100.1.29. You ping the workstation by name and by IP address, but the `ping` command times out. Upon further inspection, you find that the IP address that is returned to you is 10.100.3.29. This is the IP address that CAD01 had before it was moved to the 10.100.1.0 subnet.
>
> You check the WINS database, and the IP address associated with CAD01 is listed in the database as 10.100.1.29.
>
> **Master It Solution**   You will need to refresh the WINS cache so the correct entry will resolve (and check the LMHOSTS file for an incorrect IP assignment). You can accomplish this by using the commands `nbtstat -r` and `nbtstat -RR`.

Chapter 17: Troubleshooting Problems Related to the Active Directory Database

Problems with the AD DS database can cause a multitude of issues in your environment. Determining what is causing a problem with the database can be difficult. Being prepared with a wide array of tools will help you narrow down the issues and come to a quick resolution.

Troubleshoot database replication   Keeping information current and in sync is very important to the health of your AD DS database. Replication is the technology that keeps all domain controllers up-to-date with changes from other domain controllers.

> **Master It**   Marcus is the administrator of a large nationwide distribution company. He receives a call that states that Joe Davis from the sales department has been fired and that his account must be disabled as soon as possible.
>
> Marcus disables the account, but because Joe is a traveling employee, he could log in from anywhere on the domain. Instead of waiting for replication to occur at its regularly scheduled time, what should Marcus do to trigger replication to ensure the change propagates through the network immediately?
>
> **Master It Solution**   Marcus should use the `RepAdmin` utility to force replication immediately. To perform the immediate replication, Marcus should run the command `repadmin /syncall domain_controller_FQDN directory_partition /P`.
>
> The /P option is used because Active Directory replication is, by default, *pull replication*, meaning that the domain controller will request the data from its partners. You can change that behavior by using the /P switch, which forces the domain controller to push its objects to it partner domain controllers.

Troubleshoot FSMO roles   FSMO roles are unique in an Active Directory environment because they are the only domain controllers that are not fault-tolerant. The roles that these domain controllers host could be lost if a domain controller were to fail. You must plan specifically to ensure you can recover these special roles quickly.

Master It   Low is the Active Directory administrator of a medium-size bank. While installing a new server on the domain, The dcpromo task fails when Low tries to promote it to a domain controller. After some investigation, Low finds that the domain controller that holds the RID Master FSMO role is down and it cannot be recovered. What should he do next?

Master It Solution   Low must seize the RID Master FSMO role. When the original role holder is down and a transfer cannot be completed, the only other option is to seize the role manually. To seize the role, Low will have to run the NTDSUtil utility and run the command `seize rid master`.

Troubleshoot logon failures   FSMO roles are unique in an Active Directory environment because they are the only domain controllers that are not fault-tolerant. The roles that these domain controllers host could be lost if a domain controller were to fail. You must plan specifically to ensure you can recover these special roles quickly.

Master It   Ginger is the administrator of a large robotics-manufacturing company. Her company is often the target of hackers who are interested in trade secrets and intellectual property.

Ginger starts receiving a lot of help-desk tickets for locked-out accounts. She determines that someone is trying to log into the network using known usernames. She must determine where the login attempts are coming from.

Master It Solution   Ginger should check the domain controller that holds the PDC Emulator role. Whenever a bad password attempt is made, the PDC Emulator is updated with the attempted login information, including the name of the workstation from which the attempts are coming.

Another option for Ginger would be to install and use `LockoutStatus.exe`, which will also display the name of the workstation that attempted the login.

Chapter 18: ADSI Primer

Connect to Active Directory using VBScript   Writing Active Directory scripts for your users will increase your productivity and lighten your workload. The first step is to connect to the current domain. A portable script does not reference a particular domain, but rather uses Active Directory itself to connect to the current domain.

Master It   Develop a script that connects to the current domain using the RootDSE object. Display the default naming context and current time of the domain.

Master It Solution

```
Dim RootDSE
Set RootDSE = GetObject("LDAP://RootDSE")
WScript.Echo RootDSE("defaultNamingContext")
WScript.Echo RootDSE("currentTime")
```

Read and write the properties available in Active Directory objects   Being able to read and write the property values of objects in Active Directory is an important skill for a scripting administrator. After connecting to a given object in Active Directory, the script writer must know the name of the property as defined in the schema. The script writer must also remember to save any property changes to Active Directory.

Master It   Develop a script that connects to an object with the distinguished path CN=User1, DC=zygort,DC=com. First display the first and last name of the user. Next change the last name property to *Smith* and save the change to Active Directory.

Master It Solution

```
Dim User
Set User = GetObject("LDAP://CN=User1,DC=zygort,DC=com")
WScript.Echo User.Get("givenName")
WScript.Echo User.Get("sn")
User.Put "sn", "Smith"
User.SetInfo
```

Develop an LDAP query to retrieve objects from Active Directory   An LDAP query's format is different from the SQL queries you've probably seen before. The ability to write an effective LDAP query takes practice and requires a familiarity with the schema of your Active Directory domain.

Master It   Write an LDAP query to retrieve all objects of the OU class. Next narrow down the search to OUs beginning with *Sales*.

Write another LDAP query to find all objects of the user class that have a surname beginning with the letter *S*.

Master It Solution

Search filter 1: (objectClass=organizationalUnit)

Search filter 2: (&(objectclass=organizationalUnit)(name=Sales*))

Search filter 3: (&(objectClass=user)(sn=S*))

Chapter 19: Active Directory Scripts

Use the Windows Script File to incorporate the functionality of an existing VBScript class into a new script   When developing scripts, especially a lot of scripts, it makes sense to avoid reinventing code you've already written. Code reuse in VBScript used to be a copy-and-paste operation. With the Windows Script File (WSF) this is not the case. The script code that exists in another file can be referenced by the WSF script, which saves time and unneeded duplication.

Master It   You are writing a new script to perform some user maintenance. Your script needs to create a password based on a key value. A function named CreatePassword has already been written to create the password and exists in the file Password.vbs. Create a new WSF file that can use the existing function. Display the password that would be generated by the key value John Smith.

Master It Solution

```
<job>
<script language="VBScript" src="Password.vbs"></script>
<script>
WScript.Echo CreatePassword("John Smith")
</script>
</job>
```

Use VBScript classes to encapsulate Active Directory and other application functionality
A class is simply a blueprint for creating an object. In VBScript we create our own classes using
VBScript code. A number of functions deal specifically with Active Directory objects, such as
users and groups. By grouping those functions into a class based on the particular object, we can
accomplish two things: we can keep our main script clean and focused on the task at hand, and
we can reuse the same class code in several different scripts (with the help of WSF files).

Master It In this chapter we created a class to represent an Active Directory user. The class
is named UserClass and is contained in a file named UserClass.vbs. Create a new script
that creates a new instance of an Active Directory user (you can pick the user) and display
the user's first name, last name, and telephone properties.

Master It Solution

```
<job>
<script language="VBScript" src="includes\UserClass.vbs" />
<script>
Option Explicit
Dim UserObject
Set UserObject = New UserClass
UserObject.BindToUser "CN=ScriptUser,CN=Users,DC=zygort,DC=com"
Dim PropertyList
Set PropertyList = UserObject.PropertyList
WScript.Echo "First Name: " & PropertyList("givenName")
WScript.Echo "Last Name: " & PropertyList("sn")
WScript.Echo "Phone: " & PropertyList("telephoneNumber")
</script>
</job>
```

Develop Visual Basic scripts to read and manage Microsoft Active Directory Writing scripts
to manage Active Directory has some clear benefits. First, a script can perform several operations
on Active Directory in one fell swoop, saving the administrator time. Second, a script performs the
operations the same way every time the script is running, keeping Active Directory objects consistent and uniform. Finally, a script runs at any time of day or night, weekday or weekend. This
allows the administrator to offload routine maintenance tasks—many of which are best performed during off-hours—to the script.

Master It Using the classes presented in this chapter, develop a script that queries Active
Directory for all groups. Export a list of all groups to Excel. Save the workbook with the
name GroupList.xls.

Master It Solution

```
<job>
<script language="VBScript" src="includes\RootDSEClass.vbs" />
<script language="VBScript" src="includes\QueryClass.vbs" />
<script language="VBScript" src="includes\ExcelClass.vbs" />
<script>
Dim RootDSE
Set RootDSE = New RootDSEClass
Dim Query
```

```
Set Query = New QueryClass
Query.SearchRoot = "CN=Users,DC=zygort,DC=org"
Query.Attributes = "cn,AdsPath"
Query.Scope = "subtree"
Query.FilterText = "(&(objectClass=group)(objectCategory=group))"
Dim Results
Set Results = Query.ExecuteQuery
Set Excel = New ExcelClass
Excel.NewWorkbook
Do Until Results.eof
    Excel.CellValue = Results.Fields(0)
    Excel.CellForeColor = vbRed
    Excel.CellBackColor = vbBlue
    Excel.NextColumn
    Excel.CellValue = Results.Fields(1)
    Excel.CellFont = "Arial Narrow"
    Excel.StartNewRow
    Results.MoveNext
Loop
Excel.SetColumnForeColor 1,vbRed
Excel.SetRowHeight 2,20
Excel.SaveWorkbook "GroupList.xls"
Set Query = Nothing
Set RootDSE = Nothing
</script>
</job>
```

Chapter 20: Monitoring Active Directory

Use WMI to monitor the health of Active Directory servers   Windows Management Instrumentation (WMI) services provide a wide range of pertinent performance information for a given server. Active Directory relies on the performance and availability of several Windows services, such as File Replication Service (FRS), Intersite Messaging Service (IsmServ), Kerberos Key Distribution Center (KDC), NetLogon service (NetLogon), and Windows Time (W32Time) service. Monitoring these services is a key step in maintaining your Active Directory infrastructure.

Master It   Develop a script that queries the current status of the FRS, Netlogon, and W32Time services. The script should query three different servers named AD_Server1, AD_Server2, and AD_Server3. Report the results for each server.

Master It Solution

```
<job>
<script language="VBScript" src="..\includes\OutputClass.vbs" />
<script language="VBScript" src="..\includes\WMIClass.vbs" />
<script language="VBScript" src="..\includes\DomainClass.vbs" />
<script>
Option Explicit
Dim Output
```

```
         Set Output = New OutputClass
         Dim WMI
         Set WMI = New WMIClass
         Dim Servers, Server
         Set Servers = WScript.CreateObject("Scripting.Dictionary")
         Ô Add additional servers to this dictionary as needed
         Servers.Add "AD_Server1", Nothing
         Servers.Add "AD_Server2", Nothing
         Servers.Add "AD_Server3", Nothing
         Dim StateList, State
         For Each Server In Servers.Keys
            Output.Display "Checking Active Directory Services on " & Server
            Set StateList = _
               WMI.GetServiceState(Server, _
                      Array("ntfrs","Netlogon","w32time"))
            For Each State In StateList.Keys
               Output.Display State & " " & StateList(State)
                  If Not(StateList(State) = "Running") Then
                      Output.ModalAlert Server & " - " & _
                      State & " is not running!"
               End If
            Next
         Next
         </script>
         </job>
```

Write scripts to monitor the health of Active Directory   Microsoft's System Center Operations Manager (SCOM)—one of several methods for monitoring Active Directory—features an AD Management Pack specifically for monitoring the health of Active Directory. When actively monitoring several Microsoft products and services, SCOM is an ideal product. But for simply monitoring Active Directory we can replicate the functionality of SCOM's AD Management Pack with our own set of scripts.

Master It   Develop a script that monitors a specific Active Directory server named AD_Server1. Query the status of the FRS and Netlogon services. Check the available disk space of the drives.

Master It Solution

```
<job>
<script language="VBScript" src="..\includes\OutputClass.vbs" />
<script language="VBScript" src="..\includes\WMIClass.vbs" />
<script language="VBScript" src="..\includes\DomainClass.vbs" />
<script language="VBScript" src="..\includes\RegistryClass.vbs" />
<script>
Option Explicit
Dim Output
Set Output = New OutputClass
Dim WMI
```

```
Set WMI = New WMIClass
Dim Server
Server = "AD_Server1"
Dim StateList, State

Output.Display "Checking Active Directory Services on " & Server
Set StateList = _
  WMI.GetServiceState(Server, _
          Array("ntfrs","Netlogon"))
For Each State In StateList.Keys
  Output.Display State & " " & StateList(State)
    If Not(StateList(State) = "Running") Then
      Output.ModalAlert Server & " - " & State & _
                      " is not running!"
  End If
Next
' Check database drive Space
' Adjust thresholds to your minimum DB and Log free space.
' It currently uses Gigabytes as the unit of measure.
Const DBThreshold = 1
Const LogThreshold = 1
' Registry keys pointing to the AD Database and log file locations.
Const ADKey = "HKLM\System\CurrentControlSet\Services\NTDS\Parameters"
Const DBValue = "DSA Database file"
Const LogValue = "Database log files path"
' Number of bytes in a kilobyte, megabyte, and gigabyte.
Const KB = 1024
Const MB = 1048576
Const GB = 1073741824
Dim DBFreeSpace, LogFreeSpace
Registry.Server = Server
Registry.Connect
DBDrive = Left _
  (Registry.GetValue(ADKey,DBValue,Registry.REG_SZ),2)
LogDrive = Left _
  (Registry.GetValue(ADKey,LogValue,Registry.REG_SZ),2)
DBFreeSpace = FormatNumber _
  (WMI.GetAvailableSpace(Server,DBDrive) / GB)
If DBDrive = LogDrive Then
  LogFreeSpace = DBFreeSpace
Else
  LogFreeSpace = FormatNumber _
    (WMI.GetAvailableSpace(Server,LogDrive) / GB)
End If
Output.Display Server
Output.Display "DBDrive = " & DBFreeSpace
Output.Display "LogDrive = " & LogFreeSpace
If DBFreeSpace < DBThreshold Then
  Output.ModalAlert _
```

```
          Server & " is low on DB space (" & DBFreeSpace & ")"
End If
If LogFreeSpace < LogThreshold Then
  Output.ModalAlert _
      Server & " is low on log space (" & LogFreeSpace & ")"
End If
</script>
</job>
```

Chapter 21: Managing Active Directory with PowerShell

Use PowerShell cmdlets, piping them together to produce a result set   Piping the output from one cmdlet to the input stream of another is one of the most powerful features of PowerShell. Effectively piping cmdlets together is an essential skill of a PowerShell user.

Master It   Using the standard set of PowerShell cmdlets, create a command that counts the number of entries in the current directory. Show at least two commands to get the information.

Master It Solution

```
Dir | Measure-Object | Select Count
(Dir | Measure-Object).Count
Get-ChildItem | Measure-Object | Select Count
(Get-ChildItem | Measure-Object).Count
```

Use the Quest Active Directory Management cmdlets   The Quest Active Directory Management cmdlets make easy work of managing Active Directory from the command line. You must understand what each cmdlet does to accomplish the management task at hand quickly and efficiently.

Master It   First create a command to find all locked accounts in the domain. Then expand the command to unlock those accounts.

Master It Solution

```
Get-QADUser -Locked | Unlock-QADUser
```

Manage Active Directory using the Quest Active Directory Management and PowerShell cmdlets   Combining the Quest Active Directory Management cmdlets with the standard set of PowerShell cmdlets gives you a much wider range of solutions to management tasks. It is important to understand how these cmdlets can function together in a command.

Master It   First create a list of security groups on the server. Then find the number of users that belong to each group.

Master It Solution

```
Get-QADGroup -GroupType "Security" |
    Foreach {"$_.Name : $((
        (Get-QADGroupMember -Identity $_.DN)
            | Measure-Object).Count"}
```

Index

Note to the reader: Throughout this index **boldfaced** page numbers indicate primary discussions of a topic. *Italicized* page numbers indicate illustrations.

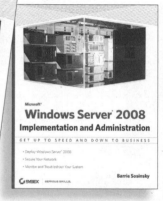

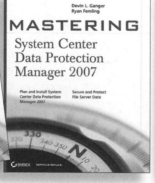
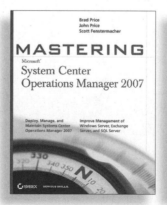